LONDON

TOP SIGHTS, AUTHENTIC EXPERIENCES

Emilie Filou
Peter Dragicevich, Steve Fallon, Damian Harper

Lonely Planet's
London

d
gton
ee a
ght

King's Cross

East London
Ground-zero for multi-cultural London, plus the highlights of Queen Elizabeth Olympic Park.
(Map p255)

ovent
arden

St Paul's
Cathedral

The City
Two thousand years of history and architecture packed into just one square mile.
(Map p245)

haring
ross

River Thames

Shakespeare's
Globe

Tower
of London

Tate Modern

Borough
Market

Tower
Bridge

London
Bridge

Waterloo

Houses of
Parliament

The South Bank
A must-visit area for art lovers, theatre-goers and culture hounds, with Thames views to boot.
(Map p245)

Welcome to London

One of the world's most visited cities, London has something for everyone, from history and culture to fine wine and good times. Its energy is intoxicating and its sheer diversity inspiring.

With a third of all Londoners foreign born, representing 270 different nationalities, London is marvellously multicultural. These cultures infuse the cuisine, fashion and music offerings of the capital – it's all delightfully international.

A tireless innovator of art and culture, London is a city of ideas and the imagination; the city's creative milieu is streaked with left-field attitude, from ground-breaking theatre to contemporary art, pioneering music, writing and design. No matter how often you come, there is always something new to eat, visit or experience.

Contrasting with the up-to-the-minute restaurant and arts scene, London is also a city immersed in history, with more than its share of mind-blowing antiquity. London's buildings are eye-catching milestones in the city's compelling biography, and its museums have collections as varied as they are magnificent. Of course, London is as much about leafy spaces and wide-open parklands as about high-density, sight-packed exploration and there is always a glorious green escape waiting to soothe the senses.

London is a city immersed in history, with more than its share of mind-blowing antiquity

London skyline

★ LONDON ★

North Lond[e]
Parks, mark[ets,]
Camden an[d]
after dark g[ive]
glorious da[ys]
out. *(Map p[.)]*

Kings Cross
⊙

Euston ⊖ St Par[ncras]
Interna[tional]
(Euros[tar)]

Clerkenwell, Shoreditch & Spitalfields
Good food and a great
night out in one of Lon-
don's trendiest areas.
(Map p253)

British Museum

The West End
The beating heart of
London, with iconic
sights, shopping and
nightlife. *(Map p248)*

SOHO
⊙

**Leices[ter]
Squa[re]**
⊙

🅰 Hyde
Park

National Gallery

Trafalgar Squar[e]

**Buckingham
Palace**
🏛

**Westminst[er]
Abb[ey]**

**Design
Museum**
🏛

**Natural History
Museum**
🏛

**Victoria &
Albert Museum**
🏛

🅥 Victoria

**T[ower
Bri[dge]**

Kensington & Hyde Park
Three world-class mu-
seums and the largest
of the royal parks in
a well-heeled district.
(Map p250)

Plan Your Trip
This Year in London

BMENWORLDTRAVEL/SHUTTERSTOCK ©

London

London has a busy year ahead: there are festivals and cultural events galore. A few key sights are reopening after extensive renovations too: whether you have seen them before or not, a visit is definitely in order!

Clockwise from above: New Year's Celebrations at Big Ben (p17); Trooping the Colour (p11); Notting Hill Carnival (p13)

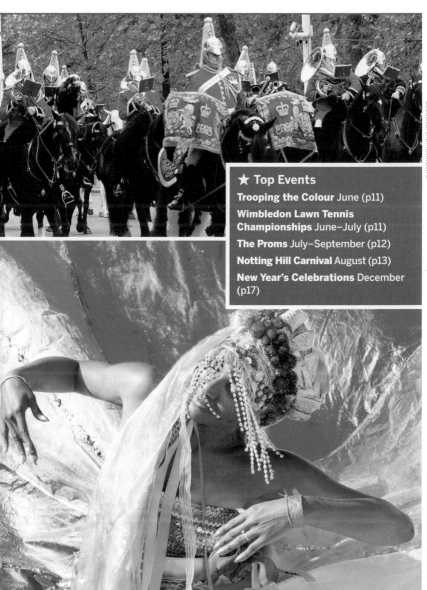

2018

★ **Top Events**

Trooping the Colour June (p11)

Wimbledon Lawn Tennis Championships June–July (p11)

The Proms July–September (p12)

Notting Hill Carnival August (p13)

New Year's Celebrations December (p17)

MEUNIERD/SHUTTERSTOCK ©

MS JANE CAMPBELL/SHUTTERSTOCK ©

Plan Your Trip
This Year in London

January

January in London kicks off with a big bang at midnight. London is in the throes of winter, with short days: light appears at 8am and is all but gone by 4pm.

☆ London International Mime Festival   10 Jan–3 Feb

Held over the month of January, this festival (www.mimelondon.com) is a must for lovers of originality, playfulness, physical talent and the unexpected.

◉ London Art Fair   17–21 Jan

Over 100 major galleries participate in this contemporary art fair (www.londonartfair.co.uk; pictured above), now one of the largest in Europe, with thematic exhibitions, special events and the best emerging artists.

☆ A Night at the Opera   Jan

The nights are long and cold so what better way to cosy up than inside the stunning Royal Opera House to revel in world-class opera or ballet? (Plus, it's a great opportunity to dress up.)

◉ Visit the Natural History Museum   Jan

The museum (p104) unveiled its new-look Hintze Hall in summer 2017: it now features the skeleton of a blue whale set in dramatic diving position, as well as brand new exhibits.

2018

MANUEL SECHI/SHUTTERSTOCK ©

02

February

February is usually chilly, wet and sometimes even snowy. The Chinese New Year (Spring Festival) is fun and Londoners lark about with pancakes on Shrove Tuesday.

🏃 Pancake Races   13 Feb
On Shrove Tuesday, you can catch pancake races and associated silliness at various venues around town (Old Spitalfields Market, in particular).

🎎 St Valentine's Day   14 Feb
Whether you're single or part of a loved-up group, you'll be able to choose from themed and alternative parties, special movie nights and dedicated menus. Book ahead as it's a popular night.

🎎 Chinese New Year   16 Feb
To usher in the year of the dog, Chinatown fizzes, crackles and pops in this colourful street festival (pictured above), which includes a Golden Dragon parade, eating and partying.

☆ BAFTAs   18 Feb
The British Academy of Film and Television Arts (BAFTA; www.bafta.org) rolls out the red carpet to hand out its annual cinema awards, the BAFTAs (the British Oscars, if you will). Expect plenty of celebrity glamour.

This Year in London

ANDREW COWIE/STRINGER/GETTY IMAGES ©

March

03

March sees spring in the air, with trees beginning to flower and daffodils emerging across parks and gardens. London is getting in the mood to head outdoors again.

✣ St Patrick's Day Parade & Festival 18 Mar

This is the top festival for the Irish in London, held on the Sunday closest to 17 March (the actual St Patrick's date), with a colourful parade through central London (pictured above) and other festivities in and around Trafalgar Sq.

☆ Flare late Mar

This LGBT film festival, organised by the British Film Institute (www.bfi.org.uk/flare), runs a packed two-week program of film screenings, along with club nights, talks and events.

☉ Kew's Chinese Pagoda Reopens Mar

The distinctive 50m octogonal pagoda tower reopens to the public after renovations. Built in 1762, it's been restored to its initial splendour and now features the 80 gold-leafed winged dragons that were part of the initial design.

☆ Head of the River Race 11 Mar

Some 400 crews take part in this colourful boat race, held over a 7km course on the Thames, from Mortlake to Putney.

April

April sees London in bloom, with warmer days and a spring in everyone's step. British summer time starts late March, so it's now light until 7pm. Some sights previously shut for winter reopen.

🌸 Easter 1 Apr

With Good Friday and Easter Monday both being public holidays, Easter is the longest bank holiday in the UK. Chocolate, which you'll find in many shapes and flavours, is a traditional Easter treat, as are hot cross buns, a spiced, sticky-glazed fruit bun.

☆ Oxford & Cambridge Boat Race early Apr

Crowds line the banks of the Thames for the country's two most famous universities going oar-to-oar from Putney to Mortlake (www.theboatraces.org).

☆ London Marathon mid-Apr

Some 35,000 runners – most running for charity – pound through London in one of the world's biggest road races (www.virginmoneylondonmarathon.com; pictured above), heading from Blackheath to the Mall.

☆ Udderbelly Festival Apr–Jul

Housed in a temporary venue in the shape of a purple upside-down cow on the South Bank, this festival of comedy, circus and general family fun (www.udderbelly.co.uk) has become a spring favourite. Events run from April to July.

👁 Southbank Centre Reopens Apr

Shut for the past two years for extensive refurbishment, the brutalist wing of the Southbank Centre, which contains the Hayward Gallery and Queen Elizabeth Centre, are finally unveiling their shiny new selves, along with the floating glass box linking them to the art-deco-inspired Royal Festival Hall.

Plan Your Trip
This Year in London

VISITBRITAIN/ERIC NATHAN/GETTY IMAGES ©

05

May

A delightful time to be in London: days are warming up and Londoners begin to start lounging around in parks, popping sunshades on and enjoying the month's two bank holiday weekends (the first and the last).

☆ Shakespeare's Globe Theatre   late Apr–Oct

Watch the work of the world's most famous playwright in a faithful reproduction of a 17th-century theatre (p191). The theatre is outdoors and most of the audience is standing.

◉ Museums at Night   mid-May

For one weekend in May, numerous museums across London open after-hours (www.culture24.org.uk/museumsatnight), with candlelit tours, spooky atmospheres, sleepovers and special events such as talks and concerts.

✿ Chelsea Flower Show   22–26 May

The world's most renowned horticultural event attracts London's green-fingered and flower-mad gardeners. Expect talks, presentations and spectacular displays from the cream of the gardening world.

☆ Regent's Park Open Air Theatre   May

A popular and very atmospheric summertime fixture in London, this 1250-seat outdoor auditorium (www.openairtheatre.com; pictured above) plays host to four productions a year – famous plays (Shakespeare often features), new works, musicals and usually one production aimed at families.

2018

June

The peak season begins with long, warm days (it's light until 10pm), the arrival of Wimbledon and other alfresco events (concerts and music festivals especially).

🎺 Trooping the Colour mid-Jun
The Queen's official birthday (www.trooping-the-colour.co.uk; pictured above) is celebrated with much flag-waving, parades, pageantry and noisy flyovers. The royal family usually attends in force.

👁 London Festival of Architecture Jun
This month-long celebration of London's built environment (www.londonfestivalofarchitecture.org) explores the significance of architecture and design and how London has become a centre for innovation in those fields.

👁 Open Garden Squares Weekend mid-Jun
Over one weekend, more than 200 gardens in London that are usually inaccessible to the public fling open their gates for exploration (www.opensquares.org).

☆ Wimbledon Lawn Tennis Championships 27 Jun–10 Jul
For two weeks a year, the quiet South London village of Wimbledon falls under a sporting spotlight as the world's best tennis players gather to battle for the championships (p203).

Plan Your Trip
This Year in London

BIKEWORLDTRAVEL/SHUTTERSTOCK ©

07

July

This is the time to munch on strawberries, drink in beer gardens and join in the numerous outdoor activities, including big music festivals.

◉ Royal Academy Summer Exhibition
mid-Jun–mid-Aug

Beginning in June and running through August, this exhibition at the Royal Academy of Arts (p49) showcases works submitted by artists from all over Britain; the 12,000 or so submissions are distilled to a thousand pieces for the final exhibit.

✿ Pride in London
early Jul

The gay community paints the town pink in this annual extravaganza (www.prideinlondon.org; pictured above), featuring a smorgasbord of experiences from talks to live events and culminating in a huge parade across London.

☆ Wireless
early Jul

One of London's top music festivals, with an emphasis on dance and R & B, Wireless (www.wirelessfestival.co.uk) takes place in Finsbury Park in northeast London. It is extremely popular, so book in advance.

☆ The Proms
mid-Jul–mid-Sep

The BBC Promenade Concerts, or Proms as they are universally known, offer two months of outstanding classical concerts (www.bbc.co.uk/proms) at various prestigious venues, centred on the Royal Albert Hall.

☆ Lovebox
mid-Jul

This two-day music extravaganza (www.loveboxfestival.com) in Victoria Park in East London was created by dance duo Groove Armada in 2002. Although its raison d'être is dance music, there are plenty of other genres, too, including indie, pop and hip-hop.

2018

PETER MACDIARMID/STAFF/GETTY IMAGES ©

08

August

Schools have broken up for summer, families are holidaying and the hugely popular annual Caribbean carnival dances into Notting Hill. The last weekend is a bank holiday weekend.

🏊 Outdoor Swimming   Aug

London may not strike you as the place to go for an alfresco swim but you can enjoy a dip in the Serpentine in Hyde Park or in the ponds at Hampstead Heath. The water quality is tested daily and they are extremely popular on warm days.

🍷 Great British Beer Festival   mid-Aug

Organised by CAMRA (Campaign for Real Ale), this boozy festival (www.gbbf.org.uk; pictured above) cheerfully cracks open casks of ale from the UK and abroad at the Olympia exhibition centre.

🎉 Notting Hill Carnival   25–27 Aug

Europe's biggest – and London's most vibrant – outdoor carnival is a celebration of Caribbean London, featuring music, dancing and costumes.

MS JANE CAMPBELL/SHUTTERSTOCK ©

☆ Summer Screen at Somerset House   early Aug

For a fortnight, Somerset House (p63) turns its stunning courtyard into an open-air cinema screening an eclectic mix of film premieres, cult classics and popular requests.

Plan Your Trip
This Year in London

September

The end of summer and start of autumn is a lovely time to be in town, with a chance to look at London properties normally shut to the public.

⚘ The Mayor's Thames Festival   Sep
Celebrating the River Thames, this month-long cosmopolitan festival (www.totallythames.org) sees fairs, street theatre, music, food stalls, fireworks and river races, culminating in the superb Night Procession.

◉ Open House London   mid-Sep
For one weekend, the public is invited in to see over 700 heritage buildings throughout the capital that are normally off-limits (www.openhouselondon.org.uk). Some require advance booking.

☆ Great Gorilla Run   mid-Sep
It looks bananas, but this gorilla-costume charity run (www.greatgorillarun.org; pictured above) along an 8km route from the City to Bankside and back again is all in aid of gorilla conservation.

🔒 London Fashion Week   Sep
If you love fashion, don't miss out on this ultimate fashion experience. Highlights include exclusive access to catwalk shows, curated talks, designer shopping and trend presentations.

SVEN HANSCHE/SHUTTERSTOCK ©

10

October

The weather is getting colder, but London's parklands are splashed with gorgeous autumnal colours. Clocks go back to winter time on the last weekend of the month.

🏃 Autumn Walks   Oct
London's parks look truly glorious on a sunny day when the trees have turned a riot of yellows and reds. Hyde Park and Greenwich Park are beautiful at this time of year and offer great views of London's landmarks.

☆ Dance Umbrella   mid-Oct
London's annual festival of contemporary dance (www.danceumbrella.co.uk) features two weeks of performances by British and international dance companies at venues across London.

🎨 Affordable Art Fair   mid-Oct
For four days, Battersea Park turns into a giant art fair (www.affordableartfair.com), where more than 100 galleries offer works of art from just £100. There are plenty of talks and workshops too.

☆ London Film Festival   early Oct
The city's premier film event (www.bfi.org.uk/lff) attracts big overseas names and you can catch over 100 British and international films before their cinema release. Masterclasses are given by world-famous directors.

Plan Your Trip
This Year in London

STUART C WILSON/STRINGER/GETTY IMAGES ©

UNDERGROUND

11

November

London nights are getting longer. It's the last of the parks' autumn colours – enjoy them on a walk and relax by an open fire in a pub afterwards.

✿ Guy Fawkes Night (Bonfire Night)   5 Nov

Bonfire Night commemorates Guy Fawkes' foiled attempt to blow up parliament in 1605. Bonfires and fireworks light up the night across the country. In London, Primrose Hill, Highbury Fields, Alexandra Palace, Clapham Common and Blackheath have the best firework displays.

☆ London Jazz Festival   mid-Nov

Musicians from around the world swing into town for 10 days of jazz (www.efglondonjazzfestival.org.uk). World influences are well represented, as are more conventional strands.

✿ Lighting of the Christmas Tree & Lights   mid-Nov

A celebrity is normally carted in to switch on all the festive lights that line Oxford, Regent and Bond streets, and a towering Norwegian spruce is set up in Trafalgar Sq.

✿ Lord Mayor's Show   mid-Nov

In accordance with the Magna Carta of 1215, the newly elected Lord Mayor of the City of London travels in a state coach from Mansion House to the Royal Courts of Justice to make an oath of allegiance to the Crown. The floats, bands and fireworks that accompany the mayor were added later (www.lordmayorsshow.london; pictured above).

2018

DISTINCTIVE SHOTS/SHUTTERSTOCK ©

12

December

A festive mood reigns as Christmas approaches and shops are dressed up to the nines. Days are increasingly shorter. Christmas Day is the quietest day of the year, with all shops and museums closed and the tube network shut.

🏃 Ice-Skating   mid-Nov–Jan
From mid-November until January, open-air ice-rinks pop up across the city, including one in the exquisite courtyard of Somerset House (p63; pictured above) and another one in the grounds of the Natural History Museum (p104).

🎁 Christmas Shopping   Dec
London has everything you could possibly want and more. Hamleys, with its five storeys of toys, will mesmerise children. Harrods will wow you with its extravagant window display and over-the-top decorations (and prices!). The festive atmosphere should put a spring in your step.

🎇 New Year's Celebrations   31 Dec
The famous countdown to midnight with Big Ben is met with terrific fireworks from the London Eye and massive crowds. There are parties in every pub and bar in town.

RAY WISE/GETTY IMAGES ©

🎁 Boxing Day   26 Dec
Boxing Day used to be the opening day of the winter sales and one of the busiest days of the year for shops. Pre-Christmas sales have somewhat dampened the rush but it remains a lively day.

Need to Know

Daily Costs

Budget
Less than £85

- Dorm bed: £10–32

- Market-stall lunch: £5; supermarket sandwich: £3.50–4.50

- Many museums: free

- Standby theatre tickets: £5–25

- Santander Cycles daily rental fee: £2

Midrange
£85–185

- Double room in a mid-range hotel: £90–160

- Two-course dinner with a glass of wine: £35

- Theatre ticket: £15–60

Top End
More than £185

- Four-star/boutique hotel room: £200

- Three-course dinner in a top restaurant with wine: £60–90

- Black cab trip: £30

- Top theatre ticket: £65

Advance Planning

Three months before Book weekend performances of top shows; make dinner reservations for renowned restaurants with celebrity chefs; snatch up tickets for must-see temporary exhibitions; book accommodation at boutique properties.

One month before Check listings for fringe theatre, live music and festivals on entertainment sites such as Time Out, and book tickets.

A few days before Check the weather on the Met Office website (www.metoffice.gov.uk).

Useful Websites

- **Lonely Planet** (www.lonelyplanet.com/london) Bookings, traveller forum and more.

- **Time Out London** (www.timeout.com/london) Up-to-date and comprehensive listings.

- **Londonist** (www.londonist.com) A website about London and everything that happens in it.

- **Transport for London** (www.tfl.gov.uk) Essential tool for staying mobile in the capital.

Currency
Pound sterling (£)

Language
English

Visas
Not required for US, Canadian, Australian, New Zealand or South African visitors for stays of up to six months. EU nationals can stay indefinitely for now (Brexit may change that).

Money
ATMs are widespread. Major credit cards are accepted everywhere. The best place to change money is in post office branches, which do not charge a commission.

Mobile Phones
Buy local SIM cards for European and Australian phones, or a pay-as-you-go phone. Set other phones to international roaming.

Time
London is on GMT; during British Summer Time (BST; late March to late October), London clocks are one hour ahead of GMT.

Tourist Information
Visit London (p232) can fill you in on everything you need to know.

When to Go

Summer is peak season: days are long and festivals are afoot, but expect crowds. Spring and autumn are cooler, but delightful. Winter is cold, but quieter.

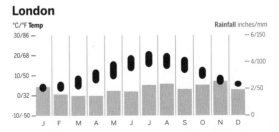

London

Arriving in London

Heathrow Airport Trains, London Underground (tube) and buses to central London from just after 5am to before midnight (night buses run later and 24-hour tube runs Friday and Saturday) £5.70 to £21.50; taxi £45 to £85.

Gatwick Airport Trains to central London from 4.30am to 1.35am £10 to £20; hourly buses to central London around the clock from £5; taxi £100.

Stansted Airport Trains to central London from 5.30am to 1.30am £23.40; round-the-clock buses to central London from £12; taxi from £130.

Luton Airport Trains to central London from 7am to 10pm from £14; round-the-clock buses to central London £10; taxi £110.

London City Airport DLR trains to central London from 5.30am to 12.30am Monday to Saturday, 7am to 11.15pm Sunday from £2.80; taxi around £30.

St Pancras International Train Station In central London (for Eurostar train arrivals from Europe) and connected by many Underground lines to other parts of the city.

Digital London

There are scores of cool apps for travellers. Here are some of our favourite free ones – from inspirational to downright practical. Many museums and attractions also have their own.

○ **Streetmuseum** Historical images (photographs, paintings, drawings etc) superimposed on modern-day locations.

○ **Street Art Tours London** Hand-picked graffiti and other street-art locations.

○ **Soho Stories** Social history of London's most bohemian neighbourhood, told through poems and extracts from novels and newspapers.

○ **CityMapper** The best app to work out how to get from A to B.

○ **Hailo** Summons the nearest black cab right to the curb.

○ **Uber** A taxi, private car or rideshare at competitive prices.

○ **London Bus Live** Real-time route finder and bus arrivals for a stop of your choice.

○ **Santander Cycles** Find a bike, a route and a place to return it.

Sleeping

Hanging your hat (and anything else you care to remove) in London can be painfully expensive and you'll almost always need to book your room well in advance. Decent, central hostels are easy enough to find and also offer reasonably priced double rooms. Bed and breakfasts are a dependable and inexpensive, if rather simple, option. Hotels range from cheap, no-frills chains through boutique choices to luxury five-star historic hotels.

For more, see the **Survival Guide** (p228).

Plan Your Trip
Top Days in London

EURASIA PRESS / GETTY IMAGES ©

The West End & the South Bank

Plunge into the heart of the West End for some of London's top sights. This itinerary also spans the River Thames to the South Bank, taking in Westminster Abbey, Buckingham Palace, Trafalgar Square, the Houses of Parliament and the London Eye.

❶ Westminster Abbey (p36)

Begin at Westminster Abbey to steep yourself in British history back to 1066.

⤷ Westminster Abbey to Buckingham Palace

🚶 Cross the road to Storey's Gate and walk west along Birdcage Walk.

❷ Buckingham Palace (p46)

Peer through the gates, go on a tour of the interior (summer only) or catch the Changing of the Guard at 11.30am.

⤷ Buckingham Palace to Cafe Murano

🚶 Stroll through St James's Park and across the Mall to St James's St.

❸ Lunch at Cafe Murano (p147)

In the heart of St James's, this busy restaurant cooks superb northern Italian fare.

⤷ Cafe Murano to Trafalgar Square

🚶 Walk along Jermyn St and down Haymarket to Trafalgar Square.

Day

FENLIOQ / SHUTTERSTOCK ©

❹ Trafalgar Square (p56)

Visit London's epicentre (all distances are measured from here) and explore the National Gallery (p54).

➲ Trafalgar Square to Houses of Parliament

🚶 Walk down Whitehall.

❺ Houses of Parliament (p50)

Dominating the east side of Parliament Sq is the Palace of Westminster, with one of London's ultimate sights, Big Ben.

➲ Houses of Parliament to London Eye

🚶 Cross Westminster Bridge.

❻ London Eye (p94)

Hop on a 'flight' on the London Eye. Pre-book tickets online or grab a fast-track ticket to shorten wait times.

➲ London Eye to Scootercaffe

🚶 Walk down to Waterloo station, cross the Leake St graffiti tunnel under the tracks and turn right on Lower Marsh.

❼ Drinks at Scootercaffe (p179)

Tucked behind Waterloo station, this atmospheric bar is perfect for winding down after traipsing across the city.

From left: Interior of Westminster Abbey (p36); London Eye (p94)

Plan Your Trip
Top Days in London

GAGLIARDIIMAGES / SHUTTERSTOCK©

History, Views & a Spot of Shakespeare

Get set for more of London's top sights – once again on either side of the Thames. Visit the British Museum in Bloomsbury, climb the dome of St Paul's Cathedral, explore the Tower of London and soak up some Shakespeare.

❶ British Museum (p42)

Begin with a visit to the British Museum and ensure you tick off the highlights, including the Rosetta Stone, the Egyptian mummies and the Parthenon Marbles.

➔ British Museum to St Paul's Cathedral

⊖ Take the Central Line from Holborn to St Paul's.

❷ St Paul's Cathedral (p86)

Enjoy a light lunch at Café Below (p145) before exploring the cathedral. Don't miss climbing the dome for its astounding views of London and save plenty of time for visiting the fascinating crypt.

➔ St Paul's Cathedral to Tower of London

🚌 Hop on bus 15 from the cathedral to the Tower of London.

❸ Tower of London (p64)

The millennium of history contained within the Tower of London, including the Crown Jewels, Traitors' Gate, the White Tower and its armour collection, and the all-important

Day

02

OLI SCARFF / GETTY IMAGES ©

resident ravens, deserves at least a couple of hours to fully explore.

🡒 Tower of London to Tower Bridge

🡅 Walk along Tower Bridge Approach from the Tower of London to Tower Bridge.

❹ Tower Bridge (p80)

Cross the Thames via elegant Tower Bridge. Check the website for bridge lift times if you want to see it open and close.

🡒 Tower Bridge to Oblix at the Shard

🡅 Stroll west along the river to the Shard; the entrance is on St Thomas St.

❺ Drinks at Oblix (p179)

Round off the day with drinks, live music and fabulous views of London from the 32nd floor of the Shard, London's most spectacular skyscraper.

🡒 Oblix at the Shard to Shakespeare's Globe

🡅 Walk through Borough Market and then follow the Thames west to Shakespeare's Globe.

❻ A Play at Shakespeare's Globe (p191)

Watch one of Shakespeare's famous plays in a theatre as it would have been in Shakespeare's day: outdoors in summer months in the Globe, or by candlelight in the Playhouse.

From left: Tower Bridge (p80); Shakespeare's Globe (p191)

Plan Your Trip
Top Days in London

Kensington Museums, Knightsbridge Shopping & the West End

Passing through some of London's most attractive and well-heeled neighbourhoods, this route takes in three of the city's best museums and a world-famous department store before delivering you to the bright lights of the West End.

Day 03

❶ Victoria & Albert Museum (p100)

Start your day in South Kensington, home to several of the best museums in the city. Cross off some of the Victoria & Albert's 146 galleries, but leave a little time for the huge Natural History Museum (p104) or the interactive Science Museum (p107).

➲ Victoria & Albert Museum to Kensington Gardens & Hyde Park

🚶 Walk north along Exhibition Rd to Kensington Gardens.

❷ Kensington Gardens & Hyde Park

Follow the museums with an exploration of Kensington Gardens (p99) and Hyde Park (p96). Make sure you take a look at the Albert Memorial (p99), take a peek inside Kensington Palace (p98) and stroll along the Serpentine.

➲ Kensington Gardens & Hyde Park to Magazine

🚶 Stroll through Hyde Park to Magazine, in the middle of the park by the Serpentine Sackler Gallery.

ANTHONY SHAW PHOTOGRAPHY / SHUTTERSTOCK ©

❸ Lunch at Magazine (p141)

Dine on lovely modern European food in the other-wordly undulating building designed by the late prize-winning architect Zaha Hadid. Afternoon tea is another great option.

➲ Magazine to Harrods

🏃 Walk down West Carriage Dr and then across Knightsbridge to reach Harrods.

❹ Harrods (p160)

A visit to Harrods is both fun and fascinating, even if you don't plan to buy anything. The food court is a great place for edible souvenirs.

➲ Harrods to Piccadilly Circus

🚇 Walk to Knightsbridge station, then take the Piccadilly Line three stops to Piccadilly Circus.

❺ Piccadilly Circus (p108)

Jump off the tube at this busy roundabout to have a look at the famous statue (Eros' brother) and enjoy a night out in Soho (p131).

➲ Piccadilly Circus to Yauatcha

🏃 Walk up Shaftesbury Ave and turn left onto Rupert St, which becomes Berwick St, then left into Broadwick St.

❻ Dinner at Yauatcha (p147)

For the most sophisticated and exquisite dim sum, Yauatcha is unrivalled. The selection of tea is second to none. Bookings are essential.

➲ Yauatcha to LAB

🏃 Turn right on Broadwick St, then right on Wardour St, then left on Old Compton St to Swift.

❼ Drinks at Swift (p181)

Ease further into the evening with drinks at this new cocktail bar.

From left: Hyde Park (p96); Statue of Anteros at Piccadilly Circus (p108)

Top Days in London

Greenwich to Camden

You don't want to neglect sights further afield and this itinerary makes a big dent in what's on offer. Lovely Greenwich has a whole raft of stately sights, while a visit to the East End and Camden will help to develop a feel for Londoners' London.

❶ Royal Observatory & Greenwich Park (p114)

Start the day in riverside Greenwich and make sure you visit Greenwich Park and the Royal Observatory, checking out the Cutty Sark (p117) clipper ship. A browse through Greenwich Market (p159) always turns up surprises.

➲ Greenwich Park & Royal Observatory to Tayyabs

🚌 & ⊖ Take the DLR from Cutty Sark station to Bow Church and change for the District or Hammersmith & City underground lines to Whitechapel.

❷ Lunch at Tayyabs (p139)

Dip into the multicultural East End with lunch at this classic Punjabi restaurant. After your meal, wander around Whitechapel, soaking up its atmosphere and visiting the ground-breaking Whitechapel Gallery (p72).

➲ Tayyabs to Old Spitalfields Market

🚶 Walk north from Whitechapel Rd up Osborn St and Brick Lane to Old Spitalfields Market.

ELENA ROSTUNOVA / SHUTTERSTOCK ©

❸ Old Spitalfields Market (p71)

Wander along Brick Lane and explore absorbing Georgian Spitalfields before browsing through Old Spitalfields Market. The best days for the market are Thursday, Friday and Sunday.

➲ Old Spitalfields Market to Worship St Whistling Shop

🚶 Walk west from the market along Spital Sq, then north up Bishopgate to Worship St.

❹ Worship St Whistling Shop (p175)

Sample the edgy, creative and offbeat Shoreditch atmosphere: drop in on this basement drinking den to try one of their curious cocktails (Undyed Bloodshed, anyone?).

➲ Worship St Whistling Shop to Market

🚇 Stroll to Old St station, then jump on a Northern Line tube to Camden Town.

❺ Dinner at Market (p143)

End the day in North London by dining on modern British cuisine at the excellent Market before turning to the riveting choice of local bars, pubs and live-music venues in this invigorating neighbourhood.

From left: View of Canary Wharf from Greenwich Park (p115); A stall at Old Spitalfields Market (p71)

Plan Your Trip
Hotspots For...

GLITZ & GLAMOUR

◉ **Buckingham Palace** Pomp, pageantry and a lot of gilded ceilings in the Queen's main residence. (p46)

☆ **Royal Opera House** Ballet or opera in the glittering surroundings of London's premier opera house. (p194)

☆ **Ronnie Scott's** Legendary jazz venue where all the big names have played. (p194)

🔒 **Harrods** Egyptian-themed elevator, stratospheric prices and opulent displays – it's London's most extravagant department store. (p160; pictured above)

🍷 **Dukes Bar** Drink where Ian Fleming of James Bond fame drank. (p179)

CULTURE VULTURES

◉ **V&A** Fashion, sculpture, jewellery, photography – there isn't a decorative art the V&A doesn't cover. (p100)

◉ **Royal Observatory** Learn how 18th-century luminaries solved the longitude problem and how GMT came to be. (p114; pictured below)

☞ **Thames River Services** Hop on a boat for a scenic and informative cruise about London's highlights. (p200)

✕ **Dinner by Heston Blumenthal** Splendid gastronomy blending traditional and experimental techniques. (p141)

🍷 **Draughts** Spend a night at London's first board-game bar – there are some 500 games to choose from. (p176)

HISTORY BUFFS

⊙ **Tower of London** From executions to the dazzling Crown Jewels, the Tower has seen it all. (p64)

⊙ **Westminster Abbey** Virtually every monarch has been crowned here since 1066, and many are also buried here. (p36)

🍷 **Ye Olde Mitre** One of the city's oldest pubs, with no music to spoil the drinking and chatting. (p174)

☞ **Guide London** Hire a Blue Badge guide for a tailor-made historical tour of the capital. (p200)

🍷 **Princess Louise** A Victorian stunner of fine tiles, etched mirrors and a horse-shoe bar. (p182)

BARGAIN HUNTERS

⊙ **Borough Market** All the free samples will easily make a starter – you can buy the mains from your favourite stall. (p76; pictured above)

⊙ **British Museum** Most museums of this calibre charge admission fees, but not this one. Tours are free too. (p42)

🍷 **Sky Pod** For the price of a coffee or cocktail, they throw in the panoramic views and tropical roof gardens. (p143)

🏠 **Burberry Outlet Store** Genuine Burberry, just 30% cheaper. (p159)

🏠 **Sunday UpMarket** Plenty of vintage stalls to browse for that unique piece. Happy haggling! (p158)

NIGHT OWLS

⊙ **Tate Modern** This outstanding modern art gallery opens until 10pm on Friday and Saturday nights. (p82; pictured above)

🍷 **XOYO** Regularly open until the small hours and one of the best clubs in town. (p174)

✕ **Brick Lane Beigel Bake** Whatever the time of day or night, this bagel shop will sort you out. (p71)

✕ **Duck & Waffle** Eating in style can now be done round the clock. (p145)

☆ **Comedy Store** The 11pm shows on Fridays and Saturdays are just as funny as the 8pm ones. (p194)

Plan Your Trip
What's New

EUGENE REGIS / SHUTTERSTOCK ©

Tate Modern Extension, Switch House

At long last, the Tate Modern (p82) can spread its expansive collection into Switch House. The views from the 10th floor are second to none (and free).

Fourth Plinth Gets Geopolitical

In 2018 artist Michael Rakowitz takes over the Fourth Plinth (p59) on Trafalgar Sq with *The Invisible Enemy Should Not Exist*, a recreation of a sculpture destroyed by Isis.

Architecture for Science

The Science Museum (p107) has unveiled its new mathematics gallery; its stunning look is courtesy of the late and much acclaimed architect Zaha Hadid.

Bigger & Better Design Museum

The Design Museum (p126; pictured above) moved to its new premises in Holland Park, West London, in November 2016. The building itself is a 1960s design icon and the museum has three times more space than in its previous location by the Thames.

Blue Whale Greetings at the Natural History Museum

In summer 2017 the Natural History Museum (p104) unveiled its new look Hintze Hall, the heart of the gallery, which is now spectacularly adorned by the plunging skeleton of a blue whale.

Plan Your Trip
For Free

Museums

The permanent collections of all state-funded museums and galleries are open to the public free of charge; temporary exhibitions cost extra.

Changing of the Guard

London's most famous open-air freebie, the Changing of the Guard in the forecourt of Buckingham Palace (p46) takes place at 11.30am from April to July (and alternate days, weather permitting, August to March). Alternatively, catch the changing of the mounted guard at Horse Guards Parade (p49) at 11am (10am on Sundays).

Houses of Parliament

When parliament (p50) is in session, it's free to attend and watch UK parliamentary democracy in action.

Concerts at St Martin-in-the-Fields

This magnificent church (p59) hosts free concerts at 1pm on Monday, Tuesday and Friday.

Walking in London

Walking around town is possibly the best way to get a sense of the city and its history. Try our walking tours: East End Eras, and Northern Point of View.

Architecture & Interiors

For one weekend in September, **Open House London** opens the doors to more than 700 buildings for free.

Best for Free

o National Gallery (p54; pictured above)

o British Museum (p42)

o Victoria & Albert Museum (p100)

o Natural History Museum (p104)

o Tate Modern (p82)

Plan Your Trip
Family Travel

KOTSOVOLOS PANAGIOTIS / SHUTTERSTOCK ©

Need to Know

º **Babysitters** Find a babysitter or nanny at Greatcare (www.greatcare.co.uk).

º **Cots** Available in most hotels, but always request them in advance.

º **Public transport** Under-16s travel free on buses, under-11s travel free on the tube, and under-5s ride free on trains.

Museums

London's museums are particularly child friendly. You'll find story telling at the National Gallery for children aged three years and over, arts-and-crafts workshops at the Victoria & Albert Museum, train-making workshops at the Transport Museum, plenty of finger-painting opportunities at the Tate Modern and Tate Britain, and performance and handicraft workshops at Somerset House. What's more, they're all free (check websites for details).

Other excellent activities for children include sleepovers at the British, Science and Natural History Museums, though you'll need to book months ahead. The last two are definitive children's museums, with interactive displays and play areas.

Other Attractions

Kids love the London Zoo, London Eye and London Dungeon. Ice rinks glitter around London in winter at the Natural History Museum and Somerset House. There's also a seasonal rink further afield at Hampton Court Palace.

In addition there are the exciting climbs up the dome of St Paul's Cathedral or the Monument and watching the performers in Trafalgar Square, Covent Garden Piazza or along the South Bank. Many arts and cultural festivals aimed at adults also cater for children. London's parks burst with possibilities: open grass, playgrounds, wildlife, trees and, in the warmer weather, ice-cream trucks.

Most attractions offer family tickets and discounted entry for kids under 15 or 16 years (children under five usually go free).

WILL RODRIGUES / SHUTTERSTOCK ©

Eating & Drinking with Kids

Most of London's restaurants and cafes are child friendly and offer baby-changing facilities and high chairs. Note that high-end restaurants and small, quiet cafes may be less welcoming, particularly if you have toddlers or small babies.

The one place that isn't traditionally very welcoming for those with children is the pub. By law, minors aren't allowed into the main bar (though walking through is fine), but many pubs have areas where children are welcome, usually a garden or outdoor space. Things are more relaxed during the day on Sunday.

Getting Around with Kids

When it comes to getting around, buses are better for children than the tube, which is often very crowded and hot in summer. As well as being big, red and iconic, buses in London are usually the famous double-decker ones; kids love to sit on the top deck and get great views of the city.

Best Activities for Kids

Natural History Museum (p104)

Changing of the Guard (p49)

Hamleys (p129)

Cutty Sark (p117)

Golden Hinde (p79)

Another excellent way to get around is simply to walk.

Hopping on a boat is another way to put fun (and sightseeing!) into getting from A to B.

From left: An animatronic T-rex in the Natural History Museum (p104); Changing of the Guard (p47)

TOP EXPERIENCES

The very best to see and do

Figure adorning the interior of Westminster Abbey

Westminster Abbey

Westminster Abbey is such an important commemoration site that it's hard to overstate its symbolic value or imagine its equivalent anywhere else in the world. With a couple of exceptions, every English sovereign has been crowned here since William the Conqueror in 1066, and most of the monarchs from Henry III (died 1272) to George II (died 1760) are buried here.

Great For...

🛈 Need to Know

Map p248; ☎020-7222 5152; www. westminster-abbey.org; 20 Dean's Yard, SW1; adult/child £20/9, verger tours £5, cloister & gardens free; ⏰9.30am-4.30pm Mon, Tue, Thu & Fri, to 7pm Wed, to 2.30pm Sat; ⊖Westminster

★ **Top Tip**

The abbey gets incredibly busy, even at opening, so come armed with patience.

There is an extraordinary amount to see at the Abbey. The interior is chock-a-block with ornate chapels, elaborate tombs of monarchs and grandiose monuments to sundry luminaries throughout the ages. First and foremost, however, it is a sacred place of worship.

A Regal History

Though a mixture of architectural styles, the Abbey is considered the finest example of Early English Gothic (1190–1300). The original church was built in the 11th century by King (later St) Edward the Confessor, who is buried in the chapel behind the sanctuary and main altar. Henry III (r 1216–72) began work on the new building, but didn't complete it; the French Gothic nave was finished by Richard II in 1388. Henry

VII's huge and magnificent Lady Chapel was added in 1519.

The Abbey was initially a monastery for Benedictine monks and many of the building's features attest to this collegial past (the octagonal Chapter House, the Quire and four cloisters). In 1536 Henry VIII separated the Church of England from the Roman Catholic Church and dissolved the monastery. The king became head of the Church of England and the Abbey acquired its 'royal peculiar' status, meaning it is administered directly by the Crown and exempt from any ecclesiastical jurisdiction.

North Transept, Sanctuary & Quire

Entrance to the Abbey is via the Great North Door. The North Transept is often referred to as Statesmen's Aisle: politicians

Exterior of Westminster Abbey

and eminent public figures are commemorated by large marble statues and imposing marble plaques.

At the heart of the Abbey is the beautifully tiled **sanctuary** (or sacrarium), a stage for coronations, royal weddings and funerals. George Gilbert Scott designed the ornate **high altar** in 1873. In front of the altar is the **Cosmati marble pavement** dating back to 1268. It has intricate designs of small pieces of marble inlaid into plain marble, which predicts the end of the world in AD 19,693. At the entrance to the lovely

GRZEGORZ FAKULA / SHUTTERSTOCK ©

Chapel of St John the Baptist is a sublime Virgin and Child bathed in candlelight.

The **Quire**, a magnificent structure of gold, blue and red Victorian Gothic by Edward Blore, dates back to the mid-19th century. It sits where the original choir for the monks' worship would have been, but bears no resemblance to the original. Nowadays, the Quire is still used for singing, but its regular occupants are the Westminster Choir – 22 boys and 12 'lay vicars' (men) who sing the daily services.

Chapels & Chairs

The sanctuary is surrounded by chapels. **Henry VII's Lady Chapel**, in the easternmost part of the Abbey, is the most spectacular, with its fan vaulting on the ceiling, colourful banners of the Order of the Bath and dramatic oak stalls. Behind the chapel's altar is the elaborate sarcophagus of Henry VII and his queen, Elizabeth of York.

Beyond the chapel's altar is the **Royal Air Force Chapel**, with a stained-glass window commemorating the force's finest hour, the Battle of Britain (1940), and the 1500 RAF pilots who died. A stone plaque on the floor marks the spot where Oliver Cromwell's body lay for two years (1658) until the Restoration, when it was disinterred, hanged and beheaded. Two bodies, believed to be those of the child princes allegedly murdered in the Tower of London in 1483, were buried here almost two centuries later in 1674.

There are two small chapels either side of Lady Chapel with the tombs of famous monarchs: on the left (north) is where **Elizabeth I** and her half-sister

✖ **Take a Break**

Part of the original 14th-century Benedictine monastery, **Cellarium** (Map p245; ☎020-7222 0516; www.benugo.com/restaurants/cellarium-cafe-terrace; Westminster Abbey, 20 Dean's Yard, SW1; mains £10.50-14.50; ☺8am-6pm Mon-Fri, 9am-5pm Sat, 10am-4pm Sun) has stunning views of the Abbey's architectural details.

Mary I (aka Bloody Mary) rest. On the right (south) is the tomb of **Mary Queen of Scots**, beheaded on the orders of her cousin Elizabeth.

The vestibule of the Lady Chapel is the usual place for the rather ordinary-looking **Coronation Chair**, upon which every monarch since the early 14th century has been crowned.

Shrine of St Edward the Confessor

The most sacred spot in the Abbey lies behind the high altar; access is generally restricted to protect the 13th-century flooring. St Edward was the founder of the Abbey and the original building was consecrated a few weeks before his death. His tomb was slightly altered after the original was destroyed during the Reformation, but it still contains Edward's remains – the only complete saint's body in Britain. Ninety-minute **verger-led tours** of the Abbey include a visit to the shrine.

Outer Buildings & Gardens

The oldest part of the cloister is the East Cloister (or East Walk), dating to the 13th century. Off the cloister are three museums. The octagonal **Chapter House** has one of Europe's best-preserved medieval tile floors and retains traces of religious murals on the walls. It was used as a meeting place by the House of Commons in the second half of the 14th century. To the right of the entrance to Chapter House is what is claimed to be the oldest door in Britain – it's been there for 950 years.

The adjacent **Pyx Chamber** is one of the few remaining relics of the original Abbey and holds the Abbey's treasures and liturgical objects. It contains the pyx, a chest with standard gold and silver pieces for testing coinage weights in a ceremony called the Trial of the Pyx.

Next door in the vaulted undercroft, the **Westminster Abbey Museum** (Map p248; www.westminster-abbey.org; Westminster Abbey; 10.30am-4pm; Westminster) exhibits the death masks of generations of royalty, wax

effigies representing Charles II and William III (who is on a stool to make him as tall as his wife, Mary II), armour and stained glass. Highlights include the graffiti-inscribed Mary Chair (used for the coronation of Mary II) and the Westminster Retable, England's oldest altarpiece, from the 13th century.

To reach the 900-year-old **College Garden** (Map p248; 10am-6pm Tue-Thu Apr-Sep, to 4pm Oct-Mar; Westminster), enter Dean's Yard and the Little Cloisters off Great College St.

South Transept & Nave

The south transept contains **Poets' Corner**, where many of England's finest writers are buried and/or commemorated by monuments or memorials.

Westminster Abbey seen from the cloister

In the nave's north aisle is **Scientists' Corner**, where you will find **Sir Isaac Newton's tomb** (note the putto holding a prism to the sky while another feeds material into a smelting oven). Just ahead of it is the north aisle of the Quire, known as **Musicians' Aisle**, where baroque composers Henry Purcell and John Blow are buried, as well as more modern music-makers such as Benjamin Britten and Edward Elgar.

The two towers above the west door are the ones through which you exit. These were designed by Nicholas Hawksmoor and completed in 1745. Just above the door, perched in 15th-century niches, are the additions to the Abbey unveiled in 1998: 10 stone statues of international 20th-century martyrs who died for their Christian faith. These include American pacifist Dr Martin Luther King, the Polish priest St Maximilian Kolbe, who was murdered by the Nazis at Auschwitz, and Wang Zhiming, publicly executed during the Chinese Cultural Revolution.

New Museum for 2018

In the works are the **Queen's Diamond Jubilee Galleries**, a new museum and gallery space located in the medieval triforium and due to open in 2018.

GIMAS / SHUTTERSTOCK ©

CLAUDIO DIVIZIA / SHUTTERSTOCK ©

British Museum

Britain's most visited attraction – founded in 1753 when royal physician Hans Sloane sold his 'cabinet of curiosities'– is an exhaustive and exhilarating stampede through 7000 years of human civilisation.

The British Museum offers a stupendous selection of tours, many of them free. There are 15 free 30- to 40-minute eyeOpener tours of individual galleries per day. The museum also has free daily gallery talks, a highlights tour (adult/child £12/free, 11.30am and 2pm Friday, Saturday and Sunday) and excellent multimedia iPad tours (adult/child £5/3.50), offering six themed one-hour tours and a choice of 35-minute children's trails.

Great Court

Covered with a spectacular glass-and-steel roof designed by Norman Foster in 2000, the Great Court is the largest covered public square in Europe. In its centre is the world-famous **Reading Room**, formerly the British Library, which has been frequented by all the big brains of history, from Mahatma Gandhi to Karl Marx. It is currently used for temporary exhibits.

Great For...

☑ **Don't Miss**

The Rosetta Stone, the Mummy of Katebet and the marble Parthenon sculptures.

Bust of Ramesses the Great

CHAMELEONSEYE / SHUTTERSTOCK ©

ℹ Need to Know

Map p254; ☏020-7323 8299; www.britishmu-seum.org; Great Russell St, WC1; ⏱10am-5.30pm Sat-Thu, to 8.30pm Fri; ⊖Russell Sq or Tottenham Court Rd FREE

✕ Take a Break

Just around the corner from the museum in a quiet, picturesque square is one of London's most atmospheric pubs, the Queen's Larder (p181).

> ### ★ Top Tip
> The museum is huge, so pick your interests and consider the free tours.

Ancient Egypt, Middle East & Greece

The star of the show here is the Ancient Egypt collection. It comprises sculptures, fine jewellery, papyrus texts, coffins and mummies, including the beautiful and intriguing **Mummy of Katebet** (room 63). The most prized item in the collection (and the most popular postcard in the shop) is the **Rosetta Stone** (room 4), the key to deciphering Egyptian hieroglyphics. In the same gallery is the enormous bust of the pharaoh **Ramesses the Great** (room 4).

Assyrian treasures from ancient Mesopotamia include the 16-tonne **Winged Bulls from Khorsabad** (room 10), the heaviest object in the museum. Behind it are the exquisite **Lion Hunt Reliefs from Ninevah** (room 10) from the 7th century BC, which influenced Greek sculpture. Such antiquities

are all the more significant after the Islamic State's bulldozing of Nimrud in 2015.

A major highlight of the museum is the **Parthenon sculptures** (room 18). The marble frieze is thought to be the Great Panathenaea, a blown-out version of an annual festival in honour of Athena.

Roman & Medieval Britain

Upstairs are finds from Britain and the rest of Europe (rooms 40 to 51). Many items go back to Roman times, when the empire spread across much of the continent, such as the **Mildenhall Treasure** (room 49), a collection of pieces of 4th-century Roman silverware from Suffolk with both pagan and early Christian motifs.

Lindow Man (room 50) is the well-preserved remains of a 1st-century man (comically dubbed Pete Marsh) discovered in a bog near Manchester in northern England in 1984. Equally fascinating are artefacts from the **Sutton Hoo Ship-Burial** (room 41), an elaborate Anglo-Saxon burial site from Suffolk dating back to the 7th century.

Perennial favourites are the lovely **Lewis Chessmen** (room 40), 12th-century game pieces carved from walrus tusk and whale teeth that were found on a remote Scottish island in the early 19th century. They served as models for the game of Wizard Chess in the first Harry Potter film.

Enlightenment Galleries

Formerly known as the King's Library, this stunning neoclassical space (room 1) was built between 1823 and 1827 and was the first part of the new museum building as it is seen today. The collection traces how disciplines such as biology, archaeology, linguistics and geography emerged during the Enlightenment of the 18th century.

What's Nearby?

Sir John Soane's Museum   Museum

(Map p245; www.soane.org; 13 Lincoln's Inn Fields, WC2; ⊙10am-5pm Tue-Sat & 6-9pm 1st Tue of month; ⊖Holborn) FREE This little museum is one of the most atmospheric and fascinating in London. The building is the beautiful, bewitching home of architect Sir John Soane (1753–1837), which he left brimming with surprising personal effects and curiosities; the museum represents his exquisite and eccentric taste.

Soane, a country bricklayer's son, is most famous for designing the Bank of England.

The heritage-listed house is largely as it was when Soane died and is itself a main part of the attraction. It has a canopy dome that brings light right down to the crypt, a colonnade filled with statuary and a picture

Great Court

gallery where paintings are stowed behind each other on folding wooden panes. This is where Soane's choicest artwork is displayed, including *Riva degli Schiavoni, looking West* by Canaletto, architectural drawings by Christopher Wren and Robert Adam, and the original *Rake's Progress*, William Hogarth's set of satirical cartoons of late-8th-century London lowlife. Among Soane's more unusual acquisitions are an Egyptian hieroglyphic sarcophagus, a mock-up of a monk's cell and slaves' chains.

Squares of Bloomsbury   Square

The Bloomsbury Group, they used to say, lived in squares, moved in circles and loved in triangles. **Russell Square** (Map p254; ⊖Russell Square) sits at the very heart of the district. It was originally laid out in 1800; a striking facelift a decade ago spruced it up and gave the square a 10m-high fountain. The centre of literary Bloomsbury was **Gordon Square** (Map p254; ⊖Russell Sq, Euston Sq), where some of the buildings are marked with blue plaques. Lovely **Bedford Square** (Map p254; ⊖Tottenham Court Rd) is the only completely Georgian square still surviving in Bloomsbury.

At various times, Bertrand Russell (No 57), Lytton Strachey (No 51) and Vanessa and Clive Bell, Maynard Keynes and the Woolf family (No 46) lived in Gordon Sq, and Strachey, Dora Carrington and Lydia Lopokova (the future wife of Maynard Keynes) all took turns living there at No 41.

Charles Dickens Museum   Museum

(Map p254; www.dickensmuseum.com; 48 Doughty St, WC1; adult/child £9/4; ⊙10am-5pm, last admission 4pm; ⊖Chancery Lane or Russell Sq) A £3.5 million renovation made this museum, located in a handsome four-storey house that was the great Victorian novelist's sole surviving residence in London, bigger and better than ever. The museum showcases the family drawing room (restored to its original condition), a period kitchen and a dozen rooms containing various memorabilia.

SONGQUAN DENG / SHUTTERSTOCK ©

ŁUKASZ PAJOR / SHUTTERSTOCK ©

Buckingham Palace

The palace has been the Royal Family's London lodgings since 1837, when Queen Victoria moved in from Kensington Palace as St James's Palace was deemed too old-fashioned.

Great For...

☑ Don't Miss

Peering through the gates, going on a tour of the interior (summer only) or catching the Changing of the Guard at 11.30am.

The State Rooms are only open in August and September, when Her Majesty is holidaying in Scotland. The Queen's Gallery and the Royal Mews are open year-round however.

State Rooms

The tour starts in the **Grand Hall** at the foot of the monumental **Grand Staircase**, commissioned by George IV in 1828. It takes in John Nash's Italianate **Green Drawing Room**, the **State Dining Room** (all red damask and Regency furnishings), the **Blue Drawing Room** (which has a gorgeous fluted ceiling by Nash) and the **White Drawing Room**, where foreign ambassadors are received.

The **Ballroom**, where official receptions and state banquets are held, was built between 1853 and 1855 and opened with

ℹ Need to Know

Map p248; ☏020-7766 7300; www.
royalcollection.org.uk; Buckingham Palace Rd,
SW1; adult/child/under-5 £21.50/12.30/free;
🕑9.30am-7.30pm late Jul–Aug, to 6.30pm
Sep; ⊖St James's Park, Victoria or Green Park

✕ Take a Break

During the summer months, you can
enjoy light refreshments in the **Garden
Café** on the Palace's West Terrace.

★ Top Tip

Come early for front-row views of the
Changing of the Guard.

a ball a year later to celebrate the end of
the Crimean War. The **Throne Room** is
rather anticlimactic, with his-and-hers pink
chairs initialled 'ER' and 'P', sitting under a
curtained theatre arch.

Picture Gallery & Garden

The most interesting part of the tour is
the 47m-long Picture Gallery, featuring
splendid works by such artists as Van Dyck,
Rembrandt, Canaletto, Poussin, Claude
Lorrain, Rubens, Canova and Vermeer.

Wandering the 18 hectares of gardens is
another highlight. You'll get beautiful views
of the palace and a peek of its famous lake;
you can also listen to the many birds and
admire some of the 350 species of flowers
and plants.

Changing of the Guard

At 11.30am daily from April to July (on
alternate days, weather permitting, for
the rest of the year), the old guard (Foot
Guards of the Household Regiment) comes
off duty to be replaced by the new guard on
the forecourt of Buckingham Palace.

Crowds come to watch the carefully
choreographed marching and shouting of
the guards in their bright-red uniforms and
bearskin hats. It lasts about 40 minutes
and is very popular, so arrive early if you
want to get a good spot.

Queen's Gallery

Since the reign of Charles I, the Royal
Family has amassed a priceless collection
of paintings, sculpture, ceramics, furniture
and jewellery. The splendid **Queen's Gal-
lery** (Map p248; www.royalcollection.org.uk;
Southern wing, Buckingham Palace, Buckingham
Gate, SW1; adult/child £10.30/5.30, with Royal
Mews £17.70/9.70; 🕑10am-5.30pm;

St James's Park, Victoria or Green Park) show-cases some of the palace's treasures on a rotating basis.

The gallery was originally designed as a conservatory by John Nash. It was converted into a chapel for Queen Victoria in 1843, destroyed in a 1940 air raid and reopened as a gallery in 1962. A £20-million renovation for Elizabeth II's Golden Jubilee in 2002 added three times as much display space.

Royal Mews

Southwest of the palace, the **Royal Mews** (Map p248; www.royalcollection.org.uk; Buckingham Palace Rd, SW1; adult/child £9.30/5.50, with Queen's Gallery £17.70/9.70; ⊙10am-5pm daily Apr-Oct, to 4pm Mon-Sat Nov-March; ⊖Victoria) started life as a falconry, but is now a working stable looking after the royals' three dozen immaculately groomed horses, along with the opulent vehicles – motorised and horse-driven – the monarch uses for transport. The Queen is well known for her passion for horses; she names every horse that resides at the mews.

Nash's 1820 stables are stunning. Highlights of the collection include the enormous and opulent Gold State Coach of 1762, which has been used for every coronation since that of George III; the 1911 Glass Coach used for royal weddings and the Diamond Jubilee in 2012; Queen Alexandra's State Coach (1893), used to transport the Imperial State Crown to the official opening of Parliament; and a Rolls-Royce Phantom VI from the royal fleet.

Royal Mews

What's Nearby?

St James's Park   Park

(Map p248; www.royalparks.org.uk; The Mall, SW1; deckchairs per hour/day £1.50/7; ☉5am-midnight, deckchairs daylight hours Mar-Oct; ⊖St James's Park or Green Park) At just 23 hectares, St James's is one of the smallest but best-groomed royal parks in London. It has brilliant views of the London Eye, Westminster, St James's Palace, Carlton Tce and the Horse Guards Parade; the sight of Buckingham Palace from the footbridge spanning the central lake is photo-perfect and the best you'll find.

> **❶ Did You Know?**
> The State Rooms represent a mere 19 of the palace's 775 rooms.

PUN_85 / SHUTTERSTOCK ©

Royal Academy of Arts   Gallery

(Map p248; www.royalacademy.org.uk; Burlington House, Piccadilly, W1; adult/child £10/6, prices vary for exhibitions; ☉10am-6pm Sat-Thu, to 10pm Fri; ⊖Green Park) Britain's oldest society devoted to fine arts was founded in 1768, moving to Burlington House exactly a century later. The collection contains drawings, paintings, architectural designs, photographs and sculptures by past and present Academicians such as Joshua Reynolds, John Constable, Thomas Gainsborough, JMW Turner, David Hockney and Norman Foster.

The famous **Summer Exhibition** (Map p248; Burlington House, Piccadilly, W1; ☉Jun–mid-Aug; ⊖Green Park), which has showcased contemporary art for sale by unknown as well as established artists for nearly 250 years, is the Academy's biggest annual event.

Horse Guards Parade   Historic Site

(Map p248; www.changing-the-guard.com/london-programme.html; Horse Guards Parade, off Whitehall, W1; ☉11am Mon-Sat, 10am Sun; ⊖Westminster or St James's Park) In a more accessible version of Buckingham Palace's **Changing of the Guard** (Map p248; www.royalcollection.org.uk; Buckingham Palace Rd, Buckingham Palace, SW1; ⊖St James's Park or Victoria), the mounted troops of the Household Cavalry change guard here daily, at the official vehicular entrance to the royal palaces. A slightly less pompous version takes place at 4pm when the dismounted guards are changed. On the Queen's official birthday in June, the Trooping the Colour is staged here.

> **❶ Did You Know?**
> At the centre of Royal Family life is the Music Room, where four royal babies have been christened – the Prince of Wales (Prince Charles), the Princess Royal (Princess Anne), the Duke of York (Prince Andrew) and the Duke of Cambridge (Prince William) – with water brought from the River Jordan.

DAN BRECKWOLDT / SHUTTERSTOCK ©

Houses of Parliament

Both the House of Commons and the House of Lords sit in the sumptuous Palace of Westminster, a neo-Gothic confection dating from the mid-19th century.

Great For...

☑ **Don't Miss**

Westminster Hall's hammer-beam roof, the Palace's Gothic Revival interior and Big Ben striking the hours.

Towers

The most famous feature of the Houses of Parliament is the Clock Tower, officially named Elizabeth Tower to mark the Queen's Diamond Jubilee in 2012, but commonly known as **Big Ben** (Map p248; ⊖Westminster). Ben is actually the bell hanging inside and is named after Benjamin Hall, the over-6ft-tall commissioner of works when the tower was completed in 1858. Ben has rung in the New Year since 1924.

At the base of the taller **Victoria Tower** at the southern end is the **Sovereign's Entrance**, which is used by the Queen.

Westminster Hall

One of the most stunning elements of the Palace of Westminster, the seat of the English monarchy from the 11th to the

Sculpture in the Palace of Westminster

KIEV VICTOR / SHUTTERSTOCK©

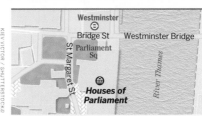

ⓘ Need to Know

Map p248; www.parliament.uk; Parliament Sq, SW1; ⊖Westminster FREE

✕ Take a Break

The **Jubilee Café** (10am-5:30pm Mon-Fri, to 6pm Sat) near the north door of Westminster Hall serves hot drinks and snacks.

★ Top Tip

There is airport-style security to enter the Houses of Parliament.

early 16th centuries, is Westminster Hall. Originally built in 1099, it is the oldest surviving part of the complex; the awesome hammer-beam roof was added around 1400. It has been described as 'the greatest surviving achievement of medieval English carpentry'. The only other part of the original palace to survive a devastating 1834 fire is the **Jewel Tower** (Map p248; ☎020-7222 2219; www.english-heritage.org.uk/visit/places/jewel-tower; Abingdon St, St James's Park, SW1; adult/child £4.70/2.80; ⊙10am-5pm daily Apr-Oct, 10am-4pm Sat & Sun Nov-Mar; ⊖Westminster), built in 1365 and used to store the monarch's valuables.

Westminster Hall was used for coronation banquets in medieval times and also served as a courthouse until the 19th century. The trials of William Wallace (1305), Thomas More (1535), Guy Fawkes

(1606) and Charles I (1649) all took place here. In the 20th century, monarchs and Sir Winston Churchill lay in state here after their deaths.

House of Commons

The **House of Commons** (Map p248; www.parliament.uk/business/commons; Parliament Sq, SW1; ⊙2.30-10pm Mon & Tue, 11.30am-7.30pm Wed, 10.30am-6.30pm Thu, 9.30am-3pm Fri; ⊖Westminster) is where Members of Parliament (MPs) meet to propose and discuss new legislation and to grill the prime minister and other ministers.

The layout of the Commons Chamber is based on St Stephen's Chapel in the original Palace of Westminster. The chamber, designed by Giles Gilbert Scott, replaced the one destroyed by a 1941 bomb.

Although the Commons is a national assembly of 650 MPs, the chamber has seating for only 437. Government members sit to the right of the Speaker and Opposition members to the left.

House of Lords

The **House of Lords** (Map p248; www.
parliament.uk/business/lords; Parliament Sq,
SW1; ⏱2.30-10pm Mon & Tue, 3-10pm Wed,
11am-7.30pm Thu, 10am-close of session Fri;
⊖Westminster) is visited via the amusingly
named Strangers' Gallery. The intricate
'Tudor Gothic' interior led its poor architect,
Augustus Pugin (1812–52), to an early
death from overwork and nervous strain.

Most of the 780-odd members of the
House of Lords are life peers (appointed
for their lifetime by the monarch); there
is also a small number – 92 at the time of
writing – of hereditary peers and a group of
'crossbench' members (numbering 179, not
affiliated to the main political parties), and
26 bishops.

Tours

On Saturdays year-round and on most
weekdays during Parliamentary recesses
including Easter, summer and Christmas,
visitors can join a 90-minute **guided tour**
(Map p248; ☏020-7219 4114; www.parliament.
uk/visiting/visiting-and-tours; adult/child
£25.50/11), conducted by qualified Blue
Badge Tourist Guides in seven languages, of
both chambers, Westminster Hall and other
historic buildings.

What's Nearby?

Tate Britain   Gallery
(www.tate.org.uk; Millbank, SW1; ⏱10am-6pm,
to 10pm 1st Fri of month; ⊖Pimlico) `FREE`
Splendidly refurbished with a stunning new
art-deco inspired staircase and a rehung
collection, the more elderly and venerable

Palace of Westminster

of the two Tate siblings celebrates paintings from 1500 to the present, with works from Blake, Hogarth, Gainsborough, Barbara Hepworth, Whistler, Constable and Turner, as well as vibrant modern and contemporary pieces from Lucian Freud, Francis Bacon, Henry Moore and Tracey Emin. Join free 45-minute **thematic tours** (⊘11am) and 15-minute **Art in Focus talks** (Millbank, SW1; ⊘1.15pm Tue, Thu & Sat). Audioguides (£3.50) are also available.

The star of the show at Tate Britain is, undoubtedly, the light-infused visions of JMW Turner. After he died in 1851, his es-

tate was settled by a decree declaring that whatever had been found in his studio – 300 oil paintings and about 30,000 sketches and drawings – would be bequeathed to the nation. The collection at the Tate Britain constitutes a grand and sweeping display of his work, including classics like *The Scarlet Sunset* and *Norham Castle, Sunrise*.

Tate Britain hosts the prestigious and often controversial Turner Prize for contemporary art from October to early December every year.

Churchill War Rooms   Museum

(Map p248; www.iwm.org.uk; Clive Steps, King Charles St, SW1; adult/child £17.25/8.60; ⊘9.30am-6pm, last entry 5pm; ⊜Westminster) Winston Churchill coordinated the Allied resistance against Nazi Germany on a Bakelite telephone from this underground military HQ during WWII. The Cabinet War Rooms remain much as they were when the lights were flicked off in 1945, capturing the drama and dogged spirit of the time, while the multimedia **Churchill Museum** affords intriguing insights into the resolute, cigar-smoking wartime leader.

No 10 Downing Street   Historic Building

(Map p248; www.number10.gov.uk; 10 Downing St, SW1; ⊜Westminster) The official office of British leaders since 1732, when George II presented No 10 to Robert Walpole, this has also been the prime minister's London residence since refurbishment in 1902. For such a famous address, No 10 is a small-looking Georgian building on a plain-looking street, hardly warranting comparison with the White House, for example. Yet it is actually three houses joined into one and boasts roughly 100 rooms plus a 2000-sq-metre garden with a lovely L-shaped lawn.

> **❶ Did You Know?**
>
> The House of Lords contains Lords Spiritual, linked with the established church, and Lords Temporal, who are both appointed and hereditary.

PATRYK KOSMIDER / SHUTTERSTOCK ©

> **★ Top Tip**
>
> When Parliament is in session, visitors are welcome to attend the debates in both houses. Enter via Cromwell Green Entrance. Expect queues.

JATIN GANDHI / SHUTTERSTOCK ©

National Gallery

With some 2300 European paintings on display, this is one of the world's richest art collections, including works by Leonardo da Vinci, Michelangelo, Titian, Van Gogh and Renoir.

The National Gallery's collection spans seven centuries of European painting displayed in sumptuous, airy galleries. All are masterpieces, but some stand out for their iconic beauty and brilliance. Don't overlook the astonishing floor mosaics in the main vestibule inside the entrance to the gallery.

Sainsbury Wing

The modern Sainsbury Wing on the gallery's western side houses paintings from 1250 to 1500. Here you will find largely religious paintings commissioned for private devotion, such as the *Wilton Diptych*, as well as more unusual masterpieces, such as Botticelli's *Venus & Mars* and Van Eyck's *Arnolfini Portrait*.

Great For...

☑ **Don't Miss**

Venus & Mars by Botticelli, *Sunflowers* by Van Gogh and *Rokeby Venus* by Velázquez.

Interior of the National Gallery

ℹ Need to Know

Map p248; www.nationalgallery.org.uk; Trafalgar Sq, WC2; ⊘10am-6pm Sat-Thu, to 9pm Fri; ⊖Charing Cross FREE

✕ Take a Break

The **National Dining Rooms** (Map p248; ☑020-7747 2525; www.peytonandbyrne.co.uk; 1st fl, Sainsbury Wing, National Gallery, Trafalgar Sq, WC2; mains £14.50-21.50; ⊘10am-5.30pm Sat-Thu, to 8.30pm Fri; 🛜; ⊖Charing Cross) have high-quality British food and splendid afternoon teas.

★ Top Tip

Take a free tour to learn the stories behind the gallery's most iconic works.

West Wing & North Wing

Works from the High Renaissance (1500–1600) embellish the West Wing where Michelangelo, Titian, Raphael, Correggio, El Greco and Bronzino hold court; Rubens, Rembrandt and Caravaggio grace the North Wing (1600–1700). Notable are two self-portraits of Rembrandt (age 34 and 63) and the beautiful *Rokeby Venus* by Velázquez.

East Wing

Many visitors flock to the East Wing (1700–1900), where they can see works by 18th-century British artists such as Gainsborough, Constable and Turner, and seminal Impressionist and post-Impressionist masterpieces by Van Gogh, Renoir and Monet.

Visiting

The comprehensive audio guides (£4) are highly recommended, as are the free one-hour taster tours that leave from the information desk in the Sainsbury Wing daily.

What's Nearby?

National Portrait Gallery   Gallery
(Map p248; www.npg.org.uk; St Martin's Pl, WC2; ⊘10am-6pm Sat-Wed, to 9pm Thu & Fri; ⊖Charing Cross or Leicester Sq) FREE What makes the National Portrait Gallery so compelling is its familiarity; in many cases you'll have heard of the subject (royals, scientists, politicians, celebrities) or the artist (Andy Warhol, Annie Leibovitz, Lucian Freud). Highlights include the famous 'Chandos' portrait of William Shakespeare, the first artwork the gallery acquired (in 1856) and believed to be the only likeness made during the playwright's lifetime, and a touching sketch of novelist Jane Austen by her sister.

Trafalgar Square

In many ways Trafalgar Sq is the centre of London, where tens of thousands congregate for anything from Christmas celebrations to political protests. The great square was neglected over many years, until a scheme was launched in 2000 to pedestrianise it and transform it into the kind of space John Nash had intended when he designed it in the 19th century.

Great For...

❶ Need to Know

Map p248; ⊖Charing Cross

★ **Top Tip**

Check www.london.gov.uk for events happening in the square during your stay, from street artists to open-air screens.

The Square

The square commemorates the 1805 victory of the British navy at the Battle of Trafalgar against the French and Spanish navies during the Napoleonic wars. The main square contains two beautiful fountains, which are dramatically lit at night. At each corner of the square is a plinth; three are topped with statues of military leaders and the fourth, in the northeast corner, is now an art space called the Fourth Plinth.

Note the much overlooked, if not entirely ignored, 19th-century brass plaques recording the precise length of imperial units – including the yard, the perch, pole, chain and link – set into the stonework and steps below the National Gallery (p55).

Nelson's Column

Standing in the centre of the square since 1843, the 52m-high Dartmoor granite Nelson's Column honours Admiral Lord Horatio Nelson, who led the fleet's heroic victory over Napoleon. The good (sandstone) admiral gazes down Whitehall toward the Houses of Parliament, his column flanked by four enormous bronze statues of lions sculpted by Sir Edwin Landseer and only added in 1867. The battle plaques at the base of the column were cast with seized Spanish and French cannons.

The Fourth Plinth

Three of the four plinths at Trafalgar Sq's corners are occupied by notables: King George IV on horseback and military men General Sir Charles Napier and Major

The Trafalgar Square Christmas tree

General Sir Henry Havelock. The fourth, originally intended for a statue of William IV, has largely remained vacant for the past 150 years (although some say it is reserved for an effigy of Queen Elizabeth II, on her death).

The Royal Society of Arts conceived the unimaginatively titled **Fourth Plinth Project** (Map p248; www.london.gov.uk/fourthplinth) in 1999, deciding to use the empty space for works by contemporary artists. They commissioned three works: *Ecce Homo* by Mark Wallinger (1999), a life-size statue of Jesus, which appeared

tiny in contrast to the enormous plinth; Bill Woodrow's *Regardless of History* (2000); and Rachel Whiteread's *Monument* (2001), a resin copy of the plinth, turned upside down.

The mayor's office has since taken over what's now called the Fourth Plinth Commission, continuing with the contemporary-art theme. In 2018 the plinth will be occupied by *The Invisible Enemy Should Not Exist*, by Michael Rakowitz, a recreation of a sculpture destroyed by Isis.

Admiralty Arch

To the southwest of Trafalgar Sq stands Admiralty Arch, from where the ceremonial Mall leads to Buckingham Palace. It is a grand Edwardian monument, a triple-arched stone entrance designed by Aston Webb in honour of Queen Victoria in 1910 and earmarked for transformation into a five-star hotel. The large central gate is opened only for royal processions and state visits.

What's Nearby?

St Martin-in-the-Fields   Church
(Map p248; ☎020-7766 1100; www.stmartin-in-the-fields.org; Trafalgar Sq, WC2; ◷8.30am-1pm & 2-6pm Mon, Tue, Thu & Fri, 8.30am-1pm & 2-5pm Wed, 9.30am-6pm Sat, 3.30-5pm Sun; ⊖Charing Cross) The 'royal parish church' is a delightful fusion of classical and baroque styles. It was completed by James Gibbs in 1726 and serves as a model for many churches in New England. The church is well known for its excellent classical music concerts, many by candlelight, and its links to the Chinese community (services in English, Mandarin and Cantonese). It usually closes for one hour at 1pm.

> ☑ **Don't Miss**
>
> Every year, Norway gives London a huge Christmas tree, which is displayed on Trafalgar Sq, to commemorate Britain's help during WWII.

DIEGO SHRUBERRY / SHUTTERSTOCK ©

> ✗ **Take a Break**
>
> Gordon's Wine Bar (p182) has a wonderful selection of wines and serves great platters of cheese and cold meats.

Covent Garden Piazza (p62)

Covent Garden

London's first planned square is now mostly the preserve of visitors, who flock here to shop among the quaint old arcades, enjoy the many street artists' performances or visit some of the excellent nearby sights.

Great For...

ⓘ Need to Know

Map p248; ⊖ Covent Garden

★ **Top Tip**

Covent Garden tube station gets unpleasantly busy at weekends – walk to Leicester Sq instead.

History

Covent Garden was originally pastureland that belonged to a 'convent' associated with Westminster Abbey in the 13th century. The site was converted in the 17th century by architect Inigo Jones, who designed the elegant Italian-style piazza, which was dominated by a fruit and vegetable market. The market remained here until 1974 when it moved to South London.

The Piazza

Covent Garden seems to heave whatever the time of day or night. The arcades are chock-a-block with boutiques, market stalls, cafes, ice-cream parlours and restaurants. They're a magnet for street artists too.

The streets around the piazza are full of top-end boutiques, including famous British designers. Covent Garden is also home to the Royal Opera House and a number of theatres.

Sights

London Transport Museum
Museum

(Map p248; www.ltmuseum.co.uk; Covent Garden Piazza, WC2; adult/child £17/free; ⊙10am-6pm Sat-Thu, 11am-6pm Fri; ⊖Covent Garden) This entertaining and informative museum looks at how London developed as a result of better transport. It contains everything from horse-drawn omnibuses, early taxis, underground trains you can drive yourself, a forward look at Crossrail (a high-frequency rail service linking Reading with east London, southeast

London Transport Museum

London and Essex, due to open in 2018), plus everything in between. Check out the museum shop for imaginative souvenirs, including historical tube posters and 'Mind the Gap' socks.

London Film Museum · Museum

(Map p248; www.londonfilmmuseum.com; 45 Wellington St, WC2; adult/child £14.50/9.50; ⊙10am-5pm; ⊖Covent Garden) Recently moved from County Hall, south of the Thames, this museum's star attraction is its signature *Bond in Motion* exhibition. Get shaken and stirred at the largest official collection of 007 vehicles, including Bond's submersible Lotus Esprit (*The Spy Who*

☑ Don't Miss

Clambering over old tramways at the London Transport Museum, and street artist performances.

GOGA18126 / SHUTTERSTOCK ©

Loved Me), the iconic Aston Martin DB5, Goldfinger's Rolls Royce Phantom III and Timothy Dalton's Aston Martin V8 (*The Living Daylights*).

Royal Opera House · Historic Building

(Map p248; ☎020-7304 4000; www.roh. org.uk; Bow St, WC2; adult/child general tours £9.50/7.50, backstage tours £12/8.50; ⊙general tour 4pm daily, backstage tour 10.30am, 12.30pm & 2.30pm Mon-Fri, 10.30am, 11.30am, 12.30pm & 1.30pm Sat; ⊖Covent Garden) On the northeastern flank of Covent Garden piazza is the gleaming Royal Opera House. The 'Velvet, Gilt & Glamour Tour' is a general 45-minute turn around the auditorium; more distinctive are the 1¼-hour backstage tours taking you through the venue – a much better way to experience the preparation, excitement and histrionics before a performance.

What's Nearby?

Somerset House · Historic Building

(Map p245; www.somersethouse.org.uk; The Strand, WC2; ⊙galleries 10am-6pm, Safra Courtyard 7.30am-11pm; ⊖Charing Cross, Embankment or Temple) Designed by William Chambers in 1775 for royal societies, Somerset House now contains two fabulous galleries. Near the Strand entrance, the **Courtauld Gallery** (Map p245; www. courtauld.ac.uk; Somerset House, The Strand, WC2; adult/child Tue-Sun £7/free, temporary exhibitions an additional £1.50; ⊙10am-6pm; ⊖Charing Cross, Embankment or Temple) displays a wealth of 14th- to 20th-century art, including masterpieces by Rubens, Botticelli, Cézanne, Degas, Renoir, Seurat, Manet, Monet, Léger and others. Downstairs, the Embankment Galleries are devoted to temporary (mostly photographic) exhibitions; prices and hours vary.

✕ Take a Break

Join the tons of noodle diners at Shoryu (p147) and try the *tonkotsu* ramen.

Tower of London

With a history as bleak as it is fascinating, the Tower of London is now one of the city's top attractions, thanks in part to the Crown Jewels.

Begun during the reign of William the Conqueror (1066–87), the Tower is in fact a castle containing 22 towers.

Tower Green

The buildings to the west and the south of this verdant patch have always accommodated Tower officials. Indeed, the current constable has a flat in Queen's House built in 1540. But what looks at first glance like a peaceful, almost village-like slice of the Tower's inner ward is actually one of its bloodiest.

Scaffold Site & Beauchamp Tower

Those 'lucky' enough to meet their fate here (rather than suffering the embarrassment of execution on Tower Hill, observed by tens of thousands of jeering and cheering onlookers) numbered but a handful

---

Great For...

☑ Don't Miss

The colourful Yeoman Warders (or Beefeaters), the spectacular Crown Jewels, the soothsaying ravens and armour fit for a king.

Royal Armouries, White Tower

ANTON_IVANOV / SHUTTERSTOCK ©

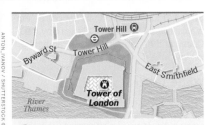

ⓘ Need to Know

Map p245; 📞0844 482 7777; www.hrp.org. uk/toweroflondon; Tower Hill, EC3; adult/child £25/12, audio guide £4/3; ⏱9am-5.30pm Tue-Sat, 10am-5.30pm Sun & Mon Mar-Oct, 9am-4.30pm Tue-Sat, 10am-4.30pm Sun & Mon Nov-Feb; ⊖Tower Hill

✕ Take a Break

The Wine Library (p145) is a great place for a light but boozy lunch opposite the Tower.

★ Top Tip

Book online for cheaper rates for the Tower.

and included two of Henry VIII's wives (and alleged adulterers), Anne Boleyn and Catherine Howard; 16-year-old Lady Jane Grey, who fell foul of Henry's daughter Mary I by attempting to have herself crowned queen; and Robert Devereux, Earl of Essex, once a favourite of Elizabeth I.

Just west of the scaffold site is brick-faced Beauchamp Tower, where high-ranking prisoners left behind unhappy inscriptions and other graffiti.

Chapel Royal of St Peter ad Vincula

Just north of the scaffold site is the 16th-century Chapel Royal of St Peter ad Vincula (St Peter in Chains), a rare example of ecclesiastical Tudor architecture. The church can be visited on a Yeoman Warder tour, or during the first and last hour of normal opening times.

Crown Jewels

To the east of the chapel and north of the White Tower is **Waterloo Block**, the home of the Crown Jewels, which are said to be worth up to £20 billion but are in a very real sense priceless. Here, you file past film clips of the jewels and their role through history, and of Queen Elizabeth II's coronation in 1953, before you reach the vault itself.

Once inside you'll be greeted by lavishly bejewelled sceptres, church plates, orbs and, naturally, crowns. A moving walkway takes you past the dozen or so crowns and other coronation regalia, including the platinum crown of the late Queen Mother, Elizabeth, which is set with the 106-carat Koh-i-Noor (Mountain of Light) diamond, and the State Sceptre with Cross topped with the 530-carat First Star of Africa (or Cullinan I) diamond. A bit further on, exhibited on its own, is the centrepiece: the Imperial State Crown, set with 2868 diamonds (including the 317-carat Second

Star of Africa, or Cullinan II), sapphires, emeralds, rubies and pearls. It's worn by the Queen at the State Opening of Parliament in May/June.

White Tower

Built in stone as a fortress in 1078, this was the original 'Tower' of London – its name arose after Henry III whitewashed it in the 13th century. Standing just 30m high, it's not exactly a skyscraper by modern standards, but in the Middle Ages it would have dwarfed the wooden huts surrounding the castle walls and intimidated the peasantry.

Most of its interior is given over to a **Royal Armouries** collection of cannon, guns and suits of mail and armour for men and horses. Among the most remarkable exhibits on the entrance floor are Henry VIII's two suits of armour, one made for him when he

was a dashing 24-year-old and the other when he was a bloated 50-year-old with a waist measuring 129cm. You won't miss the oversize codpiece. Also here is the fabulous **Line of Kings**, a late-17th-century parade of carved wooden horses and heads of historic kings. On the 1st floor, check out the 2m suit of armour once thought to have been made for the giant like John of Gaunt and, alongside it, a tiny child's suit of armour designed for James I's young son, the future Charles I. Up on the 2nd floor you'll find the block and axe used to execute Simon Fraser at the last public execution on Tower Hill in 1747.

Medieval Palace & the Bloody Tower

The Medieval Palace is composed of three towers: St Thomas's, Wakefield and Langthorn. Inside **St Thomas's Tower**

(1279) you can look at what the hall and bedchamber of Edward I might once have been like. Here, archaeologists have peeled back the layers of newer buildings to find what went before. Opposite St Thomas's Tower is **Wakefield Tower**, built by Edward's father, Henry III, between 1220 and 1240. Its upper floor is entered from St Thomas's Tower and has been even more enticingly furnished with a replica throne and other decor to give an impression of how it might have looked as an anteroom in

ALICE PHOTO / SHUTTERSTOCK ©

a medieval palace. During the 15th-century Wars of the Roses between the Houses of York and Lancaster, King Henry VI was murdered as (it is said) he knelt in prayer in this tower. A plaque on the chapel floor commemorates this Lancastrian king. The **Langthorn Tower**, residence of medieval queens, is to the east.

Below St Thomas's Tower along Water Lane is the famous **Traitors' Gate**, the portal through which prisoners transported by boat entered the Tower. Opposite Traitors' Gate is the huge portcullis of the Bloody Tower, taking its nickname from the 'princes in the Tower' – Edward V and his younger brother, Richard – who were held here 'for their own safety' and later murdered to annul their claims to the throne. An exhibition inside looks at the life and times of Elizabethan adventurer Sir Walter Raleigh, who was imprisoned here three times by the capricious Elizabeth I and her successor James I.

East Wall Walk

The huge inner wall of the Tower was added to the fortress in 1220 by Henry III to improve the castle's defences. It is 36m wide and is dotted with towers along its length. The East Wall Walk allows you to climb up and tour its eastern edge, beginning in the 13th-century **Salt Tower**, which was probably used to store saltpetre for gunpowder. The walk also takes in **Broad Arrow Tower** and **Constable Tower**, each containing small exhibits. It ends at the **Martin Tower**, which houses an exhibition about the original coronation regalia. Here you can see some of the older crowns, with their precious stones removed. It was from this tower that Colonel Thomas Blood attempted to steal the Crown Jewels in 1671 disguised as a clergyman. He was caught but – surprisingly – Charles II gave him a full pardon.

ℹ Local Knowledge

Over the years, the tower has served as a palace, an observatory, an armoury, a mint and even a zoo.

Yeoman Warders

A true icon of the Tower, the Yeoman Warders have been guarding the fortress since at least the early 16th century. There can be up to 40 – they number 37 at present – and, in order to qualify for the job, they must have served a minimum of 22 years in any branch of the British Armed Forces. They all live within the Tower walls and are known affectionately as 'Beefeaters', a nickname they dislike.

There is currently just one female Yeoman Warder, Moira Cameron, who in 2007 became the first woman to be given the post. While officially they guard the Tower and Crown Jewels at night, their main role is as tour guides. Free tours leave from the bridge near the entrance every 30 minutes; the last tour is an hour before closing.

What's Nearby?

All Hallows by the Tower   Church

(Map p245; ☎020-7481 2928; www.ahbtt. org.uk; Byward St, EC3; ⊘8am-5pm Mon-Fri, 10am-5pm Sat & Sun; ⊖Tower Hill) All Hallows (meaning 'all saints'), which dates to AD 675, survived virtually unscathed by the Great Fire, only to be hit by German bombs in 1940. Come to see the church itself, by all means, but the best bits are in the atmospheric undercroft (crypt), where you'll discover a pavement of 2nd-century Roman tiles and the walls of the 7th-century Saxon church.

Monument   Tower

(Map p245; www.themonument.org.uk; Junction of Fish Street Hill & Monument St, EC3; adult/child £4.50/2.30, incl Tower Bridge Exhibition £11/5; ⊘9.30am-6pm Apr-Sep, to 5.30pm Oct-Mar; ⊖Monument) Sir Christopher Wren's 1677 column, known simply as the Monument, is a memorial to the Great Fire of London of 1666, whose impact on London's history cannot be overstated. An immense Doric column made of Portland stone, the Monument is 4.5m wide and 60.6m tall – the exact distance it stands from the bakery in Pudding Lane where the fire is thought to have started.

The Monument is topped with a gilded bronze urn of flames that some think looks like a big gold pincushion. Although Lilliputian by today's standards, the Monument would have been gigantic when built, towering over London.

Climbing up the column's 311 spiral steps rewards you with some of the best 360-degree views over London (due to its central location as much as to its height). And after your descent, you'll also be the proud owner of a certificate that commemorates your achievement.

Leadenhall Market   Market

(Map p245; www.cityoflondon.gov.uk/things-to-do/leadenhall-market; Whittington Ave, EC3; ⊘10am-6pm Mon-Fri; ⊖Bank or Monument) A visit to this covered mall off Gracechurch St is a step back in time. There's been a mar-

All Hallows by the Tower

ket on this site since the Roman era, but the architecture that survives is all cobblestones and late-19th-century Victorian ironwork. Leadenhall Market appears as Diagon Alley in *Harry Potter and the Philosopher's Stone*; an optician's shop was used for the entrance to the Leaky Cauldron wizarding pub in *Harry Potter and the Goblet of Fire*.

30 St Mary Axe   Notable Building
(Gherkin; Map p245; www.30stmaryaxe.info; 30 St Mary Axe, EC3; ⊖Aldgate) Nicknamed 'the Gherkin' for its unusual shape, 30 St Mary Axe is arguably the City's most distinctive skyscraper, dominating the skyline despite actually being slightly smaller than the neighbouring NatWest Tower. Built in 2003 by award-winning Norman Foster, the Gherkin's futuristic exterior has become an emblem of modern London – as recognisable as Big Ben and the London Eye.

The building is closed to the public, though in the past it has opened its doors over the **Open House London** (☏020-7383 2131; www.openhouselondon.org.uk) weekend in September.

> ### ❶ Local Knowledge
> Common ravens, which once feasted on the corpses of beheaded traitors, have been here for centuries. Nowadays, they feed on raw beef and biscuits.

> ### ❶ Did You Know?
> Yeoman Warders are nicknamed Beefeaters. It's thought to be due to the rations of beef – then a luxury food – given to them in the past.

A stall at Old Spitalfields Market

ELENA ROSTUNOVA / SHUTTERSTOCK ©

A Sunday in the East End

The East End has a colourful and multicultural history. Waves of migrants (French Protestant, Jewish, Bangladeshi) have left their mark on the area, which, added to the Cockney heritage and the 21st-century hipster phenomenon, has created an incredibly vibrant neighbourhood.

Great For...

☑ **Don't Miss**

There is plenty of graffiti to admire in the area but if you'd like to see a famous Banksy artwork, make a small detour to **Cargo** (Map p245; www.cargo-london.com; 83 Rivington St, EC2A; ☺noon-1am Sun-Thu, to 3am Fri & Sat; ☺Shoreditch High St).

On Sundays, this whole area feels like one giant, sprawling market. It is brilliant fun, but pretty exhausting, so pace yourself – there are plenty of cafes and restaurants to sit down, relax and take in the atmosphere.

Columbia Road Flower Market

A wonderful explosion of colour and life, this weekly **market** (Map p253; www.columbiaroad.info; Columbia Rd, E2; ☺8am-3pm Sun; ☺Hoxton) sells a beautiful array of flowers, pot plants, bulbs, seeds and everything you might need for the garden. It's a lot of fun and the best place to hear proper Cockney barrow-boy banter ('We got flowers cheap enough for ya muvver-in-law's grave' etc).

The chimney of the Old Truman's Brewery building (p73)

CHRISDORNEY / SHUTTERSTOCK ©

Brick Lane Markets

Head south towards **Brick Lane Market** (Map p253; www.visitbricklane.org; Brick Lane, E1; ☺9am-5pm Sun; ⊖Shoreditch High St), which spills out into the surrounding streets with everything from household goods to bric-a-brac, secondhand clothes, cheap fashion and ethnic food. The best range and quality of products are to be found in the beautiful Old Truman Brewery's markets: Sunday UpMarket (p158) and Backyard Market (p158), where young designers sell their creations, along with arts and crafts and cracking food stalls.

Brick Lane's Famous Bagel

A relic of the Jewish East End, **Brick Lane Beigel Bake** (Map p253; 159 Brick Lane, E2; bagels £1-4.10; ☺24hr; ⊖Shoreditch High St)

❶ Need to Know

The area is at its best on Sundays, when the markets are in full swing.

✕ Take a Break

If you've worked up an appetite, Tayyabs (p139) does stupendous Pakistani food.

★ Top Tip

To avoid market overdose on a Sunday, choose between Brick Lane or Old Spitalfields Market.

still makes a brisk trade serving dirt-cheap homemade bagels (filled with salmon, cream cheese and/or salt beef).

Old Spitalfields Market

Traders have been hawking their wares here since 1638 and it's still one of London's best markets. Today's covered **market** (Map p253; www.oldspitalfieldsmarket.com; Commercial St, E1; ☺10am-5pm Mon-Fri & Sun, 11am-5pm Sat; ⊖Liverpool St) was built in the late 19th century, with the more modern development added in 2006. Sundays are the biggest and best days, but Thursdays are good for antiques and Fridays for independent fashion. There are plenty of food stalls, too.

Brick Lane Great Mosque

After lunch, walk over to this fascinating **mosque** (Brick Lane Jamme Masjid; Map p253; www.bricklanejammemasjid.co.uk; 59 Brick Lane, E1; ⊖Liverpool St). No building symbolises the different waves of immigration to Spitalfields quite as well as this one. Built in 1743 as the New French Church for the Huguenots, it was a Methodist chapel from 1819 until it was transformed into the Great Synagogue for Jewish refugees from Russia and central Europe in 1898. In 1976 it changed faiths yet again, becoming the Great Mosque. Look for the sundial, high up on the Fournier St frontage.

Whitechapel Gallery

From Brick Lane Mosque, continue on to **Whitechapel Gallery** (Map p245; ☎020-7522 7888; www.whitechapelgallery.org; 77-82 Whitechapel High St, E1; ☺11am-6pm Tue, Wed & Fri-Sun, to 9pm Thu; ⊖Aldgate East) **FREE**. A firm favourite of art students and the avant-garde *cognoscenti,* this ground-breaking gallery doesn't have a permanent collection, but is devoted to hosting edgy exhibitions of contemporary art. It made its name by staging exhibitions by both established and emerging artists, including the first UK shows by Pablo Picasso, Jackson Pollock, Mark Rothko and Frida Kahlo.

What's Nearby?

Geffrye Museum   Museum

(Map p253; www.geffrye-museum.org.uk; 136 Kingsland Rd, E2; ☺10am-5pm Tue-Sun; ⊖Hoxton) **FREE** If you like nosing around other people's homes, you'll love this museum, entirely devoted to middle-class domestic interiors. Built in 1714 as a home for poor pensioners, these beautiful ivy-clad almshouses have been converted into a series of living rooms, dating from 1630 to the present day. The rear garden is also organised by era, mirroring the museum's exploration of domesticity through the centuries. There's also a very impressive walled herb garden, featuring 170 different plants.

Columbia Road Flower Market (p70)

Dennis Severs' House   Museum

(Map p253; ☎020-7247 4013; www.
dennissevershouse.co.uk; 18 Folgate St, E1; day/
night £10/15; ⊙noon-2pm & 5-9pm Mon, 5-9pm
Wed & Fri, noon-4pm Sun; ⊖Liverpool St) This
extraordinary Georgian house is set up as if
its occupants had just walked out the door.
There are half-drunk cups of tea, lit candles
and, in a perhaps unnecessary attention
to detail, a full chamber pot by the bed.
More than a museum, it's an opportunity
to meditate on the minutiae of everyday
Georgian life through silent exploration.

> ### ⓘ Local Knowledge
> The area's food offering is as diverse
> as its population, from curry houses
> to modern British cuisine.

Old Truman Brewery   Historic Building

(Map p253; www.trumanbrewery.com; 91 Brick
Lane, E1; ⊖Shoreditch High St) Founded here
in the 17th century, Truman's Black Eagle
Brewery was, by the 1850s, the largest
brewery in the world. Spread over a series
of brick buildings and yards straddling both
sides of Brick Lane, the complex is now
completely given over to edgy markets,
pop-up fashion stores, vintage clothes
shops, indie record hunters, cafes, bars and
live-music venues. Beer may not be brewed
here any more, but it certainly is consumed.

After decades of decline, Truman's
Brewery finally shut up shop in 1989 –
temporarily as it turned out, with the brand
subsequently resurrected in 2010 in new
premises in Hackney Wick. In the 1990s the
abandoned brewery premises found new
purpose as a deadly cool hub for boozy
Britpoppers and while it may not have
quite the same cachet today, it's still plenty
popular.

Several of the buildings are heritage
listed, including the Director's House at 91
Brick Lane (built in the 1740s); the old Vat
House directly opposite, with its hexagonal
bell tower (c 1800); and the Engineer's
House right next to it (at 150 Brick Lane),
dating from the 1830s.

DAVID BURROWS / SHUTTERSTOCK ©

✗ Take a Break

In the evening, check out **93 Feet East**
(Map p245; www.93feeteast.co.uk; 150
Brick Lane, E1; ⊙5-11pm Thu, to 1am Fri &
Sat, 3-10.30pm Sun; ⊖Liverpool St) on Brick
Lane for DJs and cocktails.

Walking Tour: East End Eras

This route offers an insight into the old and new of East London. Wander through and soak up the unique character of its neighbourhoods.

Start ⊖ Bethnal Green
Distance 3.6 miles
Duration 2½ hours

2 On beautifully preserved **Cyprus St** you'll get a taste of what Victorian Bethnal Green would have looked like.

1 The **Old Ford Rd** area was bombed during WWII and tower blocks were subsequently erected on the bomb sites.

3 Just over Regent's Canal lies **Victoria Park**. Take the left path along the lake to the **Dogs of Alcibiades** howling on plinths.

5 Cross Cadogan Tce and pick up the much-graffitied **canal path**; this area is artistic **Hackney Wick**.

6 Cross the canal at the hooped footbridge, follow Roach Rd, then turn left to cross the bridge and enter **Queen Elizabeth Olympic Park**.

Take a Break...
Formans (p139) smokes fish on its premises and serves it in a stunning, panoramic dining room.

Classic photo: The ArcelorMittal Orbit at Queen Elizabeth Park

4 Head to the eastern section of the park and see the **Burdett-Coutts Memorial** drinking fountain (1862). Then, pass **East Lake** and exit at the park's eastern tip.

7 Keep the main stadium on your right, cross the River Lea and walk through the playground towards the **ArcelorMittal Orbit**.

Fresh fruit on display at a Borough Market stall

Borough Market

Overflowing with food lovers, inveterate gastronomes, wide-eyed visitors and Londoners in search of inspiration for their next dinner party, this fantastic market has become a sight in its own right.

Great For...

ℹ Need to Know

Map p245; www.boroughmarket.org.uk; 8 Southwark St, SE1; ⏱10am-5pm Wed & Thu, 10am-6pm Fri, 8am-5pm Sat; ⊖London Bridge

★ **Top Tip**

To avoid the worst of the crowds, avoid lunch times on Friday and Saturday.

Located here in some form or another since the 13th century, 'London's Larder' has enjoyed an astonishing renaissance in the past 15 years.

The market specialises in high-end fresh products, so you'll find the usual assortment of fruit and vegetable stalls, cheesemongers, butchers, fishmongers, bakeries and delis, as well as gourmet stalls selling spices, nuts, preserves and condiments. Prices tend to be high, but many traders offer free samples, a great perk for visitors and locals alike.

Food window-shopping (and sampling) over, you'll be able to grab lunch from one of the myriad takeaway stalls – anything from sizzling gourmet sausages to chorizo sandwiches and falafel wraps. There also seems to be an unreasonable number of cake stalls – walking out without a treat

will be a challenge! Many of the lunch stalls cluster in Green Market (the area closest to Southwark Cathedral). If you'd rather eat indoors, there are some fantastic cafes and restaurants, too.

If you'd like some elbow space to enjoy your takeaway, walk five minutes in either direction along the Thames for river views.

Note that although the full market runs from Wednesday to Saturday, some traders and takeaway stalls do open Mondays and Tuesdays.

What's Nearby?
Southwark Cathedral Church
(Map p245; ☎020-7367 6700; www.cathedral.
southwark.anglican.org; Montague CI, SE1;
☺8am-6pm Mon-Fri, 8.30am-6pm Sat & Sun;
☻London Bridge) The earliest surviving
parts of this relatively small cathedral are

Cupcakes and macaroons for sale at Borough Market

the retrochoir at the eastern end – which contains four chapels and was part of the 13th-century Priory of St Mary Overie – some ancient arcading by the southwest door and an arch that dates to the original Norman church. But most of the cathedral is Victorian. Inside are monuments galore, including a Shakespeare memorial. Catch evensong at 5.30pm on Tuesdays, Thursdays and Fridays, 4pm on Saturdays and 3pm on Sundays.

Shard   Notable Building
(Map p245; www.theviewfromtheshard.com; 32 London Bridge St, SE1; adult/child £30.95/24.95; ☺10am-10pm; ⊜London Bridge) Puncturing

> ☑ **Don't Miss**
> Grazing on the free samples or eating takeaway by the river.

the skies above London, the dramatic splinter like form of the Shard has rapidly become an icon of London. The viewing platforms on floors 68, 69 and 72 are open to the public and the views are, as you'd expect from a 244m vantage point, sweeping, but they come at a hefty price – book online at least a day in advance to save £5.

HMS Belfast   Ship
(Map p245; www.iwm.org.uk/visits/hms-belfast; Queen's Walk, SE1; adult/child £14.50/7.25; ☺10am-5pm; ⊜London Bridge) HMS *Belfast* is a magnet for naval-gazing kids of all ages. This large, light cruiser – launched in 1938 – served in WWII, helping to sink the German battleship *Scharnhorst* and shelling the Normandy coast on D-Day, and later participated in the Korean War. Her 6in guns could bombard a target 14 land miles distant. Displays offer a great insight into what life on board was like, in peace times and during military engagements.

Golden Hinde   Ship
(Map p245; ☎020-7403 0123; www.goldenhinde.com; St Mary Overie Dock, Cathedral St, SE1; self-guided tours adult/child £6/4.50, events adult/child £7/5; ☺10am-5.30pm; ⛐; ⊜London Bridge) Stepping aboard this replica of Sir Francis Drake's famous Tudor ship will inspire genuine admiration for the admiral and his rather short (average height: 1.6m) crew, which counted between 40 and 60. It was in a tiny five-deck galleon just like this that Drake and his crew circumnavigated the globe from 1577 to 1580. Visitors can explore the ship by themselves or join a guided tour led by a costumed actor – children love these.

✕ Take a Break
Arabica Bar & Kitchen (p145) serves up contemporary Middle Eastern fare.

MAPICS / SHUTTERSTOCK ©

Tower Bridge

One of London's most familiar sights, Tower Bridge doesn't disappoint up close. There's something about its neo-Gothic towers and blue suspension struts that makes it quite enthralling.

Great For...

☑ Don't Miss

The bridge lifting and the view from the top (as well as down through the new glass floor).

History & Mechanics

Built in 1894 by Horace Jones (who designed many of London's markets) as a much-needed crossing point in the east, Tower Bridge was equipped with a then-revolutionary bascule (see-saw) mechanism that could clear the way for oncoming ships in just three minutes. Although London's days as a thriving port are long over, the bridge still does its stuff, lifting largely for pleasure craft around 1000 times a year.

Tower Bridge Exhibition

Housed within is the **Tower Bridge Exhibition** (Map p245; ☎020-7403 3761; www.towerbridge.org.uk; Tower Bridge, SE1; adult/child £9/3.90, incl Monument £11/5; ⊘10am-6pm Apr-Sep, 9.30am-5.30pm Oct-Mar, last admission 30min before closing; ⊖Tower Hill), which

City Hall

PAJOR PAWEL / SHUTTERSTOCK ©

❶ Need to Know

Map p245; ⊖Tower Hill

✕ Take a Break

The Watch House (p146), on the South Bank, sells fabulous sandwiches and cakes from local bakers. It does great coffee too.

★ Top Tip

For the best views of the bridge, pop over to the southern bank of the river.

---

explains the nuts and bolts of it all. If you're not technically minded, it's still fascinating to get inside the bridge and look along the Thames from its two walkways. A lift takes you to the top of the structure, 42m above the river, from where you can walk along the east- and west-facing walkways, lined with information boards.

The 11m-long glass floor, made of a dozen see-through panels, is stunning – acrophobes can take solace in knowing that each weighs a load-bearing 530kg. There are a couple of stops on the way down before you exit and continue on to the **Victorian Engine Rooms**, which house the beautifully maintained steam engines that powered the bridge lifts, as well as some excellent interactive exhibits and a couple of short films.

What's Nearby?

City Hall   Notable Building

(Map p245; www.london.gov.uk/city-hall; Queen's Walk, SE1; ⏰8.30am-5.30pm Mon-Fri; ⊖London Bridge) Home to the Mayor of London, bulbous City Hall was designed by Foster and Partners and opened in 2002. The 45m, glass-clad building has been compared to a host of objects – from an onion, to Darth Vader's helmet, a woodlouse and a 'glass gonad'. The scoop amphitheatre outside the building is the venue for a variety of free entertainment in warmer weather, from music to theatre. Parts of the building are open to the public on weekdays.

Tate Modern

This phenomenally successful gallery combines stupendous architecture and a seminal collection of 20th-century modern art. A huge extension opened in summer 2016, dramatically increasing its display space.

Great For...

ⓘ Need to Know

Map p245; www.tate.org.uk; Bankside, SE1; ⓒ10am-6pm Sun-Thu, to 10pm Fri & Sat; ⊛; ⊖Blackfriars, Southwark or London Bridge FREE

★ Top Tip

Take the **Tate Boat** (Map p245; www.
tate.org.uk/visit/tate-boat; one-way adult/
child £8/4) **shuttle between Tate Britain
(p52) and Tate Modern.**

Boiler House

The original gallery lies in what was once Bankside Power Station. Now called Boiler House, it is an imposing sight: a 200m-long building, made of 4.2 million bricks. Its conversion into an art gallery was a masterstroke of design.

Turbine Hall

The first thing to greet you as you pour down the ramp off Holland St (the main entrance) is the astounding 3300-sq-metre Turbine Hall. Originally housing the power station's humongous electricity generators, this vast space has become the commanding venue for large-scale installation art and temporary exhibitions.

Switch House

The new Tate Modern extension got its name from the former electrical substation that still occupies the southeast end of the site. To echo its sister building, it is also constructed of brick, although these are slightly lighter and artistically laid out as a lattice to let light in (and out – the building looks stunning after dark).

The Tanks

The three huge subterranean tanks once stored fuel for the power station. These unusual circular spaces are now dedicated to showing live art, performance, installation and film, or 'new art' as the Tate calls it.

Viewing Gallery: Level 10

The views from level 10 are, as you would expect, sweeping. The river views are per-

Switch House

haps not quite as iconic as the full frontal St Paul's view you get from Boiler House, but you get to see Boiler House itself, and a lot more in every direction. The views of the Shard looking east are especially good. And best of all, they are free.

Permanent Collection

Tate Modern's permanent collection is arranged on levels 2 and 4 of Boiler House and levels 0, 2, 3 and 4 of Switch House. The emphasis in the latter is on art from the 1960s onwards.

☑ Don't Miss

Turbine Hall, special exhibitions, the view of St Paul's from the Level 3 balconies of Boiler House and the Viewing Gallery on Level 10 of Switch House.

JANSOS / ALAMY STOCK PHOTO ©

More than 60,000 works are on constant rotation. The curators have at their disposal paintings by Georges Braque, Henri Matisse, Piet Mondrian, Andy Warhol, Mark Rothko and Jackson Pollock, as well as pieces by Joseph Beuys, Damien Hirst, Rebecca Horn, Claes Oldenburg and Auguste Rodin.

A great place to start is the **Start Display** on level 2 of Boiler House: this small, specially curated 'taster' display features some of the best-loved works in the collection and gives visitors useful pointers for how to go about tackling unfamiliar (and an overwhelming amount of) art.

Special Exhibitions

With the opening of Switch House, the Tate Modern has increased the number of special exhibitions it hosts. You will find them on levels 3 and 4 of Boiler House and level 2 of Switch House; all are subject to an admission charge (£12.50 to £18.50; children go free). Blockbusters to look forward to in 2018 include a retrospective on Amedeo Modigliani and an exhibition looking at Picasso in 1932, a pivotal year for the artist.

What's Nearby?

Shakespeare's Globe　　　　　　Historic Building

(Map p245; www.shakespearesglobe.com; 21 New Globe Walk, SE1; adult/child £16/9; ⊙9am-5pm; ⛵; ⊖Blackfriars or London Bridge) Unlike other venues for Shakespearean plays, the new Globe was designed to resemble the original as closely as possible, which means having the arena open to the fickle London skies, leaving the 700 'groundlings' to stand in London's spectacular downpours. Visits to the Globe include tours of the theatre (half-hourly, generally in the morning from 9.30am, with afternoon tours on Monday too) as well as access to the exhibition space, which has fascinating exhibits about Shakespeare and theatre in the 17th century.

✕ Take a Break

Enjoy a taste of Eastern Europe at the exquisite Baltic (p145).

St Paul's Cathedral

St Paul's Cathedral is one of the most majestic buildings in London. Despite the far higher skyscrapers of the Square Mile, it still manages to gloriously dominate the skyline.

Great For...

❶ Need to Know

Map p245; ☎020-7246 8350; www.stpauls.co.uk; St Paul's Churchyard, EC4; adult/child £18/8; ⊙8.30am-4.30pm Mon-Sat; ⊖St Paul's

★ **Top Tip**

A visit to the church's hallowed ground must be made to fully appreciate its sublime architecture.

There has been a place of Christian worship on this site for over 1400 years. St Paul's Cathedral as we know it is the fifth Christian church to be erected here; it was completed in 1711 and sports the largest church dome in the capital.

Dome

Despite the cathedral's rich history and impressive (and uniform) English baroque interior, many visitors are more interested in climbing the dome for one of the best views of London. It actually consists of three parts: a plastered brick inner dome, a nonstructural lead outer dome visible on the skyline and a brick cone between them holding it all together, one inside the other. This unique structure, the first triple dome ever built and second only in size to St Peter's in the Vatican, made the cathedral Christopher Wren's tour de force. It all weighs 59,000 tonnes.

Some 528 stairs take you to the top, but it's a three-stage journey. Through a door on the western side of the southern transept, and some 30m and 257 steps above, you reach the interior walkway around the dome's base. This is the **Whispering Gallery**, so called because if you talk close to the wall it carries your words around to the opposite side, 32m away. Climbing even more steps (another 119) you reach the **Stone Gallery**, an exterior viewing platform 53m above the ground, obscured by pillars and other suicide-preventing measures. The remaining 152 iron steps to the **Golden Gallery** are steeper and narrower than below, but are really worth the effort. From here, 85m above London, you can enjoy superb 360-degree views of the city.

Interior dome of St Paul's Cathedral

Interior

Just beneath the dome is an **epitaph** written for Wren by his son: *Lector, si monumentum requiris, circumspice* (Reader, if you seek his monument, look around you). In the north aisle you'll find the grandiose **Duke of Wellington Memorial** (1912), which took 54 years to complete – the Iron Duke's horse Copenhagen originally faced the other way, but it was deemed unfitting that a horse's rear end should face the altar.

In the north transept chapel is William Holman Hunt's celebrated painting **The Light of the World**, which depicts Christ knocking at a weed-covered door that, symbolically, can only be opened from within. Beyond, in the cathedral's heart, you'll find the spectacular **quire** (or chancel) – its ceilings and arches dazzling with green, blue, red and gold mosaics telling the story of creation – and the **high altar**. The ornately carved choir stalls by Dutch–British sculptor Grinling Gibbons on either side of the quire are exquisite, as are the ornamental wrought-iron gates, separating the aisles from the altar, by Huguenot Jean Tijou (both men also worked on Hampton Court Palace).

Walk around the altar, with its massive gilded oak **baldacchino** – a kind of canopy with barley-twist columns – to the **American Memorial Chapel**, commemorating the 28,000 Americans based in Britain who lost their lives during WWII. Note the Roll of Honour book turned daily, the state flags in the stained glass and American flora and fauna in the carved wood panelling.

In the south quire aisle, Bill Viola's new and very poignant **video installation** *Martyrs (Earth, Air, Fire, Water)* depicts four figures being overwhelmed by natural forces. A bit further on is an **effigy of John Donne** (1573–1631), metaphysical poet and one-time dean of Old St Paul's that survived the Great Fire.

Crypt

On the eastern side of both the north and south transepts are stairs leading down to the crypt and the **OBE Chapel**, where services are held for members of the Order of the British Empire. The crypt has memorials to around 300 of the great and the good, including Florence Nightingale,

---

☑ Don't Miss

Climbing the dome, witnessing the quire ceiling mosaics and visiting the tombs of Admiral Nelson and the Duke of Wellington.

EUGENE REGIS / SHUTTERSTOCK ©

✕ Take a Break

The **Crypt Cafe** (Map p245; Crypt, St Paul's Cathedral, EC4; dishes £5.65-8.25; ◷9am-5pm Mon-Sat, 10am-4pm Sun; ◉St Paul's) is open for light meals from 9am.

TE Lawrence (of Arabia) and Winston Churchill, while both the Duke of Wellington and Admiral Nelson are actually buried here. On the surrounding walls are plaques in memory of those from the Commonwealth who died in various conflicts during the 20th century, including Gallipoli and the Falklands War.

Wren's tomb is also in the crypt, and many others, notably painters such as Joshua Reynolds, John Everett Millais, JMW Turner and William Holman Hunt, are remembered here, too.

The **Oculus**, in the former treasury, projects four short films onto its walls (you'll need the iPad audio tour to hear the sound). If you're not up to climbing the dome, experience it here audiovisually.

Exterior

Just outside the north transept, there's a simple **monument to the people of London**, honouring the 32,000 civilians killed (and another 50,000 seriously injured) in the city during WWII. Also to the north, at the entrance to Paternoster Sq, is **Temple Bar**, one of the original gateways to the City of London. This medieval stone archway once straddled Fleet St at a site marked by a silver dragon, but was removed to Middlesex in 1877. It was placed here in 2004.

Tours

The easiest way to explore the cathedral is by joining a free 1½-hour guided tour, which grants you access to the Geometric Staircase, the Chapel of St Michael and St George, and the quire. These usually take place four times a day (10am, 11am, 1pm and 2pm) Monday to Saturday – head to the desk just past the entrance to check times and book a place. You can also enquire here about the shorter introductory 15- to 20-minute talks.

What's Nearby?

Museum of London Museum

(Map p245; www.museumoflondon.org.uk; 150 London Wall, EC2; ⊗10am-6pm; ⊖Barbican) FREE One of the capital's best museums, this is a fascinating walk through the various incarnations of the city, from Roman Londinium and Anglo-Saxon Ludenwic to 21st-century metropolis, contained in two-dozen galleries. There are a lot of interactive displays with an emphasis on experience rather than learning.

Highlights include a video on the 1348 Black Death, a section of London's old Roman wall, the graffitied walls of a prison cell (1750), a glorious re-creation of a Victorian street, a 1908 taxi cab, a 1928 art-deco lift from Selfridges and moving WWII testimonies from ordinary Londoners.

Interior of St Paul's Cathedral

Free half-hour highlights tours depart daily at 11am, noon, 3pm and 4pm.

Millennium Bridge   Bridge

(Map p245; St Paul's or Blackfriars) The elegant steel, aluminium and concrete Millennium Bridge staples the south bank of the Thames, in front of Tate Modern, to the north bank, at the steps of Peter's Hill below St Paul's Cathedral. The low-slung frame designed by Sir Norman Foster and Antony Caro looks spectacular, particularly when lit up at night with fibre optics, and the view of St Paul's from the South Bank has become one of London's iconic images.

St Mary-le-Bow   Church

(Map p245; 020-7248 5139; www. stmarylebow.co.uk; Cheapside, EC2; 7.30am-6pm Mon-Wed, to 6.30pm Thu, to 4pm Fri; St Paul's, Bank) One of Wren's great churches,

St Mary-le-Bow (1673) is famous as the church with the bells that still dictate who is – and who is not – a true Cockney: it's said that a true Cockney has to have been born within earshot of Bow Bells. The church's delicate steeple showing the four classical orders is one of Wren's finest works.

❶ Local Knowledge

The cathedral underwent a major clean-up in 2011. To see the difference, check the section of unrestored wall under glass by the Great West Door.

★ Top Tip

If you'd rather explore on your own, pick up one of the free 1½-hour multimedia tours available at the entrance.

KOTSOVOLOS PANAGIOTIS / SHUTTERSTOCK ©

View of Big Ben from beneath the London Eye (p94)

The South Bank

Ever since the London Eye came up in 2000, the South Bank has become a magnet for visitors and the area is always a buzz of activity. A roll call of riverside sights stretches along the Thames, commencing with the London Eye, running past the cultural enclave of the Southbank Centre and on to the Tate Modern.

Great For...

❶ Need to Know

Waterloo or Southwark

★ **Top Tip**

Book online for the London Eye and London Dungeon to skip queues.

NICOLA FERRARI / GETTY IMAGES ©

The South Bank has a great vibe. As well as top attractions, there is plenty to take in whilst enjoying a stroll: views of the north bank of London (including great views of the Houses of Parliament and Big Ben), street artists, office workers on their lunchtime run, and boats toing and froing along the Thames.

South Bank Sights

London Eye   Viewpoint

(Map p245; 0871-222 4002; www.londoneye.com; adult/child £23.45/18.95; 11am-6pm Sep-May, 10am-8.30pm Jun-Aug; Waterloo or Westminster) Standing 135m high in a fairly flat city, the London Eye affords views 25 miles in every direction, weather permitting. Interactive tablets provide great information (in six languages) about landmarks as they come up in the skyline. Each rotation takes a gracefully slow 30 minutes. At peak times (July, August and school holidays) it may seem like you'll spend more time in the queue than in the capsule, so save time and money by buying tickets online.

Southbank Centre   Arts Centre

(Map p245; 020-7960 4200; www.southbankcentre.co.uk; Belvedere Rd, SE1; Waterloo or Embankment) The flagship venue of the Southbank Centre, Europe's largest centre for performing and visual arts, is the **Royal Festival Hall**. Its gently curved facade of glass and Portland stone is more humane than its 1970s Brutalist neighbours. It is one of London's leading music venues and the epicentre of life on this part of the South Bank, hosting cafes, restaurants, shops and bars.

View from the London Eye

Just north, the austere Queen Elizabeth Hall is a Brutalist icon and the second-largest concert venue in the centre, hosting chamber orchestras, quartets, choirs, dance performances and sometimes opera. Underneath its elevated floor is a graffiti-decorated **skateboarders' hang-out**.

The opinion-dividing 1968 **Hayward Gallery** (Map p245; www.southbankcentre. co.uk; Belvedere Rd, SE1; ⊖Waterloo), another Brutalist beauty, is a leading contemporary-art exhibition space.

The QEH and Hayward Gallery are both closed until April 2018 for 21st-century facelifts.

☑ **Don't Miss**

The astounding views from the London Eye.

PAWEL LIBERA / GETTY IMAGES ©

London Dungeon   Historic Building

(Map p245; www.thedungeons.com/london; County Hall, Westminster Bridge Rd, SE1; adult/child £30/24; ⊙10am-5pm Mon-Fri, to 6pm Sat & Sun; 🚼; ⊖Waterloo or Westminster) Older kids tend to love the London Dungeon, as the terrifying queues during school holidays and weekends testify. It's all spooky music, ghostly boat rides, macabre hangman's drop-rides, fake blood and actors dressed up as torturers and gory criminals (including Jack the Ripper and Sweeney Todd). Beware the interactive bits.

What's Nearby?

Roupell Street   Street

(Map p245; Roupell St, SE1; ⊖Waterloo) Waterloo station isn't exactly scenic, but wander around the back streets of this transport hub and you'll find some amazing architecture. Roupell St is an astonishingly pretty row of workers' cottages, all dark bricks and coloured doors, dating back to the 1820s. The street is so uniform it looks like a film set.

Imperial War Museum   Museum

(www.iwm.org.uk; Lambeth Rd, SE1; ⊙10am-6pm; ⊖Lambeth North) FREE Fronted by a pair of intimidating 15in naval guns, this riveting museum is housed in what was the Bethlehem Royal Hospital, also known as Bedlam. Although the museum's focus is on military action involving British or Commonwealth troops largely during the 20th century, it rolls out the carpet to war in the wider sense. The highlight of the collection is the state-of-the-art **First World War Galleries**, opened in 2014 to mark the centenary of the war's outbreak.

The museum is a short tube or bus ride from the South Bank and well worth the effort for anyone interested in WWI or WWII.

✕ **Take a Break**

For tip-top coffee in a bohemian setting, head to Scootercaffe (p179).

The Serpentine

I WEI HUANG / SHUTTERSTOCK ©

Hyde Park

London's largest royal park spreads itself over 142 hectares of neat gardens, wild grasses and glorious trees. Not only is it a fantastic green space in the middle of London, it is also home to a handful of fascinating sights.

Henry VIII expropriated Hyde Park from the church in 1536, after which it emerged as a hunting ground for kings and aristocrats; later it became a popular venue for duels, executions and horse racing. It was the first royal park to open to the public in the early 17th century, the famous venue of the Great Exhibition in 1851 and became a vast potato bed during WWII. These days, as well as being an exquisite park, it is an occasional concert and music-festival venue.

Great For...

☑ **Don't Miss**

The Albert Memorial and Kensington Palace.

Green Spaces

The eastern half of the park is covered with expansive lawns, which become one vast picnic-and-frolic area on sunny days. The western half is more untamed, with plenty of trees and areas of wild grass.

Albert Memorial (p99)

MKOS83 / SHUTTERSTOCKS ©

❶ Need to Know

Map p250; www.royalparks.org.uk/parks/
hyde-park; ⊙5am–midnight; ⊖Marble Arch,
Hyde Park Corner or Queensway

✕ Take Break

Stop off at the Orangery (p142), in
the grounds of Kensington Palace, for
afternoon tea or a pastry.

★ Top Tip

Being so central, Hyde Park is an ideal
picnic stop between sights.

p250; ⊖Knightsbridge or South Kensington), a
small lake.

The Serpentine Galleries

Straddling the Serpentine lake, the
Serpentine Galleries (Map p250; www.
serpentinegalleries.org; Kensington Gardens,
W2; ⊙10am–6pm Tue–Sun; ⊖Lancaster Gate
or Knightsbridge) FREE may look like quaint
historical buildings, but they are one of London's most important contemporary-art
galleries. Damien Hirst, Andreas Gursky,
Louise Bourgeois, Gabriel Orozco, Tomoko
Takahashi and Jeff Koons have all exhibited
here.

The original exhibition space is the 1930s
former tea pavillion located in Kensington
Gardens. In 2013 the gallery opened the
Serpentine Sackler Gallery within the Magazine, a former gunpowder depot, across
the Serpentine Bridge in Hyde Park. Built in
1805, it has been augmented with a daring,
undulating extension designed by Pritzker
Prize–winning architect Zaha Hadid.

Speakers' Corner

Frequented by Karl Marx, Vladimir Lenin,
George Orwell and William Morris, **Speak-
ers' Corner** (Map p250; Park Lane; ⊖Marble
Arch) in the northeastern corner of Hyde
Park is traditionally the spot for oratorical
acrobatics and soapbox ranting.

It's the only place in Britain where dem-
onstrators can assemble without police
permission, a concession granted in 1872
after serious riots 17 years before when
150,000 people gathered to demonstrate
against the Sunday Trading Bill before Parliament, only to be unexpectedly ambushed
by police concealed within Marble Arch.

The Serpentine

Hyde Park is separated from Kensington
Gardens by the L-shaped **Serpentine** (Map

Diana, Princess of Wales Memorial Fountain

This **memorial fountain** (Map p250; ⊖Knightsbridge or Lancaster Gate) is dedicated to the late Princess of Wales. Designed by Kathryn Gustafson as a 'moat without a castle', the circular double stream is composed of 545 pieces of Cornish granite, its waters drawn from a chalk aquifer more than 100m below ground. Unusually, visitors are actively encouraged to splash about, to the delight of children.

Gun Salutes

Royal Gun Salutes are fired in Hyde Park on 10 June for the Duke of Edinburgh's birthday and on 14 November for the Prince of Wales' birthday. The salutes are fired at midday and include 41 rounds (21 is stand-

ard, but being a royal park, Hyde Park gets a bonus 20 rounds).

What's Nearby?

Kensington Palace
Palace

(Map p250; www.hrp.org.uk/kensingtonpalace; Kensington Gardens, W8; adult/child £16.30/free; ⊙10am-6pm Mar-Oct, to 5pm Nov-Feb; ⊖High St Kensington) Built in 1605, the palace became the favourite royal residence under William and Mary of Orange in 1689 and remained so until George III became king and relocated to St James's Palace. Today, it is still a royal residence, with the likes of the Duke and Duchess of Cambridge (Prince William and his wife Catherine) and Prince Harry living there. A large part of the palace is open to the public, however, including the King's and Queen's State Apartments.

The Serpentine Galleries (p97)

The **King's State Apartments** are the most lavish, starting with the **Grand Staircase**, a dizzying feast of trompe l'oeil. The beautiful **Cupola Room**, once the venue of choice for music and dance, is arranged with gilded statues and a gorgeous painted ceiling. The **Drawing Room** is beyond, where the king and courtiers would entertain themselves with cards.

Visitors can also access **Victoria's apartments** where Queen Victoria (1819–1901) was born and lived until she became Queen. An informative narrative about her life is told through a few personal effects, extracts from her journals and plenty of visual props.

Kensington Gardens   Park
(Map p250; www.royalparks.org.uk/parks/kensington-gardens; ☉6am-dusk; ☻Queensway or Lancaster Gate) Immediately west of Hyde Park and across the Serpentine lake, these picturesque 275-acre gardens are technically part of Kensington Palace. The park is a gorgeous collection of manicured lawns, tree-shaded avenues and basins. The largest is the **Round Pond**, close to the palace. Also worth a look are the lovely fountains in the **Italian Gardens** (Map p250; Kensington Gardens; ☻Lancaster Gate), believed to be a gift from Albert to Queen Victoria.

Albert Memorial   Monument
(Map p250; ☎tours 020-8969 0104; Kensington Gardens; tours adult/concession £8/7; ☉tours 2pm & 3pm 1st Sun of month Mar-Dec; ☻Knightsbridge or Gloucester Rd) This splendid Victorian confection on the southern edge of Kensington Gardens is as ostentatious as the subject. Queen Victoria's German husband Albert (1819–61) was purportedly humble. Albert explicitly insisted he did not want a monument; ignoring the good prince's wishes, the Lord Mayor instructed George Gilbert Scott to build the 53m-high, gaudy Gothic memorial in 1872.

☑ **Don't Miss**

An architect who has never built in the UK is annually commissioned to build a 'Summer Pavilion' (June to October) for the Serpentine Galleries.

RON ELLIS / SHUTTERSTOCK ©

★ **Top Tip**

Deckchairs are available for hire (1/4 hours £1.60/4.60) throughout the park from March to October.

John Madejski Garden, Victoria & Albert Museum

Victoria & Albert Museum

The Museum of Manufactures, as the V&A was known when it opened in 1852, was part of Prince Albert's legacy to the nation in the aftermath of the successful Great Exhibition of 1851. Its aims were the 'improvement of public taste in design' and 'applications of fine art to objects of utility'. It's done a fine job so far.

Great For...

Victoria & Albert Museum

Exhibition Rd

Cromwell Rd

Thurloe Pl

Thurloe Pl

Thurloe Pl

South Kensington

❶ Need to Know

V&A; Map p250; www.vam.ac.uk; Cromwell Rd, SW7; ⏱10am-5.45pm Sat-Thu, to 10pm Fri; ⊖South Kensington **FREE**

★ **Top Tip**
The V&A's temporary exhibitions are reliably fantastic, so factor some time to check them out.

Collection

Through 146 galleries, the museum houses the world's greatest collection of decorative arts, from ancient Chinese ceramics to modernist architectural drawings, Korean bronze and Japanese swords, cartoons by Raphael, gowns from the Elizabethan era, ancient jewellery, a Sony Walkman – and much, much more.

Tours

Several free one-hour guided tours leave the main reception area every day. Times are prominently displayed; alternatively, check the website for details.

Level 1

The street level is mostly devoted to art and design from India, China, Japan, Korea and Southeast Asia, as well as European art. One of the museum's highlights is the **Cast Courts** in rooms 46a and 46b, containing staggering plaster casts collected in the Victorian era, such as Michelangelo's *David*, acquired in 1858.

The **T.T. Tsui Gallery** (rooms 44 and 47e) displays lovely pieces, including a beautifully lithe wooden statue of Guanyin seated in *lalitasana* pose from AD 1200; also check out a leaf from the *Twenty Views of the Yuanmingyuan Summer Palace* (1781–86), revealing the Haiyantang and the 12 animal heads of the fountain (now ruins) in Beijing. Within the subdued lighting of the **Japan Gallery** (room 45) stands a fearsome suit of armour in the Domaru style. More than 400 objects are within the **Islamic Middle East Gallery** (room 42), including ceramics, textiles, carpets, glass and woodwork

Ceramics and glass works on display

from the 8th-century up to the years before WWI. The exhibition's highlight is the gorgeous mid-16th-century **Ardabil Carpet**.

For fresh air, the landscaped **John Madejski Garden** is a lovely shaded inner courtyard. Cross it to reach the original **Refreshment Rooms** (Morris, Gamble and Poynter Rooms), dating from the 1860s and redesigned by McInnes Usher McKnight Architects (MUMA), who also renovated the **Medieval and Renaissance galleries** (1350–1600) to the right of the Grand Entrance.

> ☑ **Don't Miss**
>
> The temporary exhibitions, Chinese ceramics and Elizabethan gowns.

ANTON IVANOV / SHUTTERSTOCK ©

Levels 2 & 4

The **British Galleries**, featuring every aspect of British design from 1500 to 1900, are divided between levels 2 (1500–1760) and 4 (1760–1900). Level 4 also boasts the **Architecture Gallery** (rooms 127 to 128a), which vividly describes architectural styles via models and videos, and the spectacular brightly illuminated **Contemporary Glass Gallery** (room 129).

Level 3

The **Jewellery Gallery** (rooms 91 to 93) is outstanding; the mezzanine level – accessed via the glass-and-perspex spiral staircase – glitters with jewel-encrusted swords, watches and gold boxes. The **Photographs Gallery** (room 100) is one of the nation's best, with access to over 500,000 images collected since the mid-19th century. **Design Since 1946** (room 76) celebrates design classics from a 1985 Sony credit-card radio to a 1992 Nike 'Air Max' shoe, Peter Ghyczy's Garden Egg Chair from 1968 and the now-ubiquitous selfie stick.

Level 6

Among the pieces in the **Ceramics Gallery** (rooms 136 to 146) – the world's largest – are standout items from the Middle East and Asia. The **Dr Susan Weber Gallery** (rooms 133 to 135) celebrates furniture design over the past six centuries.

✕ Take a Break

Stop for a coffee at the **V&A Cafe** (Map p250; Victoria & Albert Museum, Cromwell Rd, SW7; mains £6.95-11.50; ⊙10am-5.15pm Sat-Thu, to 9.30pm Fri; ☏; ⊜South Kensington), if only to admire the magnificent Refreshment Rooms, which date from the 1860s.

JAN KRANENDONK / SHUTTERSTOCK ©

Natural History Museum

This colossal building is infused with the irrepressible Victorian spirit of collecting, cataloguing and interpreting the natural world. The museum building is as much a reason to visit as the world-famous collection within. Seasonal events and excellent temporary exhibitions complete the package to make this one of the very best museums in London, especially for families.

Great For...

☑ Don't Miss

Its thunderous, animatronic Tyranno-saurus rex, fascinating displays about planet earth, the outstanding Darwin Centre and architecture straight from a Gothic fairy tale.

Hintze Hall

This grand central hall resembles a cathe-dral nave – quite fitting for a time when the natural sciences were challenging the bibli-cal tenets of Christian orthodoxy. Naturalist and first superintendent of the museum Richard Owen celebrated the building as a 'cathedral to nature'.

Since summer 2017, the hall has been dominated by the skeleton of a blue whale, displayed in a diving position for dramatic effect. It replaced 'Dippy' the diplodocus skeleton cast, which had been the hall's main resident since the 1960s. The hall also features new displays giving a taster of what the museum holds in store.

Blue Zone

Undoubtedly the museum's star attraction, the **Dinosaurs Gallery** takes you on an

Gems in the Vault

DAVE M BENETT / GETTY IMAGES ©

Natural History Museum
Cromwell Rd
Thurloe Pl
South Kensington

ℹ Need to Know

Map p250; www.nhm.ac.uk; Cromwell Rd, SW7; ⏱10am-5.50pm; ⊖South Kensington
`FREE`

✕ Take a Break

The Queen's Arms (p177) beckons with a cosy interior and a right royal selection of ales and ciders on tap.

★ Top Tip

Families can borrow an 'explorer backpack' or buy a themed discover trail (£1).

impressive overhead walkway, past a dromaeosaurus (a small and agile meat eater) before reaching a roaring animatronic T-rex and then winding its way through skeletons, fossils, casts and fascinating displays about how dinosaurs lived and died.

Another highlight of this zone is the **Mammals & Blue Whale Gallery**, with its life-sized blue whale model and extensive displays on cetaceans.

Green Zone

While children love the Blue Zone, adults may prefer the Green Zone, especially the **Treasures in Cadogan Gallery**, on the 1st floor, which houses the museum's most prized possessions, each with a unique history. Exhibits include a chunk of moon rock, an Emperor Penguin egg collected by Captain Scott's expedition and a 1st

edition of Charles Darwin's *On the Origin of Species*.

Equally rare and exceptional are the gems and rocks held in the **Vault**, including a Martian meteorite and the largest emerald ever found.

Take a moment to marvel at the trunk section of a 1300-year-old **giant sequoia tree** on the 2nd floor: its size is mind boggling.

Back on the ground floor, the **Creepy Crawlies Gallery** is fantastic, delving into every aspect of insect life and whether they are friend or foe (both!).

Red Zone

This zone explores the ever-changing nature of our planet and the forces shaping it. The **earthquake simulator** (in the **Volcanoes & Earthquakes Gallery**), which recreates the 1995 Kobe earthquake in a grocery store (of which you can see footage) is a favourite, as is the **From the Beginning Gallery**, which retraces earth's history.

In **Earth's Treasury**, you can find out more about our planet's mineral riches and how they are being used in our everyday lives – from jewellery to construction and electronics.

Access to most of the galleries in the Red Zone is via **Earth Hall** and a very tall escalator that disappears into a large metal sculpture of earth. The most intact **stegosaurus fossil skeleton** ever found is displayed at the base.

Orange Zone

The **Darwin Centre** is the beating heart of the museum: this is where the museum's millions of specimens are kept and where its scientists work. The top two floors of the amazing '**cocoon**' building are dedicated to explaining the kind of research the museum does (and how) – windows allow you to see the researchers at work.

If you'd like to find out more, pop into the **Attenborough studio** (named after famous naturalist and broadcaster David Attenborough) for one of the daily talks with the museum's scientists. The studio also shows films throughout the day.

Exhibitions

The museum hosts regular exhibitions (admission fees apply), some of them on a recurrent basis. **Wildlife Photographer of the Year** (adult £10.50-13.50, child £6.50-8, family £27-36.90; ⊙Oct-Sep), with its show-stopping images, recently celebrated its 50th year, and **Sensational Butterflies**, a tunnel tent on the East Lawn that swarms with what must originally have been called 'flutter-bys', has become a firm summer

Stegosaurus skeleton on display

favourite. In winter, the same lawn turns into a very popular **ice-skating rink**.

Gardens

A slice of English countryside in SW7, the beautiful **Wildlife Garden** next to the West Lawn encompasses a range of British lowland habitats, including a meadow with farm gates and a bee tree where a colony of honey bees fills the air.

In 2018 the eastern grounds are also due to be redesigned to feature a geological and palaeontological walk, with a bronze sculpture of Dippy as well as ferns and cycads.

> ★ **Top Tip**
>
> As well as the obligatory dinosaur figurines and animal soft toys, the museum's shop has a fantastic collection of children's books.

What's Nearby?

Science Museum   Museum

(Map p250; www.sciencemuseum.org.uk; Exhibition Rd, SW7; ⊙10am-6pm; ⊜South Kensington) **FREE** With seven floors of interactive and educational exhibits, this scientifically spellbinding museum will mesmerise adults and children alike, covering everything from early technology to space travel. A perennial favourite is **Exploring Space**, a gallery featuring genuine rockets and satellites and a full-sized replica of *Eagle*, the lander that took Neil Armstrong and Buzz Aldrin to the moon in 1969. The **Making the Modern World Gallery** next door is a visual feast of locomotives, planes, cars and other revolutionary inventions.

The fantastic **Information Age Gallery** on level 2 showcases how information and communication technologies – from the telegraph to smartphones – have transformed our lives since the 19th century. Standout displays include wireless sent by a sinking *Titanic,* the first BBC radio broadcast and a Soviet BESM 1965 supercomputer.

The 3rd-floor **Flight Gallery** (free tours 1pm most days) is a favourite place for children, with its gliders, hot-air balloons and aircraft, including the *Gipsy Moth,* which Amy Johnson flew to Australia in 1930. This floor also features a **Red Arrows 3D flight simulation theatre** (adult/children £6/5) and **Fly 360 degree flight simulator capsules** (£12 per capsule). **Launchpad**, on the same floor, is stuffed with (free) hands-on gadgets exploring physics and the properties of liquids.

If you've got kids under the age of five, pop down to the basement and the **Garden**, where there's a fun-filled play zone, including a water-play area besieged by tots in orange waterproof smocks.

> ❶ **Did You Know?**
>
> The museum and its gardens cover a huge 5.7 hectares; the museum contains 80 million specimens from across the natural world.

ANDREI TUDORAN / SHUTTERSTOCK ©

Statue of Anteros at the centre of Piccadilly Circus

BENJAMIN B / SHUTTERSTOCK ©

Leicester Square & Piccadilly Circus

This duo of squares make up in buzz what they lack in cultural cachet. It's all flashing signs and crowds, yet no visit to London would be complete without passing through these iconic places.

Great For...

☑ **Don't Miss**

Celebrity-spotting at film premieres on Leicester Sq.

Piccadilly Circus

John Nash had originally designed Regent St and Piccadilly in the 1820s to be the two most elegant streets in town but, curbed by city planners, couldn't realise his dream to the full. He may be disappointed, but suitably astonished, with Piccadilly Circus today: a traffic maelstrom, deluged with visitors and flanked by flashing advertisement panels.

At the centre of the circus stands the famous aluminium statue, Anteros, twin brother of Eros, dedicated to the philanthropist and child-labour abolitionist Lord Shaftesbury. Through the years, the figure has been mistaken for Eros, the God of Love, and the misnomer has stuck (you'll even see signs for 'Eros' from the Underground).

Leicester Square

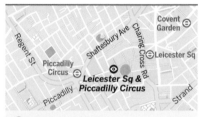

SYLVAIN SONNET / GETTY IMAGES ©

❶ Need to Know

Map p245; ⊖Leicester Square or Piccadilly Circus

✕ Take a Break

For delicious Levantine food with attitude, head to Palomar (p147).

★ Top Tip

Tkts Leicester Sq (www.tkts.co.uk/leicester-square; ⊙10am-7pm Mon-Sat, 11am-4.30pm Sun; ⊖Leicester Sq) **is the place to grab bargain tickets to West End performances.**

Leicester Square

Although Leicester Sq was very fashionable in the 19th century, more recent decades won it associations with pickpocketing, outrageous cinema-ticket prices and the nickname 'Fester Sq' during the 1979 Winter of Discontent, when it was filled with refuse. As part of the Diamond Jubilee and 2012 Olympics celebrations, the square was given an extensive £15.5 million makeover to turn it once again into a lively plaza. Today a sleek, open-plan design replaces the once-dingy little park.

It retains its many cinemas and night-clubs, and as a glamorous premiere venue it still attracts celebrities and their spotters. Pickpocketing used to be rife around Leicester Sq; things have improved but do keep a very close eye on your belongings.

What's Nearby?
Chinatown   Area

(Map p248; www.chinatownlondon.org; ⊖Leicester Sq) Immediately north of Leicester Sq – a world away in atmosphere – are Lisle and Gerrard Sts, a focal point for London's growing Chinese community. Although not as big as Chinatowns in many other cities – it's just two streets really – this is a lively quarter with oriental gates, Chinese street signs, red lanterns, restaurants, great Asian supermarkets and shops. The quality of food varies enormously, but there's a good choice of places for dim sum and other cuisine from across China.

To see it at its effervescent best, time your visit for Chinese New Year in mid-February. Twenty years ago you would only hear Cantonese but these days you'll hear Mandarin and other dialects, from places as far afield as Fujian, Sichuan and Shanghai. London's original Chinatown was further east at Limehouse but moved here after heavy bombardments in WWII.

Day Trip: Hampton Court Palace

London's most spectacular Tudor palace is a 16th-century icon that concocts an imposing sense of history, from the huge kitchens and grand living quarters to the spectacular gardens, complete with a 300-year-old maze. Tag along with a themed tour led by a costumed historian or grab one of the audio tours to delve into Hampton Court and its residents' tumultuous history.

Great For...

❶ Need to Know

www.hrp.org.uk/hamptoncourtpalace; adult/child/family £19/9.50/47; ⊘10am-6pm Apr-Oct, to 4.30pm Nov-Mar; ☀Hampton Court Palace, ᵲHampton Court

★ **Top Tip**

Ask one of the red-tunic-garbed warders for anecdotes and information.

Hampton Court Palace was built by Cardinal Thomas Wolsey in 1515, but was coaxed from him by Henry VIII just before Wolsey (as chancellor) fell from favour. It was already one of the most sophisticated palaces in Europe when, in the 17th century, Sir Christopher Wren was commissioned to build an extension. The result is a beautiful blend of Tudor and 'restrained baroque' architecture.

Entering the Palace

Passing through the magnificent main gate, you arrive first in the **Base Court** and beyond that the **Clock Court**, named after its 16th-century astronomical clock. The panelled rooms and arched doorways in **Young Henry VIII's Story** upstairs from Base Court provide a rewarding introduction: note the Tudor graffiti on the fireplace.

Henry VIII's Apartments

The stairs inside Anne Boleyn's Gateway lead up to Henry VIII's Apartments, including the stunning **Great Hall**. The **Horn Room**, hung with impressive antlers, leads to the **Great Watching Chamber**, where guards controlled access to the king. Henry VIII's dazzling gemstone-encrusted **crown** has been recreated – the original was melted down by Oliver Cromwell – and sits in the **Royal Pew** (open 10am to 4pm Monday to Saturday and 12.30pm to 1.30pm Sunday), which overlooks the beautiful **Chapel Royal** (still a place of worship after 450 years).

Tudor Kitchens & Great Wine Cellar

Also dating from Henry's day are the delightful Tudor kitchens, once used to rustle

The gardens

up meals for a royal household of some 1200 people. Don't miss the Great Wine Cellar, which handled the 300 barrels each of ale and wine consumed here annually in the mid-16th century.

Cumberland Art Gallery

The Cumberland Suite off Clock Court is the venue for a staggering collection of artworks from the Royal Collection, including Rembrandt's *Self-portrait in a Flat Cap* (1642) and Sir Anthony van Dyck's *Charles I on Horseback* (c 1635–6).

> ☑ **Don't Miss**
>
> The Great Hall, the Chapel Royal, William III's apartments, the gardens and maze, and Henry VIII's crown.

PLUSONE / SHUTTERSTOCK ©

William III's & Mary II's Apartments

A tour of William III's Apartments, completed by Wren in 1702, takes you up the grand **King's Staircase**. Highlights include the **King's Presence Chamber**, dominated by a throne backed with scarlet hangings. The sumptuous **King's Great Bedchamber**, with a bed topped with ostrich plumes, and the **King's Closet** (where His Majesty's toilet has a velvet seat) should not be missed. Restored and reopened in 2014, the unique **Chocolate Kitchens** were built for William and Mary in around 1689.

William's wife Mary II had her own apartments, accessible via the fabulous **Queen's Staircase** (decorated by William Kent).

Georgian Private Apartments

The Georgian Rooms were used by George II and Queen Caroline on the court's last visit to the palace in 1737. Do not miss the fabulous Tudor **Wolsey Closet** with its early 16th-century ceiling and painted panels, commissioned by Henry VIII.

Garden & Maze

Beyond the palace are the stunning gardens; keep an eye out for the **Real Tennis Court**, dating from the 1620s. Originally created for William and Mary, the **Kitchen Garden** is a magnificent, recently opened re-creation.

No one should leave Hampton Court without losing themselves in the 800m-long **maze** (adult/child/family £4.40/2.80/13.20; ⏰10am-5.15pm Apr-Oct, to 3.45pm Nov-Mar; ⛴Hampton Court Palace, 🚉Hampton Court), also accessible to those not entering the palace.

> ★ **Top Tip**
>
> Between April and September, **Westminster Passenger Services Association** (Map p248; ☎020-7930 2062; www.wpsa.co.uk; return to Hampton Court adult/child £25/12.50; ⊖Westminster) runs boat services between Westminster and Hampton Court.

Royal Observatory

LUKASZ PAJOR / SHUTTERSTOCK ©

Royal Observatory & Greenwich Park

The Royal Observatory is where the study of the sea, the stars and time converge. The prime meridian charts its line through the grounds of the observatory, dividing the globe into the eastern and western hemispheres. The observatory sits atop a hill within leafy and regal Greenwich Park with fabulous views.

Great For...

☑ **Don't Miss**

Straddling hemispheres and time zones as you stand astride the actual meridian line in the Meridian Courtyard.

Royal Observatory

Unlike most other attractions in Greenwich, the Royal Observatory contains free-access areas (Weller Astronomy Galleries, Great Equatorial Telescope) and ones you pay for (Meridian Line, Flamsteed House).

Flamsteed House & Meridian Courtyard

Charles II ordered construction of the Christopher Wren–designed Flamsteed House, the original observatory building, on the foundations of Greenwich Castle in 1675 after closing the observatory at the Tower of London. Today it contains the magnificent **Octagon Room** and the rather simple apartment where the Astronomer Royal, John Flamsteed, lived with his family. Here you'll also find the brilliant new **Time Galleries**, explaining how the longitude

The Time Ball at the top of the Royal Observatory

❶ Need to Know

Map p256; www.rmg.co.uk; Greenwich Park, Blackheath Ave, SE10; adult/child £9.50/5, with Cutty Sark £18.50/8.50; ⏱10am-5pm Sep-Jun, to 6pm Jul-Aug; 🚈DLR Cutty Sark, 🚊DLR Greenwich, 🚊Greenwich

✕ Take a Break

Enjoy a drink with river views on the side at the Cutty Sark Tavern (p177).

★ Top Tip

Get here before 1pm on any day of the week to see the red Time Ball at the top of the Royal Observatory drop.

problem – how to accurately determine a ship's east–west location – was solved through astronomical means and the invention of the marine chronometer.

In the Meridian Courtyard, where the globe is decisively sliced into east and west, visitors can delightfully straddle both hemispheres, with one foot on either side of the meridian line. Every day the red **Time Ball** at the top of the Royal Observatory drops at 1pm, as it has done ever since 1833.

Astronomy Centre & Planetarium

The southern half of the observatory contains the highly informative (and free) **Weller Astronomy Galleries**, where you can touch the oldest object you will ever encounter: part of the Gibeon meteorite, a mere 4.5 billion years old. Other engaging exhibits include an orrery (a mechanical

model of the solar system, minus the as-yet-undiscovered Uranus and Neptune) from 1780, astronomical documentaries, a first edition of Newton's *Principia Mathematica* and the opportunity to view the Milky Way in multiple wavelengths. To take stargazing further, pick up a Skyhawk telescope from the shop.

The state-of-the-art **Peter Harrison Planetarium** (Map p256; 📞020-8312 6608; www.rmg.co.uk/whats-on/planetarium-shows; adult/child £7.50/5.50; 🚊Greenwich, 🚈DLR Cutty Sark) – London's only planetarium – can cast entire heavens on to the inside of its roof. It runs at least five informative shows a day. Bookings advised.

Greenwich Park

The **park** (Map p256; www.royalparks.org.uk; King George St, SE10; ⏱6am-6pm winter, to 8pm spring & autumn, to 9pm summer; 🚈DLR Cutty Sark, 🚊Greenwich or Maze Hill) is one of London's loveliest expanses of green, with a rose garden, picturesque walks,

Anglo-Saxon tumuli and astonishing views from the crown of the hill near the Royal Observatory towards Canary Wharf, the financial district across the Thames.

Covering 74 hectares, this is the oldest enclosed royal park and is partly the work of André Le Nôtre, the landscape architect who designed the palace gardens of Versailles.

Ranger's House (Werhner Collection)

This elegant Georgian **villa** (EH; Map p256; ☎020-8294 2548; www.english-heritage. org.uk; Greenwich Park, Chesterfield Walk, SE10; adult/child £7.60/4.60; ☺guided tours only at 11.30am & 2pm Sun-Wed late Mar-Sep; ☒Greenwich, ☒DLR Cutty Sark), built in 1723, once housed the park's ranger and now contains a collection of 700 works of fine and applied art (medieval and Renaissance paintings, porcelain, silverware, tapestries) amassed by Julius Wernher (1850–1912), a German-born railway engineer's son who struck it rich in the diamond fields of South Africa in the 19th century.

What's Nearby?

Old Royal Naval College   Historic Building

(Map p256; www.ornc.org; 2 Cutty Sark Gardens, SE10; ☺grounds 8am-6pm, to 11pm in summer; ☒DLR Cutty Sark) FREE Designed by Christopher Wren, the Old Royal Naval College is a magnificent example of monumental classical architecture. Parts are now used by the University of Greenwich and Trinity College of Music, but you can still visit the

View of the Royal Observatory from Greenwich Park

chapel and the extraordinary **Painted Hall** (shut until 2019 for renovations), which took artist Sir James Thornhill 19 years to complete. Hour-long, yeomen-led tours (£6) of the complex leave at noon daily, taking in areas not otherwise open to the public.

Cutty Sark
Museum

(Map p256; ☎020-8312 6608; www.rmg.co.uk/cuttysark; King William Walk, SE10; adult/child £13.50/7, with Royal Observatory £18.50/8.50; ☻10am-5pm Sep-Jun, to 6pm Jul-Aug; ⍐DLR Cutty Sark) This Greenwich landmark, the last of the great clipper ships to sail between China and England in the 19th

> ℹ **Local Knowledge**
>
> In autumn Greenwich Park is one of the best places to collect chestnuts in the capital.

BBA PHOTOGRAPHY / SHUTTERSTOCK ©

century, is now fully operational after six years and £25 million of extensive renovations largely precipitated by a disastrous fire in 2007. The exhibition in the ship's hold tells her story as a tea (and then wool and mixed cargo) clipper at the end of the 19th century.

Launched in 1869 in Scotland, she made eight voyages to China in the 1870s, sailing out with a mixed cargo and coming back with a bounty of tea. As you make your way up, there are films, interactive maps and plenty of illustrations and props to convey what life on board was like. Sleepovers for kids are available.

National Maritime Museum
Museum

(Map p256; www.rmg.co.uk/national-maritime-museum; Romney Rd, SE10; ☻10am-5pm; ⍐DLR Cutty Sark) **FREE** Narrating the long and eventful history of seafaring Britain, the museum's exhibits are arranged thematically and highlights include *Miss Britain III* (the first boat to top 100mph on open water) from 1933, the 19m-long golden state barge built in 1732 for Frederick, Prince of Wales, the huge ship's propeller and the colourful figureheads installed on the ground floor. Families will love these, as well as the ship simulator and the children's gallery on the 2nd floor.

Adults are likely to prefer the fantastic (and slightly more serene) galleries such as **Voyagers: Britons and the Sea** on the ground floor, or the award-winning **Nelson, Navy, Nation 1688–1815**, which focuses on the history of the Royal Navy during the conflict-ridden 17th century. It provides an excellent look at the legendary national hero; the coat in which Nelson was fatally wounded during the Battle of Trafalgar takes pride of place.

> ✕ **Take a Break**
>
> If you've had enough of sightseeing, pop into the small but atmospheric Greenwich Market (p140) for street food and independent designer stalls.

Granary Square

RON ELLIS / SHUTTERSTOCK ©

King's Cross

Formerly a dilapidated red-light district, King's Cross used to be a place better avoided. Fast forward a couple of decades, though, and the area has metamorphosed, now boasting cool hang-outs and luxury hotels.

Great For...

☑ Don't Miss

The Sir John Ritblatt Gallery at the British Library and the fountain on Granary Square.

Granary Square Square
(Map p254; www.kingscross.co.uk; Stable St, N1; ⊖King's Cross St Pancras) Positioned by a sharp bend in the Regent's Canal north of King's Cross Station, Granary Sq is at the heart of a major redevelopment of a 27-hectare expanse once full of abandoned freight warehouses. Its most striking feature is a fountain made of 1080 individually lit water jets, which pulse and dance in sequence. On hot spring and summer days, it becomes a busy urban beach.

British Library Library
(Map p254; www.bl.uk; 96 Euston Rd, NW1; ⊙galleries 9.30am-6pm Mon & Fri, to 8pm Tue-Thu, to 5pm Sat, 11am-5pm Sun; ⊖King's Cross St Pancras) **FREE** Consisting of low-slung red-brick terraces and fronted by a large plaza featuring an oversized statue of Sir Isaac Newton, Colin St John Wilson's British

The Platform 9¾ sign inside King's Cross Station

C007 / SHUTTERSTOCK ©

❶ Need to Know

Map p245; ⊖King's Cross St Pancras

✕ Take a Break

Grain Store (p143), with its creative European cuisine, is a good example of King's Cross regeneration.

★ Top Tip

Harry Potter fans will want to seek out the Platform 9¾ sign inside King's Cross Station.

St Pancras Station & Hotel
Historic Building

(Map p254; ☑020-8241 6921; info@ luxuryvacationsuk.com; Euston Rd, NW1; ⊖King's Cross St Pancras) Looking at the jaw-dropping Gothic splendour of St Pancras, it's hard to believe that the 1873 Midland Grand Hotel languished empty for years and even faced demolition in the 1960s. Now home to a five-star hotel, 67 luxury apartments and the Eurostar terminal, the entire complex has been returned to its former glory. Tours take you on a fascinating journey through the building's history from its inception as the southern terminus for the Midlands Railway line.

Library building is a love-it-or-hate-it affair (Prince Charles once famously likened it to a secret-police academy). Completed in 1998 it's home to some of the greatest treasures of the written word, including the *Codex Sinaiticus* (the first complete text of the New Testament), Leonardo da Vinci's notebooks and a copy of the *Magna Carta* (1215).

The most precious manuscripts are held in the **Sir John Ritblatt Gallery**, including the stunningly illustrated Jain sacred texts, explorer Captain Scott's final diary and Shakespeare's *First Folio* (1623). Music fans will love the Beatles' handwritten lyrics and original scores by Bach, Handel, Mozart and Beethoven.

Walking Tour: A Northern Point of View

This walk takes in North London's most interesting locales, including celebrity-infested Primrose Hill and chaotic Camden Town, home to loud guitar bands and the last of London's cartoon punks.

Start ⊖ Chalk Farm
Distance 2.5 miles
Duration 2 hours

Classic photo: London's skyline from atop Primrose Hill

2 In **Primrose Hill**, walk to the top of the park where you'll find a classic view of central London's skyline.

1 Affluent **Regent's Park Rd** is home to many darlings of the women's mags, so keep your eyes open for famous faces.

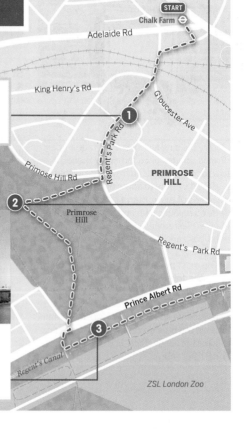

3 Walk downhill to Regent's Canal, where you'll pass the large aviary at **London Zoo**, quaint boats, superb mansions and converted industrial buildings.

START
Chalk Farm ⊖

Adelaide Rd

King Henry's Rd

Gloucester Ave

Regent's Park Rd

Primrose Hill Rd

PRIMROSE HILL

Primrose Hill

Regent's Park Rd

Prince Albert Rd

Regent's Canal

ZSL London Zoo

4 At **Camden Lock** turn left into buzzing **Camden Lock Market** (p162), with its original fashion, ethnic art and food stalls.

5 Exit onto **Camden High St** and turn right onto bar-lined **Inverness St**, which hosts its own little market.

6 At **Gloucester Cres** turn left and walk past the glorious Georgian townhouses.

Take a Break...
Enjoy excellent British cuisine at **Market** (p143), where a two-course lunch will set you back only £11.50.

7 Head toward Delancey St and make a beeline for the **Edinboro Castle** (p178), where this walk ends with a well-deserved drink!

Palm House (p124)

Day Trip:
Kew Gardens

The 121-hectare gardens at Kew are the finest product of the British botanical imagination and really should not be missed. No worries if you don't know your quiver tree from your alang-alang, a visit to Kew is a journey of discovery for all.

Great For...

ⓘ Need to Know

www.kew.org; Kew Rd; adult/child £15/3.50; ⏰10am-6.30pm Apr-Aug, closes earlier Sep-Mar; 🚢Kew Pier, 🚉Kew Bridge, ⊖Kew Gardens

★ **Top Tip**

Kew is a big place so if you're pressed for time, or getting tired, take the **Kew Explorer** (adult/child £5/2), a hop-on/hop-off road train that takes in the main sights.

As well as being a public garden, Kew is also a pre-eminent research centre that maintains its reputation as the most exhaustive botanical collection in the world.

Conservatories

Assuming you travel by tube and enter via Victoria Gate, you'll come almost immediately to the enormous and elaborate 700-glass-paned **Palm House**, a domed hothouse of metal and curved sheets of glass dating from 1848, enveloping a splendid display of exotic tropical greenery; an aerial walkway offers a parrot's-eye view of the lush vegetation. Just northwest of the Palm House stands the tiny and irresistibly steamy **Waterlily House** (☉Mar-Dec), sheltering the gigantic *Victoria cruziana* waterlily, whose vast pads can support the weight of a small adult.

In the southeast of Kew Gardens, **Temperate House** (built in 1860) is the world's largest surviving Victorian glasshouse, covering 4880 sq metres. It has been closed for vital restoration work since 2013 and is set to reopen in 2018.

The angular **Princess of Wales Conservatory** houses plants in 10 different climatic zones – everything from a desert to a mangrove swamp. Look out for stone plants, which resemble pebbles (to deter grazing animals), carnivorous plants, gigantic waterlilies, cacti and a collection of tropical orchids.

Chinese Pagoda

Kew's 49.5m-tall eight-sided Chinese Pagoda (1762), designed by William Chambers (the architect of Somerset House), is one of the gardens' architectural icons. During

Chinese Pagoda

WWII, the pagoda withstood the blast from a stick of Luftwaffe bombs exploding nearby and was also secretly employed by the Ministry of Defence to test bomb trajectories (which involved cutting holes in each floor!).

The pagoda is set to reopen to the public in early 2018 after extensive renovations, which include the reinstatement of 80 winged dragons. They were part of the original design but disappeared shortly after the tower's inauguration.

☑ **Don't Miss**

The Palm House, Rhizotron and Xstrata Treetop Walkway, Chinese Pagoda, Temperate House and the numerous vistas.

ALEXEY FEDORENKO / SHUTTERSTOCK ©

Kew Palace

The adorable red-brick **Kew Palace** (www.hrp.org.uk/kewpalace; with admission to Kew Gardens; ◷10.30am-5.30pm Apr-Sep), in the northwest of the gardens was built in 1631 and is the smallest of the royal palaces. This former royal residence was once known as Dutch House. It was the favourite home of George III and his family; his wife, Queen Charlotte, died here in 1818 (you can see the very chair in which she expired). Don't miss the restored **Royal Kitchens** next door.

Rhizotron & Xstrata Treetop Walkway

This fascinating walkway in the **Arboretum** first takes you underground and then 18m up in the air into the tree canopy (a big hit with kids).

Other Highlights

Several long vistas (**Cedar Vista**, **Syon Vista** and **Pagoda Vista**) are channelled by trees from vantage points within Kew Gardens. The idyllic, thatched **Queen Charlotte's Cottage** (◷11am-4pm Sat & Sun Apr-Sep) in the southwest of the gardens was popular with 'mad' George III and his wife; the carpets of bluebells around here are a drawcard in spring. The **Marianne North Gallery** displays the botanical paintings of Marianne North, an indomitable traveller who roamed the continents from 1871 to 1885, painting plants along the way.

✕ Take a Break

The aptly named **Glasshouse** (✆020-8940 6777; www.glasshouserestaurant.co.uk; 14 Station Pde, TW9; 2/3-course lunch Mon-Sat £24.50/29.50, 3-course lunch Sun £32.50, 3-course dinner £47.50; ◷noon-2.30pm & 6.30-10.30pm Mon-Sat, 12.30-3pm & 7-10pm Sun; 🛜♿; Ⓡ Kew Gardens, Ⓔ Kew Gardens) restaurant, with its Michelin star, is the perfect conclusion to a day exploring the gardens.

The central atrium of the Design Museum

EUGENE REGIS / SHUTTERSTOCK ©

Design Museum

Relocated in 2016 from its former Thames location to a stunning new home by Holland Park, this slick museum is a crucial pit stop for anyone with an eye for modern and contemporary aesthetics.

Great For...

☑ **Don't Miss**

The Designer Maker User gallery and the museum's architecture.

Collections & Exhibitions

Dedicated to popularising the importance and influence of design in everyday life, the Design Museum has a revolving program of special exhibitions. Most exhibitions are ticketed (from £10), but the extensive 2nd-floor **Designer Maker User** gallery is free. Exploring the iconography of design classics, the gallery contains almost 1000 objects that trace the history of modern design, from 1980s Apple computers, to water bottles, typewriters, floppy disks and a huge advert for the timeless VW Beetle.

Iconic Building

Until 2016 the museum was housed in a former 1930s banana warehouse that had been given a 1930s modernist makeover by museum founder Terence Conrad. The building, located by the Thames in

Kyoto Garden, Holland Park

❶ Need to Know

Map p250; ☎020-7940 8790; www.design-museum.org; 224-238 Kensington High St, W8; ⏱10am-5.45pm; 🚇High St Kensington

✖ Take a Break

For a delicious, modern take on Greek cuisine, head to Mazi (p151).

★ Top Tip

Choose a sunny day to visit and relax in Holland Park afterwards.

Bermondsey, was a design success but it became too small for the museum's growing collection. For its new home, the museum chose another design jewel: the former Commonwealth Institute building, a listed 1960s beauty, which was given a 21st-century, £83 million facelift for the occasion.

What's Nearby?

Holland Park   Park

(Map p250; Ilchester Pl; ⏱7.30am-dusk; 🚇High St Kensington or Holland Park) This handsome park divides into dense woodland in the north, spacious and inviting lawns by Holland House, sports fields for the beautiful game and other exertions in the south, and some lovely gardens, including the restful Kyoto Garden. The park's many splendid peacocks are a gorgeous sight and an

adventure playground keeps kids occupied. Holland House – largely bombed to smithereens by the Luftwaffe in 1940 – is the venue of Opera Holland Park (p195) in summer.

Portobello Road Market   Clothing, Antiques

(Map p250; www.portobellomarket.org; Portobello Rd, W10; ⏱8am-6.30pm Mon-Wed, Fri & Sat, to 1pm Thu; 🚇Notting Hill Gate or Ladbroke Grove) Lovely on a warm summer's day, Portobello Road Market is an iconic London attraction with an eclectic mix of street food, fruit and veg, antiques, curios, collectables, vibrant fashion and trinkets. Although the shops along Portobello Rd open daily and the fruit and veg stalls (from Elgin Cres to Talbot Rd) only close on Sunday, the busiest day by far is Saturday, when antique dealers set up shop (from Chepstow Villas to Elgin Cres).

Oxford St adorned with Christmas decorations

IR STONE / SHUTTERSTOCK ©

Shopping in the West End

Shopping is part and parcel of a trip to London and the West End, with shop-lined Regent St and Oxford St, is probably the most high-profile shopping destination in the capital.

Great For...

☑ Don't Miss

The Christmas lights on Regent St and the sheer number of toys at Hamleys.

The shopping nerve centre of the West End are the elegantly curving Regent St and the dead-straight east–west artery of Oxford St.

Regent Street

The handsome border dividing the hoi polloi of Soho from the Gucci-two-shoed of Mayfair, Regent St was designed by John Nash as a ceremonial route linking the Prince Regent's long-demolished city dwelling with the 'wilds' of Regent's Park. Nash had to downscale his plan but Regent St is today a well-subscribed shopping street (as is pedestrian Carnaby St, which runs parallel to it, a block east) and a beautiful curve of listed architecture.

Its most famous tenant is undoubtedly Hamleys, London's premier toy and game store. Regent St is also famous for its

Light installation above Regent St

BDRONE / SHUTTERSTOCK ©

Shopping in the West End

ⓘ Need to Know

Map p245; ⊖Marble Arch, Bond St, Oxford Circus, Tottenham Court Rd or Piccadilly Circus

✕ Take a Break

Yauatcha (p147) in Soho does the best dim-sum in town; it's not for nothing they have a Michelin star.

★ Top Tip

Shops in the West End open until 9pm on Thursdays (otherwise they usually close at 7pm or 8pm).

Christmas light displays, which get glowing with great pomp earlier and earlier (or so it seems) each year (usually around mid-November).

Hamleys
Toys

(Map p248; www.hamleys.com; 188-196 Regent St, W1; ⊙10am-9pm Mon-Fri, 9.30am-9pm Sat, noon-6pm Sun; ⊖Oxford Circus) Claiming to be the world's oldest (and some say largest) toy store, Hamleys moved to its address on Regent St in 1881. From the ground floor – where staff glide UFOs and foam boomerangs through the air with practised nonchalance – to Lego World and a cafe on the 5th floor, it's a layer cake of playthings.

Liberty
Department Store

(Map p248; www.liberty.co.uk; Great Marlborough St, W1; ⊙10am-8pm Mon-Sat, noon-6pm Sun; ⊖Oxford Circus) An irresistible blend of contemporary styles in an old-fashioned mock-Tudor atmosphere, Liberty has a huge cosmetics department and an accessories floor, along with a breathtaking lingerie section, all at very inflated prices. A classic London souvenir is a Liberty fabric print, especially in the form of a scarf.

We Built This City
Gifts & Souvenirs

(Map p248; www.webuilt-thiscity.com; 56-57 Carnaby St, W1; ⊙10am-7pm Mon-Wed, to 8pm Thu-Sat, noon-6pm Sun; ⊖Oxford Circus) Taking a commendable stand against Union Jack hats and black cab key rings, We Built This City is a shop selling London-themed souvenirs that the recipient might actually want. The products are artistic and thoughtful and celebrate the city's creative side.

Oxford Street

Oxford St is all about chains, from Marks & Spencer to H&M, Top Shop to Gap, with large branches of department stores, the most famous of which is Selfridges. The small lanes heading south towards Mayfair are a favourite for designer boutiques.

Selfridges Department Store

(Map p250; www.selfridges.com; 400 Oxford St, W1; ⊘9.30am-10pm Mon-Sat, 11.30am-6pm Sun; ⊖Bond St) Selfridges loves innovation – it's famed for its inventive window displays by international artists, gala shows and, above all, its amazing range of products. It's the trendiest of London's one-stop shops, with labels such as Boudicca, Luella Bartley, Emma Cook, Chloé and Missoni. It has an unparalleled food hall and Europe's largest cosmetics department.

Stella McCartney Fashion & Accessories

(Map p248; ☑020-7518 3100; www.stellamccartney.com; 30 Bruton St, W1;

⊘10am-7pm Mon-Sat; ⊖Bond St) ✔ Stella McCartney's sharp tailoring, floaty designs, accessible style and 'ethical' approach to fashion (no leather or fur) is very of-the-moment. This three-storey terraced Victorian home is a minimalist showcase for the designer's current collections. Depending on your devotion and wallet, you'll either feel at ease or like a trespasser.

Topshop Clothing

(Map p248; ☑020-7927 0000; www.topshop.co.uk; 214 Oxford St, W1; ⊘9am-9pm Mon-Sat, 11.30am-6pm Sun; ⊖Oxford Circus) The 'it' store when it comes to clothes and accessories, venturing boldly into couture in recent years, Topshop encapsulates London's supreme skill at bringing catwalk fashion to the youth market affordably and quickly.

Selfridges

Browns   Clothing

(Map p250; 📞020-7629 1416; www.
brownsfashion.com; 23-27 South Molton St, W1;
⏰10am-7pm Mon-Wed & Sat, to 8pm Thu & Fri,
noon-6pm Sun; 🚇Bond St) Edgy and exciting,
this parade of shops on upscale South
Molton St is full of natty and individual
clothing ideas, and shoes from Asish, Stella
Jean, Natasha Zinko and other creative
designers.

> ★ **Top Tip**
>
> Non-EU visitors should look out for
> 'tax free' signs in shop windows for
> the opportunity to claim back 20%
> value-added tax (VAT).

ELENA ROSTUNOVA / SHUTTERSTOCK ©

What's Nearby?

Soho   Area

(Map p248; 🚇Tottenham Court Rd, Leicester
Sq) In a district that was once pastureland,
the name Soho is thought to have evolved
from a hunting cry. While the centre of London nightlife has shifted east and Soho has
recently seen landmark clubs and music
venues shut down, the neighbourhood definitely comes into its own in the evenings
and remains a proud gay neighbourhood.
During the day you'll be charmed by the
area's bohemian side and its sheer vitality.

At Soho's northern end, leafy **Soho
Square** (Map p248; 🚇Tottenham Court Rd,
Leicester Sq) is the area's back garden. It
was laid out in 1681 and originally named
King's Sq; a statue of Charles II stands
in its northern half. In the centre is a tiny
half-timbered mock-Tudor cottage built as
a gardener's shed in the 1870s. The space
below it was used as an underground bomb
shelter during WWII.

South of the square is **Dean Street**,
lined with bars and restaurants. No 28 was
the home of Karl Marx and his family from
1851 to 1856; they lived here in extreme
poverty as Marx researched and wrote *Das
Kapital* in the Reading Room of the British
Museum.

Old Compton Street is the epicentre of
Soho's gay village. It's a street loved by all,
gay or otherwise, for its great bars, risqué
shops and general good vibes.

Seducer and heartbreaker Casanova and
opium-addicted writer Thomas de Quincey
lived on nearby Greek St, while the parallel
Frith Street housed Mozart at No 20 for a
year from 1764.

> ℹ **Local Knowledge**
>
> Independent music stores find it
> difficult to keep going nowadays, but
> they seem to thrive in Soho, with its long
> rock-and-roll tradition.

DINING OUT

Top-notch restaurants, gastropubs,
afternoon tea and more

Dining Out

Once the laughing stock of the cooking world, London has got its culinary act together in the last 20 years and is today an undisputed dining destination. There are plenty of top-notch, Michelin-starred restaurants, but it is the sheer diversity on offer that is head-spinning: from Afghan to Vietnamese, London is a virtual A to Z of world cuisine.

You'll find that there are restaurants to suit every budget – and every occasion. Dinner in a fabulous restaurant is part and parcel of a great trip to London, but make sure you also sample the cheap and cheerful fare on offer in market stalls and sit down in one of the capital's tip-top cafes.

In This Section

Price Ranges & Tipping

These symbols indicate the average cost per main course at the restaurant in question.

£ less than £10

££ £10–20

£££ more than £20

Most restaurants automatically tack a 'discretionary' service charge (12.5%) onto the bill. If you feel the service wasn't adequate, you can tip separately (or not at all).

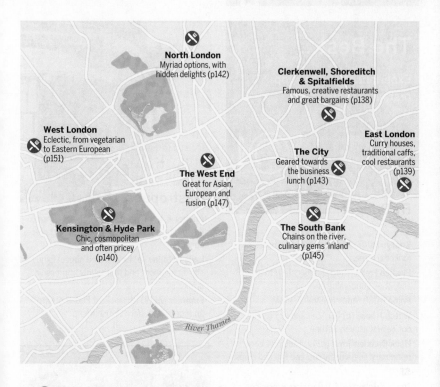

North London
Myriad options, with hidden delights (p142)

Clerkenwell, Shoreditch & Spitalfields
Famous, creative restaurants and great bargains (p138)

West London
Eclectic, from vegetarian to Eastern European (p151)

East London
Curry houses, traditional caffs, cool restaurants (p139)

The City
Geared towards the business lunch (p143)

The West End
Great for Asian, European and fusion (p147)

Kensington & Hyde Park
Chic, cosmopolitan and often pricey (p140)

The South Bank
Chains on the river, culinary gems 'inland' (p145)

River Thames

Useful Websites

Time Out London (www.timeout.com/london) Has the most up-to-date listings of restaurants as well as information on harder-to-track pop-up eateries and food trucks.

Open Table (www.opentable.co.uk) Bookings for numerous restaurants, as well as meal deals with excellent discounts.

Wine Pages (www.wine-pages.com) Keeps a useful directory of BYO restaurants.

Classic Dishes

Pie & Mash Once a staple lunch – pie (usually beef) served with mashed potatoes, liquor (a parsley sauce) and jellied eels (we dare you!).

English Breakfast This champion's breakfast usually includes bacon, sausages, eggs, baked beans, tomatoes and mushrooms.

Sunday Roast Your choice of meat (lamb, beef etc) smothered in gravy and served with ballooning Yorkshire pudding, roast potatoes and a smorgasbord of vegetables.

The Best...

Experience London's top
restaurants and cafes

By Budget

£

Shoryu (p147) Perfectly executed bowls of *tonkotsu* ramen.

Pimlico Fresh (p140) Perky cafe with an accent on good-value fine food.

Polpo (p138) Addictive Italian tapas.

Watch House (p146) Ace sandwiches, fine coffee and a lovely setting.

Hook Camden Town (p144) Fabulous, contemporary, sustainably sourced fish and chips.

££

Tom's Kitchen (p140) Relaxing ambience, warm staff, excellent food: you can't go wrong.

Palomar (p147) Excellent Jerusalem food for sharing with a foodie friend.

Rabbit (p140) Champions of modern British food and drink.

Baltic (p145) Authentic flavours from Eastern Europe in elegant decor.

Cafe Murano (p147) Northern Italian fare cooked to perfection and without fuss.

£££

Dinner by Heston Blumenthal (p141) A supreme fusion of perfect British food, eye-catching design and celeb stature.

Hawksmoor (p138) An essential destination for carnivores.

Arabica Bar & Kitchen (p145) Forget kebabs and belly-dancers: this is contemporary Middle Eastern cuisine at its best.

Ledbury (p151) A long-standing, scintillating culinary stalwart in West London.

Gastropubs

Anchor & Hope (p146) Flying the gastropub flag on the South Bank for the best part of a decade.

Lady Ottoline (p149; pictured above) Exquisite dining room and thoroughly impressive drinks list.

Empress (p139) Choice East End spot with an excellent modern British menu.

For Views

Duck & Waffle (p145) Hearty British dishes from the top of Heron Tower, round the clock.

Min Jiang (p142) Breathtaking panoramas over Kensington Gardens.

Portrait (p150) Classic views to Nelson's Column and beyond, down Whitehall to Big Ben.

British

St John (p138; pictured above) The restaurant that inspired the revival of British cuisine.

Rabbit (p140) Make it to King's Rd for some of the best British food in London.

Market (p143) A modern British decor for a modern British menu in Camden.

Great Queen St (p150) Quality roasts, stews and other British staples in relaxed atmosphere.

Indian

Tayyabs (p139; pictured above) Long-standing Punjabi favourite in the East End.

Dishoom (p149) Bombay cafe food as it really is served and eaten.

Gymkhana (p149) Splendid club-style Raj environment, top cuisine.

Celebrity Chef Restaurants

Dinner by Heston Blumenthal (p141) Molecular gastronomy at its very best.

Tom's Kitchen (p140; pictured above) Tom Aikens' relaxed Chelsea brasserie remains ever popular.

Cafes

Towpath (p139) Canal-side alfresco lattes: welcome to London.

Sky Pod (p143) The views and surroundings trump the coffee, but how could they not?

Tomtom Coffee House (p141; pictured above) No one takes their coffee more seriously than these guys.

Nude Espresso (p139) Kings of the single-origin coffee.

🍴 British Cuisine in a Nutshell

England might have given the world baked beans on toast, mushy peas and chip butties (French fries between two slices of buttered and untoasted white bread), but that's hardly the whole story.

Modern British food has become a cuisine in its own right, by championing traditional (and sometimes underrated) ingredients such as root vegetables, smoked fish, shellfish, game, sausages and black pudding (a kind of sausage stuffed with oatmeal, spices and blood). Dishes can be anything from game served with a traditional vegetable such as Jerusalem artichoke, to seared scallops with orange-scented black pudding, or roast pork with chorizo on rosemary mash.

England does a mean dessert and establishments serving British cuisine revel in these indulgent treats. Favourites include bread-and-butter pudding, sticky toffee pudding (a steamed pudding that contains dates and is topped with a divine caramel sauce), the alarmingly named spotted dick (a steamed suet pudding with currants and raisins), Eton mess (meringue, cream and strawberries mixed into a gooey, heavenly mess) and seasonal musts such as Christmas pudding (a steamed pudding with candied fruit and brandy) and fruity crumbles (rhubarb, apple etc).

Scotch eggs at Maltby Street Market (p146)
ELENACHAYKINAPHOTOGRAPHY / SHUTTERSTOCK ©

✖ Clerkenwell, Shoreditch & Spitalfields

Polpo   Italian £

(Map p253; ☑020-7250 0034; www.polpo.co.uk; 3 Cowcross St, EC1M; dishes £4-12; ☺11.30am-11pm Mon-Sat, to 4pm Sun; ⊖Farringdon) Occupying a sunny spot on semi-pedestrianised Cowcross St, this sweet little place serves rustic Venetian-style meatballs, *pizzette,* grilled meat and fish dishes. Portions are larger than your average tapas but a tad smaller than a regular main – the perfect excuse to sample more than one of the exquisite dishes. Exceptional value for money.

Hawksmoor   Steak £££

(Map p253; ☑020-7426 4850; www.the-hawksmoor.com; 157 Commercial St, E1; mains £20-50; ☺noon-2.30pm & 5-10.30pm Mon-Sat, noon-9pm Sun; ⓐ; ⊖Liverpool St) You could easily miss this discreetly signed Hawksmoor, but confirmed carnivores will find it worth seeking out. The dark wood, bare bricks and velvet curtains make for a handsome setting in which to gorge yourself on the best of British beef. The Sunday roasts (£20) are legendary.

Morito   Tapas ££

(Map p253; ☑020-7278 7007; www.morito.co.uk; 32 Exmouth Market, EC1R; dishes £6.50-9.50; ☺noon-4pm & 5-11pm Mon-Sat, noon-4pm Sun; ⓐ; ⊖Farringdon) This diminutive eatery is a wonderfully authentic take on a Spanish tapas bar and has excellent eats. Seats are at the bar, along the window, or on one of the small tables inside or out. It's relaxed, convivial and often completely crammed; reservations are taken for lunch, but dinner is first come, first served, with couples generally going to the bar.

St John   British ££

(Map p253; ☑020-7251 0848; www.stjohngroup.uk.com/spitalfields; 26 St John St, EC1M; mains £14.80-24.90; ☺noon-3pm & 6-11pm Mon-Fri, 6-11pm Sat, 12.30-4pm Sun; ⊖Farringdon) Whitewashed brick walls, high ceilings and simple wooden furniture don't make for a cosy dining space but they do keep diners free to concentrate on St John's famous nose-to-tail dishes. Serves are big, hearty and a celebration of England's culinary past. Don't miss the signature roast bone marrow and parsley salad (£8.90).

Nude Espresso   Cafe £

(Map p253; www.nudeespresso.com; 26 Hanbury St, E1; dishes £4.50-12; ⏰7am-6pm Mon-Fri, 9.30am-5pm Sat & Sun; ⊖Liverpool St) A simply styled, cosy cafe serving top-notch coffee (roasted across the street). Along with the standard blend, it has rotating single-origin coffees and filter as well as espresso-based brews. The sweet treats are delicious, as are the cooked breakfasts, brunch items and light lunches.

✪ East London

Empress   Modern British ££

(Map p255; ☎020-8533 5123; www.empresse9.co.uk; 130 Lauriston Rd, E9; mains £16-18; ⏰10am-9.30pm Sun, 6-10.15pm Mon, noon-3.30pm & 6-10.15pm Tue-Sat; 🚌277) This up-market pub conversion belts out excellent modern British cuisine in very pleasant surroundings. On Mondays there's a £10 main-plus-drink deal and on weekends it serves an excellent brunch.

Brawn   British, French ££

(Map p253; ☎020-7729 5692; www.brawn.co; 49 Columbia Rd, E2; mains £11.50-28; ⏰noon-3pm Tue-Sat, 6-10.30pm Mon-Sat, noon-4pm Sun; ⊖Hoxton) There's a Parisian bistro feel to this relaxed corner restaurant, yet the menu walks a fine line between British and French traditions. Hence oxtail and veal kidney pie sits alongside plaice Grenobloise, and souffles are filled with Westcombe cheddar. Try its legendary spicy Scotch-egg starter – a Brit classic delivered with French finesse. The three-course Sunday lunch is £28.

Corner Room   Modern British ££

(Map p255; ☎020-7871 0460; www.townhall-hotel.com/cornerroom; Patriot Sq, E2; mains £13-14, 2-/3-course lunch £19/23; ⏰7.30-10am, noon-3pm & 6-9.45pm; ⊖Bethnal Green) Some-

one put this baby in the corner, but we're certainly not complaining. Tucked away on the 1st floor of the Town Hall Hotel, this relaxed restaurant serves expertly crafted dishes with complex yet delicate flavours, highlighting the best of British seasonal produce.

Towpath   Cafe £

(Map p253; ☎020-7254 7606; rear 42-44 De Beauvoir Cres, N1; mains £6.50-9; ⏰9am-5.30pm Tue-Sun; ⊖Haggerston) Occupying four small units on the Regent's Canal towpath, this simple cafe is a super place to sip a cuppa and watch the ducks and narrowboats glide by. The food's excellent too, with delicious frittatas and brownies on the counter and cooked dishes chalked up on the blackboard daily.

Mangal Ocakbasi   Turkish ££

(Map p255; ☎020-7275 8981; www.mangal1.com; 10 Arcola St, E8; mains £8-18; ⏰noon-midnight; 🖊; ⊖Dalston Kingsland) Mangal is the quintessential Turkish *ocakbasi* (open-hooded charcoal grill, the mother of all BBQs): cramped, smoky and serving superb mezze, grilled vegetables, lamb chops, quail and a lip-smacking assortment of kebabs. BYO alcohol.

Formans   Modern British ££

(Map p255; ☎020-8525 2365; www.formans.co.uk; Stour Rd, E3; mains £15-19.50, brunch £6-10; ⏰7-11pm Thu & Fri, 10am-3pm & 7-11pm Sat, noon-5pm Sun; 📶; ⊖Hackney Wick) Curing fish since 1905, riverside Formans boasts prime views over the Olympic stadium, with a gallery overlooking its smokery. The menu includes a delectable choice of smoked salmon (including its signature 'London cure'), plenty of other seafood and a few nonfishy things, as well as delicious sticky puddings. There's a great selection of British wines and spirits, too.

Tayyabs   Punjabi ££

(☎020-7247 9543; www.tayyabs.co.uk; 83-89 Fieldgate St, E1; mains £5.60-16; ⏰noon-11.30pm; 🖊; ⊖Whitechapel) This buzzing (OK, crowded) Punjabi restaurant is in another league to its Brick Lane equivalents. *Seekh*

¶◯¶ Celebrity Chefs

London's food renaissance was partly led by a group of telegenic chefs who built food empires around their names and their TV programs. **Gordon Ramsay** is the most (in)famous of the lot and his London venues are still standard-bearers for top-quality cuisine. Other big names include campaigning star **Jamie Oliver; Tom Aikens**, who champions British products; and **Heston Blumenthal** (p141), whose mad-professor-like experiments with food (molecular gastronomy, as he describes it) have earned him rave reviews.

Tom Aikens
HOMER SYKES / ALAMY STOCK PHOTO ©

kebabs, masala fish and other starters served on sizzling hot plates are delicious, as are accompaniments such as dhal, naan and raita. On the downside, it can be noisy, service can be haphazard and queues often snake out the door.

Randy's Wing Bar   American £
(Map p255; ☑020-8555 5971; www.randyswingbar.co.uk; 28 East Bay Ln, E15; ☺noon-11pm Tue-Wed, to 11.30pm Thu-Sun, 6pm-11pm Mon; ☒Hackney Wick) What began life as a street-food cart has developed into a fully fledged restaurant; happily, the flavours have been unaffected by the presence of a roof. Chicken is the order of the day and, unsurprisingly, the wings are the signature dish, with an excellent variety on offer, from Indian to Korean to good old Americana.

❽ Greenwich & South London

Greenwich Market   Market £
(Map p256; www.greenwichmarketlondon.com/food-and-drink; College Approach, SE10; ☺9am-5.30pm; ℗☒; ☒DLR Cutty Sark) Perfect for snacking your way through a world atlas of food while browsing the other market stalls. Come here for delicious food to go, from Spanish tapas and Thai curries to sushi, Ethiopian vegetarian, French crêpes, dim sum, Mexican burritos and lots more.

❽ Kensington & Hyde Park

Rabbit   Modern British ££
(Map p250; ☑020-3750 0172; www.rabbit-restaurant.com; 172 King's Rd, SW3; mains £6-24, set lunch £13.50; ☺noon-midnight Tue-Sat, 6-11pm Mon, noon-6pm Sun; ☒; ☒Sloane Sq) Three brothers grew up on a farm. One became a farmer, another a butcher, while the third worked in hospitality. So they pooled their skills and came up with Rabbit, a breath of fresh air in upmarket Chelsea. The restaurant rocks the agri-chic (yes) look and the creative, seasonal modern British cuisine is fabulous.

Tom's Kitchen   Modern European ££
(Map p250; ☑020-7349 0202; www.tomskitchen.co.uk/chelsea; 27 Cale St, SW3; mains £16-30, 2-/3-course lunch menu £16.50/19.50; ☺8am-2.30pm & 6-10.30pm Mon-Fri, 9.30am-3.30pm & 6-10.30pm Sat, to 9.30pm Sun; ☒☒; ☒South Kensington) ✪ Recipe for success: mix one part relaxed and smiling staff, one part light and airy decor to two parts divine food and voilà, you have Tom's Kitchen. Classics such as grilled steaks, burgers, slow-cooked pork belly and chicken schnitzel are cooked to perfection, whilst seasonal choices such as the homemade ricotta or pan-fried scallops are sublime.

Pimlico Fresh   Cafe £
(☑020-7932 0030; 86 Wilton Rd, SW1; mains from £4.50; ☺7.30am-7.30pm Mon-Fri, 9am-6pm Sat & Sun; ☒Victoria) This friendly two-room

cafe will see you right whether you need breakfast (French toast, bowls of porridge laced with honey or maple syrup), lunch (homemade quiches and soups, 'things' on toast) or just a good old latte and cake.

Dinner by Heston Blumenthal   Modern British £££

(Map p250; ☎020-7201 3833; www. dinnerbyheston.com; Mandarin Oriental Hyde Park, 66 Knightsbridge, SW1; 3-course set lunch £45, mains £28-44; ☻noon-2pm & 6-10.15pm Mon-Fri, noon-2.30pm & 6-10.30pm Sat & Sun; ☞; ☻Knightsbridge) Sumptuously presented Dinner is a gastronomic tour de force, taking diners on a journey through British culinary history (with inventive modern inflections). Dishes carry historical dates to convey context, while the restaurant interior is a design triumph, from the glass-walled kitchen and its overhead clock mechanism to the large windows looking onto the park. Book ahead.

Tomtom Coffee House   Cafe

(Map p250; ☎020-7730 1771; www.tomtom. co.uk; 114 Ebury St, SW1; ☻8am-5pm Mon-Fri, 9am-6pm Sat & Sun; ☞; ☻Victoria) Tomtom has built its reputation on its amazing coffee: not only are the drinks fabulously presented (forget ferns and hearts in your latte, here it's peacocks fanning their tails), the selection is dizzying, from the usual espresso-based suspects to filter, and a full choice of beans. You can even spice things up with a bonus tot of cognac or Scotch (£3).

The cafe also serves lovely food throughout the day, from breakfast and toasties on sourdough bread to homemade pies (mains £5 to £10).

Magazine   International ££

(Map p250; ☎020-7298 7552; www.magazine-restaurant.co.uk; Serpentine Sackler Gallery, West Carriage Dr, W2; mains £13-24, 2-/3-course lunch menu £17.50/21.50; ☻9am-6pm Tue-Sat; ☞; ☻Lancaster Gate, Knightsbridge) Located in the elegant extension of the Serpentine Sackler Gallery, Magazine is no ordinary museum cafe. The food is as contemporary and elegant as the building, and artworks from current exhibitions add yet another dimension. The afternoon tea (£25, with

Magazine

one cocktail) is particularly original: out with cucumber sandwiches, in with gin-cured sea trout, goat's curd and coconut granita.

Magazine opens for dinner on Fridays and Saturdays from April to September, with the added bonus of live music.

Min Jiang — Chinese £££

(Map p250; ☑020-7361 1988; www.minjiang. co.uk; Royal Garden Hotel, 10th fl, 2-24 Kensington High St, W8; mains £12-68, lunch set menu £40-55, dinner set menu £70-88; ◷noon-3pm & 6-10.30pm; ☑; ⊖High St Kensington) Min Jiang serves up seafood, excellent wood-fired Peking duck (*běijīng kǎoyā*; half/whole £33/60), *dim sum* (from £4.80) and sumptuously regal views over Kensington Palace and Gardens. The menu is diverse, with a sporadic accent on spice (the Min Jiang is a river in Sichuan).

Orangery — Cafe ££

(Map p250; www.orangerykensingtonpalace. co.uk; Kensington Palace, Kensington Gardens, W8; mains £12.50-16.50, afternoon tea £27.50; ◷10am-5pm; ☑; ⊖Queensway or High St Kensington) The Orangery, housed in an 18th-century conservatory on the grounds of Kensington Palace (p98), is lovely for a late breakfast or lunch, but the standout experience here is English afternoon tea. Book ahead to bag a table on the beautiful terrace.

⊗ North London

Ottolenghi — Bakery, Mediterranean ££

(☑020-7288 1454; www.ottolenghi.co.uk; 287 Upper St, N1; breakfast £5.50-10.50, mains lunch/dinner from £12.90/11; ◷8am-10.30pm Mon-Sat, 9am-7pm Sun; ☑; ⊖Highbury & Islington) Mountains of meringues tempt you through the door of this deli-restaurant, where you will be greeted by a sumptuous array of baked goods and fresh salads. Meals are as light and bright as the brilliantly white interior design, with a strong influence from the eastern Mediterranean.

Chin Chin Labs — Ice Cream £

(Map p254; www.chinchinlabs.com; 49-50 Camden Lock Pl, NW1; ice cream £4-5; ◷noon-

Ottolenghi

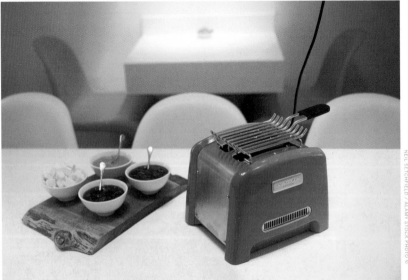

NEIL SETCHFIELD / ALAMY STOCK PHOTO ©

7pm Sun-Thu, to 10pm Fri & Sat; ⊖Camden Town) This is food chemistry at its absolute best. Chefs prepare the ice-cream mixture and freeze it on the spot by adding liquid nitrogen. Flavours change regularly and match the seasons (spiced hot cross bun, passionfruit and coconut, for instance). Sauces and toppings are equally creative. Try the ice-cream sandwich if you can: ice cream wedged inside gorgeous brownies or cookies.

Grain Store International ££
(Map p254; ☑020-7324 4466; www.grainstore. com; 1-3 Stable St, N1C; mains £13-20.50; ☺10am-11.30pm Mon-Sat, 10.30am-3.30pm Sun; ☑; ⊖King's Cross St Pancras) Fresh seasonal vegetables take top billing at Bruno Loubet's bright and breezy Granary Sq restaurant. Meat does appear but it lurks coyly beneath leaves, or adds crunch to mashes. The creative menu gainfully plunders from numerous cuisines to produce dishes that are simultaneously healthy and delicious.

Caravan International ££
(Map p254; ☑020-7101 7661; www. caravanrestaurants.co.uk; 1 Granary Sq, N1C; mains £7-19.50; ☺8am-10.30pm Mon-Fri, 10am-10.30pm Sat, 10am-4pm Sun; ☜☑; ⊖King's Cross St Pancras) Housed in the lofty Granary Building, Caravan is a vast industrial-chic destination for tasty fusion bites from around the world. You can opt for several small plates to share tapas style, or stick to main-sized plates. The outdoor seating area on Granary Sq is especially popular on warm days.

Market Modern British ££
(Map p254; ☑020-7267 9700; www.marketrestaurant.co.uk; 43 Parkway, NW1; 2-course lunch menu £11.50, mains £15-20; ☺noon-2.30pm & 6-10.30pm Mon-Sat, 11am-3pm Sun; ⊖Camden Town) This fabulous restaurant is an ode to great, simple British food, with a measure of French sophistication thrown in. The light and airy space (bare brick walls, steel tables and basic wooden chairs) reflects this stripped-back approach.

🍽 Afternoon Tea

Afternoon tea has become all the rage in the last few years. This indulgent treat usually includes a selection of savoury sandwiches (such as smoked salmon or cucumber), cakes (anything from macarons to Battenberg), scones (the pièce de résistance) served with jam and clotted cream, and a pot of tea (or, if you're feeling decadent, a glass of sparkling wine).

It's convivial, fun but generally overpriced (£20 to £40 per person). It is usually served in top-end restaurants and hotels at weekends, between 3pm and 6pm. It's best to skip lunch (and you probably won't need much dinner either). Bookings are essential pretty much everywhere, especially in winter.

The best places to try it are Claridge's Foyer & Reading Room (p149), Portrait (p150), Delaunay (p148), Orangery (p142) and Wallace (p150).

Afternoon tea spread
MICHAEL BLANN / GETTY IMAGES ©

⊗ The City

Sky Pod Bar
(Map p245; ☑0333-772 0020; http://skygarden. london/sky-pod-bar; 20 Fenchurch St, EC3; ☺7am-1am Mon, 7am-2am Tue-Fri, 8am-2am Sat, 9am-midnight Sun; ⊖Monument) One of the best places in the City to get high is the Sky Pod in the Sky Garden on level 35 of the so-called Walkie Talkie. The views are nothing short of phenomenal – especially from the open-air South Terrace – the gardens

London on a Plate

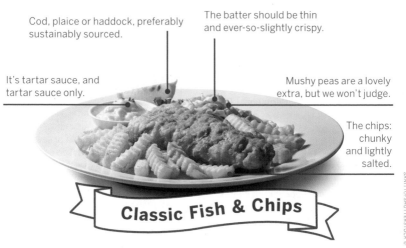

Cod, plaice or haddock, preferably sustainably sourced.

The batter should be thin and ever-so-slightly crispy.

It's tartar sauce, and tartar sauce only.

Mushy peas are a lovely extra, but we won't judge.

The chips: chunky and lightly salted.

SANITTO/SHUTTERSTOCK ©

Classic Fish & Chips

Fish & Chips in London

Fish and chips isn't fancy and is best enjoyed straight out of the takeaway wrapper while sitting on a park bench on a sunny day. Alternatively, fish and chips 'shops' (as they're usually called) tend to be simple, busy cafes, often offering little more than formica tables and wafts from the deep-fryer. Luckily, London standards are high and the best fish and chips restaurants are rather lovely.

A London fish and chips shop
PAWEL LIBERA / GETTY IMAGES ©

★ Top Three Fish & Chips Restaurants

Hook Camden Town (Map p254; www.hookrestaurants.com; 65 Parkway, NW1; mains £8-12; ⊘noon-3pm & 5-10pm Mon-Thu, noon-10.30pm Fri & Sat, to 9pm Sun; 🚼; ⊖Camden Town) ☞ **Works entirely with sustainable small fisheries and local suppliers.**

Poppie's (Map p253; www.poppiesfishandchips.co.uk; 6-8 Hanbury St, E1; mains £12.20-15.90; ⊘11am-11pm; ⊖Liverpool St) **A glorious re-creation of a 1950s East End chippy.**

Geales (Map p250; ☎020-7727 7528; www.geales.com; 2 Farmer St, W8; 2-course express lunch £9.75, mains £9-39.50; ⊘noon-3pm & 6-10.30pm Tue-Fri, noon-10.30pm Sat, noon-4pm Sun; ⊖Notting Hill Gate) **Frying since 1939, Geales has endured with its quiet location on the corner of Farmer St in Hillgate Village.**

are lush and it's the only place where this obstructive and clumsy-looking building won't be in your face.

Enjoy a cocktail or a light meal (breakfast, Bircher muesli £4, sandwiches and salads from £5). More substantial meals are available above in the Sky Garden's **Darwin Brasserie** (level 36) and the **Fenchurch Seafood Bar & Grill** (level 37). But we prefer this cafe and bar where the seating is free and the atmosphere relaxed. The only drawback is that without a restaurant reservation, entry is ticketed (see website) from 10am to 6pm weekdays and 11am to 9pm on Saturday and Sunday. Outside those hours, be prepared to queue (and perhaps be disappointed).

Wine Library   Modern European **££**

(Map p245; 020-7481 0415; www.winelibrary. co.uk; 43 Trinity Sq, EC3; set meal £18; 10am-6pm Mon, to 8pm Tue-Fri; Tower Hill) This is a great place for a light but boozy lunch opposite the Tower. Buy a bottle of wine at retail price (no mark-up, £8 corkage fee) from the large selection on offer at the vaulted-cellar restaurant and then snack on a set plate of delicious pâtés, cheeses and salads. Reservations recommended at lunch.

Duck & Waffle   Brasserie **££**

(Map p245; 020-3640 7310; www.duckandwaf-fle.com; 40th fl, Heron Tower, 110 Bishopsgate, EC2; mains £10-18; 24hr; ; Liverpool St) If you like your views with sustenance round the clock, this is the place for you. Perched atop Heron Tower, just down from Liverpool St station, it serves European and British dishes (shellfish, roast chicken, some unusual seafood concoctions such as pollack meatballs) in small and large sizes by day, waffles by night, and round-the-clocktails.

Café Below   Cafe **£**

(Map p245; 020-7329 0789; www.cafebelow. co.uk; St Mary-le-Bow, Cheapside, EC2; mains £8-15.50; 7.30am-2.30pm Mon-Fri, to 9.30pm Wed-Fri; ; Mansion House or St Paul's) This very atmospheric cafe-restaurant, in the crypt of one of London's most famous

churches, offers excellent value and a tasty range of international fare, with as many vegetarian choices as meat choices. Summer sees tables outside in the shady courtyard. Occasional set dinners are available, but check the website or phone in for details.

The South Bank

Arabica Bar & Kitchen   Middle Eastern **£££**

(Map p245; 020-3011 5151; www. arabicabarandkitchen.com; 3 Rochester Walk, Borough Market, SE1; dishes £6-14; 11am-11pm Mon-Fri, 8.30am-11.30pm Sat, 11am-9pm Sun; ; London Bridge) Pan–Middle Eastern cuisine is a well-rehearsed classic these days, but Arabica Bar & Kitchen has managed to bring something fresh to its table: the decor is contemporary and bright, the food delicate and light, and there's an emphasis on sharing (two to three small dishes per person). The downside of this tapas approach is that the bill adds up quickly.

Baltic   Eastern European **££**

(Map p245; 020-7928 1111; www. balticrestaurant.co.uk; 74 Blackfriars Rd, SE1; mains £10.50-19, 2-course lunch menu £17.50; noon-3pm & 5.30-11.15pm Tue-Sun, 5.30-11.15pm Mon; ; Southwark) In a bright and airy, high-ceilinged dining room with glass roof and wooden beams, Baltic is travel on a plate: dill and beetroot, dumplings and blini, pickle and smoke, rich stews and braised meat. From Polish to Georgian, the flavours are authentic and the dishes beautifully presented. The wine and vodka lists are equally diverse.

Padella   Italian **£**

(Map p245; www.padella.co; 6 Southwark St, SE1; dishes £5-11; noon-4pm & 5-10pm Mon-Sat, noon-5pm Sun; ; London Bridge) Yet another fantastic addition to the foodie enclave of Borough Market, Padella is a small, energetic bistro specialising in handmade pasta dishes, inspired by the owners' extensive culinary adventures in Italy. The portions are small, which means that, joy of joys, you can (and should!) have more than one dish. Outstanding.

Watch House   Cafe £

(Map p245; www.watchhousecoffee.com; 193 Bermondsey St, SE1; mains from £4.95; ☺7am-6pm Mon-Fri, 8am-6pm Sat, 9am-5pm Sun; 🖉; ⊖Borough or London Bridge) 🍃 Saying that the Watch House nails the sandwich wouldn't really do justice to this tip-top cafe: the sandwiches really are delicious and feature artisan breads from a local baker. There is also great coffee and treats for the sweettoothed. The small but lovely setting is a renovated 19th-century watch-house from where guards looked out for grave robbers in the cemetery next door.

Anchor & Hope   Gastropub ££

(Map p245; www.anchorandhopepub.co.uk; 36 The Cut, SE1; mains £12-20; ☺noon-2.30pm Tue-Sat, 6-10.30pm Mon-Sat, 12.30-3pm Sun; ⊖Southwark) A stalwart of the South Bank food scene, the Anchor & Hope is a quintessential gastropub: elegant but not formal, and utterly delicious (European fare with a British twist). The menu changes daily but think salt marsh lamb shoulder cooked for seven hours; wild rabbit with anchovies, almonds and rocket; and panna cotta with rhubarb compote.

Maltby Street Market   Market £

(Map p245; www.maltby.st; Maltby St, SE1; dishes £5-10; ☺9am-4pm Sat, 11am-4pm Sun; ⊖London Bridge) Started as an alternative to the juggernaut that is Borough Market, Maltby Street Market is becoming a victim of its own success, with brick and mortar shops and restaurants replacing the old workshops, and throngs of visitors. That said, it boasts some original – and all topnotch – food stalls selling smoked salmon from east London, African burgers, seafood and lots of pastries.

Maltby Street Market

⊗ The West End

Yauatcha   Chinese £
(Map p248; ☑020-7494 8888; www.yauat-cha.com; 15 Broadwick St, W1; dishes £5-30; ⏰noon-11.30pm Mon-Sat, to 10.30pm Sun; ⊖Piccadilly Circus, Oxford Circus) London's most glamorous dim-sum restaurant has a Michelin star and is divided into two: the ground-floor dining room offers a delightful blue-bathed oasis of calm from the chaos of Berwick St Market, while downstairs has a smarter feel, with constellations of 'star' lights. Both serve exquisite dim sum and have a fabulous range of teas. Cakes here are creations to die for.

Cafe Murano   Italian ££
(Map p248; ☑020-3371 5559; www.cafemurano.co.uk; 33 St James's St, SW1; mains £18-25, 2/3-course set meal £19/23; ⏰noon-3pm & 5.30-11pm Mon-Sat, 11.30am-4pm Sun; ⊖Green Park) The setting may seem somewhat demure at this superb and busy restaurant, but with such a sublime North Italian menu on offer, it sees no need to be flash and of-the-moment. You get what you come for and the lobster linguini, pork belly and cod with mussels and samphire are as close to culinary perfection as you'll get.

Palomar   Israeli ££
(Map p248; ☑020-7439 8777; http://thepalomar.co.uk; 34 Rupert St, W1; mains £7-16.50; ⏰noon-2.30pm & 5.30-11pm Mon-Sat, 12.30-3.30pm & 6-9pm Sun; 🛜; ⊖Piccadilly Circus) The buzzing vibe at this good-looking celebration of modern-day Jerusalem cuisine (in all its permutations) is infectious, but the noise in the back dining room might drive you mad. Choose instead the counter seats at the front. The 'Yiddish-style' chopped chicken liver pate, the Jerusalem-style polenta and the 'octo-hummus' are all fantastic, but portions are smallish, so you'll need to share.

Shoryu   Noodles £
(Map p248; ☑none; www.shoryuramen.com; 9 Regent St, SW1; mains £9.50-14.90; ⏰11.15am-midnight Mon-Sat, to 10.30pm Sun;

🍽 Food Markets

The boom in London's eating scene has extended to its markets, which come in three broad categories: food stalls that are part of a broader market and appeal to visitors keen to soak up the atmosphere, such as **Old Spitalfields** (p71), **Borough** (p76) or **Camden** (Map p254; www.camdenmarket.com; Camden High St, NW1; ⏰10am-6pm; ⊖Camden Town or Chalk Farm); farmers markets, which sell pricey local and/or organic products (check out www.lfm.org.uk for a selection of the best); and the many colourful food markets, where the oranges and lemons come from who knows where and the barrow boys and girls speak with perfect Cockney accents (such as Berwick St in Soho).

Old Spitalfields Market

⊖Piccadilly Circus) Compact, well-mannered and central noodle-parlour Shoryu draws in reams of noodle diners to feast at its wooden counters and small tables. It's busy, friendly and efficient, with helpful and informative staff. Fantastic *tonkotsu* pork-broth ramen is the name of the game here, sprinkled with *nori* (dried, pressed seaweed), spring onion, *nitamago* (soft-boiled eggs) and sesame seeds. No bookings.

Barrafina   Spanish ££
(Map p248; ☑020-7440 1456; www.barrafina.co.uk; 10 Adelaide St, WC2; tapas £6.50-15.80; ⏰noon-3pm & 5-11pm Mon-Sat, 1-3.30pm & 5.30-10pm Sun; ⊖Embankment or Leicester Sq) With no reservations, you may need to get in

🍽️ Gastropubs

While not so long ago the pub was where you went for a drink, with maybe a packet of potato crisps to soak up the alcohol, the birth of the gastropub in the 1990s means that today just about every establishment serves full meals. The quality varies widely, from defrosted-on-the-premises to Michelin-star worthy.

A meal in a traditional English pub
EKATERINA POKROVSKY / SHUTTERSTOCK ©

line for an hour or so at this restaurant that does a brisk service in some of the best tapas in town. Divine mouthfuls are served on each plate, from the stuffed courgette flower (£7.80) to the suckling pig's ears (£6.80) and crab on toast (£8), so would-be diners prepare to wait.

There's a maximum group size of four. There are a couple of tables on the pavement.

Spuntino   American £

(Map p248; 🍴none; www.spuntino.co.uk; 61 Rupert St, W1; mains £6-12.50; ☺11.30am-midnight Mon-Wed, to 1am Thu-Sat, to 11pm Sun; 🛜; ☻Piccadilly Circus) Offering an unusual mix of speakeasy decor and surprisingly creative American food, Spuntino is a delight at every turn. Try old favourites such as macaroni cheese (from £6), cheeseburger with jalapeño peppers (£8) and, as a dessert, peanut butter and jelly sandwich. Seating is at the bar or counters at the back with two-dozen stools.

Delaunay   Brasserie ££

(Map p245; 🍴020-7499 8558; www.thedelaunay. com; 55 Aldwych, WC2; mains £7.50-35; ☺7am-11.30pm Mon-Fri, 8am-midnight Sat, 9am-11pm Sun; 🛜; ☻Temple, Covent Garden) This smart brasserie southeast of Covent Garden is a kind of Franco-German hybrid, where schnitzels and wieners sit happily beside croque-monsieurs and *choucroute alsacienne* (Alsace-style sauerkraut). Even more relaxed is the adjacent **Counter at the Delaunay** (Map p245; soups & sandwiches £4.5-10; ☺7am-8pm Mon-Wed, 7am-10.30pm Thu & Fri, 10.30am-10.30pm Sat, 11am-5.30pm Sun), where you can drop in for chicken noodle soup and a New York–style hot dog.

Brunch is from 11am to 5pm at the weekend and afternoon tea (£19.75, or £29.75 with Champagne) is available daily from 3pm.

Kanada-Ya   Noodles £

(Map p248; 🍴020-7240 0232; www.kanada-ya. com; 64 St Giles High St, WC2; mains £10.50-14; ☺noon-3pm & 5-10pm Mon-Sat; ☻Tottenham Court Rd) With no reservations taken, queues can get impressive outside this tiny and enormously popular canteen, where ramen cooked in *tonkotsu* (pork-bone broth) draws in diners for its three types of noodles delivered in steaming bowls, steeped in a delectable broth and highly authentic flavours. The restaurant also serves up *onigiri* (dried seaweed-wrapped rice balls, £2).

Brasserie Zédel   French ££

(Map p248; 🍴020-7734 4888; www. brasseriezedel.com; 20 Sherwood St, W1; mains £13.50-25.75; ☺11.30am-midnight Mon-Sat, to 11pm Sun; 🛜; ☻Piccadilly Circus) This brasserie in the renovated art deco ballroom of a former hotel is the Frenchest eatery west of Calais. Favourites include *choucroute alsacienne* (sauerkraut with sausages and charcuterie, £15.50) or a straight-up *steak haché* (chopped steak) with pepper sauce and *frites* (£9.95). Set menus (£9.75/12.75 for two/three courses) and plats du jour (£15.50) offer excellent value in a terrific setting.

Gymkhana — Indian ££

(Map p248; ☑020-3011 5900; www.
gymkhanalondon.com; 42 Albemarle St, W1; mains
£10-38, 2/3-course lunch £25/30; ⊙noon-2.30pm
& 5.30-10.30pm Mon-Sat; 🛜; ⊖Green Park) The
rather sombre setting is all British Raj: ceiling
fans, oak ceiling, period cricket photos and
hunting trophies; the menu is lively, bright
and inspiring. For lovers of variety, try the
six-course tasting meat/vegetarian menu
(£70/£65). The bar is open to 1am.

Dishoom — Indian £

(Map p248; ☑020-7420 9320; www.dishoom.
com; 12 Upper St Martin's Lane, WC2; mains
£4.50-16.50; ⊙8am-11pm Mon-Thu, 8am-
midnight Fri, 9am-midnight Sat, 9am-11pm
Sun; 🛜; ⊖Covent Garden) This branch of a
highly successful minichain takes the fast-
disappearing Iranian cafe of Bombay and
gives it new life. Distressed with a modern
twist (all ceiling fans, stained mirrors and
sepia photos), you'll find yummy favourites
like *seekh* kebab and spicy chicken
ruby, okra fries and snack foods such as
bhel (Bombay mix and puffed rice with
pomegranate, onion, lime and mint).

Claridge's Foyer & Reading Room — British £££

(Map p250; ☑020-7107 8886; www.claridges.
co.uk; 49-53 Brook St, W1; afternoon tea £68, with
champagne £79; ⊙afternoon tea 2.45-5.30pm;
🛜; ⊖Bond St) Extend that pinkie finger to
partake in afternoon tea within the classic
art-deco Foyer and Reading Room of this
landmark hotel, whose gentle clink of
fine porcelain and champagne glasses
could be a defining memory of your trip to
London. The setting is gorgeous and dress
is elegant, smart casual (ripped jeans and
baseball caps won't get served).

Lady Ottoline — Gastropub ££

(Map p254; ☑020-7831 0008; www.theladyottoline.
com; 11a Northington St, WC1; mains £14-17;
⊙noon-11pm Mon-Sat, to 5pm Sun; ⊖Chancery
Lane) Bloomsbury can sometimes seem a bit
of a culinary wasteland, but this gastropub
(named after a patron of the Bloomsbury
Set) is a pleasant exception. You can eat in
the buzzy pub downstairs, but the cosy dining
room above is more tempting. Favourites
such as beer-battered fish and chips and
pork with apple ketchup are excellent.

Delaunay

¡O¡ Vegetarians & Vegans

London has been one of the best places for vegetarians to dine out since the 1970s, initially due mostly to its many Indian restaurants, which, for religious reasons, always cater for people who don't eat meat. A number of dedicated vegetarian restaurants have since cropped up, offering imaginative, filling and truly delicious meals. Most nonvegetarian places generally offer a couple of dishes for those who don't eat meat; vegans, however, will find it harder outside Indian or dedicated establishments.

Some 95 gins are on offer as well as Lady Ottoline's own in-house vermouth.

Wallace   Modern European ££

(Map p250; ☑020-7563 9505; www.wallacecollection.org/visiting/thewallacerestaurant; Hertford House, Manchester Sq, W1; mains £14-22.50; ☺10am-5pm Sun-Thu, to 11pm Fri & Sat; ⊖Bond St) There are few more idyllically placed restaurants than this spot in the enclosed courtyard of the **Wallace Collection** (Map p250; www.wallacecollection.org; Hertford House, Manchester Sq, W1; ☺10am-5pm; ⊖Bond St) **FREE**. The emphasis is on seasonal French-inspired dishes, with the daily menu offering two- or three-course meals for £22.50/25.50. Afternoon tea is £18.50.

Great Queen Street   British ££

(Map p248; ☑020-7242 0622; www.greatqueenstreetrestaurant.co.uk; 32 Great Queen St, WC2; mains £15.80-19.80; ☺noon-2.30pm & 5.30-10.30pm Mon-Sat, noon-3.30pm Sun; ⊖Holborn) The menu at one of Covent Garden's best places to eat is seasonal (and changes daily), with an emphasis on quality, hearty dishes and fine ingredients – there are always delicious stews, roasts and simple fish dishes. The atmosphere is lively, with the small **Cellar Bar** (5pm to 11pm Tuesday to Saturday) open for cocktails and drinks. Booking is essential.

La Fromagerie   Cafe ££

(Map p250; ☑020-7935 0341; www.lafromagerie.co.uk; 2-6 Moxon St, W1; mains £7-18; ☺8am-7.30pm Mon-Fri, 9am-7pm Sat, 10am-6pm Sun; 🛜; ⊖Baker St) ✔ This deli-cafe has bowls of delectable salads, antipasto, peppers and beans scattered about the long communal table. Huge slabs of bread invite you to tuck in while the heavenly waft from the cheese room beckons. Cheese boards come in small and large (£9.25 and £16) and breakfast is always a good choice.

Pollen Street Social   Modern European £££

(Map p248; ☑020-7290 7600; www.pollenstreetsocial.com; 8-10 Pollen St, W1; mains £33-38; ☺noon-2.45pm & 6-10.45pm Mon-Sat; ⊖Oxford Circus) Jason Atherton's cathedral to haute cuisine would be beyond reach of anyone not on a hefty expense account, but the excellent-value set lunch (£32/37 for two/three courses) makes it fairly accessible to all. A generous two-hour slot allows ample time to linger over such delights as lime-cured salmon, braised West Country ox cheek and a choice from the dessert bar.

Portrait   Modern European £££

(Map p248; ☑020-7312 2490; www.npg.org.uk/visit/shop-eat-drink.php; 3rd fl, National Portrait Gallery, St Martin's Pl, WC2; mains £19.50-26, 2/3-course menu £27.50/31.50; ☺10-11am, 11.45am-3pm & 3.30-4.30pm daily, 6.30-8.30pm Thu, Fri & Sat; 🛜; ⊖Charing Cross) This stunningly located restaurant above the excellent National Portrait Gallery (p55) comes with dramatic views over Trafalgar Sq and Westminster. It's a fine choice for tantalising food and the chance to relax after a morning or afternoon of picture-gazing at the gallery. The breakfast/brunch (10am to 11am) and afternoon tea (3.30pm to 4.30pm) come highly recommended. Booking is advisable.

West London

Mazi Greek ££
(Map p250; 020-7229 3794; www.mazi.co.uk; 12-14 Hillgate St, W8; mains £9-24; noon-3pm Tue-Sun, 6.30-10.30pm Mon-Sat & 6.30-10pm Sun; ; Notting Hill Gate) Where long-standing Costa's Grill did business for decades, Mazi has shaken up the Greek tradition along pretty Hillgate St, concocting a lively menu of modern and innovative (and many of sharing size) platters in a bright and neat setting, with a small back garden (for summer months) and an all-Greek wine list. It's both small and popular, so reservations are important.

Ledbury French £££
(Map p250; 020-7792 9090; www.theledbury.com; 127 Ledbury Rd, W11; 4-course set lunch £70, 4-course dinner £115; noon-2pm Wed-Sun & 6.30-9.45pm daily; ; Westbourne Park or Notting Hill Gate) Two Michelin stars and swooningly elegant, Brett Graham's artful French restaurant attracts well-heeled diners in jeans with designer jackets. Dishes – such as hand-dived scallops, Chinese water deer, smoked bone marrow, quince and red leaves or Herdwick lamb with salt-baked turnips, celery cream and wild garlic – are simply triumphant. London gastronomes have the Ledbury on speed-dial, so reservations well in advance are crucial.

Taquería Mexican £
(Map p250; www.taqueria.co.uk; 139-143 Westbourne Grove; tacos £6.50-9; noon-11pm Mon-Thu, to 11.30pm Fri & Sat, to 10.30pm Sun; ; Notting Hill Gate) You won't find fresher, limper (they're not supposed to be crispy!) tacos anywhere in London because these ones are made on the premises. Recently refurbished, it's a small casual place with a great vibe. Taquería is also a committed environmental establishment: the eggs, chicken and pork are free-range, the meat British, the fish MSC-certified and the milk and cream organic.

The kitchen of Pollen Street Social

TRAVELCOLLECTION / ALAMY STOCK PHOTO ©

TREASURE HUNT

Begin your shopping adventure

Treasure Hunt

From charity-shop finds to designer bags, there are thousands of ways to spend your hard-earned cash in London. Many of the big-name shopping attractions, such as Harrods, Hamleys, Camden Market and Old Spital-fields Market, have become must-sees in their own right. Chances are that with so many temptations, you'll give your wallet a full workout.

Perhaps the biggest draw for visitors are the capital's famed markets. These treasure troves of small designers, unique jewellery pieces, original framed photographs and posters, colourful vintage pieces and bric-a-brac are the antidote to impersonal, carbon-copy shopping centres.

In This Section

Taxes & Refunds

In certain circumstances visitors from non-EU countries are entitled to claim back the 20% value-added tax (VAT) they have paid on purchased goods. The rebate applies only to items purchased in stores displaying a 'tax free' sign. For more information, see www.gov.uk/tax-on-shopping/taxfree-shopping.

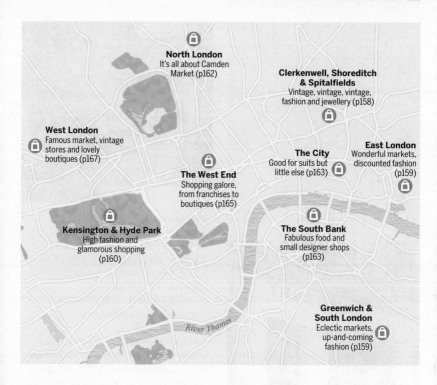

North London
It's all about Camden Market (p162)

Clerkenwell, Shoreditch & Spitalfields
Vintage, vintage, vintage, fashion and jewellery (p158)

West London
Famous market, vintage stores and lovely boutiques (p167)

The West End
Shopping galore, from franchises to boutiques (p165)

The City
Good for suits but little else (p163)

East London
Wonderful markets, discounted fashion (p159)

Kensington & Hyde Park
High fashion and glamorous shopping (p160)

The South Bank
Fabulous food and small designer shops (p163)

River Thames

Greenwich & South London
Eclectic markets, up-and-coming fashion (p159)

Opening Hours

Shops generally open from 9am or 10am to 6pm or 7pm Monday to Saturday.

The majority of stores in the most popular shopping strips also open on Sunday, typically from noon to 6pm but sometimes from 10am to 4pm.

Shops in the West End open late (to 9pm) on Thursday.

Sales

With the popularity of online shopping, sales now often start earlier and last longer, but there are two main sales seasons in the UK, both of which last about a month:

Winter sales Start on Boxing Day (26 December)

Summer sales July

The Best...

Experience London's best shopping

Best Markets

Broadway Market (p159) Local market known for its food but with plenty else besides.

Camden Lock Market (p162; pictured above) Authentic antiques to tourist tat – and everything in between.

Portobello Road Market (p127) Classic Notting Hill sprawl, perfect for vintage everything.

Sunday UpMarket (p158) Up-and-coming designers, cool tees, terrific food and vintage.

Old Spitalfields Market (p71) One of London's best for young fashion designers.

Best Fashion Shops

Selfridges (p130) Everything from streetwear to high fashion under one roof.

Burberry Outlet Store (p159) A slightly cheaper take on the classic Brit brand.

Harvey Nichols (p162) The best denim range in town.

Best for Vintage

Blitz London (p158) A massive selection of just about everything.

Beyond Retro (p159; pictured above) A London vintage empire with a rock 'n' roll heart.

British Red Cross (p162) Kensington cast-offs of exceptional quality.

Best for Music

Rough Trade East (p158; pictured above) An excellent selection of vinyl and CDs, plus in-store gigs.

Sister Ray (p167) Just what you'd expect from a store whose name references the Velvet Underground.

Casbah Records (p160) Classic vinyl and memorabilia.

Reckless Records (p167) A superb selection of secondhand CDs and vinyls.

Best Department Stores

Selfridges (p130) Over 100 years of retail innovation.

Liberty (p129; pictured above) Fabric, fashion and much, much more.

Harrods (p160) Enormous, overwhelming and indulgent, with a world-famous food hall.

Fortnum & Mason (p165) A world of food in luxuriously historic surroundings.

Harvey Nichols (p162) Fashion, food, beauty and lifestyle over eight floors.

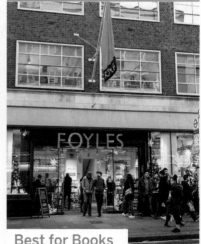

Best for Books

Hatchards (p165) The oldest, and still one of the best, independent bookshops.

Stanford's (p166) Guidebooks and maps galore, with a great range of books on London.

Foyles (p165; pictured above) Four miles of shelving in light, airy settings; you'll be there for hours.

Gay's The Word (p166) A literary institution for the LGBT community.

Gosh! (p166) A compulsory stop for lovers of graphic novels.

★ Lonely Planet's Top Choices

Sunday Upmarket (p158) Up-and-coming designers, cool tees and terrific food.

Silver Vaults (p163) The world's largest collection of silver, from cutlery to jewellery.

Fortnum & Mason (p165) The world's most glamorous grocery store.

Harrods (p160) Garish, stylish, kitsch, yet perennially popular department store.

Sister Ray (p167) A top independent music shop, with an ever-changing selection of vinyls and CDs.

ⓔ Clerkenwell, Shoreditch & Spitalfields

Sunday UpMarket   Market
(Map p253; www.sundayupmarket.co.uk; Old Truman Brewery, 91 Brick Lane, E1; ☉11am-6pm Sat, 10am-5pm Sun; ⊖Shoreditch High St) The Sunday Upmarket (which in fact opens Saturdays and Sundays) sprawls within the beautiful red-brick buildings of the Old Truman Brewery. You'll find young designers in the Backyard Market (p158), a drool-inducing array of food stalls in the Boiler House, antiques and bric-a-brac in the Tea Rooms and a huge range of vintage clothes in the basement across the street.

Rough Trade East   Music
(Map p253; www.roughtrade.com; Old Truman Brewery, 91 Brick Lane, E1; ☉9am-9pm Mon-Thu, to 8pm Fri, 10am-8pm Sat, 11am-7pm Sun; ⊖Shoreditch High St) It's no longer directly associated with the legendary record label (home to The Smiths, The Libertines and The Strokes, among many others), but this huge record shop is still the best for music of an indie, soul, electronica and alternative persuasion. In addition to an impressive selection of CDs and vinyl, it also dispenses coffee and stages promotional gigs.

Backyard Market   Market
(Map p253; www.backyardmarket.co.uk; 146 Brick Lane, E1; ☉11am-6pm Sat, 10am-5pm Sun; ⊖Shoreditch High St) Just off Brick Lane, the Backyard Market fills a large brick warehouse (part of the Old Truman Brewery complex) with stalls selling designer clothes, ceramics, jewellery, unique prints and funky furniture titbits.

Blitz London   Vintage
(Map p253; www.blitzlondon.co.uk; 55-59 Hanbury St, E1; ☉11am-7pm; ⊖Liverpool St) One of the capital's best secondhand clothes stores, with more than 20,000 hand-selected items of men's and women's clothing, shoes and accessories spanning four decades since the 1960s. You'll find anything from mainstream brands such as Nike to designer labels such as Burberry.

John Sandoe Books (p160)

⊙ East London

Broadway Market   Market

(Map p255; www.broadwaymarket.co.uk; Broadway Market, E8; ⊗9am-5pm Sat; ⛴394) There's been a market down this pretty street since the late 19th century. The focus these days is artisan food, arty knick-knacks, books, records and vintage clothing. Stock up on edible treats then head to **London Fields** (Map p255; Richmond Rd, E8; ⊖Hackney Central) for a picnic.

Pringle of Scotland
Outlet Store   Clothing

(Map p255; ☎020-8533 1158; www.pringlescotland.com; 90 Morning Lane; ⊗10am-6.30pm Mon-Sat, 11am-5pm Sun; ⊖Hackney Central) There are proper bargains to be had at this excellent outlet store that stocks seconds and end-of-line items from the Pringle range. Expect high-quality merino, cashmere and lambswool knitwear for both men and women.

Burberry Outlet Store   Clothing

(Map p255; www.burberry.com; 29-31 Chatham Pl, E9; ⊗10am-5pm; ⊖Hackney Central) This outlet shop has excess international stock from the reborn-as-trendy Brit brand's current and last-season collections. Prices are around 30% lower than those in the main shopping centres – but still properly pricey.

Beyond Retro   Vintage

(Map p255; ☎020-7923 2277; www.beyondretro.com; 92-100 Stoke Newington Rd, N16; ⊗10am-7pm Mon-Sat, 11.30am-6pm Sun; ⊖Dalston Kingsland) A riot of colour, furbelow, frill, feathers and flares, this vast store has every imaginable type of vintage clothing for sale, from hats to shoes. When it all gets too overwhelming, retreat to the licensed cafe. There's a smaller but even cheaper outlet branch in **Bethnal Green** (Map p255; ☎020-7613 3636; www.beyondretro.com; 110-112 Cheshire St, E2; ⊗10am-7pm Mon-Sat, 11.30am-6pm Sun; ⊖Shoreditch High St).

British Designers

British designers are well established in the fashion world, and **Stella McCartney** (p130), Vivienne Westwood, Paul Smith, Burberry and Alexander McQueen (the design house behind Princess Catherine's wedding dress) are now household names. For the best selection, head to Selfridges (p130); otherwise most designers have their own boutique.

Vivienne Westwood store on Bond St
VISITBRITAIN/BRITAIN ON VIEW/GETTY IMAGES ©

Traid   Clothing

(Map p255; ☎020-7923 1396; www.traid.org.uk; 106-108 Kingsland High St, E8; ⊗11am-7pm Mon-Sat, to 5pm Sun; ⊖Dalston Kingsland) Banish every preconception you have about charity shops, for Traid is nothing like the ones you've seen before: big and bright, with not a whiff of mothball. The offerings aren't necessarily vintage but rather quality, contemporary secondhand clothes for a fraction of the usual prices. It also sells its own creations made from offcuts.

⊙ Greenwich &
South London

Greenwich Market   Market

(Map p256; www.greenwichmarketlondon.com; College Approach, SE10; ⊗9.30am-5pm; ⛴DLR Cutty Sark) Greenwich Market is one of the smallest of London's ubiquitous markets, but it holds its own in quality. On Tuesdays, Wednesdays, Fridays and weekends, stallholders tend to be small, independent artists, offering original prints, wholesome beauty products, funky jewellery and accessories, cool fashion pieces and so on. On Tuesdays, Thursdays and Fridays, you'll find vintage, antiques and collectables. Loads of street food too.

Casbah Records   Music
(Map p256; ☎020-8858 1964; www.
casbahrecords.co.uk; 320-322 Creek Rd, SE10;
☺11.30am-6pm Mon, 10.30am-6pm Tue-Fri,
10.30am-6pm Sat & Sun; ☒DLR Cutty Sark) This
funky meeting ground of classic, vintage
and rare vinyl (Bowie, Rolling Stones, soul,
rock, blues, jazz, indie etc) – as well as CDs,
DVDs and memorabilia – originally traded
at Greenwich Market before upgrading to
this highly browsable shop.

Arty Globe   Gifts & Souvenirs
(Map p256; ☎020-7998 3144; www.artyglobe.
com; 15 Greenwich Market, SE10; ☺11am-6pm;
☒DLR Cutty Sark) The unique fisheye-view
drawings of various areas of London (and
other cities, including New York, Paris and
Berlin) by architect Hartwig Braun are
works of art and appear on the shopping
bags, place mats, notebooks, coasters,
mugs and jigsaws available in this tiny
shop. They make excellent gifts.

ⓖ Kensington & Hyde Park

Harrods   Department Store
(Map p250; ☎020-7730 1234; www.harrods.com;
87-135 Brompton Rd, SW1; ☺10am-9pm Mon-Sat,
11.30am-6pm Sun; ☻Knightsbridge) Garish
and stylish in equal measures, perennially
crowded Harrods is an obligatory stop for
visitors, from the cash-strapped to the big
spenders. The stock is astonishing, as are
many of the price tags. High on kitsch, the
'Egyptian Elevator' resembles something
out of an Indiana Jones epic, while the
memorial fountain to Dodi and Di (lower
ground floor) merely adds surrealism.

Many visitors don't make it past the
ground floor where designer bags, the
myriad scents from the perfume hall and
the mouth-watering counters of the food

hall provide plenty of entertainment. The
latter actually makes for an excellent, and
surprisingly affordable, option for a picnic
in nearby Hyde Park. From 11.30am to midday on Sunday, it's browsing time only.

John Sandoe Books   Books
(Map p250; ☎020-7589 9473; www.johnsandoe.
com; 10 Blacklands Tce, SW3; ☺9.30am-
6.30pm Mon-Sat, 11am-5pm Sun; ☻Sloane Sq)
The perfect antidote to impersonal book
superstores, this atmospheric three-storey
bookshop in 18th-century premises is a
treasure trove of literary gems and hidden
surprises. It's been in business for six
decades and loyal customers swear by it,
while knowledgeable booksellers spill forth
with well-read pointers and helpful advice.

Pickett   Gifts & Souvenirs
(Map p250; ☎020-7823 5638; www.pick-
ett.co.uk; cnr Sloane St & Sloane Tce, SW1;
☺9.30am-6.30pm Mon-Tue & Thu-Fri, 10am-7pm
Wed, 10am-6pm Sat; ☻Sloane Sq) ✐ Walking
into Pickett as an adult is a bit like walking
into a sweets shop as a child: the exquisite
leather goods are all so colourful and beautiful, you don't really know where to start.
Choice items include the perfectly finished
handbags, the exquisite roll-up backgam-
mon sets and the men's grooming sets. All
leather goods are made in Britain.

Jo Loves   Cosmetics
(Map p250; ☎020-7730 8611; www.joloves.com;
42 Elizabeth St, SW1; ☺10am-6pm Mon-Wed &
Fri-Sat, to 7pm Thu, noon-5pm Sun; ☻Victoria)
Famed British scent-maker Jo Malone
opened Jo Loves in 2013 on a street where
she once had a Saturday job as a young
florist. The shop features the entrepreneur's
signature candles, fragrances and bath
products in a range of delicate scents –
Arabian amber, white rose and lemon leaves,
oud and mango. All products come exqui-
sitely wrapped in red boxes with black bows.

Conran Shop   Design
(Map p250; ☎020-7589 7401; www.conranshop.
co.uk; Michelin House, 81 Fulham Rd, SW3;
☺10am-6pm Mon, Tue & Fri, to 7pm Wed & Thu, to
6.30pm Sat, noon-6pm Sun; ☻South Kensington)

★ Vintage Fashion

The realm of vintage apparel has moved from being sought out by those looking for something off-beat and original, to an all-out mainstream shopping habit. Vintage designer garments and odd bits and pieces from the 1920s to the 1980s are all gracing the rails in some surprisingly upmarket boutique vintage shops.

The less self-conscious charity shops – especially those in areas such as Chelsea, Kensington and Islington – are your best bets for real bargains on designer wear (usually, the richer the area, the better the secondhand shops).

Clockwise from top: A classic car boot sale; Camden Lock Market (p162); Vintage clothes stall at Broadway Market (p159)

The original design store (going strong since 1987), the Conran Shop is a treasure trove of beautiful things – from radios to sunglasses, kitchenware to children's toys and books, bathroom accessories to greeting cards. Browsing bliss. Spare some time to peruse the magnificent art nouveau/deco Michelin House the shop belongs to.

Harvey Nichols   Department Store
(Map p250; www.harveynichols.com; 109-125 Knightsbridge, SW1; ☺10am-8pm Mon-Sat, 11.30am-6pm Sun; ⊖Knightsbridge) At London's temple of high fashion, you'll find Chloé and Balenciaga bags, the city's best denim range, a massive make-up hall with exclusive lines and great jewellery. The food hall and in-house restaurant, **Fifth Floor**, are, you guessed it, on the 5th floor. From 11.30am to midday, it's browsing time only.

British Red Cross   Vintage
(☎020-7376 7300; 69-71 Old Church St, SW3; ☺10am-6pm Mon-Sat; ⊖Sloane Sq) The motto 'One man's rubbish is another man's treasure' couldn't be truer in this part of London, where the 'rubbish' is made up of designer gowns, cashmere jumpers and perhaps a

first edition or two. Obviously the price tags are a little higher than in your run-of-the-mill charity shop (£40 rather than £5 for a jumper or jacket) but it's still a bargain for the quality and browsing is half the fun.

🅰 North London

Camden Lock Market   Market
(Map p254; www.camdenmarket.com; 54-56 Camden Lock Pl, NW1; ☺10am-6pm; ⊖Camden Town) Right next to the canal lock, this is the original Camden Market, with diverse food stalls, ceramics, furniture, oriental rugs, musical instruments and clothes.

Stables Market   Market
(Map p254; www.camdenmarket.com; Chalk Farm Rd, NW1; ☺10am-6pm; ⊖Chalk Farm) Connected to the Lock Market, the Stables is the best part of the Camden Market complex, with antiques, Asian artefacts, rugs, retro furniture and clothing. As the name suggests, it used to be an old stables complex, complete with horse hospital, where up to 800 horses (who worked hauling barges on Regent's Canal) would have been housed.

From left: Cambridge Satchel Company (p165); Harvey Nichols; Harry Potter Shop at Platform 9¾; South Bank Book Market (p165)

Harry Potter Shop at Platform 9¾
Gifts & Souvenirs

(Map p254; www.harrypotterplatform934.com; King's Cross Station, N1; ⊗8am-10pm Mon-Sat, 9am-9pm Sun; ⊖King's Cross St Pancras) With Pottermania refusing to wind down and Diagon Alley impossible to find, take your junior witches and wizards to King's Cross Station instead. This little wood-panelled store also stocks jumpers sporting the colours of Hogwarts' four houses (Gryffindor having pride of place) and assorted merchandise, including, of course, the books.

🅖 The City

Silver Vaults
Arts & Crafts

(Map p245; ☎020-7242 3844; http:// silvervaultslondon.com; 53-63 Chancery Lane, WC2; ⊗9am-5.30pm Mon-Fri, to 1pm Sat; ⊖Chancery Lane) The 30-odd shops that work out of these secure subterranean vaults make up the world's largest collection of silver under one roof in the world. The different businesses tend to specialise in particular types of silverware –

from cutlery sets to picture frames and lots of jewellery.

🅖 The South Bank

Lovely & British
Gifts & Souvenirs

(Map p245; ☎020-7378 6570; www.facebook. com/LovelyandBritish; 132a Bermondsey St, SE1; ⊗10am-6pm; ⊖London Bridge) As the name suggests, this gorgeous Bermondsey boutique prides itself on stocking prints, jewellery and homewares (crockery especially) from British designers. It's an eclectic mix of wares, with very reasonable prices, which make lovely presents or souvenirs.

Southbank Centre Shop
Homewares

(Map p245; www.southbankcentre.co.uk; Festival Tce, SE1; ⊗10am-9pm Mon-Fri, to 8pm Sat, noon-8pm Sun; ⊖Waterloo) This is the place to come for quirky London books, '50s-inspired homewares, original prints and creative gifts for children. The shop is eclectic but you're sure to find unique gifts or souvenirs to take home.

Top Five London Souvenirs

Tea

The British drink par excellence, with plenty of iconic names to choose from. For lovely packaging too, try Fortnum & Mason (p165; pictured above) or Harrods (p160).

Vintage Clothes & Shoes

Your London vintage fashion finds will forever be associated with your trip to the city. Start your search at the Sunday UpMarket (p158).

British Design

With its cool and understated chic, British design has made a name for itself worldwide. Try the Conran Shop (p160; pictured above) or Monocle (p167).

London Toys

Double-decker buses, Paddington bears, guards in bearskin hats – London's icons make for great souvenirs. Hamleys (p129; pictured above) is the place to go.

Music

The city that produced legends from The Clash to Amy Winehouse is a brilliant place to buy records. Try Rough Trade East (p158) or Sister Ray (p167; pictured above).

South Bank Book Market Market

(Map p245; Riverside Walk, SE1; ⊗11am-7pm, shorter hours winter; ⊖Waterloo) The South Bank Book Market sells prints and secondhand books daily under the arches of Waterloo Bridge. You'll find anything here, from fiction to children's books, comics to classics.

⓵ The West End

For more, see Shopping in the West End (p128).

Fortnum & Mason Department Store

(Map p248; ☎020-7734 8040; www. fortnumandmason.com; 181 Piccadilly, W1; ⊗10am-8pm Mon-Sat, 11.30am-6pm Sun; ⊖Piccadilly Circus) With its classic eau-de-Nil (pale green) colour scheme, 'the Queen's grocery store' established 1707 refuses to yield to modern times. Its staff – men and women – still wear old-fashioned tailcoats and its glamorous food hall is supplied with hampers, cut marmalade, speciality teas, superior fruitcakes and so forth. Fortnum and Mason remains the quintessential London shopping experience.

Hatchards Books

(Map p248; ☎020-7439 9921; www.hatchards. co.uk; 187 Piccadilly, W1; ⊗9.30am-8pm Mon-Sat, noon-6.30pm Sun; ⊖Green Park or Piccadilly Circus) London's oldest bookshop dates to 1797. Holding three royal warrants, it's a stupendous bookshop now in the Waterstones stable, with a solid supply of signed editions and bursting at its smart seams with very browsable stock. There's a strong selection of first editions on the ground floor and regularly scheduled literary events.

Cadenhead's Whisky & Tasting Shop Drinks

(Map p250; ☎020-7935 6999; www. whiskytastingroom.com; 26 Chiltern St, W1; ⊗10.30am-6.30pm Mon-Thu, 11am-8.30 Fri, 10.30am-6pm Sat; ⊖Baker St) This shop is Scotland's oldest independent bottler of pure, nonblended whisky from local distilleries and a joy for anyone with a passion for *uisge-beatha* ('water of life', the

Scots Gaelic word for 'whisky'), though don't expect a warm welcome. All bottled whiskies derive from individually selected casks, without any filtrations, additions or colouring. Regular whisky tastings are held downstairs.

Cambridge Satchel Company Fashion & Accessories

(Map p248; ☎020-3077 1100; www. cambridgesatchel.com; 31 James St, WC2; ⊗10am-7pm Mon-Sat, 11am-6pm Sun; ⊖Covent Garden) The classic British leather satchel concept has morphed into a trendy and colourful array of backpacks, totes, clutches, work and music bags, mini satchels and more for men and women.

Skoob Books Books

(Map p254; ☎020-7278 8760; www.skoob.com; 66 The Brunswick, off Marmont St, WC1; ⊗10.30am-8pm Mon-Sat, to 6pm Sun; ⊖Russell Sq) Skoob (you work out the name) has got to be London's largest secondhand bookshop, with some 60,000 titles spread over 2000 sq ft of floor space (plus more than a million further books in a warehouse outside town). If you can't find it here, it probably doesn't exist.

Penhaligon's Perfume

(Map p248; ☎020-7629 1416; www.penhaligons. com; 16-17 Burlington Arcade, W1; ⊗10am-6pm Mon-Fri, 9.30am-6.30pm Sat, 11.30am-5.30pm Sun; ⊖Piccadilly Circus, Green Park) Located in the historic Burlington Arcade, Penhaligon's is a classic British perfumery. Attendants inquire about your favourite smells, take you on an exploratory tour of the shop's signature range and help you discover new scents in their traditional perfumes, home fragrances and bath and body products. Everything is produced in England.

Foyles Books

(Map p248; ☎020-7434 1574; www.foyles.co.uk; 107 Charing Cross Rd, WC2; ⊗9.30am-9pm Mon-Sat, 11.30am-6pm Sun; ⊖Tottenham Court Rd) This is London's most legendary bookshop, where you can bet on finding even the most obscure of titles. Once synonymous with chaos, Foyles got its act together and in 2014 moved just down the road into the spacious former home of Central St Martins art school. Thoroughly redesigned, its stunning new home is a joy to explore.

Stanford's
Books, Maps

(Map p248; ☑020-7836 1321; www.stanfords. co.uk; 12-14 Long Acre, WC2; ⊙9am-8pm Mon-Sat, 11.30am-6pm Sun; ⊜Leicester Sq or Covent Garden) Trading from this address since 1853, this granddaddy of travel bookshops and seasoned seller of maps, guides, globes and literature is a destination in its own right. Ernest Shackleton and David Livingstone and, more recently, Michael Palin and Brad Pitt have all popped in and shopped here.

Molton Brown
Cosmetics

(Map p248; ☑020-7240 8383; www.moltonbrown. co.uk; 18 Russell St, WC2; ⊙10am-7pm Mon-Sat, 11am-6pm Sun; ⊜Covent Garden) A fabulously fragrant British natural beauty range, Molton Brown is *the* choice for boutique hotel, posh restaurant and 1st-class airline bathrooms. Its skincare products offer plenty of pampering for both men and women. In this store you can also pick up home accessories.

Gay's the Word
Books

(Map p254; ☑020-7278 7654; www.gaystheword. co.uk; 66 Marchmont St, WC1; ⊙10am-6.30pm Mon-Sat, 2-6pm Sun; ⊜Russell Sq) This London gay institution has been selling books nobody else stocks since 1979, with a superb range of gay- and lesbian-interest books and magazines plus a real community spirit. Used books available as well.

Cath Kidston
Fashion & Accessories

(Map p250; ☑020-7935 6555; www.cathkidston. com; 51 Marylebone High St, W1; ⊙10am-7pm Mon-Sat, 11am-5pm Sun; ⊜Baker St) If you favour the preppy look, you'll love Cath Kidston's signature floral prints and vintage-inspired fashion. There is also a range of homewares and some delightful London-branded gift items.

Gosh!
Books

(Map p248; ☑020-7636 1011; www.goshlondon. com; 1 Berwick St, W1; ⊙10.30am-7pm; ⊜Piccadilly Circus) Make your way here for graphic novels, manga and children's books, such as the Tintin and Asterix series. It's also the perfect place for finding presents for kids and teenagers.

Reckless Records

Reckless Records   Music

(Map p248; ☎020-7437 4271; www.reckless.
co.uk; 30 Berwick St, W1; ⊙10am-7pm; ⊖Oxford
Circus, Tottenham Court Rd) This outfit hasn't
really changed in spirit since it first opened
its doors in 1984. It still stocks secondhand
records and CDs, from punk, soul, dance
and independent to mainstream.

Moomin Shop   Gifts & Souvenirs

(Map p248; ☎020-7240 7057; www.
themoominshop.com; 43 Market Bldg. Covent
Garden, WC2; ⊙10am-8pm Mon-Sat, to 7pm Sun;
⊖Covent Garden) This tiny shop in Covent
Garden's central market building is a temple
to all things Moomin, that weird hippo-like
character created by Finnish artist Tove
Jansson. Trays, coasters, enamel mugs,
plates, towels, lunchboxes – the whole works.

Monocle Shop   Fashion & Accessories

(Map p250; ☎020-7486 8770; www.monocle.
com; 2a George St, W1; ⊙11am-7pm Mon-Sat,
noon-5pm Sun; ⊖Bond St) Run by the people
behind the design and international
current-affairs magazine *Monocle,* this tiny
(and attitudy) shop stocks very costly clothing, bags, umbrellas and books (including
their own guides). But if you are a fan of
minimalist quality design, you'll want to
stop by. There's also the **Monocle Cafe**
(Map p250; http://cafe.monocle.com; 18 Chiltern
St, W1; mains from £5.50; ⊙7am-7pm Mon-Wed,
7am-8pm Thu & Fri, 8am-8pm Sat, 8am-7pm Sun;
🛜; ⊖Baker St) not far away on Chiltern St.

Sister Ray   Music

(Map p248; ☎020-7734 3297; www.sisterray.
co.uk; 75 Berwick St, W1; ⊙10am-8pm Mon-Sat,
noon-6pm Sun; ⊖Oxford Circus, Tottenham
Court Rd) If you were a fan of the late John
Peel on the BBC, this specialist in innovative, experimental and indie music is just
right for you. Those of you who have never
heard of him will probably also like the shop
that 'sells music to the masses'.

Benjamin Pollock's Toy Shop   Toys

(Map p248; ☎: 020-7379 7866; www.pol-
locks-coventgarden.co.uk; 1st fl, 44 Market Bldg,
Covent Garden, WC2; ⊙10.30am-6pm Mon-Wed,
10.30am-6.30pm Thu-Sat, 11am-6pm Sun;

Chain Stores

Many bemoan the fact that chains have
taken over the main shopping centres,
leaving independent shops struggling
to balance the books. But since these
stores are cheap, fashionable and
always conveniently located, Londoners
(and others) keep going back for more.
As well as familiar overseas retailers,
such as Gap, H&M, Urban Outfitters and
Zara, you'll find plenty of home-grown
chains, including luxury womenswear
brand **Reiss** (www.reiss.com) and shoe
designer **L.K. Bennett** (www.lkben-
nett.com) – both regularly worn by
Catherine, Duchess of Cambridge – and
global giant Topshop (p130), for whom
super model Kate Moss has designed a
number of limited-edition collections.

Topshop on the Strand
ELENA ROSTUNOVA/SHUTTERSTOCK ©

⊖Covent Garden) This traditional toy shop
is stuffed with the things that kids of all
ages love: Victorian paper theatres, wooden
marionettes and finger puppets, and antique teddy bears (that look far too fragile
to cuddle, much less play with).

ⓐ West London

Rough Trade West   Music

(Map p250; ☎020-7229 8541; www.roughtrade.
com; 130 Talbot Rd, W11; ⊙10am-6.30pm Mon-
Sat, 11am-5pm Sun; ⊖Ladbroke Grove) With
its underground, alternative and vintage
rarities, this home of the eponymous punk-
music label remains a haven for vinyl junkies.

STUART MONK/SHUTTERSTOCK ©

BAR OPEN

Afternoon pints, all-night clubbing and beyond

Bar Open

There is little Londoners like to do more than drink: from Hogarth's 18th-century Gin Lane prints to former mayor Boris Johnson's decision to ban all alcohol on public transport in 2008, the capital's history has been shot through with the population's desire to imbibe as much alcohol as possible and party into the night.

The metropolis offers a huge variety of venues at which to wet your whistle, from neighbourhood pubs to all-night clubs and everything in between. Note that when it comes to clubbing, a little planning will help you keep costs down and skip queues.

In This Section

Opening Hours

Pubs usually open at 11am or midday and close at 11pm, with a slightly earlier closing on a Sunday. On Friday and Saturday, some bars and pubs remain open to around 2am or 3am.

Clubs generally open at 10pm and close between 3am and 7am.

North London
Atmospheric pubs and
live music (p178)

**Clerkenwell, Shoreditch
& Spitalfields**
Edgy clubs and
hip bars (p174)

West London
Traditional pubs, river
views, relaxed evenings
(p183)

East London
Increasingly trendy,
with excellent
bars (p175)

The City
Post-work punters,
quiet after 10pm
(p178)

The West End
Legendary establishments,
up-for-it crowds (p179)

The South Bank
Franchises and
good ol' boozers
(p179)

**Greenwich &
South London**
Vibrant parties and
old-school pubs
(p177)

River Thames

Costs & Tipping

Many clubs are free or cheaper mid-week. If you want to go to a famous club on a Saturday night (the night for clubbing), expect to pay around £20. Some places are considerably cheaper if you arrive earlier in the night.

Tipping isn't customary.

Useful Websites

London on the Inside (www.londontheinside.com)

Skiddle (www.skiddle.com) Comprehensive info on nightclubs, DJs and events.

Time Out (www.timeout.com/london) Has details of bars, pubs and nightlife.

The Best...

Experience London's finest drinking establishments

Best Cocktail Bars

Worship St Whistling Shop (p175) Molecular cocktails at a Victorian-style drinking den.

Dukes London (p179) Bond-perfect martinis in gentleman's-club surroundings.

Swift (p181) Bespoke cocktails at a new Soho favourite.

Zetter Townhouse Cocktail Lounge (p174) Wonderfully quirky boudoir surroundings and devilishly good drinks.

Best Pubs

Dove Freehouse (p176) Great beers, great atmosphere – just how a pub should be.

Dove Freehouse bar(p174) A delightfully cosy 16th-century pub in a hidden alleyway.

Prospect of Whitby (p175; pictured above) London's oldest river pub, with Thames views and an open fire in winter.

Princess Louise (p182) A splendid Victorian pub with decorated tiles, etched mirrors and wood panelling.

Best for Clubbing

XOYO (p174) Excellent and varied gigs, club nights and art events.

Dalston Superstore (p176) Part bar, part club, straight and gay. It works.

Heaven (p182; pictured above) A long-standing favourite on the gay clubbing circuit.

Roof Gardens (p183) Clubbing cum roof gardens and flamingos. Obviously.

Best for Views

Madison (p178) Look into the heart of St Paul's and beyond from One New Change.
Oblix (p179) It's not even halfway up the Shard, but the views are legendary.
Netil360 (p175) Fab city views from hip rooftop bar – croquet, anyone?

Best Bars

Gordon's Wine Bar (p182) A classic and long-standing London institution in darkened vaults.
Bar Pepito (p178) A delightful, pocket-sized Andalusian bar dedicated to lovers of sherry.
French House (p182) Soho's best boozer, with a steady supply of pastis and local eccentrics.

Best Beer Gardens

Windsor Castle (p183; pictured above) Come summer, regulars abandon the Windsor's historic interior for the chilled-out garden.
Edinboro Castle (p178) A festive place to stretch out on a summer evening.
Greenwich Union (p177) Work your way through the Meantime brews from a garden table.

★ Lonely Planet's Top Choices

Princess Louise (p182) A stunner of a Victorian pub with snugs and a riot of etched glass.
Worship St Whistling Shop (p175) Fine-dining sophistication in liquid form.
Cat & Mutton (p175) Simultaneously traditional and hip, and always up for a party.
Trafalgar Tavern (p177) Riverside tavern oozing history.

The Pub

The pub (public house) is at the heart of London life and is one of the capital's great social levellers. Virtually every Londoner has a 'local' and looking for your own is a fun part of any visit.

Pubs in central London are mostly after-work drinking dens, busy from 5pm onwards with the postwork crowd during the week and revellers at weekends. In more residential areas, pubs come into their own at weekends, when long lunches turn into sloshy afternoons and groups of friends settle in for the night. Many also run popular quizzes on week nights. Other pubs entice punters through the doors with live music or comedy. Some have developed such a reputation for the quality of their food that they've been dubbed 'gastropubs'.

You'll be able to order almost anything you like in a pub, from beer to wine, soft drinks, spirits and sometimes hot drinks too. Some specialise in craft beer, offering drinks from local microbreweries, including real ale, fruit beers, organic ciders and other rarer beverages. Others, particularly the gastropubs, have invested in a good wine list.

In winter, some pubs offer mulled wine; in summer the must-have drink is Pimms and lemonade (if it's properly done it should have fresh mint leaves, citrus, strawberries and cucumber).

Clerkenwell, Shoreditch & Spitalfields

Ye Olde Mitre   Pub
(Map p253; www.yeoldemitreholborn.co.uk; 1 Ely Ct, EC1N; ⊙11am-11pm Mon-Fri; ; Farringdon) A delightfully cosy historic pub with an extensive beer selection, tucked away in a backstreet off Hatton Garden. Ye Olde Mitre was built in 1546 for the servants of Ely Palace. There's no music, so rooms echo only with amiable chit-chat. Queen Elizabeth I danced around the cherry tree by the bar, they say.

Zetter Townhouse Cocktail Lounge   Cocktail Bar
(Map p253; 020-7324 4545; www. thezettertownhouse.com; 49-50 St John's Sq, EC1V; ⊙7.30am-12.45am; ; Farringdon) Tucked away behind an unassuming door on St John's Sq, this ground-floor bar is decorated with plush armchairs, stuffed animal heads and a legion of lamps. The cocktail list takes its theme from the area's distilling history – recipes of yesteryear plus homemade tinctures and cordials are used to create interesting and unusual tipples. House cocktails are all £10.50.

Fabric   Club
(Map p253; www.fabriclondon.com; 77a Charterhouse Street, EC1M; £5-25; 11pm-7am Fri-Sun; Farringdon or Barbican) London's leading club, Fabric's three separate dance floors in a huge converted cold store opposite Smithfield meat market draws impressive queues (buy tickets online). FabricLive (on selected Fridays) rumbles with drum and bass and dubstep, while Fabric (usually on Saturdays but also on selected Fridays) is the club's signature live DJ night. Sunday's WetYourSelf! delivers house, techno and electronica.

XOYO   Club
(Map p253; www.xoyo.co.uk; 32-37 Cowper St, EC2A; ⊙9pm-4am Fri & Sat, hours vary Sun-Thu; Old St) This fantastic Shoreditch warehouse club throws together a pulsing and popular mix of gigs, club nights and

Dove Freehouse (p176)

art events. It has a varied line-up of indie bands, hip hop, electro, dub-step and much in between, and attracts a mix of clubbers, from skinny-jeaned hipsters to more mature hedonists (but no suits).

Worship St Whistling Shop
Cocktail Bar

(Map p253; ☑020-7247 0015; www. whistlingshop.com; 63 Worship St, EC2A; ☺5pm-midnight Mon & Tue, to 1am Wed & Thu, to 2am Fri & Sat; ⊖Old St) While the name is Victorian slang for a place selling illicit booze, this subterranean drinking den's master mixologists explore the experimental limits of cocktail chemistry and aromatic science, and they also concoct the classics. Many ingredients are made with rotary evaporators in the on-site lab. Also runs cocktail masterclasses.

⊖ East London

Netil360
Bar

(Map p255; www.netil360.com; 1 Westgate St, E8; ☺10am-10pm Wed-Fri, noon-11pm Sat & Sun Apr-

Nov; �; ☑55) Perched atop Netil House, this uber-hip rooftop cafe/bar offers incredible views over London, with brass telescopes enabling you to get better acquainted with workers in the Gherkin. In between drinks you can knock out a game of croquet on the AstroTurf, or perhaps book a hot tub for you and your mates to stew in.

Cat & Mutton
Pub

(Map p255; ☑020-7249 6555; www. catandmutton.com; 76 Broadway Market, E8; ☺noon-midnight Sun-Fri, 10am-1pm Sat; ☑394) At this fabulous Georgian pub, Hackney hipsters sup pints under the watchful eyes of hunting trophies, black-and-white photos of old-time boxers and a large portrait of Karl Marx. If it's crammed downstairs, as it often is, head up the spiral staircase to the comfy couches. DJs spin funk, disco and soul on the weekends.

Prospect of Whitby
Pub

(57 Wapping Wall, E1; ☺noon-11pm; �; ⊖Wapping) Once known as the Devil's Tavern, the Whitby is said to date from 1520, making it the oldest riverside pub in London.

From left: Trafalgar Tavern; Counting House (p178); Cutty Sark Tavern

Famous patrons have included Charles Dickens and Samuel Pepys so it's firmly on the tourist trail. There's a smallish terrace overlooking the Thames, a restaurant upstairs, open fires in winter and a pewter-topped bar.

Dove Freehouse   Pub

(Map p255; ☎020-7275 7617; www.dovepubs. com; 24-28 Broadway Market, E8; ⏱noon-11pm Sun-Fri, 11am-11pm Sat; ☏; 🚌394) Alluring at any time, the Dove has a rambling series of rooms and a wide range of Belgian Trappist, wheat and fruit-flavoured beers. Drinkers spill on to the street in warmer weather, or hunker down in the low-lit back room with board games when it's chilly.

Carpenter's Arms   Pub

(Map p255; ☎020-7739 6342; www.carpentersarmsfreehouse.com; 73 Cheshire St, E2; ⏱4-11.30pm Mon-Wed, noon-11.30pm Thu-Sun; ☏; ⊖Shoreditch High St) Once owned by infamous gangsters the Kray brothers (who bought it for their old ma to run), this chic yet cosy pub has been beautifully restored and its many wooden surfaces positively

gleam. A back room and small yard provide a little more space for the convivial drinkers. There's a huge range of draught and bottled beers and ciders.

Draughts   Bar

(Map p253; www.draughtslondon.com; 337 Acton Mews, E8; ⏱10am-5pm & 6pm-11pm Mon-Thu & Sun, to midnight Fri, 10am-midnight Sat; 🚉Haggerston) London's first board-game theme bar – it has over 500 to choose from – offers a delightfully geeky way to while away an afternoon. Food, wine and ale are served all day and there is even a 'game guru' on hand to explain rules and advise which games are best suited to your group's wants.

Dalston Superstore   Gay

(Map p255; ☎020-7254 2273; www. dalstonsuperstore.com; 117 Kingsland High St, E8; ⏱11.45am-late; ⊖Dalston Kingsland) Bar, club or diner? Gay or straight? Dalston Superstore is hard to pigeonhole, which we suspect is the point. This two-level industrial space is open all day but really comes into its own after dark when there are club nights in the basement.

D HALE SUTTON/ALAMY STOCK PHOTO ©

🔵 Greenwich & South London

Cutty Sark Tavern — Pub

(Map p256; 📞020-8858 3146; www.cuttysarkse10.co.uk; 4-6 Ballast Quay, SE10; ⏰11.30am-11pm Mon-Sat, noon-10.30pm Sun; 📶; 🚉DLR Cutty Sark) Housed in a delightful bow-windowed, wood-beamed Georgian building directly on the Thames, the Cutty Sark is one of the few independent pubs left in Greenwich. Half a dozen cask-conditioned ales on tap line the bar, there's an inviting riverside seating area opposite and an upstairs dining room looking out on to glorious views. It's a 10-minute walk from the DLR station.

Greenwich Union — Pub

(Map p256; www.greenwichunion.com; 56 Royal Hill, SE10; ⏰noon-11pm Mon-Fri, 10am-11pm Sat, 10am-10.30pm Sun; 🚉DLR Greenwich) The award-winning Union plies six or seven Meantime microbrewery beers, including raspberry and wheat varieties, and has a strong list of ales and bottled international brews. It's a handsome place, with duffed-up leather armchairs and a welcoming long, narrow aspect that leads to a conservatory and beer garden at the rear.

Trafalgar Tavern — Pub

(Map p256; 📞020-8858 2909; www.trafalgartavern.co.uk; 6 Park Row, SE10; ⏰noon-11pm Mon-Thu, noon-midnight Fri, 10am-midnight Sat, 10am-11pm Sun; 🚉DLR Cutty Sark) This elegant tavern with big windows overlooking the Thames is steeped in history. Dickens apparently knocked back a few here – and used it as the setting for the wedding breakfast scene in *Our Mutual Friend* – and prime ministers Gladstone and Disraeli used to dine on the pub's celebrated whitebait.

🔵 Kensington & Hyde Park

Queen's Arms — Pub

(Map p250; www.thequeensarmskensington.co.uk; 30 Queen's Gate Mews, SW7; ⏰noon-11pm Mon-Sat, to 10.30pm Sun; 🚇Gloucester Rd) Just around the corner from the Royal Albert Hall, this godsend of a blue-grey painted pub in an adorable cobbled mews setting off bustling Queen's Gate beckons with a cosy interior and a right royal selection of ales – including selections from small, local cask brewers – and ciders on tap. In warm weather, drinkers stand outside in the mews (only permitted on one side).

⊖ North London

Bar Pepito   Wine Bar
(Map p254; www.barpepito.co.uk; 3 Varnishers Yard, The Regent's Quarter, N1; ⊘5pm-midnight Mon-Sat; ⊖King's Cross St Pancras) This tiny, intimate Andalusian bodega specialises in sherry and tapas. Novices fear not: the staff are on hand to advise. They're also experts at food pairings (top-notch ham and cheese selections). To go the whole hog, try a tasting flight of selected sherries with snacks to match.

Proud Camden   Bar
(Map p254; www.proudcamden.com; Stables Market, Chalk Farm Rd, NW1; ⊘11am-1.30am Mon-Sat, to midnight Sun; ⊖Chalk Farm) Proud occupies a former horse hospital within Stables Market, with private booths in the old stalls, fantastic artworks on the walls (the main bar acts as a gallery during the day) and a kooky garden terrace complete with a hot tub. It's also one of Camden's best music venues, with live bands and DJs most nights (entry free to £15).

Edinboro Castle   Pub
(Map p254; www.edinborocastlepub.co.uk; 57 Mornington Tce, NW1; ⊘11am-11pm; ⊛; ⊖Camden Town) Large and relaxed Edinboro offers a refined atmosphere, gorgeous furniture perfect for slumping into, a fine bar and a full menu. The highlight, however, is the huge beer garden, complete with warm-weather BBQs and lit up with coloured lights on long summer evenings. Patio heaters come out in winter.

⊖ The City

Madison   Cocktail Bar
(Map p245; ☎020-3693 5160; www.madisonlondon.net; Rooftop Terrace, One New Change, EC4; ⊘11am-midnight Mon-Wed, to 1am Thu-Sat, to 9pm Sun; ⊖St Paul's) Perched atop One New Change with a drop-dead view of St Paul's and beyond, Madison offers one of the largest public open-air roof terraces you'll ever encounter. There's a full restaurant and bar on one side and a cocktail bar with outdoor seating on the other. We come for the latter. Drinkers must be over 21; dress code is smart casual.

Blackfriar   Pub
(Map p245; ☎020-7236 5474; www.nicholsonspubs.co.uk/theblackfriarblackfriarslondon; 174 Queen Victoria St, EC4V; ⊘9am-11pm Mon-Fri, noon-10.30pm Sun; ⊖Blackfriars) It may look like the corpulent friar above the entrance just stepped out of this olde-worlde pub just north of Blackfriars station, but the interior is actually an art-nouveau makeover from 1905. Built on the site of a monastery of Dominicans (who wore black robes), the theme is appealingly celebrated throughout the pub. It has a good selection of ales.

Ye Olde Cheshire Cheese   Pub
(Map p245; ☎020-7353 6170; Wine Office Court, 145 Fleet St, EC4; ⊘11.30am-11pm Mon-Fri, noon-11pm Sat; ⊖Chancery Lane) The entrance to this historic pub is via a narrow alley off Fleet St. Over its long history, locals have included Dr Johnson, Thackeray and Dickens. Despite (or possibly because of) this, the Cheshire can feel a bit like a museum. Nevertheless it's one of London's most famous and historic pubs and well worth popping in for a pint.

Counting House   Pub
(Map p245; ☎020-7283 7123; www.the-counting-house.com; 50 Cornhill, EC3; ⊘10am-11pm Mon-Fri; ⊛; ⊖Bank) With its counters and basement vaults, this award-winning pub certainly looks and feels comfortable in the former headquarters of NatWest Bank (1893) with its domed skylight and beautifully appointed main bar. This is a favourite of City boys and girls, who come for the good range of real ales and the speciality pies (from £12).

⊖ The South Bank

Oblix
Bar

(Map p245; www.oblixrestaurant.com; 32nd fl, Shard, 31 St Thomas St, SE1; ⊙noon-11pm; ⊖London Bridge) On the 32nd floor of the Shard (p79), Oblix offers mesmerising vistas of London. You can come for anything from a coffee (£3.50) to a cocktail (from £10) and enjoy virtually the same views as the official viewing galleries of the Shard (but at a reduced cost and with the added bonus of a drink). Live music every night from 7pm.

Little Bird Gin
Cocktail Bar

(Map p245; www.littlebirdgin.com; Maltby St, SE1; ⊙10am-4pm Sat, from 11am Sun; ⊖London Bridge) This South London–based distillery opens a pop-up bar in a workshop at Maltby Street Market (p146) to ply merry punters with devilishly good cocktails (£5 to £7), served in jam jars or apothecary's glass bottles.

Scootercaffe
Bar

(Map p245; 132 Lower Marsh, SE1; ⊙8.30am-11pm Mon-Fri, 10am-midnight Sat, to 11pm Sun; 🛜; ⊖Waterloo) A well-established fixture on the up-and-coming Lower Marsh road, this funky cafe-bar and former scooter repair shop with a Piatti scooter in the window serves killer hot chocolates, coffee and decadent cocktails. Unusually, you're allowed to bring in takeaway food. The tiny patio at the back is perfect for soaking up the sun.

⊖ The West End

Dukes London
Cocktail Bar

(Map p248; ☎020-7491 4840; www.dukeshotel.com/dukes-bar; Dukes Hotel, 35 St James's Pl, SW1; ⊙2-11pm Mon-Sat, 4-10.30pm Sun; 🛜; ⊖Green Park) Sip to-die-for martinis in a gentleman's-club-like ambience at this tucked-away classic bar where white-jacketed masters mix up some awesomely good preparations. Ian Fleming used to frequent the place, perhaps perfecting his 'shaken, not stirred' James Bond maxim. Smokers can ease into the secluded Cognac and Cigar Garden to light up cigars purchased here.

Beer

The *raison d'être* of a pub is first and foremost to serve beer – be it lager, ale or stout in a glass or a bottle. On draught (drawn from the cask), it is served by the pint (570mL) or half-pint (285mL) and, more occasionally, third-of-a-pint for real ale tasting.

Pubs generally serve a good selection of lager (highly carbonated and drunk cool or cold) and a smaller selection of real ales or 'bitter' (still or only slightly gassy, drunk at room temperature, with strong flavours). The best-known British lager brand is Carling, although you'll find everything from Fosters to San Miguel.

Among the multitude of ales on offer in London pubs, London Pride, Courage Best, Burton Ale, Adnam's, Theakston (in particular Old Peculier) and Old Speckled Hen are among the best. Once considered something of an old man's drink, real ale is enjoying a renaissance among young Londoners keen to sample flavours from the country's brewing tradition. Staff at bars serving good selections of real ales are often hugely knowledgeable, just like a sommelier in a restaurant with a good cellar, so ask them for recommendations if you're not sure what to order.

Stout, the best known of which is Irish Guinness, is a slightly sweet, dark beer with a distinct flavour that comes from malt that is roasted before fermentation.

London in a Glass

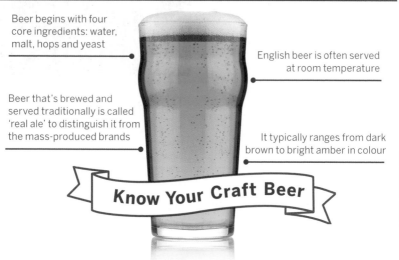

Beer begins with four core ingredients: water, malt, hops and yeast

English beer is often served at room temperature

Beer that's brewed and served traditionally is called 'real ale' to distinguish it from the mass-produced brands

It typically ranges from dark brown to bright amber in colour

BEER PINT/GETTY IMAGES ©

Know Your Craft Beer

Craft beer in London

The growing interest in small-batch or artisan beer over the past five to 10 years has been spectacular. It is now de rigueur for virtually every pub to serve at least a couple of craft beers. London has also a raft of microbreweries, many of which you can visit; popular brews to try include Camden Town, Beavertown, London Fields, Redchurch and Meantime.

Equipment in a boutique microbrewery
ZSTOCK/SHUTTERSTOCK ©

★ Top Three Places for a Pint

Anspach & Hobday (Map p245; www. anspachandhobday.com; 118 Druid St, SE1; ☺5-9pm Fri, 10.30am-5.30pm Sat, 12.30-5pm Sun; ⊖London Bridge) **Beer aficionados will also love trying brews from the experimental range.**

Howling Hops (Map p255; www. howlinghops.co.uk; Queen's Yard, White Post Lane, E9; ☺noon-11pm Mon-Thurs & Sun, noon-midnight Fri & Sat; ⓡHackney Wick) **The tank bar at the Howling Hops brewery is the first of its kind in the UK, and as such serves arguably the freshest beer not just in London, but the country.**

Euston Tap (Map p254; ☎020-3137 8837; www.eustontap.com; 190 Euston Rd, NW1; ☺noon-11pm; ⊖Euston) **At this specialist boozery, craft beer devotees can choose between seven cask ales, 20 keg beers and 150 by the bottle.**

American Bar
Cocktail Bar

(Map p248; ☏020-7836 4343; www.fairmont.
com/savoy-london/dining/americanbar; Savoy,
The Strand, WC2; ⊗11.30am-midnight Mon-Sat,
noon-midnight Sun; ⊖Covent Garden) Home
of the Hanky Panky, White Lady and other
classic infusions created en situ, the
seriously dishy and elegant American Bar
is an icon of London, with soft blue and rust
art-deco lines and live piano music. Cocktails
start at £16.50 and peak at a stupefying
£5000 (The Original Sazerac, containing
Sazerac de Forge cognac from 1857).

Dog & Duck
Pub

(Map p248; ☏020-7494 0697; www.
nicholsonspubs.co.uk/restaurants/london/
thedoganducksoholondon; 18 Bateman St,
W1; ⊗11am-11pm Mon-Sat, noon-10pm Sun;
⊖Tottenham Court Rd) With a fine array of
real ales, some stunning Victorian glazed
tiling and garrulous crowds spilling onto the
pavement, the Dog & Duck has attracted a
host of famous regulars, including painters
John Constable and pre-Raphaelite Dante
Gabrielle Rossetti, dystopian writer George
Orwell and musician Madonna.

She Soho
Lesbian

(Map p248; ☏020-7287 5041; www.she-soho.
com; 23a Old Compton St, W1D; ⊗4-11.30pm
Mon-Thu, noon-midnight Fri & Sat, noon-10.30pm
Sun; ⊖Leicester Sq) This intimate and dimly
lit basement bar has DJs, comedy, cabaret,
burlesque, live music and party nights.
Open till 3am on the last Friday and Saturday of the month. Everybody is welcome at
this friendly place.

Draft House
Bar

(Map p248; ☏020-7323 9361; www.drafthouse.
co.uk; 43 Goodge St, W1; ⊗noon-11pm Mon-Thu,
to midnight Fri & Sat; ☏; ⊖Goodge St) Although
you can line your tummy with decent nosh,
Draft House (and its nine other branches
strewn throughout London) is largely about
the beer choice it crams into its pea-sized
premises. This is a public house for ale
aficionados, where you can happily corner
Sambook's from Battersea or choose from
several cask and a dozen keg ales.

Terroirs
Wine Bar

(Map p248; ☏020-7036 0660; www.
terroirswinebar.com; 5 William IV St, WC2;
⊗noon-11pm Mon-Sat; ☏; ⊖Charing Cross Rd)
A fab two-floor spot for a pretheatre glass
and some expertly created charcuterie,
with informative staff, tempting and
affordable £10 lunch specials, a lively,
convivial atmosphere and a breathtaking
list of organic, natural and biodynamic
wines.

Swift
Cocktail Bar

(Map p248; ☏020-7437 7820; www.barswift.
com; 12 Old Compton St, W1; ⊗3pm-midnight
Mon-Sat, to 10.30pm Sun; ⊖Leicester Sq or Tottenham Court Rd) Our favourite new place for
cocktails, Swift (as in the bird) has a black-
and-white, candlelit Upstairs Bar designed
for those who want a quick tipple before
dinner or the theatre, while the Downstairs
Bar (open from 5pm), with its sit-down bar
and art deco sofas, is a place to hang out.
There's live jazz and blues at the weekend.

Queen's Larder
Pub

(Map p254; ☏020-7837 5627; www.queenslarder.
co.uk; 1 Queen Sq, WC1; ⊗11.30am-11pm Mon-Fri,
noon-11pm Sat, noon-10.30pm Sun; ⊖Russell
Sq) In a lovely square southeast of Russell
Sq is this cosy pub, so called because
Queen Charlotte, wife of 'Mad' King George
III, rented part of the pub's cellar to store
special foods for her husband while he
was being treated nearby for what is now
believed to have been the genetic disease
porphyria. There are benches outside and a
dining room upstairs.

Lamb & Flag
Pub

(Map p248; ☏020-7497 9504; www.
lambandflagcoventgarden.co.uk; 33 Rose St,
WC2; ⊗11am-11pm Mon-Sat, noon-10.30pm Sun;
⊖Covent Garden) Everybody's favourite pub
in central London, pint-sized Lamb & Flag
is full of charm and history. It's on the site
of a pub that dates to at least 1772. Rain
or shine, you'll have to elbow your way to
the bar through the merry crowd drinking
outside. Inside are brass fittings and creaky
wooden floors.

Clubbing

When it comes to clubbing, London is up there with the best of them. You'll probably know what you want to experience – it might be big clubs or sweaty shoebox clubs with the freshest DJ talent – but there's plenty to tempt you to branch out from your usual tastes and try something new.

There are clubs across town. The East End is the top area for cutting-edge clubs, especially Shoreditch. Dalston and Hackney are popular for makeshift clubs in restaurant basements and former shops – so it's great for night-fun hunters. Camden Town still favours the indie crowd, while King's Cross has a bit of everything. The gay party crowd mainly gravitates to the south of the river, especially Vauxhall, although gay clubs still maintain a toehold in the West and East End.

Fabric (p174)

Gordon's Wine Bar   Bar

(Map p248; 020-7930 1408; www.
gordonswinebar.com; 47 Villiers St, WC2; 11am-
11pm Mon-Sat, noon-10pm Sun; Embankment
or Charing Cross) Cavernous, candlelit
and atmospheric, Gordon's (founded in
1890) is a victim of its own success – it's
relentlessly busy and unless you arrive
before the office crowd does (around
6pm), forget about landing a table. The
French and New World wines are heady and
reasonably priced; buy by the glass, the
beaker (12cl), the schooner (15cl) or the
bottle.

Princess Louise   Pub

(Map p248; 020-7405 8816; http://
princesslouisepub.co.uk; 208 High Holborn, WC1;
11am-11pm Mon-Fri, noon-11pm Sat, noon-6.45pm
Sun; Holborn) The ground-floor saloon of
this pub dating from 1872 is spectacularly
decorated with a riot of fine tiles, etched
mirrors, plasterwork and a stunning central
horseshoe bar. The old Victorian wood
partitions give drinkers plenty of nooks and
alcoves to hide in and the frosted-glass 'snob
screens' add further period allure.

French House Soho   Pub

(Map p248; 020-7437 2477; www.
frenchhousesoho.com; 49 Dean St, W1; noon-
11pm Mon-Sat, to 10.30pm Sun; Leicester
Sq) French House is Soho's legendary
boho boozer with a history to match: this
was the meeting place of the Free French
Forces during WWII. De Gaulle is said to
have drunk here often, while Dylan Thomas,
Peter O'Toole and Francis Bacon all ended
up on the wooden floor at least once.

Heaven   Club, Gay

(Map p248; http://heaven-live.co.uk; Villiers
St, WC2; 11pm-5am Mon, Thu & Fri, 10pm-5am
Sat; Embankment or Charing Cross) This perennially popular gay club under the arches
beneath Charing Cross station since 1979
is host to excellent live gigs and club nights.
Monday's Popcorn (mixed dance party,
all-welcome door policy) offers some of the
best weeknight clubbing in the capital. The
celebrated G-A-Y takes place here on Thursday (G-A-Y Porn Idol), Friday (G-A-Y Camp
Attack) and Saturday (plain ol' G-A-Y).

Lamb   Pub

(Map p254; 020-7405 0713; www.thelamblondon.
com; 94 Lamb's Conduit St, WC1; 11am-11pm
Mon-Wed, to midnight Thu-Sat, noon-10.30pm Sun;
Russell Sq) The Lamb's central mahogany
bar with beautiful Victorian 'snob screens'
(so-called as they allowed the well-to-do to
drink in private) has been a favourite with locals since 1729. Nearly three centuries later,
its popularity hasn't waned, so come early to
bag a booth and sample its good selection of
Young's bitters and genial atmosphere.

Yard   Gay

(Map p248; ☎020-7437 2652; www.yardbar.
co.uk; 57 Rupert St, W1; ⊘4-11.30pm Mon & Tue,
noon-11.30pm Wed & Thu, noon-midnight Fri &
Sat, 1-10.30pm Sun; ⊖Piccadilly Circus) This
Soho favourite attracts a cross-section of
the great and the good. It's fairly attitude-
free, perfect for preclub drinks or just an
evening out. There are DJs upstairs in the
renovated Loft Bar most nights as well as
a friendly crowd in the open-air (heated in
season) Courtyard Bar below.

❽ West London

Roof Gardens   Club

(Map p250; www.roofgardens.virgin.com; 99
Kensington High St, W8; club £20, gardens free;
⊘club 10pm-2am Fri & Sat, garden 9am-5pm (on
selected dates); ☞; ⊖High St Kensington) Atop
the former Derry and Toms building is this
enchanting venue – a nightclub with 0.6
hectares of gardens and resident flamingos. The wow-factor requires £20 entry,
you must register on the guest list (http://
gls.roofgardens.com/) before going and

drinks are £10 a pop. Open to over-21s, the
dress code is 'no effort, no entry' (leave the
onesie at home).

Windsor Castle   Pub

(Map p250; www.thewindsorcastlekensington.
co.uk; 114 Campden Hill Rd, W11; ⊘noon-11pm
Mon-Sat, to 10.30pm Sun; ☞; ⊖Notting Hill Gate)
A classic tavern on the brow of Campden
Hill Rd, this place has history, nooks and
charm on tap. It's worth the search for its
historic compartmentalised interior, roaring fire (in winter), delightful beer garden
(in summer) and affable regulars (most
always). According to legend, the bones of
Thomas Paine (author of *Rights of Man*) are
in the cellar.

Notting Hill Arts Club   Club

(Map p250; www.nottinghillartsclub.com; 21
Notting Hill Gate, W11; ⊘6pm-late Mon-Fri, 4pm-
late Sat & Sun; ☞; ⊖Notting Hill Gate) London
simply wouldn't be what it is without places
like NHAC. Cultivating the underground
music scene, this small basement club attracts a musically curious and experimental crowd. Dress code: no suits and ties.

Windsor Castle pub

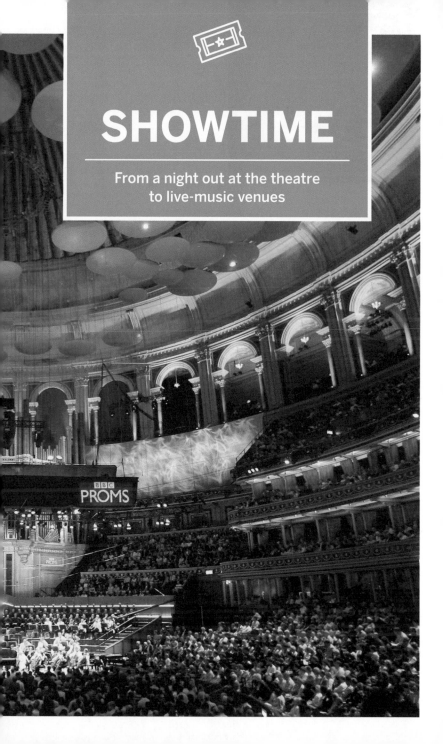

SHOWTIME

From a night out at the theatre
to live-music venues

BBC
PROMS

Showtime

Whatever it is that sets your spirits soaring or your booty shaking, you'll find it in London. The city's been a world leader in theatre ever since a young man from Stratford-upon-Avon set up shop here in the 16th century. And if London started swinging in the 1960s, its live rock and pop scene has barely let up since.

The trick to bag tickets to high-profile events and performances is to book ahead – or hope there will be standby tickets on the day. And don't worry if you miss out: there are literally hundreds of smaller gigs and performances every night and the joy is to stumble upon them.

In This Section

Tickets

Book well ahead for live performances and if you can, buy directly from the venue.

On the day of performance, you can buy discounted tickets, sometimes up to 50% off, for West End productions from **Tkts Leicester Sq** (www.tkts.co.uk/leicester-square).

All Time Low perform at the O2 Brixton Academy

The Best...

Theatre

Shakespeare's Globe (p190) Shakespeare, as it would have been 400 years ago.

National Theatre (p191) Contemporary theatre on the South Bank.

Wilton's (p188) The Victorian music-hall tradition lives on.

Live Music

Royal Albert Hall (p189) Gorgeous, grand and spacious, yet strangely intimate.

KOKO (p189) Fabulously glitzy venue showcasing original indie rock.

O2 Academy Brixton (p188) Legendary concert hall.

Royal Opera House (p194) One of the world's great opera venues.

✪ Clerkenwell, Shoreditch & Spitalfields

Sadler's Wells   Dance
(Map p253; ☎020-7863 8000;
www.sadlerswells.com; Rosebery Ave, EC1R;
⊖Angel) A glittering modern venue that
was, in fact, first established in 1683,
Sadler's Wells is the most eclectic
modern-dance and ballet venue in town,
with experimental dance shows of all
genres and from all corners of the globe.
The Lilian Baylis Studio stages smaller
productions.

✪ East London

Vortex Jazz Club   Jazz
(Map p255; ☎020-7254 4097; www.vortexjazz.
co.uk; 11 Gillet Sq, N16; ☉8pm-midnight;
ℝDalston Kingsland) With a fantastically
varied menu of jazz, the Vortex hosts an
outstanding line-up of musicians, singers
and songwriters from the UK, US, Europe,
Africa and beyond. It's a small venue so
make sure you book if there's an act you
particularly fancy.

Wilton's   Theatre
(Map p245; ☎020-7702 2789; www.wiltons.
org.uk; 1 Graces Alley, E1; tour £6; ☉tours 6pm
most Mon, bar 5-11pm Mon-Sat; ⊖Tower Hill)
A gloriously atmospheric example of one
of London's Victorian public-house music
halls, Wilton's hosts a variety of shows,
from comedy and classical music to
theatre and opera. One-hour guided tours
offer an insight into its fascinating history.
The Mahogany Bar is a great way to get a
taste of the place if you're not attending a
performance.

Hackney Empire   Theatre
(Map p255; ☎020-8985 2424; www.
hackneyempire.co.uk; 291 Mare St, E8;
⊖Hackney Central) One of London's
most beautiful theatres, this renovated
Edwardian music hall (1901) offers an
extremely diverse range of performances
– from hard-edged political theatre to
musicals, opera and comedy. It's one of the
very best places to catch a pantomime at
Christmas.

✪ Greenwich & South London

O2 Academy Brixton   Live Music
(www.o2academybrixton.co.uk; 211 Stockwell Rd,
SW9; ☉doors open 7pm most nights; ⊖Brixton)
It's hard to have a bad night at the Brixton
Academy, even if you leave with your
soles sticky with beer, as this cavernous
former-5000-capacity art-deco theatre
always thrums with bonhomie. There's a
properly raked floor for good views, as well
as plenty of bars and an excellent mixed bill
of established and emerging talent. Most
shows are 14-plus.

Up the Creek   Comedy
(Map p256; www.up-the-creek.com; 302 Creek
Rd, SE10; admission £5-15; ☉7-11pm Thu & Sun,
to 2am Fri & Sat; ℝDLR Cutty Sark) Bizarre-
ly enough, the hecklers can be funnier
than the acts at this great club. Mischief,
rowdiness and excellent comedy are the
norm, with the Blackout open-mic night on
Thursdays (www.the-blackout.co.uk, £5)
and Sunday specials (www.sundayspecial.
co.uk, £7). There's an after-party disco on
Fridays and Saturdays.

O2 Arena   Live Music
(www.theo2.co.uk; Peninsula Sq, SE10; ☎;
⊖North Greenwich) One of the city's major
concert venues, hosting all the biggies –
the Rolling Stones, Paul Simon and Sting,
One Direction, Ed Sheeran and many
others – inside the 20,000-capacity arena.
It's also a popular venue for sporting
events.

✪ Kensington & Hyde Park

606 Club   Blues, Jazz
(☎020-7352 5953; www.606club.co.uk; 90 Lots
Rd, SW10; ☉7-11.15pm Sun-Thu, 8pm-12.30am
Fri & Sat; ℝImperial Wharf) Named after its

old address on King's Rd that cast a spell over jazz lovers London-wide back in the '80s, this fantastic, tucked-away basement jazz club and restaurant gives centre stage to contemporary British-based jazz musicians nightly. The club can only serve alcohol to nonmembers who are dining and it is highly advisable to book to get a table.

Royal Albert Hall   Concert Venue
(Map p250; ☎0845 401 5034; www. royalalberthall.com; Kensington Gore, SW7; ⊖South Kensington) This splendid Victorian concert hall hosts classical-music, rock and other performances, but is famously the venue for the BBC-sponsored Proms. Booking is possible, but from mid-July to mid-September Proms punters queue for £5 standing (or 'promenading') tickets that go on sale one hour before curtain-up. Otherwise, the box office and prepaid-ticket collection counter are through door 12 (south side of the hall).

✪ North London

Cecil Sharp House   Traditional Music
(Map p254; www.cecilsharphouse.org; 2 Regent's Park Rd, NW1; ⊖Camden Town) If you've ever fancied clog stamping, hanky waving or bell jingling, this is the place for you. Home to the English Folk Dance and Song Society, this institute keeps all manner of wacky folk traditions alive, with performances and classes held in its gorgeous mural-covered Kennedy Hall. The dance classes are oodles of fun; no experience necessary.

KOKO   Live Music
(Map p254; www.koko.uk.com; 1a Camden High St, NW1; ⊖Mornington Cres) Once the legendary Camden Palace, where Charlie Chaplin, the Goons and the Sex Pistols performed, and where Prince played surprise gigs, KOKO is maintaining its reputation as one of London's better gig venues. The theatre has a dance floor

Live Music

Musically diverse and defiantly different, London is a hotspot of musical innovation and talent. It leads the world in articulate indie rock, in particular, and tomorrow's guitar heroes are right this minute paying their dues on sticky-floored stages in Camden Town, Shoreditch and Dalston.

Monster international acts see London as an essential stop on their transglobal stomps, but be prepared for tickets selling out faster than you can find your credit card. The city's beautiful old theatres and music halls play host to a constant roster of well-known names in more intimate settings. In summer, giant festivals take over the city's parks, while smaller, more localised events such as the **Dalston Music Festival** (www.dalstonmusicfestival.com) showcase up-and-comers in multiple spaces.

If jazz or blues are your thing, London has some truly excellent clubs and pubs where you can catch classics and contemporary tunes. The city's major jazz event is the **London Jazz Festival** (www.londonjazzfestival.org.uk) in November.

Ice-T and Ron McCurdy perform at the London Jazz Festival
JOSEPH OKPAKO / CONTRIBUTOR / GETTY IMAGES ©

and decadent balconies, and attracts an indie crowd. There are live bands most nights and hugely popular club nights on Saturdays.

Scala
Live Music

(Map p254; ☎020-7833 2022; www.scala.co.uk; 275 Pentonville Rd, N1; ⊖King's Cross St Pancras) Opened in 1920 as a salubrious golden-age cinema, Scala slipped into porn-movie hell in the 1970s only to be reborn as a club and live-music venue in the noughties. It's one of the best places in London to catch an intimate gig and is also a great dance space that hosts a diverse range of club nights.

Regent's Park Open Air Theatre
Theatre

(Map p254; ☎0844 826 4242; www.openairtheatre.org; Queen Mary's Gardens, Regent's Park, NW1; ⊗May-Sep; ⊛; ⊖Baker St) A popular and very atmospheric summertime fixture in London, this 1250-seat outdoor auditorium plays host to four productions a year: famous plays (Shakespeare often features), new works, musicals and usually one production aimed at families.

Roundhouse
Concert Venue

(www.roundhouse.org.uk; Chalk Farm Rd, NW1; ⊖Chalk Farm) Built as a railway-repair shed in 1847, this unusual Grade II–listed round building became an arts centre in the 1960s and hosted legendary bands before falling into near-dereliction in 1983. Its 21st-century resurrection as a creative hub has been a great success and it now hosts everything from big-name concerts to dance, circus, stand-up comedy, poetry slam and improvisation.

✪ The City

Barbican
Performing Arts

(Map p253; ☎box office 020-7638 8891; www.barbican.org.uk; Silk St, EC2; ⊗box office 10am-8pm Mon-Sat, from 11am Sun; ⊖Barbican) Home to the wonderful London Symphony Orchestra and its associate orchestra, the lesser-known BBC Symphony Orchestra, the arts centre also hosts scores of other leading musicians, focusing in particular on jazz, folk, world and soul artists. Dance is another strong point here, while film covers recent releases as well as film festivals and seasons.

From left: Scala (p189); 100 Club (p194); Royal Festival Hall; London Wonderground

❂ The South Band

Shakespeare's Globe   Theatre
(Map p245; ☎020-7401 9919; www.
shakespearesglobe.com; 21 New Globe Walk,
SE1; seats £20-45, standing £5; ⊖Blackfriars
or London Bridge) If you love Shakespeare
and the theatre, the Globe (p85) will knock
your theatrical socks off. This authentic
Shakespearean theatre is a wooden 'O'
without a roof over the central stage area,
and although there are covered wooden
bench seats in tiers around the stage, many
people (there's room for 700) do as 17th-
century 'groundlings' did, standing in front
of the stage.

Because the building is quite open to
the elements, you may have to wrap up.
Groundlings note: umbrellas are not allowed, but cheap raincoats are on sale. Unexpected aircraft noise is unavoidable, too.

The theatre season runs from late April
to mid-October and includes works by
Shakespeare and his contemporaries such
as Christopher Marlowe.

If you don't like the idea of standing in
the rain or sitting in the cold, opt for an
indoor candlelit play in the **Sam Wanamak-
er Playhouse**, a Jacobean theatre similar
to the one Shakespeare would have used
in winter. The programming also includes
opera.

National Theatre   Theatre
(Royal National Theatre; Map p245; ☎020-7452
3000; www.nationaltheatre.org.uk; South Bank,
SE1; ⊖Waterloo) England's flagship theatre
showcases a mix of classic and contemporary plays performed by excellent casts
in three theatres (Olivier, Lyttelton and
Dorfman). Artistic director Rufus Norris,
who started in April 2015, made headlines
in 2016 for announcing plans to stage a
Brexit-based drama.

Southbank Centre   Concert Venue
(Map p245; ☎0844 875 0073; www.
southbankcentre.co.uk; Belvedere Rd, SE1;
⊖Waterloo) The Southbank Centre
comprises several venues – **Royal Festival
Hall** (Map p245; ☎020-7960 4200; www.
southbankcentre.co.uk; Southbank Centre,
Belvedere Rd, SE1; 🛜; ⊖Waterloo), Queen
Elizabeth Hall and Purcell Room – hosting
a wide range of performing arts. As well

as regular programming, it organises fantastic festivals, including **London Wonderground** (circus and cabaret), **Udderbelly** (a festival of comedy in all its guises) and **Meltdown** (a music event curated by the best and most eclectic names in music).

Old Vic   Theatre
(Map p245; ☎0844 871 7628; www.oldvictheatre. com; The Cut, SE1; ⊖Waterloo) American actor Kevin Spacey took the theatrical helm of this London theatre in 2003, giving it a new lease of life. He was succeeded in April 2015 by Matthew Warchus (who directed *Matilda the Musical* and the film *Pride*), whose aim is to bring an eclectic programming to the theatre: expect new writing, as well as dynamic revivals of old works and musicals.

Young Vic   Theatre
(Map p245; ☎020-7922 2922; www.youngvic.org; 66 The Cut, SE1; ⊖Southwark or Waterloo) This ground-breaking theatre is as much about showcasing and discovering new talent as it is about people discovering theatre. The Young Vic features actors, directors and plays from across the world, many tackling contemporary political and cultural issues, such as the death penalty, racism or corruption, and often blending dance and music with acting.

✪ The West End

Pizza Express Jazz Club   Jazz
(Map p248; ☎020-7439 4962; www. pizzaexpresslive.com/venues/soho-jazz-club; 10 Dean St, W1; admission £15-40; ⊖Tottenham Court Rd) Pizza Express has been one of the best jazz venues in London since opening in 1969. It may be a strange arrangement, in a basement beneath a branch of the chain restaurant, but it's highly popular. Lots of big names perform here and promising artists such as Norah Jones, Gregory Porter and the late Amy Winehouse played here in their early days.

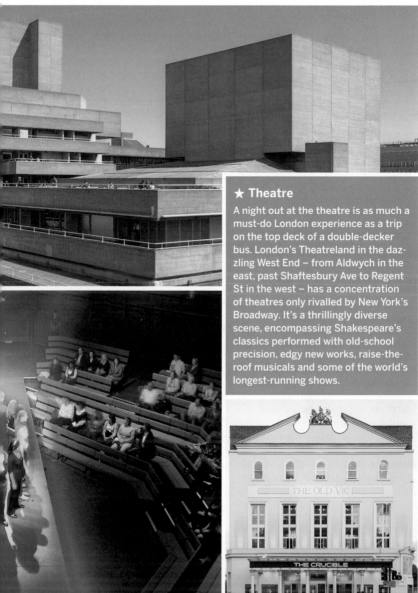

★ Theatre

A night out at the theatre is as much a must-do London experience as a trip on the top deck of a double-decker bus. London's Theatreland in the dazzling West End – from Aldwych in the east, past Shaftesbury Ave to Regent St in the west – has a concentration of theatres only rivalled by New York's Broadway. It's a thrillingly diverse scene, encompassing Shakespeare's classics performed with old-school precision, edgy new works, raise-the-roof musicals and some of the world's longest-running shows.

Clockwise from top: National Theatre (p191); Old Vic; A performance at Young Vic

Classical Music, Ballet & Opera

With multiple world-class orchestras and ensembles, quality venues, reasonable ticket prices and performances covering the whole musical gamut from traditional crowd-pleasers to innovative compositions, London will satisfy even the fussiest classical music buff. The Southbank Centre (p191), Barbican (p190) and Royal Albert Hall (p189) all maintain an alluring program of performances, further gilding London's outstanding reputation as a cosmopolitan centre for classical music. The Proms (p12) is the festival calendar's biggest event.

Opera and ballet lovers should make an evening at the **Royal Opera House** a priority – the setting and quality of the programming are truly world class.

Paul Hamlyn Hall, Royal Opera House
CHRISTIAN MUELLER / SHUTTERSTOCK ©

Wigmore Hall   Classical Music
(Map p250; www.wigmore-hall.org.uk; 36 Wigmore St, W1; ⊖Bond St) This is one of the best and most active (more than 400 concerts a year) classical-music venues in town, not only because of its fantastic acoustics, beautiful art-nouveau hall and great variety of concerts and recitals, but also because of the sheer standard of the performances. Built in 1901, it has remained one of the world's top places for chamber music.

Prince Charles Cinema   Cinema
(Map p248; www.princecharlescinema.com; 7 Leicester Pl, WC2; tickets £8-16; ⊖Leicester Sq) Leicester Sq cinema-ticket prices

are very high, so wait until the first-runs have moved to the Prince Charles, central London's cheapest cinema, where non-members pay only £9 to £11.50 for new releases. Also on the cards are minifestivals, Q&As with film directors, classics, sleepover movie marathons and exuberant sing-along screenings of films like *Frozen*, *The Sound of Music* and *Rocky Horror Picture Show* (£16).

Royal Opera House   Opera
(Map p248; ☑020-7304 4000; www.roh.org.uk; Bow St, WC2; tickets £4-270; ⊖Covent Garden) Classic opera in London has a fantastic setting on Covent Garden Piazza and coming here for a night is a sumptuous – if pricey – affair. Although the program has been fluffed up by modern influences, the main attractions are still the opera and classical ballet – all are wonderful productions and feature world-class performers.

Ronnie Scott's   Jazz
(Map p248; ☑020-7439 0747; www.ronniescotts.co.uk; 47 Frith St, W1; ⊖7pm-3am Mon-Sat, 1-4pm & 8pm-midnight Sun; ⊖Leicester Sq or Tottenham Court Rd) Ronnie Scott's jazz club opened at this address in 1965 and became widely known as Britain's best. Support acts are at 7pm, with main gigs at 8.15pm (8pm Sunday) and a second house at 11.15pm Friday and Saturday (check though). The more informal Late, Late Show runs from 1am till 3am.

Comedy Store   Comedy
(Map p248; ☑0844 871 7699; www.thecomedystore.co.uk; 1a Oxendon St, SW1; admission £8-22.50; ⊖Piccadilly Circus) This is one of the first (and still one of the best) comedy clubs in London. Wednesday and Sunday night's Comedy Store Players is the most famous improvisation outfit in town, with the wonderful Josie Lawrence, now a veteran of two decades. On Thursdays, Fridays and Saturdays, Best in Stand Up features the best on London's comedy circuit.

Prince Charles Cinema

100 Club
Live Music

(Map p248; 020-7636 0933; www.the100club. co.uk; 100 Oxford St, W1; admission £8-20; check website for gig times; Oxford Circus or Tottenham Court Rd) This heritage London venue at the same address for over a half-century started off as a jazz club but now leans toward rock. Back in the day it showcased Chris Barber, BB King and the Rolling Stones, and it was at the centre of the punk revolution and the '90s indie scene. It hosts dancing gigs, the occasional big name, where-are-they-now bands and top-league tributes.

Amused Moose Soho
Comedy

(Map p248; box office 020-7287 3727; www. amusedmoose.com; Sanctum Soho Hotel, 20 Warwick St, W1; Piccadilly Circus, Oxford Circus) One of the city's best clubs, the peripatetic Amused Moose (the cinema in the Sanctum Soho Hotel is just one of its hosting venues) is popular with audiences and comedians alike, perhaps helped along by the fact that heckling is 'unacceptable' and all the acts are 'first-date friendly' (ie unlikely to humiliate the front row).

☺ West London

Electric Cinema
Cinema

(Map p250; 020-7908 9696; www. electriccinema.co.uk; 191 Portobello Rd, W11; tickets £8-22.50; Ladbroke Grove) Having notched up its first centenary in 2011, the Electric is one of the UK's oldest cinemas, updated. Avail yourself of the luxurious leather armchairs, sofas, footstools and tables for food and drink in the auditorium, or select one of the six front-row double beds! Tickets are cheapest on Mondays.

Opera Holland Park
Opera

(Map p250; 0300 999 1000; www. operahollandpark.com; Holland Park, W8; tickets £18-77; High St Kensington, Holland Park) Sit under the 1000-seat canopy, temporarily erected every summer for a nine-week season in the middle of Holland Park (p127) for a mix of crowd pleasers and rare (even obscure) works. Five operas are generally performed each year.

ACTIVE
LONDON

Exploring the city on two wheels and more

Active London

The 2012 Olympic Games put a spring in London's step and left the city with a sudden embarrassment of world-class sports facilities in the east of town, some of which are now open to the public. The rest of London boasts a well-developed infrastructure for participatory and spectator sports to get your heart racing and the endorphins flowing.

Many events are free to watch; and if you've missed out on expensive ones, you can always watch in the pub or on a big screen somewhere. Active types will love the Santander Cycle Hire Scheme, which allows you to explore the city easily (and cheaply!) on two wheels.

In This Section

Sports Seasons

Football The season runs from mid-August to May.

Rugby The Six Nations (www.www.rbssixnations.com) is rugby's big annual tournament, spread over five weekends in February and March.

Tennis London is gripped by tennis fever during Wimbledon (July).

People watching Wimbledon on an outdoor screen

The Best...

Free Spectator Sports

London Marathon (April) Watch runners pound the pavement from Blackheath to Buckingham Palace.

Oxford & Cambridge Boat Race (early April) Features the arch-rival universities on a course from Putney to Mortlake.

Head of the River Race (late March) Held along the same course as the Boat Race, but in reverse and with international crews.

Big-Screen Locations

Outdoor screens usually operate between April and October.

Trafalgar Square If there is anything big happening, you can be guaranteed there will be a big screen to watch it on at London's prime square.

Queen Elizabeth Olympic Park Given its legacy, it's hardly surprising big sporting events are broadcast here.

⊕ Walking Tours

Guide London   Tours
(Association of Professional Tourist Guides; ☎020-7611 2545; www.guidelondon.org.uk; half-/full-day £160/272) Hire a prestigious Blue Badge Tourist Guide: these know-it-all guides have studied for two years and passed a dozen written and practical exams to do their job. They can tell you stories about the sights that you'd only hear from them, or whisk you on a themed tour – from royalty and the Beatles to parks and shopping. Go by car, public transport, bike or on foot.

Unseen Tours   Walking
(☎07514 266 774; www.sockmobevents.org.uk; £12) See London from an entirely different angle on one of these award-winning neighbourhood tours led by the London homeless covering Camden Town, Brick Lane, Shoreditch and London Bridge. Sixty percent of the tour price goes to the guide.

London Walks   Walking
(☎020-7624 3978; www.walks.com; adult/child £10/free) A huge choice of themed walks, including Jack the Ripper, the Beatles, Sherlock Holmes, Harry Potter and ghost walks. Check the website for schedules – there are walks every day.

⊕ Bus Tours

Original Tour   Bus
(www.theoriginaltour.com; adult/child £30/15; ◷8.30am-8.30pm) A 24-hour hop-on, hop-off bus service with a river cruise thrown in, as well as three themed walks: Changing of the Guard, Rock 'n' Roll and Jack the Ripper. Buses run every five to 20 minutes; you can buy tickets on the bus or online. There's also a 48-hour ticket available (adult/child £40/19), with an extended river cruise.

Big Bus Tours   Bus
(☎020-7808 6753; www.bigbustours.com; adult/child £30/12.50; ◷every 20min 8.30am-6pm Apr-Sep, to 5pm Oct & Mar, to 4.30pm

Nov-Feb) Informative commentaries in 12 languages. The ticket includes a free river cruise with City Cruises and three thematic walking tours (Royal London, film locations, mysteries). Good online booking discounts available. Onboard wi-fi. The ticket is valid for 24 hours; for an extra £8 (£5 for children), you can upgrade to a 48-hour ticket.

⊕ Boat Tours

Thames River Services   Boating
(Map p256; ☎020-7930 4097; www.thamesriverservices.co.uk; adult/child 1-way £12.50/6.25, return £16.50/8.25) These cruise boats leave Westminster Pier for Greenwich, stopping at the Tower of London. Every second service from April to October continues on from Greenwich to the Thames Barrier (from Westminster, one-way adult/child £14/7, return £17/8.50, hourly 11.30am to 3.30pm) but does not land there; it passes the **O2** (www.theo2.co.uk; Peninsula Sq, SE10; ⊖North Greenwich) along the way.

Lee & Stort Boats   Boating
(Map p255; ☎0845 116 2012; www.leeandstortboats.co.uk; Stratford Waterfront Pontoon, E20; adult/child £9/4; ◷Sat & Sun Mar, daily Apr-Sep, selected days Oct-Feb; ⊖Stratford) Lee & Stort offers 45-minute tours on the waterways through Queen Elizabeth Olympic Park. Check the display boards in the park for departure times, which are usually on the hour from midday onwards.

Thames Rockets   Boating
(Map p245; ☎020-7928 8933; www.thamesrockets.com; Boarding Gate 1, London Eye, Waterloo Millennium Pier, Westminster Bridge Rd, SE1; adult/child £43.50/29.50; ◷10am-6pm; ⊕) Feel like James Bond – or David Beckham en route to the 2012 Olympic Games – on this high-speed inflatable boat that flies down the Thames at 30 to 35 knots. Thames Rockets also does a Captain Kidd–themed trip between the London Eye and Canary Wharf for the same price.

London Waterbus Company Cruise

(Map p250; ☎020-7482 2550; www.
londonwaterbus.co.uk; 32 Camden Lock Pl, NW1;
adult/child one-way £9/7.50, return £14/12;
⏱hourly 10am-5pm Apr-Sep, weekends only
and less frequent departures other months;
⊖Warwick Ave or Camden Town) This enclosed
barge runs enjoyable 50-minute trips on
Regent's Canal between Little Venice and
Camden Lock, passing by Regent's Park
and stopping at London Zoo. There are
fewer departures outside high season –
check the website for schedules. One-way
tickets (adult/child £25/18), including
entry to London Zoo, are also available
for passengers to disembark within the
zoo grounds. Buy tickets aboard the
narrowboats.

⊕ Pool & Spa

Hampstead Heath Ponds Swimming

(www.cityoflondon.gov.uk; Hampstead Heath,
NW5; adult/child £2/1; ⊖Hampstead Heath)
Set in the midst of the gorgeous heath,
Hampstead's three bathing ponds (men's,
women's and mixed) offer a cooling dip
in murky brown water. Despite what you
might think from its appearance, the water
is tested daily and meets stringent quality
guidelines.

Porchester Spa Spa

(Map p250; ☎020-7313 3858; www.
porchesterspatreatments.co.uk; Porchester
Centre, Queensway, W2; admission £28.55;
⏱10am-10pm; ⊖Bayswater, Royal Oak)
Housed in a gorgeous art-deco building,
the Porchester is a no-frills spa run
by Westminster Council. With a 30m
swimming pool, a large Finnish-log sauna,
two steam rooms, three Turkish hot rooms
and a massive plunge pool, there are
plenty of affordable treatments on offer
including massages and male and female
pampering/grooming sessions.

It's women only on Tuesdays, Thursdays and Fridays all day and between

Football

Football is at the very heart of English
culture, with about a dozen league
teams in London and usually around
five or six in the Premier League.
Tickets for Premier League fixtures
(August to mid-May) can be impossible to secure for visitors. Stadiums
where you can watch matches (or,
more realistically, take tours) include
the city's landmark national stadium, **Wembley** (☎0800 169 9933;
www.wembleystadium.com; tours adult/
child £19/11; ⊖Wembley Park); **Arsenal
Emirates Stadium** (☎020-7619 5000;
www.arsenal.com/tours; Hornsey Rd, N5;
tours self-guided adult/child £20/10, guided
£40; ⏱10am-6pm Mon-Sat, to 4pm Sun;
⊖Holloway Rd); **Chelsea** (☎0871 984
1955; www.chelseafc.com; Stamford Bridge,
Fulham Rd, SW6; tours adult/child £21/15;
⏱museum 9.30am-5pm, tours 10am-3pm;
⊖Fulham Broadway); and the **London
Stadium**, formerly known as the Olympic Stadium and now home of West
Ham United.

Numerous pubs across the capital
show Premier League games (as well as
international fixtures) and watching a
football game in a pub is an experience
in itself.

London Stadium
BBA PHOTOGRAPHY / SHUTTERSTOCK ©

10am and 2pm on Sundays; men only on
Mondays, Wednesdays and Saturdays.
Couples are welcome from 4pm to 10pm
on Sundays.

🚲 Santander Cycles

Like Paris and other European cities, London has its own cycle-hire scheme, called Santander Cycles (p235), also variously referred to as 'Barclays Bikes' after their former sponsor, or 'Boris bikes' after the city's mayor, Boris Johnson (2008–16), who launched the initiative. The bikes have proved as popular with visitors as with Londoners.

The idea is simple: pick up a bike from one of the 700 docking stations dotted around the capital. Cycle. Drop it off at another docking station.

The access fee is £2 for 24 hours. All you need is a credit or debit card. The first 30 minutes are free. It's then £2 for any additional period of 30 minutes.

You can take as many bikes as you like during your access period (24 hours), leaving five minutes between each trip.

The pricing structure is designed to encourage short journeys rather than longer rentals; for those, go to a hire company. You'll also find that although easy to ride, the bikes only have three gears and are quite heavy. You must be 18 to buy access and at least 14 to ride a bike.

Santander Cycles docking station at Canary Wharf
SIXPIXX / SHUTTERSTOCK ©

Serpentine Lido   Swimming
(Map p250; ☎020-7706 3422; Hyde Park, W2; adult/child £4.80/1.80; ☺10am-6pm daily Jun-Aug, 10am-6pm Sat & Sun May; ⊜Hyde Park Corner, Knightsbridge) Perhaps the ultimate London pool inside the Serpentine lake, this fabulous lido is open May to August. Sun loungers are available for £3.50 for the whole day.

London Aquatics Centre   Swimming
(www.londonaquaticscentre.org; Queen Elizabeth Olympic Park, E20; adult/child £4.95/2.50; ☺6am-10.30pm; ⊜Stratford) The sweeping lines and wave-like movement of Zaha Hadid's award-winning Aquatics Centre make it the architectural highlight of Olympic Park. Bathed in natural light, the 50m competition pool beneath the huge undulating roof (which sits on just three supports) is an extraordinary place to swim. There's also a second 50m pool, a diving area, gym, creche and cafe.

⊙ Cycling

Lee Valley VeloPark   Cycling
(Map p255; ☎0300 0030 610; www.visitleevalley.org.uk/velopark; Abercrombie Rd, E20; 1hr taster adult/child £40/30, pay & ride weekend/weekday £5/4, bike & helmet hire from £8; ☺9am-10pm; ⊜Hackney Wick) An architectural highlight of Olympic Park, the cutting-edge velodrome is open to the public – either to wander through and watch the pros tear around the steep-sloped circuit, or to have a go yourself. Both the velodrome and the attached BMX park offer taster sessions. Mountain bikers and road cyclists can attack the tracks on a pay-and-ride basis.

London Bicycle Tour   Cycling
(Map p245; ☎020-7928 6838; www.londonbicycle.com; 1 Gabriel's Wharf, 56 Upper Ground, SE1; tour incl bike from adult/child £24.95/21.95, bike hire per day £20; ⊜Southwark or Waterloo) Three-hour tours begin in the South Bank and take in London's highlights on both sides of the river; the classic tour is available in eight languages. A night ride is available. You can also hire traditional or speciality bikes, such as tandems and folding bikes, by the hour or day.

London Aquatics Centre

⊕ Tennis

Wimbledon Championships — Spectator Sport

(☏020-8944 1066; www.wimbledon.com; Church Rd, SW19; grounds admission £8-25, tickets £41-190) For a few weeks each June and July, the sporting world's attention is fixed on the quiet southern suburb of Wimbledon, as it has been since 1877. Most show-court tickets for the Wimbledon Championships are allocated through public ballot, applications for which usually begin in early August of the preceding year and close at the end of December.

Entry into the ballot does not mean entrants will get a ticket. A quantity of show-court, outer-court, ground tickets and late-entry tickets are also available if you queue on the day of play, but if you want a show-court ticket it is recommended you camp the night before in the queue. See www.wimbledon.com for details.

⊕ Climbing

Up at The O2 — Adventure Sports

(www.theo2.co.uk/upattheo2; The O2, Greenwich Peninsula, SE10; from £28; ⊙hours vary; ⊖North Greenwich) London isn't exactly your thrill-seeking destination, but this ascent of the O2 is not for the faint-hearted. Equipped with climbing suit and harness, you'll scale the famous entertainment venue to reach a viewing platform perched 52m above the Thames with sweeping views of Canary Wharf, the river, Greenwich and beyond. Hours vary depending on the season (sunset and twilight climbs also available).

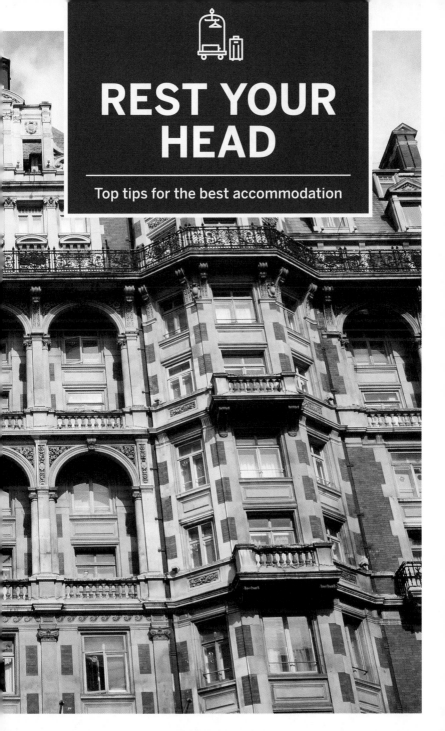

REST YOUR HEAD

Top tips for the best accommodation

Rest Your Head

Landing the right accommodation is integral to your London experience, and there's no shortage of choice. There's some fantastic accommodation about – from party-oriented hostels to stately top-end hotels – so it's worth spending a little time ahead of your trip researching your options.

Budget is likely to be your number one consideration, given how pricey accommodation is in London, but you should also think about the neighbourhood you'd like to stay in. Are you a culture vulture? Would you like to be able to walk (or hop a quick cab ride) home after a night out? Are you after village charm or cool cachet? Make sure you think your options through and book ahead: London is busy year-round.

In This Section

Prices & Tipping

A 'budget hotel' in London generally costs up to £100 for a standard double room with bathroom. For a midrange option, plan on spending £100 to £200. Luxury options run £200 and higher.

Tipping isn't expected in hotels in London, except perhaps for porters in top-end hotels (although it remains discretionary).

The Ritz Hotel

Reservations

○ Book rooms as far in advance as possible, especially for weekends and holiday periods.

○ The British Hotel Reservation Centre (www.bhrconline.com) has desks at airports and major train stations.

○ Visit London (www.visitlondon.com) offers a free accommodation booking service and has a list of gay-friendly accommodation.

Useful Websites

Lonely Planet (www.lonelyplanet.com/london) Hundreds of properties, from budget hostels to luxury apartments.

London Town (www.londontown.com) Excellent last-minute offers on boutique hotels and B&Bs.

Alastair Sawdays (www.sawdays.co.uk) Hand-picked selection of bolt-holes in the capital.

Good to Know

Value-added tax (VAT; 20%) is added to hotel rooms. Some hotels include this in their advertised rates, some don't.

Breakfast may be included in the room rate. Sometimes this is a continental breakfast; full English breakfast might cost extra.

Hotels

London has a grand roll call of stately hotels and many are experiences in their own right. Standards across the top end and much of the boutique bracket are high, but so are prices. Quirkiness and individuality can be found in abundance, alongside dyed-in-the-wool traditionalism. A wealth of budget boutique hotels has exploited a lucrative niche, while a rung or two down in overall quality and charm, midrange chain hotels generally offer good locations and dependable comfort. Demand can often outstrip supply – especially on the bottom step of the market – so book ahead, particularly during holiday periods and in summer.

B&Bs

Housed in good-looking old properties, bed and breakfasts come in a tier below hotels, often promising boutique-style charm and a more personal level of service. Handy B&B clusters appear in Paddington, South Kensington, Victoria and Bloomsbury.

Hostels

After B&Bs the cheapest form of accommodation are hostels: both the official Youth Hostel Association (YHA) ones and the usually hipper, more party-orientated independent ones. Hostels vary in quality so select carefully; most offer twins as well as dorms.

Rates & Booking

Deluxe hotel rooms will cost from around £350 per double but there's good variety at the top end, so you should find a room from about £200 offering superior comfort without the prestige. Some boutique hotels also occupy this bracket. There's a noticeable dip in quality below this price. Under £100 and you're at the more serviceable, budget end of the market. Look out for weekend deals that can put a better class of hotel within reach. Rates often slide in winter. Book through the hotels' websites for the best online deals or promotional rates.

Long-Term Rentals

If you're in London for a week or more, a short-term or serviced apartment may make sense: rates at the bottom end are comparable to a B&B, you can manage your budget more carefully by eating in, and you'll get to feel like a local.

Great neighbourhoods to consider for their vibe include Notting Hill, Hackney, Bermondsey, Pimlico and Camden, where you'll find plenty of food markets, great local pubs and lots of boutiques. **Airbnb** (www.airbnb.co.uk/london) is the go-to source for finding a London pad, but you can also try **Holiday Lettings** (www.holidaylettings.co.uk/london).

For something a little more hotel-like, serviced apartments are a great option. Try the following, which are all in the centre: **196 Bishopsgate** (☎020-7621 8788; www.196bishopsgate.com; 196 Bishopsgate, EC2; apt from £183; ✷⬢; ◉Liverpool St), **Number 5 Maddox Street** (☎020-7647 0200; www.living-rooms.co.uk/hotel/no-5-maddox-st; 5 Maddox St, W1; ste £250-925; ✷⬢; ◉Oxford Circus) and **Beaufort House** (☎020-7584 2600; www.beauforthouse.co.uk; 45 Beaufort Gardens, SW3; 1-4 bedroom apt £443-1350; ✷⬢; ◉Knightsbridge).

Where to Stay

Neighbourhood	Atmosphere
The West End	At the heart of London, with excellent transport links. Fantastic range of options, but expensive and busy. Numerous eating and nightlife options.
The City	Central and well connected, but geared toward business clientele; very quiet at weekends. Expensive on week nights, but good deals to be found at weekends.
The South Bank	Cheaper than the West End, but choice and transport connections more limited. Close to great sights such as the Tate Modern and Borough Market.
Kensington & Hyde Park	Stylish area, with gorgeous hotels, but expensive and with limited nightlife. Good transport links and easy connection to Heathrow.
Clerkenwell, Shoreditch & Spitalfields	Trendy area with great boutique hotels; excellent for restaurants and nightlife, but few top sights and transport options somewhat limited.
East London	Limited sleeping options, but great multicultural local feel; some areas less safe at night.
North London	Leafy area, with great sleeping options and a vibrant nightlife, but further from main sights and with fewer transport options.
West London	Lovely neighbourhood with village charm, great vibe at weekends; plenty of cheap but average hotels. Light on top sights.
Greenwich & South London	Village feel, but limited sleeping and transport options; great for Greenwich sights, but inconvenient for everything else.
Richmond, Kew & Hampton Court	Smart riverside hotels, semirural pockets, but sights spread out and far from central London.

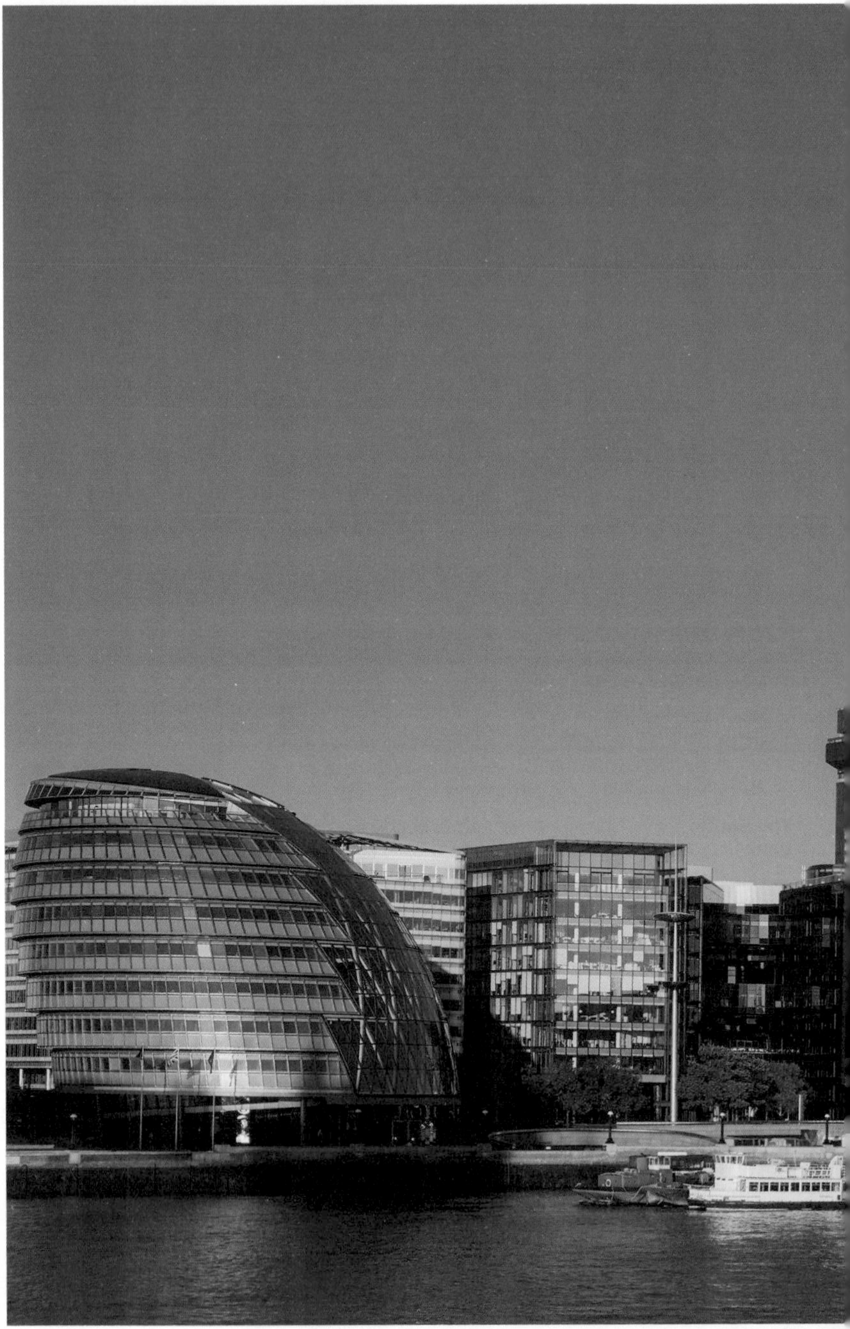

In Focus

The financial district of London

London Today

Britain's exit from the EU (Brexit) has put a damper on London's spirit. With its multicultural population, thriving financial sector and firm links with the continent, the capital seems at odds ideologically with the rest of the country. Its energy, however, remains second to none; its creative juices are still in full flow with a lot of exciting developments, such as the new Crossrail Line and the regeneration of Battersea and King's Cross.

London v the Rest?

London is the world's leading financial centre for international business and commerce and the fifth-largest city economy in the world. As the economic downturn of the last decade fades into memory, the UK is increasingly a nation of two halves: London (and the southeast) and the rest of the country. The capital generates more than 20% of Britain's income, a percentage that has been rising over the last 10 years. Employment in London is rosier than for the rest of the nation, with the jobless rate at just under 6%; the price of property is double the national average; and incomes are 30% higher in London than elsewhere in the country. Tourism continues to grow at 3.5% a year. There's a flip side, however: 28% of Londoners are living in poverty compared with just 21% in the rest of England.

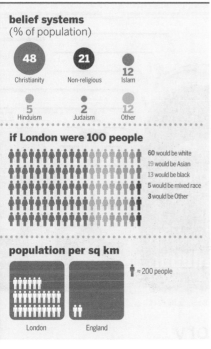

belief systems
(% of population)

48 Christianity
21 Non-religious
12 Islam
5 Hinduism
2 Judaism
12 Other

if London were 100 people

60 would be white
19 would be Asian
13 would be black
5 would be mixed race
3 would be Other

population per sq km

≈ 200 people

London   England

Ethnicity & Multiculturalism

London is one of the most cosmopolitan place in which to live. According to the last census (2011), almost 37% of London's population is foreign born – with almost a quarter born outside Europe. Today an estimated 270 different ethnic groups speak 300 different languages and, despite some tensions, most get along well.

Building Boom

The huge rise in population – London is expected to have 9 million inhabitants by 2020, up from 8.3 million today – has led to a building boom not seen since the end of WWII. Church spires are now dwarfed by a forest of construction cranes working to build more than 230 high-rise condos and office buildings. East London is where most of the activity is taking place these days, but the building boom is evident along the entire stretch of the Thames. New landmark skyscrapers in the City include the 37-storey Walkie Talkie (20 Fenchurch St) and the 225m-tall Cheesegrater (Leadenhall Building), with many more on the cards or under construction south of the river.

All Change in Politics

Virtually no one foresaw the outcome of the 2015 national elections, in which the Conservative Party soundly beat Labour, gaining 28 seats and a narrow majority in Parliament. Always bucking the trend, however, London elected Labour candidate Sadiq Khan as its mayor a year later, convincingly defeating Conservative golden boy Zac Goldsmith.

Goodbye to Europe

On June 24 2016, Britain awoke to monumental news. By a slim referendum vote the UK had opted to leave the EU, cutting ties stretching back 43 years. Within hours of the so-called 'Brexit' (British exit) result, Prime Minister David Cameron, who'd campaigned to remain within the EU, announced his resignation.

Nationally, the referendum result was very close: 52% voted to leave the EU against 48% to remain, although unsurprisingly, the capital was strongly in favour of 'remain' (60%).

Brexit became law in March 2017, when Prime Minister Theresa May formally launched the two-year disentanglement process. Depending on the outcome of the negotiations, Brexit could have an enormous impact on London, especially the financial services industry and the millions of EU nationals living in the capital.

BENSON HE / SHUTTERSTOCK ©

History

London's history is a long and turbulent narrative spanning more than two millennia. Over those years there have been good times of strength and economic prosperity and horrific times of plague, fire and war. But even when down on its knees, London has always been able to get up, dust itself off and move on, constantly re-inventing itself along the way.

AD 43

The Romans invade Britain, led by Emperor Claudius; they mix with the local Celtic tribespeople and stay for almost four centuries.

852

Vikings settle in London; a period of great struggle between the kingdoms of Wessex and Denmark begins.

1066

Following his decisive victory at the Battle of Hastings, William, Duke of Normandy, is crowned in Westminster Abbey.

Statue of King George V, Westminster Abbey (p36)

Londinium

The Celts were the first to arrive in the area that is now London, some time around the 4th century BC. It was the Romans, however, who established a real settlement in AD 43, the port of Londinium. They slung a wooden bridge over the Thames (near the site of today's London Bridge) and created a thriving colonial outpost before abandoning British soil for good in 410.

Saxon & Norman London

Saxon settlers, who colonised the southeast of England from the 5th century onwards, established themselves outside the city walls due west of Londinium in Lundenwic. This infant trading community grew in importance and attracted the attention of the Vikings in Denmark. They attacked in 842 and again nine years later, burning Lundenwic to the ground. Under the leadership of King Alfred the Great of Wessex, the Saxon population fought back, driving the Danes out in 886.

1215
King John signs the Magna Carta, an agreement forming the basis of constitutional law in England.

1348
Rats on ships from Europe bring the 'Black Death', a plague that eventually wipes out almost two-thirds of the city's residents.

1605
A Catholic plot to blow up James I is foiled; Guy Fawkes, one of the alleged plotters, is executed the following year.

Hampton Court Palace (p110)

★ **Best for Royal History**

Hampton Court Palace (p110)

Westminster Abbey (p36)

Buckingham Palace (p46)

Tower of London (p64)

Kensington Palace (p98)

PLUSONE/SHUTTERSTOCK ©

Saxon London grew into a prosperous and well-organised town segmented into 20 wards, each with its own alderman and resident colonies of German merchants and French vintners. But attacks by the Danes continued apace and the Saxon leadership was weakening; in 1016 Londoners were forced to accept the Danish leader Canute as king of England. With the death of Canute's brutal son Harthacanute in 1042, the throne passed to the Saxon Edward the Confessor, who went on to found a palace and an abbey at Westminster.

On his deathbed in 1066, Edward anointed Harold Godwinson, the Earl of Wessex, as his successor. This enraged William, Duke of Normandy, who claimed that Edward had promised him the throne. William mounted a massive invasion from France, and on 14 October defeated (and killed) Harold at the Battle of Hastings, before marching on London to claim his prize. William, now dubbed 'the Conqueror', was crowned king of England in Westminster Abbey on 25 December 1066, ensuring the Norman conquest was complete.

Medieval & Tudor London

Successive medieval kings were happy to let the City of London keep its independence as long as its merchants continued to finance their wars and building projects. During the Tudor dynasty, which coincided with the discovery of the Americas and thriving world trade, London became one of the largest and most important cities in Europe. Henry VIII reigned from 1509 to 1547, built palaces at Whitehall and St James's, and bullied his lord chancellor, Cardinal Thomas Wolsey, into giving him the one at Hampton Court.

The most momentous event of his reign, however, was his split with the Catholic Church in 1534 after the Pope refused to annul his marriage to Catherine of Aragon, who had borne him only one surviving daughter after 24 years of marriage.

The 45-year reign (1558–1603) of Henry's daughter Elizabeth I is still regarded as one of the most extraordinary periods in English history. During these four decades English literature reached new heights and religious tolerance gradually grew. With the defeat of the Spanish Armada in 1588, England became a naval superpower and London established itself as the premier world trade market with the opening of the Royal Exchange in 1570.

1666	1708	1838
The Great Fire of London burns for five days, leaving four-fifths of the metropolis in smoking ruins.	The last stone of Sir Christopher Wren's masterpiece, St Paul's Cathedral, is laid by his son and the son of his master mason.	The coronation of Queen Victoria ushers in a new era for London; the British capital becomes the economic centre of the world.

Civil Wars, Plague & Fire

Elizabeth was succeeded by her second cousin James I and then his son Charles I. The latter's belief in the 'divine right of kings' set him on a collision course with an increasingly confident parliament at Westminster and a powerful City of London. The latter two rallied behind Oliver Cromwell against Royalist Troops. Charles was defeated in 1646 and executed in 1649.

Cromwell ruled the country as a republic for the next 11 years. Under the Commonwealth of England, as the English republic was known, Cromwell banned theatre, dancing, Christmas and just about anything remotely fun.

After Cromwell's death, parliament restored the exiled Charles II to the throne in 1660. Charles II's reign witnessed two great tragedies in London: the Great Plague of 1665, which decimated the population, and the Great Fire of London, which swept ferociously through the city's densely packed streets the following year. The wreckage of the inferno at least allowed master architect Christopher Wren to build his 51 magnificent churches. The crowning glory of the 'Great Rebuilding' was his St Paul's Cathedral, completed in 1708. A masterpiece of English baroque architecture, it remains one of the city's most prominent and iconic landmarks.

Great Fire of London

The Great Fire of London broke out in Thomas Farriner's bakery in Pudding Lane on the evening of 2 September 1666. Initially dismissed by London's lord mayor as 'something a woman might pisse out', the fire spread uncontrollably and destroyed 89 churches and more than 13,000 houses, raging for days. Amazingly, fewer than a dozen people died. The fire destroyed medieval London, changing the city forever. Many Londoners left for the countryside or to seek their fortunes in the New World, while the city itself rebuilt its medieval heart with grand buildings such as Wren's St Paul's Cathedral. Wren's magnificent Monument (1677) near London Bridge stands as a memorial to the fire and its victims.

Georgian & Victorian London

While the achievements of the 18th-century Georgian kings were impressive (though 'mad' George III will forever be remembered as the king who lost the American colonies), they were overshadowed by those of the dazzling Victorian era, dating from Queen Victoria's ascension to the throne in 1837.

During the Industrial Revolution, London became the nerve centre of the largest and richest empire the world had ever witnessed, in an imperial expansion that covered a quarter of the earth's surface area and ruled over more than 500 million people. Queen Victoria lived to celebrate her Diamond Jubilee in 1897, but died four years later aged 81 and was laid to rest beside her beloved consort, Prince Albert, at Windsor. Her reign is seen as the climax of Britain's world supremacy, when London was the de facto capital of the world.

1851	1940–41	1953
The Great Exhibition, the brainchild of Victoria's consort, Albert, opens to great fanfare in the Crystal Palace in Hyde Park.	London is devastated by the Blitz, although St Paul's Cathedral and the Tower of London escape largely unscathed.	Queen Elizabeth II's coronation is broadcast live around the world on television; many English families buy their first TV.

★ **Best Historic Pubs & Bars**

Princess Louise (p182)

Ye Olde Mitre (p174)

Dukes London (p179)

Lamb (p182)

The World Wars

WWI broke out in August 1914 and became known as the Great War. The first German bombs fell from zeppelins near the Guildhall a year later, killing 39 people. Planes were soon dropping bombs on the capital, killing in all some 670 Londoners (half the national total of civilian deaths).

In the 1930s Prime Minister Neville Chamberlain's policy of appeasing Adolf Hitler eventually proved misguided, as the German Führer's lust for expansion appeared insatiable. When Nazi Germany invaded Poland on 1 September 1939, Britain declared war, having signed a mutual-assistance pact with Poland only a few days before. World War II (1939–45), which would prove to be Europe's darkest hour, had begun.

Winston Churchill, prime minister from 1940, orchestrated much of the nation's war strategy from the Cabinet War Rooms deep below Whitehall, lifting the nation's spirit from here with his stirring wartime speeches. By the time Nazi Germany capitulated in May 1945, up to a third of the East End and the City of London had been flattened, almost 30,000 Londoners had been killed and a further 50,000 seriously wounded.

Postwar London

Once the celebrations of Victory in Europe (VE) Day had died down, the nation began to confront the war's appalling toll and to rebuild. The years of austerity had begun, with rationing of essential items and high-rise residences sprouting up from bomb sites. Rationing of most goods ended in 1953, the year Elizabeth II was crowned following the death the year before of her father King George VI.

Immigrants from around the world – particularly the former colonies – flocked to post-war London, where a dwindling population had generated labour shortages, and the city's character changed forever. The place to be during the 1960s, 'Swinging London' became the epicentre of cool in fashion and music, its streets awash with colour and vitality.

1981	2000	2005
Brixton sees the worst race riots in London's history.	Ken Livingstone is elected mayor of London as an independent.	A day after London is awarded the 2012 Olympics, 52 people are killed in a series of suicide bombings on London's transport network.

The ensuing 1970s brought glam rock, punk, economic depression and the country's first female prime minister in 1979. In power for the entire 1980s and pushing an unprecedented program of privatisation, the late Margaret Thatcher is easily the most significant of Britain's postwar leaders. Opinions about 'Maggie' still polarise the Brits today.

While poorer Londoners suffered under Thatcher's significant trimming back of the welfare state, things had rarely looked better for the wealthy, as London underwent explosive economic growth. In 1992, much to the astonishment of most Londoners, the Conservative Party was elected for their fourth successive term in government, despite Mrs Thatcher being jettisoned by her party a year and a half before. By 1995 the writing was on the wall for the Conservative Party, as the Labour Party, apparently unelectable for a decade, came back with a new face.

The Blitz

The Blitz (from the German Blitzkrieg, meaning 'lightning war') struck England between September 1940 and May 1941, when London and other parts of Britain were heavily bombed by the German Luftwaffe. Londoners responded with legendary resilience and stoicism. Underground stations were converted into giant bomb shelters, although this was not always safe – one bomb rolled down the escalator at Bank station and exploded on the platform, killing more than 100 people. Buckingham Palace took a direct hit during a bombing raid early in the campaign, famously prompting Queen Elizabeth (the present monarch's late mother) to announce that 'now we can look the East End in the face'.

London in the New Century

Invigorated by its sheer desperation to return to power, the Labour Party elected the thoroughly telegenic Tony Blair as its leader, who in turn managed to ditch some of the more socialist-sounding clauses in the party credo and reinvent it as New Labour, leading to a huge landslide win in the May 1997 general election. The Conservatives atomised nationwide; the Blair era had begun in earnest.

Most importantly for London, Labour recognised the demand the city had for local government and created the London Assembly and the post of mayor. In Ken Livingstone, London elected a mayor who introduced a congestion charge and sought to update the ageing public transport network. In 2008 he was defeated by his arch-rival, Conservative Boris Johnson.

Johnson won his second term in 2012, the year of the Olympic Games (overwhelmingly judged an unqualified success) and the Queen's Diamond Jubilee (the 60th anniversary of her ascension to the throne).

2008
Boris Johnson, a Conservative MP and journalist, beats Ken Livingstone to become London's new mayor.

2012
Boris Johnson narrowly beats Ken Livingstone to win his second mayoral election; London hosts the 2012 Olympics and Paralympics.

2014
The southern half of the Olympic site opens to the public as Queen Elizabeth Olympic Park.

Millennium Bridge before St Paul's Cathedral (p86)

Architecture

Unlike many other world-class cities, London has never been methodically planned. Rather, it has developed in an organic fashion. London retains architectural reminders from every period of its long history. This is a city for explorers; seek out part of a Roman wall enclosed in the lobby of a modern building, for example, or a coaching inn dating to the Restoration tucked away in a courtyard off Borough High St.

Ancient London Architecture

Traces of medieval London are hard to find thanks to the devastating Great Fire of 1666, but several works by the architect Inigo Jones (1573–1652) have endured, including Covent Garden Piazza in the West End.

There are a few even older treasures scattered around – including the mighty Tower of London in the City, parts of which date back to the late 11th century. Westminster Abbey and Temple Church are 12th- to 13th-century creations. Few Roman traces survive outside museums, though the Temple of Mithras, built in AD 240, was relocated to the eastern end of Queen Victoria St in the City when the Bloomberg headquarters were completed at Walbrook Sq in 2016. Stretches of the Roman wall remain as foundations to a medieval wall outside Tower Hill tube station and in a few sections below Bastion high walk, next to the Museum of London, all in the City.

The Saxons, who moved into the area after the decline of the Roman Empire, found Londinium too small, ignored what the Romans had left behind and built their communities further up the Thames. The best place to see in situ what the Saxons left behind is the church of All Hallows by the Tower, northwest of the Tower of London. The church boasts an important archway, the walls of a 7th-century Saxon church and fragments from a Roman pavement.

Noteworthy medieval secular structures include the 1365 Jewel Tower, opposite the Houses of Parliament, and Westminster Hall; both are surviving chunks of the medieval Palace of Westminster.

After the Great Fire

After the 1666 fire, Sir Christopher Wren was commissioned to oversee reconstruction, but his vision of a new city layout of broad, symmetrical avenues never made it past the planners. His legacy lives on, however, in St Paul's Cathedral (1708), in the maritime precincts at Greenwich and in numerous City churches.

Nicholas Hawksmoor joined contemporary James Gibb in taking Wren's English baroque style even further; one great example is St Martin-in-the-Fields in Trafalgar Sq.

Like Wren before him, Georgian architect John Nash aimed to impose some symmetry on unruly London and was slightly more successful in achieving this, through grand creations such as Trafalgar Sq and the elegantly curving arcade of Regent St. Built in similar style, the surrounding squares of St James's remain some of the finest public spaces in London – little wonder then that Queen Victoria decided to move into the recently vacated Buckingham Palace in 1837.

Toward Modernity

Pragmatism replaced grand vision with the Victorians, who desired ornate civic buildings that reflected the glory of empire but were open to the masses, too. The style's turrets, towers and arches are best exemplified by the flamboyant Natural History Museum (Alfred Waterhouse), St Pancras Chambers (George Gilbert Scott) and the Houses of Parliament (Augustus Pugin and Charles Barry), the latter replacing the Palace of Westminster that had largely burned down in 1834.

The Victorians and Edwardians were also ardent builders of functional and cheap terraced houses, many of which became slums but today house London's urban middle classes.

A flirtation with art deco and the great suburban residential building boom of the 1930s was followed by a utilitarian modernism after WWII, as the city rushed to build new housing to replace terraces lost in the Blitz. Low-cost developments and unattractive high-rise housing were thrown up on bomb sites; many of these blocks still fragment the London horizon today.

Brutalism – a hard-edged and uncompromising architectural style that flourished from the 1950s to the 1970s, favouring concrete and reflecting socialist utopian principles – worked better on paper than in real life, but made significant contributions to London's architectural melange. Denys Lasdun's National Theatre, begun in 1966, is representative of the style.

30 St Mary Axe (p69)

BJORN HOLLAND / GETTY IMAGES ©

Postmodernism & Beyond

The next big wave of development arrived in the derelict wasteland of the former London docks, which were emptied of their terraces and warehouses and rebuilt as towering skyscrapers and 'loft' apartments. Taking pride of place in the Docklands was Cesar Pelli's 244m-high 1 Canada Square (1991), commonly known as Canary Wharf and easily visible from central London. The City was also the site of architectural innovation, including the centrepiece 1986 Lloyd's of London: Sir Richard Rogers' 'inside-out' masterpiece of ducts, pipes, glass and stainless steel.

Contemporary Architecture

There followed a lull in new construction until around 2000, when a glut of millennium projects unveiled new structures and rejuvenated others: the London Eye, Tate Modern and the Millennium Bridge all spiced up the South Bank, while Norman Foster's iconic 30 St Mary Axe, better known as the Gherkin, started a new wave of skyscraper construction in the City. Even the once-mocked Millennium Dome won a new lease on life as the 02 concert and sports hall.

By the middle of the decade, London's biggest urban development project ever was under way: the 200-hectare Queen Elizabeth Olympic Park in the Lea River Valley near Stratford in East London, where most of the events of the 2012 Summer Olympics and Paralympics took place. But the park would offer few architectural surprises – except for Zaha Hadid's stunning Aquatics Centre, a breathtaking structure suitably inspired by the fluid geometry of water; and the ArcelorMittal Orbit, a zany public work of art with viewing platforms designed by the sculptor Anish Kapoor.

The spotlight may have been shining on East London, but the City and South London have undergone energetic developments, too. Most notable is the so-called Shard, the EU's tallest building at 310m, completed in 2012. In the City, the Walkie Talkie has divided opinions, but its jungle-like Sky Garden on levels 35 to 37 are universally loved.

British Library (p118)

RON ELLIS / SHUTTERSTOCK ©

Literary London

For over six centuries, London has been the setting for works of prose. Indeed, the capital has been the inspiration for the masterful imaginations of such eminent wordsmiths as Shakespeare, Defoe, Dickens, Orwell, Conrad, Eliot, Greene and Woolf (even though not all were native to the city, or even British).

It's hard to reconcile the bawdy portrayal of London in Geoffrey Chaucer's *Canterbury Tales* with Charles Dickens' bleak hellhole in *Oliver Twist,* let alone Daniel Defoe's plague-ravaged metropolis in *Journal of the Plague Year* with Zadie Smith's multiethnic romp *White Teeth.* Ever-changing, yet somehow eerily consistent, London has left its mark on some of the most influential writing in the English language.

Chaucerian London

The first literary reference to London appears in Chaucer's *Canterbury Tales,* written between 1387 and 1400: the 29 pilgrims of the tale gather for their trip to Canterbury at the

Shakespeare's Globe (p190)

KAMIRA / SHUTTERSTOCK ©

Tabard Inn in Talbot Yard, Southwark, and agree to share stories on the way there and back. The inn burned down in 1676; a blue plaque marks the site of the building today.

Shakespearian London

Born in Warwickshire, William Shakespeare spent most of his life as an actor and playwright in London around the turn of the 17th century. He trod the boards of several theatres in Shoreditch and Southwark and wrote his greatest tragedies, among them *Hamlet, Othello, Macbeth* and *King Lear,* for the original Globe theatre on the South Bank. Although London was his home for most of his life, Shakespeare set nearly all his plays in foreign or imaginary lands. Only *Henry IV: Parts I & II* include a London setting – a tavern called the Boar's Head in Eastcheap.

Dickensian & 19th-Century London

Two early 19th-century Romantic poets drew inspiration from London. John Keats, born above a Moorgate public house in 1795, wrote 'Ode to a Nightingale' while living near Hampstead Heath in 1819 and 'Ode on a Grecian Urn' reportedly after viewing the Parthenon frieze in the British Museum the same year. William Wordsworth discovered inspiration for the poem 'Upon Westminster Bridge' while visiting London in 1802.

Charles Dickens was the definitive London author. When his father and family were interned at Marshalsea Prison in Southwark for not paying their debts, the 12-year-old Charles was forced to fend for himself on the streets. That grim period provided a font of experiences on which to draw. His novels most closely associated with London are *Oliver Twist,* with its gang of thieves led by Fagin in Clerkenwell, and *Little Dorrit,* whose hero was born in the Marshalsea. The house in Bloomsbury where he wrote *Oliver Twist* and two other novels now houses the expanded Charles Dickens Museum (p45).

Sir Arthur Conan Doyle (1858–1930) portrayed a very different London, his pipe-smoking, cocaine-snorting sleuth, Sherlock Holmes, coming to exemplify a cool and unflappable Englishness. Letters to the mythical hero and his admiring friend, Dr Watson, still arrive at 221b Baker St, where there's a **museum** (☏020-7224 3688; www.sherlock-holmes.co.uk; 221b Baker St, NW1; adult/child £15/10; ⊗9.30am-6pm; ⊖Baker St) to everyone's favourite Victorian detective.

London at the end of the 19th century appears in many books, but especially those of Somerset Maugham. His first novel, *Liza of Lambeth,* was based on his experiences as an intern in the slums of South London, while *Of Human Bondage* provides a portrait of late-Victorian London.

American Writers & London in the 20th Century

Of Americans who wrote about London at the turn of the century, Henry James, who settled here, stands supreme with his *Daisy Miller* and *The Europeans*. St Louis–born TS Eliot moved to London in 1915, where he published his poems 'The Love Song of J Alfred Prufrock' and 'The Waste Land', in which London is portrayed as an 'unreal city'.

Interwar Developments

Between the world wars, PG Wodehouse depicted London high life with his hilarious lampooning of the English upper classes in the Jeeves stories. George Orwell's experience of living as a beggar in London's East End coloured his book *Down and Out in Paris and London* (1933).

The Modern Age

This period is marked by the emergence of multicultural voices. Hanif Kureishi explored London from the perspective of young Pakistanis in his best-known novels *The Black Album* and *The Buddha of Suburbia,* while Timothy Mo's *Sour Sweet* is a poignant and funny account of a Chinese family in the 1960s trying to adjust to English life.

The decades leading up to the turn of the millennium were great ones for British literature, bringing a dazzling new generation of writers to the fore, such as Martin Amis *(Money, London Fields)*, Julian Barnes *(Metroland, Talking it Over)*, Ian McEwan *(Enduring Love, Atonement)* and Salman Rushdie *(Midnight's Children, The Satanic Verses)*.

Millennium London

Helen Fielding's *Bridget Jones's Diary* and its sequel, *Bridget Jones: The Edge of Reason*, launched the 'chick lit' genre, one that transcended the travails of a young single Londoner to become a worldwide phenomenon.

Peter Ackroyd named the city as the love of his life; *London: the Biography* was his inexhaustible paean to the capital.

The Current Scene

Home to most of the UK's major publishers and its best bookshops, London remains a vibrant place for writers and readers alike. New London writers in recent years include Monica Ali *(Brick Lane),* Zadie Smith *(NW),* Jake Arnott *(The Long Firm)* and Gautam Malkani *(Londonstani)*.

Every bookshop in town has a London section, where you will find many of these titles and lots more.

National Gallery (p54)

PHOTOICONIX / SHUTTERSTOCK ©

Art

*When it comes to art, London has traditionally been
overshadowed by other European capitals. Yet many
of history's greatest artists have spent time in London,
including the likes of Monet and Van Gogh, and in terms
of contemporary art, there's a compelling argument for
putting London at the very top of the European pack.*

Holbein to Turner

It wasn't until the rule of the Tudors that art began to take off in London. The German Hans Holbein the Younger (1497–1543) was court painter to Henry VIII; one of his finest works, *The Ambassadors* (1533), hangs in the National Gallery. A batch of great portrait artists worked at court during the 17th century, the best being Anthony Van Dyck (1599–1641), who painted *Charles I on Horseback* (1638), also in the National Gallery.

Local artists began to emerge in the 18th century, including landscapists Thomas Gainsborough (1727–88) and John Constable (1776–1837).

JMW Turner (1775–1851), equally at home with oils and watercolours, represented the pinnacle of 19th-century British art. His later works, including *Snow Storm – Steam-boat off a Harbour's Mouth* (1842) and *Rain, Steam and Speed – the Great Western Railway* (1844), now in the Tate Britain and the National Gallery, later inspired the Impressionist works of Claude Monet.

★ **Best for British Art**

Tate Britain (p52)

National Gallery (p54)

National Portrait Gallery (p55)

Fourth Plinth Project (p58)

The Pre-Raphaelites to Hockney

The brief but splendid flowering of the Pre-Raphaelite Brotherhood (1848–54) with the likes of William Holman Hunt and John Everett Millais took its inspiration from the Romantic poets. Tate Britain has the best selection of works from this period.

Sculptors Henry Moore (1898–1986) and Barbara Hepworth (1903–1975) both typified the modernist movement in British sculpture (you can see examples of their work in Kensington Gardens).

After WWII, art transformed yet again. In 1945, the tortured, Irish-born painter Francis Bacon (1909–92) caused a stir when he exhibited his *Three Studies for Figures at the Base of a Crucifixion* – now on display at the Tate Britain – and afterwards continued to spook the art world with his repulsive yet mesmerising visions.

Australian art critic Robert Hughes eulogised Bacon's contemporary, Lucian Freud (1922–2011), as 'the greatest living realist painter'. Freud's early work was often surrealist, but from the 1950s the bohemian Freud exclusively focused on pale, muted portraits.

London in the swinging 1960s was perfectly encapsulated by pop art, the vocabulary of which was best articulated by the brilliant David Hockney (b 1937). Two of his most famous works, *Mr and Mrs Clark and Percy* (1971) and *A Bigger Splash* (1974), are displayed at the Tate Britain.

Brit Art & Beyond

Brit Art sprang from a show called *Freeze*, which was staged in a Docklands warehouse in 1988, organised by artist and showman Damien Hirst and largely featuring his fellow graduates from Goldsmiths' College. Influenced by pop culture and punk, Brit Art was brash, decadent, ironic, easy to grasp and eminently marketable. Hirst's *Mother & Child (Divided)*, a cow and her calf sliced into sections and preserved in formaldehyde, and Tracey Emin's *My Bed*, the artist's unmade bed and the mess next to it, are seminal works from this era.

The best way to take the pulse of the British contemporary art scene is to attend the annual Summer Exhibition at the Royal Academy of Arts, which features works by established as well as unknown artists.

Canary Wharf underground station

CLAUDIO DIVIZIA / SHUTTERSTOCK ©

Survival Guide

Directory A–Z

Customs Regulations

The UK distinguishes between goods bought duty-free outside the EU and those bought in another EU country, where taxes and duties will have already been paid.

If you exceed your duty-free allowance, you will have to pay tax on the items. For European goods, there is officially no limit to how much you can bring but customs use certain guidelines to distinguish between personal and commercial use.

Discount Cards

Of interest to visitors who want to take in lots of paid sights in a short time is the **London Pass** (www.londonpass.com; 1/2/3/6 days £59/79/95/129). The pass offers free entry and queue-jumping to all major attractions and can be altered to include use of the Underground and buses. Check the website for details. Child passes are available too.

Electricity

**Type G
230V/50Hz**

Emergency

Dial 999 to call the police, fire brigade or ambulance in the event of an emergency.

Gay & Lesbian Travellers

Protection from discrimination is enshrined in law, but that's not to say homophobia does not exist. Always report homophobic crimes to the **police** (☎999).

Useful Websites

o **60by80** (www.60by80.com/london)

o **Ginger Beer** (www.gingerbeer.co.uk)

o **Jake** (www.jaketm.com)

o **Time Out London LGBT** (www.timeout.com/london/lgbt)

Health

EU nationals can obtain free emergency treatment (and, in some cases, reduced-cost healthcare) on presentation of a **European Health Insurance Card** (www.ehic.org.uk).

Reciprocal arrangements with the UK allow Australians, New Zealanders and residents and nationals of several other countries to receive free emergency medical treatment and subsidised dental care through the **National Health Service** (NHS; ☎111; www.nhs.uk). They can use hospital emergency departments, GPs and dentists. For a full list click on 'Services near you' on the NHS website.

Hospitals

The following hospitals have 24-hour accident and emergency departments:
Guy's Hospital (☎020-7188 7188; www.guysandstthomas.nhs.uk; Great Maze Pond, SE1; ⦿London Bridge) One of central

Practicalities

Smoking Forbidden in all enclosed public places nationwide. Most pubs have some sort of smoking area outside.

Weights & Measures The UK uses a confusing mix of metric and imperial systems.

London's busiest hospitals, near London Bridge.

University College London Hospital (☏020-3456 7890, 0845 155 5000; www.uclh. nhs.uk; 235 Euston Rd, NW1; ⊖Warren St or Euston) A large hospital in Euston.

Insurance

Travel insurance is advisable for non-EU residents as it offers greater flexibility over where and how you're treated and covers expenses for an ambulance and repatriation that will not be picked up by the NHS.

Pharmacies

The main pharmacy chains in London are Boots and Superdrug; a branch of either – or both – can be found on virtually every high street.

The **Boots** (☏020-7734 6126; www.boots.com; 44-46 Regent St, W1; ⊗8am-11pm Mon-Fri, 9am-11pm Sat, 12.30-6.30pm Sun; ⊖Piccadilly Circus) in Piccadilly Circus is one of the biggest and most centrally located and has extended opening times.

Internet Access

❂ Virtually every hotel in London now provides wi-fi free of charge (only a couple of budget places have it as an add-on).

❂ A huge number of cafes and an increasing number of restaurants offer free wi-fi to customers, including chains such as Starbucks, Costa, Pret A Manger and McDonald's. Cultural venues such as the Barbican or the Southbank Centre also have free wi-fi.

Legal Matters

Should you face any legal difficulties while in London, visit a branch of the Citizens Advice Bureau (www. citizensadvice.org.uk), or contact your embassy.

Drugs

Illegal drugs of every type are widely available in London, especially in clubs. Nonetheless, all the usual drug warnings apply. If you're caught with pot today, you're likely to be arrested. Possession of harder drugs, including heroin and cocaine, is always treated seriously. Searches on entering clubs are common.

Fines

In general you rarely have to pay on the spot for an offence. The exceptions are trains, the tube and buses, where people who can't produce a valid ticket for the journey when asked to by an inspector can be fined then and there.

Money

❂ The pound sterling (£) is the unit of currency.

❂ One pound sterling is made up of 100 pence (called 'pee', colloquially).

❂ Notes come in denominations of £5, £10, £20 and £50, while coins are 1p ('penny'), 2p, 5p, 10p, 20p, 50p, £1 and £2.

ATMs

ATMs are everywhere and will generally accept Visa, MasterCard, Cirrus or Maestro cards, as well as more obscure ones. There is almost always a transaction surcharge for cash withdrawals with foreign cards.

Changing Money

○ The best place to change money is in any local post-office branch, where no commission is charged.

○ You can also change money in most high-street banks and some travel agencies, as well as at the numerous bureaux de change throughout the city.

Credit & Debit Cards

○ Credit and debit cards are accepted almost universally in London, in restaurants, bars, shops and even by some taxis.

○ American Express and Diners Club are far less widely used than Visa and MasterCard.

○ Contactless cards and payments (which do not require a chip and pin or a signature) are increasingly widespread (watch for the wi-fi-like symbol on cards and in shops). Transactions are limited to a maximum of £30.

Opening Hours

The following are standard opening hours:

Banks 9am–5pm Monday to Friday

Pubs & Bars 11am–11pm

Restaurants noon–2.30pm & 6–11pm

Sights 10am–6pm

Shops 9am–7pm Monday to Saturday, noon–6pm Sunday

Public Holidays

Most attractions and businesses close for a couple of days over Christmas and sometimes Easter. Places that normally shut on Sunday will probably close on bank-holiday Mondays.

New Year's Day 1 January

Good Friday Late March/April

Easter Monday Late March/April

May Day Holiday First Monday in May

Spring Bank Holiday Last Monday in May

Summer Bank Holiday Last Monday in August

Christmas Day 25 December

Boxing Day 26 December

Safe Travel

London is a fairly safe city for its size, so exercising common sense should keep you secure.

If you're getting a cab after a night's clubbing, make sure you go for a black cab or a licensed minicab firm.

Pickpocketing does happen in London, so keep an eye on your handbag and wallet, especially in bars and nightclubs and in crowded areas such as the Underground.

Telephone

Mobile Phones

Buy local SIM cards for European and Australian phones, or a pay-as-you-go phone. Set other phones to international roaming.

Useful Numbers

Directory Enquiries (International) 118 505

Directory Enquiries (Local & National) 118 118, 118 500

International dialing code 00

Premium rate applies 09

Reverse Charge/Collect Calls 155

Special rates apply 084 and 087

Toll-free 0800

Time

London is on GMT; during British Summer Time (BST; late March to late October), London clocks are one hour ahead of GMT.

Toilets

It's an offence to urinate in the streets. Train stations, bus terminals and attractions generally have good facilities, providing also for people with disabilities and those with young children.

You'll also find public toilets across the city; most charge 50p.

Tourist Information

City of London Information Centre (www.visitthecity.co.uk; St Paul's Churchyard, EC4; ☺9.30am-5.30pm Mon-Sat, 10am-4pm Sun; ☎; ⊜St Paul's) Multilingual tourist information, fast-track tickets to City attractions and guided walks (adult/ child £7/6).

Greenwich Tourist Office (☑0870 608 2000; www. visitgreenwich.org.uk; Pepys House, 2 Cutty Sark Gardens, SE10; ☺10am-5pm; ®DLR Cutty Sark) Has a wealth of information about Greenwich and the surrounding areas. Free daily guided walks leave at 12.15pm and 2.15pm.

Visit London (www.visitlondon. com) Visit London can fill you in on everything from tourist attractions and events (such as the Changing of the Guard and Chinese New Year parade) to river trips and tours, accommodation, eating, theatre, shopping, children's London, and gay and lesbian venues. There are helpful kiosks at **Heathrow Airport** (www. visitlondon.com/tag/tourist-information-centre; Terminal 1, 2 & 3 Underground station concourse; ☺7.30am-8.30pm), **King's Cross St Pancras Station** (www.visitlondon. com/tag/tourist-information-centre; Western Ticket Hall, Euston Rd N1; ☺8am-6pm), **Liverpool Street Station** (www. visitlondon.com/tag/tourist-information-centre; Liverpool Street Station; ☺8am-6pm), **Piccadilly Circus Underground Station** (www.visitlondon.com/ tag/tourist-information-centre; Piccadilly Circus Underground Station; ☺9.30am-4pm), The City, Greenwich and **Victoria Station** (www.visitlondon.com/ tag/tourist-information-centre; Victoria Station; ☺7.15am-9.15pm Mon-Sat, 8.15am-8.15pm Sun).

Travellers with Disabilities

For travellers with disabilities, London is an odd mix of user-friendliness and downright disinterest. New hotels and modern tourist attractions are legally required to be accessible to people in wheelchairs, but many historic buildings are hard to adapt.

Transport is equally hit and miss, but slowly improving:

● Only 66 of London's 270 tube stations have step-free access; the rest have escalators or stairs.

● The above-ground DLR is entirely accessible for wheelchairs.

● All buses can be lowered to street level when they stop; wheelchair users travel free.

● Guide dogs are universally welcome on public transport and in hotels, restaurants, attractions etc.

Transport for London (www.tfl.gov.uk) publishes the *Getting Around London* guide, which contains the latest information on accessibility for passengers with disabilities.

Download Lonely Planet's free Accessible Travel guide from http://lptravel.to/ accessibletravel.

Climate Change & Travel

Every form of transport that relies on carbon-based fuel generates CO_2, the main cause of human-induced climate change. Modern travel is dependent on aeroplanes, which might use less fuel per kilometre per person than most cars but travel much greater distances. The altitude at which aircraft emit gases (including CO_2) and particles also contributes to their climate change impact. Many websites offer 'carbon calculators' that allow people to estimate the carbon emissions generated by their journey and, for those who wish to do so, to offset the impact of the greenhouse gases emitted with contributions to portfolios of climate-friendly initiatives throughout the world. Lonely Planet offsets the carbon footprint of all staff and author travel.

Visas

Visas are not required for US, Canadian, Australian, or New Zealand visitors for stays of up to six months. European Union nationals can stay indefinitely for the time being (Brexit pending). Check the website of the **UK Border Agency** (www.gov. uk/check-uk-visa) or with your local British embassy or consulate for the most up-to-date information.

Women Travellers

Female visitors to London are unlikely to have many problems, provided they take the usual big-city precautions. Don't get into an Underground carriage with no one else in it or with just one or two men. And if you feel unsafe, you should take a taxi or licensed minicab.

Transport

Arriving in London

Most people arrive in London by air, but an increasing number of visitors coming from Europe let the Eurostar (the Channel Tunnel train) take the strain, while buses from across the continent are a further option.

The city has five airports: Heathrow, Gatwick, Stansted, Luton and London City. Most transatlantic flights land at Heathrow and Gatwick. Visitors from Europe are more likely to arrive at Gatwick, Stansted or Luton (the latter two are used exclusively by low-cost airlines such as easyJet and Ryanair).

Flights, cars and tours can be booked online at lonelyplanet.com.

Heathrow Airport

Some 15 miles west of central London, **Heathrow** (LHR; www.heathrowairport. com) is one of the world's busiest international airports and counts four terminals (numbered 2 to 5).

Train

Underground (www.tfl.gov.uk; one-way £5.10) Three Underground stations on the Piccadilly line serve Heathrow: one for Terminals 2 and 3, another for Terminal 4, and the terminus for Terminal 5. The Underground, commonly referred to as 'the tube', is the cheapest way of getting to Heathrow (from central London one hour, every three to nine minutes). It runs from around 5am to midnight. Buy tickets at the station.

Crossrail (www.crossrail.co.uk) The western branch of this new line is due to open in May 2018, linking London Paddington with Heathrow Terminal 4 in 30 minutes.

Heathrow Express (www. heathrowexpress.com; 1-way/ return £22/36) This high-speed train whisks passengers from Heathrow Central station (serving Terminals 2 and 3) and Terminal 5 to Paddington in 15 minutes. Terminal 4 passengers should take the free interterminal shuttle train to Heathrow Central and board there. Trains run every 15 minutes from just after 5am in both directions to between 11.25pm (from Paddington) and 11.40pm (from the airport).

Bus

National Express (www.nationalexpress.com) coaches (one-way from £6, 35 to 90 minutes, every 30 minutes to one hour) link the Heathrow Central bus station with Victoria coach station.

Taxi

A metered black-cab trip to/from central London will cost between £45 and £85 and take 45 minutes to an hour, depending on traffic and your departure point.

Gatwick Airport

Located some 30 miles south of central London, **Gatwick** (LGW; www. gatwickairport.com) is Britain's number-two airport. The North and South Terminals are linked by a 24-hour shuttle train, with the journey time about three minutes.

Train

Gatwick Express (www.gatwickexpress.com; 1-way/return adult £19.90/34.90, 1-way/return child £9.95/17.45) This dedicated train service links the station near the South Terminal with Victoria station in central London every 15 minutes. From the airport, there are services between 4.35am and 12.50am. From Victoria, they leave between 3.30am and 12.32am. The journey takes 30 minutes.

National Rail (www.nationalrail.co.uk) has regular train services to/from London Bridge (30 minutes, every 15 to 30 minutes), London King's Cross (55 minutes, every 15 to 30 minutes) and London Victoria (30 minutes, every 10 to 15 minutes). Fares vary depending on the time of travel and the train company, but allow £10 to £20 for a single.

Bus

National Express (www.nationalexpress.com) coaches (one-way from £6, 80 minutes to two hours) run throughout the day from Gatwick to Victoria Coach station. Services leave hourly around the clock.

Taxi

A metered black-cab trip to/from central London costs around £100 and takes just over an hour. Minicabs are usually cheaper.

Stansted Airport

Stansted (STN; www.stanstedairport.com) is 35 miles northeast of central London in the direction of Cambridge.

Train

Stansted Express (☎0845 8500150; www.stanstedexpress.com; one-way/return £19/32) This rail service (one-way/return £19.10/31, 45 minutes, every 15 to 30 minutes) links the airport and Liverpool St station. From the airport, the first train leaves at 5.30am, the last at 12.30am. Trains depart Liverpool St station from 3.40am to 11.25pm.

Bus

National Express (www.nationalexpress.com) Run around the clock, offering well over 100 services per day. The A6 runs to Victoria coach station (one-way from £12, 85 minutes to more than two hours, every 20 minutes) via North London. The A9 runs to Liverpool St station (one-way from £10, 60 to 80 minutes, every 30 minutes).

EasyBus (www.easybus.co.uk) Runs services to Baker St and Old St tube stations every 15 minutes. The journey (one-way from £4.95) takes one hour from Old St, 1¼ hour from Baker St.

Terravision (www.terravision.eu) Coaches link Stansted to both Liverpool St train station (bus A51, one-way/return from £8/14, 55 minutes) and Victoria coach station (bus A50, one-way/return from £9/15, 75 minutes) every 20 to 40 minutes between 6am and 1am.

Taxi

A metered black-cab trip to/from central London costs around £130. Minicabs are cheaper.

Luton Airport

A smallish airport 32 miles northwest of London, **Luton** (LTN; www.london-luton.co.uk) generally caters for cheap charter flights and discount airlines.

Train

National Rail (www.nationalrail.co.uk) services (one-way from £10, 35 to 50 minutes, every six to 30 minutes, from 7am to 10pm) run from London Bridge and London King's Cross stations to Luton Airport Parkway station, from where an airport shuttle bus (one-way £1.60) will take you to the airport in 10 minutes.

Bus

EasyBus (www.easybus.co.uk) minibuses run between Victoria coach station and Luton (one-way from £4.95) every half-hour round the clock. Another route links the airport with Liverpool St station (buses every 15 to 30 minutes).

Taxi

A metered black-cab trip to/from central London costs about £110.

London City Airport

Its proximity to central London, which is just 6 miles to the west, as well as to the commercial district of the Docklands, means **London City Airport** (LCY; www.londoncityairport.com; 🛜) is predominantly a gateway airport for business travellers.

Train

The **Docklands Light Railway** (DLR; www.tfl.gov.uk/dlr) stops at the London City Airport station (one-way £2.80 to £3.30). The journey to Bank takes just over 20 minutes.

Taxi

A metered black-cab trip to or from the City/Oxford St/Earl's Court costs about £25/35/50.

St Pancras International Train Station

St Pancras International, the arrival point for **Eurostar** (✆03432 186186; www.eurostar.com) trains from Europe is connected by many underground lines to other parts of the city.

Getting Around

Public transport in London is extensive, often excellent and always pricey. It is managed by **Transport for London** (www.tfl.gov.uk),

Oyster Card & Contactless

The Oyster Card is a smart card on which you can store credit towards 'prepay' fares, as well as Travelcards valid for periods from a day to a year. Oyster Cards are valid across the entire public transport network in London. All you need to do when entering a station is touch your card on one of the readers (which have a yellow circle with the image of an Oyster Card on them) and then touch again on your way out. The system will then deduct the appropriate amount of credit from your card, as necessary. For bus journeys, you only need to touch once upon boarding.

Oyster Cards can be bought (£5 refundable deposit required) and topped up at any Underground station, travel information centre or shop displaying the Oyster logo. To get your deposit back along with any remaining credit, simply return your Oyster Card at a ticket booth.

Contactless cards (which do not require chip and pin or a signature) can now be used directly on Oyster Card readers and are subject to the same Oyster fares. The advantage is that you don't have to bother with buying, topping up and then returning an Oyster Card, but bear in mind the cost of card transactions.

which has a user-friendly, multilingual website with a journey planner, maps, detailed information on every mode of transport in the capital and live updates on traffic.

The cheapest way to get around London is with an Oyster Card or a UK contactless card (foreign card holders should check for contactless charges first). Paper tickets still exist but aren't as cheap or convenient.

The tube, DLR and Overground network are ideal for zooming across different parts of the city; buses and the **Santander**

Cycles (✆0343 222 6666; www.tfl.gov.uk/modes/cycling/santander-cycles) are great for shorter journeys.

Left-luggage facility **Excess Baggage** (www.left-baggage.co.uk) operates at London's main train stations and airports. The pricing structure varies but allow £10 per 24-hour slot.

London Underground

The London Underground ('the tube'; 11 colour-coded lines) is part of an integrated-transport system that also includes the Docklands Light Railway (a driverless overhead train operating in the eastern part of the city) and Overground network (mostly outside of Zone 1 and sometimes underground). It is the quickest and easiest way of getting around the city, if not the cheapest.

The first trains operate from around 5.30am Monday to Saturday and 6.45am Sunday. The last trains leave around 12.30am Monday to Saturday and 11.30pm Sunday.

Additionally, selected lines (the Victoria and Jubilee lines, plus most of the Piccadilly, Central and Northern lines) run all night on Fridays and Saturdays to get revellers home, with trains every 10 minutes or so.

During weekend closures, schedules, maps and alternative route suggestions are posted in every station and staff are at hand to help redirect you.

Some stations, most famously Leicester Sq and Covent Garden, are much closer in reality than they appear on the map.

Fares

○ London is divided into nine concentric fare zones.

○ It will always be cheaper to travel with an Oyster Card or a contactless card than a paper ticket.

○ Children under the age of 11 travel free; 11- to 15-year-olds are half-price if regis-

tered on an accompanying adult's Oyster Card (register at Zone 1 or Heathrow tube stations).

Bus

London's ubiquitous red double-decker buses afford great views of the city but be aware that the going can be slow. Bus services normally operate from 5am to 11.30pm.

There are excellent bus maps at every stop detailing all routes and destinations served from that particular area.

Night Bus

○ More than 50 night-bus routes (prefixed with the letter 'N') run from around 11.30pm to 5am.

○ There are also another 60 bus routes operating 24 hours; the frequency decreases between 11pm and 5am.

Fares

○ Cash cannot be used on London's buses. Pay with an Oyster Card, Travelcard or a contactless payment card.

○ Bus fares are a flat £1.50, no matter the distance travelled.

○ Children under 11 travel free; 11- to 15-year-olds are half-price if registered on an accompanying adult's Oyster Card (register at Zone 1 or Heathrow tube stations)

Taxi

Black Cabs

The **black cab** is as much a feature of the London cityscape as the red double-decker bus.

○ Cabs are available for hire when the yellow sign above the windscreen is lit; just stick your arm out to signal one.

○ Fares are metered, with the flagfall charge of £2.60 (covering the first 248m during a weekday), rising by increments of 20p for each subsequent 124m.

○ Fares are more expensive in the evenings and overnight.

○ Apps such as **Hailo** (www. hailocab.com) use your smartphone's GPS to locate the nearest black cab. You only pay the metered fare.

Minicabs

○ Minicabs, which are licensed, are cheaper (usually) competitors of black cabs.

○ Unlike black cabs, minicabs cannot be hailed on the street; they must be hired by phone or through a dispatcher.

○ Minicabs don't have meters; there's usually a fare set by the dispatcher. Make sure you ask before setting off.

○ Your hotel or host will be able to recommend a

reputable minicab company in the neighbourhood. Or phone a large 24-hour operator such as **Addison Lee** (☏020-7387 8888; www. addisonlee.com).

○ Apps such as **Uber** (www. uber.com) or **Kabbee** (www. kabbee.com) allow you to book a minicab in double-quick time.

Boat

Thames Clippers (www. thamesclippers.com; all zones adult/child £8.20/4.10) One of several companies operating boats along the River Thames, Thames Clippers offers proper commuter services. It's fast, pleasant and you're almost always guaranteed a seat and a view. Boats run every 20 minutes from 6am to between 10pm and 11pm. The route goes from London Eye Millennium Pier to Woolwich Arsenal Pier, with boats west to Putney too.

Bicycle

The Santander Cycle Hire Scheme is a great and affordable way to get around London.

Behind the Scenes

Acknowledgements

Climate map data adapted from Peel MC, Finlayson BL & McMahon TA (2007) 'Updated World Map of the Köppen-Geiger Climate Classification', *Hydrology and Earth System Sciences*, 11, 163344.

This Book

This book was curated by Emilie Filou, who also researched and wrote for it along with Peter Dragicevich, Steve Fallon and Damian Harper.

The previous edition was also researched and written by Emilie Filou, Peter Dragicevich, Steve Fallon and Damian Harper.

This guidebook was produced by the following:

Destination Editor James Smart

Product Editor Will Allen

Senior Cartographer Mark Griffiths

Book Designer Michael Buick

Assisting Editors Imogen Bannister, Katie Connolly, Kellie Langdon, Kathryn Rowan, Maja Vatrić

Assisting Book Designer Virginia Moreno

Cover Researcher Wibowo Rusli

Thanks to Grace Dobell, Sasha Drew, Victoria Harrison, Anne Mason, Lauren O'Connell, Lyahna Spencer

Send Us Your Feedback

We love to hear from travellers – your comments keep us on our toes and help make our books better. Our well-travelled team reads every word on what you loved or loathed about this book. Although we cannot reply individually to postal submissions, we always guarantee that your feedback goes straight to the appropriate authors, in time for the next edition. Each person who sends us information is thanked in the next edition, the most useful submissions are rewarded with a selection of digital PDF chapters.

Visit lonelyplanet.com/contact to submit your updates and suggestions or to ask for help. Our award-winning website also features inspirational travel stories, news and discussions.

Note: We may edit, reproduce and incorporate your comments in Lonely Planet products such as guidebooks, websites and digital products, so let us know if you don't want your comments reproduced or your name acknowledged. For a copy of our privacy policy visit lonelyplanet.com/privacy.

Index

ENGEL CHING / SHUTTERSTOCK ©

London Maps

City & South Bank

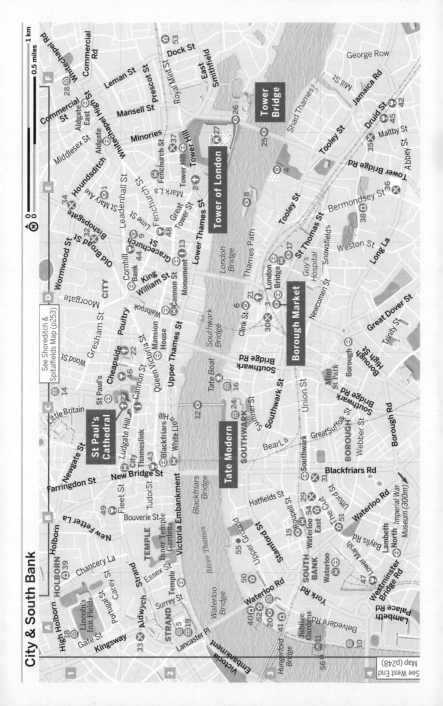

1 km
0.5 miles

Commercial Rd
Whitechapel Rd
Dock St
53
George Row
East Smithfield
Commercial St
Leman St
Prescot St
Royal Mint St
Mill St
Jamaica Rd
Aldgate East St
Mansell St
28
Minories
37
26
Tower Bridge
Shad Thames
Druid St
42
45
Middlesex St
Whitechapel High St
Fenchurch St
Tower Hill
27
25
Maltby St
35
Abbey St
Houndsditch
St Mary Axe
1
Aldgate
Leadenhall St
Mark La
Tower of London
Tooley St
Tower Bridge Rd
Bermondsey St
36
Bishopsgate
34
Lime St
Fenchurch St
8
Tooley St
38
Weston St
Long La
Wormwood St
Old Broad St
32
Cornhill
St Mary Axe
48
Great Tower St
Lower Thames St
London Bridge
Thames Path
St Thomas St
Guy's Hospital
Snowsfields
Newcomen St
Moorgate
CITY
Gracechurch St
44
13
Monument
17
London Bridge
3
Great Dover St
Gresham St
Poultry
Bank
King William St
Walbrook
Cannon St
6
21
Clink St
30
Trinity St
Wood St
See Shoreditch & Spitalfields Map (p253)
Cheapside
22
46
Mansion House
Queen Victoria St
Upper Thames St
Southwark Bridge
Tate Boat
Southwark Bridge Rd
Borough Market
Union St
Mint St Park
Borough High St
Southwark Bridge Rd
Borough Rd
BOROUGH
Webber St
14
St Paul's
23
Cannon St
16
24
12
Summer St
SOUTHWARK
Bear La
Great Suffolk St
St Paul's Cathedral
Ludgate Hill
City Thameslink
43
Blackfriars
White Lion
Southwark
Southwark St
Southwark
Blackfriars Rd
Tate Modern
Little Britain
Newgate St
New Bridge St
Blackfriars Bridge
Hatfields St
29
54
31
Union St
Farringdon St
Fleet St
Tudor St
Bouverie St
49
Roupell St
15
The Cut
51
Waterloo Rd
HOLBORN
39
Chancery La
New Fetter La
TEMPLE
Inner Temple Gardens
Victoria Embankment
Blackfriars Bridge
River Thames
Upper Ground
55
Waterloo East
50
SOUTH BANK
Waterloo
Lower Marsh
Baylis Rd
Imperial War Museum (300m)
North
High Holborn
8
Lincoln's Inn Fields
Portugal St
Carey St
Essex St
Temple
Surrey St
Stamford St
York Rd
Westminster Bridge Rd
Lambeth North
Lambeth Palace Rd
33
5
19
Aldwych
STRAND
Lancaster Pl
Waterloo Bridge
Waterloo Rd
40
52
20
41
Jubilee Gardens
56
47
10
11
Gate St
Kingsway
Chancery La
Holborn
HOLBORN
Temple
Belvedere Rd
Hungerford Bridge
Victoria Embankment

See West End Map (p248)

City & South Bank

◉ Sights
1 30 St Mary Axe...E1
2 All Hallows by the Tower...........................E2
3 Borough Market..D3
4 City Hall..E3
5 Courtauld Gallery.......................................A2
6 Golden Hinde..D3
7 Hayward Gallery..A3
8 HMS Belfast..E3
9 Leadenhall Market.....................................E2
10 London Dungeon A4
11 London Eye..A3
12 Millennium Bridge.......................................C2
13 Monument D2
14 Museum of London.....................................C1
15 Roupell St...B3
16 Shakespeare's Globe C3
17 Shard D3
18 Sir John Soane's Museum.........................A1
19 Somerset House..A2
20 Southbank Centre.......................................A3
21 Southwark Cathedral.................................D3
22 St Mary-le-Bow D2
23 St Paul's Cathedral....................................C2
24 Tate Modern..C3
25 Tower Bridge...F3
26 Tower Bridge Exhibition.............................F3
27 Tower of London...E2
28 Whitechapel Gallery F1

⊗ Eating
29 Anchor & Hope..B3
30 Arabica Bar & Kitchen...............................D3
31 Baltic..B3
Café Below..(see 22)
32 City Social...E1
33 Counter at the Delaunay...........................A2
Crypt Café..(see 23)

Delaunay..(see 33)
34 Duck & Waffle E1
35 Maltby Street Market.................................E4
Padella...(see 3)
36 Watch House E4
37 Wine Library..E2

⊙ Shopping
38 Lovely & British E4
39 Silver Vaults..A1
40 South Bank Book Market...........................A3
41 Southbank Centre Shop.............................A3

◉ Drinking & Nightlife
42 Anspach & Hobday F4
43 Blackfriar..B2
44 Counting House...D2
45 Jensen...F4
Little Bird Gin ....(see 35)
46 Madison..C2
Oblix...(see 17)
47 Scootercaffe...A4
48 Sky Pod...E2
49 Ye Olde Cheshire Cheese..........................B1

◉ Entertainment
50 National Theatre A3
51 Old Vic...B4
52 Queen Elizabeth Hall.................................A3
Royal Festival Hall.............................(see 20)
Shakespeare's Globe........................(see 16)
Southbank Centre.............................(see 20)
53 Wilton's...F2
54 Young Vic B3

◉ Activities, Courses & Tours
55 London Bicycle Tour...................................B3
56 Thames Rockets A4

West End

⊚ Sights

⊗ Eating

⊜ Shopping

⊝ Drinking & Nightlife

⊕ Entertainment

⊕ Activities, Courses & Tours

West End

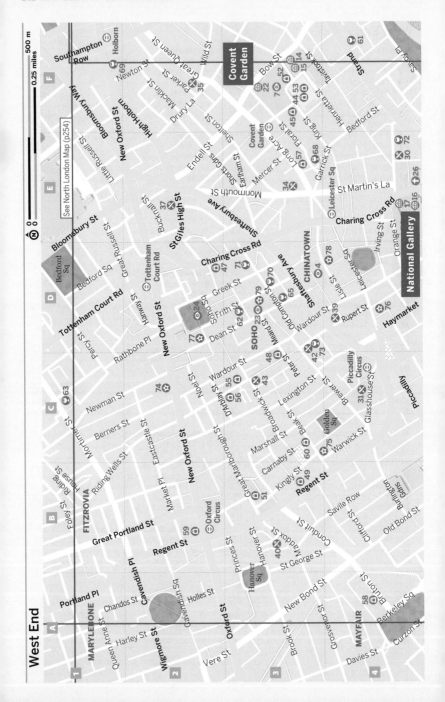

500 m
0.25 miles

See North London Map (p254)

MARYLEBONE

FITZROVIA

BLOOMSBURY

SOHO

CHINATOWN

MAYFAIR

Covent Garden

Charing Cross Rd

National Gallery

Piccadilly Circus

Oxford Circus

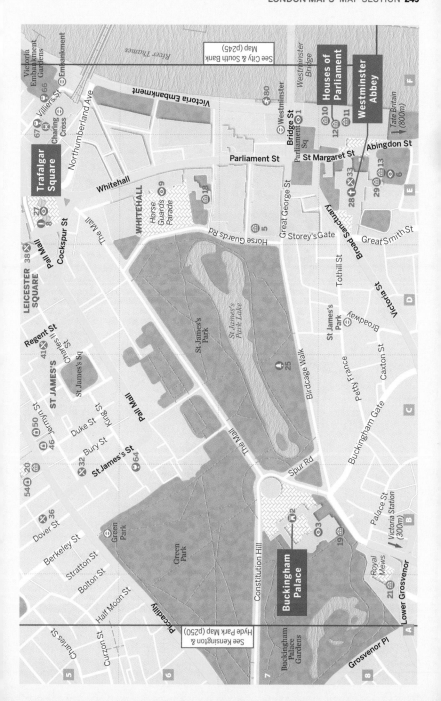

Kensington & Hyde Park

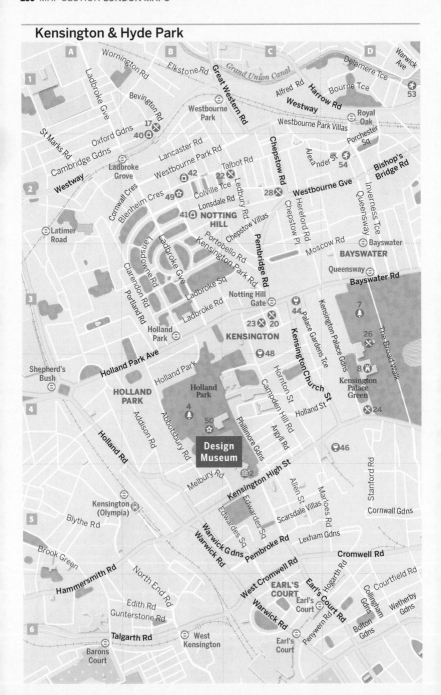

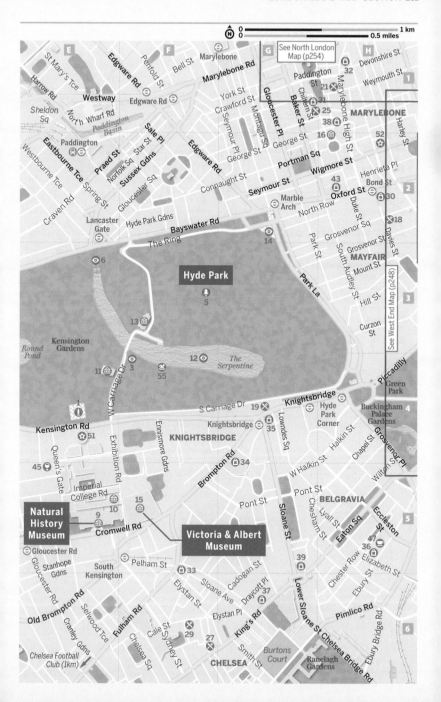

N

0 _____ 1 km
0 _____ 0.5 miles

See North London
Map (p254)

St Mary's Tce

Harrow Rd

E

Edgware Rd

Pentold St

Bell St

F

Marylebone

Marylebone Rd

G

32

H

Devonshire St

Weymouth St

1

Westway

North Wharf Rd

Sheldon
Sq

Paddington
Basin

Edgware Rd

York St

Crawford St

Montagu St

George St

Gloucester Pl

Baker St

Paddington
St 21

Chiltern St

25

31

38

16

Marylebone High St

MARYLEBONE

52

Harley St

Eastbourne Tce

Westbourne Tce

Paddington

Praed St

Spring St

Norfolk Sq

Star St

Sale Pl

Sussex Gdns

Gloucester Sq

Edgware Rd

George St

Portman Sq

Wigmore St

43

Henrieta Pl

Bond St

30

2

Craven Rd

Lancaster
Gate

Hyde Park Gdns

Connaught St

Seymour St

Marble
Arch

North Row

Oxford St

Duke St

Grosvenor Sq

Davies St

18

Bayswater Rd

The Ring

14

Park St

South Audley St

Grosvenor St

MAYFAIR

Mount St

See West End Map (p248)

3

6

Hyde Park

5

Park La

Hill St

Curzon
St

13

Kensington
Gardens

Round
Pond

11

3

55

12

The
Serpentine

Piccadilly

Green
Park

W Carriage Dr

S Carriage Dr

19

Knightsbridge

Hyde
Park
Corner

Buckingham
Palace
Gardens

4

1

Kensington Rd

51

Exhibition Rd

Ennismore Gdns

Knightsbridge

35

Lowndes Sq

KNIGHTSBRIDGE

Halkin St

Chapel St

Grosvenor Pl

Wilton Pl

45

Queen's Gate

Imperial
College Rd

Brompton Rd

34

Pont St

W Halkin St

Pont St

BELGRAVIA

Eccleston St

Eaton Sq

5

Natural
History
Museum

Gloucester Rd

Stanhope
Gdns

South
Kensington

9

10

Cromwell Rd

Pelham St

15

Victoria & Albert
Museum

Sloane St

Cadogan St

Chesham St

Lyall St

Chester Row

47

36

Elizabeth St

Ebury St

Gloucester Rd

Cranley Gdns

Old Brompton Rd

Selwood Tce

Fulham Rd

Cale St

33

Elystan St

Sloane Ave

Draycott Pl

37

Elystan Pl

King's Rd

39

Lower Sloane St

Pimlico Rd

Chelsea Bridge Rd

Ebury Bridge Rd

6

Chelsea Football
Club (1km)

Sydney St

Chelsea Sq

29

27

Smith St

CHELSEA

Burtons
Court

Ranelagh
Gardens

Kensington & Hyde Park

Sights
1 Albert Memorial E4
2 Design Museum C5
3 Diana, Princess of Wales
  Memorial Fountain....................................F4
4 Holland Park...B4
5 Hyde Park F3
6 Italian Gardens...E3
7 Kensington Gardens................................. D3
8 Kensington Palace..................................... D4
9 Natural History Museum E5
10 Science Museum E5
11 Serpentine Galleries...................................E4
12 Serpentine Lake...F4
13 Serpentine Sackler Gallery.......................F3
14 Speakers' Corner...................................... G2
15 Victoria & Albert Museum F5
16 Wallace Collection H2

Eating
17 Acklam Village Market B1
18 Claridge's Foyer and
  Reading Room...H2
19 Dinner by Heston
  Blumenthal..G4
20 Geales...C3
21 La Fromagerie..H1
22 Ledbury...C2
  Magazine...(see 13)
23 Mazi...C3
24 Min Jiang.. D4
25 Monocle Cafe G1
26 Orangery.. D3
27 Rabbit..F6
28 Taquería..C2
29 Tom's Kitchen..F6

V&A Café...(see 15)
  Wallace ....(see 16)

Shopping
30 Browns..H2
31 Cadenhead's Whisky & Tasting Shop G1
32 Cath Kidston..H1
33 Conran Shop...F5
34 Harrods.. G4
35 Harvey Nichols G4
36 Jo Loves..H5
37 John Sandoe Books G6
38 Monocle Shop...H1
39 Pickett.. G5
40 Portobello Green Arcade B2
41 Portobello Road Market............................B2
42 Rough Trade West B2
43 Selfridges..H2

Drinking & Nightlife
44 Notting Hill Arts Club................................C3
45 Queen's Arms E5
46 Roof Gardens... D4
47 Tomtom Coffee House...............................H5
48 Windsor Castle...C3

Entertainment
49 Electric Cinema B2
50 Opera Holland Park....................................B4
51 Royal Albert Hall..E4
52 Wigmore Hall H2

Activities, Courses & Tours
53 London Waterbus Company D1
54 Porchester Spa...D2
55 Serpentine Lido..F4

Shoreditch & Spitalfields

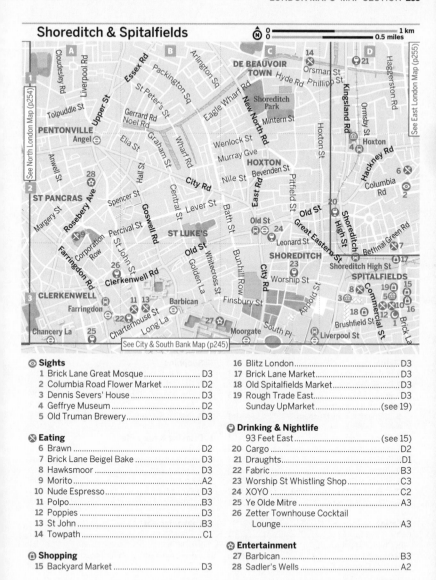

⊚ Sights
1 Brick Lane Great Mosque	D3
2 Columbia Road Flower Market	D2
3 Dennis Severs' House	D3
4 Geffrye Museum	D2
5 Old Truman Brewery	D3

⊗ Eating
6 Brawn	D2
7 Brick Lane Beigel Bake	D3
8 Hawksmoor	D3
9 Morito	A2
10 Nude Espresso	D3
11 Polpo	B3
12 Poppies	D3
13 St John	B3
14 Towpath	C1

⊟ Shopping
15 Backyard Market	D3

16 Blitz London	D3
17 Brick Lane Market	D3
18 Old Spitalfields Market	D3
19 Rough Trade East	D3
Sunday UpMarket	(see 19)

⊜ Drinking & Nightlife
93 Feet East	(see 15)
20 Cargo	D2
21 Draughts	D1
22 Fabric	B3
23 Worship St Whistling Shop	C3
24 XOYO	C2
25 Ye Olde Mitre	A3
26 Zetter Townhouse Cocktail Lounge	A3

✪ Entertainment
27 Barbican	B3
28 Sadler's Wells	A2

North London

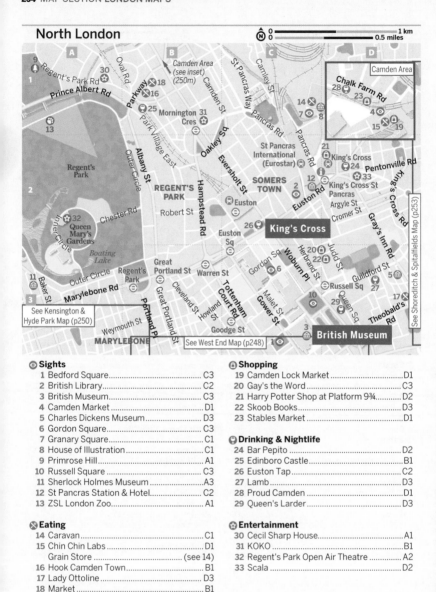

Sights
1 Bedford Square..C3
2 British Library..C2
3 British Museum..C3
4 Camden Market..D1
5 Charles Dickens Museum...........................D3
6 Gordon Square..C3
7 Granary Square..C1
8 House of Illustration...................................C1
9 Primrose Hill..A1
10 Russell Square..C3
11 Sherlock Holmes Museum.......................A3
12 St Pancras Station & Hotel.....................C2
13 ZSL London Zoo..A1

Eating
14 Caravan..C1
15 Chin Chin Labs..D1
   Grain Store..(see 14)
16 Hook Camden Town.......................................B1
17 Lady Ottoline..D3
18 Market..B1

Shopping
19 Camden Lock Market...................................D1
20 Gay's the Word..C3
21 Harry Potter Shop at Platform 9¾............D2
22 Skoob Books..D3
23 Stables Market..D1

Drinking & Nightlife
24 Bar Pepito..D2
25 Edinboro Castle..B1
26 Euston Tap..C2
27 Lamb..D3
28 Proud Camden..D1
29 Queen's Larder..D3

Entertainment
30 Cecil Sharp House...A1
31 KOKO..B1
32 Regent's Park Open Air Theatre................A2
33 Scala..D2

East London

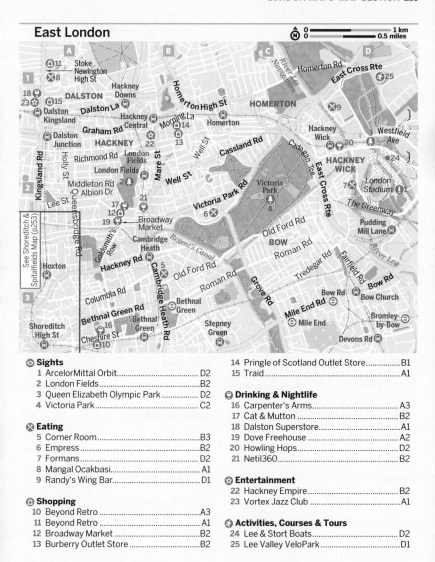

◎ Sights

1 ArcelorMittal Orbit	D2
2 London Fields	B2
3 Queen Elizabeth Olympic Park	D2
4 Victoria Park	C2

⊗ Eating

5 Corner Room	B3
6 Empress	B2
7 Formans	D2
8 Mangal Ocakbasi	A1
9 Randy's Wing Bar	D1

ⓐ Shopping

10 Beyond Retro	A3
11 Beyond Retro	A1
12 Broadway Market	B2
13 Burberry Outlet Store	B2
14 Pringle of Scotland Outlet Store	B1
15 Traid	A1

⊙ Drinking & Nightlife

16 Carpenter's Arms	A3
17 Cat & Mutton	B2
18 Dalston Superstore	A1
19 Dove Freehouse	A2
20 Howling Hops	D2
21 Netil360	B2

✪ Entertainment

22 Hackney Empire	B2
23 Vortex Jazz Club	A1

⊕ Activities, Courses & Tours

24 Lee & Stort Boats	D2
25 Lee Valley VeloPark	D1

Greenwich

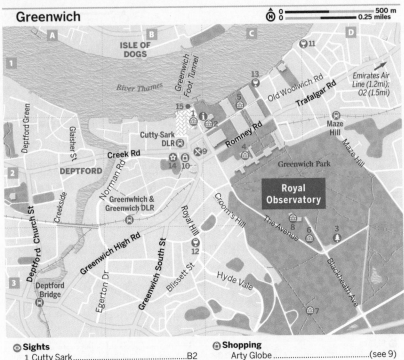

DANS LA MÊME COLLECTION

Henry BAUCHAU : *Mao Zedong.*
Nicole BARRY : *Pauline Viardot, l'amie de Sand et l'égérie de Tourgueniev.*
André BILLY : *L'Abbé Prévost.*
Monica CHARLOT : *Victoria, le pouvoir partagé.*
Michel CROUZET : *Stendhal ou Monsieur Moi-Même.*
Dominique DESANTI : *Drieu La Rochelle.*
Hortense DUFOUR : *La Comtesse de Ségur, née Sophie Rostopchine.*
Pierre GASCAR : *Montesquieu.*
Pierre GAXOTTE : *Molière.*
Anna GAYLOR : *Marie Dorval.*
GEORGES-ROUX : *Napoléon III.*
Henry GIDEL : *Feydeau.*
Roger GREAVES : *Nadar.*
Frédéric GRENDEL : *Beaumarchais.*
René GUERDAN : *François Ier.*
Paul GUTH : *Mazarin.*
Hubert JUIN : *Victor Hugo.*
    1. *1802-1843.*
    2. *1844-1870.*
    3. *1871-1885.*
Emmanuel HAYMANN : *Courteline.*
Jean HAMBURGER : *Monsieur Littré.*
Françoise MALLET-JORIS : *Jeanne Guyon.*
André MAUROIS : *Balzac.*
Pierre MOINOT : *Jeanne d'Arc, le pouvoir et l'innocence.*
Jean ORIEUX :
— *Bussy-Rabutin.*
— *Catherine de Médicis.*
— *La Fontaine.*
— *Talleyrand.*
— *Voltaire.*
Roland PENROSE : *Picasso.*
Gesnette PISANI-FERRY : *Le Général Boulanger.*
François PORCHÉ : *Baudelaire.*
R.E. SHIKES et P. HARPER : *Pissarro.*
Enid STARKIE : *Rimbaud.*
Henri TROYAT :
— *Gogol.*
— *Gorki.*
— *Catherine la Grande.*
— *Pierre le Grand.*
— *Alexandre Ier.*
— *Ivan le Terrible.*
— *Tchekhov.*
— *Tourgueniev.*
— *Flaubert.*
— *Maupassant.*
— *Alexandre II, le tsar libérateur.*
Dimitri VOLKOGONOV : *Staline, triomphe et tragédie.*
Georges WALTER : *Edgar Allan Poe.*
Jacques WEYGAND : *Weygand, mon père.*

CHÈRE GEORGE SAND

DU MÊME AUTEUR

Le Mauvais Genre, Le Seuil.
Les Plaisirs infinis, Le Seuil.
L'Honneur de plaire, Le Seuil.
Les Amours imaginaires, Gallimard.
Les Couples involontaires, Flammarion.
Les Bonheurs défendus, Flammarion.
Ouvrir une maison de rendez-vous, Fayard.
Un éternel amour de trois semaines, Fayard.
Une jeune femme de soixante ans, Fayard.
Les Paradis provisoires, Fayard.
Portrait d'une séductrice, Stock et Presses-Pocket (prix Cazes et prix Sévigné en 1976).
L'avenir est à ceux qui s'aiment ou l'Alphabet des sentiments, Stock.
L'École des arbres, Mercure de France.
Un amour d'arbre, Plon.
La Maison de miroirs, Éditions Pierre-André Benoit.
Les Petites Solitudes, Éditions Marc Pessin.
Zizou artichaut coquelicot oiseau, Grasset-Jeunesse, en collaboration avec Alain Gauthier.
Narcisse, Ipomée, en collaboration avec Martine Delerm.
Le Lumineux Destin d'Alexandra David-Néel, Librairie académique Perrin et Presses-Pocket (prix Fémina Vacaresco, prix Kléber-Haedens-Mumm et l'un des grands prix de l'Académie française en 1985).
Florence et Louise les Magnifiques (Florence Jay-Gould et Louise de Vilmorin), Éditions du Rocher.
Chère Marie-Antoinette, Librairie académique Perrin et Presses-Pocket (prix Gabrielle-d'Estrées en 1988).

JEAN CHALON

CHÈRE GEORGE SAND

FLAMMARION

BIBLIOGRAPHIE ET DÉDICACE

L'usage veut qu'on place la bibliographie à la fin d'une biographie. Je suis obligé de placer la mienne au début, afin de prévenir le lecteur que toutes les citations, y compris les exergues, qui sont placées entre guillemets, sans autre précision, ont été extraites des vingt-quatre volumes de la *Correspondance* de George Sand, édition de Georges Lubin, collection « Classiques Garnier », et des deux volumes *Œuvres autobiographiques* de George Sand, chez Gallimard, collection « La Pléiade », œuvres présentées et annotées par Georges Lubin.

C'est en 1964 que j'ai lu le premier volume de cette *Correspondance* et depuis, jusqu'en 1990, j'ai suivi l'édification de ce monument que l'on doit à la patience et à l'érudition de Georges Lubin. Je crois avoir salué chaque parution d'un article, me trouvant parfois en panne de superlatif devant un tel travail ! Car Georges Lubin, seulement aidé par son épouse Mady, a accompli le labeur de toute une équipe de chercheurs. C'est donc à Georges et à Mady Lubin que sont dédiées les pages qui vont suivre, en signe de profonde reconnaissance pour la constance de leur aide.

Les sujets ne sont à personne : ils sont à tout le monde. Personne ne les déflore parce que personne ne les complète. Ils sont inépuisables, et chaque artiste leur donne une vie nouvelle...

Je suis ainsi faite que je supporte longtemps, très longtemps ce qui est intolérable. Il est vrai que quand ma patience est lassée, je brise tout d'un coup et pour jamais.

Mon cher ami, j'ai fait une quarantaine de livres de confitures de prunes (...) J'en ferai d'autres à ton intention. Les femmes que tu m'enverrais ne me serviraient à rien, car on ne peut pas confier cette besogne. Il faut la faire soi-même et ne pas la quitter d'un instant. C'est aussi sérieux que de faire un livre.

LES AURORES D'AURORE

À coup sûr, j'étais très heureuse, car
j'étais très aimée ; nous étions pauvres, et je ne m'en apercevais nullement.

Prenant les hommes qu'elle aime pour des anges avec qui elle partage ce qu'elle nomme « un embrasement céleste », George Sand puise, dans chacune de ses passions, si courte soit-elle, le sentiment d'une résurrection qu'elle croit éternelle, le sentiment d'un renouveau à l'infini. Pourtant, personne n'est plus fidèle que Sand à l'évidence de ses goûts profonds. Si elle est allergique aux épinards, et à sa fille Solange, elle s'épanouit en présence de son fils Maurice, de ses amis les arbres, dans la fabrication de romans et de confitures, dans l'exercice quotidien d'une inépuisable générosité. Sa bourse et sa plume sont au service de tous. Elle donne tout aux autres et ne réserve à son usage que le strict nécessaire, avec quelques indispensables superflus comme les cigarettes, ou les parfums. Avec l'un de ses premiers amants, Alfred de Musset, elle se parfume au patchouli. Avec l'un de ses derniers, Alexandre Manceau, elle se parfume à l'ylang-ylang. Entre ces deux parfums, et ces deux compagnons, sa vie s'est écoulée.

Une vie qui commence à Paris le 1er juillet 1804 [1], à une heure de l'après-midi, au 15, rue Meslay

---

1. À ce propos, à la page 21 du premier tome de la *Correspondance*, Georges Lubin écrit : « G.S. fut longtemps abusée sur la date exacte de sa naissance : dans *Hist. vie*, III, pp. 236 et 238, elle répète encore qu'elle est née le 5 juillet 1804. Sans doute avait-on mal traduit la date du calendrier révolutionnaire : 12 messidor an XII, qui correspond au 1er juillet 1804. Jusqu'à la fin de sa vie, et même lorsqu'elle fut détrompée, on célébra son anniversaire le 5 juillet. »

(actuellement le 46). Celle qui aimera tant la musique, et les musiciens, naît aux sons du violon que joue son père, Maurice, tandis que sa mère, Sophie-Victoire, danse.

Pendant une contredanse, Sophie-Victoire, qui est vêtue d'« une jolie robe de couleur rose », murmure qu'elle est « un peu souffrante » et se retire dans sa chambre, accompagnée de sa sœur, Lucie. Maurice continue à jouer sa contredanse. Aux dernières notes, Lucie survient en s'écriant : « Venez, venez, Maurice, vous avez une fille. » Elle ajoute : « Elle est née en musique et dans le rose, elle aura du bonheur. » Réponse de Maurice : « Elle s'appellera Aurore, comme ma pauvre mère qui n'est pas là pour la bénir, mais qui la bénira un jour. »

Dès le lendemain, en l'église Saint-Nicolas-des-Champs, la nouvelle-née est baptisée Amandine-Aurore-Lucie tandis qu'elle est déclarée à la mairie Amantine-Aurore-Lucie. Amandine ou Amantine, elle est surtout Aurore, comme en a décidé son père qui, en novembre de cette même année, envoie à sa mère ce triomphant bulletin de santé : « Mon Aurore se porte à merveille. » À dix mois, Aurore marche. À deux ans, elle est blessée au front. C'est son premier souvenir, celui d'une blessure, due à la négligence d'une bonne que l'on renvoie aussitôt, et non à la turbulence d'Aurore qui est une enfant tranquille, pouvant passer des heures dans la contemplation des plis des rideaux, des fleurs de la tapisserie ou de la flamme des bougies qui éclairent le nouvel appartement de ses parents qui ont quitté la rue Meslay pour le 22, rue de la Grange-Batelière (actuellement le 13).

À quatre ans, Aurore sait lire. Elle apprend par cœur ses prières et des fables de La Fontaine, sans en comprendre un mot. En revanche, elle comprend parfaitement sa première chanson d'enfant que chante sa mère :

Allons dans la grange
Voir la poule blanche
Qui pond un bel œuf d'argent
Pour ce cher petit enfant

Aurore croit en cet œuf d'argent comme elle croit
en ce père Noël qui, au matin de chaque 25 décembre, dépose dans ses souliers une orange ou une
pomme rouge. Fruits si beaux, si précieux qu'elle
ose à peine les manger.

Enfin, Aurore a son premier accès de mélancolie
en entendant ce refrain :

Nous n'irons plus au bois
Les lauriers sont coupés

Elle ne parvient pas à s'expliquer cette tristesse
précoce qui ne tarde pas à être effacée par le plaisir
qu'elle prend au spectacle des ombres chinoises, ou
des féeries que l'on joue sur les Boulevards. Plaisir
aussi d'entendre sa mère raconter les histoires de la
mythologie, et parler des trois Grâces, ou des neuf
Muses, comme s'il s'agissait de personnes réelles.
Les anges et les amours, les fées et la Sainte Vierge,
tout cela se mêle dans sa tête livrée très tôt aux jeux
de l'imagination. À quatre ans, comme à quarante
ou à soixante-dix, la fille de Maurice et de Sophie-
Victoire se livre à ses deux occupations que rien, ni
les pires malheurs, ni les plus impérieux bonheurs,
ne parvient à interrompre : occuper ses mains à
quelque ouvrage et son esprit à bâtir des romans.

À quatre ans donc, Aurore s'applique à enlever
une à une les pailles des chaises pendant qu'elle
compose à haute voix « d'interminables contes que
ma mère appelait des romans ». Elle pourra ainsi
affirmer, en décembre 1842, à l'une de ses correspondantes : « Née romancier, je fais des romans. »
C'est l'évidence même. George Sand est née George
Sand. Elle n'est pas, comme on l'a cru jusqu'à
maintenant, « devenue » George Sand. Elle est née

George Sand, comme la rose naît rose et contient en son bouton son futur épanouissement. On n'a jamais vu une rose se changer en chardon !

Enfant, Aurore, comme George plus tard, enfourche des coursiers imaginaires, chevauche des nuées et se livre, sans retenue, aux plaisirs de la rêverie : « Tout ce que j'apprenais par les yeux et par les oreilles entrait en ébullition dans ma petite tête, et j'y rêvais au point de perdre souvent la notion de réalité et du milieu où je me trouvais. »

À ce goût de la rêverie dont elle mesure déjà le pouvoir, puisqu'elle peut transformer à sa guise un canapé de velours vert en forêt ou en champ de bataille, s'ajoute par hasard la découverte du monde de la musique, en écoutant une mélodie tombant du haut d'une mansarde et qui semble venir du ciel. Désormais, ciel et musique sont à jamais liés pour Aurore.

Ce précoce amour des contes, des romans et de la musique va de pair avec l'amour de la campagne, celle de Chaillot, où sa tante Lucie possède une maison et un jardin. Ce jardin est « un lieu de délices » avec ses légumes et ses fleurs, d'immenses tournesols qui paraissent à la petite fille comme autant de géants bienveillants. Au fond de ce jardin, une terrasse sablée. C'est là qu'Aurore joue, avec sa cousine Clotilde, à « de grands jeux de fuite et de poursuite ». Quand Clotilde se fâche, elle transforme le prénom d'Aurore en « horreur ». Ce qui exaspère « l'horreur », qui se met à bouder. Jamais longtemps.

Quand elle ne cède pas aux vertiges de son imagination qui l'entraîne à voir des géants dans les tournesols et des forêts dans le velours vert, Aurore est une petite fille comme les autres qui casse ses poupées pour voir ce qu'il y a dedans. Son jouet de prédilection demeure une petite Vénus en biscuit de Sèvres portant deux colombes entre ses mains. C'est un surtout de table qui a déjà servi de jouet à son père. Aurore joue avec Vénus en attendant d'être, à son tour, le jouet de Vénus comme l'ont été son père, sa mère et leurs ancêtres.

LES ANCÊTRES D'AURORE

Donc, le sang des rois se trouva mêlé
dans mes veines au sang des pauvres
et des petits.

Il s'en est fallu de peu qu'Aurore Dupin ne soit une bâtarde. Ce n'est que le 5 juin 1804, juste vingt-cinq jours avant la naissance de leur fille, que Maurice Dupin qui a vingt-six ans épouse Sophie-Victoire Delaborde qui en a trente et un. Mariage civil comme il y en a beaucoup en cette période de transition qui voit l'Empire succéder au Consulat.

La bâtardise n'a pas de quoi effrayer Maurice Dupin puisque lui-même descend d'un illustre bâtard, Maurice de Saxe, fils naturel de Frédéric-Auguste de Saxe qui devint le roi Auguste II de Pologne et d'Aurore de Kœnigsmark dont la séduction était telle qu'elle effrayait certains hommes, et non des moindres, comme Charles XII de Suède, qui, dit-on, la redoutait autant qu'une armée et refusa de la recevoir.

Maurice de Saxe, grand homme de guerre et grand coureur de jupons, eut de Marie Rainteau, présentée pudiquement par Sand comme une « dame d'opéra », une fille, Marie-Aurore.

Née en 1748, Marie-Aurore fut reconnue, en 1766, par un décret du Parlement, comme « fille naturelle de Maurice, comte de Saxe ». Marie-Aurore pouvait considérer la nièce de Maurice, Marie-Josèphe de Saxe, qui avait épousé le Dauphin et serait la mère de trois rois, Louis XVI, Louis XVIII et Charles X, comme sa cousine germaine. Marie-Aurore, qui sera la grand-mère de Sand, est donc cousine par alliance de Marie-Antoinette, et par conséquent sa petite-fille l'est aussi. Oublieuses de cette parenté, Marie-Aurore de Saxe et Aurore Dupin se firent l'écho souvent complaisant des calomnies dont on accabla celle qui fut la reine la plus diffamée de l'histoire. Car on cousina fort peu, et même, pas du tout.

Entre Marie-Aurore et Marie-Josèphe, le cousinage se borna à des échanges de placets et à des demandes de pension. La Dauphine ne pouvait recevoir, ni fréquenter, une bâtarde, fût-elle reconnue par le Parlement comme « fille naturelle de Maurice, comte de Saxe » !

Élevée à Saint-Cyr, grâce à la protection lointaine et efficace de Marie-Josèphe, Marie-Aurore ne quitta cette institution que pour épouser en 1766 le capitaine d'infanterie Antoine de Horn, et se retrouver, cinq mois plus tard, veuve à dix-huit ans. La jeune veuve se réfugia chez sa mère, Marie, et chez sa tante Geneviève, qui passaient pour de « modernes Aspasies », autrement dit des courtisanes. Marie et Geneviève Rainteau avaient pris, selon l'usage, un nom de guerre galante et se faisaient appeler Marie et Geneviève de Verrières. Ces deux « dames d'opéra », à l'exemple de leurs consœurs, considéraient la scène comme un tremplin où l'on pouvait, entre deux roulades, aguicher les riches amateurs qui se pressaient dans les loges.

Sagement, la protégée de la Dauphine, l'élève de Saint-Cyr, préféra le mariage à l'aventure dans ces milieux de libertinage. Marie-Aurore épousa en 1778 un fermier général, ami des philosophes et amant de Mme d'Épinay, Louis-Claude Dupin de Francueil. Dupin avait soixante et un ans et Marie-Aurore, trente ans. De cette union naîtra, un an après, Maurice, le père de Sand. Mme Dupin de Francueil idolâtre son fils, comme plus tard Sand idolâtrera le sien. À noter que, dans cette famille, on est naturellement porté aux sentiments extrêmes et qu'aimer ne suffit pas, il faut idolâtrer. À noter aussi l'utilisation persistante des prénoms illustres dans cette même famille : Maurice pour les garçons, en souvenir de Maurice de Saxe, et Aurore pour les filles, en souvenir d'Aurore de Kœnigsmark.

Le sang des Saxe et des Kœnigsmark coule dans les veines de George Sand, qui n'en sera pas plus fière pour cela : « Frédéric-Auguste, électeur de Saxe et roi de Pologne, fut le plus étonnant débauché de son temps. Ce n'est pas un honneur bien rare que d'avoir un peu de son sang dans les veines, car il eut, dit-on, plusieurs centaines de bâtards. »

Voilà pour les ancêtres du côté paternel : un roi débauché (Frédéric-Auguste), une coquette (Aurore de Kœnigsmark), un séducteur (Maurice de Saxe), une dame d'opéra (Marie Rainteau de Verrières), une protégée des dames d'opéra (Marie-Aurore) et un fermier général (Louis-Claude Dupin de Francueil). Tous, à l'exception de Marie-Aurore, ont été les jouets de Vénus et ont allègrement sacrifié aux autels de la déesse.

L'asservissement à Vénus comporte des degrés. Avec les Saxe, les Kœnigsmark, les Rainteau, les Dupin, on tient le haut du pavé. On est à la cour ou dans ses alentours, les milieux de la haute finance ou de l'opéra.

Côté maternel des ancêtres de Sand, on tombe sur la Vénus des carrefours. Sophie-Victoire Delaborde, fille d'Antoine Delaborde, qui vendait des oiseaux à Paris, quai de la Mégisserie, et de Marie-Anne Cloquart, est, d'après l'aveu de sa propre fille, « moins que danseuse » : « Elle était danseuse, moins que danseuse, comparse sur le dernier des théâtres du boulevard de Paris, lorsque l'amour du riche vint la tirer de cette abjection pour lui en faire subir de plus grandes encore. Mon père la connut lorsqu'elle avait déjà trente ans, et au milieu de quels égarements ! Il avait un grand cœur, lui ; il comprit que cette belle créature pouvait encore aimer, et il l'épousa contre le gré et presque sous le coup de la malédiction de sa famille. Longtemps pauvre avec elle, il aima jusqu'aux enfants qu'elle avait eus avant lui. »

Pour qui sait lire entre ces lignes écrites par Sand le 23 décembre 1843, et traduire le langage de l'époque en termes modernes, il est facile de comprendre ce que signifient cette « abjection » et ces « égarements ». Mlle Delaborde a fait commerce de ses charmes, comme les demoiselles Rainteau. Hélas, elle ne comptait pas parmi ses clients des fermiers généraux, mais des obscurs, des sans-grade. De ces liaisons multiples resta une fille, Caroline, qui est la demi-sœur de Sand. Caroline est née, de père inconnu, le 10 mars 1799 à Paris, tandis que le 5 mai de cette même année naissait à La Châtre Hyppolite Chatiron, fils naturel non reconnu de Maurice Dupin, et donc demi-frère de Sand.

En ce dix-huitième siècle finissant, les liaisons dangereuses sont à la mode. Laclos a fait école. Il en résulte, dans la vie quotidienne, des bâtards comme Caroline et Hyppolite, des filles perdues comme Sophie-Victoire. L'amour considéré comme une rédemption — et on retrouve là l'un des thèmes majeurs du roman au dix-neuvième siècle — change la fille perdue, Sophie-Victoire, quand elle aime enfin et qu'elle est fidèle à son amour, Maurice, en une dame qui se veut respectable et respectée.

L'horreur que Sand portera à la prostitution, fût-elle la plus légitime, la prostitution conjugale, se justifie aisément quand on sait que son arrière-grand-mère, Marie Rainteau de Verrières, et sa mère, Sophie-Victoire Delaborde, la pratiquèrent avec des fortunes diverses. La première avec éclat et dans un hôtel de la Chaussée-d'Antin acheté grâce aux libéralités de ses protecteurs. La seconde, moins chanceuse, dans la rue et dans les armées. Car c'est à l'armée, où il parvint à l'arracher à un général, que le lieutenant Maurice Dupin connut, en 1800, en Italie, celle qui allait devenir la mère de son Aurore.

Mme Dupin de Francueil ne voulut pas entendre parler de cette liaison, encore moins de mariage. À Saint-Cyr, Marie-Aurore avait appris que l'on ne mélangeait pas les serviettes et les torchons. Elle se refusait à un mélange des serviettes Rainteau et des torchons Delaborde. La galanterie a toujours eu ses classes et ses castes. Au début de notre siècle, il n'était pas non plus question de confondre une Liane de Pougy qui recevait dans son lit les rois de l'Europe avec la fille publique qui recevait dans le sien le bourgeois en goguette ou le soldat en permission. Bref, Mme Dupin de Francueil n'assista pas au mariage de son fils bien-aimé avec la Delaborde, et encore moins à la naissance qui s'ensuivit, vingt-cinq jours après. Elle s'efforça, sans y parvenir, de faire dissoudre ce mariage civil.

De toute façon, aucune femme n'aurait trouvé grâce aux yeux de Marie-Aurore, qui voyait en sa belle-fille une triomphante rivale et s'en plaignait amèrement à son fils : « Tu aimes une femme plus que moi, donc tu ne m'aimes plus ! Que ne suis-je morte comme tant d'autres en 93 ! Je n'aurais jamais eu de rivale dans ton cœur ! » Mme Dupin de Francueil n'en continuait pas moins d'idolâtrer son fils. Après bien des refus, elle consentit à voir sa petite-fille, qui avait reçu en héritage les beaux yeux des Kœnigsmark et des Saxe, les beaux yeux de la première Aurore et du premier Maurice, les yeux de Maurice, son Maurice. Vaincue par cette ressemblance qui établissait de manière irréfutable la paternité de son fils, Mme Dupin de Francueil consentit alors à assister au mariage religieux du couple.

En 1808, Maurice Dupin, devenu colonel, était nommé, à Madrid, aide de camp de Murat. Dès le mois d'avril de cette année-là, Sophie-Victoire, bien qu'enceinte de sept mois, partit, avec sa fille Aurore, rejoindre son mari. Sophie-Victoire connaissait trop, et pour cause, les faciles galanteries de la vie de garnison pour laisser longtemps son époux exposé aux tentations madrilènes. Sophie-Victoire était jalouse, comme savent l'être parfois les prêtresses de Vénus...

Plus épouse que mère, Sophie-Victoire ne songe pas un instant à épargner à sa fille de quatre ans les inconvénients d'un voyage dans une Espagne au bord du soulèvement contre l'occupant français. Les routes sont peu sûres. Il en faut davantage pour effrayer une amoureuse comme Sophie-Victoire. Le sang des Delaborde draine dans ses veines autant de passion que le sang des Kœnigsmark et des Saxe. Comme on dit familièrement, Aurore a de qui tenir et saura, en amour, montrer la même intrépidité que sa mère en ce printemps 1808.

LE VOYAGE EN ESPAGNE
(printemps 1808)

Nous arrivâmes à Madrid dans le
courant de mai (...) déjà l'Espagne
était soulevée sur plusieurs points et
partout grondait l'orage prêt à éclater.

Comme son épouse, Maurice Dupin a du courage à revendre. Il a débuté comme simple soldat et clame : « Je suis invulnérable. » Dépensier de son argent, quand il en a, et de ses forces physiques, Maurice est, comme sa mère, avec qui il correspond assidûment, un infatigable épistolier. Sand héritera de leur amour fou pour la correspondance.

Nature d'artiste qui voit dans son violon l'idéal compagnon de sa vie, Maurice manie aussi bien l'archet que la plume ou l'épée. Fier, il refuse de faire des courbettes pour obtenir de l'avancement. En août 1804, il a reconnu que « le nouveau régime est sous ce rapport pire que l'ancien ». Par « sous ce rapport », Maurice désigne, et flétrit, l'influence des courtisans qui, à la cour de Napoléon, sont encore plus puissants qu'à la cour de Versailles, sous l'Ancien Régime. Qu'importe ? Maurice adore son épouse — « Tu es mon dieu, l'ange tutélaire que j'invoque » — et sa fille, à qui il offre, comme friandise, du vermicelle cuit dans du lait sucré et pour qui il fabrique des pantins avec sa serviette. Ce qui provoque les gronderies de Sophie-Victoire qui trouve que son mari gâte trop leur enfant.

Entre Maurice et Aurore, Sophie-Victoire peut croire que son sort s'est aplani et qu'elle a enfin atteint les rivages de la tranquillité familiale qu'elle n'a guère goûtée jusqu'à maintenant. Ayant perdu son père en 1781 et sa mère en 1790, Sophie-Victoire est une fleur du pavé parisien. Au commencement de la Révolution, elle a connu un instant de gloire : elle a, pour sa beauté, été élue « perle du district » et offert une couronne de fleurs à La Fayette, héros du jour. Puis la « perle » est arrêtée pour avoir chanté une chanson séditieuse et enfermée dans la prison des Anglaises où devait séjourner aussi sa future belle-mère, Mme Dupin de Francueil. Libérée, Sophie-Victoire s'octroie toutes les libertés, se refusant aux « grands dîners » et aux « visites banales ». Comme sa mère, Aurore aimera le coin du feu ou la promenade « rapide et folâtre ».

Les parents d'Aurore vivent très retirés. Si la conduite de la colonelle Dupin est irréprochable, il est difficile de faire oublier les frasques de Mlle Delaborde. Le couple formé par le colonel et par son épouse, qui fut une femme entretenue par des militaires, appartient, à ces couples que la société dite bonne tient à l'écart. Cet ostracisme ne pèse guère à Maurice et à Sophie-Victoire, à qui leur amour suffit, et qui fuient un monde qui les fuit. Ils lèguent à Aurore « cette secrète sauvagerie qui m'a toujours rendu le monde insupportable et le *home* nécessaire ».

L'isolement du couple Dupin souffre une exception en faveur de Pierret, « l'ami Pierret », qui est, en tout bien tout honneur, l'ami du ménage. Son extrême laideur et ses tics incessants en font le moins compromettant des amis. Pierret est employé au Trésor. Il a vu naître Aurore et a aidé à la sevrer. Depuis, il se considère comme son second père. Ce qu'admet Maurice qui, avant de partir en Espagne, fait à Pierret cette recommandation solennelle : « Je te recommande ma femme et mes enfants, et si je ne reviens pas, c'est pour toute ta vie. »

C'est Pierret qui organise les préparatifs du départ en Espagne. Mme Dupin s'en va avec la femme d'un fournisseur de l'armée, Mme Fontanier, qui lui offre une place dans sa calèche. Et en route pour Madrid !

Jusqu'aux montagnes des Asturies, Aurore ne se rappelle plus rien. À partir de ces montagnes dont la hauteur l'étonne et la terrorise, elle se souvient de tout, et surtout des enseignements de sa mère qui, devant un beau nuage, un effet de soleil, une eau claire, dit aussitôt à sa fille : « Voilà qui est joli, regarde. » Pendant ce voyage en Espagne, Aurore apprend à regarder et à admirer. Elle ne pourra plus voir des liserons sans entendre la voix de sa mère répéter : « Respire-les, cela sent le bon miel ; et ne les oublie pas. » Aurore n'oubliera pas non plus les frayeurs de Sophie-Victoire qui prend trois ours sur le bord du chemin pour trois bandits, ce qui provoque les rires de Mme Fontanier : « Oh ! mon Dieu, madame Dupin, que vous êtes drôle avec votre petite fille ! »

L'Espagne sombre dans une guerre dont Goya s'apprête à graver les désastres tandis que Mme Dupin et sa fille n'observent que des liserons et des ours. Elles ne se plaignent que de la chaleur, déjà suffocante en ce mois d'avril 1808, et de n'avoir à manger, dans les auberges, que des oignons crus.

Dès qu'elle arrive à Madrid et retrouve Maurice, Sophie-Victoire oublie les fatigues du voyage. Quant à Aurore, elle n'a d'yeux que pour les splendeurs du palais où elle est installée. C'est le palais de Godoy, le prince de la Paix, le favori de Marie-Louise, reine d'Espagne. La reine et sa famille sont en fuite : Sophie-Victoire et sa fille pourraient dire, comme Mme Sans-Gêne : « Maintenant, c'est nous qu'on sont les princesses. » À elles les appartements damassés de soie cramoisie, les glaces immenses où Aurore se contemple, pour la première fois, des pieds à la tête et ne se reconnaît pas. Elle croit reconnaître en la personne du prince Murat, « doré et empanaché », le prince Fanfarinet, héros de l'un des contes de Mme d'Aulnoy qu'elle aime particulièrement. Sa mère a toutes les peines du monde à l'empêcher d'appeler Murat « prince Fanfarinet ». Amusé, et bon prince, Murat prend en amitié Aurore à qui l'on fait revêtir, taillé à sa mesure, l'uniforme du régiment, dolman blanc et pantalon de casimir amarante. Voilà Aurore, à quatre ans, portant déjà le pantalon...

Le séjour à Madrid dure plus de deux mois pendant lesquels le colonel Dupin et son épouse doivent sacrifier aux devoirs de leur charge et abandonner leur fille aux soins d'une domestique espagnole que l'on dit sûre, et d'un domestique allemand, Weber. « Weber, je t'aime bien, va-t'en », ordonne Aurore à l'Allemand qui obéit.

Aurore savoure alors dans le palais désert les plaisirs d'un moment de solitude dont elle ne pourra plus se passer, sa vie durant. « Je connus donc pour la première fois le plaisir, étrange pour un enfant, mais vivement senti par moi, de me trouver seule, et, loin d'en être contrariée ou effrayée, j'avais comme du regret en voyant revenir la voiture de ma mère. » C'est que les instants de solitude passent vite pour Aurore qui va et vient à sa guise, prend, devant les glaces, des poses, se drape dans des mantilles, et invite à danser son double, « alors j'oubliais complètement que cette figure dansant dans la glace fût la mienne et j'étais étonnée qu'elle s'arrêtât quand je m'arrêtais ».

Ce précoce Narcisse féminin découvre, sur le haut d'une terrasse, l'écho. Elle dit le nom de sa mère, et l'écho renvoie ce nom. Elle grossit sa voix, et l'écho grossit la sienne. Narcisse et Écho en une même personne, Aurore est dans le ravissement.

Un ravissement interrompu par l'accouchement de Sophie-Victoire qui met au monde un petit garçon auquel Aurore fait à peine attention. Elle ne regarde que sa mère couchée, pâlie, et, croit-elle, mourante. Elle se met à pleurer, sans plus s'intéresser à son frère qui est né aveugle. Cécité que l'on réussit à cacher à Sophie-Victoire qui, deux semaines après son accouchement, se remet « en route pour la France à travers l'Espagne en feu ».

LA PREMIÈRE ARRIVÉE À NOHANT
(été 1808)

C'est la première fois que nous
étions à Nohant, ma mère et moi.

C'est vraiment toute l'Espagne qui est en feu maintenant. Le 2 mai 1808, le soulèvement du peuple de Madrid contre l'occupant français ne s'est pas limité à la capitale et s'est étendu au reste du pays. Murat retourne en France. Le 12 juin, Maurice annonce à sa mère que lui aussi revient, à la suite du prince, et qu'il espère être à Nohant vers le 20 juillet. Il pense rester à Nohant « le plus longtemps possible » et ce sera « le bonheur complet ». Les dissensions entre Mme Dupin de Francueil et son fils sont oubliées, ou semblent l'être. Maurice est sûr que sa mère ne manquera pas d'admirer ces trois merveilles que sont sa femme, sa fille et son fils. On peut espérer que les médecins français sauront guérir ce dernier de sa cécité. Et, quatrième merveille, un cheval d'Andalousie, « l'indomptable Leopardo », offert par le prince des Asturies à Maurice. Sophie-Victoire déteste d'emblée ce cheval et souhaite que son époux s'en défasse. Il refuse, malgré les supplications de sa bien-aimée qui prétend voir en Leopardo un cheval de mort, un cheval qui donnera la mort à son maître.

Maurice, qui se croit toujours invulnérable, rit de ces craintes. Sophie-Victoire ne prétend-elle pas aussi que le chirurgien madrilène qui l'a accouchée a appuyé ses pouces sur les yeux du nouveau-né en disant : « Celui-là ne verra pas le soleil d'Espagne » ? Faiblesses d'une femme qui vient d'accoucher...

Début juillet, la famille Dupin quitte Madrid. De ce voyage de retour avec les colonnes de l'armée,

Aurore gardera le souvenir de la soif, de la faim, de la fièvre et d'une « dévorante chaleur ». On avance lentement à travers les champs de bataille, les cadavres, l'air infecté. On se nourrit des inévitables oignons crus auxquels s'ajoutent des citrons verts et des graines de tournesol. Aurore, affamée, dévore une soupe faite avec des bouts de chandelle et offerte à discrétion par des soldats, au hasard d'une rencontre.

Aurore et son frère Louis attrapent la gale. À Sophie-Victoire qui s'en désole, les cantinières répondent en riant : « Bah ! ma petite dame, ce n'est rien, c'est un brevet de santé pour toute la vie de vos enfants ; c'est le véritable baptême des *enfants de la giberne*. »

Un baptême dont Aurore et Louis se seraient bien passés ! Enfin, on arrive à la frontière, à Fontarabie. Les enfants sont baignés puis enduits de soufre des pieds à la tête. Ils doivent avaler des « boulettes de soufre pulvérisé dans du beurre et du sucre ». La gale ne devrait pas résister à un pareil traitement. Elle résiste. À partir de là, Aurore sombre dans la fièvre, devient une masse inerte et brûlante. C'est ainsi que fin juillet, elle arrive, pour la première fois, à Nohant. « Je repris mes sens en entrant dans la cour de Nohant. Ce n'était pas aussi beau, à coup sûr, que le palais de Madrid, mais cela me fit le même effet, tant une grande maison est imposante pour les enfants élevés dans de petites chambres. »

Aurore trouve aussi imposante sa grand-mère, « quoiqu'elle n'eût que cinq pieds ». Mais, avec son bonnet de dentelle et sa robe de soie prune, Mme Dupin de Francueil incarne en sa personne l'Ancien Régime et ses façons impeccables.

M. Dupin de Francueil est mort en 1788. Sa veuve paye les dettes du défunt et ne s'en retrouve pas moins à la tête de 60 000 livres de rente. Ce qui ne l'empêche pas de s'estimer, tout est relatif, « ruinée ».

Acquise aux idées nouvelles qui conduisirent à la

prise de la Bastille, Mme Dupin de Francueil avait vu « sans terreur » s'approcher la Révolution qui dégénère en Terreur. En août 1793, elle acquiert dans le Berry, où M. Dupin de Francueil avait des intérêts dans les manufactures de drap de Châteauroux, la « terre de Nohant », qui comporte une bâtisse suffisamment vaste pour se donner des allures de château, un jardin, un verger, des fermes, des champs.

Le 3 décembre 1793, Mme Dupin de Francueil, qui trouve de moins en moins de charme aux idées nouvelles, est arrêtée à Paris, vraisemblablement pour avoir souscrit à un fonds en faveur des princes émigrés. Incarcérée à la prison des Anglaises, comme le fut sa belle-fille, elle n'est libérée qu'après Thermidor, le 21 août 1794. Peu après, dès le mois d'octobre, elle s'installe à Nohant avec Maurice et son précepteur, Deschartres.

Nourrie de Voltaire et de Rousseau, Mme Dupin de Francueil prend sa retraite avec philosophie et trouve en Nohant un goût de paradis terrestre puisqu'elle ne croit guère en l'autre, le céleste.

Son éducation à Saint-Cyr, son passage chez les dames d'opéra, son état d'épouse de fermier général avaient doté Mme Dupin de Francueil d'un savoir-vivre capable de s'adapter aux cas les plus difficiles, comme, en cette fin juillet 1808, l'arrivée de son fils idolâtré, de son indigne belle-fille et de leurs deux enfants galeux.

En mondaine accomplie, Mme Dupin de Francueil surmonte son aversion pour Sophie-Victoire, qu'elle veut embrasser et qui s'y refuse en expliquant : « Ah ! ma chère maman, ne touchez ni à moi ni à ces pauvres enfants. Vous ne savez pas quelles misères nous avons subies, nous sommes tous malades. — Figure-toi, intervient Maurice, que ces enfants ont une petite éruption de boutons et que Sophie s'imagine qu'ils ont la gale. — Gale ou non, je me charge de celui-là », répond Mme Dupin de Francueil en prenant dans ses bras Aurore qui n'oubliera jamais ce geste. « Elle m'emporta dans sa chambre, et, sans aucun dégoût de l'état horrible où j'étais, cette excellente femme, si délicate et si recherchée, me déposa sur son lit. » Telle qu'elle est, fiévreuse et galeuse, Aurore a conquis sa grand-mère. On peut considérer Mme Dupin de Francueil comme la première à inscrire sur une liste d'innombrables conquêtes...

Ensuite, Aurore est présentée à son demi-frère[1], Hyppolite Chatiron, qui a neuf ans. Tous deux ignorent, pour le moment, les liens de parenté qui les unissent. Avec une simplicité patriarcale, Maurice conduit son Hyppolite, fruit de ses amours de jeune homme avec une jeune servante de Nohant, à Sophie-Victoire qui, avec une égale simplicité, accepte cet enfant d'un : « Eh bien, il est à moi aussi, comme Caroline est à toi. » Sophie-Victoire « adopte » Hyppolite, comme Maurice avait « adopté » Caroline, la demi-sœur d'Aurore.

Enfin, Aurore est présentée au personnage qui, dans la hiérarchie de Nohant, vient immédiatement après Mme Dupin de Francueil, François Deschartres, qui a alors soixante-sept ans. Avant d'être le précepteur de Maurice, Deschartres a été professeur à Paris, au collège du Cardinal-Lemoine. Il sait tout, ou croit tout savoir. On l'a surnommé « le grand homme ». Pendant la Terreur, Deschartres, aidé par Maurice, a, certainement au péril de sa vie, sauvé Mme Dupin de Francueil en détruisant des papiers compromettants. Il a du courage, un cœur excellent, un caractère impossible, et des connaissances en physique, chimie, chirurgie. Il est à la fois le médecin et le pharmacien de Nohant. Il examine Aurore et diagnostique immédiatement la gale.

Le bon air de Nohant, la bonne nourriture suffisent à guérir Aurore tandis que Louis, son frère,

---

1. Leur vie durant, Hyppolite et Aurore se considéreront comme frère et sœur à part entière ; nous ferons de même.

dépérit à vue d'œil. C'est une révélation pour la petite fille : « Je commençais à l'aimer en le voyant souffrir. » Ainsi, dès sa quatrième année, Aurore trouve au malheur, à la souffrance, d'étranges attraits. Sa vocation d'infirmière, son besoin de secourir l'autre, naît pendant cet été 1808, dans le jardin de Nohant, face à cet enfant étendu sur les genoux de sa mère.

Louis meurt le 8 septembre. On l'enterre le lendemain. Pendant la cérémonie, Hyppolite est chargé de distraire Aurore à qui l'on veut épargner les pleurs de ses parents.

La nuit qui succède à l'enterrement, Sophie-Victoire persuade Maurice que leur fils n'est pas mort et qu'il faut aller le reprendre au cimetière. Le couple ramène le cercueil à Nohant, en secret, et constate l'inévitable. Toujours en secret, Maurice et Sophie-Victoire enterrent leur fils au pied d'un poirier. (Aurore n'apprendra que plus tard, et de la bouche de sa mère, les détails de ces scènes macabres.)

Au pied du poirier, le couple Dupin plante des reines-marguerites, élève une butte de gazon où Aurore et Hyppolite peuvent jouer. Ces travaux occupent Maurice et Sophie-Victoire, et les distraient un peu de leur chagrin.

Le vendredi 16 septembre 1808, Maurice monte l'indomptable Leopardo et s'en va à La Châtre dîner chez des amis, les Duvernet.

LA TRAGÉDIE À NOHANT
(septembre 1808-février 1809)

Je vois encore dans quel endroit de
la chambre où nous étions. C'est celle
que j'habite encore et dans laquelle
j'écris le récit de cette lamentable
histoire.

À peine Maurice est-il parti pour La Châtre que Sophie-Victoire laisse éclater sa jalousie envers ces Duvernet qu'elle ne connaît pas et qui, visiblement, ne veulent pas la connaître ! Mme Dupin de Francueil calme, du mieux qu'elle peut, sa belle-fille qui va se coucher, abandonnant son projet d'attendre le retour de son mari sur la route. Attendre son mari sur la route, comme une paysanne ! Mme Dupin de Francueil en frémit et trouve l'argument suprême : Sophie-Victoire doit dormir pour rester belle afin de plaire à Maurice. L'ancienne perle du district ne demande qu'à se laisser convaincre et ne tarde pas à s'endormir.

Vers minuit, Mme Dupin de Francueil s'inquiète du retard de son fils, mais ne dit rien à Deschartres, avec qui elle termine une partie de piquet. Elle se retire dans sa chambre quand sonnent les douze coups de minuit. Soudain, elle entend des bruits que l'on s'efforce d'étouffer. Personne n'ose dire à la châtelaine de Nohant que Maurice a eu un accident en sortant de La Châtre. Comme une flèche, Deschartres est déjà parti. Également comme une flèche, dès qu'elle est prévenue, et sans penser à réveiller sa belle-fille, Mme Dupin de Francueil s'élance, seule. Cette femme de soixante ans, qui ne quitte guère son salon et que le tour de son jardin fatigue à l'extrême, trouve la force de courir de Nohant à La Châtre d'une traite, et de s'écrouler sur le cadavre de son fils. Maurice est mort.

Dans l'obscurité, au détour de la route, l'indomptable Leopardo a heurté un tas de pierres et désarçonné son maître qui s'est rompu les vertèbres du cou. Avant d'expirer, Maurice a juste eu le temps de crier à son fidèle Weber qui l'accompagnait : « À moi, Weber, je suis mort. »

Mme Dupin de Francueil ressemble à une morte. Pendant le retour à Nohant, cadavre agrippé au cadavre de son fils, elle fait entendre, selon le témoignage de Deschartres, « un râle semblable à celui de l'agonie ».

À six heures du matin, Aurore est levée, sa mère s'habille, quand Deschartres entre dans leur chambre. En voyant ce visage décomposé, Sophie-Victoire pressent un malheur et demande : « Maurice ! Où est Maurice ? » Deschartres parvient à articuler : « Il est tombé... Non, n'y allez pas, restez ici, pensez à votre fille... Oui, c'est grave, très grave. » Puis, avec un accent qui frappe Aurore, il murmure : « Il est mort » et éclate en sanglots. Sophie-Victoire pousse des cris déchirants. Aurore couvre de baisers les mains de sa mère. Deschartres dit : « Voyez donc cette enfant et vivez pour elle. »

Le deuil s'abat sur Nohant. Aurore répugne à porter des vêtements noirs, surtout des bas qui lui inspirent « une grande terreur ». Mais sa grand-mère, sa mère, Deschartres, Hyppolite, tous sont en noir « à cause de la mort de son père », explique-t-on à Aurore qui ne peut pas comprendre que la mort soit un état définitif et qui, chaque jour, interroge : « Mon papa est donc encore mort aujourd'hui ? » Devant la persistante absence de son père, elle renouvelle son interrogation et répète à sa mère : « Quand mon papa aura fini d'être mort, il reviendra bien te voir ? »

Puis Aurore se tait. Elle reste des heures entières, assise sur un tabouret, les yeux fixes, la bouche entrouverte. Sa grand-mère s'alarme de cet excès de calme. « Je l'ai toujours vue ainsi, explique Sophie-Victoire, c'est sa nature ; ce n'est pas bêtise. Soyez sûre qu'elle rumine toujours quelque chose. Autrefois, elle parlait tout haut en rêvassant, mais, comme disait son pauvre père, elle n'en pense pas moins. » « C'est probable, répond Mme Dupin de Francueil, mais il n'est pas bon pour les enfants de tant rêver. Il faut que cette petite soit distraite, et secouée malgré elle. Nos chagrins la feront mourir, si on n'y prend garde ; elle les ressent, bien qu'elle ne les comprenne pas. Ma fille, il faut vous distraire aussi, ne fût-ce que physiquement. Vous êtes naturellement robuste, l'exercice vous est nécessaire. Il faut reprendre votre travail de jardinage, l'enfant y reprendra goût avec vous. »

Sophie-Victoire obéit. Elle est la proie de cette atonie qui succède à l'intensité du malheur. Cet état de soumission à sa belle-mère ne peut pas durer longtemps. Pourtant, dans les semaines qui suivent la mort de Maurice, les deux femmes, que tout sépare, observent une trêve et en profitent pour se connaître mieux.

Drapée dans son calme et sa dignité, Mme Dupin de Francueil s'étonne de la passion que Sophie-Victoire met jusque dans l'exécution des plus petites choses. Broderie, robe, chapeau, Sophie-Victoire sait tout faire. « C'est une fée », doit admettre Mme Dupin de Francueil qui reconnaît les mérites de sa belle-fille : « Elle est charmante. Elle est généreuse et donnerait sa chemise aux pauvres. » En écho, Sophie-Victoire reconnaît que sa belle-mère « est une femme supérieure. Elle est si douce et si bien élevée qu'il n'y a jamais moyen de se fâcher avec elle, et si elle vous dit quelquefois une parole qui pique, au moment où la colère vous prend, elle vous en dit une autre qui vous donne envie de l'embrasser. Si on pouvait la débarrasser de ses vieilles comtesses, elle serait adorable ».

Ces « vieilles comtesses », amies de Mme Dupin de Francueil, habitent Paris, séjournent parfois à Nohant et portent des noms sonores, Mme de Pardaillan, Mme de La Marlière, Mme de Bérenger, Mme de Ferrières. Elles regardent de haut Sophie-

Victoire et appellent Aurore « ma pauvre enfant ». Ces grands airs, ces petits soupirs exaspèrent Sophie-Victoire qui ne cache pas qu'elle est peuple, et fière de l'être ! Aurore, qui a choisi le camp de sa mère, sera, elle se le jure, peuple.

Quand des orages éclatent entre la belle-mère et la belle-fille, les compliments se changent en invectives. Mme Dupin de Francueil trouve que sa belle-fille est une folle et un démon. Sophie-Victoire traite sa belle-mère de prude et d'hypocrite. La « fée » devient une sorcière et la « femme supérieure », une mesquine.

Mme Dupin de Francueil et Sophie-Victoire se disputent Aurore, comme elles se sont disputé Maurice. La première séduit et gâte. La seconde, qui a « la parole vive et la main leste » et qui met en pratique la maxime « Qui aime bien, châtie bien », est celle que préfère Aurore.

Mme Dupin de Francueil s'attache de jour en jour davantage à cette Aurore dont la ressemblance avec son Maurice est de plus en plus frappante. Et la grand-mère ne peut s'empêcher d'appeler parfois sa petite-fille « Maurice » ou « mon fils »...

Devant une telle ressemblance, Mme Dupin de Francueil peut penser que le drame n'a pas eu lieu à Nohant et que les beaux jours d'autrefois sont revenus... Pour ressusciter ce passé, elle est prête à mettre le prix qu'il faudra pour obtenir la garde d'Aurore. Laquelle comprend confusément qu'elle constitue, entre les deux femmes, un enjeu financier. Mme Dupin de Francueil promet à Sophie-Victoire une rente, si elle lui laisse l'entière responsabilité de l'éducation d'Aurore.

Aurore supplie sa mère de ne pas la donner à sa grand-mère « pour de l'argent ». C'est exactement ce que fait Sophie-Victoire qui, le 28 janvier 1809, se désiste de la tutelle de sa fille en faveur de Mme Dupin de Francueil. La crainte de retomber dans sa misère première, la certitude d'assurer son propre avenir, et celui d'Aurore, ont certainement déterminé Sophie-Victoire à accomplir cet abandon. En fin de compte, Aurore a été vendue par sa mère et en conçoit un inusable mépris pour cette chose mystérieuse que les adultes semblent adorer : l'argent.

LA GUERRE DE SIX ANS
(février 1809-décembre 1817)

(...) Car toute ma vie, j'ai été le jouet
des passions d'autrui, par conséquent
leur victime. Pour ne parler que du
commencement de ma vie, ma mère et
ma grand-mère, avides de mon affection, s'arrachèrent les lambeaux de
mon cœur.

LA GUERRE DE SIX ANS
(février 1865-décembre 1871)

De 1809 à 1817, la France et les autres États de l'Europe vivent une période des plus agitées. Des peuples s'éveillent, des trônes basculent, des empires tombent en miettes.

Mme Dupin de Francueil et Sophie-Victoire traversent ces événements, sans y participer. Après les excès de la Révolution, Mme Dupin de Francueil ne cache pas sa nostalgie de l'Ancien Régime et regrette d'avoir recopié, et peut-être même composé, des libelles « sanglants » contre Marie-Antoinette. Elle n'aime pas l'Empereur, ce parvenu corse, cet ogre qui dévore les hommes et qui aurait fini par engloutir son Maurice. Sophie-Victoire vénère Napoléon qui est la preuve même que l'on peut partir de rien et arriver à tout. De ce point de vue-là, Sophie-Victoire n'a pas trop mal réussi. La voilà devenue, à trente-six ans, veuve d'un colonel et rentière.

Force est de constater, une fois de plus, que le chagrin ne tue pas. Mme Dupin de Francueil et Sophie-Victoire, que la mort de Maurice avait rendues agonisantes, récupèrent leurs forces vitales pour se disputer le cœur d'Aurore et discuter chiffres. Le 3 février 1809, Mme Dupin de Francueil signe une promesse de rente de 1 500 livres[1] à laquelle s'ajoutent 1 000 autres francs provenant du revenu d'un domaine de Westphalie qui avait été accordé en majorat à Maurice. Mme Dupin de

1. Voir à ce sujet la note de Georges Lubin dans les *Œuvres autobiographiques*, tome I, Gallimard, « La Pléiade », p. 1388.

Francueil se chargeant d'acquitter les dettes de son fils, Sophie-Victoire ne recevra, pendant les six années à venir, qu'une rente de 1 000 livres.

Il ne reste plus à Sophie-Victoire qu'à regagner Paris, sous prétexte de s'occuper de son autre fille, Caroline, oubliée dans une pension. Pauvre Caroline, qui n'a pas de bonne-maman pour la gâter !

Si Aurore était en âge de comprendre ces choses, Sophie-Victoire démontrerait aisément que mieux vaut être vendue à une vraie bonne-maman qu'à un faux bon-papa libidineux... Et puis, quoi, ce n'est qu'une séparation. On se reverra bientôt, c'est promis.

Pendant six ans, Aurore vivra dans l'espérance de l'accomplissement de cette promesse. Pendant six ans, alors que la guerre change la face de l'Europe, Mme Dupin de Francueil et Sophie-Victoire, à Nohant, comme à Paris, se livrent à une incessante guerre d'usure. « Ma mère et ma grand-mère, avides de mon affection, s'arrachèrent les lambeaux de mon cœur », se plaindra plus tard George Sand. Ce cœur saura quand même garder son intégrité et battre à l'unisson d'autres cœurs.

Avec l'aide de Julie, sa femme de chambre, et celle de Deschartres, bonne-maman s'efforce de changer en une demoiselle accomplie Aurore, à qui elle donne une compagne de son âge, Ursule, fille d'un chapelier de Châteauroux. Ursule a dix mois de plus qu'Aurore. Après quelques bonnes, et secrètes, bagarres, les deux petites filles s'entendent comme larronnes en foire. C'est Ursule qui console Aurore du départ de sa mère, en vantant les avantages de la vie à Nohant : « C'est pourtant gentil d'avoir une grande maison et un grand jardin comme ça pour se promener, et des voitures, et des robes, et des bonnes choses à manger tous les jours. » À moitié convaincue, Aurore sèche ses larmes et se laisse entraîner par Ursule dans le « grand jardin » qui retentit bientôt de leurs jeux et de leurs cris.

À cinq ans, Aurore apprend à écrire et à lire. Elle se délecte des contes de Mme d'Aulnoy ou de Perrault, et de l'*Abrégé de la mythologie grecque*. À Nohant, dans sa chambre, sur la tapisserie, parmi les guirlandes, figurent une Flore dansante et une grave Bacchante. La Flore et la Bacchante deviennent pour la petite fille des « personnes naturelles ». À part Deschartres et Hyppolite, l'univers réel, et imaginaire, d'Aurore est exclusivement féminin : bonne-maman, maman, Ursule, Caroline, Clotilde, les fées, les nymphes, les Bacchantes. Pour Aurore, l'univers ne peut être que féminin. Ne dit-on pas *la* terre ? Cette bonne terre où il est si doux de se rouler. Dès qu'elle touche terre, Aurore reprend des forces ! George gardera cette bienfaisante habitude.

Née une première fois à Paris, Aurore renaît à Nohant pendant ces six années et se métamorphose en une authentique Berrichonne qui sait parler berrichon aussi bien qu'Ursule et Hyppolite. Pour enrayer un peu ces influences provinciales, Mme Dupin de Francueil entraîne, de temps en temps, sa petite-fille à Paris.

Pendant un premier séjour dans la capitale, de février à avril 1810, et un deuxième pendant l'hiver 1811-1812, Mme Dupin de Francueil constate, sans aucun plaisir, que l'emprise de Sophie-Victoire sur Aurore est intacte. La petite ne voit qu'avec les yeux de sa mère. Elle rend visite à sa tante, Lucie Maréchal, et à sa cousine Clotilde. Elle admire, au passage, les nouvelles boutiques des boulevards. Et, comme autrefois devant les liserons des routes d'Espagne, sa mère dit : « Regarde, c'est joli. » Agacée par cette aveugle admiration, compréhensible chez la fille d'un boutiquier, bonne-maman introduit sa petite-fille dans ce qui sera plus tard, espère-t-elle, son vrai milieu, celui des salons et des vieilles comtesses.

Aurore rend visite à l'oncle Beaumont, aux cousins René et Auguste de Villeneuve. Elle se lie d'amitié avec Pauline de Pontcarré, fille d'une amie de bonne-maman. Pauline est aussi blonde qu'Aurore est brune. Pauline a déjà acquis cette tenue, ce maintien, ces manières que bonne-maman voudrait tant voir se développer chez sa petite-fille qui n'en a cure, encouragée dans son refus des bons usages du monde par Sophie-Victoire.

La guerre entre la belle-mère et la belle-fille reprend de plus belle. L'entourage compte les points. Les vieilles comtesses, Julie et Deschartres sont pour bonne-maman. Rose, la bonne d'Aurore, Ursule et Hyppolite sont pour maman.

Quand, en mai 1812, Mme Dupin de Francueil et sa petite-fille retournent à Nohant, Sophie-Victoire décide de s'installer définitivement à Paris. Elle ne viendra plus dans le Berry qu'en visiteuse. À chacune de ses trop rares, et trop courtes, visites, Aurore espère repartir avec sa mère. À chaque fois, son espoir est déçu. Julie se moque de la déception de l'enfant, à qui elle dit : « Vous voulez donc retourner dans votre petit grenier manger des haricots ? » Aurore ne demanderait pas mieux que de retourner dans le petit appartement de sa mère, si injustement qualifié de « grenier », pour y manger non pas des haricots, mais un pot-au-feu que Sophie-Victoire réussit comme personne.

En 1812, en sa septième année, Aurore « subit » le préceptorat de Deschartres. Avec Deschartres, elle apprend l'histoire, la géographie, un peu de ce latin qui l'ennuie tant et un peu de cette arithmétique qu'elle déteste. Elle apprend mieux la musique avec bonne-maman. Elle apprend surtout, en cet été 1812, à s'amuser, le dimanche, avec Ursule et ses trois sœurs, à des jeux en vogue dans le Berry d'alors comme l'aveuglat (le colin-maillard) ou les évalines (les osselets).

Quand Aurore revient de ces jeux dominicaux, Mme Dupin de Francueil, sur un ton sans réplique, prodigue reproches et conseils : « Ma fille, vous marchez comme une paysanne, vous avez encore perdu vos gants, vous êtes trop grande pour faire des choses pareilles. »

Aurore est assez grande pour prendre conscience qu'elle ne doit plus mettre les pieds à la cuisine, ni tutoyer les domestiques, afin qu'ils perdent l'habitude de la tutoyer. Et ne plus dire « vous » à bonne-maman, à qui elle doit parler à la troisième personne du singulier : « Ma bonne-maman veut-elle me permettre d'aller au jardin ? »

Bonne-maman veut par-dessus tout que sa petite-fille acquière les grâces en vogue sous l'Ancien Régime. Point de grâce naturelle, mais des grâces acquises, une certaine façon de s'asseoir, de se lever, de marcher, de tenir sa fourchette, de présenter un objet, tout cela devient, à force de pratique, comme une seconde nature. Tout cela est pour Sophie-Victoire le comble du ridicule et du démodé ! Forte de l'approbation maternelle, Aurore déclare : « Je voudrais être un bœuf ou un âne ; on me laisserait marcher à ma guise et brouter comme je l'entendrais au lieu qu'on veut faire de moi un chien savant. » Mme Dupin de Francueil et ses vieilles comtesses en frémissent d'horreur ; Aurore veut être une sauvage. La sauvage qu'elle sait être, en cachette, celle qui saute par la fenêtre pour courir la campagne et cuire des pommes de terre sous la cendre.

Avril 1814. Sophie-Victoire passe ce mois à Nohant, et c'est peut-être pendant ce mois-là que se situe l'un des plus désagréables épisodes de la guerre de six ans.

Afin de ne pas perdre un instant de la divine présence de sa mère, Aurore la rejoint dans son lit pour dormir la tête sur son épaule. Et cela, malgré l'interdiction formelle de bonne-maman qui, avertie par Julie, survient une nuit, comme la statue de la justice. La statue de la justice et la déesse-mère échangent « des paroles assez vives ».

Mme Dupin de Francueil assure qu'une telle habitude n'est ni saine ni chaste. Aurore se demande ce que veut dire « chaste » quand elle entend sa mère répondre : « Si quelqu'un manque de chasteté, c'est vous pour avoir de pareilles idées. C'est en parlant trop tôt de cela aux enfants qu'on leur ôte l'innocence de leur esprit, et je vous assure bien que si c'est comme cela que vous comptez élever ma fille, vous auriez mieux fait de me la laisser. Mes caresses sont plus honnêtes que vos pensées. »

Mme Dupin de Francueil en perd la respiration. Elle subit un insupportable affront, une affreuse défaite. Elle devra subir pire. Après cette bataille nocturne, quand bonne-maman veut prendre son Aurore sur ses genoux et l'embrasser, celle-ci se dégage d'un : « Puisque ce n'est pas chaste, je ne veux pas embrasser. »

Septembre-octobre 1815. Le nouveau séjour de Sophie-Victoire à Nohant se termine par une escarmouche encore plus pénible que la précédente. Il n'y est plus question de chasteté, mais d'intérêt. En 1815, l'année de Waterloo, Aurore a onze ans. Sa mère ne peut plus la tromper par des promesses, des « à bientôt » qui se traduisent par des mois et des mois d'interminable absence. Sa mère ne cherche plus à la tromper. La veille de son départ, Sophie-Victoire ne cache pas à Aurore qu'elle étouffe dans ce Berry rigoriste et puritain, qu'elle doit s'occuper de Caroline, et qu'elle ne viendra plus à Nohant que de loin en loin. Ce qui signifie, en clair, qu'elle n'y viendra plus. Aurore croit entendre un arrêt de mort. Elle se roule par terre, supplie sa mère de l'emmener à Paris, et, devant son refus, déclare qu'elle ira la rejoindre, à pied s'il le faut. Atterrée par une telle détermination, Sophie-Victoire explique sa situation financière. Si Aurore suivait sa mère à Paris, Mme Dupin de Francueil réduirait la rente qu'elle verse à sa bru à 1 500 francs. Aurore assure que cette somme suffirait amplement. « Nous serons si pauvres que tu ne pourras pas le supporter, et tu me redemanderas ton Nohant et tes quinze mille livres de rente »[1], réplique sa mère. « Jamais, s'écrie Aurore, nous serons pauvres, mais nous serons ensemble. » Et elle développe le thème « Je veux être pauvre avec toi, on n'est pas heureuse sans sa mère » avec une telle passion que Sophie-Victoire, ébranlée, se plaît à rêver tout haut. Elle échafaude un brillant avenir dans lequel, enfin réunie avec Aurore et Caroline, elle ouvrirait un magasin de modes. Ne sait-elle pas faire des chapeaux et des bonnets ? Emportée par son rêve, elle décrit la boutique qu'elle ouvrira à Orléans où elle a déjà travaillé. Oui, à Orléans, avec, à l'entrée de la boutique, en grosses lettres, « Madame Veuve Dupin, marchande de modes ».

Sophie-Victoire se rend aux raisons d'Aurore qui ne sera jamais à sa place dans le milieu de Mme Dupin de Francueil : « On ne t'y pardonnera pas d'être ma fille et d'avoir eu pour grand-père un marchand d'oiseaux. » Aurore exulte et montre au dîner une excitation extrême dont bonne-maman s'alarme et que maman doit calmer. À la fin de ce dîner, toute joie semble avoir abandonné Sophie-Victoire, qui montre un visage préoccupé. La boutique à Orléans est en train de s'envoler en fumée...

Préoccupée à son tour, Aurore monte se coucher et, craignant de ne plus voir sa mère avant son départ, et surtout de « ne plus pouvoir s'épancher avec l'objet de mon amour », elle lui écrit une longue lettre. « L'objet de mon amour » désigne évidemment Sophie-Victoire. Aurore aime tant sa mère que c'est à sa mère que s'adresse sa première lettre d'amour, écrite dans la fièvre, les larmes, à la lueur d'une bougie. La correspondance de Sand, qui comptera tant de lettres écrites dans la passion, dans la nuit, à la lueur de bougies qui s'éteignent et de la lune qui arrive à point pour servir de flambeau,

---

1. Cf. note de Georges Lubin dans les *Œuvres autobiographiques*, tome I, Gallimard, « La Pléiade », p. 1402.

commence là, avec cette première lettre à Sophie-Victoire.

Aurore place cette lettre derrière un portrait de son grand-père Dupin de Francueil avec cette recommandation : « Place ta réponse derrière ce même portrait du vieux Dupin. Je la trouverai demain, quand tu seras partie. » Sur le bonnet de nuit de sa mère, elle dépose un mot au crayon : « Secoue le portrait. » Aurore a tout prévu, sauf que sa mère changerait d'avis. Dans la nuit, elle rejoint Sophie-Victoire qu'elle trouve en train de lire sa lettre, et de pleurer sur leur rêve perdu de vie commune et de boutique. Aurore doit s'habituer à vivre à Nohant en compagnie de sa grand-mère. Ce serait une folie de partir. Ces paroles de raison prodiguées par sa mère, « c'étaient des coups de poignards froids comme la mort dans mon pauvre cœur ». Aurore exige quand même une réponse à sa lettre. Sa mère promet et renvoie sa fille se coucher.

Après avoir écrit sa première lettre d'amour, Aurore connaît, à onze ans, sa première nuit « de douleur et d'insomnie ». Ultime coup de poignard : après le départ de sa mère, elle secoue vainement le portrait du vieux Dupin, aucune lettre n'en tombe. « Ce fut pour moi le dernier coup. (...) Je ne pleurais plus, je n'avais plus de larmes, et je commençais à souffrir d'un mal plus profond et plus déchirant que l'absence. Je me disais que ma mère ne m'aimait pas autant qu'elle était aimée de moi. »

Mal aimée par sa mère qui ne voit en elle qu'une bonne rente, mal aimée par sa grand-mère qui ne voit en elle qu'un autre Maurice, c'est le destin sentimental de Sand la mal-aimée qui se joue dans le cœur de cette Aurore de onze ans. Aussi indomptable que Leopardo, elle n'en décide pas moins de mener à bien ses projets de fuite à Paris et amasse un trésor de guerre, un collier d'ambre, un peigne en corail, une bonbonnière en écaille, objets qu'elle vendra, ou échangera, chemin faisant, contre le gîte et le couvert.

Ces projets sont anéantis par une crise qui saisit sa grand-mère ; elle a un étourdissement et reste « pétrifiée pendant une heure ». Deschartres s'en effraye et communique sa peur à Aurore qui se jure de renoncer à la fuite si sa bonne-maman guérit. Son instinct d'infirmière, sa sensibilité à tout ce qui souffre provoquent ce revirement. De toute façon, Aurore doit se résigner à vivre à Nohant. Sa mère semble avoir complètement oublié leurs projets « romanesques » dont elle ne parle plus dans ses très rares lettres qui abondent en conseils du genre « Cours, marche, reprends tes bonnes joues roses, ne pense à rien que de gai ».

Entre les somnolences de bonne-maman, les insolences de Julie qui en profite pour régenter Nohant, les turbulences d'Hyppolite, les exigences de Deschartres, Aurore se dégoûte de tout, boude ou pleure pour un rien. À ces calamités, il faut ajouter les violences de sa bonne, Rose, qui, elle aussi, met à profit les « absences » de Mme Dupin de Francueil pour brutaliser Aurore. Oui, Aurore est battue pour avoir déchiré sa robe ou cassé son sabot, et encore plus si elle crie. Elle supporte ces duretés de Rose parce que Rose est, à Nohant, la seule personne avec qui elle puisse parler de sa mère. Et tout simplement parce qu'elle aime Rose et qu'elle a besoin d'aimer. En rapportant cet épisode dans *Histoire de ma vie*, Sand l'accompagne de ces lignes révélatrices : « Je suis ainsi faite que je supporte longtemps, très longtemps, ce qui est intolérable. Il est vrai que quand ma patience est lassée, je brise tout d'un coup et pour jamais. »

Ces lignes présagent, et expliquent, les futures, les éclatantes ruptures avec ses amants, ses amies, ses éditeurs qui marqueront la vie de Sand. À onze ans, Aurore sait qu'elle est « ainsi faite » pour supporter « l'humiliation » de son esclavage par « une sorte de stoïcisme naturel ».

Stoïcisme qui ne la rend guère heureuse. Et ce ne sont pas les visites à Nohant de son cousin, René de

Villeneuve, ou des vieilles comtesses, comme Mme de La Marlière ou Mme de Pardaillan, qui atténueront ses tristesses.

Autre sujet de peine, en mars 1816, Hyppolite, qui a dix-sept ans, s'enrôle au troisième hussard. Voilà Aurore réduite à la seule compagnie de sa grand-mère, de Deschartres, de Julie et de Rose. Elle trouve un remède à sa solitude dans l'étude de l'histoire dont elle apprécie « les grands caractères, les belles actions, les étranges aventures, les détails poétiques ». Peu à peu, en rendant compte, par écrit, de certains épisodes de l'histoire, elle arrive à glisser au milieu de son récit « une petite description ». Elle fait intervenir « le soleil ou l'orage, les fleurs, les ruines, les monuments » dont elle fera un grand usage dans son œuvre romanesque. George Sand perce déjà en cette Aurore qui, à douze ans, compose deux textes, l'un sur la vallée Noire, l'autre sur une nuit d'été avec clair de lune [1].

Éblouie, bonne-maman déclare à qui veut l'entendre qu'il s'agit là d'authentiques chefs-d'œuvre. Nettement moins admirative, maman se moque de ces balbutiements littéraires : « Tes belles phrases m'ont bien fait rire, j'espère que tu ne vas pas te mettre à parler comme ça. » Aurore, qui, comme Sand, est indifférente aux critiques, répond : « Sois tranquille, ma petite maman, je ne deviendrai pas une pédante, et quand je voudrai te dire que je t'aime, que je t'adore, je te le dirai tout bonnement comme le voilà dit. » Décidément, bonne-maman et maman ne s'accorderont jamais, même pas pour reconnaître les talents de leur Aurore !

Trouvant consolation et inspiration dans l'histoire, dans la lecture d'œuvres comme l'*Iliade* et *La Jérusalem délivrée*, Aurore, prise entre les dieux païens de cette *Iliade* et les dieux chrétiens de cette

___
1. Quand je vous disais que George Sand était née George Sand, en voilà encore une preuve.

Jérusalem, s'invente une divinité. « Puisqu'on ne m'enseignait aucune divinité, je m'aperçus qu'il m'en fallait une, et je m'en fis une. (...) Et voilà qu'en rêvant la nuit, il me vint une figure et un nom. Le nom ne signifiait rien que je sache ; c'était un assemblage fortuit de syllabes comme il s'en forme dans les songes. Mon fantôme s'appelait Corambé et ce nom lui resta. Il devint le titre de mon roman et le dieu de ma religion. »

Corambé est la première créature qui jaillit de ce cerveau de douze ans. Il est Jésus, il est Orphée, elle est Pallas Athénée, elle est Diane, Corambé ne se limitant pas à un sexe. Au gré de l'imagination d'Aurore, Corambé est tantôt dieu, tantôt déesse, ou, encore mieux, « c'était ma mère ». On ne saurait pousser plus loin l'adoration, la divinisation de sa mère !

À ce, ou à cette, Corambé, Aurore dresse un autel secret dans les profondeurs d'un petit bois du parc de Nohant, des fourrés où personne ne pénètre. Elle bâtit un autel de cailloux, de coquilles, de mousses. Elle offre à sa divinité des papillons, des lézards, des oiseaux. Elle se souvient alors d'un pauvre fou qui venait à Nohant et à qui l'on demandait ce qu'il voulait. « Je cherche la tendresse », répondait-il. Commentaire d'Aurore : « Je crois que j'étais devenue un peu comme ce pauvre fou qui cherchait la tendresse. Je la demandais aux bois, aux plantes, au soleil, aux animaux, et à je ne sais quel être invisible qui n'existait que dans mes rêves. »

Un jour, son asile est découvert par l'un de ses compagnons de jeu qui s'exclame : « Ah ! mam'selle, le joli petit reposoir de la Fête-Dieu. » Adieu asile, adieu tendresse, adieu Corambé, le charme est rompu. Aurore enterre les cailloux, les mousses, les coquilles au pied de trois érables. Corambé, émanation de l'esprit de la terre, revient à la terre...

Aux bouillonnements de l'esprit s'ajoutent les effervescences physiques propres à la douzième année. Quand elle n'est pas immobile en train de dévorer un livre, Aurore se livre à la passion de l'action. Avec des Fanchon, des Liline, des Sylvain, des Pierrot, elle court les champs, traverse les ruisseaux, garde les troupeaux, boit le lait des chèvres, déguste les mûres des buissons, tout devient alors régal. Quelle mélancolie résisterait à une bouchée de galette, ou à une glissade sur une meule de foin ?

À l'époque des moissons, la généreuse Aurore arrache des épis des gerbes pour les donner aux glaneuses, ce qui ne manque pas de provoquer les gronderies de Deschartres, très strict sur les droits des propriétaires. « C'est de cette époque particulièrement que datent les grandes et fastidieuses instructions que le bon Deschartres entreprit de me faire goûter sur les avantages et les plaisirs de la propriété. » Par réaction, Aurore décrète l'égalité des fortunes et le partage des propriétés. Deschartres, à qui elle expose son utopie, lève les yeux au ciel et déclare : « Il faut combattre en vous ces instincts de prodigalité que vous tenez de votre père. »

Deschartres essaie d'initier Aurore au fonctionnement d'un domaine comme Nohant. Devant les bâillements, ou les folies, que débite Aurore, il soupire : « C'est absolument comme son père ; de l'intelligence pour certaines choses inutiles et brillantes, mais néant en fait de notions pratiques ! Pas de logique, pas un grain de logique ! »

Le dialogue entre Deschartres et Aurore tourne vite au dialogue de sourds. Quand Deschartres évoque le rendement d'une terre, Aurore ne voit que « poésie des scènes champêtres ». Elle enrage : « Me sentant devenir chaque jour artiste, avec des instincts de poésie et de tendresse, je maudissais le sort qui m'avait fait naître dame et châtelaine contre mon gré. »

Aurore la révoltée doit pourtant sacrifier aux convenances et faire tardivement, en 1817, sa première communion. Bonne-maman, qui a gardé l'esprit philosophe du dix-huitième siècle, prie sa petite-fille d'accomplir « cet acte de bienséance » sans y croire et sans aller « jusqu'à croire que j'allais " manger mon Créateur " ».

Aurore se confesse « avec une extrême répugnance » et, le jour de sa première communion, ne montre guère de recueillement. Ensuite, et c'est plus important, elle assiste à des opéras à La Châtre et en est transportée. Avec Charles, fils de ces Duvernet chez qui son père a pris son dernier repas, elle se déguise et improvise des spectacles.

Corambé, les charmes de la campagne berrichonne, les lectures, les jeux, la première communion, les opéras, les déguisements et autres amusements ne parviennent pas à distraire complètement Aurore de sa passion, malheureuse s'il en fut, pour sa mère. Elle persiste à vouloir être « ignorante, laborieuse et pauvre avec elle ». Elle ne s'en cache plus, elle jette ses livres et ses cahiers à terre pour bien montrer son inexorable volonté. Elle est surprise dans son accès de colère par Julie qui la menace aussitôt : « Par mauvaise volonté, vous mécontentez votre bonne-maman, vous mériteriez qu'elle vous renvoyât chez votre mère. » Aurore bondit sur l'occasion et lance à Julie : « Me renvoyer chez ma mère, mais c'est tout ce que je désire ! » Julie rapporte ces propos, en les envenimant certainement, à bonne-maman qui s'en irrite et consigne sa petite-fille trois jours dans sa chambre.

Trois jours qui passent vite pour Aurore qui se voit déjà, et enfin, dans les bras de sa mère. Après ces trois jours sur les cimes du rêve, elle est plongée dans l'abîme de la réalité. Bonne-maman, fille du maréchal de Saxe et mère d'un colonel, quitte ses somnolences et retrouve ses instincts belliqueux pour se venger de la défaite infligée par sa belle-fille Avoir été accusée de manquer de chasteté par celle qui en manqua tant, cela n'est plus supportable ! Aurore doit savoir la vérité sur sa mère, et sans mesurer les ravages que peut causer un pareil aveu,

Mme Dupin de Francueil « lâcha le grand mot, l'affreux mot : ma mère était une femme perdue, et moi un enfant aveugle qui voulait s'élancer dans un abîme ».

Aurore croit vivre un cauchemar. Après avoir écouté ces paroles de dévastation et bu le calice jusqu'à la lie, elle quitte sa grand-mère, sans un mot. Elle rencontre dans le couloir Rose, qui demande : « Eh bien, est-ce fini, tout cela ? » « Oui, c'est bien fini, fini pour toujours », répond Aurore, qui s'enferme dans sa chambre pour se livrer « aux convulsions du désespoir », et aux horreurs du raisonnement suivant : « Si ma mère était méprisable et haïssable, moi, le fruit de ses entrailles, je l'étais aussi. »

Au bout de quelques jours « d'une indicible souffrance », Aurore se rend à l'évidence : elle continue à adorer sa mère, et à aimer sa grand-mère, « heureusement pour moi, le Bon Dieu m'avait faite pour aimer et pour oublier. On m'a souvent reproché d'être oublieuse du mal ; puisque je devais tant en subir, c'est un état de grâce. »

La grâce n'empêche pas que quelque chose soit brisé en cette Aurore de treize ans qui se met à vivre « comme une machine ». Elle rêve de s'échapper en Inde, ou en Amérique, si sa mère ne veut plus d'elle à Paris. Pour étouffer ses tourments intérieurs, elle se livre à des jeux de plus en plus bruyants que sa bonne-maman qui aime le silence supporte de moins en moins, et qui mettent la maison sens dessus dessous. Aurore « tourne à l'enfant terrible », selon Rose, sa bonne, qui n'ose plus la battre. Mlle Dupin a suffisamment grandi pour être de taille à rendre coup pour coup.

Constatant que sa petite-fille refuse d'être une demoiselle, Mme Dupin de Francueil accable la coupable d'un minutieux réquisitoire : « Ma fille, vous n'avez plus le sens commun. Vous aviez de l'esprit, et vous faites tout votre possible pour devenir ou pour paraître bête. Vous pourriez être agréable, et vous vous faites laide à plaisir. Votre teint est noirci, vos mains gercées, vos pieds vont se déformer dans les sabots. Votre cerveau se déforme et se dégingande comme votre personne. Tantôt vous répondez à peine et vous avez l'air d'un esprit fort qui dédaigne tout. Tantôt vous parlez à tort et à travers comme une pie qui babille pour babiller. Vous avez été une charmante petite fille, il ne faut pas devenir une jeune personne absurde. Vous n'avez point de tenue, point de grâce, point d'à-propos. Vous avez un bon cœur et une tête pitoyable. Il faut changer tout cela. J'ai donc résolu de vous mettre au couvent, et nous allons à Paris à cet effet. »

Réponse de la condamnée au couvent parisien : « Et je vais voir ma mère ? »

LA HONTE DU COUVENT
(1818-1820)

Ô honte! s'écria la mère Alippe,
vous riez pendant le catéchisme?

Cette guerre de six ans se termine par l'incontestable victoire de maman sur bonne-maman. À cette réplique, « Et je vais revoir ma mère ? », Mme Dupin de Francueil peut mesurer l'étendue de sa défaite : elle n'a pas réussi à extirper du cœur d'Aurore cette obsession, cette idolâtrie pour Sophie-Victoire. Mais la principale victime de ce conflit, c'est Aurore, à jamais marquée par cette lutte et à qui le couvent apparaît comme un paradis après les enfers familiaux qu'elle vient de traverser. « Je me réjouis d'être au couvent ; j'éprouvais un impérieux besoin de me reposer de tous ces déchirements intérieurs ; j'étais lasse d'être comme une pomme de discorde entre deux êtres que je chérissais. »

Avant d'entrer au couvent des Augustines Anglaises situé rue des Fossés-Saint-Victor, et placé sous la protection de Notre-Dame-de-Sion, Aurore a revu sa mère. Décevantes retrouvailles. Aurore pensait que sa mère jugerait ce séjour au couvent « inutile et ridicule ». Pas du tout. Maman, pour une fois d'accord avec bonne-maman, démontre à sa fille l'avantage d'acquérir des manières et des grâces. Aurore n'en croit pas ses oreilles. Tout ce dont sa mère s'était tant moquée devient estimable. Pour un peu, Sophie-Victoire conseillerait à Aurore de prendre le ton, et les façons, des vieilles comtesses ! Et puis, un couvent, ce n'est pas une prison ! Sa mère et sa grand-mère savent de quoi elles parlent, puisque c'est dans ce couvent, changé en prison par la Terreur, la prison des Anglaises, que toutes deux furent alors enfermées. Mlle Dupin ira donc chez les

Anglaises comme Mme Dupin de Francueil et Mlle Delaborde y sont déjà allées...

Le 12 janvier 1818, revêtue de « l'uniforme de sergette amarante », Aurore entre au couvent et se sépare de bonne-maman sur un dernier malentendu. Fervente admiratrice de Greuze, de Gluck et de Mme de Genlis, ces trois « G » qui ont donné au dix-huitième siècle le goût des larmes et des scènes larmoyantes, Mme Dupin de Francueil comptait fermement sur des adieux déchirants. Aurore retient ses pleurs afin de ne pas peiner sa grand-mère, qui, se trompant sur cette apparence de froideur, s'écrie : « Ah ! insensible cœur, vous me quittez sans aucun regret, je le vois bien. »

Aurore en reste stupéfaite, et peinée. Une religieuse, la mère Alippe, la console puis l'entraîne à une leçon de catéchisme. « Où vont les enfants morts sans baptême ? » demande la mère Alippe à Aurore qui ne sait pas. « Dans les limbes », souffle l'une de ses compagnes. « Dans l'Olympe », répète Aurore qui a mal entendu et qui, comprenant sa bévue, éclate de rire. « Ô honte ! s'écrie la mère Alippe, vous riez pendant le catéchisme. »

Promue, dès son arrivée, la honte du collège, Aurore ne peut que s'engager dans le « camp des diables », qui rassemble celles qui ne veulent pas être des dévotes. Ces dernières sont appelées « les sages ». Entre les « sages » et les « diables », les « bêtes ». Parmi ces sages, ces diables et ces bêtes, figurent Laurence de Montmorency, Cordélia de Greffulhe, Alicia et Alix de Mortemart, Anne de Chabot. La grandeur de ces noms laisse Mlle Dupin indifférente, comme elle l'est aussi aux plaisanteries de son nom que l'on change en « du pain ». Comme Aurore est la première à en rire, elle est immédiatement populaire chez les diables et participe à leurs jeux qui les entraînent à délivrer « une victime » à travers le couvent, un vrai dédale de couloirs obscurs, d'escaliers tortueux, de galeries sans issue, de cours, de cloîtres, de jardins, d'allées de marronniers. Avec Mary Gillibrand, une Irlandaise de onze ans, un vrai garçon manqué, Aurore se trouve vite à la tête des diables.

Diables, sages ou bêtes n'ont droit qu'à deux sorties par mois. Bonne-maman a exigé de maman qu'elle renonce à prendre Aurore pendant ces sorties. Ce serait encore retomber dans l'esprit boutiquier. Les cousins Villeneuve qui représentent l'esprit salon offrent de s'occuper de la pensionnaire, qui refuse. Ou elle sort avec sa mère, ou elle ne sort pas. Elle ne sortira donc pas. À l'étonnement d'Aurore, Mme Dupin de Francueil approuve sa décision.

Dans une lettre du 18 juin 1818, bonne-maman renouvelle ses recommandations : « J'ai tant envie de te voir parfaite au moral et au physique », et termine son homélie par : « Je t'embrasse avec toute ma raison, et toute ma tendresse. »

À treize ans, si elle n'est pas encore en état d'entendre le langage de la raison, Aurore comprend celui de la tendresse. Une tendresse qui l'unit peu à peu à cette grand-mère à qui elle envoie lettres et dessins. Mme Dupin de Francueil annonce, avec une satisfaction non dissimulée, qu'elle fait encadrer ces dessins tellement jolis. Voilà qui console un peu Aurore de l'éloignement manifesté par sa mère depuis qu'elle est au couvent. Elle se résigne à cet inexplicable changement puisque, en amitié, elle est comblée par Mary Gillibrand, Isabelle Clifford, Fanelly de Brissac, Anna Vié et Helena de Narbonne, à qui elle doit son surnom de « Calepin » parce qu'elle a toujours un carnet en poche sur lequel elle prend inlassablement des notes, s'affirmant par ce perpétuel besoin d'écrire qu'elle est un écrivain-né.

Au couvent des Anglaises, la coutume veut que les religieuses choisissent parmi les pensionnaires une « fille » dont elles s'occupent particulièrement. Aurore, qui ne peut agir comme tout le monde, va au-devant de ce choix en prenant pour « mère » la

« perle du couvent », Mme Mary Alicia Spring,
Mme Alicia.

La trentaine, des yeux bleus bordés de cils noirs,
Mme Alicia, qui semble représenter l'idéal de la
beauté féminine pour Aurore, s'étonne de ce choix :
« Vous, le plus grand diable du couvent ? Mais
voulez-vous donc me faire faire pénitence ? Que
vous ai-je donc fait pour que vous m'imposiez le
gouvernement d'une aussi mauvaise tête que la
vôtre ? » La « honte du couvent » explique tranquillement : « J'ai besoin d'une mère. J'en ai deux en
réalité qui m'aiment trop, et nous ne nous faisons
que du mal les unes aux autres. » Mme Alicia doit
se résigner à être une troisième « mère ». Grisée par
cette acceptation, Aurore voit en cette religieuse
« mon idéal, mon saint amour, la mère de mon
choix ».

Quand elle a joué au diable le jour durant, Aurore,
le soir venu, joue à l'ange, en se glissant dans la
cellule de Mme Alicia qui soupire : « Voilà encore
mon cher tourment. » Le « cher tourment » raconte
ses dernières bêtises, ses fous rires, ses chagrins, ses
engelures. Mme Alicia écoute, conseille, suggère, et
souvent gronde. Aurore ne dissimule pas son plaisir
d'être grondée par Mme Alicia...

Au couvent des Anglaises, Aurore commence à
écrire des vers, des alexandrins, ou prétendus tels.
Puis elle passe à la prose, compose un roman
« chrétien », puis un autre roman, « pastoral » celui-
là, et tellement mauvais qu'elle s'en sert pour
allumer le poêle, un jour d'hiver. Deux romans,
même mauvais, Aurore montre déjà les signes d'une
fécondité qui deviendra légendaire.

À quatorze ans, Aurore obtient une cellule, « la
plus mauvaise du couvent », pour elle seule. C'est
une mansarde située au bout du bâtiment qui
touche à l'église. C'est un four en été, une glacière en
hiver, Aurore y est heureuse parce qu'elle y satisfait
son goût de l'isolement et qu'elle y jouit d'un
superbe paysage : Paris s'étend au-dessus des mar-

ronniers. Elle ne se lasse pas de regarder « les nuages, les branches des arbres, le vol des hirondelles ».

À quinze ans, Aurore aspire à l'absolu. Un *Abrégé de la vie des saints* et un tableau qu'elle attribue au Titien et qui, placé dans un coin de la chapelle, représente Jésus au montdes Oliviers, décident de sa dévotion. L'air, les parfums du jasmin et du chèvrefeuille, l'atmosphère du sanctuaire, les prosternations des religieuses devant l'autel éclairé par une petite lampe, la lueur de cette lampe, tout porte Aurore au recueillement, puis à l'extase. Subitement elle croit. Elle n'en dit rien à personne, pas même à Mme Alicia. À partir de cet instant de révélation, un soir, dans la chapelle, « toute lutte cessa, ma dévotion eut le caractère d'une passion. » Elle fait une confession générale et reçoit l'absolution. Sans l'habileté de son confesseur, l'abbé de Prémord, Aurore serait devenue « folle, ou religieuse cloîtrée à l'heure qu'il est ».

Le 15 août 1819, elle communie avec une ferveur qui tranche avec l'indifférence de sa première communion. Ensuite, elle communie chaque dimanche. Elle se prend pour sainte Thérèse d'Avila. Elle ne dort plus, elle ne mange plus, elle ne marche plus, elle plane, elle vit dans l'extase. Excessive Aurore qui, sans transition, passe de l'état de diable à celui de sainte. Elle devient « sage, obéissante et laborieuse ». Elle passe l'été 1819 dans une béatitude complète. Elle reconnaît, certes, qu'elle s'abrutit de dévotion, mais que, grâce à cette pratique, « j'apprenais à aimer autre chose que moi-même ». Un tel revirement ne saurait passer inaperçu. La mère supérieure et Mme Alicia s'en inquiètent.

Au couvent des Anglaises, on ne sait que faire de cette petite sainte et on charge l'abbé de Prémord de la ramener dans le droit chemin. « Je savais bien que vous étiez folle, et c'est de cela que je veux vous gronder. Vos parents s'inquiètent de votre exaltation. Votre mère pense que le régime du couvent vous tue ; votre grand-mère écrit que l'on vous fanatise et que vos lettres se ressentent d'un grand trouble de l'esprit. Vous savez bien qu'au contraire on cherche à vous calmer », dit, en souriant, l'abbé à Aurore, à qui il inflige une douce pénitence : retourner à la récréation avec les diables. La petite sainte obéit et retrouve sa gaieté, ses amies, son calepin. Suivent six mois de bonheur. Aurore est citée en exemple, elle entraîne les classes, elle est l'enfant chérie des Dames Anglaises. Elle improvise des scénarios que jouent ses compagnes, on réclame l'auteur, Mlle Dupin... Elle est la gloire du couvent, après en avoir été la honte. Et comme un bonheur ne vient jamais seul, elle se fait deux nouvelles amies, Chérie et Jane Bazouin, qui prennent place, dans le vaste cœur d'Aurore, entre Isabelle Clifford et Pauline de Pontcarré.

C'est certainement par la mère de Pauline que Mme Dupin de Francueil a appris que son Aurore était « toute confite en Dieu », et n'hésiterait pas à entrer en religion. Bonne-maman voit l'état religieux avec les yeux de Diderot et porte ce jugement sur l'éducation reçue par sa petite-fille au couvent des Anglaises : « On l'élève dans la dévotion qui se passera, ou se modifiera, j'espère, le bal est un péché, la comédie un crime, que de sottise dans le siècle présent ! » Il est temps d'arracher Aurore à ces damnées Anglaises et de la ramener à Nohant !

Cette décision de bonne-maman tombe comme la foudre sur Aurore, elle qui se croyait déjà au paradis, elle qui était « l'amie de tout le monde, le conseil et le meneur de tous les plaisirs, l'idole des petites ». Dire qu'il faut abandonner cela pour retourner à Nohant, y être une pomme de discorde et recommencer la guerre. Elle décide de se soumettre, « sans murmure ». Elle est, une fois de plus, « brisée ». Elle dit adieu à Mme Alicia, aux petites, aux diables, aux sages, aux bêtes, aux marronniers, à sa cellule. Elle quitte le couvent au printemps 1820 pour une autre prison bien plus redoutable : le mariage. Mme Dupin de Francueil, dont la santé décline et qui envisage la mort avec « un calme philosophique », est fermement décidée à marier Aurore le plus vite possible.

UNE VRAIE FILLE DES BOIS
(mai 1820-décembre 1821)

> Je me sens de la race de ces bohé-
> miens dont Béranger a dit : « Voir,
> c'est avoir. »

Bonne-maman doit constater que le couvent n'a guère amélioré Aurore, qui continue à se comporter comme une vraie fille des bois : elle marche au lieu de glisser, elle s'assoit au lieu de se poser. Et des rêveries perpétuelles, ce désir d'être religieuse, ces silences. Un seul remède à ces excentricités : un mari et une ribambelle d'enfants. Le mariage est la panacée que le dix-neuvième siècle offre aux jeunes filles, aux sages comme aux folles. Avant de mourir, Mme Dupin de Francueil pourrait avoir l'ultime joie de choisir pour sa petite-fille un mari qui aurait l'approbation des vieilles comtesses, des cousins Villeneuve et qui aurait ainsi toutes les chances de déplaire à Sophie-Victoire. Un tel mari délivrerait Aurore de sa tentation du peuple, de son envie d'être du côté Delaborde.

Mme Dupin de Francueil prévient Aurore de ces intentions : « Ma fille, il faut que je te marie bien vite, car je m'en vais. Songe que je finirai épouvantée et désespérée, si je te laissais sans guide et sans appui dans la vie. »

Deux ou trois prétendants se présentent. Mlle Dupin ne s'en aperçoit même pas. Elle reconnaît qu'elle a gardé « un cerveau d'enfant » dans un corps de jeune fille de seize ans. Aurore et George garderont toujours cet esprit d'enfance. Et vers la fin de sa vie, Sand avouera être « restée enfant à bien des égards... ». En attendant, ce « cerveau d'enfant » ne fait guère avancer les projets matrimoniaux de Mme Dupin de Francueil. Trop fine pour ne pas se rendre compte que sa petite-fille n'est pas prête pour les noces, elle accorde à Aurore six mois, ou peut-être un an, de répit que l'on passera à Nohant. Inutile donc de séjourner davantage à Paris.

Aurore espère que sa mère les suivra dans le Berry. Sophie-Victoire détruit cet espoir avec une brutalité sans appel : « Je ne retournerai à Nohant que quand ma belle-mère sera morte. » Cette allusion à la mort prochaine de bonne-maman chagrine Aurore qui n'en assure pas moins sa mère de son entière soumission. Elle n'épousera personne sans avoir obtenu le consentement de Sophie-Victoire qui ricane : « Je ne m'inquiète guère de cela. Est-ce que tu ne sais pas qu'on ne peut pas te marier sans mon consentement ? » Aurore se demande sérieusement si sa mère est bien cette déesse qui prêtait parfois son visage à Corambé.

Le chagrin d'avoir quitté le couvent, la peine causée par les paroles de sa mère ne résistent pas au printemps de 1820 qui, à Nohant, est superbe. Ce ne sont qu'arbres en fleurs, chants de rossignol et cantilènes de laboureurs. Le « parler berrichon » sonne aux oreilles d'Aurore comme « une musique aimée ». Elle s'émerveille de retrouver son Deschartres, son Ursule, ses arbres, ses chiens. Tous et toutes célèbrent à l'envi le retour de la fille prodigue. Ah, que c'est bon de se sentir aimée, admirée et de courir les bois avec une liberté dont on avait perdu le goût. Aurore savoure les petits plaisirs d'une pensionnaire hors de sa cage. Elle dort jusqu'à neuf heures du matin sans encourir de punition, et arrange ses cheveux à sa guise sans être accusée d'indécence.

Peu après ce retour, Hyppolite revient, lui aussi, à Nohant. C'est maintenant un fringant maréchal des logis qui aime les chevaux et communique à sa demi-sœur son goût de l'équitation. « Cet exercice physique devait influer beaucoup sur mon caractère et mes habitudes d'esprit », reconnaîtra Sand.

Aurore apprend à monter avec une jument de quatre ans, Colette, avec laquelle elle s'entend tellement bien qu'elle la gardera pendant quatorze ans...

Au bout de huit jours d'apprentissage, Aurore et Colette sautent les haies et traversent les rivières...

La supérieure du couvent des Anglaises avait décrété que Mlle Dupin était une « eau qui dort ». Ce sommeil se termine, Aurore s'éveille à la vie et se déclare, après ces courses, « plus robuste qu'un paysan » et « plus téméraire qu'un hussard ». Ce n'est pas exactement ce qu'avait souhaité Mme Dupin de Francueil ! Qu'importe. Entre la grand-mère qui achève sa vie et la petite-fille qui commence la sienne, une intimité, une complicité s'établissent enfin.

Pendant l'automne 1820 et l'hiver 1821, elles lisent ensemble le *Génie du christianisme*. Mais Aurore considère la conversation de bonne-maman comme « le meilleur des livres ». Mme Dupin de Francueil parle, sa petite-fille écoute, recueillant avec passion les souvenirs de l'Ancien Régime et de sa douceur de vivre : « C'est qu'on savait vivre et mourir dans ce temps-là. (...) On jouissait de la vie et, quand l'heure de la perdre était venue, on ne cherchait pas à dégoûter les autres de vivre. Le dernier adieu de mon vieux mari fut de m'engager à lui survivre longtemps et à me faire une vie heureuse. C'était la vraie manière de se faire regretter que de montrer un cœur si généreux. »

Mme Dupin de Francueil ne doute pas que, quand elle ne sera plus là, sa petite-fille la regrettera infiniment. Aurore s'efforce de mieux comprendre sa grand-mère, pour qui elle ressent « une tendresse des entrailles qui ressemblait aux sollicitudes de la maternité ».

Entre une page de Chateaubriand et une partie de cartes, Mme Dupin de Francueil avoue à sa petite-fille que, sans la consulter, elle a repoussé un prétendant proposé par leur cousin, René de Villeneuve, le baron Rottier de Laborde, parce qu'elle l'a jugé trop vieux : quarante-deux ans. Aurore remercie avec effusion. Bonne-maman en profite pour faire le point de la situation : « Je suis tranquille sur ton compte à présent. Je te vois pieuse, tolérante, et conservant les goûts de l'intelligence. » Pour conserver ces goûts, Aurore se remet à l'étude avec Deschartres, qui l'accuse d'être « d'une ignorance crasse ».

Un soir, saisie d'illumination, Aurore comprend qu'elle peut réunir ses « deux mères rivales dans un même amour ». Elle se rend compte qu'elle aime également maman et bonne-maman. Elle se flatte de leur faire accepter cette égalité. Trop tard. Le lendemain de cette illumination, Deschartres vient réveiller Aurore avec l'annonce d'une triste nouvelle. Dans la nuit, Mme Dupin de Francueil a été prise « d'une crise d'apoplexie et de paralysie ».

Conscient de cet irrémédiable déclin et prévoyant le pire, Deschartres exige que son élève tienne la comptabilité de la maison et que les ordres viennent désormais de « Mademoiselle Aurore ». Il amène ainsi les domestiques et les fermiers à considérer Mlle Aurore comme la maîtresse de Nohant.

Malgré la gravité de la situation, Aurore se sent libre comme elle ne l'a jamais été. Le danger du mariage étant écarté, elle peut s'appartenir : « Il était décidé par le sort que dès l'âge de dix-sept ans (...) je m'appartiendrais entièrement pendant près d'une année, pour devenir, en bien ou en mal, ce que je devais être à peu près tout le reste de ma vie. » En effet, elle prend l'habitude de lire, et d'écrire, de dix heures du soir jusqu'à deux ou trois heures du matin. Elle ne dort que quatre ou cinq heures. Elle joue de la harpe et de la guitare. Elle dessine. Elle correspond avec ses amies de couvent comme Jane Bazouin, Émilie de Wismes ou Appolonie de Bruges. Elle discute à perte de vue avec Deschartres sur Dieu, la religion, la philosophie, les Grecs opprimés par les Turcs. Elle veut comprendre le monde par les livres et dévore, pêle-mêle, Aristote, Pascal, La Bruyère, Dante, Virgile, Montaigne, Bossuet, Shakespeare. La fréquentation des grands esprits la porte à douter du Saint-Esprit des catholiques. Sa foi est battue en brèche par le triste spectacle qu'offrent les messes dominicales à La Châtre : bourgeoises médisantes, glapissements des collégiens, « tripotage de pain bénit et de gros sous ». Aurore en vient à souhaiter qu'il pleuve pour ne pas aller à la messe et mener, sans interruption aucune, sa vie de fille des bois, peu conforme aux usages en vigueur. Elle est poussée à ces singularités par Deschartres qui n'y voit pas malice et qui lui suggère de mettre des pantalons pour monter à cheval, et chasser, plus commodément.

Bonne-maman, en voyant Aurore ainsi accoutrée, se met à pleurer et dit : « Tu ressembles trop à ton père. Habille-toi comme cela pour courir, mais rhabille-toi en femme en rentrant pour que je ne m'y trompe pas, car cela me fait un mal affreux, et il y a des moment où j'embrouille si bien le passé avec le présent que je ne sais plus à quelle époque j'en suis de ma vie. »

Bonne-maman n'est pas la seule à être frappée par l'accoutrement d'Aurore. À La Châtre et dans les alentours, on commence à juger « bizarre » cette demoiselle du château qui s'habille en monsieur et qui étudie l'ostéologie et la chirurgie avec Deschartres qui passe pour un vieux fou. Comble de l'indécence, Mlle Aurore étudie l'anatomie avec le fils d'un ami de Deschartres, Stéphane Ajasson de Grandsagne, qui a dix-neuf ans. Né à La Châtre, fils du comte de Grandsagne, Stéphane s'intéresse plus aux sciences qu'à la littérature et suit, à Paris, les cours de Cuvier.

Qu'une jeune fille de dix-sept ans prenne des cours d'anatomie avec un jeune homme de dix-neuf ans, cela paraît, dans le Berry de 1821, absolument scandaleux !

Aurore, qui sait qu'elle n'a rien à se reprocher, va partout la tête haute, sans souci aucun de l'opinion. L'opinion publique se venge de ce mépris en stigmatisant ces façons trop libres et en propageant les bruits les plus absurdes sur Mlle Aurore : elle se livre aux sciences occultes, elle entre à cheval à l'église, elle fait semblant de communier et emporte, dans son mouchoir, l'hostie qu'elle livre comme cible à Stéphane et à ses frères, elle déterre, la nuit, les cadavres dans les cimetières, elle s'amuse à tirer des coups de pistolet sur les enfants des paysans. Bref, il s'en faut de peu que Mlle Dupin ne soit présentée, comme le fut sa cousine par alliance, Marie-Antoinette, comme « une tigresse altérée de sang », et cela, avec autant de fondement !

Il faut bien constater que dès 1821, en sa dix-septième année, la fille de Maurice et de Sophie-Victoire a mauvaise réputation dans le Berry. Rien ne va plus vite que la rumeur et « rien n'est plus bêtement méchant que l'habitant des petites villes ».

À la fin de l'été 1821, Mme Dupin de Francueil donne des signes d'épuisement tels qu'il faut songer aux derniers sacrements. Qui sera capable de les administrer à celle qui n'y croit pas ? C'est alors qu'arrive à Nohant celui que Sand nomme « mon oncle par bâtardise », Mgr Leblanc de Beaulieu, archevêque d'Arles. « Il était né des amours très passionnées et très divulguées de mon grand-père Francueil et de la célèbre Mme d'Épinay. » Encore un bâtard dans la famille : Mme Dupin de Fran-cueil s'en est occupée maternellement, ce qui en dit long sur l'esprit de tolérance de l'Ancien Régime.

Avec une irrésistible rondeur, Mgr Leblanc de Beaulieu amène l'ancienne élève de Saint-Cyr à se confesser et à recevoir l'extrême-onction. Aurore est navrée de voir « fourrer » les sacrements à quel-qu'un qui, depuis Saint-Cyr, les a fuis. Bonne-maman apaise les scrupules de sa petite-fille d'un « Aie l'esprit tranquille, je sais ce que je fais. » Elle le fait pour éviter tout remords de conscience à Aurore et parce que la châtelaine de Nohant doit donner jusqu'au bout l'exemple du bon ton. Après quoi, Mme Dupin de Francueil retombe dans ses somnolences et doit être veillée, surveillée, vingt-quatre heures sur vingt-quatre.

Aurore s'épuise à soigner sa grand-mère et sombre dans une mélancolie qu'encouragent l'automne et la lecture de *René*, de Chateaubriand. Elle s'identifie complètement à ce héros et à ses désenchantements. Elle ne peut pas discuter de son malaise avec Stéphane, qui ne croit pas en Dieu. « Cela creusait un abîme entre nous et notre amitié épistolaire en était glacée. » Stéphane est retourné à Paris et à ses cours de sciences.

Aurore est livrée à elle-même, c'est-à-dire à la mélancolie. Elle finit par trouver un attrait certain au suicide. Elle voudrait s'ôter la vie, cela prend la forme d'une idée fixe, particulièrement devant une eau profonde, en pensant : « Comme c'est aisé. Je n'aurais qu'un pas à faire. » Une fois, une seule, en compagnie de Deschartres et de Colette, Aurore manque se noyer volontairement dans l'Indre. Elle échoue. Elle avoue son affreuse tentation à Deschartres, qui lui révèle que Maurice Dupin avait aussi des tendances suicidaires.

Désenchantement, mélancolie, tentative de suicide ne durent qu'un moment. Ce qui compte pour Aurore, comme pour Sand, c'est de vivre à la campagne, comme elle l'explique dans une lettre à Émilie de Wismes. « Eh bien, je suis assez bête pour préférer ma solitude à tous les plaisirs mondains. (...) Quelle conversation vaut celle de mes livres ? Quelle société, quels plaisirs, seront aussi doux pour moi qu'une belle campagne ? (...) Non, je ne pourrais plus vivre à la ville. J'y mourrais d'ennui. J'aime ma solitude passionnément. (...) Mais tu vas me prendre pour une sauvage. Sans ta politesse, tu me qualifierais presque d'ours mal léché[1]. »

Fille des bois, ourse mal léchée, Aurore est trop

---

1. Sand, à quelques variantes près, répétera, sa vie durant, cette profession de foi de sa dix-septième année.

différente des autres pour ne pas provoquer l'incompréhension et les critiques. Même sa mère se met de la partie et reproche à Aurore de négliger sa grand-mère pour « courir les champs », ou pis encore, puisqu'elle a reçu, paraît-il, Stéphane Ajasson de Grandsagne dans sa chambre, sans chaperon. Réponse indignée d'Aurore : « Où voudriez-vous que je reçusse les personnes qui me viennent voir ? Il me semble que ma grand-mère dans ses souffrances ou dans son sommeil serait très importunée par une visite. »

Bonne-maman ne sera plus importunée. Elle meurt le 26 décembre 1821, à l'âge de soixante-treize ans, en disant à Aurore : « Tu perds ta meilleure amie. »

L'APRÈS-BONNE-MAMAN
(janvier-mars 1822)

Mlle Lucie-Amantine-Aurore Dupin de Nohant a l'honneur de vous faire part de la perte qu'elle vient de faire en la personne de Dame Marie-Aurore Du Pin, née de Saxe, sa grand-mère, décédée en son château de Nohant le 26 décembre 1821. Prenez part à sa douleur profonde.

À la mort de Mme Dupin de Francueil, Aurore et Deschartres ne peuvent plus pleurer. Ils n'ont plus de larmes, tant ils en ont versé pendant ces jours d'agonie... Julie fait une ultime toilette à sa maîtresse qu'elle pare de dentelles et de rubans.

Le soir de l'enterrement, Aurore se retire dans la chambre de sa grand-mère. Elle y met de l'ordre, allume la veilleuse, ranime le feu et s'imagine que bonne-maman est encore là, avec son odeur de benjoin, son parfum préféré. Elle s'endort dans un fauteuil et ne s'éveille qu'au matin. Enfin, elle pleure sur l'oreiller qui garde l'empreinte de la tête de celle qui fut sa « meilleure amie », elle en est bien persuadée maintenant ! Puis elle quitte la chambre, à laquelle on appose des scellés. C'est la fin d'une époque.

L'après-bonne-maman commence avec l'ouverture de son testament dont Aurore connaît la principale disposition, puisque c'est en mai 1821 que Mme Dupin de Francueil l'avait rédigé, pendant un séjour de René de Villeneuve à Nohant. René sera le tuteur d'Aurore.

Fils d'une fille que M. Dupin de Francueil avait eue d'un premier mariage, M. de Villeneuve est entiché de noblesse, ultraconservateur, chambellan du roi de Hollande. Avec son frère, Auguste, il représente ce monde dans lequel Mme Dupin de Francueil souhaite voir s'épanouir sa petite-fille. Aurore a accepté de bon cœur ce tuteur de quarante-quatre ans qui ignore les préjugés provinciaux, qui ne trouve en rien excentrique le comportement de sa pupille et qui, après avoir lu certains de ses textes, l'encourage à écrire. On ne saurait rêver tuteur plus compréhensif, et qui ne se moque pas de ses « belles phrases » comme Sophie-Victoire.

Aurore s'est aperçue qu'elle ne reconnaît plus sa mère en cette personne fantasque qui vient de lui apprendre le mariage de Caroline avec un M. Cazamajou par un sec : « Caroline est lasse de vivre avec moi. Je crois, après tout, que je serai plus libre et plus heureuse quand je vivrai seule. » À bon entendeur, salut. Sophie-Victoire n'a plus besoin de ses deux filles pour être heureuse.

Début janvier 1822, Sophie-Victoire, accompagnée de sa sœur Lucie et de son beau-frère Maréchal, arrive, triomphante, dans ce Nohant où elle avait juré de ne revenir que sa belle-mère morte. Le premier quart d'heure entre la mère et la fille se passe bien. Elles s'embrassent avec une chaleur qui ne semble pas feinte. Puis, lassée par les fatigues du voyage, irritée par les airs renfrognés de Deschartres et par la présence de René de Villeneuve accouru pour l'ouverture du testament, Sophie-Victoire se met à lancer contre la défunte d'insupportables invectives qui consternent, et glacent, Aurore. La chaleur des premiers embrassements n'a pas duré.

L'ouverture du testament provoque de nouvelles tempêtes, soigneusement orchestrées par Sophie-Victoire qui, prévenue par on ne sait qui, savait que M. de Villeneuve était nommé tuteur d'Aurore et que celle-ci était d'accord. Avec l'assurance de celle qui n'ignore pas ses droits, elle invoque la nullité d'une telle clause qui ferait d'elle une mère indigne. Elle reprend ses invectives contre sa belle-mère, et contre Deschartres qu'elle accuse d'avoir « corrompu » le cœur d'Aurore. Elle reproche à sa fille de n'avoir plus pour elle cette passion manifestée pendant une nuit de l'automne 1815. « Que ne m'avez-vous prise au mot dans ce temps-là ! Je n'aurais rien regretté alors. J'aurais tout quitté pour vous. Pourquoi m'avez-vous trompée dans mes espérances et abandonnée si complètement ? » s'écrie Aurore.

Plus de sept ans ont passé depuis cette nuit de l'automne 1815 avec ses rêves de boutique de mode à Orléans, plus de sept ans de craintes, de tristesse et de désespoirs pour en arriver là ! Aurore, qui avait tant souhaité vivre avec sa mère, y est maintenant condamnée contre son gré. René de Villeneuve s'incline devant la volonté de Sophie-Victoire et quitte Nohant le 17 janvier.

Le lendemain, Aurore et sa mère s'en vont à leur tour. Aurore obtient, à grand-peine, d'emmener à Paris sa femme de chambre, son chien Pluchon et quelques livres. Elle a la ferme intention de regagner, au plus vite, le couvent des Anglaises. À sa demande, Mme Alicia répond qu'il n'y a pas de place. Les excentricités d'Aurore dans le Berry auraient-elles déjà gagné la capitale ? Dans sa correspondance avec ses amies de couvent, Aurore n'a pas caché qu'elle s'habillait en homme pour chasser et monter à cheval. Et ces mêmes amies ont pu rapporter ces nouvelles « diableries » aux Augustines Anglaises qui ne les ont guère appréciées...

À Paris, Aurore et sa mère, qui devaient habiter l'appartement que Mme Dupin de Francueil possédait rue Neuve-des-Mathurins, ne peuvent pas s'y installer, les scellés n'ayant pas encore été levés, et se réfugient chez les Maréchal, rue de Bourgogne. Aurore y retrouve sa cousine Clotilde, avec qui elle se sent en harmonie et avec qui elle joue du piano.

La musique n'adoucit pas les humeurs de Sophie-Victoire qui, ayant constaté que les fermages de Nohant n'avaient pas été réglés par Deschartres depuis trois ans, ce qui représente une dette de 18 000 francs, convoque une assemblée de famille, avec un avoué.

Sophie-Victoire va enfin pouvoir se venger des mépris de Deschartres, qui n'avait jamais caché son aversion pour l'ancienne « perle du district ». C'est compter sans Aurore, qui sait que Nohant ne rapporte plus rien et que l'on y vivait de « quelques rentes sur l'État ». Deschartres ne pouvant fournir, et pour cause, de quittances s'entend menacer de « prison pour dettes » et entend Aurore annoncer tranquillement qu'elle a reçu les 18 000 francs de la main à la main. Sophie-Victoire n'en croit rien et exige que sa fille donne sa parole d'honneur. Aurore, prête à tout pour sauver son « grand homme » à qui elle doit tant, jure, déchaînant les insultes de sa mère.

En représailles, Sophie-Victoire chasse la femme de chambre et le chien de sa fille et met à la porte M. de Villeneuve, venu transmettre à Aurore une invitation à dîner. Sophie-Victoire estime que Mme de Villeneuve aurait dû, en personne, venir faire cette invitation. M. de Villeneuve répond que jamais son épouse ne mettra les pieds chez Mme Dupin.

Les ponts sont coupés avec les Villeneuve et le seront pendant vingt ans.

Aurore a confirmation de sa disgrâce par son autre cousin, Auguste de Villeneuve, qui explique que Mme Dupin, son M. Pierret, les Maréchal sont des « gens impossibles ». Il conseille à Aurore de se marier avant que sa réputation ne soit perdue par de telles fréquentations. Aurore prend bonne note de cette idée de mariage présentée par Auguste comme un moyen d'échapper à la tyrannie de Sophie-Victoire. Mais elle défend sa mère, son bon Pierret et les Maréchal, dont le seul crime est d'appartenir au « monde moyen » avec lequel les Villeneuve ne peuvent s'abaisser à frayer...

La mésentente entre Aurore et sa mère n'en demeure pas moins complète. Sophie-Victoire s'obstine à voir en sa fille une ennemie dont elle jure de briser la « sournoiserie ». Un jour, elle brandit une lettre venue de La Châtre, une lettre contenant toutes les calomnies circulant sur Mlle Dupin et que Mme Dupin prend pour argent comptant. Dégoûtée, Aurore ne répond rien et se sent mourir.

« TIENS, VOILÀ CASIMIR »
(avril-septembre 1822)

Je ne pouvais pas ne point regarder
Casimir comme le meilleur et le plus
sûr des amis.

Aurore ne meurt pas, mais elle ne dort plus et perd l'appétit. C'est qu'il faudrait être une sainte pour supporter les changements d'humeur de sa mère. Et bien que Sophie-Victoire ait surnommé sa fille sainte Tranquille, Aurore ignore la tranquillité et s'éloigne de la sainteté. Elle ne supporte plus que les confesseurs s'immiscent dans ses affaires de famille, et, en ce printemps 1822, fait des Pâques sans ferveur.

Dans la vie quotidienne, Sophie-Victoire donne le spectacle du désordre et de l'agitation, tout ce que déteste Aurore. Mme Dupin veut sans cesse changer de logement, de restaurant, de chemise, de chapeaux, de perruque. Elle veut être où elle n'est pas.

Aurore se refuse à juger sa mère : « Elle m'aimait cependant, ou du moins, elle aimait en moi le souvenir de mon père et celui de mon enfance. »

Une nuit d'insomnie, Sophie-Victoire appelle sa fille qu'elle initie « au secret de toutes ses infortunes ». On pourrait considérer cette confession de 1822 comme la défense contre les accusations portées par Mme Dupin de Francueil, une nuit de 1817. « Tout mon crime, c'est d'avoir aimé », avoue Sophie-Victoire qui s'inquiète ensuite de l'effet produit par l'aveu de ses turpitudes. « Pour moi, votre passé est sacré », répond la magnanime Aurore.

Une paix est signée qui dure trois jours. Après quoi, Sophie-Victoire reprend ses invectives, ses accusations, ses agitations. Elle ne tolère plus sous son toit la présence de celle qui est exactement son contraire, cette sainte Tranquille qu'elle conduit chez des amis, les Roëttiers du Plessis, dans leur domaine du Plessis-Picard, près de Melun. « Tu n'es pas bien portante : l'air de la campagne te fera du bien. Je viendrai te chercher la semaine prochaine », dit-elle à Aurore. Sophie-Victoire ne reviendra chercher sa fille que cinq mois plus tard.

Voilà Aurore à nouveau abandonnée par sa mère. Elle ne s'en plaint pas et ne se roule pas à terre, comme autrefois. À dix-huit ans, elle se réjouit de la disparition de Sophie-Victoire et apprécie la compagnie de ses amis, Jacques et Angèle Roëttiers du Plessis. Jacques et Angèle l'adoptent comme une nouvelle fille, ils en ont déjà cinq. Ils reçoivent beaucoup et préviennent Aurore que, si parmi tant d'invités elle remarque un possible prétendant, elle n'aura qu'à en informer ses protecteurs. En attendant, Mlle Dupin profite de la bibliothèque, du piano, du parc et d'un cheval.

Lecture, musique, arbres et équitation, c'est tout ce qu'il faut pour assurer le bonheur d'Aurore qui se sent renaître au Plessis. Elle comprend qu'elle est faite pour la vie de famille et le grand air, et non pour passer le reste de ses jours dans une cellule. Adieu couvent, adieu dévotion. Aurore veut connaître une union aussi paisible que celle de Jacques et d'Angèle. Ce couple s'aperçoit que leur invitée n'est pas « la pédante », « l'originale », « l'esprit fort » dénoncé par Mme Dupin. Aurore s'amuse avec leurs cinq petites filles comme si elle-même était une enfant de leur âge...

Au Plessis, tout plaît à Aurore, sauf les prétendants. Elle en repousse deux, « un brave officier de marine » et un fils de médecin. Elle accepte le troisième, François Dudevant, dit Casimir, né le 5 juillet 1795 dans le Lot-et-Garonne, fils naturel d'une servante, Augustine Soulé, mais reconnu par Jean-François Dudevant, colonel-baron.

Entré à l'école de Saint-Cyr en 1813, Casimir en sort sous-lieutenant. Il étudie ensuite le droit. En 1821, il obtient le « diplôme de licence ».

C'est en mai 1822, à Paris, au café Tortoni, qu'Aurore aperçoit pour la première fois son futur mari, un ami de Jacques et Angèle. « Tiens, voilà Casimir », dit Angèle. Et Aurore voit « un jeune homme mince, assez élégant, d'une figure gaie et d'une allure militaire ». Casimir demande tout bas à Angèle qui est Aurore. « C'est ma fille », répond Angèle. « Alors, c'est donc ma femme ? Vous savez que vous m'avez promis la main de votre fille aînée. Je croyais que ce serait Wilfrid, mais comme celle-ci me paraît d'un âge mieux assorti au mien, je l'accepte si vous voulez me la donner », réplique Casimir. Il ne s'agit pas d'un coup de foudre, mais d'une plaisanterie. Casimir qui a vingt-sept ans ne saurait épouser Wilfrid qui en a huit...

Quelques jours plus tard, Casimir Dudevant vient au Plessis et se mêle aux jeux d'Aurore et de Wilfrid. Il s'établit entre Aurore et Casimir « une camaraderie tranquille ». Casimir confesse à Angèle « votre fille est bon garçon ». Et comme Casimir passe pour le gendre d'Angèle, Aurore, de son côté, reconnaît : « Votre gendre est bon enfant. »

Le « bon garçon » et le « bon enfant » se traitent de « mari » et de « femme », par jeu, sans embarras ni passion. Cette « douce camaraderie » est, à peine, troublée par la demande en mariage de Casimir qui, bravant les convenances, dit à Aurore : « Cela n'est peut-être pas conforme aux usages, mais je ne veux obtenir le premier consentement que de vous seule, en toute liberté d'esprit. » Voilà qui plaît à Aurore. Elle prévient, comme convenu, Jacques et Angèle, qui estiment qu'il est temps d'avertir la mère d'Aurore et le père de Casimir. On arrange une entrevue entre la veuve du colonel et le colonel. Sophie-Victoire trouve que son gendre n'est pas assez beau : « J'aurais voulu un beau gendre pour me donner le bras. » Le colonel-baron ne cache pas à Aurore qu'il la trouve extrêmement plaisante.

On en reste là, et quinze jours après, Sophie-Victoire tombe comme une bombe au Plessis. Elle prétend avoir découvert que Casimir a mené une existence « désordonnée » et qu'il a été garçon de café. Tout cela est faux. Mais Casimir sait habilement déjouer l'antipathie que Sophie-Victoire manifeste à son endroit, et en consoler celle qu'il considère déjà comme son Aurore. Ce qu'Aurore apprécie le plus en Casimir, ce sont ses prévenances, sa bonté, sa générosité. Agréablement surprise, elle avoue : « Je n'avais jamais été l'objet de ces soins exclusifs, de cette soumission volontaire et heureuse qui étonnent et touchent un jeune cœur. Je ne pouvais pas ne point regarder bientôt Casimir comme le meilleur et le plus sûr de mes amis. »

Pendant que Casimir et Aurore s'apprécient mutuellement, les discussions d'intérêt vont bon train entre le colonel et la veuve du colonel. Sophie-Victoire n'est pas sans faire remarquer que sa fille peut être considérée comme un riche parti puisqu'elle possède à Paris l'hôtel de Narbonne, en Berry le domaine de Nohant, et des rentes d'État. Casimir, lui, n'est riche que d'espérances. En effet, deux ans après la naissance de son fils, M. Dudevant a épousé une demoiselle de Saint-James qui ne lui a pas donné de descendance, et à qui il a légué l'usufruit de ses biens, représenté par le domaine de Guillery et des rentes. Ce n'est qu'à la mort de Mme Dudevant que Casimir héritera de la fortune familiale. Pour le moment, M. Dudevant père ne donne à M. Dudevant fils que 60 000 francs de dot.

Sophie-Victoire pousse de hauts cris et réclame le régime dotal, qu'Aurore juge offensant pour Casimir. Aurore cède devant l'évident plaisir de sa mère à exercer, une dernière fois, son autorité.

Le 24 août 1822, le contrat de mariage est établi sous le régime dotal. Sophie-Victoire ne cache pas une satisfaction qui est de courte durée. Elle apprend que le mariage est fixé au 17 septembre, date anniversaire de la mort de Maurice Dupin. Elle tempête, en vain, accuse Aurore d'être, comme d'habitude, une mauvaise fille. Sans résultat.

Le 17 septembre, à Paris, le mariage d'Aurore et Casimir est célébré religieusement à l'église Saint-Louis d'Antin, et civilement à la mairie du premier arrondissement.

Les noces terminées, quelques formalités restent à accomplir. Le 5 octobre, Sophie-Victoire rend ses comptes de tutelle. Casimir donne sa démission à l'armée qui l'accepte, le 18 octobre. Alors Aurore et Casimir prennent la route de Nohant.

DEUX CAMARADES EN LUNE DE MIEL
(17 septembre 1822-5 juillet 1825)

D'ailleurs mon mari ne m'inspirait aucun dégoût instinctif, il ne m'inspirait pas non plus d'aversion morale. Je ne demandais qu'à l'aimer fraternellement comme je m'y étais sentie disposée en recevant la première offre de notre association.

On a beaucoup épilogué sur ce qu'a dû être la nuit de noces d'Aurore et de Casimir, dont on ignore tout, en se fondant uniquement sur l'avertissement que Sand lance, en février 1843, à son frère, Hyppolite Chatiron qui marie sa fille, Léontine. « Empêche que ton gendre ne brutalise ta fille la première nuit de ses noces. (...) Rien n'est affreux comme l'épouvante, la souffrance et le dégoût d'une pauvre enfant qui ne sait rien et qui se voit violée par une brute. Nous les élevons tant que nous pouvons comme des saintes, et puis nous les livrons comme des pouliches. »

Ces conseils ne suffisent pas à prouver qu'Aurore a été « violée » par cette « brute » de Casimir. En tout cas, « l'épouvante, la souffrance et le dégoût » d'Aurore, s'ils ont existé, auront été éphémères ! Dès sa première séparation avec Casimir, en juillet 1823, Aurore est comme une âme, et un corps, en peine. Le 29 juillet, elle adresse à son mari une lettre qui commence par : « Comme c'est triste, mon bon petit ange, mon cher amour, de t'écrire au lieu de te parler, de ne plus te savoir là près de moi » et qui se termine par : « Adieu, bon ami, cher ange, adieu, mon petit amour. Tu sais comme je t'aime, comme je te chéris, comme je t'attends... reviens, je t'en prie à genoux, reviens. »

À d'autres hommes qu'à Casimir, Aurore n'écrira pas autrement. Il a droit au même vocabulaire, aux mêmes mots que les futurs amants de son épouse. Il est un « cher ange », le premier d'une interminable cohorte. Aurore aime prendre l'homme pour un ange, et feint d'oublier qu'il est aussi une bête. La découverte de la « bête » aura été des plus supportables. Ce n'est pas avec Casimir qu'Aurore connaîtra le plaisir dans son intensité. Ce n'est pas avec Casimir qu'elle atteindra cet « embrasement céleste » qu'elle pratiquera avec d'autres anges. Le mariage des Dudevant est un mariage de raison, et non de passion. Aurore et Casimir sont d'accord là-dessus. Ni l'un ni l'autre ne sont aveuglés par le désir. Ce sont deux camarades qui se mettent au lit et qui essaient d'être agréables l'un à l'autre. Aurore, dès le début, insiste beaucoup sur ce terme : « J'ai ici un camarade que j'aime beaucoup. » Camaraderie voluptueuse qui conduit à un certain bonheur. Là-dessus, le témoignage de Deschartres est capital qui, dans une lettre du 24 novembre 1822, note que le « jeune baron (...) aime sa jolie femme, comme il en est aimé, et entre nous, il peut se flatter d'avoir trouvé une maîtresse de maison très agréable, et susceptible de le devenir plus encore avec de l'expérience ». Et de conclure : « Le spectacle de leur bonheur augmente ma tristesse. » Faut-il que le bonheur d'Aurore et de Casimir, à Nohant, soit éclatant pour que Deschartres, qui ne s'est jamais consolé de la mort de Maurice Dupin, ni de celle de Mme Dupin de Francueil, en prenne ombrage !

Dès son arrivée à Nohant, Aurore a constaté qu'elle était enceinte. Motif de joie supplémentaire même si sa grossesse est pénible, avec vomissements, migraines, étourdissements. Émilie de Wismes s'inquiète de ces maux, Aurore la rassure d'un : « Ces peines-là ne sont pas grandes (...), il n'est pas de souffrance plus douce que celle qui vous annonce un enfant. »

Sur les conseils de Deschartres, pour éviter un accident, Aurore garde le lit pendant six semaines. Elle profite de son oisiveté forcée pour se livrer à des travaux d'aiguilles pour lesquels elle se croit peu douée. Avec l'aide de la chère Ursule, Aurore devient rapidement experte en ourlet et en broderie. Pendant que Casimir chasse, elle prépare la layette.

La neige est si épaisse, cet hiver-là, que les oiseaux, mourant de faim, se laissent prendre à la main. On en apporte à Aurore qui transforme sa chambre en volière. Elle est entourée d'autant de pinsons, de moineaux, de rouges-gorges que l'était son grand-père Delaborde dans sa boutique.

Autre sujet de satisfaction pour Aurore, Deschartres s'entend bien avec Casimir dont il célèbre « le caractère très doux » et qui « a un peu de la pétulance gasconne sans en avoir la jactance ». Malgré cette entente, Deschartres est décidé à quitter Nohant à la prochaine Saint-Jean. Il n'aspire plus qu'à la solitude et à la tranquillité. Après avoir servi trois générations de Dupin, la mère, le fils, la petite-fille, son désir est justifié.

Fin mai 1823, Aurore et Casimir regagnent Paris et séjournent au Plessis afin de montrer leur félicité à Jacques et à Angèle qui en sont un peu les auteurs. La rencontre chez Tortoni, avec son « Tiens, voilà Casimir », porte ses fruits : le 30 juin, Aurore accouche, à Paris, d'un fils, Maurice. De son propre aveu, elle tient ce moment pour le plus beau de sa vie. Pour son dix-neuvième anniversaire, quel magnifique cadeau que ce fils qu'elle allaite elle-même, se singularisant ainsi — une femme de sa condition devrait avoir recours à une nourrice.

Le jeudi 24 juillet 1823, Jean-François Maurice Arnault est baptisé en l'église Saint-Louis d'Antin. Il a pour parrain le père de Casimir, et pour marraine, la mère d'Aurore. Une marraine qu'il ne verra pas beaucoup. Estimant qu'elle n'est pas traitée avec les égards qui lui sont dus, Sophie-Victoire s'éloigne irrémédiablement de sa fille et de son gendre.

Pendant cet été-là, les Dudevant séjournent au Plessis. Aurore qui, décidément, voit des anges partout, baptise « Angel » son amie Angèle. Au Plessis, les Dudevant « donnent dans les plaisirs », c'est-à-dire qu'ils jouent la comédie et courent les

103

bals. Aurore n'aime pas danser et, l'ennui la laissant sans voix, les dames de Melun la surnomment « la muette ». Une muette qui sait parfaitement s'exprimer avec sa plume et qui, revenue à Nohant pour y passer l'hiver, écrit à Émilie de Wismes, devenue vicomtesse de Cornulier : « Mon cher Casimir est le plus agissant de tous les hommes, il ne fait qu'entrer, sortir, chanter, jouer avec son enfant ; à peine si le soir je puis obtenir une ou deux heures de lecture. »

On a voulu voir dans ces lignes les premiers signes de la mésentente entre Aurore et Casimir. La mésentente, si elle existe, n'est pas grave. Casimir est un rat des champs, et non un rat de bibliothèque. Casimir dépense ses forces physiques, ce n'est pas un pur esprit. Pendant l'hiver 1823-1824, à Émilie encore, Aurore fait la confidence suivante : « Je vis toujours dans la solitude, si l'on peut se croire seule quand on est tête à tête avec un mari que l'on adore. » Quand elle ne joue pas avec Maurice, ou avec ce mari adoré, Aurore relit les *Essais* de Montaigne. Mais ni les jeux familiaux ni Montaigne ne peuvent éviter à la jeune châtelaine de Nohant d'être contaminée par le mal de son temps, le spleen, qui peut être considéré comme une phtisie mentale et qui semble aussi inguérissable que la phtisie l'était alors. Le spleen du dix-neuvième siècle a son équivalent au vingtième : la dépression.

Au printemps 1824, un matin, sans aucun motif, Aurore éclate en sanglots dont la violence étonne Casimir. Grande explication entre les deux époux. Aurore dévoile à Casimir qu'il ne partage aucun de ses goûts. Joue-t-elle du piano ? Il s'enfuit. Essaie-t-il de lire pour plaire à son épouse ? Il s'endort. Parlent-ils littérature, poésie ou morale ? Casimir traite les idées d'Aurore de « folies, de sentiments exaltés et romanesques ». Le silence, le terrible silence des couples qui n'ont rien à se dire s'installe entre Aurore et Casimir. Mme Dudevant s'aperçoit que les connaissances engrangées en compagnie de sa grand-mère et des Dames Anglaises ne servent à rien. Son époux, M. Dudevant, ne s'intéresse qu'à l'art militaire et au droit.

Aurore se rend à l'évidence : « Mes connaissances étaient perdues, tu ne les partageais pas. (...) Je te pressais dans mes bras, j'étais aimée de toi. » Mais presser quelqu'un entre ses bras ne suffit pas à remplir les nuits, et encore moins les jours. Aurore s'ennuie. Et Casimir aussi. L'ennui, le formidable ennui du dix-neuvième siècle, n'épargne personne. Casimir n'aime pas le Berry et s'ennuie dans ce Nohant où il a voulu mettre de l'ordre. Il a vendu les vieux chevaux, congédié les vieux domestiques, abattu les vieux arbres, les vieux chiens, le vieux paon qui mangeait dans la main de Mme Dupin de Francueil. Aurore ne reconnaît plus son Nohant. Ces changements ne suffisent pas à expliquer sa crise de sanglots et la profondeur de sa dépression. Inquiet, Casimir sacrifie généreusement la moitié de sa dot, 30 000 francs, pour distraire Aurore et l'emmener passer l'été au Plessis.

Aurore la mélancolique s'efface devant Aurore la joyeuse qui joue avec les enfants, et comme une enfant : « Mon mari, comme beaucoup d'autres, s'étonnait un peu de me voir devenue tout à coup si vivante et si folle. » Elle se livre à sa passion des « amusements innocents », tellement innocents que Casimir se demande sérieusement s'il n'a pas épousé une idiote. « Certaines gens prirent de moi l'opinion que j'étais tout à fait bizarre. Mon mari, plus indulgent, me jugea idiote. »

Une fois, elle fait trop l'enfant et jette des grains de sable dans les tasses de café. Casimir gifle légèrement, mais publiquement, son épouse qui, sur le moment, ne s'offense pas trop de cette marque d'autorité conjugale. Elle saura s'en souvenir plus tard, à bon escient. Non, vraiment, quoi qu'en pense Casimir, Aurore n'est pas une idiote.

Début 1825, Mme Dudevant fait une retraite au couvent des Dames Anglaises. N'étant plus une célibataire excentrique mais une baronne légitime, elle est à nouveau *persona grata* et reçue comme telle. Elle revoit la mère Alicia, à qui elle confie ses tourments intérieurs, son spleen. Mme Alicia ne veut pas entendre parler de ces chagrins abstraits et essaie de remettre son ancien « tourment » dans le chemin de la réalité : « Vous avez un charmant enfant, c'est tout ce qu'il faut pour votre bonheur en ce monde. La vie est courte. »

De cette brièveté, Aurore n'est que trop persuadée. À vingt ans, elle estime n'avoir pas vécu. Un mari, un enfant, cela ne compte pas pour qui aspire à l'infini... Sans perdre plus de temps au couvent des Anglaises, elle retourne à Nohant à la rencontre du printemps, et de son frère Hyppolite qui s'est marié et a une petite fille, Léontine, qui a à peu près le même âge que Maurice.

Hyppolite a une nouvelle compagne qui causera sa perte : la boisson. Il promet de ne pas boire pour aider Aurore à recevoir dignement ses amies de pension, Aimée et Jane Bazouin. Des trois sœurs Bazouin, Chérie, Aimée et Jane, c'est Jane qui est la préférée d'Aurore. Aussi, quand Aimée et Jane annoncent leur départ pour Cauterets, c'est sans peine que Jane obtient d'Aurore la promesse de les rejoindre.

Le 5 juillet 1825, Aurore fête son vingt et unième anniversaire en prenant avec Casimir le chemin des Pyrénées. Ce jour-là, ni l'un ni l'autre ne savent que se termine leur lune de miel.

APPARITION D'UN ANGE
ET NAISSANCE D'UN ÉCRIVAIN
(6 juillet-15 novembre 1825)

> Voilà dix-huit pages que j'écris, il
> semblerait que je t'ai tout conté. Eh
> bien ! je ne t'ai encore rien dit...
> Guillery, le 15 novembre 1825

Le voyage dans les Pyrénées prend les allures d'une expédition — les Dudevant emmènent leur fils, Maurice, sa bonne, Fanchon, un domestique, Vincent — et débute sous de mauvais auspices. Aurore croit voir dans l'opiniâtreté d'une toux qui l'afflige « quelques symptômes de phtisie ». Elle s'estime mourante et note dans son Journal intime qu'elle ne reverra plus Nohant...

À Périgueux, elle se dit « triste à la mort » et corrige cette constatation d'un : « À quoi sert de pleurer ? Il faut s'habituer à avoir la mort dans l'âme et le visage riant » qui se veut stoïque. Et puis, adieu la mort, adieu le stoïcisme, la beauté des Pyrénées saisit Mme Dudevant : elle en suffoque de surprise et d'admiration.

M. Dudevant trouve que son épouse est bien excessive et en manifeste de l'humeur.

À Cauterets, Jane et Aimée sont là qui prennent sagement les eaux. Les amies s'embrassent follement. Aurore ne prendra pas les eaux, mais une leçon de vie. À Cauterets, elle découvre le vaste monde, les curistes, et non des moindres, comme la princesse de Condé ou le général Foy. Grisée de nouveaux paysages et de nouveaux visages, elle ne tousse plus.

Dès le lendemain de leur arrivée, M. Dudevant se livre à sa passion dominante : la chasse. Avec une inhabituelle causticité, Mme Dudevant note dans son Journal : « Il tue des chamois et des aigles. Il se lève à deux heures du matin et rentre à la nuit. Sa femme s'en plaint. Il n'a pas l'air de prévoir qu'un temps peut venir où elle s'en réjouira. »

Mme Dudevant chasse un autre gibier. Par l'intermédiaire de Zoé Leroy, une Bordelaise de vingt-huit ans rencontrée à Cauterets, Aurore fait la connaissance d'Aurélien de Sèze, vingt-six ans, neveu de l'un des défenseurs de Louis XVI et étoile du barreau de Bordeaux. En avril 1823, il a été nommé substitut au tribunal de cette ville. Ce séduisant magistrat est attiré par les irrésistibles changements d'humeur d'Aurore dont seul un mari peut prendre ombrage, et par les beaux yeux des Saxe et des Kœnigsmark. Ces yeux fascinent tellement Aurélien qu'il en oublie qu'il est fiancé à une Mlle Le Hoult.

À Aurore charmée, Aurélien découvre ce qu'elle croyait cacher à tous : les ardeurs de son regard et de son cœur, la beauté de son âme, la supériorité de son esprit et l'étendue de son instruction. Il conclut sa déclaration par un : « Vous seriez laide que je vous aimerais » qui laisse Aurore médusée. Elle écoute cette musique comme on écoute la musique des anges, ou comme Ève écoutait les promesses du serpent.

En ancienne élève du couvent des Dames Anglaises, en digne fille adoptive de Mme Alicia, elle repousse la tentation. Et peut-être aussi parce qu'elle ne veut pas tomber dans les galanteries des dames d'opéra qu'elle a pour ancêtres, ou dans les turpitudes d'une Sophie-Victoire, sans en avoir les excuses. Aurore résiste, ignorant que sa résistance attise les feux d'Aurélien qui se consume et qui boude. Pendant trois jours, il n'adresse plus la parole à Mme Dudevant. Pendant trois interminables jours, Mme Dudevant attend un mot, un geste. Et puis, ces trois jours passés dans la vaine espérance d'un signe quelconque, Aurore court après Aurélien à qui elle demande raison d'une telle attitude.

Aux déclarations d'amour fou qu'elle reçoit, elle oppose les avantages de la tendresse, de l'amitié et de la pureté. En réponse à ces propositions, Aurélien « imprime un baiser de feu sur son cou ». Ce « baiser de feu » trouble assez Mme Dudevant pour que M. Dudevant s'en aperçoive, s'en émeuve et parle durement à son épouse qui se « singularise » de plus en plus. Le Tout-Cauterets, comme le Tout-La Châtre, s'émeut de ces « singularités ». Et comment respecter les normes quand les montagnes, les lacs, les forêts incitent à la démesure ?

Pour ne pas perdre l'incomparable Aurore, Aurélien est prêt à tout, et à se soumettre aux nécessités d'une flamboyante pureté. Oui, ils seront irréprochables et n'auront à rougir de rien ! C'est à la grotte de Lourdes qu'Aurélien fait ses adieux à Aurore : « C'est à la face de cette nature imposante que je veux, en te disant adieu, te faire le serment solennel de t'aimer toute ma vie, comme une mère, comme une sœur, et de te respecter comme elles. » Ce « frère » qui se refuse à être incestueux peut presser sa « sœur » contre sa poitrine. Mme Dudevant entrevoit à cet instant ce que peut être le paradis sur terre : la cime des montagnes jointe au sommet des sentiments. Elle atteint le sublime et le sublime sera désormais sa drogue.

Mme Dudevant consent à descendre de telles hauteurs pour suivre son époux en Gascogne, à Guillery, chez M. Dudevant père. Dans les alentours de Nérac, Guillery est une bastide perdue dans les forêts de pins et de chênes-lièges. On y chasse les loups et les lièvres et on se gave de poulardes farcies, de canards truffés, le tout noyé dans des sauces à la graisse qu'Aurore ne supporte pas. Parmi les palombes et les ortolans, elle meurt de faim et maigrit à vue d'œil. Elle n'a pour compagnie que « d'importuns campagnards » et se réfugie dans sa chambre pour y écrire, ou dessiner. Elle écrit des lettres interminables à Zoé Leroy : « On me trouve l'être le plus maussade de la terre, et on s'étonne d'entendre dire que j'étais le boute-en-train des Pyrénées. J'ai perdu toute ma vivacité et toutes les grâces de mon esprit. » Elle écrit aussi à Aurélien pour qui elle retrouve la vivacité et les grâces de son esprit, et qu'elle appelle « mon tendre frère », « mon ange protecteur ». Dans le rôle d'ange, Aurélien remplace Casimir, qui, repu de jambon et de galette au maïs, dort en bas, dans le salon de Guillery.

Le voyage dans les Pyrénées a brisé le cercle de famille. Aurore s'aperçoit que Nohant n'est pas le centre de l'univers, que Casimir n'est pas le seul homme qu'elle peut avoir dans sa vie et que des étrangers sont plus proches que ceux que l'on nomme, à la légère, ses proches.

En octobre, invités à la Brède par Zoé, les Dudevant s'arrêtent à Bordeaux. Aurore a pris la décision d'arracher de son cœur « une affection non criminelle, mais trop vive pour être légitime ». Seule avec Aurélien, elle appuie la tête sur l'épaule de son ami et fond en larmes. Le sacrifice est trop dur. Aurélien tombe à genoux et supplie Aurore d'expliquer la raison de ces larmes. À ce moment précis, comme dans une comédie de boulevard, survient Casimir. Aurélien se relève et s'éclipse. Aurore s'évanouit et, quand elle reprend ses esprits, elle retrouve d'instinct l'esprit d'une Ninon de Lenclos qui, surprise en galante compagnie par un amant jaloux, protesta de son innocence et, devant l'incrédulité du jaloux, déclara sévèrement : « Ah, je le vois bien, vous ne m'aimez plus, vous croyez ce que vos yeux voient, vous ne croyez plus ce que je vous dis. »

Sans prétendre égaler la virtuosité d'une Ninon de Lenclos, Aurore s'en tire avec les honneurs de la guerre. Casimir est persuadé que son épouse n'est coupable que d'un instant d'égarement et qu'elle n'a pas franchi le pas.

Mme Dudevant pousse très loin ses avantages et fait admettre à M. Dudevant la possibilité d'un idéal ménage à trois. Puisque ses relations avec Aurélien sont pures, Aurore demande à Casimir le droit d'aimer Aurélien platoniquement. Casimir renâcle.

·En novembre 1825, isolée à Guillery, Aurore multiplie les lettres passionnées à Aurélien, et d'autres, plus calmes, à Casimir, en voyage d'affaires du côté de Périgueux. À Aurélien, des descriptions de crépuscule, de « quelques peupliers jaunis par l'automne » et de la mélancolie qu'ils engendrent. À Casimir, des considérations sur les « dures nécessités de la vie », l'achat de bas de laine pour Maurice, et un accès de colique. C'est le premier accès de colique que mentionne Aurore qui en sera frappée aux moments les plus inopportuns...

Le 12 novembre, elle exprime sa gratitude à Aurélien et doit s'arrêter net : il n'y a plus d'encre dans son encrier. Le 15 novembre, ayant rempli son encrier, elle assure aussi Casimir de sa gratitude : « Mon ami, mon généreux époux, je sens tout ce que je te dois. » Duplicité d'Aurore ? Non, sincère avec Aurélien, sincère avec Casimir, elle voudrait l'impossible. Elle voudrait Aurélien pour ami et Casimir pour époux. Tendre amitié et amour conjugal ne font pas bon ménage.

Il faut s'arrêter à cette lettre du 15 novembre 1825 qui, dans le premier volume de la *Correspondance*, va de la page 262 à la page 292, exactement trente pages imprimées. Ces trente pages marquent le véritable début d'Aurore comme écrivain. Le ton George Sand est trouvé, un sombre lyrisme, des élans fiévreux, un besoin forcené d'aveux qu'elle doit tenir de ses lectures de Rousseau, le sentiment de la nature et la passion des beaux sentiments, et cette extraordinaire fécondité qui la fait s'exclamer : « Voilà dix-huit pages que j'écris, il semblerait que je t'ai tout conté. Eh bien ! je ne t'ai encore rien dit de ce que j'ai à te demander. »

Suit un plan de conduite touchant et puéril. Les Dudevant n'iront pas à Bordeaux, cet hiver, les blessures sont trop fraîches. Mme Dudevant n'écrira jamais en secret à M. de Sèze et M. Dudevant pourra lire, s'il le veut, la lettre mensuelle qu'elle enverra à leur ami. Casimir doit s'engager à partager les études d'Aurore et à lui faire la lecture quand elle

dessinera. Plus de fâcherie de la part de M. Dudevant, plus de colère de la part de Mme Dudevant. Ils
ne se causeront plus de « chagrins mutuels ». Ce
sont de bonnes résolutions comme chaque ménage
en prend, après la tempête, et en attendant la
prochaine.

Ce qui importe, en ce 15 novembre 1825, c'est la
confirmation pour Aurore d'écrire comme elle respire. Elle ne cessera plus de noircir du papier. Le
papier, la plume et l'encre seront ses fidèles compagnons. Elle n'est pas encore totalement consciente
du pouvoir de sa prose qui étonne Casimir et fascine
Aurélien qui, lui, en plus, admire les yeux de
l'épistolière.

LES MORTES SAISONS
DE MME DUDEVANT
(16 novembre 1825-13 septembre 1828)

> (...) Et je pourrai à mon aise ne
> penser à rien. À rien ! Quand ne pense-
> t-on à rien ? Qu'on serait heureux si un
> quart d'heure dans la vie on pouvait
> ne penser à rien !

Au dix-neuvième siècle, en Italie, les épouses pouvaient avoir, sans que cela porte atteinte à leur réputation, un sigisbée, c'est-à-dire un chevalier servant, un confident. À la même époque, cette notion de sigisbée est inconnue en Gascogne, comme dans le Berry. À Guillery, comme à Nohant, Mme Dudevant ne saurait avoir un sigisbée, un double idéal, un Aurélien, sans que sa réputation ni celle de M. Dudevant n'en souffrent.

Casimir qui, dans la lettre-confession du 15 novembre, est présenté comme « un ange de bonté », Casimir qui devrait aimer Aurélien « comme un frère » trouve que la complaisance a des limites. C'est aussi l'avis d'Hyppolite, son beau-frère, qui a pris son parti et adresse de durs reproches à Aurore qui répond vertement : « Et si j'étais une femme inconséquente, oubliant tout à fait la dignité d'une mère de famille, si j'étais le petit monstre dont tu fais le portrait, tu n'en serais pas moins mon frère, tu ne m'en devrais pas moins secours, consolation, protection. »

Ni Casimir ni Hyppolite ne sont capables de partager cette utopie des sentiments qui fait les délices d'Aurore et d'Aurélien. « Ma pauvre femme a perdu l'esprit », gémit Casimir, complètement dépassé par ces subtilités sentimentales. Hyppolite recommande à Casimir de ne pas confondre bonté et bêtise. Hyppolite ne manque jamais une occasion de nuire à Aurore, qui, chaque fois, pardonne. Dans sa famille, dans ses amitiés, dans ses amours, Aurore est vouée au drame. En cette fin 1825, sa seule consolation, c'est Maurice qui, à deux ans, est déjà « un petit homme gai et caressant qui vient m'embrasser et me tenir compagnie quand je suis malade ».

Fin 1825 et début 1826, Mme Dudevant est en effet malade. Et comment ne pas l'être quand on vit avec ses dissemblables, dans ce Guillery, « pays de loups et de brigands » ? Mme Dudevant cesse brusquement d'être souffrante pour aller à Bordeaux, avec Casimir, retrouver ce qu'elle appellera, dans *Histoire de ma vie*, « l'agréable société des eaux de Cauterets ». Aimable euphémisme qui cache deux personnes précises, Aurélien et Zoé, le sigisbée et la confidente. Charmantes retrouvailles qui permettent à Aurore de constater que son emprise sur Aurélien est intacte, et qu'interrompt, un jour, et toujours inopportun, Casimir qui clame, sans ménagement aucun : « Il est mort. » Mme Dudevant, croyant qu'il s'agit de Maurice, tombe à genoux, terrassée de douleur. Quand elle apprend qu'il ne s'agit que de son beau-père, elle n'en donne pas moins quelques marques de chagrin : « J'aimais véritablement mon vieux papa et je fondis en larmes. »

Casimir et Aurore retournent précipitamment à Guillery où la veuve Dudevant, « personne glacée autant que glaciale », les reçoit, l'œil sec, fermement décidée à s'en tenir aux clauses du testament établi en sa faveur. Il ne reste plus au baron et à la baronne Dudevant qu'à s'enterrer, faute de mieux et de moyens financiers, à Nohant.

Casimir se résigne à être l'époux d'un phénix dont la réputation à Bordeaux (Aurélien et Zoé doivent y être pour quelque chose) est des plus grandes. Lors d'un séjour dans cette ville, M. Dudevant écrit à madame, ne cachant pas sa stupéfaction : « Tu jouis ici d'une réputation extraordinaire. »

À Nohant, Aurore s'applique à être une parfaite maîtresse de maison, commandant du rhum pour son époux, de l'huile d'Aix, du chocolat à la vanille, des bougies ordinaires, veillant à la dépense : « Nous sommes fort " crasseux " cette année (...) et la succession ne nous a pas fort enrichis. » L'éducation de Maurice l'occupe aussi, ainsi que le plaisir d'être à Nohant, en été. En juin 1826, elle écrit à Zoé — mais écrire à Zoé, c'est aussi écrire à Aurélien — son attachement pour la campagne au moment du solstice : « Il est un temps dans l'année où je suis toute animal. Ces mois de mai et de juin exercent sur moi une influence dont je ne saurais me défendre. (...) Je deviens oiseau, ou chien, ou lièvre. (...) Mais n'est-ce pas une grâce d'état ? » Elle se délecte du chant des grenouilles, comme s'en délectera, et presque dans les mêmes termes, quelques années plus tard, en Amérique du Nord, Henry David Thoreau...

Déchiffrer le chant des grenouilles, ou le langage de la lune, suffit au contentement d'Aurore. Elle épanche son lyrisme dans des lettres dont les « descriptions ravissantes » enchantent ses amies qui déplorent de ne pouvoir les égaler. La seule qui soit insensible à la magie de sa prose, c'est sa mère, qui ne désarme pas et refuse de venir à Nohant. Sophie-Victoire n'en consent pas moins à se charger de petites commissions pour sa fille, ou pour son gendre, qui veut acheter un collier d'or à Aurore.

L'achat de ce collier montre bien que Casimir s'efforce de plaire à Aurore et de l'arracher par de tangibles babioles aux séductions intellectuelles d'Aurélien. Mais le grand rival de M. Dudevant, c'est le spleen, l'ennui qui ronge intérieurement Mme Dudevant.

Casimir, ne sachant plus qu'inventer pour distraire sa mélancolique épouse, l'entraîne en janvier 1827, pour une quinzaine de jours à Paris, puis, en août, en Auvergne, au Mont-Dore. Aurore qui a lu Sénèque sait que voyager n'est pas guérir son âme. Le 12 août, au Mont-Dore, elle laisse courir sa plume sur le papier, et surgissent, dans cet essai d'écriture automatique, des aveux révélateurs. Elle voudrait d'abord ne penser à rien, « qu'on serait heureux si un quart d'heure dans la vie on pouvait ne penser à rien ! », puis pense à sa mère : « Ô ma mère, que vous ai-je fait ? Pourquoi ne m'aimez-vous pas ? », et entreprend un plan de ses Mémoires dans lequel on peut voir l'esquisse de ce que sera *Histoire de ma vie*. Après quoi, elle s'examine et se trouve vieille. Vieille, à vingt-trois ans ! Vieille et vide comme le néant. Néant qu'elle supporte grâce à Aurélien, qui remplace Corambé.

Elle rêve, loin de ce monde des réalités représenté par La Châtre, qui, une fois l'an, s'anime pour le Carnaval. Aurore s'y amuse, ou fait semblant, avec des camarades de son âge que tolère son camarade-mari, comme Charles Duvernet, un ami d'enfance, Alexis Duteil, Fleury dit le Gaulois parce qu'il ressemble à un homme des cavernes, Néraud dit le Malgache parce qu'il est allé à Madagascar. L'assiduité de ce quatuor à fréquenter la jeune dame de Nohant fait jaser La Châtre. Les excentricités de Mme Dudevant confirment celles de Mlle Dupin, et les surpassent. On plaint ce pauvre Casimir qui se console avec Hyppolite, en partageant son penchant pour la boisson. On boit, on danse, on aboie sur le passage de son prochain, on passe comme on peut de mornes saisons. Aurore se sent de plus en plus étrangère à son entourage et à ces divertissements. Il se peut qu'elle entrevoie l'adultère comme un possible moyen de rompre un peu la monotonie de son existence. L'adultère, oui, mais avec qui ? Le quatuor Duvernet-Fleury-Duteil-Néraud ne demanderait pas mieux que de jouer les grands airs de la consolation. Mais le quatuor n'est pas autorisé à passer les limites d'un facile compagnonnage : bals, promenades, chevauchées.

Prise au piège de son angélisme, Aurore ne peut demander à Aurélien de s'abaisser à de vulgaires étreintes. Leurs sentiments s'essoufflent à vouloir rester sur les cimes, et leur correspondance en souffre. Des silences s'installent dont on s'excuse poliment de part et d'autre. Aurélien ose avouer à Aurore qui ne cesse de penser et d'avoir des idées sur tout : « Je n'ai, je l'avoue à ma honte, d'idées arrêtées sur rien, personne n'a moins réfléchi que moi. Les trois quarts de ma vie se sont écoulés sans penser à rien. » En lisant cet aveu, Aurore doit se demander si elle a fait le bon choix, et si Aurélien est bien le frère chéri, l'ange qu'elle souhaite !

En cet été 1827, le quatuor s'enrichit d'une recrue et se change en quintette, avec un revenant, Stéphane Ajasson de Grandsagne. Il vient d'entrer au Museum pour y être le collaborateur de Cuvier. Il est « moitié poitrinaire, moitié fou ». Tout ce qu'il faut pour plaire à Aurore, pour qui la maladie et la folie sont autant d'excitants. Il est maigre à faire peur et se dit mourant. Aurore ne demande qu'à aider à sa résurrection. Soigner son ancien professeur d'anatomie, et aller plus loin dans la connaissance de leurs propres anatomies, voilà une occasion idéale pour Aurore, lassée de la camaraderie de Casimir et du platonisme d'Aurélien, de suivre les traces d'une Aurore de Kœnigsmark !

Avec M. Dudevant, Mme Dudevant a perdu son innocence et appris ce que Mlle Dupin ignorait. Avec Stéphane, Mme Dudevant n'a plus à tenir compte des scrupules de Mlle Dupin.

De cette liaison avec Stéphane Ajasson de Grandsagne, qui fut, en son temps, la fable du Berry, on ne sait pas grand-chose. Il n'en reste que les tardives confidences de Paul-Émile Ajasson de Grandsagne, fils de Stéphane, qui, en 1900, se disait détenteur de cent vingt-trois lettres de Sand adressées à « celui qui fut tout pour elle, celui auquel elle devait une partie de son savoir et de son immense talent d'écrivain ». Paul-Émile n'a jamais publié ces cent vingt-trois lettres, qui, pour le moment, n'ont pas été retrouvées. Attribuer à Stéphane une « partie » du talent de l'écrivain, c'est pousser la piété filiale un peu loin !

Comme on ne prête qu'aux riches, on a aussi attribué à Stéphane la paternité de Solange qui, légalement, est la fille de Casimir et d'Aurore. Évidemment, les dates sont là. Le 13 décembre 1827, Aurore est à Paris avec Stéphane, et c'est le 13 septembre 1828, neuf mois après, jour pour jour, que Mme Dudevant accouche de Solange. Elle est revenue à Nohant le 21 décembre. À quelques jours près, rien ne prouve que Solange n'a pas été conçue dans la hâte des retrouvailles entre époux, dans une rapide étreinte destinée à combler une absence commencée le 3 décembre, puisque c'est le 3 qu'Aurore a quitté Nohant pour se rendre à Paris, en compagnie de Jules, frère de Stéphane, afin d'y consulter des médecins, et non des moindres.

Broussais, médecin chef du Val-de-Grâce, diagnostique une irritation du cœur et de l'estomac. Landré-Beauvais, doyen de la faculté de médecine, estime que Mme Dudevant est phtisique. Quant à Rostan, médecin de la Salpêtrière, il trouve que sa patiente « n'a rien du tout ». Des trois[1], c'est certainement Rostan qui a raison. Fille de Stéphane ou fille de Casimir, Solange, en tout cas, n'est pas la fille d'Aurélien qui surgit à Nohant quelques jours avant l'accouchement de Mme Dudevant. Il montre sa « consternation déchirante » devant ce qu'il considère comme une trahison des serments de pureté et de chasteté qui avaient eu pour témoins les cimes des Pyrénées. Le sublime des sentiments qu'il portait à sa « sœur chérie » se brise devant le berceau et finit dans les langes. Les vagissements de Solange remplacent les musiques angéliques

---

1. Mme Dudevant est tellement occupée par ses médecins, ou par Stéphane, qu'elle néglige d'aller voir Deschartres, retiré à la Maison royale de santé, rue du Faubourg-Saint-Denis. Négligence qu'elle regrettera amèrement quand, en mars 1828, elle apprendra la mort de son « grand homme » ruiné et solitaire. Seule l'implacable Sophie-Victoire exultera en apprenant ce décès : « Enfin, Deschartres n'est plus de ce monde. »

qui unissaient l'étoile du barreau de Bordeaux au phénix de Nohant. Les astres lumineux qu'ils rêvaient d'être l'un pour l'autre se brisent et leurs débris s'en vont rejoindre les vieilles lunes et les mortes saisons.

UNE « VIEILLE » DE VINGT-SIX ANS
(14 septembre 1828-30 juillet 1830)

> Vous avez la tournure d'une femme de dix-huit ans, et moi celle d'une femme de quarante.
>
> Nohant, le 3 avril 1830

Un mari, deux enfants, un amant, quatre amis, voilà de quoi combler n'importe quelle jeune femme. Mais Mme Dudevant n'est pas n'importe quelle jeune femme qui se satisfait de n'importe quoi. Elle a le plaisir difficile, en tout, même pour le tabac. Peu après la naissance de Solange, le 25 octobre 1828, apparaît pour la première fois, dans la *Correspondance*, un appel qui sera suivi de nombreux autres : « Mon bon ami, apporte-moi du tabac, celui d'ici ne vaut rien. Choisis-le-moi bien fin et à odeur de rose. »

Ce « bon ami », c'est Casimir, qui est à Paris, pour affaires. Mari qui a appris à être complaisant pour sauvegarder la paix du ménage, M. Dudevant est un père attentif qui s'inquiète de la santé de Solange, en proie à une convulsion nerveuse. Il ne semble pas douter qu'il soit le père de Solange. Avec une conviction méritoire, la petite-fille de Sand, Aurore Lauth-Sand, déclarera plus tard . « Il est certain qu'en 1827-1828, ma grand-mère avait fait une dernière tentative de complète conciliation avec son mari. » Cette tentative aurait porté ses fruits, Solange, que Mme Dudevant trouve « jolie comme une miniature », dans une lettre du 22 octobre 1828 adressée à M. Dudevant. Dans cette même lettre éclate déjà la préférence pour Maurice. Si Solange est jolie, Maurice est « toujours le plus beau des amours ». Et il le restera jusqu'à la mort de sa mère à jamais éblouie d'avoir pu enfanter pareille merveille.

La tentative de réconciliation, tant admirée par

Aurore Lauth-Sand, n'aura pas de lendemain. Car, aux lendemains de la naissance de Solange, Mme Dudevant fait chambre à part et renvoie M. Dudevant à des amours ancillaires. Cette pratique, à l'époque, n'a rien d'original. Les épouses, lassées par des maternités consécutives, n'ont pas d'autres moyens de contraception que le renoncement. Comme Mme Dudevant ne renoncera pas à ces plaisirs, mais avec d'autres que son époux, on peut imaginer qu'elle sut, à sa façon, éviter d'importunes grossesses. À moins que la fragilité de certains de ses amants, ou l'habileté de certains autres, n'aient empêché la taille d'Aurore de trop s'alourdir...

S'ils font chambre à part, les Dudevant n'en gardent pas moins des rapports de camaraderie établis dès leurs fiançailles. Chacun a renoncé à changer l'autre. Casimir, qui sait qu'il n'est pas un oiseau rare, supporte de vivre avec ce phénix qu'est Aurore. Et puis, avec l'imprévisible Aurore, Casimir ne s'ennuie pas. Mme Dudevant ne sait pas quoi inventer pour défrayer la chronique de La Châtre. En janvier 1829, n'imagine-t-elle pas de persuader leurs amis, M. de Perigny, sous-préfet à La Châtre, et son épouse, de donner une soirée où seraient « amalgamées » les sept ou huit sociétés qui forment la ville et qui ne se mêlent point ?

La France de 1829 est séparée en classes aussi distinctes, et aussi jalouses de leur identité, que le sont les castes en Inde. Le scandale causé à La Châtre par cette soirée est immense. Mme Dudevant, qui en est à l'origine, est unanimement mise au ban. Elle hausse les épaules devant tant d'incompréhension et s'en console en lisant les nouveautés littéraires commandées à Paris, les poésies de Victor Hugo et les derniers ouvrages de Benjamin Constant.

À force de lire des nouveautés, elle en compose une, *le Voyage de M. Blaise*, qu'elle dédie, le 12 mars 1829, à Jules Néraud. Texte nettement autobiographique, où l'on retrouve Colette, la jument, Duteil,

Blaise Duplomb, dont le fils, Adolphe, est un ami d'Aurore. En août, elle écrit *le Voyage en Auvergne* encore plus autobiographique que *le Voyage de M. Blaise.* Elle s'y peint sans complaisance aucune : « Je n'ai jamais pu comprendre comment on a fait attention à moi. Mes yeux qu'on a vantés souvent me semblent froids et bêtes. » À ces deux premiers textes succède un troisième, *le Voyage en Espagne,* qui retrace quelques épisodes de son équipée ibérique, en 1808, avec sa mère.

L'écriture, la musique, le dessin occupent assez Mme Dudevant pour qu'elle ne puisse plus se consacrer entièrement à ses enfants. Début octobre, elle engage un précepteur pour Maurice, Jules Boucoiran, un Nîmois de vingt et un ans pour qui elle ressent une amitié immédiate, et partagée. M. Boucoiran sera l'un de ses plus fidèles confidents, et, en deux mois, il devient « mon cher petit Jules ». Honni soit qui mal y pense.

Le « cher petit Jules » doit s'occuper du « cher petit Maurice » pendant que Mme Dudevant galope vers Périgueux et que M. Dudevant est à Paris, où il apporte à Jane Bazouin la dernière œuvre de sa femme, *la Marraine,* écrite à la demande de cette même Jane qui s'extasie : « Tout cela est excellent. » Malgré les compliments de Jane, *la Marraine,* et les trois autres textes précédents, ne seront publiés qu'après la mort de leur auteur.

Si *le Voyage de M. Blaise, le Voyage en Auvergne, le Voyage en Espagne* et *la Marraine* avaient été publiés sitôt écrits, Mme Dudevant aurait été la muse du département. Elle a évité le pire en gardant dans ces tiroirs ces feuillets trop intimes pour être livrés à un public non encore préparé à recevoir, par livres interposés, les confidences de George Sand. L'intensité de la production littéraire de Mme Dudevant en cette année 1829 présage celle de Mme Sand qui ne terminera un roman que pour en commencer un autre.

L'infatigable Mme Dudevant commence, le

19 décembre 1829, une carrière artistique en commandant deux planchettes de houx pour écrans portatifs. Songerait-elle déjà à s'évader de Nohant et à gagner sa vie en décorant des écrans, des tabatières ? Ou en exécutant ces aquarelles qu'admirait tant bonne-maman ? Il serait temps de s'assurer de nouveaux revenus, de gagner de l'argent frais, puisque Casimir se révèle incapable d'en gagner, et même en perd en se faisant berner dans une affaire de vins. On doit restreindre les frais et on ne peut plus garder Jules Boucoiran, qui s'en va le 21 décembre.

Les consolations prodiguées par Stéphane ne suffisent pas à faire oublier à Mme Dudevant les pesants défauts de M. Dudevant, à qui elle reproche, entre autres, à la fin décembre, son manque de sobriété : « On ne doit pas conclure d'affaires à la suite d'un repas quand on a le malheur de n'être pas sobre et je suis persuadée que tu as fait celle-là le verre à la main. (...) Ne te fâche pas de ce que je te dis. Le droit de dire la vérité est réciproque, autrement il est tyrannique. D'ailleurs, je suis mère avant tout et j'ai du caractère quand il en faut. » Là, c'est la bourgeoise irritée qui parle en Mme Dudevant, qui, bonne fille quand même, recommande à M. Dudevant : « En attendant que tu puisses revenir, je t'ordonne de t'amuser (...). J'ai beaucoup de plaisir à te savoir dans une société où il y a des femmes, là tu es toujours bien et raisonnable. »

On ne saurait rêver couple plus moderne, plus actuel que le ménage Dudevant. La tolérance de madame a quand même des limites. En février 1830, elle met à la porte Pepita, la bonne de Solange et la maîtresse de Casimir. Madame ne supporte pas d'être trompée sous son toit. Monsieur n'a qu'à suivre son exemple et courir à Paris, à Bordeaux, ou à La Châtre. Il faut absolument respecter le toit de Nohant, ce toit qui abrite leurs deux chérubins, Solange, « douce comme un agneau », et Maurice qui, à sept ans, montre déjà une vocation de peintre. Eh oui, le temps passe, Maurice a sept ans et sa mère, vingt-six. Mme Dudevant confie alors à l'une de ses amies, Mme Gondouin Saint-Agnan : « Vous avez la tournure d'une femme de dix-huit ans, et moi celle d'une femme de quarante. » Cette « vieille » de vingt-six ans décide de pratiquer une cure de rajeunissement à Paris et d'y conduire, en avril, Maurice, qui doit connaître la ville natale de sa mère. Mme Dudevant aura ainsi l'illusion de redevenir Mlle Dupin, pensionnaire au couvent des Dames Augustines Anglaises... Elle retrouve sa mère, l'ami Pierret et montre à son fils les Boulevards, le jardin des Plantes, le Louvre. Et puis, brusquement, Mme Dudevant annonce à M. Dudevant, resté à Nohant, que, cédant aux instances de Zoé Leroy et fuyant les disputes avec Sophie-Victoire qui est vraiment insupportable, elle s'en va, le 13 mai, à Bordeaux. Elles ont bon dos, les instances de Zoé et les insultes de Sophie-Victoire ! Mme Dudevant court à Bordeaux pour retrouver Aurélien. Elle quitte Bordeaux le 17. Les ardeurs d'Aurore auraient-elles enfin couronné les flammes d'Aurélien, pendant cette brève escapade ? Les deux anges auraient-ils fait la bête ? Ce contact entre leurs deux épidermes n'ayant pas eu le résultat escompté, les deux forçats du sublime optent pour « un divorce tranquille ». Peu après, en 1833, Aurélien épouse l'une de ses parentes, Louise de Villeminot.

Aux tempêtes des sentiments succèdent les tempêtes politiques. Les 27, 28, 29 juillet, l'état de siège est proclamé à Paris. À la suite de ces trois journées d'émeute, les Trois Glorieuses, Charles X abdique et est remplacé par Louis-Philippe. Mme Dudevant vit cette révolution de 1830 à travers Jules Boucoiran qui est à Paris et à qui elle écrit, le 31 juillet, à onze heures du soir : « Je vous remercie d'avoir pensé à moi au milieu de ces horreurs. Ô mon Dieu, que de sang ! que de larmes ! (...) J'ai peur mais je n'en dis rien. »

Elle ne dit pas non plus que la veille, au château de Coudray, chez ses amis Duvernet, elle a rencontré

131

un jeune homme de dix-neuf ans, Jules Sandeau, et que le lendemain, ce même 31 juillet, elle l'a invité à dîner, surmontant ainsi ses craintes de la révolution et invitant aussi ses fidèles, comme Fleury le Gaulois.

Ce nouveau petit Jules sera bientôt un « cher petit Jules », autrement cher que Jules Boucoiran, que l'opinion publique range pourtant parmi les amants de Mme Dudevant, qui se fait l'écho de ces bruits : « À Paris, à Bordeaux, au Havre, partout j'avais des amants. Tous mes amis étaient des compagnons de débauche, et quant à vous, c'était un passe-temps de plus de vous déniaiser. »

Les dix-neuf printemps de Jules Sandeau feront oublier ces vilaines rumeurs à Mme Dudevant, qui en oubliera même qu'elle est une « vieille » de vingt-six ans.

LES RÉVOLUTIONS
DE SAINTE TRANQUILLE
(juillet-décembre 1830)

Je ne suis pas une sainte.

En cet été 1830, la révolution est à Paris comme en province, dans les esprits comme dans les cœurs. Mme Dudevant, pour une fois, suit la mode. Le 15 août, elle écrit à l'un de ses amis, Charles Meure, procureur du roi, à Clamecy : « Moi, je vous l'avoue, mon cher magistrat, je suis républicaine, comme tous les diables. » Le petit diable des Dames Augustines Anglaises ne s'est guère assagi. Que la baronne Dudevant soit républicaine, cela défie le bon sens ! Là-haut, bonne-maman, et son père, Maurice de Saxe, doivent en frémir.

La républicaine Aurore ne dissimule pas son mépris pour Charles X, et son exécration pour « un Polignac imbécile, lâche et cruel ». Lucide, elle voit « avec dégoût s'élever des nuées d'ambitieux et de serviles qui se disaient hier ennemis du pouvoir et qui l'encensent aujourd'hui ». Elle trotte à La Châtre pour avoir des nouvelles de ses amis, elle s'inquiète pour Aurélien qui veut donner sa démission, elle ne tient pas en place, elle va, elle vient, elle ne cache pas ses opinions puisqu'elle est... une femme. « Je suis si bien connue pour un être sans conséquence, faible d'esprit et un peu lunatique, que je ne crains pas d'influencer les gens qui m'entourent et de les entraîner dans des erreurs dangereuses. Une femme est toujours une femme et ne croyez-pas que je m'en plaigne. C'est si commode au contraire ! C'est si doux de faire un roman de la vie, de s'entourer de fantômes, de n'avoir pas le sens commun, de battre la campagne à son aise et de ne pas aller en prison pour cela... »

Ce bonheur d'être une femme ne se limite pas à profiter des avantages de sa condition, ou à s'avouer républicaine. Ce bonheur est aussi celui d'aimer, et d'être aimée, de Jules Sandeau, « ce pauvre enfant ». Elle a été séduite « dès le premier jour » par « son regard expressif, ses manières brusques et franches », sa « gaucherie timide ».

Étudiant en droit à Paris, Jules Sandeau passe ses vacances à La Châtre, chez son père, modeste fonctionnaire. Jules est blond, a le teint blanc et se singularise en portant un cordon rouge à son chapeau alors que tous ses amis, de Charles Duvernet à Néraud, portent des cordons bleus. « Il n'y avait pas jusqu'au lacet rouge de ce chapeau qui ne me fît tressaillir de joie. (...) Aussi je l'ai gardé comme une relique, ce petit cordon. Il y a pour moi, dans son aspect, une vie de souvenirs, d'agitation et de bonheur », se souviendra plus tard Sand.

Pour la petite-fille de l'oiselier, Sandeau est un colibri : « Et toi, petit Sandeau ! Aimable et léger comme le colibri des savanes parfumées. » Ce besoin de miniaturiser, ou de grandir, les hommes qu'elle aime fait qu'Aurore voit rarement ses amants dans leur dimension réelle. Cette confusion engendre bien des désillusions...

La liaison du colibri de La Châtre et du phénix de Nohant déchaîne les commérages. « Les cancans vont leur train à La Châtre plus que jamais. Ceux qui ne m'aiment guère disent que j'aime " Sandot " (vous comprenez la portée du mot), ceux qui ne m'aiment pas du tout disent que j'aime Sandot et Fleury à la fois ; ceux qui me détestent disent que Duvernet et vous ne me font pas peur », écrit-elle à Jules Boucoiran, le 27 octobre 1830.

Les vives passions, les révolutions intenses ne détournent jamais longtemps Aurore de son centre de gravité, Nohant, auquel elle accorde ses soins vigilants. Elle a voulu, un temps, se charger de la gestion du domaine. Catastrophe : elle a dépensé plus que prévu. Casimir, qu'elle accusait de mauvaise gestion, triomphe. Et son triomphe, même modeste, agace Aurore.

Sainte Tranquille, comme l'avait surnommée sa mère, ne le reste jamais longtemps. Est-ce l'exemple des Trois Glorieuses, et du peuple de Paris qui a su se libérer de Charles X et de Polignac ? Mme Dudevant veut s'affranchir de M. Dudevant. Elle avait essayé d'être financièrement indépendante en se créant « quelque petit métier ». Mais les portraits qu'elle avait peints manquent de ressemblance et ne trouvent pas acquéreur. Forte de sa facilité d'écriture, manifestée dans ses lettres et dans ses quatre œuvres inédites, *le Voyage de M. Blaise, le Voyage en Auvergne, le Voyage en Espagne, la Marraine*, elle envisage la littérature comme un gagne-pain, ou un gagne-brioche, puisque sa sobriété est telle qu'elle peut se contenter pour dîner d'une brioche. Elle se sent capable de faire des romans comme sa mère faisait des chapeaux. Elle veut être un artisan des lettres, rien de plus. Et pourquoi pas ? Pourquoi ne pas vendre ces textes qu'admirent ces amis ? Pourquoi ne pas mettre à profit ce don de raconter aux autres les histoires qu'elle se raconte à elle-même depuis son enfance ? Être libre, être indépendante, comme elle le fut, pendant sa dix-septième année, Aurore est prête, pour y parvenir, à faire feu de tout bois, y compris du testament de Casimir, qu'elle découvre, fin novembre, dans un tiroir, par hasard. Un hasard que Mme Dudevant a dû un peu aider... L'enveloppe porte la mention « Ne l'ouvrez qu'après ma mort ». Aurore, qui n'a pas la patience d'attendre d'être veuve, ouvre l'enveloppe et lit le testament. Quel testament ! Tout ce que Casimir n'a jamais osé dire à sa fantasque épouse est là, noir sur blanc, les malédictions y alternent avec de dures réflexions sur ce qu'il considère comme des perversités. Mme Dudevant estime aussitôt qu'elle ne saurait vivre davantage avec M. Dudevant, qui ne l'estime pas.

Avec « un aplomb et un sang-froid » qui pétrifient

M. Dudevant, Mme Dudevant déclare de façon irrévocable : « Je veux une pension et j'irai à Paris pour toujours, mes enfants resteront à Nohant. » Elle se dit inébranlable. Casimir pleure. Aurore transige. Elle consent à partager sa vie entre Nohant et Paris, et, sans l'avouer à Casimir, espère fermement trouver un moyen de garder ses enfants auprès d'elle, à Nohant comme à Paris. Mme Dudevant fait admettre à M. Dudevant qu'il n'aura plus en elle qu'une « compagne libre ». Casimir, qui n'en croit pas ses oreilles, accepte de verser une rente de 1 500 francs à la descendante de ces dames d'opéra qui savaient monnayer leurs faveurs à des prix nettement plus élevés. Aurore remporte sa première victoire. La fin justifie les moyens. Et puis, comme Sand le reconnaîtra elle-même dans *Histoire de ma vie*, « je ne suis pas une sainte ».

LES LIBERTÉS
D'UNE CHÂTELAINE RÉPUBLICAINE
(janvier-décembre 1831)

> Pour moi, ma chère maman, la
> liberté de penser et d'agir est le pre-
> mier des biens.
>   Nohant, le 31 mai 1831

Dans ces moments de rupture, et d'extrême exaltation, Mme Dudevant ne cesse pas d'être une femme pratique. Elle veut bien quitter Nohant, à condition que tout y soit en ordre, et que son précieux Maurice ne souffre pas trop de son absence. Une seule personne est capable d'assurer l'éducation de son fils, c'est Jules Boucoiran qui est maintenant précepteur des enfants du général Bertrand et à qui Aurore écrit : « Si vous êtes à Nohant, je puis respirer et dormir tranquille (...). Si je laisse mon fils livré à son père, il sera gâté aujourd'hui, battu demain, négligé toujours. » Boucoiran ne résiste pas aux appels de la sirène et reprend ses fonctions de précepteur de Maurice, le 20 janvier 1831.

Mme Dudevant espère pouvoir emmener Solange à Paris, ce qui provoque les sarcasmes d'Hyppolite : « Tu t'imagines vivre à Paris avec un enfant moyennant 250 francs par mois ! C'est trop risible, toi qui ne sais pas ce que coûte un poulet ! » À ces moqueries, Aurore oppose une détermination de vivre à Paris selon les conditions passées avec Casimir, « deux fois trois mois, avec 250 francs par mois d'absence ». À cette mensualité s'ajoute une pension de 1 500 francs. Ce qui porte à 3 000 francs le budget parisien annuel d'Aurore. C'est peu.

Casimir est persuadé qu'il s'agit là d'un caprice de courte durée, et Hyppolite aussi qui prête à sa sœur un appartement dans la maison qu'il possède à Paris. C'est là que Mme Dudevant s'installe, au 31, rue de Seine-Saint-Germain, dès son arrivée, le 6 janvier 1831.

Le lendemain, sa première lettre est pour Maurice : « J'ai fait un bon voyage et je me porte bien. (...) Prends aussi bien garde de t'enrhumer. » Jusqu'à la fin de sa vie, George Sand vivra dans l'obsession des rhumes de Maurice.

Le 8 janvier, c'est Casimir qui a droit à des nouvelles aussi banales que celles envoyées à Maurice : elle a fait bon voyage et se porte bien. C'est à son confident Boucoiran qu'Aurore réserve, le 12, l'aveu suivant : « Je m'embarque sur la mer orageuse de la littérature. Il faut vivre. Je ne suis pas riche maintenant. » S'embarquer sur la mer orageuse de la littérature, cela veut dire pour Aurore qu'elle a été reçue, en ce même 12 janvier, par M. de Latouche, qui avait pris la direction du *Figaro*. *Le Figaro*, fondé en 1826, était un petit journal comptant peu de rédacteurs et peu d'abonnés. **Mais** ce petit journal pratiquant l'opposition systématique faisait grand bruit et était régulièrement poursuivi par le gouvernement.

Latouche travaille dans son appartement, au coin du feu, avec ses collaborateurs. Dès février, Aurore, la frileuse Aurore, a sa place dans ce *Figaro* d'appartement, près de la cheminée où elle jette régulièrement une dizaine de feuillets qu'elle a barbouillés sur un sujet donné par Latouche et qui ne valent rien.

Latouche est sans pitié pour la débutante dont il lit les articles, et les manuscrits, avec son habituelle causticité. Dès leur première rencontre, il a prévenu Aurore qu'elle n'aurait pas à compter sur sa bienveillance. « La bienveillance n'est que trop souvent la paresse de l'amitié, n'est-ce pas », lui a-t-il dit.

Les amis de Latouche, comme Marceline Desbordes-Valmore et Honoré de Balzac, sont là pour témoigner que le patron du *Figaro* n'a pas l'amitié paresseuse...

Latouche n'a pas caché à Aurore qu'il avait trouvé détestable son premier roman, *Aimée*, dont le manuscrit prend, lui aussi, le chemin de la cheminée. « Il faut vivre pour connaître la vie. Le roman, c'est la vie racontée avec art », enseigne-t-il à la romancière qui n'oubliera pas le conseil.

Mme Dudevant est entrée au *Figaro* sur intervention de la mère de son ami Charles Duvernet, cousine de Latouche, lequel est né à La Châtre en 1785. Entre le Latouche de La Châtre et la Dudevant de Nohant, on est entre Berrichons, et on peut, sur les bords de la Seine, évoquer la douceur des bords de l'Indre.

Dans sa lettre de remerciements à Charles Duvernet, le 19 janvier, Aurore précise : « Je n'ai pas parlé de Sandeau à M. Delatouche. » Elle écrira toujours « de Latouche » en un seul mot. À Duvernet, elle annonce qu'elle forme avec Sandeau « une association littéraire ». Jules et Aurore écrivent ensemble des textes qu'ils placent dans des revues comme *la Revue de Paris*, pour gagner quelque argent. Vraiment, 3 000 francs pour vivre à Paris, c'est peu. Balzac ne prétend-il pas que l'on ne peut être femme à Paris à moins d'avoir 25 000 francs de rente ? Aurore est loin du compte. Et puisqu'elle ne peut être femme et qu'elle se ruine en blanchissage, elle se déguise en garçon, sur les conseils de sa mère : « Quand j'étais jeune et que ton père manquait d'argent, il avait imaginé de m'habiller en garçon, fais-en autant. » Aurore obéit à Sophie-Victoire et commande ce qui est alors l'uniforme à la mode, une redingote-guérite en gros drap gris, pantalons et gilet assortis. Avec un chapeau gris et une grosse cravate de laine, elle a l'air d'un étudiant de première année et peut suivre partout ses copains berrichons qu'elle a retrouvés à Paris et avec qui elle court les théâtres, les concerts, les expositions. On dîne chez Pinson, rue de l'Ancienne-Comédie, où se réunissent les membres les plus éminents du club des Berrichons de Paris.

Toutes ces sorties occasionnent plus de dépenses que Mme Dudevant n'en avait prévues, et si elle veut éviter un retour piteux à Nohant, elle doit, à tout prix, vendre sa prose comme un artisan vend ses produits, « et comme je n'ai nulle ambition d'être connue, je ne le serai point », écrit-elle à Boucoiran le 12 février 1831.

Aurore va être connue, et plus tôt que prévu. En mars, elle écrit, dans *le Figaro*, une « bigarrure », c'est-à-dire un bref article qui brocarde les précautions que prend le gouvernement pour prévenir les rassemblements. Le gouvernement s'en irrite, et fait saisir *le Figaro*. Aurore jubile, tout en minimisant l'incident : « On me blâme, à ce qu'il paraît, d'écrire dans *le Figaro*. Je m'en moque encore. Il faut bien vivre et je suis assez fière de gagner mon pain moi-même. *Le Figaro* est un moyen comme un autre d'arriver. »

Sans illusions sur le journalisme, et sur le goût du public, Mme Dudevant s'aperçoit que « la littérature est dans le même chaos que la politique. (...) On veut du neuf et pour en faire, on fait du hideux. Balzac est au pinacle pour avoir peint l'amour d'un soldat pour une tigresse (...). Les monstres sont à la mode. Faisons des monstres. »

Petite-bourgeoise aux grandes idées, Mme Dudevant est prête, pour gagner son indépendance, à enfanter des monstres et à suivre les traces de Balzac. Brouillé avec Latouche, l'auteur des *Chouans*, paru en 1829, accorde son amitié à Aurore et à Jules, avec une préférence pour le « cher petit Jules ».

Sa permission de trois mois à Paris terminée, Mme Dudevant revient à Nohant le 12 avril. Elle retrouve ses enfants « beaux comme des amours et caressants pour moi seule ». Ces caresses ne suffisent plus à Aurore qui connaît avec Sandeau une résurrection totale : « Il a réchauffé mon cœur glacé, il a ranimé ma vie prête à s'éteindre, avec l'amour qu'il m'a inspiré. » Mais la vraie passion d'Aurore, ce n'est pas Jules Sandeau, c'est la passion d'écrire, qu'elle découvre en ce printemps 1831 : « J'ai un but, une tâche, disons le mot, une passion. Le métier

144

d'écrire en est une violente, presque indestructible. Quand elle s'est emparée d'une pauvre tête, elle ne peut plus la quitter. »

Cette passion d'écrire prévaudra sur les autres et aura l'avantage de n'avoir pas à être cachée. Car Aurore vit dans la hantise du flagrant délit. À Paris, sa mère, sa tante, sa sœur, son frère, et peut-être même son mari peuvent surgir à l'improviste et la surprendre « embrassant le petit Jules ». Il est nécessaire de trouver un logis à double issue afin que « le petit Jules » puisse s'échapper sans dommage. « Je tuerai celui qui porterait la main sur lui, fût-ce mon mari, fût-ce mon frère », jure Aurore qui, pour n'être pas acculée à une telle extrémité, s'installe, à la mi-juillet, dans un petit appartement au 25, quai Saint-Michel.

La disposition de cet appartement permet d'éviter les mauvaises surprises et d'y vivre en toute liberté. Cette liberté à laquelle Mme Dudevant a goûté et qu'elle considère comme « le premier des biens ». Prendre ses repas à l'heure qu'elle veut, se promener où elle veut, se coucher quand, et avec qui, elle veut, voilà qui vaut pour Aurore les plus grandes richesses du monde. Que chacun suive son exemple et soit libre, y compris Casimir qui, depuis qu'il ne contrarie plus les aspirations d'Aurore, a retrouvé « l'estime et la confiance » de sa singulière moitié. À condition qu'il ne se montre pas trop curieux et ne tombe pas à l'improviste au logis parisien de madame...

Tout semble aller selon la volonté d'Aurore en cet été 1831, y compris ses enfants qui se portent bien et prennent son absence en patience. Maurice, qui a huit ans, est « maigre et bon ». Solange, qui a trois ans, est « belle et mauvaise ». Dans le cœur de leur mère, le « bon Maurice » l'emporte déjà sur la « mauvaise Solange ». Il est curieux de constater combien Sand, éprise de justice humanitaire, n'a jamais songé qu'une justice bien entendue commençait dans son propre foyer...

Mi-juillet 1831. Aurore et Jules se retrouvent à Paris et s'installent au 25, quai Saint-Michel. Ils sont dans « cet état parfait d'imbécillité » que d'autres appellent le bonheur : « Nous y sommes encore et nos journées se passent à nous regarder et à nous demander si ce n'est pas un rêve que nous faisons. »

Aurore exagère un peu. Elle passe aussi ses journées, et une partie de ses nuits, à écrire, le besoin d'argent aux trousses. Elle n'a plus un sou, doit emprunter à ses amis berrichons de Paris et menace Casimir de se suicider s'il ne l'aide pas à payer des « dettes urgentes » au tapissier, à l'ébéniste, au cordonnier. Hyppolite avance 500 francs à sa sœur, pour éviter « une extrémité dont nous ne nous consolerions jamais ».

Ni Casimir ni Hyppolite n'auront à se reprocher la mort d'Aurore qui revient à Nohant, en septembre, débordante de vitalité, puisqu'elle écrit « un volume en cinq nuits ». Il s'agit du premier volume de *Rose et Blanche,* qui en comptera cinq. Sandeau qui est à Niort écrit, de son côté, deux volumes de *Rose et Blanche.* En l'absence du manuscrit, il est bien difficile de savoir ce qui est dû à la plume d'Aurore et à celle de Jules. Ce qui est certain, c'est que *Rose et Blanche* est un roman à quatre mains, dont la composition est interrompue du 18 au 30 septembre par Sandeau qui séjourne clandestinement au château d'Ars, près de Nohant. Aurore réussit à vaincre sa peur du flagrant délit et à recevoir Jules dans sa propre chambre.

Casimir qui, pendant la journée, a fait les vendanges, « dort comme un cochon ». Est-ce le piment du danger ? Les retrouvailles sont frénétiques. « Cette nuit encore je veux qu'il vienne. Deux fois ce n'est pas trop. (...) Je suis abîmée de morsures et de coups. Je ne peux pas me tenir debout. Je suis dans une joie frénétique. » Ce langage n'est vraiment pas celui d'une femme que ses contemporains ont crue frigide...

Quand la fête des sens a pris fin, Aurore, tranquillement, fait des corrections au deuxième volume de *Rose et Blanche* apporté par Sandeau.

Ces transports amoureux épuisent le « cher petit Jules ». Il maigrit, il se tue de plaisir, Aurore en prend conscience et s'épouvante, aux veilles de retourner à Paris, de reprendre leur vie commune, quai Saint-Michel. « Je le tue, et les plaisirs que je lui donne sont achetés aux dépens de ses jours. Je suis sa " peau de chagrin ". »

En dépit de son lot quotidien de malaises nerveux, d'élancements au cœur, de rhumatismes et de constipation, Aurore se sent forte : « Je suis forte à vous enterrer tous. » Force de la nature, elle ne peut chérir que des faibles. Avec Sandeau, elle apprend à se refuser, science dont elle se souviendra plus tard avec Frédéric Chopin.

Apprentissage du refus, de la liberté, de la littérature et du journalisme, ces mois de 1831 sont pleins d'enseignements pour Mme Dudevant qui, le 6 novembre, en dresse un bilan positif : « Je vis tranquille, je travaille à mon aise et je me porte bien maintenant. » Elle se porte d'autant mieux que la venue, fin novembre, à Paris, de M. Dudevant ne dérange en rien ses habitudes. « Je descendrai chez Hyppolite, parce que je ne veux te gêner nullement, ni par conséquent être gêné, ce qui est bien juste », prévient Casimir. On ne saurait pousser plus loin la complaisance. Quand, fin décembre, M. Dudevant retourne à Nohant, il a droit aux compliments de son épouse enfin satisfaite : « Ton séjour ici a été un vrai temps de bombance et de débauche pour moi. Je t'en remercie. »

À cette satisfaction s'en ajoute une autre, encore plus importante, la mise en vente, dans les librairies de Paris et de province, de *Rose et Blanche*, signé par Jules Sand.

DE JULES SAND À GEORGE SAND
(janvier-décembre 1832)

> Delatouche, consulté, trancha la
> question par un compromis : Sand
> resterait intact et je prendrais un
> autre prénom qui ne servirait qu'à
> moi.

L'euphorie de la fin 1831 ne dure pas et 1832 commence mal. Aurore est à Nohant, triste et malade, ou malade parce qu'elle est triste, atteinte de ce mal de vivre qui la tourmente sans répit. À cette crise de spleen s'ajoute une crise de lucidité comme Mme Dudevant en connaît régulièrement. Elle se rend compte que l'association littéraire avec Sandeau bat de l'aide. S'il a donné pour *Rose et Blanche* son prénom, Jules, et la moitié de son nom, Sand, le « colibri » n'aime guère travailler et n'use guère ses plumes à écrire. Aurore, qui ne trouve son équilibre qu'une plume à la main, ignore la paresse. Le « cher petit Jules » est un paresseux.

Le 23 janvier 1832, Aurore s'interroge et interroge leur ami commun, le Dr Émile Regnault : « N'est-ce pas, Émile, qu'il mérite bien que je l'aime avec passion ? N'est-ce pas qu'il m'aime de toute son âme et que je fais bien de tout lui sacrifier, fortune, réputation, enfants ? » Questions qu'elle ne se posait pas pendant les nuits « frénétiques » de l'automne 1831. Elle a des suffocations, elle se croit perdue et Regnault, qui est l'un des modèles du Dr Bianchon de Balzac, s'efforce de rassurer sa patiente qui se plaint : « Le mal va vite, mon pauvre Émile, et je ne peux pas me dissimuler ses progrès. » Ces souffrances, morales et physiques, la rendent « atrabilaire comme un vieux ours ». Et ce n'est pas la teinture éthérée de digitale recommandée par le Dr Regnault, ou le sirop de pointes d'asperge préconisé par un médecin de La Châtre, qui y changeront quelque chose !

Cette femme forte est déconcertante par ces brusques accès de faiblesse, qu'elle réussit à réprimer, entreprenant, dès février 1832, un roman, sans la collaboration du « colibri » qui s'amuse à Paris avec ses compagnons berrichons. Ce sera *Indiana*, Indiana qui est le prénom de la sœur d'Aurélien de Sèze...

Pendant que sa mère travaille, Solange joue tranquillement à ses côtés. Tranquillité qui décide Aurore à emmener Solange à Paris, lors de son prochain séjour. Décision qui scandalise Émile Regnault que Mme Dudevant rassure aussitôt, « Nous nous lèverons comme elle à neuf heures, et comme elle a trois ans et demi, je vous assure qu'elle ne fera ni remarques, ni commentaires, ni questions, ni bavardages. (...) Ainsi, que votre moralité ne s'alarme pas. Je n'ai pas plus envie que la plus " vertueuse des mères " de scandaliser ma fille. »

Optimisme ou inconscience, Mme Dudevant ne craint pas de faire vivre sa fille sous le même toit que son amant, elle qui reprochait à M. Dudevant de « souiller » son foyer par sa liaison avec Pepita, la bonne de Solange... De toute façon, Sandeau a promis d'adorer Solange qui est « bête comme une oie », et qui, trop gâtée par sa bonne, doit être éduquée par sa mère.

La mère et l'amante coexistent pacifiquement, pour le moment, en Aurore et s'effacent devant la suprématie d'un troisième personnage, l'écrivain, qui se rend compte des difficultés de son métier : « Je travaille un sujet dur comme le fer et malléable comme le moellon. » Pendant que, feuillet après feuillet, naît *Indiana*, on danse à La Châtre dans des bals qui empestent, « car en province, et dans la nôtre particulièrement, hommes et femmes ont horreur de l'eau et ignorent l'usage des ablutions ».

Mme Dudevant fuit les bals et leur crasse avec une égale ardeur, et s'enfuit avec Solange à Paris, où elle arrive le 1er avril 1832. Le choléra y sévit,

Aurore en subit « une petite attaque » qu'elle noie dans du « thé bien chaud ».

En mai paraît *Indiana*, signé G. Sand. *Rose et Blanche* s'étant bien vendu, les éditeurs avaient souhaité gardé le nom de Sand sur la couverture d'*Indiana*. Jules Sandeau, n'ayant pas participé à cet ouvrage, récupère son prénom, que l'on remplace par Georges, avec un s d'abord, puis sans[1]. De J. Sand à G. Sand, le glissement pour le public est imperceptible. Pour l'auteur, ce changement est capital. Avec *Indiana*, George Sand entre sur la scène littéraire et y tient immédiatement les premiers rôles, recevant l'hommage de ceux qui vont être ses pairs, comme Balzac qui, dans *la Caricature*, porte aux nues *Indiana :* « Je ne connais rien de plus simplement écrit, de plus délicieusement conçu (...). Bref, le succès du livre est assuré. » Dans *la Revue des Deux Mondes*, le critique Gustave Planche n'hésite pas à proclamer la supériorité de Sand sur Mme de Staël. Quant à Latouche, qui, en lisant les premières pages d'*Indiana*, avait accusé George d'avoir pastiché Balzac, il fait amende honorable dans un billet : « Oubliez les niaiseries que je vous ai dites hier sur le commencement de votre livre ; votre livre est un chef-d'œuvre. »

Toute la presse est unanime. *Le Journal des débats* célèbre un « récit chaleureux et plein d'intérêt », *la Revue de Paris*, « le roman de la passion le plus attachant ».

L'héroïne, Indiana, est, comme Sand, une mal-mariée qui est à la fois déçue par son mari, le colonel Delmare, et par son amoureux, Raymon de la Ramière. Elle trouve le salut, sinon le bonheur, avec un ami d'enfance, sir Ralph. Les mal-aimées de 1832

---

1. Dans *Histoire de ma vie*, Sand explique le choix de son prénom, sans s, en une seule phrase : « Je pris vite et sans chercher celui de George qui me paraissait synonyme de Berrichon. » À ce propos, voir la note de Georges Lubin dans *Histoire de ma vie*, tome 2, Gallimard, « La Pléiade », page 1336.

s'identifient avec Indiana, et signent « Indiana » leurs billets amoureux, et leurs amants y répondent en signant Ralph. Tout cela fait un beau public. Et un beau succès, gâché par les émeutes du 6 juin. Une fois de plus, l'état de siège est proclamé à Paris.

George Sand se place immédiatement au-dessus des partis : « Moi, je m'indigne contre tous les hommes. (...) Pour les hommes de parti, il n'y a que des assassins et des victimes. Ils ne comprennent pas qu'eux tous sont victimes et assassins tour à tour. (...) J'ai horreur de la monarchie, horreur de la république, horreur de tous les hommes. (...) le 6 juin a tué Indiana pour un mois et m'a jetée si brutalement dans la vie réelle qu'il me semble impossible à présent de jamais rêver à des romans. »

Impossibilité rapidement vaincue. Comment résister aux éditeurs qui se pressent à sa porte et la supplient de leur donner un nouvel ouvrage, un autre *Indiana* ? Dans les escaliers du 25, quai Saint-Michel, « ce ne sont que romanciers, journalistes, faiseurs d'esprit et dispensateurs de gloire qui montent et descendent ». Sand découvre les inconvénients de la célébrité dans la vie quotidienne, elle est harcelée par des importuns. Elle en découvre aussi les avantages financiers. Le 26 juillet, elle vend pour 2 400 francs son deuxième roman, *Valentine*. Le 30, laissant Jules Sandeau à Paris, elle rentre à Nohant avec sa fille. Les retrouvailles avec son fils sont passionnées : « Nous sommes (...) comme deux amants qui se retrouvent, nous ne pouvons pas nous quitter d'un pas. »

« Plus beau que jamais », Maurice a de l'intelligence, de la douceur, du cœur et des dents très blanches. Il est, aux yeux de sa mère, parfait. Il fait du latin pendant que l'auteur d'*Indiana* travaille à *Valentine* et que Solange se roule sur le parquet, « quelle diable de tête ».

À Nohant, en cet été 1832, Sand se renferme « dans un abominable égoïsme ». « Tout ce qui n'est pas moi, c'est-à-dire mes enfants, mon amant et mes amis, n'est absolument rien pour moi. » Les dissensions avec Jules Sandeau rompent cet enfermement : « Je gronde Jules de vouloir ressembler à Latouche. »

Jules ne se donne plus la peine d'écrire à George, qui se plaint de son silence, et de sa paresse. Elle est écrasée de tâches diverses. Elle doit satisfaire aux besoins de la mère, de l'amante, de l'écrivain, de la châtelaine de Nohant, et cela fait beaucoup de personnes à la fois pour une jeune femme de vingt-huit ans qui, fin octobre, part brusquement à Paris et y reste jusqu'au 5 novembre.

Pendant ce bref séjour, et entre deux orages avec celui qui est de moins en moins ce « cher petit Jules », elle déménage du 25, quai Saint-Michel au 19, quai Malaquais, revient à Nohant prendre Solange et retourne à Paris le 1er décembre. À partir de cette date, elle affirme vivre comme une recluse avec sa fille, un feu dans la cheminée, un piano sur lequel elle joue des mélodies de Berlioz, et ses broderies ; elle brode — qui l'eût cru ? — des pantoufles pour Casimir. « Mon appartement est si bon, si chaud, il y fait tant de soleil et un si beau silence que je ne peux pas m'en arracher. » Elle fait de la copie, c'est-à-dire de l'argent, recevant des propositions de toutes parts.

La Revue de Paris et *la Revue des Deux Mondes* se disputent ses textes. C'est *la Revue des Deux Mondes* qui l'emporte et le 11 décembre, elle signe avec son directeur, François Buloz, son premier traité. « Enfin je me suis livrée à *la Revue des Deux Mondes* pour une rente de 4 000 francs et trente-deux pages d'écriture toutes les six semaines. »

Le temps des vaches maigres n'aura guère duré. Celui des travaux forcés littéraires commence.

RUPTURES ET CONSOLATIONS
DE PRINTEMPS
(1er janvier-1er avril 1833)

J'aime donc mieux les hommes que
les femmes, et je le dis sans malice...

Dès la publication de *Rose et Blanche*, alors qu'elle n'était encore que Jules Sand, George avait prévenu ses amis : « Ne m'appelez jamais " femme auteur " (...). Depuis que j'ai l'honneur d'être imprimée (...), je bois et je mange comme une simple particulière. » Aurore Dudevant a pris pour identité George Sand. Mais elle entend bien rester ce qu'elle est, ou ce qu'elle croit être, « une simple particulière ». Elle tient à préserver sa vie privée. Ce n'est pas parce qu'on achète son *Indiana* qu'on achète aussi le droit de venir frapper à la porte de son auteur.

Ce droit, seuls en bénéficient ses intimes, comme Jules Sandeau ou son éditeur, Émile Dupuy, avec qui, le 8 janvier 1833, elle signe le traité de cession de son prochain roman, *Lélia*. Elle commence *Lélia* tout en travaillant à deux nouvelles, *Cora* et *Lavinia*.

L'association littéraire avec Sandeau est terminée, leur compagnonnage sensuel s'achève. Ils n'habitent plus ensemble. Quand elle s'est installée au 19, quai Malaquais, Jules est allé habiter au 7, rue de l'Université. Ils voisinent, ils sont encore amants, par habitude, et sans retrouver la « frénésie » des débuts de leur liaison...

Dans sa retraite du quai Malaquais, entre son encrier, sa plume et son papier, George se croit à l'abri des tentations, quand, à la mi-janvier, elle écrit à une actrice qu'elle admire, Marie Dorval. Touchée par cette admiration, Marie accourt au quai Malaquais, sans prévenir, saute au cou de George en disant : « Me voilà, moi. » George reconnaît cette voix qui a été celle, inoubliable, de Marion de Lorme. Mince comme un « souple roseau », Marie est coiffée d'un chapeau orné d'une plume que Sandeau, qui se trouve là, compare à « l'aile de quelque fée en voyage ». Charmée, Marie invite George et Jules à dîner, le dimanche suivant.

Telle est Marie, spontanéité et passion. Elle est, à la scène, « la femme du drame nouveau », l'héroïne romantique par excellence. Jusqu'à son triomphe, en 1822, dans *les Deux Forçats*, à la Porte-Saint-Martin, Marie a mené une existence misérable de nomade. C'est une bâtarde, une bohémienne que ses succès au théâtre, et sa liaison avec le poète Alfred de Vigny, ont changée en une étoile du ciel parisien.

Quand elles se rencontrent, Marie a trente-cinq ans, et George, vingt-neuf. Ce ne sont plus des gamines. Elles n'en éprouvent pas moins l'une pour l'autre une passion de pensionnaire avec ce que cela peut comporter d'exaltations diverses. Le critique Gustave Planche, qui, après son éloge d'*Indiana*, est tombé amoureux de son auteur et en est devenu le conseiller, s'en alarme. Gustave prévient George que Mme Dorval peut manifester pour une femme « une passion de même nature que celle de Sappho pour les jeunes lesbiennes ». Cet avertissement ne suffit pas à retenir George qui, accompagnée de l'encore « cher petit Jules », dîne avec Marie et l'applaudit au théâtre.

George bombarde Marie de billets contenant des aveux comme : « Je voudrais bien que quelqu'un m'aimât comme je vous aime. » Le 18 février, Sand confesse à Dorval : « Vous, petite femme, vous avez beaucoup de choses dans votre vie. Moi, rien ! »

Ce « rien » est excessif. Nohant, un mari, un amant, deux enfants, du succès, ce n'est pas rien ! Voudrait-elle dire que sans Marie, elle n'a rien ? Ce rien est d'une imprudence à irriter les dieux. Et début mars, la rupture avec Jules Sandeau s'accomplit, brutalement.

Le 3 mars, George écrit à Marie, à propos d'un bal : « Décidément, Jules sera des nôtres, mais à l'heure où je vous écris il est près de vous sans doute, et il est plus heureux que moi. » Le 5, à la même Marie : « Rayez-nous tous de la liste du bal. Gustave Planche n'y allait qu'à cause de moi et moi je n'irai pas pour des millions. D'affreux chagrins me sont tombés sur la tête, et j'ai bien plus d'idées de mort que de plaisir. »

Que sont ces « affreux chagrins » ? George a-t-elle surpris Jules dans les bras d'une autre femme ? Ou rompent-ils parce qu'ils sont lassés l'un de l'autre au point de rompre avec violence ? À leur ami commun, Émile Regnault, elle évoque en termes graves cette nécessaire séparation : « Nous avions dévoré assez de chagrin. Il ne nous restait plus qu'à nous tuer. Sans mes enfants, nous l'aurions fait. »

Le 7 mars, George demande aide et secours à sa chère Marie : « Si vous aimez mieux venir chez moi, je vous garderai. Nous serons seules. » Marie vient et console George qui, le 9 mars, ne songe plus à la mort. Puissance de ces consolations qui ressuscitent véritablement Sand : elle trouve la force de lire à l'un de ses nouveaux amis, le critique Sainte-Beuve, une partie de *Lélia*.

Le 10 mars, elle écrit à Sainte-Beuve, à qui elle a raconté sa rupture avec Jules Sandeau et qui a proposé un consolateur en la personne d'un jeune poète, Alfred de Musset : « À propos, réflexion faite, je ne veux pas que vous m'ameniez Alfred de Musset. Il est très dandy, nous ne nous conviendrions pas, et j'avais plus de curiosité que d'intérêt à le voir. (...) À la place de celui-là, je veux donc vous prier de m'amener Dumas (...). »

En matière de prompte résurrection, Sand en remontrerait au phénix lui-même ! Ces caprices, voir Dumas plutôt que Musset, ne sont pas ceux d'une femme que la perte de son « cher petit Jules » désespère. Ce « pauvre Jules », comme dit Sand, va se consoler en Italie, fin mars. Il y part avec des lettres de recommandation obtenues par George, qui montre pour ce paresseux, ce bambocheur impénitent, une indulgence maternelle. Ainsi, Sand passe de l'état d'amante martyre à l'état de mère comblée qui voit son petit Jules partir en Italie, comme un grand.

L'affaire Sandeau se termine définitivement en juin 1833. Sand, toujours généreuse, règle le loyer de l'appartement que son amant occupait rue de l'Université. Elle n'éprouve plus pour Sandeau qu'une « compassion affectueuse ». Elle veut bien régler le loyer, mais ne veut plus revoir le locataire. Ce qui est fini est fini.

La rapidité de cette rupture n'exclut pas quelque déchirement. Trois semaines après cet orage, George écrit à l'une de ses plus anciennes amies, Laure Decerfz, fille du médecin qui soigna Mme Dupin de Francueil : « J'ai eu dans le cœur une profonde amertume. » Dans cette lettre du 1er avril 1833 à Laure se trouve, peut-être, le secret des sentiments de Sand pour Dorval : « Ensuite je vois dans une intimité tutoyante Mme Dorval, la fameuse comédienne dont je t'ai si souvent parlé. (...) Quand au sortir des coulisses, nous pouvons bavarder au coin de mon feu (...), nous regagnons le temps perdu et nous vivons beaucoup en peu d'heures. »

Chacun est libre d'interpréter à sa façon ce « nous vivons beaucoup en peu d'heures ».

FIASCO D'AVRIL
(avril 1833)

Un de ces jours d'ennui et de désespoir, je rencontrai un homme qui ne
doutait de rien, un homme calme et
fort, qui ne comprenait rien à ma
nature et qui riait de mes chagrins. La
puissance de son esprit me fascina
pendant huit jours, je crus qu'il avait
le secret du bonheur...

Rupture avec Sandeau, fantaisie avec Dorval, amitiés avec d'aussi éminents critiques que Sainte-Beuve ou Planche ont fait de George Sand, en quelques mois, un personnage parisien qui assiste à la première du drame de Hugo, *Lucrèce Borgia*, et à qui Balzac envoie son *Histoire intellectuelle de Louis Lambert*. Sand pourrait être un personnage à la mode, et passer avec cette mode, comme sa rivale, qui se dit son amie, Hortense Allart, « tranchante, politique, hommasse, femme auteur comme tous les diables ». Hortense passera, George restera. N'empêche qu'en ce printemps 1833 on se presse et on s'empresse autour de l'auteur d'*Indiana*. Voilà pour les apparences mondaines.

Dans la réalité, George souffre d'une esquinancie, « c'est-à-dire d'une inflammation de la gorge », et pâtit encore plus, le 17 avril, de voir Maurice amené par Casimir à Paris pour entrer au collège Henri-IV. Maurice le bien-aimé livré aux promiscuités et aux brimades du collège ! George en pleure et se dit inconsolable. Est-ce pour oublier un peu cette insupportable nécessité d'emprisonner son fils ? Elle jette les yeux sur Prosper Mérimée, dont elle admire les livres, en attendant mieux. Ce mieux tarde.

Entre George et Prosper, ce ne sont que rendez-vous annulés sous divers prétextes. George a mal à la gorge. Prosper est enrhumé. George doit sortir. Prosper n'est pas libre. Chacun s'offre et se dérobe à la fois. Il se peut que Mérimée, comme Sainte-

165

Beuve, qui ne s'en cachait pas, éprouve une certaine frayeur pour celle que l'on confond avec son Indiana. Par ses façons d'être et de vivre, Sand a de quoi effrayer des hommes aussi conventionnels que le sont Sainte-Beuve et Mérimée.

Avec Sainte-Beuve, Sand s'en est franchement expliquée : « Après avoir écouté *Lélia*, vous m'avez dit une chose qui m'a fait de la peine. Vous m'avez dit que vous aviez peur de moi. (...) Et ne croyez pas trop à mes airs sataniques ; je vous jure que c'est un " genre " que je me donne. »

Hélas, Sand ne fournit aucune explication à Mérimée, que ces « airs sataniques » refroidissent. George, elle, est fascinée par le calme, la force de Prosper, la puissance de son esprit, pendant que, fin avril 1833, dure leur liaison, une huitaine de jours ou quarante-huit heures, on ne sait pas exactement. On ne sait que trop que cette liaison se termine par un fiasco, l'un des plus célèbres de notre histoire littéraire. Prosper a voulu persuader George qu'il peut exister « une sorte d'amour supportable aux sens, enivrant l'âme ». Il rate complètement sa démonstration. George en pleure de dégoût, comme elle le racontera peu après à son confident, Sainte-Beuve. « L'expérience manqua complètement. Je pleurai de souffrance, de dégoût et de découragement. Au lieu de trouver une affection capable de me plaindre et de me dédommager, je ne trouvai qu'une raillerie amère et frivole. Ce fut tout, et l'on a résumé toute cette histoire en deux mots que je n'ai pas dits, que Mme Dorval n'a ni trahis ni inventés, et qui font peu d'honneur à l'imagination de M. Dumas. »

Sand n'a pu se retenir de conter son échec à Dorval, qui l'aurait rapporté à Dumas, qui aurait répété au Tout-Paris ces paroles que n'aurait jamais prononcées George : « J'ai eu Mérimée hier soir, ce n'est pas grand-chose. » On éclate de rire, Sand éclate en sanglots, et regrette profondément ce qu'elle qualifie d' « ânerie ».

De ce ratage Mérimée tire l'une de ses nouvelles les plus réussies, *la Double Méprise,* dont la fin semble un écho aux aveux de Sand à Sainte-Beuve : « Ces deux cœurs qui se méconnurent étaient peut-être faits l'un pour l'autre ».

UN INCESTE IMAGINAIRE
(nuit du 28 au 29 juillet 1833)

> Tu t'étais trompée, tu t'es crue ma maîtresse, tu n'étais que ma mère ; (...) c'est un inceste que nous commettions.
>
> Musset à Sand, le 4 avril 1834

> Tu as raison, notre embrassement était un inceste, mais nous ne le savions pas.
>
> Sand à Musset, le 15 avril 1834

À quoi sert donc cette liberté si chèrement acquise, à quoi sert d'avoir abandonné Nohant et de laisser Maurice dans un collège ? Pour en arriver à cet échec humiliant et à ce terrible constat : « Ma liberté me ronge et me tue. » Sand espérait trouver en Mérimée un maître qui possédait « le secret du bonheur ». Elle n'a même pas réussi à devenir sa maîtresse. Après ce désastre d'alcôve, elle se sent d'humeur suicidaire. Mais le bon sens l'emporte sur ce ratage des sens et la porte à croire que « s'il y a des jours de froid et de fièvre, il y a aussi des jours de soleil et d'espérance ».

Et puis, il y a le travail, *Lélia* qu'il faut terminer et dont *la Revue des Deux Mondes* du 15 mai publie déjà plusieurs chapitres dont Sainte-Beuve déclare : « C'est très beau, très haut et très vrai. » Et puis, il faut soigner Maurice qui a la grippe, Solange qui a la coqueluche, et apaiser la colère de Sophie-Victoire qui accuse sa fille de ne venir la voir qu'en son absence.

George se laisse prendre aux pièges du quotidien. Elle se promet d'être bonne mère, bonne fille, bon écrivain et considère sa vie sentimentale comme finie. Elle en prévient le seul homme qui ne puisse pas passer pour son amant, un ami véritable, son Pylade, François Rollinat, avocat à Châteauroux. Le 20 mai 1833, elle épanche son cœur dans cette « âme d'élite » : « Mon cœur a vieilli de vingt ans et rien dans la vie ne me sourit plus. Il n'est plus pour moi de passions profondes, plus de joies vives. Tout est dit. J'ai doublé le cap. Je suis au port. »

Un mois après, George Sand est prête à quitter ce port, toutes voiles dehors. Un mois après cette déclaration de retraite sentimentale, George Sand rencontre Alfred de Musset, à la mi-juin, à un dîner qui réunit les collaborateurs de *la Revue des Deux Mondes*.

À ce dîner très littéraire, Alfred de Musset et George Sand, qui voisinent, ne sont que deux auteurs en vogue se faisant des grâces. Le premier parle, la seconde écoute. Alfred passe pour l'un des plus brillants causeurs de Paris. George n'a pas de conversation, elle s'est suffisamment plainte de ce manque. Le bavard et la muette se quittent enchantés l'un de l'autre. Il a parlé, elle a écouté. Dans la nuit qui suit, Musset lit *Indiana* et écrit des vers intitulés « Après la lecture d'*Indiana* » :

Sand, quand tu l'écrivais, où donc l'avais-tu vue,
Cette scène terrible où Noun, à demi nue,
Sur le lit d'Indiana s'enivre avec Raymon ?
(...)
Ces plaisirs sans bonheur, si pleins d'un vide immense,
As-tu rêvé cela, George, ou t'en souviens-tu ?

Ce sont les premiers vers inspirés par Sand à Musset. Sand y répond, le 24 juin. D'autres suivront. Sand y répond par une lettre. D'autres suivront encore, qui se terminent par cette sévère invitation : « Si dans un jour de fatigue et de dégoût de la vie active, vous étiez tentée d'entrer dans la cellule d'une recluse, vous y seriez reçue avec reconnaissance et cordialité. »

Voilà qui sent la pose, et la pose d'écrivain. Car, dans cette liaison qui a fait couler tant d'encre, il ne faut jamais oublier que ces amours sont des amours d'écrivains. Poèmes et lettres seront les seuls enfants qu'ils auront et qu'ils seront conscients d'offrir à la postérité. Au paroxysme de leur passion, ils n'oublient pas ce qu'ils sont exactement, lui, l'auteur des *Contes d'Espagne et d'Italie*, de *Namouna* et d'*À quoi rêvent les jeunes filles*, et elle, l'auteur d'*Indiana* et de cette *Lélia* dont la parution, dans *la Revue des Deux Mondes*, suscite mille et une rumeurs.

Elle a vingt-neuf ans. Il en a vingt-trois. Enfant chéri des Muses et des dames, grisettes ou duchesses, il est amateur d'Andalouses au sein bruni, d'alcool et d'opium. Si George peut passer pour une Andalouse, elle préfère le lait à l'alcool et sa seule drogue est l'encre de son encrier. Il est dans tout l'éclat de sa jeune gloire. Elle est dans tout l'éclat de sa récente célébrité. Il est blond. Elle est brune. Il n'ignore rien de la débauche, ni de ses raffinements. Elle manque d'expérience, et les partenaires qu'elle a eus, Casimir, Stéphane, Jules, ne sont pas des adeptes des plaisirs compliqués. Il se fatigue « à jouir de tout, vite et sans réflexion ». Elle a besoin de lenteur et de réflexion pour savourer sa jouissance. Comme Sandeau, Musset n'est pas un bourreau de travail. Sand, qui sait que travail rime avec argent et indépendance, pond sa copie avec une scrupuleuse, une quotidienne régularité. Musset est la fantaisie même, il est Fantasio, il se moque de tout. Elle prend tout au sérieux. Bref, Alfred de Musset et George Sand sont la preuve même que les contraires s'attirent. Il admire sa prose. Elle admire ses vers.

Après avoir lu *Indiana*, Alfred lit *Lélia* sur épreuves. Il éprouve pour *Lélia* autant d'enthousiasme que pour *Indiana*. « Il y a dans *Lélia* des vingtaines de pages qui vont droit au cœur (...) Vous voilà George Sand ; autrement vous eussiez été Mme Unetelle faisant des livres. »

Bien qu'il l'appelle cérémonieusement « madame », il aspire à une camaraderie « sans conséquence et sans droits, par conséquent sans jalousie et sans brouilles ». Il ne revendique que le droit de fumer le tabac de George et de se promener en sa compagnie. Marché conclu. Ils fument et se promènent ensemble. Le 26 juillet, abandonnant le « madame », il écrit à sa camarade : « Mon cher

George, j'ai quelque chose de bête et de ridicule à vous dire. (...) Je suis amoureux de vous. Je le suis depuis le premier jour où j'ai été chez vous. J'ai cru que je m'en guérirai tout simplement en vous voyant à titre d'ami. » Le 27 juillet, il revient à la charge avec l'un de ces arguments auxquels George est incapable de résister : « Plaignez-moi. » À lire cette lettre du 27, Alfred est une victime que George doit plaindre, un prisonnier qu'elle doit délivrer. Il termine sa missive par un : « Adieu, George, je vous aime comme un enfant. »

George ne peut être qu'attendrie par les plaintes de cet enfant et accorder le rendez-vous qu'Alfred sollicite dans une lettre du 28, pour ce même 28, à minuit. C'est donc dans la nuit du 28 au 29 juillet 1833 que George succombe à la jeunesse et aux larmes d'Alfred : « Sans ta jeunesse et la faiblesse que tes larmes m'ont causée, un matin, nous serions restés frère et sœur. » Il est jeune et il pleure. Elle se croit vieille et croit n'avoir plus de larmes. Ils devaient rester frère et sœur, ils cèdent aux emportements d'un inceste imaginaire. George est persuadée d'avoir cédé par affection plus que par amour.

Le 31 juillet, *Lélia* paraît en librairie, et début août, la chaleur écrasant Paris, les deux amants vont à Fontainebleau chercher un peu de fraîcheur, et d'isolement. Ils descendent à l'hôtel Britannique, rue de France, à une heure de marche des rochers de Franchard.

Les rochers de Franchard, les arbres de la forêt, le clair de lune, tout porte le couple à une perfection d'exaltation qui sera gâtée par une crise d'hallucination jetant Alfred à terre. Il a vu un spectre passer dans les bruyères, il a eu peur. George n'a rien vu que la peur de son amant.

Délivré de son hallucination, Alfred en plaisante, la dessine et, sous sa propre caricature, inscrit : « Perdu dans la forêt et dans l'esprit de sa maîtresse ». Et, sous la caricature de George : « Le cœur aussi déchiré que sa robe. » George n'a pourtant pas le cœur à plaisanter. Elle est inquiète. Si Alfred était vraiment à plaindre ? Et si George était aussi à plaindre d'avoir un amant sujet à de telles crises ? Questions sans réponse, ou qui trouvent une facile solution dans des étreintes assez folles pour éloigner le spectre de la folie.

Pendant ce temps, à Paris, *Lélia* fait grand bruit. Le récit des ténébreuses amours de Lélia avec le poète Stenio provoque un scandale. Un journaliste, Capo de Feuillide, donne le ton : « Le jour où vous ouvrirez *Lélia,* renfermez-vous dans votre cabinet (pour ne contaminer personne). Si vous avez une fille dont vous voulez que l'âme reste vierge et naïve, envoyez-la aux champs avec ses compagnes. » *Le Figaro,* où Latouche n'est plus pour protéger George Sand, attaque à son tour. Dans *la Revue des Deux Mondes,* Gustave Planche riposte par un éloge de *Lélia* et veut se battre en duel avec Capo de Feuillide. On parle partout du « criminel auteur » de cette *Lélia* dont George Sand donne les clés à son ami Rollinat : « Quelques-uns diront que je suis Lélia, mais d'autres pourraient se souvenir que je fus jadis Stenio. »

La romancière revendique le droit d'être tous les personnages de son roman, et non pas seulement son héroïne, cette Lélia qui, pour la première fois, ose dire tout haut ce que les femmes pensent tout bas, à savoir que les étreintes des mâles peuvent laisser de marbre celles qui les subissent. De cette frigidité avouée de Lélia, on a accusé Sand qui, elle, n'a connu que des accès de passagère impuissance à atteindre le plaisir. Une telle sincérité provoque un concert d'insultes qu'interrompent quelques bénédictions inattendues, comme celles de Chateaubriand, qui prédit à l'auteur de *Lélia* qu'elle sera « le lord Byron de la France ».

Le 25 août 1833, Sand écrit à Sainte-Beuve, que Musset surnomme Sainte-Bévue : « Je suis très insultée comme vous savez, et j'y suis fort indifférente. » Ce n'est pas pour évoquer cette indifférence aux insultes qu'elle écrit à son confident parisien, mais pour lui annoncer sa nouvelle passion : « Je me suis énamourée et cette fois très sérieusement d'Alfred de Musset (...). C'est un amour de jeune homme et une amitié de camarade. » Casimir Dudevant ne savait pas qu'en offrant à Aurore Dupin l'amour en camarade il allait faire école et que, par la suite, Aurore considérerait l'amour comme une camaraderie incandescente... C'est à M. Dudevant que Mme Dudevant annonce, le plus naturellement du monde, qu'elle part en Italie... pour y soigner ses rhumatismes !

Elle laisse en pension Maurice qui s'y « porte bien », et renvoie à Nohant Solange qui en est « enchantée ». Solange, qui a cinq ans, n'est plus « bête comme une oie » et n'est peut-être pas aussi « enchantée » que le prétend sa mère. Estimant avoir ainsi accompli ses devoirs envers sa famille, George peut se consacrer entièrement à son nouvel enfant : Alfred.

On aura compris que Sand ne part pas en Italie pour y soigner ses rhumatismes, mais s'en va avec Musset à Venise, dans l'espoir que cette ville apportera à leur passion un supplément d'exotisme, et à leur œuvre, une nouvelle source d'inspiration. Elle mène l'expédition italienne tambour battant, comme son ancêtre, le maréchal de Saxe, devait conduire ses campagnes. Elle finance cette expédition en vendant à son éditeur, François Buloz, *Metella* et *le Secrétaire intime*. Elle obtient une avance sur *Jacques*, un roman qu'elle promet de livrer en mai 1834. Elle obtient aussi le consentement de la mère de Musset, très réticente à cette escapade, en l'assurant qu'elle aura pour Alfred « une affection et des soins maternels ». Le 12 décembre 1833, elle prend place dans la malle-poste qui la conduira, avec Alfred, jusqu'à Lyon. Tous les obstacles familiaux et financiers ayant été vaincus, George peut s'accorder un soupir de soulagement.

LA « FOIRE » À VENISE
(1er janvier-29 mars 1834)

> Foire : flux de ventre.
> Littré

Il y a indéniablement un côté « enlèvement » dans les amours de Sand, un côté « fuite éperdue ». Elle s'enfuit à Paris pour y rejoindre Jules Sandeau. Elle entraîne Alfred de Musset à Venise pour y vivre sa passion à son aise, et être délivrée des importuns du quai Malaquais. Mais on ne se délivre pas aisément des importuns... À Lyon, Alfred et George quittent la malle-poste pour prendre un bateau jusqu'à Avignon. Sur le bateau, le couple rencontre Henry Beyle, dit Stendhal, qui rejoint en Italie son consulat de Civitavecchia. Alfred se réjouit de cette rencontre et s'amuse de l'esprit caustique du consul. George fait grise mine. Elle n'a pas quitté Paris pour se retrouver avec l'un des représentants de cet esprit parisien. Quelle importunité !

Délivrée de Stendhal en Avignon, George s'embarque, le 20 décembre, à Marseille, pour Gênes. Elle montre, pendant la traversée, un pied marin, ce qui n'est pas le cas de Musset, que le tangage rend malade.

Du 21 au 31 décembre, de Gênes à Livourne, de Pise à Ferrare, George joue les touristes avec une froideur qui étonne Casimir : « Tu vois d'un œil froid et tranquille, et pour ainsi dire avec les yeux d'une bonne philosophie, les monuments, les sites, et le luxe en tout genre qui a fait palpiter tant de cœurs, bouleversé tant de têtes, et dicté tant de pages de feu. »

Ce n'est pas le feu de l'inspiration, ou de la passion, qui attend les amants à Venise, mais le feu des entrailles, la dysenterie. Au dix-neuvième siècle, l'Italie est pour les Français ce qu'est l'Inde au vingtième siècle : on meurt d'abord d'extase devant les paysages et les monuments, on croit mourir ensuite d'une diarrhée due à l'impureté des eaux, ou à la nourriture infecte.

À Venise, le 1ᵉʳ janvier 1834, le couple s'installe à l'hôtel Danieli, où, d'après son frère Paul, Alfred « ne se lassait pas de contempler ces lambris sous lesquels s'était promené jadis le chef de quelque grande famille vénitienne » tandis que George, trois jours après leur installation, doit s'aliter, atteinte d'une affreuse dysenterie. La violence des crises l'empêche de quitter sa chambre dont elle se lasse vite de contempler les lambris. Ainsi, George Sand et Alfred de Musset, qui sont entrés dans la légende comme « les amants de Venise », n'ont profité de leur passion en cette ville que pendant trois jours, les trois premiers jours de 1834.

Les débâcles intestinales n'incitent guère aux étreintes. Et, exactement un mois plus tard, le 4 février, la pauvre George se plaint au fidèle Boucoiran de la persistance de son mal : « Je viens encore d'être malade cinq jours d'une dysenterie affreuse. Mon compagnon de voyage est très malade aussi. Nous ne nous en vantons pas, parce que nous avons à Paris une foule d'ennemis qui se réjouiraient en disant : " Ils ont été en Italie pour s'amuser et ils ont la foire. " (...) J'ai donc le cœur aussi barbouillé que l'estomac. »

Ce qu'elle ne dit pas à Boucoiran, et qui « barbouille » son cœur, c'est que, pendant qu'elle se tordait de coliques, Alfred, qui n'a pas la vocation de garde-malade, l'abandonnait pour courir Venise, ses églises, ses filles. Alfred craint même d'avoir attrapé en leur compagnie « une mauvaise maladie ». À cet aveu, il en ajoute un autre, pire : « George, je m'étais trompé, je t'en demande pardon, mais je ne t'aime pas. » Si elle n'était pas retenue par la plus humiliante des maladies, George partirait sans tarder. Pour couronner le tout, Alfred appelle George « l'ennui personnifié ». Il y a de quoi avoir le cœur barbouillé et l'estomac malade !

Aux malaises physiques, au désarroi moral, s'ajoutent les embarras financiers. Buloz se fait tirer l'oreille pour régler ce qu'il doit à Sand, surprise par la cherté de l'hôtel Danieli. Elle voudrait changer de logement, mais pour le moment, Alfred, qui est tombé malade à son tour, est intransportable. Ce même 4 février 1834, George apprend à Buloz, qu'elle presse d'envoyer 1 000 francs, qu'Alfred souffre « d'une fièvre nerveuse et inflammatoire ».

Musset n'est pas un malade facile. Il refuse de suivre les prescriptions d'un médecin appelé en consultation, Pietro Pagello, vingt-sept ans, blond, la peau très blanche, habile à lancer le poignard et à pousser la romance. Cet amateur de femmes, très apprécié des Vénitiennes, a déjà remarqué George à une fenêtre de l'hôtel Danieli.

Le 5 février, Sand ne cache pas au Dr Pagello l'état fébrile du malade, tâchant d'en expliquer les origines, « le vin, les fêtes, les femmes ». On le voit, Sand est sans illusion sur son enfant qui vient de passer une nuit de délire complet, « six heures d'une frénésie telle que, malgré deux hommes robustes, il courait nu dans la chambre ». Les hallucinations de la nuit de Franchard n'étaient qu'un aimable divertissement comparées aux horribles déchaînements de cette nuit vénitienne.

Musset passe de l'affection cérébrale à l'inflammation de poitrine. Sand reste huit jours et huit nuits, sans se déshabiller, à le soigner, guettant la moindre accalmie pour prendre un peu de repos. Elle n'en peut plus, elle est à bout de nerfs, elle se demande si Alfred ne va pas devenir fou et la rendre folle. Elle est seule, sans argent, sans aide aucune, dans une ville qu'elle ne connaît pas et où elle ne connaît personne, sauf ce Dr Pagello auprès de qui elle trouve un réconfort grandissant, et qu'elle trouve de plus en plus séduisant. Elle se déclare dans un billet que Pietro feint de croire adressé à un autre. George inscrit alors sur l'enveloppe « Au stupide Pagello ».

Après avoir lu des phrases comme « Je t'aime parce que tu me plais » ou « Les plaisirs d'amour te laissent-ils haletant et abruti, ou te jettent-ils dans une extase divine ? », Pagello cesse d'être stupide et montre, de la façon la plus simple et la plus efficace, son intelligence. Il a compris parfaitement ce que souhaite Sand et le prouve avec une ardeur convaincante. Il n'y a plus qu'à être prudent afin que le malade ne se doute de rien. « Aurons-nous assez de prudence et assez de bonheur, toi et moi, pour lui cacher encore notre secret pendant un mois ? Les amants n'ont pas de patience et ne savent pas se cacher. Si j'avais pris une chambre dans l'auberge, nous aurions pu nous voir sans le faire souffrir et sans nous exposer à le voir d'un moment à l'autre devenir furieux », expose Sand à Pagello. Elle doit reconnaître qu'elle est follement éprise de son Pagello, « avec ses gros baisers, son air simple, son sourire de jeune fille, ses caresses, son grand gilet, son regard doux ». Elle n'a plus qu'une envie, être seule avec Pagello qui l'enfermerait dans une chambre et qui emporterait la clé quand il sortirait. « Être heureuse un an et mourir. Je ne demande que cela à Dieu et à toi. » Elle voit Pagello « grand comme Dieu ». Stéphane Ajasson de Grandsagne, Jules Sandeau, Alfred de Musset n'étaient que des anges, Pietro Pagello, c'est Dieu.

Pietro, qui n'est pas un saint, ni un dieu, se comporte comme un simple humain et s'inquiète : « Si elle a cessé d'aimer cet homme pour m'aimer, elle pourra cesser de m'aimer pour en aimer un autre. » Réponse catégorique de Sand : « Je ne crois pas que j'en puisse aimer un autre à présent, si je cessais de t'aimer. » Les vrais amants de Venise, ce sont Pietro Pagello et George Sand.

Il est difficile de cacher longtemps un aussi éclatant coup de foudre et cette foudre tombe sur Musset quand, dans son délire, il aperçoit, ou croit apercevoir, George sur les genoux de Pietro, George donnant un baiser à Pietro, et là, sur la table, une tasse de thé, une seule, ce qui prouve que George et Pietro ont bu dans la même tasse. La violence des reproches d'Alfred surprend George : « Au premier mot, comme tu m'as traitée ! Tu voulais me souffleter, m'appeler catin devant tout le monde. » Et ce ne sont pas les plus insupportables reproches que doit essuyer George. « Tu m'as reproché dans un jour de fièvre et de délire de n'avoir jamais su te donner les plaisirs de l'amour. » Autrement dit, Musset accuse Sand d'être une catin, sans en avoir le savoir-faire et les complaisances.

George avait pardonné à Alfred ses aventures vénitiennes quand elle était malade. Alfred ne pardonne pas à George sa faiblesse pour le corps médical. Faiblesse d'une esclave qui s'échappe vers un nouveau maître. Alfred se sent frustré et furieux. Fureur que minimise George, qui explique à Pietro ce qu'est réellement Alfred : « Il est aussi incapable de constance que de ressentiment. (...) Il me tarde de lui avoir rendu sa liberté et de reprendre la mienne. » Au fond, Sand aimerait assez changer d'homme comme elle change de chemise. Malheureusement pour George, Musset ne se laisse pas enlever comme une chemise et devient une tunique de Nessus.

Début mars 1834, George Sand et Alfred de Musset quittent l'hôtel Danieli où ils devaient être tellement heureux et où ils ont tant souffert, pour un appartement calle delle Rasse. Le couple connaît un instant de répit dû à la visite d'un ami d'Alfred, Alfred Tattet, richissime dandy qui, pendant son séjour, tâche « de procurer quelques distractions à Mme Dudevant qui n'en pouvait plus ; la maladie d'Alfred l'avait beaucoup fatiguée ».

La maladie d'Alfred, les dépenses incessantes, jusqu'à 20 francs par jour en drogues diverses, les discussions d'argent avec Buloz, les excès de travail, les ardeurs de Pagello, George a des motifs d'être

« beaucoup fatiguée ». À Venise, elle travaille jusqu'à treize heures par jour. « L'amour du travail sauve de tout. Je bénis ma grand-mère qui m'a forcé d'en prendre l'habitude », écrit-elle le 6 mars à Hyppolite Chatiron à qui elle vante les charmes de cette cité, son ciel magnifique, les chants de son peuple, les chœurs des gondoliers, les sérénades sous les fenêtres. Sand, qui aime la musique, vit en musique dans cette Venise où d'excellents poulets ne valent que 6 sous. Hyppolite ne pourra plus dire que George ignore le prix des poulets !

On est confondu par la souplesse de Sand à courber sous les orages sentimentaux et à se redresser pour goûter la beauté d'une fleur, d'un oiseau ou du clair de lune sur la place Saint-Marc. À Venise, elle est prête à croire qu'elle pourrait vivre de l'air du temps. Elle se nourrit de poulet bouilli et fume des cigarettes de Maryland. Des cigarettes, et non des cigares, il est temps de le remarquer et de détruire la légende de Sand fumant le cigare comme un homme. Elle fume la cigarette comme une charmante jeune femme qui est maintenant aimée à la fois par Alfred de Musset et par Pietro Pagello.

Alfred s'attache à George plus que de raison et refuse de s'en détacher. Le 22 mars, George constate : « Il croit désirer beaucoup que nous ne nous séparions pas et il me témoigne beaucoup d'affection. » Il témoignerait aussi de l'affection, mais cela semble sujet à caution, à Pagello. Toujours est-il que, quand il quitte Venise, le 29 mars, Alfred reçoit en cadeau de départ un petit carnet offert par George et par Pietro. Sur la première page, il lit : « À son bon camarade frère et ami Alfred, sa maîtresse, George », et, à la dernière, des recommandations diverses de Pietro destinées à faciliter son retour.

À ces marques d'attention, George et Pietro en ajoutent une ultime dont Alfred se serait peut-être passé : ils l'accompagnent jusqu'à Mestre. C'est prolonger inutilement les souffrances d'une séparation nécessaire et d'une situation difficile. Sand

veut tenter de vivre avec Pagello dans cette Venise
que Musset a prise en horreur. Ni Sand, ni Musset
ne sont prêts à accepter les servitudes du ménage
à trois. Il faut se quitter et suivre chacun son
destin.

LES VRAIS AMANTS DE VENISE
(30 mars-24 juillet 1834)

On ne nous avait certainement pas assez vanté la beauté du ciel et les délices des nuits de Venise.

Délivrée de Musset, de son inconstance, de son affreux aveu — « Je m'étais trompé, je ne t'aime pas » —, de ses terribles reproches — « Tu n'as jamais su me donner les plaisirs de l'amour » —, Sand savoure le printemps vénitien. Elle sait qu'Alfred se consolera promptement avec d'autres femmes qui auront pour lui ces complaisances qu'elle n'a pas eues, et auxquelles il tenait tant, comme il l'avouera, plus tard, à l'éditeur Hetzel : « La griserie, elle ne voulait pas me la donner, la griserie, tu comprends, celle qu'on trouve chez toutes les filles. Je l'injuriais, je l'accusais de ne pas vouloir. »

Sand sait aussi qu'elle continue à régner sur cet enfant gâté, « pourri » selon Hetzel, qu'est Alfred. Elle en reçoit la confirmation dans une lettre du 4 avril. « Je t'aime encore d'amour, George (...), je t'aime, je te sais près d'un homme que tu aimes, et cependant je suis tranquille (...). Je ne suis qu'un enfant, mais j'ai deux grands amis et ils sont heureux. »

En quoi Alfred ne se trompe pas. George est heureuse avec Pietro, autant qu'elle puisse l'être après de telles épreuves. Elle vit paisiblement en compagnie de Pagello et d'un sansonnet offert par ce même Pagello. Le sansonnet boit l'encre, mange le tabac et se perche sur les genoux de Sand quand elle écrit. Un sansonnet idéal. Quant à Pagello, il est aussi idéal que son sansonnet. Il est sensible, il sait se taire, il n'est jamais importun, il est prévenant. C'est « un ange de douceur, de bonté et de dévouement ». Le contraire de Musset qui s'est comporté comme un démon de méchanceté et qui a montré une absence totale de dévouement quand Sand était malade. Sans rancune, Sand veille sur la santé de son troisième enfant qu'elle supplie « à genoux » de ne pas se jeter inconsidérément dans le vin et les filles : « C'est trop tôt. (...) Ne t'abandonne au plaisir que quand la nature viendra te le demander impérieusement, mais ne le cherche pas comme un remède à l'ennui et au chagrin, c'est le pire de tous (...). Ménage cette vie que je t'ai conservée, peut-être, par mes veilles et mes soins. »

L'infirmière Sand et le médecin Pagello ont sauvé Musset. Avec le sentiment du devoir accompli, ils peuvent se réjouir d'être ensemble, à Venise, en avril. Certes, il y a bien une maîtresse de Pietro qui manifeste sa jalousie publiquement en déchirant les vêtements du docteur et en menaçant de tuer George. Qu'importe ? Cela n'est rien comparé aux horreurs subies à l'hôtel Danieli.

Ces tourmentes n'ont pas entravé la production de Sand, qui envoie sa première *Lettre d'un voyageur* à Buloz, qui l'en complimente — « Vous serez grande dans l'avenir » —, et qui la publie, le 15 mai, dans *la Revue des Deux Mondes*.

En attendant d'être « grande dans l'avenir », George se contente des petites joies du quotidien : « Tous les vrais biens, je les ai à ma disposition. » Les vrais biens : le ciel, l'eau, le soleil et l'amour tranquille. Elle change d'appartement, et, habile comme sa mère aux travaux manuels, elle fait des rideaux, plante des clous, couvre des chaises.

Dans ce nouveau logis proche du pont dei Barcaroli, elle rêve encore à cet impossible ménage à trois, et écrit à Musset, le 24 mai 1834 : « Oh, pourquoi ne pouvais-je vivre entre vous deux et vous rendre heureux sans appartenir ni à l'un ni à l'autre ! » Pieux souhait d'angélisme dans lequel on peut voir un écho lointain de l'angélisme imposé par Aurore Dupin à Aurélien de Sèze...

Le bonheur de Sand à Venise serait parfait si elle avait de l'argent et des nouvelles de Maurice. Et puis, l'argent arrive, et les nouvelles de son fils aussi qui se porte bien et qui n'oublie pas sa mère. « Je n'ai pas encore pu me décider à voir Maurice, mais il a une paire d'yeux noirs que je ne verrais pas sans douleur », confesse Musset à Sand. Ah, les yeux, les beaux yeux de George, comme ils sont inoubliables !

La correspondance entre George et Alfred ne faiblit pas. Dès qu'ils sont séparés, ils s'aiment à l'unisson. Le 15 juin, George conseille à Alfred : « Aime et écris, c'est ta vocation, mon ami. » À sa lettre du 15, George joint un billet de Pietro qui se termine par : « Adieu, mon bon Alfred, aimez-moi comme je vous aime. »

George, dont le goût pour le sublime ne faiblit pas, est comblée. Elle se parfume au patchouli et porte des souliers de satin noir. Elle vit pleinement son intermède vénitien avec, comme à Nohant, des rossignols, des chèvrefeuilles et des roses. Où qu'elle aille, Sand est toujours environnée de fleurs et d'oiseaux, du matin au soir. Et les nuits sont dignes de cet Orient où elle brûle d'aller, et où elle n'ira pas, faute d'argent. À quoi bon courir en Orient ? Elle peut s'y croire à Venise, favorite du sultan Pagello.

Avec l'été qui arrive, Venise devient « un miroir ardent ». On prend le frais au balcon, on s'allonge sur un sofa, on va au café avec des amis de Pagello, on parle, on traîne, on chante, et à deux heures du matin, George se retrouve dans un restaurant de Sainte-Marguerite en train de manger « des soles accommodées avec du raisin de Corinthe ». On boit du vin de Bragance et on mange, au dessert, des macarons au girofle. Et puis, infatigable, George se précipite voir le soleil se lever sur Torcello. « L'air était embaumé et le chant des cigales interrompait seul le silence religieux du matin. J'avais sur la tête le plus beau ciel du monde, à deux pas de moi les meilleurs amis. »

Oui, les vrais amants de Venise, et les plus heureux, ce sont, en ces jours de juin et de juillet 1834, George Sand et Pietro Pagello.

LES AMANTS TERRIBLES
(octobre 1834-mars 1835)

J'ai entendu dire que Musset et George Sand avaient eu une liaison. George était calme, positive, travailleuse. Musset était lâche, apathique et négligent dans son travail. Tout cela a fini par une crise et une séparation, suivie d'une tentative désespérée et des regrets de Musset, profondément enlisé dans la boue ; George Sand, de son côté, avait mis de l'ordre dans ses affaires, elle s'était abîmée dans son travail et elle lui avait dit : « Il est trop tard maintenant, ce n'est plus possible. »

Vincent Van Gogh
Lettres à Théo

LES AMANTS TERRIBLES

(octobre 1834-mars 1837)

Depuis que Sand est devenue la maîtresse de Pagello, six mois ont passé. Six mois d'accord parfait entre la sirène du Berry et le dieu de Venise. Comme le Tout-La Châtre et le Tout-Paris s'étaient scandalisés de ses amours avec Jules Sandeau, le Tout-Venise stigmatise ses amours avec un médecin. Le père de Pagello fulmine. Il accuse son fils de perdre sa jeunesse avec une femme mariée, de ruiner sa carrière et de renier les principes de la morale chrétienne.

Les anciennes maîtresses de Pagello enragent également et ne désespèrent pas de voir l'étrangère succomber à une crise de colique plus forte que les autres. Bref, George et Pietro ont intérêt à quitter la Sérénissime République, où les choses pourraient se gâter pour eux s'ils continuaient à donner le spectacle d'un adultère aussi réussi.

George n'est pas femme à céder aux menaces de l'opinion publique, mais elle veut être à Paris le 15 août, afin d'assister au collège Henri-IV à la distribution des prix. Maurice, à qui elle répète qu'elle est sa « meilleure amie », espère y avoir un accessit.

Le 24 juillet 1834, George Sand et Pietro Pagello quittent Venise. Aux veilles de son départ, Pietro envoie à son père une lettre qui se veut rassurante : « Je suis au dernier stade de ma folie et je dois le courir les yeux fermés comme j'ai couru les autres. Demain je pars pour Paris où je quitterai George Sand et je reviendrai t'embrasser digne de toi. Je suis jeune et je pourrai refaire ma carrière. »

Les amants vénitiens ne seront pas des amants parisiens. Ils arrivent à Paris le 14 août, et, dès le 17, Sand reçoit Musset, un Musset toujours amoureux, et dont Pagello s'avise d'être subitement jaloux. « Lui qui comprenait tout à Venise, du moment qu'il a mis le pied en France il n'a plus rien compris, et le voilà désespéré. Tout de moi le blesse et l'irrite », se lamente George, qui voit s'effondrer ses espoirs de chaste ménage à trois. « Je l'aimais comme un père et tu étais notre enfant à nous deux », confie Sand à Musset, qui doit se demander si l'inceste imaginaire n'est pas le péché mignon de l'auteur de *Lélia*. Elle aime Musset comme un fils. Elle aime Pagello comme un père. Elle aime surtout ce qui n'existe pas et s'en rend compte : « Toujours saisir des fantômes et poursuivre des ombres, je m'en lasse. » Ce dont elle ne se lasse pas, c'est d'annoncer à Boucoiran, une fois de plus, qu'elle en a « fini avec les passions » !

Le 24 août, elle retourne à Nohant tandis que Musset part à Bade. Pagello reste à Paris, confié à Boucoiran, qui est vraiment l'homme à tout faire. Le médecin vénitien veut rencontrer des médecins parisiens et visiter des hôpitaux. Il rencontre et visite, sur intervention de George qui, bonne fille, veille à ce que Pietro ne manque de rien, et surtout pas d'argent. Comme elle avait réglé les loyers que devait Jules Sandeau, et assumé les frais du voyage à Venise, elle organise une vente fictive de quatre tableaux apportés par Pagello qui peut ainsi recevoir de l'argent de sa maîtresse sans avoir à en rougir. Comme il l'avait noté dans son Journal intime, Pagello s'aperçoit que Sand, « sobre, économe, laborieuse pour elle-même », est « prodigue pour les autres ». C'est à se demander si George ne veut pas racheter la conduite de ses ancêtres, les dames d'opéra qui se faisaient payer par les hommes. Leur descendante paye pour ses hommes...

Peu avant son retour à Nohant, Mme Dudevant décerne un certificat de bonne conduite, en tant que père, à M. Dudevant : « Si tu étais un mauvais père, je ne quitterais jamais mes enfants, tu peux en être sûr. » Il s'agit visiblement d'amadouer Casimir qui pourrait être en droit de faire remarquer à son épouse qu'elle n'a pas respecté leur pacte. Il l'avait autorisée à passer trois mois à Paris, et non six mois à Venise, fût-ce pour y soigner ses rhumatismes !

George, « craignant d'être mal reçue », se fait accompagner pour ce retour à Nohant par sa mère et par son fils. Ce dragon de Sophie-Victoire et cet agneau de Maurice en imposeront certainement à M. Dudevant. Pour éviter tout accueil désagréable, Mme Dudevant bat le rappel de ses amis qui accourent. Les Papet, Fleury, Duvernet, Duteil se pressent à Nohant pour y accueillir la voyageuse qui revient auréolée des prestiges d'un voyage en Italie. Et alors, Venise, c'était comment ?

M. Dudevant, que l'absence de madame n'a pas dû trop faire souffrir, est « devenu fort aimable » et pousse l'amabilité jusqu'à inviter ce M. Pagello qui a été si bon à Venise pour son épouse. M. Pagello refuse cette invitation. Il sait qu'il n'est plus un dieu, ni un ange, et qu'il est tombé de ce piédestal sur lequel Sand place chacun de ses amants. Il comprend qu'il n'a été qu'un caprice, un éternel amour de six mois. Il en a de la peine, juste ce qu'il faut. Le Vénitien est trop bon vivant pour se laisser aller longtemps aux chagrins inutiles.

Déçue par Pagello qu'elle croyait « généreux et romanesque » comme elle, et qui, d'après elle, n'est qu'un « être faible, soupçonneux, injuste », Sand se déclare, une fois de plus, « prête à descendre au tombeau » et charge Boucoiran, à qui rien n'est épargné, « de l'exécution de volontés sacrées ». Telle est cette George Sand de trente ans qui a vécu à Venise deux mois d'enfer avec Musset, six mois de paradis avec Pagello, et qui, maintenant, à Nohant, subit un supportable purgatoire en compagnie de son mari, de ses enfants et de ses amis. Il n'y a vraiment pas de quoi aller se jeter dans l'Indre. Mais

George, bourreau d'elle-même, s'accuse de ne pas savoir aimer. Les accusations de Musset, on le voit, ont causé de durables ravages : « Me voilà insensible, un être stérile et maudit. » Là voilà qui se prend pour Lélia, et Musset, à qui elle fait cet aveu d'insensibilité, la supplie de ne pas se croire telle.

De Bade, Alfred envoie des messages d'amour fou : « Quelle soif, mon George, ô quelle soif j'ai de toi ! » George se refuse à étancher cette soif et la seule eau qu'elle propose est celle où elle se noierait. « Adieu, mon pauvre enfant, sans mes enfants à moi, comme je me jetterais dans la rivière avec plaisir ! », écrit-elle à Musset le 7 septembre.

Début octobre, George revient à Paris. Fin octobre, Pagello repart à Venise renouer avec son père, ses maîtresses, sa carrière. Libérée de Pagello, Sand reprend sa liaison avec Musset et rencontre Franz Liszt. La romancière est troublée par le musicien qui l'est également. De cette tentation à laquelle ils ne succombent pas naît une amitié.

Départ de Pagello, retrouvailles avec Musset, rencontre avec Liszt, ces événements ne détournent pas Sand de sa table de travail et *la Revue des Deux Mondes* publie sa quatrième *Lettre d'un voyageur*.

La copie à composer, les contrats à discuter, les enfants à éduquer, cela prend du temps. George ne peut plus, ou ne veut plus, se consacrer complètement à Alfred qui, lui, jure : « Je n'ai à faire que de t'aimer. » George a d'autres occupations et ne se soucie guère de cette éternité promise par le poète qui l'assure que « la postérité répétera nos noms, comme ceux des amants immortels qui n'en ont qu'un à eux deux, comme Roméo et Juliette, comme Héloïse et Abélard. On ne parlera jamais de l'un sans l'autre ».

Cette postérité-là, Sand s'en moque. Elle n'a plus l'âge de Juliette et Alfred n'a plus celui de Roméo. Musset boit de plus en plus. Son intempérance choque Sand dont la sobriété est exemplaire. Quand il a bu, il peut dire, ou écrire, n'importe quoi. Il devait être ivre quand, à Venise, il l'a couverte d'injures.

Musset ne peut aimer qu'en souffrant et en faisant souffrir. Ce besoin s'exacerbe avec certaine révélation sur l'affaire vénitienne. Avant de quitter Paris, Pietro Pagello a commis une indiscrétion. Il a confié à Alfred Tattet qu'il avait été l'amant de Sand alors que Musset était encore à Venise. Tattet s'empresse de rapporter cet aveu à Fantasio qui se change immédiatement en un Othello furieux. Sand et Pagello avaient réussi à persuader Musset, non sans peine et on est en droit de se demander jusqu'à quel point, de la pureté de leur relation pendant qu'il était malade à Venise. Les reproches reprennent presque en même temps que la liaison. « J'en étais bien sûre que ces reproches-là viendraient dès le lendemain du bonheur rêvé et promis et que tu me ferais un crime de ce que tu avais accepté comme un droit », soupire tristement George. Mais allez faire entendre raison à un fou qui chérit sa folie, à un furieux qui se complaît dans des fureurs qu'il s'empresse de mettre en vers.

Sand est accablée. Elle a renoué avec Musset vers le 24 ou le 25 octobre et Musset a rompu, après les indiscrétions de Pagello et de Tattet, vers le 8 ou le 10 novembre, et avec quelle violence, et avec quelles injures ! Sand a pu se croire revenue aux heures noires de Venise.

Qu'ils sont rares, les moments de bonheur avec Musset, nuit du 28 au 29 juillet 1833, trois ou quatre jours à Fontainebleau, trois jours à Venise, et maintenant, une quinzaine de jours à Paris. Ces trop brefs instants sont payés par d'interminables heures de désespoir que George note dans son Journal intime qu'elle donne à lire à Alfred. « Insensé, tu me quittes dans le plus beau moment de ma vie, dans le jour le plus vrai, le plus passionné, le plus saignant, de mon amour ! »

L'insensé refuse de croire à la sincérité de ces cris et repousse celle qu'il considère comme une pécheresse, une Marie Madeleine qui se traîne à ses genoux et qui, comme Marie Madeleine, fait le sacrifice de sa chevelure. Inutile sacrifice. Pour Musset, Sand n'existe plus. Anéantie, elle crie son désespoir. « Ô mes yeux bleus, vous ne me regarderez plus ! Belle tête, je ne te verrai plus t'incliner sur moi et te voiler d'une douce langueur ! Mon petit corps souple et chaud, vous ne vous étendrez plus sur moi (...) Adieu mes cheveux blonds, adieu mes blanches épaules, adieu tout ce que j'aimais, tout ce qui était à moi. »

Entre Sand et Musset, c'est à celui qui criera le plus fort. Toute pudeur est abandonnée. Les fureurs d'Alfred, les douleurs de George retentissent à travers Paris et remplissent la place publique. Sand se confie à Buloz, à Sainte-Beuve, à Liszt, à Delacroix qui fait son portrait et immortalise ainsi ses cheveux coupés... Tout le monde se mêle de l'affaire Sand-Musset et l'emmêle à plaisir. Oui, tout le monde, y compris Jules Sandeau, que Sand revoit le 22 novembre et qu'elle accuse de colporter des calomnies à son propos. Sandeau se défend d'avoir dit un mot contre Sand qui n'en croit rien. Elle ne croit plus en rien puisque Musset ne croit plus en elle. Alfred ne répond plus à ses lettres et hausse les épaules devant une menace de départ « définitif ». « Bah ! tu ne partiras pas ! » dit-il. « Sois tranquille, je pars dans quatre jours et nous ne nous reverrons plus », répond-elle.

Le 7 décembre 1834, George Sand revient à Nohant, fermement décidée à ne plus revoir Musset, comme elle le confirme à Sainte-Beuve, dans une lettre du 15 : « Je ne désire plus le revoir, cela me fait trop de mal. »

Moins d'un mois plus tard, revenue à Paris, elle envoie, le 14 janvier 1835, ce triomphal bulletin de victoire à Alfred Tattet : « Alfred est redevenu mon amant ; comme je présume qu'il sera bien aise de vous voir chez moi, je vous engage à venir dîner avec nous au premier jour de liberté que vous aurez.

Puisse l'oubli que je fais de mon offense ramener l'amitié entre nous. » On ne saurait se venger plus joliment d'un indiscret qu'en l'invitant à contempler un bonheur détruit par son indiscrétion et qui renaît de plus belle. Pour peu de temps. Dès la fin janvier, la tension et les scènes reprennent entre les amants terribles et George propose à Alfred : « Veux-tu que nous allions nous brûler la cervelle ensemble à Franchard ? »

Ils n'iront pas à Franchard brûler leurs précieuses cervelles d'écrivains qui changeront ces sombres douleurs en pages étincelantes.

Fin février, à bout de forces, George envisage une nouvelle, et définitive, séparation : « Non, non, c'est assez ! Pauvre malheureux, je t'ai aimé comme mon fils, c'est un amour de mère, j'en saigne encore. Je te plains, je te pardonne tout, mais il faut nous quitter. » Alfred ne croit pas à ce nouveau projet d'irrémédiable rupture.

Le 6 mars, sans prévenir Musset de son départ, Sand retourne à Nohant. « Monsieur, je sors de chez Mme Sand et on m'apprend qu'elle est à Nohant. Ayez la bonté de me dire si cette nouvelle est vraie », demande Alfred, stupéfait, à Boucoiran.

Les poèmes de l'un et les lettres de l'autre, les rochers de Franchard et les lambris de l'hôtel Danieli demeurent les seuls tangibles témoins de songes définitivement évanouis.

LE ROI MICHEL
(printemps 1835-été 1836)

La première chose qui m'avait frappée en voyant Michel pour la première fois (...), c'était la forme extraordinaire de sa tête. Il semblait avoir deux crânes soudés l'un à l'autre, les signes des hautes facultés de l'âme étant aussi proéminents à la proue de ce puissant navire que ceux des généreux instincts l'étaient à la poupe.

Après son tumultueux naufrage sentimental avec Musset et son irrévocable décision de rupture définitive, George Sand considère Nohant comme une source de tranquillité où elle puise un peu de calme. « Je suis très calme », écrit-elle à Boucoiran, le 9 mars 1835. Et pour preuve de son calme, elle demande à Boucoiran de lui expédier son *houka* [1] qu'elle a oublié dans sa précipitation, ainsi que trois livres, le théâtre de Shakespeare, les œuvres de Platon et le Coran. Elle sait que la lecture aide à vaincre les douleurs sentimentales. Aux grands maux, les grands auteurs !

Elle demande aussi à Boucoiran des nouvelles de Musset, il se porte bien, merci, et, apparemment, ne montre aucun chagrin. Elle est certaine qu'il se console avec du vin et des filles. Si tel est son bon plaisir... Elle veut tellement se persuader qu'elle est calme qu'elle le répète à Sainte-Beuve, à qui elle reproche, discrètement, de l'avoir abandonnée pendant ces tourmentes et de l'avoir traitée comme « une lépreuse du malheur ». Le 11 mars, mettant à profit son calme, elle annonce à Buloz qu'il aura bientôt une nouvelle, *Mauprat*.

Ainsi, du 6 au 11 mars, en cinq jours, Sand, éternel phénix, émerge, une fois de plus, de ses cendres. Ces amours entre deux écrivains, entre Sand et Musset, ressemblent à une tempête dans un encrier. George y a perdu quelques plumes, quelques illusions et une

---

1. Sorte de narguilé.

partie de sa belle chevelure. Ses cheveux repoussent et *Mauprat* prend une ampleur inattendue, passant de l'état de nouvelle à celui de roman.

La force de résurrection de George Sand tient du prodige. Lazare se contentait de sortir du tombeau et de rendre grâces à Dieu. George veut que la terre entière participe à sa résurrection et, en avril 1835, elle compose sa *Prière d'une matinée de printemps* qui paraît dans *la Revue des Deux Mondes* et qu'elle dédie aux « êtres souffrants » afin qu'ils sachent bien « qu'il n'est pas d'éternelles douleurs, pas de blessures sans remèdes ». Elle sait de quoi elle cause, Sand !

Le 6 mars, elle a donc rompu avec Alfred de Musset et le 9 avril, entraînée à Bourges par son ami Fleury le Gaulois, elle y rencontre Louis-Chrysostome Michel, avocat, républicain résolu et militant, époux d'une riche veuve. George est aussitôt éblouie, conquise. Et si elle ne devient pas immédiatement la maîtresse de Michel, c'est que, séquelle de ses récentes contrariétés, elle est couverte de boutons des pieds à la tête. La colique à Venise, les boutons à Bourges, les liaisons de George ne débutent jamais sous d'agréables auspices...

Michel a trente-sept ans et en paraît soixante. Il souffre de la poitrine, de l'estomac et du foie. Une aubaine pour Sand qui rêve toujours d'exercer ses talents d'infirmière. Il affecte une simplicité rustique, porte une houppelande et des sabots, une casquette et un foulard. Ah, ce n'est pas un dandy comme Musset. Parmi ses crasseux confrères, Michel étincelle de propreté et se distingue par une chemise impeccablement blanche, son seul luxe. On sait combien Sand tient à la propreté corporelle. Enfin, Michel a un crâne aux prometteuses immensités. Il vient de lire *Lélia* dont il se dit « toqué ». Et comme si tant de perfections ne suffisaient pas pour conquérir Sand, Michel, lors de cette première rencontre, déploie, de sept heures du soir à quatre heures du matin, les trésors de son esprit et les feux de son éloquence justement réputée. On en oublie les splendeurs du clair de lune, la magnificence de la nuit de printemps, le silence de Bourges endormi. Michel subjugue Sand et ses amis, Fleury et Planet. On se sépare épuisé mais ravi. « Jamais je ne l'ai vu ainsi. Il y a un an que je vis à ses côtés, et je ne le connais que de ce soir. Il s'est enfin livré pour vous tout entier », dit Planet à Sand, qui comprend bien qu'elle n'est pas indifférente à Michel...

Fleury le Gaulois espère mettre fin à ces effervescences en ramenant le plus rapidement possible Mme Dudevant à Nohant. Mais, à son réveil, dans une auberge où elle a pris quelques heures de repos, George reçoit une lettre de Michel qui prolonge les enchantements de la nuit de Bourges. « Ces lettres se succèdent avec rapidité sans attendre les réponses. Cet ardent esprit avait résolu de s'emparer du mien », racontera George Sand dans *Histoire de ma vie*, œuvre dans laquelle elle a élevé l'euphémisme à la hauteur d'un art. On ne peut qu'admirer la formule « Cet ardent esprit avait résolu de s'emparer du mien ». Dans ce cas précis, les ardeurs de l'esprit présagent, ou accompagnent, les ardeurs du corps.

Le 3 mai, George part à Paris retrouver Michel qui y est déjà pour défendre les accusés du « procès monstre », ainsi nommé parce que l'on y jugeait, en même temps et en bloc, cent vingt et un ouvriers et chefs d'opposition accusés d'avoir conspiré et provoqué, l'année précédente, des troubles à Lyon et dans d'autres villes. Louis-Philippe et son gouvernement ne badinaient pas avec le maintien de l'ordre public.

Michel présente Sand à ses amis républicains parmi lesquels Emmanuel Arago, Ledru-Rollin, Armand Carrel, Raspail, Barbès, Pierre Leroux. Seule femme parmi ces hommes, la châtelaine de Nohant fait sensation et, pour n'être pas trop remarquée, reprend ce qu'elle appelle « mes habits de petit garçon ». Ce qui comble Michel qui, en lisant *Lélia* et les *Lettres d'un voyageur*, avait toujours

20

imaginé leur auteur « sous l'aspect d'un jeune garçon, d'un poète enfant dont je faisais mon fils ». En fille ou en garçon, George plaît à Michel. En avocat ou en père, Michel plaît à George, ce qu'elle traduit par : « Le charme de ses paroles me retenait des heures entières. »

À Paris, George qui loge quai Malaquais voisine avec Michel, qui habite quai Voltaire. Ils se promènent sur les bords de la Seine et discutent à perdre haleine. Parfois, Michel s'impatiente et reproche à Sand sa « légèreté d'esprit » et sa « sécheresse de cœur ». Une fois, en colère, il brise sa canne contre la balustrade du pont des Saints-Pères tandis que les Tuileries retentissent des musiques d'un bal, ou d'un concert. George est ravie.

Dès le 11 avril, dans sa sixième *Lettre d'un voyageur*, dédiée à Everard, surnom qu'elle a donné à Michel, Sand écrit : « Tu es né roi. » Sandeau et Musset avaient été des anges, Pagello l'égal de Dieu, Michel est un roi dont George se dit « le très humble et très fidèle sujet ».

George et Michel ne se quittent plus. Ils ont en commun le goût des idées, de la république et de l'eau sucrée. Comme George, Michel ne boit que de l'eau sucrée. Il adore les enfants de George et les enfants de George le chérissent. Il prend soin de Maurice pendant ses jours de sortie et conduit Solange au jardin des Plantes.

George et Michel vivent heureux au royaume de l'utopie. Ils font et défont le monde, oublieux de la réalité. Mais la réalité ne les oublie pas. Le 4 juin, Michel publie un texte attaquant la pairie avec une violence telle que son auteur est condamné à un mois de prison et à 10 000 francs d'amende. Michel en tombe malade et retourne à Bourges, se faire soigner, cette fois, par son épouse. Il a obtenu de purger sa peine pendant la vacance des tribunaux.

Le 13 juin, George Sand fait établir un passeport pour voyager en France et à l'étranger. Passeport qu'elle n'utilise pas mais qui nous permet de savoir qu'elle mesurait alors exactement un mètre cinquante-huit.

Pendant l'été 1835, Michel vient à Nohant passer deux ou trois jours en l'absence de Casimir. À cette audace, on mesurera combien Michel et George ne peuvent plus se passer l'un de l'autre. Le roi Michel a complètement conquis son unique sujette, et réciproquement. Cette passion ne rend pas George aveugle et sourde aux autres. Par Michel, elle est devenue l'amie des chefs du parti républicain comme Ledru-Rollin, Pierre Leroux, Carnot, Barbès. La descendante des rois de Pologne, la cousine par alliance de Marie-Antoinette exulte d'être liée aux défenseurs des parias de la terre. Et ces révolutionnaires sont secrètement flattés de fréquenter un auteur à succès, une châtelaine, une baronne. Le snobisme n'épargne personne...

Par Liszt, elle connaît l'abbé Félicité de Lamennais qui a rompu avec Rome. L'abbé, qui ne doute de rien, veut une Église détachée de tout pouvoir terrestre. Le Vatican, qui s'est toujours placé du côté des puissants de ce monde et du pouvoir établi, ne saurait admettre cette déviation. Lamennais rejoint, en tout bien tout honneur, la cohorte des anges qui gravite autour de la romancière.

Un autre ange, « une belle comtesse aux cheveux blonds », Marie d'Agoult, provoque l'admiration de George Sand en quittant tout, mari, enfants, position mondaine, pour suivre Liszt, en juin 1835. George déteste le titre de comtesse autant que les épinards. Elle en oublie pourtant que Marie est comtesse et ne voit que sa beauté, sa douceur, son éclat de diamant. « Vous êtes de diamant », lui écrit-elle en septembre 1835.

La politique avec Michel, la musique avec Liszt, la foi avec Lamennais, la beauté avec Marie d'Agoult : Sand, en amour comme en amitié, va droit à ce que son siècle produit de plus flamboyant. Peu importe qu'elle s'y brûle. Le feu est son élément.

Habituée aux incendies et aux orages, elle n'est

pas surprise outre mesure par la tempête familiale qui s'abat sur Nohant.

À Nohant, le 19 octobre 1835, après le dîner auquel assistaient des amis comme M. et Mme Bourgoing, Fleury, Duteil, Papet, on passe au salon où Maurice tourne autour de son père qu'il importune. M. Dudevant ne cache pas son impatience et attribue à l'influence de Mme Dudevant les nombreux défauts de Maurice le Parfait.

Voulant éviter un esclandre public, Mme Dudevant dit à son fils, « Va-t'en dans ta chambre. Tu vois bien que tu impatientes ton père et qu'il ne sait... » Mme Dudevant arrête sa phrase à temps, Maurice sort en pleurant et M. Dudevant éclate :

« Achevez votre phrase : " ... Ton père ne sait ce qu'il dit. "

— C'est possible, mais je ne l'ai pas dit. »

Le ton entre les deux époux-camarades monte rapidement. M. Dudevant menace de gifler Mme Dudevant. Les amis s'interposent. M. Dudevant quitte la pièce en criant : « Vous allez voir ce que je vais faire. » Il prend un fusil, on le désarme, on le calme, on le reconduit au salon, où Duteil s'efforce vainement de ramener la gaieté. Au bout de quelques instants, Mme Dudevant prend congé et se retire dans sa chambre.

Être ainsi menacée dans Nohant, son Nohant, c'est plus qu'elle n'en peut supporter ! Sa décision est prise, elle demande une séparation de corps et de biens. Les tempêtes conviennent à George. Dès le lendemain, elle rédige un mémoire pour Michel qui, excellent avocat, ne peut que se surpasser pour défendre sa bien-aimée. Mme Dudevant accuse, entre autres, son mari de libertinage, de concubinage notoire, et de mœurs dissolues. M. Dudevant accable madame des mêmes griefs. Mais l'habileté de Michel est telle qu'il persuade le tribunal du contraire, en mai 1836. « Le domicile conjugal a été profané et c'est vous qui l'avez profané. Vous y avez introduit la débauche et la superstition », clame

Michel qui accuse, en plus, M. Dudevant de « représenter sa femme comme la plus vile des prostituées ».

Dans la salle, George, vêtue de blanc, symbolise l'innocence que l'on ne peut persécuter plus longtemps. Elle récupère Nohant et obtient la garde de ses enfants. Oui, vraiment, Michel est un roi !

CONTES DE L'OURS BLANC
ET RÈGLEMENTS DE COMPTES
(30 juillet 1836-7 janvier 1837)

Chère maman, tout est terminé et je suis enfin libre et tranquille pour toujours. Les plaidoiries ont duré deux jours et j'en suis sortie avec tous les honneurs de la guerre.

Bourges, le 30 juillet 1836

La reconquête de Nohant n'a pas été sans mal, ni rebondissements judiciaires divers. Mais, le 30 juillet 1836, George Sand lance à sa mère ce cri de victoire : « Chère maman, tout est terminé et je suis enfin tranquille et libre pour toujours. (...) M. Dudevant me laisse à jamais libre de gouverner ma fortune et de vivre loin de lui. Je lui abandonne le revenu de l'hôtel de Narbonne, à condition qu'il payera l'éducation de Maurice et qu'à partir de l'âge de vingt ans, il lui fera cent louis de pension. Je garde Nohant et ma fille. »

George peut savourer sa victoire et jeter sur les sept mois qui viennent de s'écouler un regard satisfait. Elle avait commencé l'année 1836 par cette dure constatation : « Je suis condamnée toute cette année à une énorme activité de plume », pour faire face, entre autres, aux dépenses qu'engendre le procès.

Elle est aussi satisfaite de la façon dont Alfred de Musset a raconté leurs amours dans *la Confession d'un enfant du siècle*, qui a paru le 1er février. Elle n'a pas caché à Buloz qu'elle a trouvé ce livre « magnifique » et « très supérieur à *Adolphe*, de Benjamin Constant ». Ce qu'elle n'a pas dit à Buloz, mais qu'elle a avoué à Marie d'Agoult : « Je me suis mise à pleurer comme une bête en fermant le livre. Puis j'ai écrit quelques lignes à l'auteur pour lui dire je ne sais quoi : que je l'avais beaucoup aimé, que je lui avais tout pardonné et que je ne voulais jamais le revoir. » George confirme son irrévocable décision de ne plus revoir Musset à Liszt et, de toute façon, elle estime que le poète l'a oubliée. « Je ne crois pas qu'il pense à moi, si ce n'est quand il a envie de faire des vers et de gagner cent écus à *la Revue des Deux Mondes.* » Voilà une façon bien terre à terre de juger certaines de ces *Nuits* qu'elle a quand même inspirées...

Décidément, les premiers mois de 1836 ont été placés sous le signe du souvenir. George a reçu en mai une lettre de Zoé Leroy à laquelle elle répond avec franchise. Elle n'a pas oublié Aurélien de Sèze, plus présent dans son cœur qu'Alfred de Musset. Cette lettre à Zoé contient deux autres aveux importants : « Appelez-moi George au masculin — c'est une maladie que j'ai de ne pouvoir entendre, ni lire, l'ancien nom. » George ne veut plus entendre parler d'Aurore. À cet enterrement d'Aurore succède la glorification de Maurice, « un ange de grâce, de bonté, de tendresse. C'est mon ami, c'est mon amant. »

À quatorze ans, Maurice est désespéré par la séparation de ses parents, désespéré d'entendre ses camarades de collège traiter sa mère de « putain »...

Les camarades de Maurice ignoraient pourtant que Sand, depuis avril, avait un nouvel amant en la personne de Charles Didier, homme de lettres sans envergure aucune, auteur d'une *Rome souterraine* qui avait paru en 1833 et avait été un succès de librairie.

Né à Genève en 1805, Charles est très beau. Il a été, ce qui est une référence pour l'époque, l'amant d'Hortense Allart. Parce qu'il a « une belle chevelure blanchie longtemps avant l'âge », George l'appelle « mon ours blanc ». À propos de sa liaison avec Charles Didier, George Sand évoquera, dans *Histoire de ma vie*, « un homme de génie » et « une amitié pure et parfaite ».

Ni pure, ni parfaite, cette liaison est entrecoupée de brouilles et de réconciliations. Chaque brouille permet à George d'affirmer à son amant numéro deux l'importance de son amant numéro un, Michel.

216

« Si je voulais, demain, Michel quitterait tout pour moi et je n'aurais plus un seul ami s'il l'exigeait. » Charles doit se résigner à n'être qu'un caprice de George. Il n'est pas de taille à supplanter Michel.

En août 1836, après avoir gagné son procès, George n'a plus qu'une ambition : vivre à Nohant avec ses enfants, et avec 6 000 francs par an. Mais avant de se retirer comme elle l'espère fermement, et pour oublier les tracas du procès, elle s'offre un petit voyage en Suisse où elle rejoint ses amis, Franz Liszt et Marie d'Agoult. Elle emporte dans ses bagages Maurice, Solange, une pèlerine rose, une robe de foulard gris, des pantalons, des chemises jaune paille, et « une paire de pantoufles très aisées pour mettre en voyage avec des pieds enflés ». Prévoyante Sand...

Le 4 septembre, George et ses enfants arrivent à Genève. Franz et Marie n'y sont plus : ils se trouvent à Chamonix, où George les rejoint. Les retrouvailles de la romancière avec le musicien et la comtesse ne passent pas inaperçues. Embrassades, cris de joie, congratulations tellement théâtrales qu'on prend le trio pour des comédiens ambulants. En artistes consommés, George, Franz et Marie offrent le spectacle de leurs fantaisies aux bourgeois anglais, allemands et italiens venus admirer les beautés des Alpes. On commente les réponses de George sur le registre de l'hôtel :

> *Où ils vont :* au ciel
> *Lieu de naissance :* Europe
> *Qualités :* flâneurs

Ils flânent, ils s'amusent, ils se donnent noms et surnoms. George et ses enfants sont les Piffoëls. Franz et Marie, les Fellows.

Dans la dixième *Lettre d'un voyageur*, Sand raconte ce séjour et déclare que ce qu'elle a vu de plus beau à Chamonix, c'est sa fille, Solange, dans l'éclat de ses huit ans. Au glacier des Bossons,

Solange dit à sa mère : « Sois tranquille, mon George ; quand je serai reine, je te donnerai tout le Mont-Blanc. » À cette promesse non tenue, Maurice ajoute une prédiction dont la seconde partie se réalisera : « Elle te rendra fier *(sic)*, moi je te rendrai heureux. »

Début octobre, les Fellows et les Piffoëls, devenus les meilleurs amis du monde, se quittent. Les Fellows retournent à Genève, les Piffoëls à Nohant, en passant par Lyon.

À Lyon, Michel, qui devait les attendre, n'est pas là. George en prend de l'humeur, et quand elle apprend que Michel s'avise d'être jaloux d'un garçon de vingt ans, Gustave de Gévaudan, rencontré au hasard du voyage, elle éclate et proteste de son innocence : « Je suis pure comme le cristal. » Elle n'a pas trompé Michel avec Gustave, comme Michel le croit, et elle en a bien du mérite. « J'ai beaucoup souffert de ma chasteté, je ne vous le cache pas, j'ai eu des rêves très énervants. (...) Je suis encore jeune, quoique je dise aux autres hommes que j'ai le calme des vieillards, mon sang est brûlant (...) Les autres croient que je suis Lélia dans toute l'acception du mot et que, quand je pâlis, c'est que j'ai trop marché, et l'occasion ne m'eût pas manqué pour me soulager, vous pouvez le croire. Il y avait autour de moi beaucoup d'hommes plus jeunes que vous et à qui un seul regard eût suffi... » Qui osera encore prêter à Sand la frigidité de sa Lélia ? Après avoir énuméré ses ardeurs contenues, elle ne cache pas à Michel qu'elle l'attend « avec la soumission d'une odalisque » et que l'envie, le désir qu'elle a de son sultan la laisse sans repos, « c'est de vous que je rêve quand je m'éveille trempée de sueur ». L'odalisque invite son sultan à la rejoindre à Paris, en automne.

Michel ne vient pas rejoindre George qui s'installe, rue Laffitte, à l'hôtel de France, où son cher Franz et sa chère Marie tiennent salon. C'est là que George rencontre un jeune pianiste polonais, Frédéric Chopin, qui l'invite à une soirée qu'il donne le 5 novembre. C'est là aussi que George rencontre la femme du consul d'Espagne à Paris, Charlotte Marliani, qui l'invite à dîner le 9 novembre, en compagnie de Frédéric Chopin, de Franz Liszt et de Marie d'Agoult.

Ces premières rencontres avec Frédéric Chopin et Charlotte Marliani, qui compteront parmi ses intimes, ne semblent pas avoir laissé un impérissable souvenir à George qui, à ce moment-là, est terriblement préoccupée par la santé de Maurice. Son fils souffre d'une maladie de langueur qui se traduit par de la fièvre, des crises de larmes, des insomnies. En fait, Maurice ne veut plus retourner au lycée Henri-IV, où sa mère est constamment traitée de « putain ».

George réussit à faire partager ses alarmes à Casimir qui, très réticent d'abord, finit par accepter que Maurice soit éduqué à Nohant par des précepteurs. Cette nouvelle victoire sur Casimir console un peu George de son échec auprès d'Alfred de Musset : elle a voulu récupérer ses lettres, sans y parvenir. Elle a plaidé sa cause aussi bien que l'avocat Michel. Elle n'a pas hésité à prétexter le choc que causerait leur lecture à Maurice. « Mon fils sera bientôt un jeune homme ; il m'aime passionnément. Un jour celui qui colporterait sous ses yeux une lettre de moi risquerait bien de se la voir arracher des mains sans cérémonie. » Moins sensible que Casimir à la sauvegarde de Maurice, Alfred garde les lettres de George.

Ces incessants tracas n'ont pas empêché Sand de se changer en l'un des piliers de *la Revue des Deux Mondes* et d'être un auteur dont on réimprime les ouvrages comme *Lélia*, ou comme *André*. À la reconquête de Nohant s'est ajoutée la conquête d'un public. George Sand sait maintenant qu'elle est l'une des valeurs sûres du marché littéraire. Elle en prévient Buloz. « Je ne redeviendrai pas le George d'autrefois. Le George d'autrefois avait besoin de cent écus et vous les lui prêtiez à cinquante pour cent d'intérêts. »

Le comble, c'est que Buloz fait à Sand « une réputation d'âpreté, de caprice », et cancane sur son compte. Ce règlement de comptes, par lettre du 18 décembre 1836, a été provoqué par le retard à recevoir les épreuves d'un texte qui aurait dû être publié en mai. Mais le motif profond de cette algarade, c'est que Buloz a osé refuser une avance à Charles Didier que Sand avait fait entrer à *la Revue*. Il faut reconnaître que George sait défendre ses amis, même quand elle n'est pas satisfaite de leur conduite. Son Didier, son « ours blanc », est plus ours que jamais. C'est pourtant en sa compagnie, et dans son appartement de la rue du Regard, que Sand termine 1836 et commence 1837. Comme avec Musset, les étreintes et les querelles alternent. Dans son Journal, Didier note : « Effroyable querelle. Elle me reproche d'avoir une corde grossière dans l'âme, moi de prendre les amis à l'essai. » On ose espérer que Maurice, qui loge aussi chez Charles Didier, ne prête pas trop l'oreille à ces disputes.

Le 7 janvier 1837, après des « adieux furtifs et froids » avec Charles Didier, George retourne à Nohant avec son fils. Son bonheur avec Michel « ne tient plus qu'à un fil ». Un fil que Sand est fermement décidée à ne pas rompre. Comme signe de sa volonté de rupture, Michel a réclamé ses lettres. « Craignez-vous que je publie vos lettres et que je compromette votre réputation ? Vous me feriez rire si vous ne me faisiez pleurer, avec vos bizarreries », répond-elle.

LA PROIE DE VÉNUS
(janvier-novembre 1837)

Ce n'est plus une ardeur dans mes
[veines cachée
C'est Vénus tout entière à sa proie
[attachée.
Racine, *Phèdre*

En janvier 1837, on pourrait croire George Sand heureuse d'être à Nohant, en tête à tête avec Maurice, Solange étant restée en pension à Paris. Heureuse d'être la maîtresse d'un Nohant qui ne dépend plus de M. Dudevant. Mais à quoi sert d'être la maîtresse de Nohant si elle n'est plus la maîtresse de Michel ? Michel se dérobe à ses appels. Michel ne répond plus à ses lettres. Michel est malade et guérit sans l'aide de George. Bref, Michel ne l'aime plus et en aime une autre.

Cet autre amour, ces dérobades, ce silence, cette guérison font mesurer à George ce qu'elle est en train de perdre. Le 16 janvier, elle écrit à l'avocat : « Il n'y a qu'une réalité, qu'une certitude : c'est que je t'aime, Michel. »

Le 21 janvier, elle revient à la charge, évoquant un proche passé : « Il y a un monde invisible, inconnu, où nous avons vécu et où nous ne faisions qu'un. (...) tu es la moitié de mon être. Je vois en toi la face de ma vie qui ne s'est pas réalisée. » Elle regrette la vie qu'elle aurait pu mener, esclave soumise à son maître. Oui, elle entrevoit ce qu'aurait pu être ce bonheur dans l'esclavage, oubliant qu'elle ne supporte pas le moindre joug. L'odalisque se consume à attendre le sultan Michel qui ne vient pas. À la place, c'est Marie d'Agoult qui arrive.

Pour suppléer à l'absence de Michel, George est prête à accepter n'importe quelle compagnie, y compris celle de Frédéric Chopin. À Liszt qui s'apprête à rejoindre Marie à Nohant, elle demande, le 17 février : « Dites à Chopin que je le prie et le supplie de vous accompagner ; que Marie ne peut pas vivre sans lui, et que moi je l'adore. » Cette adoration prématurée est une pure mondanité ne signifiant pas grand-chose. Celui que Sand adore alors, c'est Michel. « Je t'aime parce que quand je me représente la grandeur, la sagesse, la force et la beauté, c'est ton image qui se présente devant moi, parce que ton nom est le seul qui me fasse tressaillir. »

Liszt vient à Nohant, sans Chopin. L'amitié de Franz et de Marie n'apaise guère les tourments intimes de George, qui doit, en plus, affronter des critiques particulièrement acerbes, provoquées par la publication dans le journal *le Monde* de ses *Lettres à Marcie*, visiblement inspirées par l'abbé de Lamennais. L'union, spirituelle, entre ce prêtre désavoué par Rome et cette romancière en qui certains bien-pensants voient l'Antéchrist provoque les brocards de Mme de Girardin dans *la Presse* du 8 mars. « L'alliance de M. de Lamennais et de George Sand fait beaucoup parler ; pour nous, à chaque amitié nouvelle de George Sand, nous nous réjouissons ; chacun de ses amis est un sujet pour elle ; chaque nouvelle relation est un nouveau roman. L'histoire de ses affections est tout entière dans le catalogue de ses œuvres. »

Ces piqûres ne sont rien comparées aux souffrances infligées par Michel. George ne supporte plus son absence, elle brûle et doit se faire saigner par un médecin. « Le médecin m'a dit que c'est un " crime ", un " suicide " que d'ailleurs cela ne me soulage pas beaucoup, qu'il faut que j'aie un amant ou que ma vie est menacée par son excès même », avoue-t-elle à Michel qu'elle interroge sur sa rivale : « Cette femme sert-elle à te soulager les reins comme ferait une fille publique ? » George ne demanderait pas mieux que de jouer les filles publiques et d'accorder ces complaisances qu'elle avait refusées à Musset, comme elle le rappelle à Michel : « Une fois que je t'avais réchauffé les sens de mon souffle, j'ai cru que j'allais mourir. » Pour mourir à nouveau de volupté, George est prête à tout, « j'accepterai tout ».

Les véhémences de George pèsent à Michel qui veut retrouver sa tranquillité d'avant leur rencontre. Son métier, la politique, ses discours l'intéressent plus qu'une heure ou deux passées avec sa maîtresse de Nohant. Pourquoi perdre son temps à courir à Nohant, puisqu'il a une maîtresse à Bourges ? À plusieurs reprises, il a essayé de faire entendre raison à George, et de lui faire comprendre que leur passion était, pour lui, terminée. « Je suis guéri, Dieu me préserve de vivre jamais avec toi ! » George ne veut rien entendre. « Je veux te porter le plaisir aussi, car tu aimes le plaisir et je sais te le donner », insiste-t-elle.

Repris par ses devoirs conjugaux et extra-conjugaux, Michel est effrayé par la passion qu'il a déclenchée chez George. Il oppose sa froideur, son sens des convenances à ce volcan capable, pour un instant de plaisir, de tout détruire.

Le 3 avril, George annonce à Michel qu'elle a manqué mourir d'une congestion cérébrale, évitée grâce à une opportune saignée, encore une. Effrayé par ces saignées successives et ne voulant pas être responsable de la mort de l'auteur de *Lélia*, Michel consent à revoir George qui accourt à Bourges, le 11 avril, et en revient plus éprise que jamais : « Moi je t'aime plus que jamais. »

Trois mois de souffrance sont effacés par quelques heures d'amour. À peine comblée par ce rendez-vous, sa frénésie renaît, et l'insatiable George veut revoir Michel : « Viens, soyons heureux, dussé-je en mourir le lendemain. » Entre deux soupirs, Sand travaille à *Mauprat*. Elle ne quitte *Mauprat* que pour multiplier les messages de passion à Michel : « Je défie qui que ce soit, homme ou femme, de t'aimer comme je t'aime. » Elle se reprend à rêver à la possibilité d'une vie quotidienne avec Michel, sans se rendre compte, la malheureuse, qu'elle se rend importune par tant d'exigence. Excédé, Michel cède au désir de sa maîtresse, en croyant, chaque fois, que c'est la dernière. Et chaque fois, George répète : « Ah ! mon amour adoré, tue-moi si tu veux, mais aime-moi en me tuant. »

Du 2 au 6 mai, George va allègrement se faire « tuer » à Bourges, et en retourne, brisée « d'une douce fatigue ». Son corps est « tout disloqué d'une autre fatigue terrible, mais délicieuse » et « porte des stigmates en mille endroits ». Comme Sandeau, Michel doit être un amant ardent et dévorant. Ses « bras de fer » font « bondir de joie » George qui, à son retour de Bourges, a une autre joie, celle de trouver à Nohant Franz Liszt et Marie d'Agoult qui viennent y passer l'été.

Le musicien et la comtesse ont dû certainement remarquer l'état d'exaltation de la romancière qui, du 12 mai à onze heures du soir au 13 mai à cinq heures et demi de l'après-midi, termine *Mauprat* et commence aussitôt *les Maîtres mosaïstes*. Sand prouve ainsi que contrairement à l'opinion répandue, l'abus du plaisir n'entrave en rien le mécanisme de la création !

Comme n'importe quelle amoureuse, George Sand scrute le ciel et craint la pluie qui pourrait déranger, ou pis encore, faire annuler un rendez-vous avec Michel à qui elle reproche de ne l'aimer que par beau temps. « Tu m'as appris à détester le mauvais temps », se plaint-elle le 20 mai.

Se souvenant que c'est en mai 1835 qu'elle est devenue la maîtresse de Michel à Paris, George exige que son amant vienne à Nohant, en mai 1837, célébrer cet événement. Accablé par cette invitation, Michel répond qu'il envisage de se retirer dans une cabane au bord de la Méditerranée. Peine perdue, George s'empresse de préciser qu'elle rejoindrait Michel, sans tarder, dans sa cabane, « comme un nègre dévoué », ou « comme un chien fidèle ». En nègre, ou en chien, George est capable de n'importe quelle métamorphose pour être avec son amant qui ne sait plus quoi faire pour se débarrasser d'une aussi pesante proie. George se rend enfin compte de cette lassitude le 1er juin : « Il est possible que tu sois las de moi [1]. »

Les 9 et 10 juin, une entrevue à Bourges entre les deux amants tourne à la rupture. Dans son journal intime, George note qu'elle a été élue « entre toutes les dupes ». La honte d'avoir été la dupe d'un homme qui ne voulait plus d'elle, ou qui n'en voulait que quelques moments de plaisir, George ne peut l'oublier. Elle a voulu être traitée comme une fille publique que l'on congédie après usage, elle l'a été. Elle en souffre et ne crie pas sa souffrance sur les toits. Pour son trente-deuxième anniversaire, elle avoue simplement, et sans plus de détails, à son Pylade, Rollinat : « Mon cher vieux, j'ai bien souffert. » Elle souffre sur fond de musique de Liszt et silhouette de Marie d'Agoult se promenant au clair de lune sur la terrasse de Nohant.

Les prétendants à la succession de Michel ne manquent pas. L'acteur Pierre-François Bocage, que Sand a connu en 1833 quand il a créé le rôle titre de l'*Antony* d'Alexandre Dumas, a surgi à Nohant, « à l'improviste » le 8 juin, et il y est encore quand survient Charles Didier, le 15 juin.

L'ours Charles est rentré en grâce dans la ménagerie sandienne. Il est accueilli avec douceur et tendresse par la châtelaine de Nohant, mais il ne se fait aucune illusion. « Elle est occupée de Bocage. Cette rivalité avec un comédien me blesse et me dégoûte, Liszt approuve mon départ. »

Avant son départ le 5 juillet, Didier confie ces dégoûts à Marie d'Agoult qui, charitablement, opine que Sand est prête à « entrer dans le monde de la galanterie ». La comtesse ne doit rien ignorer des

---

1. La dernière lettre de Sand à Michel est datée du 6 juin. À propos de ces lettres dont on n'a pas la totalité, et de cette rupture, lire la note de Georges Lubin dans le quatrième volume de la *Correspondance*, aux pages 112 et 113.

ardeurs présentes de la romancière, ni de celles, passées, des dames galantes accrochées aux branches de l'arbre généalogique de la descendante des Saxe et des Kœnigsmark. Bon sang ne saurait mentir !

Pour calmer ces ardeurs que Bocage ne suffit pas à apaiser, George a recours à son remède habituel, la saignée. Ce qui provoque les moqueries de Marie qui préconise Chopin comme remède. « À votre place, j'aimerais mieux Chopin », dit-elle, en riant, à George qui ne rit pas.

À défaut de placer Chopin, Marie d'Agoult réussit à caser l'un de ses protégés, Félicien Mallefille, un créole de vingt-quatre ans, auteur de drames comme *Glenarvon, les Sept Infants de Lara* qui ont eu quelque succès au théâtre de la Porte-Saint-Martin. Mallefille entre en juillet à Nohant comme précepteur de Maurice et secrétaire de George Sand. Il succède aussi à Bocage, ce qui fait dire à Marie d'Agoult : « Elle quitte le bossu pour le borgne, l'acteur pour le dramaturge, Bocage pour Mallefille ! »

Pauvre, cherchant des appuis, un profil superbe, « l'air d'un Velázquez descendu de sa toile », Mallefille comble de son mieux les ardeurs éveillées par Michel.

Le 24 juillet, Franz Liszt et Marie d'Agoult quittent Nohant. Les incandescences de George choquent les froideurs de Marie. Les grands airs de Marie, ses plaisanteries sur les saignées, fatiguent Sand. Les Fellows et les Piffoëls ne sont plus les meilleurs amis du monde. Le temps de l'admiration béate et réciproque est terminée.

Début août, George va à Fontainebleau, à l'hôtel Britannique, pour y retrouver Bocage. Elle a ses habitudes dans cet hôtel où elle est déjà descendue avec Musset. Comme son idylle avec Musset avait été troublée par un spectre, son idylle avec Bocage est gâchée par le spectre de l'enlèvement de Maurice par Casimir qui veut récupérer son fils. L'enlève-

ment rate, et Maurice rejoint sa mère à Fontainebleau le 15 août. Le 19, Sophie-Victoire Dupin meurt
en prononçant ces dernières paroles qui résument
une vie de frivolité : « Arrangez-moi mes cheveux. »
L'ancienne « perle du district » veut être bien coiffée
pour affronter la mort. Oraison funèbre de Sophie-
Victoire par George : « Pauvre petite femme : fine,
intelligente, artiste, colère, généreuse, un peu folle,
méchante dans les petites choses et redevenant
bonne dans les grandes. Elle m'avait fait bien
souffrir et mes plus grands maux me sont venus
d'elle. » Ainsi s'achève l'une des plus grandes
amours de George Sand.

Bien qu'il soit en procès avec Mme Dudevant[1],
M. Dudevant assiste à l'enterrement de sa belle-
mère. Sa présence ne console guère George qui, le 25
août, découvre que « vraiment le cœur est une mine
inépuisable de souffrances ». Et aussi une inépuisable source de surprises : à la mi-septembre, George
constate qu'elle n'aime plus Michel et que, pour rien
au monde, elle ne voudrait le revoir. « Je ne puis
plus désirer que ce lien terrible soit renoué. Je ne le
désire plus, je ne le peux plus, je ne le veux plus. »

Celle que sa défunte mère avait surnommée sainte
Tranquille soupire, encore une fois : « Je suis bien
tranquille. »

À peine a-t-elle goûté aux bienfaits de sa guérison,
à peine s'est-elle assurée que Michel ne pourra plus
la faire souffrir, qu'elle est frappée par de nouveaux
tourments. M. Dudevant, qui a de la suite dans les
idées, après avoir raté l'enlèvement de Maurice,
réussit celui de Solange que Mme Dudevant récupère à Guillery, avec l'aide du sous-préfet de Nérac,

---

1. Casimir étant enfin entré en possession de son héritage et
devenu propriétaire de Guillery, Sand ne voit pas pourquoi son
époux continuerait à toucher les rentes de l'hôtel de Narbonne.
Elle intente un procès qu'elle perd le 11 juillet. Et ce n'est que le
2 juillet 1838, par un acte signé devant notaire, que George
récupérera l'hôtel de Narbonne qu'elle tenait de bonne-maman.

M. Haussmann, le futur baron qui, sous Napoléon III, changera la face de Paris.

Pour se remettre de ces émotions diverses, George s'accorde un pèlerinage dans ces Pyrénées où, en 1825, elle se promenait au bras d'Aurélien de Sèze. Le souvenir d'Aurélien et celui de l'enlèvement de Solange l'empêchent de dormir. Elle ne dort pas non plus parce qu'elle revoit Michel, après avoir juré de ne plus jamais le rencontrer. Le 25 octobre, elle écrit à Frédéric Girerd, qui est le confident de ses amours avec l'avocat : « Arrivée ici[1], j'ai bientôt reçu — sans autre forme de procès — sommation de Michel de me rendre à Châteauroux pour le voir. Tu penses que je n'y suis pas allée ? Tu te trompes, j'ai fait huit lieues au galop par une nuit glacée pour le voir un instant. (...) Au reste, notre position respective est bien changée et il y a de si étranges complications que je ne puis te les dire que verbalement. »

Ces « étranges complications » n'ont pu être élucidées jusqu'à maintenant, et l'on est réduit à des suppositions. Michel aurait-il voulu imposer sa maîtresse à George ? George se serait-elle refusée à ce ménage à trois, et même à quatre, si l'on y inclut la légitime Mme Michel ? Ce qui est certain, c'est que Sand est capable de faire « huit lieues au galop par une nuit glacée » pour voir un instant cet homme auprès de qui elle connaît ce qu'elle définit, de façon révélatrice, comme un « embrasement céleste ». Et ce céleste embrasement vaut bien de galoper par une nuit glacée...

George conclut sa lettre du 25 octobre par un « Ma vie est si étrange ! » Comme elle n'en est pas à une étrangeté près, elle se réjouit, à la mi-novembre, de l'élection de Michel comme député. « Voilà Michel élu. (...) Je lui reste dévouée en tant qu'il m'appellera et qu'il aura besoin de moi. Tant qu'il

---

1. Ici, c'est-à-dire à Nohant.

m'oublie, je m'arrange pour n'en plus souffrir et je crois que j'y suis parvenue. »

Sand serait-elle devenue raisonnable ? Elle ne se plaint même pas que Michel ait annoncé sa nomination « à tout le monde », sauf à elle. Silence éloquent. Avec Michel, George n'en est plus à une humiliation près : « Au fond, je sais qu'il m'aime, mais à sa manière qui n'est pas la mienne, et dont je ne puis me contenter. » Sand serait-elle devenue sage ? Pour combien de temps ?

LA COURSE DANS LES ÉTOILES
(novembre 1837-novembre 1838)

Je crois que notre amour ne peut durer que dans les conditions où il est né, c'est-à-dire que de temps en temps, quand un bon vent nous ramènera l'un vers l'autre, nous irons encore faire une course dans les étoiles.

Fin mai 1838

Sainte Tranquille prend l'éloignement de Michel avec une philosophie qu'elle doit peut-être à sa fréquentation de celui en qui elle voit « un nouveau Platon » ou « un nouveau Christ », Pierre Leroux. Un mois après l'élection de Michel, elle claironne à Marie d'Agoult : « Je tombe dans le " Pierre Leroux ", et pour cause. Il était ici ces jours derniers. »

Né à Paris en 1797, typographe, journaliste au *Globe*, créateur avec Jean Reynaud d'une *Encyclopédie nouvelle*, il croit au progrès de l'humanité, il prêche un évangile socialiste, il préconise l'égalité véritable, et surtout l'égalité entre les sexes : tout cela ne peut qu'enthousiasmer l'auteur de *Lélia*. Il a été recommandé à George Sand par Sainte-Beuve, au printemps 1835, le printemps de ses amours avec Michel. Elle trouve Leroux « éloquent, ingénieux, sublime ». Elle a beau affirmer qu'elle en a plein le dos des grands hommes et qu'elle aime mieux les voir dans Plutarque, George est toujours prête, comme Aurore au temps d'Aurélien de Sèze, à s'élancer vers les cimes du sublime. En Pierre Leroux, qui promet « le règne du ciel sur cette même terre », elle est certaine d'avoir rencontré un envoyé de Dieu, un prophète.

Veuf, Leroux est dans la misère, avec de nombreux enfants à élever. Ses bottes sont crottées, ses propos nébuleux, ses demandes d'argent incessantes. Avec Leroux, Sand apprend à combien revient la philosophie, et l'entretien d'un philosophe. Avec sa générosité spontanée et coutumière, George aide Leroux tant qu'elle peut. C'est un gouffre sans fin dans lequel elle se jette, à fonds perdus.

En cet automne 1837, Pierre Leroux fait la pluie et le beau temps à Nohant, autant que Félicien Malefille, mais pas de la même façon... Pierre comble l'esprit de la châtelaine, et Félicien son corps. Reconnaissante, Sand essaie de persuader Buloz du génie de Leroux et du talent de Malefille. Buloz est des plus réticents à publier les textes des protégés de sa populaire feuilletoniste qui s'est mis en tête de faire écrire à Malefille « trois drames bibliques non représentables »... En attendant ces trois chefs-d'œuvre, Malefille « fait faire à Maurice sous tous les rapports des progrès étonnants et il gouverne mon lion de Solange comme un agneau ».

Avec l'aide de Leroux et de Malefille, elle a définitivement « terrassé le dragon » Michel, qui dit maintenant à qui veut l'entendre que George est « le seul amour de sa vie ». Trop tard. En Malefille, George espère avoir trouvé une affection « plus douce, moins enthousiaste, moins âpre aussi » et, elle l'espère, « plus durable ».

En janvier 1838, Sand doit défendre Malefille des griffes de Marie d'Agoult. En effet, Félicien a osé répondre quatre lignes saugrenues, six mois après avoir reçu une longue lettre affectueuse de la comtesse qui, pour avoir été mise au ban de la société, n'en est que plus à cheval sur les principes. Ce retard, ce saugrenu ont déplu à Marie qui en profite pour reprocher à George le ralentissement de leur correspondance. Sand pousse de hauts cris. Si Marie l'exige, elle écrira chaque jour. Ces protestations d'amitié mutuelle cachent mal une croissante exaspération entre George et Marie. Chacune dit tout haut ce qu'elle pense de l'autre. Ces propos rapportés par les uns et les autres enveniment les rapports de la romancière et de la comtesse. Là-dessus, en février, Honoré de Balzac, qui est alors à Issoudun chez son amie, Zulma Carraud, vient à Nohant, en pèlerinage, rencontrer celle qu'il nomme

A quatre ans, Aurore Dupin sait lire et compose à haute voix "d'interminables contes que ma mère appelait des romans". Elle aime déjà ce qu'elle aimera toute sa vie : la rêverie, la musique, les animaux et les arbres. Son jouet préféré est une petite Vénus en biscuit de Sèvres... A quatre ans, elle perd son père, le colonel Maurice Dupin, et devient aussitôt "une pomme de discorde" entre sa mère et sa grand-mère qui "s'arrachèrent les lambeaux de mon coeur".

Musée Renan Scheffer. Photo : Roger-Viollet.

Jeune fille, Aurore joue de la guitare, dessine, lit Montaigne, Pascal ou Shakespeare, et met des pantalons pour monter plus commodément à cheval. Cet accoutrement, peu conforme aux usages de l'époque, suffit à assurer sa mauvaise réputation. A dix-sept ans, dans le Berry, Aurore Dupin passe pour une excentrique qui préfère la solitude des champs aux plaisirs mondains de la ville.
Musée Carnavalet. Photo : Bulloz.

Casimir Dudevant. Ce hobereau gascon pense pratiquer avec son Aurore "une camaraderie tranquille". A la place de quoi, il ne trouve que tempêtes romantiques et subtiles complications auxquelles il ne comprend rien. Pour prix de ses infortunes conjugales, il réclame, vainement, la légion d'honneur.
Photo : D.R.

En épousant Casimir Dudevant, Aurore devient baronne Mais une baronne qui, comme sa cousine par alliance, Marie-Antoinette, refuse de se soumettre aux exigences de son rang et préfère chercher refuge dans son encrier. Elle découvre alors qu'elle écrit comme elle respire.
Aquarelle de Candide Blaize. Musée Renan Scheffer. Photo : Bulloz.

En sa personne,
Mme Dupin
de Francueil, née
Marie-Aurore
de Saxe, incarne
toutes les grâces de
l'Ancien Régime :
elle a été élevée à
Saint-Cyr. Elle ne
supporte pas sa
belle-fille,
Sophie-Victoire,
qu'elle juge trop
"peuple" et parvient
difficilement
à devenir
"la meilleure amie"
de sa petite-fille,
Aurore.
Photo : Roger - Viollet.

Sophie-Victoire Dupin,
née Delaborde. Voilà la
femme que George Sand
a le plus aimée et par qui
elle a le plus souffert :
sa mère.
Fille d'un marchand
d'oiseaux, fille galante
en sa jeunesse,
Sophie-Victoire craint
par dessus tout de
retomber dans sa misère
première et sacrifie
sa fille Aurore pour
assurer son propre
avenir.
Photo : Bulloz.

Enfants et petits-enfants

Maurice Dudevant.
Pour sa mère, Maurice
incarne toutes les
perfections. Il n'a qu'un
défaut : il s'enrhume
facilement. Quand Maurice
tousse, George a mal à la
poitrine.
*Photo : Félix Nadar/Archives
photographiques de la ville de
Paris/SPADEM.*

Solange Clésinger, née
Dudevant. Solange est
une mal aimée. Elle sait que
son frère, Maurice,
est le préféré de leur mère.
L'incompréhension entre
George et Solange
est totale, la première
finissant par déclarer
de la seconde,
"ma fille est mon pire
ennemi".
*Dessin de Auguste Clésinger.
Photo : Roger-Viollet.*

Lina Calamatta a épousé
Maurice parce qu'elle ne pouvait
pas se marier avec George.
Elle a, pour sa belle-mère, une
admiration éperdue.
Autoportrait. Photo : Bulloz

Aurore et Gabrielle, filles de Maurice et de Lina. Avec Aurore et Gabrielle, George se
console enfin de la perte effroyable de sa bien-aimée Nini, fille de Solange et du sculpteur
Clésinger.
Collection Christiane Sand. Photo : André Martin.

Les fausses passions

Aurélien de Sèze. Neveu de l'un des
défenseurs de Louis XVI et substitut au
tribunal de Bordeaux. Il est le premier à
parler d'amour à Aurore Dudevant qui
prétend ne voir en lui qu'un "tendre frère"
ou un "ange protecteur".
Photo : D.R.

Stéphane Ajasson de Grandsagne. Il
est le premier amant d'Aurore
Dudevant et passe pour le père de
Solange. Il est moitié poitrinaire,
moitié fou. La maladie et la folie
exercent d'étranges attraits sur la
baronne Dudevant.
Lithographie de Dévéria.
Photo : D.R.

Jules Sandeau. Il devient
rapidement "mon cher petit
Jules", il est "aimable et léger
comme un colibri des savanes
parfumées". Hélas, ce "colibri"
n'use guère ses plumes à écrire et
George ne supporte pas longtemps
une telle paresse !
Dessin de Jules Sandeau
par George Sand.
Photo : D.R.

Alfred de Musset. Il croit commettre avec George Sand, trop maternelle, un inceste imaginaire, ce qui ne l'empêchera pas de déclarer, après leur éclatante rupture : "C'est la femme la plus femme que j'ai jamais connue."
Photo : D.R.

Frédéric Chopin. Il répugne à l'amour physique, et George ne tarde pas à voir en Frédéric son troisième enfant, et le plus difficile des trois...
Musée de La Châtre. Collection Christiane Sand.

Les "embrasements célestes"

Pietro Pagello. Les vrais amants de Venise, ce sont George Sand et Pietro Pagello, et non George Sand et Alfred de Musset. George voit Pagello, un médecin vénitien de vingt-sept ans, "grand comme Dieu" alors que Sandeau ou Musset n'étaient que des "anges".
Photo : D.R.

Michel de Bourges. Avocat. Si Pagello est "Dieu", Michel est un "roi" dont George se veut "l'humble sujette", un "sultan" dont elle rêve d'être "l'odalisque". Elle est capable de galoper, toute une nuit, sous une pluie glacée, pour passer un moment auprès de cet homme qui provoque en elle "un embrasement céleste".
Photo : D.R.

Alexandre Manceau. Graveur. Quand, en juillet 1850, George Sand envoie à son éditeur Hetzel ce constat de bonheur, "j'ai quarante-six ans, j'ai des cheveux blancs, cela ne fait rien. On aime les vieilles femmes plus que les jeunes, je le sais maintenant", c'est à Manceau qu'elle pense, son cher compagnon, un exemple de passion discrète et efficace.
Dessin d'Auguste Lehmann. Musée Renan Scheffer. Photo : D.R.
Photo : Félix Nadar/Archives photographiques de la ville de Paris/SPADEM.

Charles Marchal. Peintre. Le dernier amour de George Sand qui, à soixante-douze ans et exactement trois mois avant sa mort, lui envoie cet ultime message : "Je t'embrasse et t'aime toujours." Marchal a été successivement "mon lapin rose", "mon lapin bleu", "mon lapin vert", sans que l'on sache ce qui a provoqué ces changements de couleurs.
Photo : D.R.

Les amis de coeur

Ci-dessous :
Gustave Flaubert. L'amitié qui unit
Flaubert et Sand atteint à la
perfection. Tous deux savent faire
de leurs multiples différences un
motif d'entente supplémentaire.
Photo : D.R.

Marie Dorval. C'est "la femme du drame
nouveau". Quand l'actrice et la romancière
se rencontrent, Marie a trente-cinq ans et
George vingt-neuf. Ce ne sont plus des
gamines. Elles n'en éprouvent pas moins
l'une pour l'autre une passion de
pensionnaires, avec ce que cela peut
comporter d'exaltations diverses. S'ensuit
une indéfectible amitié.
Aquarelle de Paul Delaroche, 1831.
Musée des Arts Décoratifs, Paris.
Photo : Giraudon.

Alexandre Dumas fils
appartient à ce que l'on
pourrait nommer les fils
imaginaires de George Sand.
Elle veille sur sa santé, ses
humeurs et essaie de le guérir
de ce fameux "spleen" qu'elle
connaît bien pour en avoir
beaucoup souffert.
Musée Carnavalet.
Photo : Bulloz.

Les éditeurs

Ci-contre :
François Buloz. C'est le premier éditeur de George Sand, il publie *Lélia* en feuilleton dans sa *Revue des Deux Mondes* et il soutient cette débutante, dont il pressent le génie, de ses conseils et de son argent. En pleine débâcle de 1870, il supplie George de continuer à envoyer sa copie : "On vous lira malgré tout". Car tout s'effondre alors en France, sauf le pouvoir de Sand sur ses lecteurs.
Photo : D.R.

Michel Lévy. Editeur en 1849 de *La Petite Fadette,* il s'assure, à partir de 1856, de la quasi-exclusivité de la production de Sand qui, en échange, reçoit de confortables revenus dont les paiements ne doivent pas être interrompus, même en cas de maladie, elle a beaucoup insisté sur ce point.
Photo : D.R.

Ci-dessus :
Pierre-Jules Hetzel. Pour Sand, Hetzel est plus qu'un éditeur, c'est un ami et son confident dans certaines affaires amoureuses. Cette confiance n'empêche pas une brouille quand Hetzel a l'imprudence, ou l'impudence, de ne guère apprécier les gravures de Maurice qui tient absolument à illustrer l'oeuvre de sa mère, et qui l'illustrera...
Photo : Roger-Viollet.

L'esprit des lieux

Au premier rang des amours de George Sand, il faut ranger Nohant. Elle en chérit la maison et le jardin comme autant de personnes. Nohant où elle installe "deux ateliers de peinture, un atelier de gravure, une petite bibliothèque, un petit théâtre avec vestiaire et magasin de décors". Nohant toujours rempli de domestiques et d'invités alors que l'un des rêves de Sand est celui de "la maison déserte". Nohant où elle reprend force et vie.
Photos : D.R. – André Martin.

La Châtre. Qu'elle soit Mademoiselle Dupin, Madame la baronne Dudevant ou Madame Sand, George a toujours scandalisé "les commères mâles et femelles de la ville de La Châtre". C'est à propos de La Châtre qu'elle écrit dans *Histoire de ma vie*, "il n'y a rien de plus bêtement méchant que l'habitant des petites villes". George compte à La Châtre d'excellents amis comme les Duvernet. *Photo : D.R.*

La Chartreuse de Valldemosa. D'abord un paradis, puis un enfer où Chopin, toujours malade, réclame plus de cataplasmes que de caresses. Il en est des amants de la Chartreuse comme des amants de l'hôtel Danieli : une légende peu conforme à la réalité.
Photo : D.R.

Le salon de Nohant. Si les murs de ce salon pouvaient parler, ils raconteraient Franz Liszt, Marie d'Agoult, Frédéric Chopin, Eugène Delacroix, Gustave Flaubert, Théophile Gautier et autres hôtes illustres venus là pour des séjours plus ou moins longs.
Photo : André Martin.

L'auteur de *Consuelo* et de *La Mare au diable* a passé plus de temps à sa table de travail que sur le divan des alcôves. C'est sur ce petit bureau que la nuit, elle écrivait, terminant un roman pour en commencer aussitôt un autre.
Photo : André Martin.

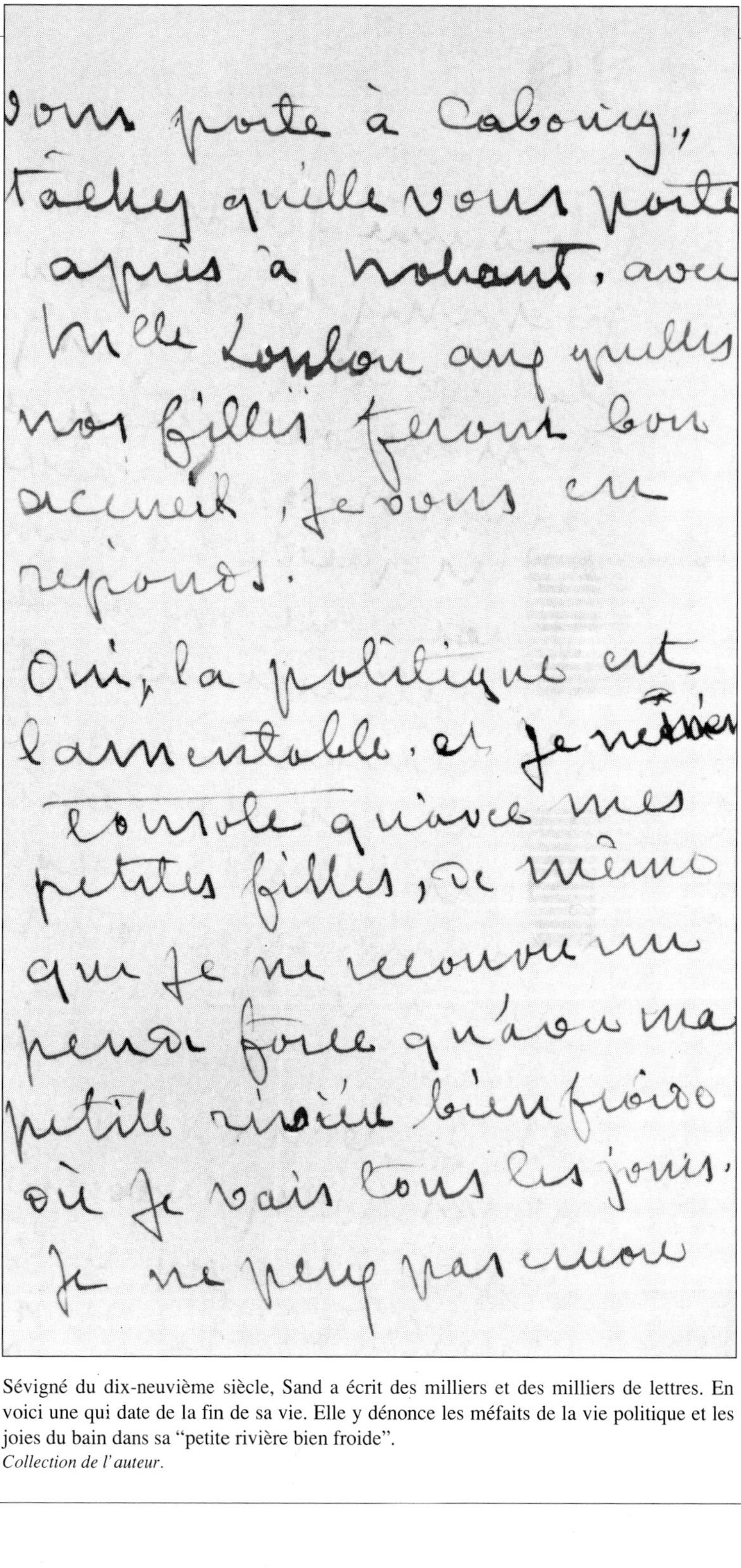

vous porte à Cabourg,
tâchez qu'elle vous porte
après à Nohant, avec
Mlle Loulou aux quelles
nos filles feront bon
accueil, je vous en
réponds.

Oui, la politique est
lamentable, et je ne me
console qu'avec mes
petites filles, de même
que je ne recouvre un
peu de force qu'avec ma
petite rivière bien froide
où je vais tous les jours.
Je ne peux pas encore

Sévigné du dix-neuvième siècle, Sand a écrit des milliers et des milliers de lettres. En voici une qui date de la fin de sa vie. Elle y dénonce les méfaits de la vie politique et les joies du bain dans sa "petite rivière bien froide".
Collection de l'auteur.

George Sand en 1863. Aux approches de la soixantaine, elle s'enchante des bienfaits de son âge : "C'est excellent d'être vieux. C'est le meilleur âge, c'est celui où l'entendement voit clair. Tant pis si les yeux s'éteignent. On approche de la belle grande lumière." Elle a acquis la sagesse, la clarté intérieure et son sourire s'apparente au sourire du Bouddah. Elle est enfin devenue celle que sa mère avait surnommée, par dérision, Sainte Tranquille.
Photo : Félix Nadar/Archives photographiques de la ville de Paris/SPADEM.

« la lionne du Berry ». Flattée, la lionne fait patte de velours et initie Balzac au *houka* et au *lataki*, qui est un tabac d'Orient.

Honoré arrive à Nohant le 24 février au soir et en repart le 2 mars avec le sujet d'un roman, *les Galériens de l'amour*, qui sera publié en septembre 1839, en feuilleton dans *le Siècle*, sous le titre de *Béatrix*, comme il l'écrit à sa future épouse, Ève Hanska : « C'est à propos de Liszt et de Mme d'Agoult qu'elle m'a donné le sujet des *Galériens ou les Amours forcés* que je vais faire, car, dans sa position, elle ne le peut pas. Gardez bien ce secret-là. »

Le secret ne fut pas bien gardé. Lors de la parution de *Béatrix*, chacun ne reconnut que trop Marie d'Agoult en Béatrix, et George Sand en Mlle des Touches. Voilà qui apprendrait à Marie à trop se moquer des saignées de George et de la prose de Félicien !

À peine interrompue par la visite de Balzac, sainte Tranquille retombe dans la routine du quotidien. Écriture, promenade, et inquiétudes pour la santé de Maurice qui, comme sa mère, souffre de rhumatismes et supporte mal les rigueurs de l'hiver à Nohant. George envisage de passer l'hiver prochain sous un ciel plus clément, bien qu'elle soit de mieux en mieux dans ce cocon de Nohant qu'elle quitte à regret quand des obligations l'appellent à Paris, comme en cette fin avril 1838. Elle doit assister au procès qui l'oppose à son mari pour récupérer les rentes de l'hôtel de Narbonne. Elle en raconte la fin à sa sœur, Caroline. « Mon procès à la veille du jugement se termine par une transaction entre M. Dudevant et moi. Je lui cède mon inscription de rentes sur l'État montant à 40 000 francs et il me rend l'hôtel de Narbonne. En même temps, il renonce à Maurice et à Solange et s'engage à ne plus me persécuter. »

Procès et transaction n'empêchent pas George Sand de se rendre à un concert de Frédéric Chopin, en compagnie de Marie Dorval. George et Marie envoient à Frédéric ce bref billet :

> *On vous adore*
> *George.*
> *Et moi aussi ! et moi aussi ! et moi aussi !!!*
> *Marie Dorval.*

Il semblerait bien que ce « On vous adore » ne s'adresse plus seulement au musicien, mais à l'homme.

Chopin est né en Pologne en 1810, d'un Français, un Lorrain venu à Varsovie en 1787, et d'une Polonaise. Comme George, Frédéric est né en musique, aux sons d'un violon. Ce n'est pas une contredanse que l'on jouait, mais une mazurka. Jeune prodige applaudi à Vienne et à Prague, il s'installe à Paris en septembre 1831 pour y chercher la consécration et y témoigner des malheurs de sa patrie ravagée par les Russes. Il joue du piano de façon inimitable et il a l'habitude du grand monde : il a été élevé avec des enfants de la noblesse polonaise auxquels son père servait de précepteur. À Paris, il devient rapidement l'idole des salons et des ambassades qui portent aux nues ses compositions quand il daigne les jouer. Il tourne la tête des femmes qui apprécient sa blondeur, sa langueur, la pâleur de son sourire, et sa façon de tousser qui fait dire à Marie d'Agoult : « Chopin tousse avec une grâce infinie. » Incapable de retenir une méchanceté, Marie ne manque pas d'ajouter : « Il n'y a chez lui que la toux de permanente. » En public, il est brillant et drôle. En privé, il est sombre et ne cache pas ses multiples tourments. Il aime le luxe et fuit les contraintes de la vie réelle. Homme d'habitudes, il ne supporte pas les dérangements. C'est un écorché vif, « le pli d'une feuille de rose, l'ombre d'une mouche le faisaient saigner », comme le rapportera Sand dans *Histoire de ma vie*. Musicien et malade, Frédéric ne peut que plaire à George qui raffole de la musique et adore soigner.

Ce « On vous adore » que Sand adresse à Chopin date de fin avril 1838. Un mois plus tard, fin mai, George Sand se déclare encore plus nettement à Frédéric Chopin par personne interposée, c'est-à-dire en s'adressant au plus cher ami du musicien, Albert Grzymala, à qui elle envoie l'une de ces interminables lettres dont elle a le secret. Elle y pèse soigneusement le pour et le contre des possibilités d'une liaison avec Chopin. Elle a trente-quatre ans, il en a vingt-huit. Ils ont chacun beaucoup vécu, et beaucoup souffert. Vont-ils se convenir ? À sa première rencontre avec Sand, chez Marie d'Agoult, pendant l'hiver 1836, Chopin a dit : « Quelle femme antipathique que cette Sand ! Est-ce vraiment une femme ? Je suis prêt à en douter... » Un an après, en octobre 1837, il n'en doute plus, c'est vraiment une femme, et il note dans son Journal : « Je l'ai revue trois fois. Elle me regardait profondément dans les yeux, pendant que je jouais. C'était de la musique un peu triste, légendes du Danube ; mon cœur dansait avec elle au pays. Et ses yeux dans mes yeux, yeux sombres, yeux singuliers, que disaient-ils ? Elle s'appuyait sur le piano et ses regards embrasants m'inondaient !... Des fleurs autour de nous. Mon cœur était pris ! Je l'ai revue deux fois depuis... Elle m'aime... »

Mais lui, l'aime-t-il ? Et son cœur est-il aussi pris qu'il le dit, son cœur toujours plein du souvenir d'une jeune, d'une belle Polonaise, Marie Wodzinska, qu'il considérait comme sa fiancée. Les fiançailles ont été rompues. Chopin est libre, mais Sand ne l'est pas. Malefille est là.

Sand expose son problème à Grzymala : peut-elle avoir Chopin et Malefille, pas ensemble, certes, mais en même temps ? Avant de se lancer à nouveau dans l'océan des passions, sainte Tranquille examine les risques de la traversée : « De même, lui sans doute se fût éloigné de mon premier baiser s'il eût su que j'étais comme "mariée". Nous ne nous sommes point trompés l'un l'autre, nous nous sommes livrés au vent qui passait et qui nous a emportés tous deux dans une autre région pour quelques instants. Mais il n'en faut pas moins que nous redescendions ici-bas, après cet embrasement céleste et ce voyage à travers l'empyrée. »

On sait exactement ce que Sand veut dire par cet « embrasement céleste » qu'elle a tant pratiqué avec Michel. Elle ne cache pas à Grzymala qu'elle est prête à recommencer avec Chopin cet « embrasement céleste » qui, le vent aidant, se changera en « une course dans les étoiles ». Mais peut-elle atteindre les étoiles avec Chopin sans trop faire souffrir Malefille qui, lui, reste à terre ? Et Chopin se prêterait-il de temps en temps à ces jeux et à ces feux ? « Nous ne nous verrons pas tous les jours, nous ne posséderons pas tous les jours le feu sacré, mais il y aura de beaux jours et de saintes flammes », prévoit la prudente Sand que la passion n'aveugle pas, pour le moment. Elle arrive à une époque de sa vie où elle ne peut plus s'engager à la légère, les yeux fermés. « J'ai connu plusieurs sortes d'amour. Amour d'artiste, amour de femme, amour de sœur, amour de mère, amour de religieuse, amour de poète, que sais-je ? (...) Je ne suis pas d'une nature inconstante. Je suis au contraire si habituée à aimer exclusivement qui m'aime bien, si peu facile à m'enflammer, si habituée à vivre avec des hommes sans songer que je suis une femme que vraiment j'ai été un peu confuse et un peu consternée de l'effet que m'a produit ce petit être. »

Elle, dont la tranquillité n'était pas troublée par le paisible Malefille, doit reconnaître qu'elle est troublée par « ce petit être » — c'est ainsi qu'elle désigne Chopin. Elle doit reconnaître aussi que quelque chose l'inquiète en ce même Chopin : il semble répugner à l'amour physique. « Il semblait faire fi, à la manière des dévots, des grossièretés humaines et rougir des tentations qu'il avait eues et craindre de souiller notre amour par un transport de plus. (...) Quelle est donc la malheureuse femme qui lui a laissé de l'amour physique de pareilles impressions ? Il a donc eu une maîtresse indigne de lui ? Pauvre ange ! »

En tout cas, Sand se dit prête à effacer ce mauvais souvenir. Et puis, à la fin de la lettre à Grzymala, la femme pratique qui est toujours en George surgit et donne quelques utiles recommandations. Si Chopin souhaite venir cet été à Nohant, qu'il prévienne à temps afin que Malefille, sous un prétexte quelconque, soit expédié à Paris, ou à Genève. Bon, a-t-elle bien tout examiné ? Oui, et elle conclut en adressant cette mise en demeure à Grzymala : « Si vous n'avez pas la solution des problèmes que je vous pose, tâchez de la tirer de lui. » On ne saurait montrer plus de précision, et moins de passion. On dirait que George prépare avec Frédéric une liaison de raison, comme elle avait accepté un mariage de raison avec Casimir. Malgré cela, elle ne néglige rien pour séduire complètement le « petit être » qui, le 8 mai, joue chez le marquis de Custine. Elle y apparaît, resplendissante dans une robe à ramages, les cheveux dans une résille rouge. Ramages et résille retiennent l'attention du Paris Élégant. Peu après, elle apprend par Marie d'Agoult que Pietro Pagello vient d'épouser une femme laide et bête. Il n'y a vraiment que Marie pour se souvenir de Pagello...

Août 1838. Pendant qu'elle envoie promener Malefille et Maurice en Normandie, George Sand se consacre à son nouveau roman, *Spiridion*, et à son nouvel amour, Frédéric Chopin, dont les répugnances à l'amour physique semblent avoir été vaincues. Il a passé, avec succès, l'examen qui change les hommes que George aime en anges. Début septembre, elle confie son ivresse à Delacroix et sa croyance en ces « anges déguisés en hommes ».

Il ne reste plus à la châtelaine de Nohant qu'à faire place nette et à se débarrasser de Malefille. Or, Félicien ne veut pas céder sa place et menace de faire un esclandre. C'est un chaos que Sand ne peut supporter ; elle charge donc Pierre Leroux d'y mettre bon ordre. Leroux doit apprendre à Malefille à voir les choses avec plus de philosophie. Félicien reste sourd aux arguments du philosophe. La situation devient rapidement intolérable et ne trouve de solution que dans la fuite.

Puisqu'elle avait envisagé, à cause de la santé de Maurice et de la sienne, de passer l'hiver sous un climat plus doux, Sand décide, fin octobre, sur les conseils de ses amis Manuel et Charlotte Marliani, d'aller aux Baléares, à l'île de Majorque. Maurice, Solange et Frédéric seront du voyage. Elle abandonne Félicien aux bons soins de Leroux qui saura le ramener « aux bons sentiments et aux bonnes études ». Elle en profite pour décerner au philosophe le titre d'ange, un ange abstrait et sans aucun embrasement céleste ! Car le seul ange qui soit sur terre, en ce moment, pour George Sand, c'est Frédéric Chopin qu'elle voit arriver à Perpignan, « frais comme une rose, et rose comme un navet ».

Par respect des convenances et souci de l'opinion parisienne, George et Frédéric n'ont pas voyagé ensemble et ont pris des chemins différents pour finalement s'embarquer à Port-Vendres, le 1er novembre 1838, sur le même bateau, le *Phénicien*.

Les convenances sont respectées et les apparences sont sauves. On va à Majorque pour raisons de santé, comme on était allé à Venise, et pour le même motif : les rhumatismes. Chopin, lui, y soignera sa toux. Selon le témoignage de Liszt, depuis l'automne 1837, Chopin éprouve « des atteintes inquiétantes d'un mal » qui ne lui laisse que « la moitié de forces vitales ». Liszt, Grzymala, Custine craignent, pour leur ami, la phtisie. Toujours selon Liszt : « L'île Majorque, où l'air de la mer, joint à un climat toujours tiède, est particulièrement salubre aux malades attaqués de la poitrine. »

Du climat de Majorque et des soins de George, Frédéric peut espérer des miracles.

UN ENFER À MAJORQUE
(8 novembre 1838-24 février 1839)

Tout alla fort bien au commencement, et j'admis éventuellement l'idée que Chopin pourrait se reposer et refaire sa santé parmi nous (...). Je n'étais pas illusionnée par une passion. J'avais pour l'artiste une sorte d'adoration maternelle très vive, très vraie (...).

Sand et sa tribu débarquent à Palma, le 8 novembre 1838, en fin de matinée, à onze heures trente exactement. Depuis Barcelone, ils ont voyagé sur le *Mallorquin*, en compagnie d'une cargaison de cochons. Sur ce bateau, ces animaux sont mieux traités que les rares passagers. Car, George l'apprend à ses dépens, la spécialité de l'île de Majorque, ce sont les cochons. C'est un pays de cochons, et depuis sa plus tendre enfance, Sand a horreur des cochons, autant que des épinards.

On oublie les cochons pour savourer la douceur de l'air : il fait aussi chaud qu'au mois de juin. C'est un enchantement qui augmente à chaque pas. Beauté des monuments et de la nature, ce n'est pas pour rien que Majorque passe alors pour « l'Eldorado de la peinture ». George Sand prédit que Majorque, dès qu'elle sera plus accessible, attirera autant de touristes que la Suisse : « C'est la verte Helvétie sous le ciel de la Calabre. »

Ce ne sont pas des touristes qui, en 1838, ont envahi l'île, mais des Espagnols qui fuient leur pays déchiré entre les partisans de la reine Christine et ceux du prétendant Don Carlos. Toujours prophétique, Sand prévoit que ce « pays est destiné à se dévorer lui-même », ce qui arrivera le siècle suivant, de 1936 à 1939, pendant la guerre civile espagnole.

Avec cet afflux de réfugiés, il est impossible de trouver un seul appartement habitable dans la ville de Palma. George, Frédéric, Maurice et Solange échouent dans une mauvaise auberge, près du port, presque un mauvais lieu, dans un quartier réservé aux gitans et à la pègre.

Le bruit, l'inconfort, les aliments pétris de poivre et d'ail provoquent la fuite des voyageurs qui s'établissent dans un village des alentours de Palma, Establisments, dans une villa, *Son Vent*, la demeure du vent. Là ils profitent de trois semaines de beau temps. Ils sont tous enchantés, y compris Chopin, qui écrit à l'un de ses amis, Julien Fontana : « Tout le monde est vêtu comme en été car il fait chaud. La nuit, on entend des chants et le son des guitares pendant des heures entières. »

Sand ne tarit pas d'éloges sur les « palais arabes, orangers, citronniers, palmiers, montagnes magnifiques, la mer comme un beau lac, les vallées délicieuses, et une population excellente ». Le 14 novembre, elle annonce triomphalement à Mme Buloz qu'elle a loué, pour 35 francs par an, une cellule dans la Chartreuse de Valldemosa, « immense et magnifique couvent désert au milieu des montagnes. Notre jardin est jonché d'oranges et de citrons, les arbres en cassent. (...) Je suis dans l'enchantement. » Elle considère la Chartreuse comme « le séjour le plus romantique de la terre ». Et elle ajoute : « Je crois que je ne sortirai plus jamais de Majorque. »

Début décembre, les pluies commencent, un vrai déluge rendant *Son Vent* inhabitable. La maison du vent se change en maison de la pluie. Pour combattre le froid et l'humidité, on allume des braseros dont la fumée provoque chez Chopin d'incessantes crises de toux. « De ce moment nous devînmes un objet d'horreur et d'épouvante pour la population. Nous fûmes atteints et convaincus de phtisie pulmonaire, ce qui équivaut à la peste dans les préjugés contagionnistes de la médecine espagnole. » Le mot terrible est prononcé, la phtisie, qui est au dix-neuvième ce que le sida est au vingtième.

Le propriétaire de *Son Vent*, M. Gomez, qui

craint la contagion, prie les locataires de déguerpir dans les plus brefs délais.

Le 15 décembre, Sand et sa tribu quittent *Son Vent* pour la Chartreuse de Valldemosa. Chemin faisant, Sand oublie les contrariétés de l'expulsion pour s'extasier sur le paysage, et particulièrement sur les « arbres tortueux, penchés, échevelés ». Pour atteindre la Chartreuse, il faut prendre un chemin qui s'insinue entre les chênes, les pins, les caroubiers, les oliviers, les cyprès. George, qui aime les arbres, est comblée par cet accueil végétal. Elle l'est moins par les trois habitants de la Chartreuse : un sacristain, un pharmacien et la Maria Antonia, une Espagnole aux allures de sorcière qui propose ses services à ceux qui s'égarent en ces parages. Sous des airs douceureux, la Maria Antonia est une voleuse qui prélève « le plus pur de vos nippes et de votre dîner ».

Dans cette sublime Chartreuse, on manque de tout et Sand doit tout faire, même la cuisine, puisque Chopin ne supporte pas la nourriture locale mijotée par Maria Antonia et ses deux acolytes, deux autres sorcières, une vieille et une jeune. « Je fais la cuisine au lieu de faire de la littérature », écrit-elle à Buloz qui attend, avec une impatience qu'il ne dissimule plus, *Spiridion*. En même temps qu'elle termine tant bien que mal ce roman, Sand soigne Chopin : « Je le soigne comme mon enfant. C'est un ange de douceur et de bonté ! »

La bonté et la douceur de Chopin sont mises à rude épreuve. Le piano commandé en France n'arrive pas et les sonorités du piano qu'il a loué à Palma l'irritent prodigieusement.

Frédéric est aussi agacé d'être regardé comme une bête curieuse par les paysans de Valldemosa. Le couple que forment le musicien et la romancière doit étonner les populations. Elle écrit pendant des heures, et pendant des heures il tape sur un piano.

Au village proche de la Chartreuse, on n'aime guère ces étrangers qui s'installent dans des lieux saints qu'ils profanent par l'excentricité de leur comportement et de leur tenue. La tribu fait scandale en se promenant à minuit dans le cimetière. Solange porte des pantalons comme sa mère. Des femmes en pantalons à la Chartreuse !

Sand ne va pas à la messe du dimanche, ignorant qu'il faut toujours sacrifier aux divinités du lieu. Pour se venger de ce mépris de leurs croyances, les paysans pratiquent des prix exorbitants pour des produits qui ne justifient pas une pareille dépense. Le vin n'est pas bon et les boudins sont assaisonnés « d'une telle profusion d'ail, de poivre, de piment et d'épices corrosives de tout genre qu'on y risque sa vie à chaque morceau ». Le poisson est « aussi plat et aussi sec que les poulets ». Les desserts sont magnifiques, « des patates de Malaga et des courges de Valence confites, et du raisin digne de la terre de Chanaan ». Mais se nourrit-on de desserts ? Heureusement que l'eau est bonne, et, en plus, blanchit les dents.

Sand comprend que l'insolite de sa tribu provoque l'hostilité générale. Repoussée, elle se sent une âme d'émigré. « Nous sommes si différents de la plupart des gens et des choses qui nous entourent, que nous nous faisons l'effet d'une pauvre colonie émigrée qui dispute son existence à une race malveillante ou stupide. » Le peuple a cessé d'être « excellent ».

Mais il en faudrait d'autres pour décourager une George Sand ! Avec un entrain et un courage méritoires, elle se charge de changer son désert en un lieu habitable. Elle aménage la Chartreuse comme elle peut et invente le chic Valldemosa avec des couvre-pieds en indienne, des nattes valenciennes, et des poteries de Felanitx. Elle arrive à créer « une sorte de bien-être. Nous avions des vitres, des portes et un poêle, un poêle unique en son genre, que le premier forgeron de Palma avait mis un mois à forger et qui nous coûta cent francs ».

Ils sont, à Majorque, aussi seuls que sur une île

déserte. Solitude qui n'empêche pas la plus franche gaieté de régner entre George, Maurice et Solange. Depuis que, entre Barcelone et Palma, Solange a eu le mal de mer, Maurice prétend que sa sœur a craché son venin et qu'elle est, presque, charmante. Seul Chopin soupire, gémit et compose sur le piano enfin arrivé de France.

Entre deux averses, George et ses enfants courent la campagne. Un jour même, la mère et le fils vont jusqu'à Palma. La crue des rivières retarde leur retour. Chopin s'en inquiète et quand il les voit revenir, il leur dit d'un air étrange : « Ah ! je le savais bien, que vous étiez morts ! » Il joue alors l'un de ses préludes[1], qu'il a composé pendant leur absence. « Sa composition de ce soir-là était bien pleine des gouttes de pluie qui résonnaient sur les tuiles sonores de la Chartreuse, mais elles s'étaient traduites dans son imagination et dans son chant par des larmes tombant du ciel sur son cœur », rapportera Sand dans *Histoire de ma vie*.

On ne se nourrit pas de gouttes d'eau, même musicales, et Sand acquiert une chèvre pour avoir du lait. La chèvre, comme George autrefois, a le spleen et ne rêve que de s'évader dans les montagnes.

Les deux seules personnes de Majorque dont la romancière gardera un bon souvenir et qu'elle nommera avec chaleur et reconnaissance, c'est la chèvre spleenitique et une jeune fille, Perica, rencontrée au hasard d'une promenade.

Après les pluies, c'est le printemps, et dès la fin janvier, les amandiers sont en fleur. George, Maurice et Solange gambadent allègrement dans les

---

1. « On a discuté pour identifier ce prélude. Liszt opinait pour *le 8ᵉ en fa dièse mineur* ; Édouard Ganche proposait le *15ᵉ en ré bémol majeur*. Nombreux sont les musicologues qui se sont prononcés pour le *6ᵉ en si mineur*. » Note de Georges Lubin, *Histoire de ma vie*, tome 2, Gallimard, « La Pléiade », page 1397.

collines. Chopin, dont les crises de toux sont de plus en plus fréquentes, reste à la Chartreuse et compose.

On est en droit de se demander où, et quand, Sand et Chopin pouvaient se livrer aux embrasements célestes. Les trois pièces que la tribu occupe à la Chartreuse imposent une promiscuité qui interdit tout ébat un peu bruyant que Maurice, quinze ans, et Solange, dix ans, ne manqueraient pas d'entendre et de remarquer. Chopin, toujours malade, réclame plus de cataplasmes que de caresses.

Il en est des amants de la Chartreuse comme des amants du Danieli. À Valldemosa, comme à Venise, Sand joue les infirmières. Comme c'est l'un de ses rôles préférés, elle ne s'en plaint pas. Elle s'effraye quand même d'avoir un troisième enfant sur les bras. Et de ses trois enfants, Frédéric est le plus difficile. Il éprouve de grands chagrins pour de petites contrariétés, un bouillon trop poivré, un pain changé en éponge par la pluie, et le voilà déprimé, malheureux, mourant...

Entre les soins accordés à Chopin, les leçons données à Maurice et à Solange, la copie pondue régulièrement — après avoir terminé *Spiridion*, elle corrige *Lélia* en vue d'une nouvelle édition —, Sand n'a pas une minute à elle. Dire qu'elle pensait se reposer à Majorque ! En fait de repos, elle balaye, cuisine, fait son lit, petite femme vaillante comme un régiment. Ses seules voluptés à Majorque, ce sont les promenades. Elle ne s'en lasse pas. Un après-midi, pour voir la mer de plus près, elle manque y tomber. Elle est sauvée de justesse par Maurice qui, pour la première fois de sa vie, réprimande sa mère pour son imprudence. Sans l'intervention de Maurice, George s'écrasait sur les rochers. Comble de l'horreur, on aurait enterré Mme Dudevant à Majorque. Après cet incident, il est temps de partir.

Sand a manqué mourir, Chopin est mourant. Il ne supporte plus l'inconfort de la Chartreuse, la rusticité de ses habitants. Sand, de son côté, n'en peut plus de ce dénuement, de ces privations diverses, de ces avanies quotidiennes. Avoir été le scandale du Tout-La Châtre, du Tout-Paris et du Tout-Venise, pour l'être encore du Tout-Majorque, non, non, et non ! C'est trop ! Pour Sand, il en est des pays comme des amants. Elle brûle ce qu'elle a adoré avec une facilité déconcertante. En novembre 1838, elle jure de ne plus quitter Majorque. En février 1839, elle fait le serment de ne plus jamais y mettre les pieds. « Je crois que je ne pourrais plus jamais revoir la figure de Valldemosa. » Il est temps de quitter cet enfer où règne « cette race stupide, voleuse et dévote ».

L'enfer ne se quitte pas aussi aisément. Sand sollicite une dizaine de personnes pour transporter sa tribu à Palma. Elle essuie une dizaine de refus polis. Personne ne veut laisser contaminer sa carriole par Chopin. George loue à prix d'or une patache si mal suspendue qu'en arrivant à Palma, le 11 février, Frédéric est pris d'un épouvantable crachement de sang. Le 13, la tribu quitte Palma pour Barcelone.

Le 24 février, accostage à la terre promise, Marseille. George Sand laisse alors éclater son ressentiment contre l'Espagne entière. « Oh, que je hais l'Espagne ! J'en suis sortie comme les anciens, à reculons, c'est-à-dire avec toutes les formules et malédictions. (...) Un mois de plus, et nous mourions en Espagne, Chopin et moi, lui de mélancolie et de dégoût, moi de colère et d'indignation. Ils m'ont blessée dans l'endroit le plus sensible de mon cœur, ils ont percé à coups d'épingle un être souffrant sous mes yeux, jamais je ne leur pardonnerai, et si j'écris sur eux, ce sera du fiel. » Ce sera *Un hiver à Majorque*, l'un de ses meilleurs textes.

LA MACHINE À DEVOIR
(printemps 1839-hiver 1840)

> Je suis une machine à devoir, et je m'hébète chaque jour davantage, mais sans regret, car le temps de ma jeunesse et de ma liberté a été plein d'amertumes et d'orages que je ne voudrais pas recommencer.
>
> Nohant, le 18 septembre 1839

De Marseille, où elle est maintenant depuis un mois avec sa tribu, Sand écrit, vers le 25 mars 1839, à Charlotte Marliani, à qui elle ne tient pas rigueur d'être à l'origine du désastre de Majorque : « J'ai trois enfants sur les bras et Chopin n'est pas celui dont je m'occupe le moins, quoique sa santé s'améliore chaque jour. »

L'avantage de ce troisième enfant, c'est qu'il représente une protection pour les deux autres. Avec Frédéric qu'elle aime d'une tendresse maternelle, George se croit à l'abri des passions. N'est-ce pas payer trop cher sa tranquillité sentimentale ? En mars 1839, une rupture serait encore possible entre George et Frédéric, du moins George le croit-elle. Leur affection n'est pas encore exclusive. Pendant ces mois d'enfer à Majorque, ils ont appris à se connaître, à s'estimer, et d'une certaine façon à s'aimer. Déjà, la force de l'habitude, ou des habitudes. Dans *Histoire de ma vie*, pour justifier la continuation de sa liaison avec Chopin, Sand invoque la destinée. « La destinée nous poussait dans les liens d'une longue association, et nous y arrivâmes tous deux sans nous en apercevoir. »

Sand aime trop la musique pour se passer de son musicien. Chopin aime trop sa vraie mère, restée en Pologne, pour se passer de cette seconde mère qu'il trouve en George. Ils pensent qu'en unissant leurs faiblesses, ils seront forts... En attendant, l'éden de Marseille a été de courte durée : Sand s'y ennuie. Marseille est une « ville de marchands et d'épiciers, où la vie de l'intelligence est parfaitement inconnue ». Marseille n'a qu'une vertu : son air vivifiant qui atténue les crises de toux de Chopin. Sand est donc encore dans cette ville en avril.

À Marseille comme à Valldemosa, la tribu mène une existence « d'une innocence et d'une simplicité primitives ». On travaille, on se promène quand le mistral et ses tourbillons le permettent. Sous les yeux attendris de George, Maurice montre de belles dispositions pour le dessin et Solange arrange Plutarque à sa façon.

Buloz se plaint que *Spiridion* n'a pas eu le succès attendu, on a trouvé cet ouvrage trop mystique. Il ose suggérer à son auteur de faire paraître « quelque chose de moins philosophique ». Sand se moque de cette recommandation et se plaint, à son tour, de la vie chère à Marseille. Cherté compensée par un avantage sans prix : Chopin a retrouvé le sommeil. Fin avril, il dort toute la nuit et une partie de la journée. En cette somnolence, approuvée par un médecin local, le Dr Cauvière, Sand voit une preuve supplémentaire de la nature angélique de son troisième enfant. Oui, « ce Chopin est un ange. Sa bonté, sa tendresse et sa patience m'inquiètent quelquefois, je m'imagine que c'est une organisation trop fine, trop exquise et trop parfaite pour vivre longtemps de notre grosse et lourde vie terrestre ».

Après une escapade en mai à Gênes, Sand et les siens arrivent à Nohant le 1er juin. Nohant plaît à Chopin qui désire « y rester le plus possible ». « Je ne le prendrai au mot qu'autant que je verrai ce séjour lui être réellement favorable », prévoit prudemment George. La passion semble bien absente des rapports établis entre George et Frédéric. En tout cas, ce n'est pas pour Frédéric que George galoperait, pendant des lieues, la nuit, sous une pluie glacée, comme elle l'a fait pour Michel... Non, simplement, Frédéric « est devenu pour moi un autre Maurice ». Quand on sait l'amour que Sand portait à son fils, cette comparaison, s'il l'avait connue, aurait rassuré Chopin.

En cet été 1839, le calme qui règne à Nohant est, à peine, troublé par un coup de tonnerre signé Marie d'Agoult. Marie ordonne à George de rompre un silence qui dure depuis dix-huit mois et dont elle s'étonne, enfin. Elle s'en serait moins étonnée si elle avait su que leur amie commune, Charlotte Marliani, n'avait pas caché à George ce que Marie pensait vraiment de George, de ses « caprices », de ses « inconstances », de ses « profanations de la sainte amitié ». Atteinte par ces révélations, George s'est réfugiée dans un silence qu'elle s'apprête à rompre, non pour obéir aux ordres de Marie, mais pour défendre cet innocent de Chopin que Marie rend aussi coupable de ce silence qui ressemble fort à une brouille. En fin de compte, l'amitié entre la blonde Marie et la brune George n'aura été qu'un feu de paille.

Le 30 novembre, les deux déesses outragées font mine de se réconcilier. Elles se tendent la main, elles s'embrassent et deviennent ainsi « des ennemies mortelles ». Marie ne tarde pas à regretter ce qu'elle nomme sa « démarche conciliatrice » et trouve que l'un de ses principes — « on ne pense jamais assez de mal des gens » — est absolument justifié par la « perfidie complète » de Sand. Dans cette perfidie, la comtesse doit inclure certainement le récit de ses amours avec Liszt que Balzac a transposées, à peine, dans *Béatrix*, qui a paru le 26 novembre.

En plus, en ce 30 novembre, la princesse Marie a dû prendre la peine de se rendre au nouveau domicile parisien de la reine George, au 16, rue Pigalle (actuellement le 20). George a prétexté une crise de rhumatismes pour n'avoir pas à aller chez Marie. Décidément, les rhumatismes auront été de commodes alliés pour Sand.

Le 15 octobre, George a aménagé son logis rue Pigalle, où elle occupe, au fond d'un jardin, deux pavillons qu'elle décore de tableaux de Delacroix, de son portrait par Luigi Calamatta, un peintre italien, disciple de Ingres, et de vases chinois débordant de fleurs. Pour préserver le secret de leur liaison qui, à Paris, est un secret de Polichinelle, Chopin loge au 5, rue Tronchet. Après avoir donné des leçons de piano à de jeunes aristocrates plus ou moins douées, Frédéric, ponctuel, arrive au 16, rue Pigalle à quatre heures de l'après-midi. C'est l'heure à laquelle, d'après Balzac, George se lève.

La tribu a quitté Nohant parce que Paris est indispensable à Chopin qui y gagne sa vie, à Maurice qui y fait des progrès en peinture, et à Solange qui y progresse en coquetterie. George aurait préféré rester à Nohant et s'est sacrifiée à ses trois enfants, bien que, elle aussi, soit obligée d'être à Paris, puisque Buloz, en plus de *la Revue des Deux Mondes*, dirige maintenant le Théâtre-Français et souhaite monter l'une de ses pièces, *Cosima*.

Pour le rôle-titre, l'auteur veut sa chère Marie Dorval. À propos de Dorval, Marie d'Agoult écrira à Franz Liszt, le 21 janvier 1841 : « Potocki m'a avoué que, lorsque j'étais partie seule pour Nohant (en 1837), il n'avait pas douté qu'il n'y eût, entre George et moi, quelque amitié à la Dorval. » On ne prête qu'aux riches...

À peine Marie d'Agoult a-t-elle quitté le cœur de George Sand que la place est presque immédiatement occupée par Pauline Garcia, cantatrice de dix-neuf ans, sœur de la Malibran. Pendant l'hiver 1839-1840, George envoie à Pauline un billet qui la sacre « reine du monde ». Si elle ne domine pas encore le monde de l'opéra, Pauline règne sur George à qui elle inspirera son personnage de Consuelo. La voix de Pauline plonge George dans un embrasement quasiment céleste. Et Delacroix croque, à la mine de plomb et sur le même feuillet, les deux nouvelles amies.

Avec Pauline, George apprend à vivre complètement l'instant présent. Et voilà que, en février 1840, le passé surgit, à l'occasion d'un dîner chez Buloz qui réunit Musset et Sainte-Beuve. Sand ne voit plus son ancien amant, ni son ancien confident. Avec ce dernier, à qui elle reprochait son goût immodéré des commérages, elle s'est brouillée voilà quatre ans. Mais George, pendant ce dîner, sait se montrer si charmante, si « bonne enfant » que Sainte-Beuve n'y résiste pas et renoue leur amitié.

Rien ne se renoue avec Musset qui, à son tour, cherche à récupérer ses lettres d'amour, vainement. Avec Musset, rencontre sans lendemain. George, qui proclame volontiers : « Je suis une machine à devoir », refuse de céder aux vertiges de la nostalgie. Rien ne vaut le présent représenté par Frédéric et par Pauline.

LES SERMONS DE SAND
(printemps 1840-hiver 1843)

Encore un sermon, c'est le tiroir aux
sermons, aujourd'hui.
Paris, le 21 janvier 1843

16 avril 1840. Pauline Garcia épouse Louis Viardot qui dirige le Théâtre Italien. Il abandonne ses fonctions pour accompagner son épouse dans des tournées de récitals à travers l'Europe. Ce mariage a de quoi satisfaire George qui aime Pauline et qui estime Louis qui partage sa passion pour Pierre Leroux et son « Catéchisme républicain ».

29 avril 1840. Tout ce que Sand compte d'ennemis se réunit au Théâtre-Français pour assurer l'insuccès de *Cosima* qui n'aura que sept représentations. À l'hostilité du public correspond celle de la presse, unanime à dénoncer « une œuvre déplorable » par son « manque d'action » et son « bavardage plein d'ennui ».

Stoïque, George constate : « J'ai été huée et sifflée comme je m'y attendais. » Elle assiste à cette catastrophe qu'elle juge « burlesque » et se dit « fort tranquille et même fort gaie ». Telle est Sand qu'aucun échec ne peut abattre, et surtout pas un échec théâtral. Elle a, comme on dit, de la ressource. Et une consolation : faire relier un exemplaire de *Cosima* pour celle qui en a été l'interprète malmenée, Marie Dorval, à qui elle propose le rire comme remède à leur échec commun.

La chute de *Cosima* n'arrange pas les éternelles difficultés financières de George Sand, qu'augmente son inlassable générosité. En juin, elle envoie 500 francs à l'un de ses nouveaux protégés, Agricol Perdiguier, dit Avignonnais la Vertu. Ce menuisier de trente-cinq ans, compagnon du tour de France, a publié en 1839 *le Livre du compagnonnage*. Il veut unifier les classes ouvrières pour les rendre plus fortes face au patronat. Ce projet intéresse Sand qui fera de Perdiguier Pierre Huguenin, le héros de son *Compagnon du tour de France*.

Est-ce l'exemple des errances d'Agricol Perdiguier à travers la France ? George se permet, en août, une escapade à Cambrai où chante Pauline Viardot. Déception : les bourgeois de Cambrai « sont bêtes, ils sont épiciers ». Le 13 août, elle envoie une lettre adressée à ses trois enfants, « à Frédéric Chopin, Maurice et Solange Dudevant ». Le ton en est familial à souhait. Chopin y devient Chip-Chip et Maurice y reçoit le surnom de Bouli. Solange reste résolument Solange, tout en devenant, à douze ans, une femme. Cette « précoce puberté » inquiète sa mère, ainsi que son humeur fantasque, et son irréductible esprit d'indépendance. Solange semble avoir hérité de la fantaisie et de l'indépendance de sa grand-mère, Sophie-Victoire Dupin...

Ayant usé la patience de sa mère et de son institutrice, Mlle Dudevant est mise en pension, en octobre, à Paris. Ses enfants ainsi casés, Solange en pension, Maurice à l'atelier de Delacroix, George Sand connaît avec Frédéric Chopin un bonheur bourgeois. Le couple va ensemble aux concerts, aux expositions, et reçoit à dîner, rue Pigalle, quelques amis choisis. À ce régime, sainte Tranquille « engraisse comme un limaçon ». Et c'est avec une vigueur accrue qu'elle administre emplâtre et tisane de gruau à Frédéric quand il est malade. Il l'est souvent...

Sand admire la facilité avec laquelle Chopin, en un seul concert, gagne 6 000 francs alors que Nohant ne rapporte que 4 000 francs par an. Les terres sont en pleine décadence, ce qui ne diminue en rien l'amour de George pour son domaine. « J'aime Nohant avec une sorte de tendresse, comme un être qui m'a toujours été salutaire, calmant et fortifiant. » Elle est indissolublement liée à Nohant qui, dans sa vie mouvementée, représente une appréciable unité de lieu.

Experte en rupture, Sand rompt, fin septembre, avec Buloz qui prétend censurer son nouveau roman, *Horace,* dont les idées sociales hardies — le prolétariat considéré comme un nouvel ordre social, et puis quoi encore ? — choqueraient à coup sûr les très conservateurs lecteurs de *la Revue des Deux Mondes.* On se sépare, sans se fâcher, comme le précise Sand. « De quoi me fâcherais-je, si vous voulez bien ne plus m'adresser de sermons inutiles ? Je ne suis pas embarrassée de mon roman, comme vous pouvez croire. Je n'y puis rien changer, j'ai assez d'estime pour vous pour être certaine qu'à ma place vous n'y changeriez rien. »

Débarrassée momentanément de Buloz et de *la Revue des Deux Mondes,* George Sand est libre de fonder, avec Pierre Leroux et Louis Viardot, *la Revue indépendante,* dont le premier numéro paraît début novembre 1841, et d'y publier *Horace,* « tableau des mœurs populaires ». Leroux prêche pour le peuple. Sand essaie de convertir son public au peuple et à Leroux. « J'ai la certitude qu'un jour on lira Leroux comme on lit le *Contrat social* », répète-t-elle. En quoi elle se trompe. Forte de son aveuglement, elle bat le rappel de ses amis et connaissances afin qu'ils souscrivent à *la Revue indépendante* et partagent sa foi en Leroux et en ses œuvres.

Sa correspondance tourne au bulletin de propagande pour la revue et au bulletin de santé. « Le Chopinet a été rhumatisé et souffre encore », écrit-elle à Delacroix, au printemps 1842. Elle est heureuse de s'affirmer comme « la plus solide de tous ». Elle travaille la nuit, monte à cheval le jour, joue au billard le soir et dort le matin, « c'est toujours la même vie ». Elle ne s'en plaint pas, au contraire. En mai, aux veilles de son trente-huitième anniversaire, elle affirme sa confiance en la bonté de Dieu : « Je trouve que Dieu est si bon, si bon de nous vieillir, de nous calmer et de nous ôter ces aiguillons de personnalité qui sont si âpres dans la jeunesse ! »

Au dix-huitième siècle, sa cousine par alliance, Marie-Antoinette, se trouvait vieille à trente ans. Au dix-neuvième, George se croit vieille à trente-huit et souffre de migraines qu'elle attribue à « l'irritation du nerf optique ».

Le 24 juin 1842, Michel tombe à Nohant, sans prévenir, en pleine crise de migraine. Sa présence n'apporte aucun adoucissement à ces maux de tête. Ce qui est fini, pour George, l'est à jamais. Michel, pas plus que Musset, n'a droit à un retour de flammes.

Ayant beaucoup brûlé, sainte Tranquille se repose de tant d'embrasements célestes. Aux « bras de fer » de Michel, elle préfère « les doigts de velours » de Chopin. Et aux exaltations de la passion, les simples joies de l'amitié. Quel bonheur de lire sous la plume de Pauline Viardot : « *Consuelo* (...) nous fait frémir, rire, pleurer, réfléchir. (...) Je ne puis pas vous dire ce qui se passe en moi depuis *Consuelo*, seulement, je sais que je vous en aime dix mille fois davantage et que je suis toute fière d'avoir été un des fragments qui vous ont servi à créer cette admirable figure. »

Consuelo paraît en feuilletons dans *la Revue indépendante*, et George finira par appeler Pauline Consuelo, ce qui veut dire, en espagnol, consolation...

La Revue indépendante paraît maintenant deux fois par mois et Sand redouble d'efforts, continuant avec acharnement *Consuelo* « comme étant destinée à faire beaucoup de numéros ». Inépuisable Consuelo !

Le 29 septembre 1842, George Sand quitte la rue Pigalle pour le 5, square d'Orléans, où elle s'installe en compagnie de Frédéric Chopin. Chacun y occupe un pavillon. Y demeurent également « la bonne et active Marliani » et son époux. Après avoir créé *la Revue indépendante*, Sand a l'illusion d'avoir inventé

266

un phalanstère : « Nous nous rapprochons, autant que faire se peut dans ce triste Paris, de la vie de Nohant. (...) Nous courons le soir des uns chez les autres, comme de bons voisins de province. Nous avons même inventé de ne faire qu'une marmite, et de manger tous ensemble, chez Mme Marliani, ce qui est plus économique, et plus enjoué de beaucoup que le chacun chez soi. C'est une espèce de phalanstère qui nous divertit (...). »

Elle vit là, comme dans un couvent, fuyant les salons et leurs causeries qui sont pour elle « une fatigue, une perte de temps et d'énergie sans aucun profit ». Elle refuse de sacrifier à ces visites qui rythment la vie de son époque, visites reçues, visites rendues. Et quand un visiteur insiste pour être admis, elle répond : « Il y a plusieurs années que je vis dans une retraite absolue, me privant des sociétés les plus agréables, et ne voyant pas mes amis bien souvent. Si je faisais une exception à cette règle de conduite, il me faudrait en faire beaucoup d'autres. » Elle remplace les visites par des lettres, édifiant ainsi, sans le savoir, feuillet par feuillet, ce monument qu'est sa *Correspondance*. Autant elle répugne à perdre son temps à des visites, autant elle n'hésite pas à écrire longuement à des inconnus qui en valent la peine. Parmi ces derniers, Charles Poncy, poète et maçon, qui a vingt et un ans, et habite sa ville natale, Toulon. Il a publié un recueil de poèmes, *Marines*.

George Sand commence l'année 1843 en sermonnant Poncy qu'elle somme de ne pas devenir un poète bourgeois et de rester ce qu'il est : un poète prolétaire. Elle termine son prêche par un vibrant : « Enfin, voulez-vous être un vrai poète ? Soyez un saint. » Elle engage également Poncy à maîtriser les ardeurs de ses vingt ans, à choisir la voie de l'amour unique et de la fidélité dans le couple. Elle n'a guère donné l'exemple jusqu'à maintenant. Honni soit qui mal y pense : revenue de tout, et sans aucune envie d'y retourner, George Sand voudrait épargner aux autres ses propres erreurs. Rien d'extraordinaire à ce comportement alors en vogue. Les courtisanes qui ont réussi veillent à ce que leurs filles soient sévèrement élevées dans des couvents. Quand on connaît les dangers du feu, on veille à ce que les personnes que l'on aime n'aient pas à en subir les effets. Et c'est certainement animée par cet esprit de compassion que Sand, peu après avoir sermonné Poncy, prodigue ses conseils à Hyppolite Chatiron. Elle adjure son frère, qui marie sa fille Léontine, de demander à son futur gendre de ne pas se comporter comme une brute pendant ce viol légal qu'est la nuit de noces.

Maurice aurait pu épouser sa cousine Léontine. Mais il est trop jeune, il a juste vingt ans, et il est trop sage. Sagesse qui réjouit sa mère, scandalise son oncle Hyppolite et ses amis. Il est dit que la famille Dudevant fera toujours scandale dans le Berry, les uns par leur sagesse, les autres par leurs folies.

Pendant l'été 1843, dans les alentours de Nohant, George Sand et Frédéric Chopin se livrent à des voluptés qui ne déçoivent jamais, celles de la promenade, lui sur une ânesse, elle à pied. Un jour, les charmes de l'ânesse attirent un baudet entreprenant, et voilà Sand qui défend Chopin, et la vertu de sa monture, à coups d'ombrelle. Cris et éclats de rire. À peine les gaietés de cette scène sont-elles terminées que Sand, saisie par son nouveau démon du sermon, reproche à Solange le style « maniéré » de ses lettres. « Tout le monde n'a pas ton style », répond Solange qui, du haut de ses quinze printemps, se croit tous les droits, y compris celui d'exercer sur Frédéric Chopin ses coquetteries. « Dis à Chopin que je l'embrasse s'il veut m'écrire des bourrées. » Un baiser pour une bourrée, voilà qui promet !

À Nohant, Chopin et Delacroix discutent pour savoir exactement à quoi ressemblent les belles jambes de Solange. Pour Chopin, ce sont des tilleuls.

Pour Delacroix, ce sont des cèdres du Liban. Pour Sand qui se mêle à la conversation, ce sont des « futailles ». On peut rêver, un instant, à cette réunion, à Nohant, de ces trois êtres tellement différents, en cet été 1843. La musique, la peinture et la littérature discourant sur les jambes d'une nymphe de quinze ans. De quoi inspirer une allégorie.

Après avoir sermonné Poncy et Hyppolite, George Sand conjure Charlotte Marliani de ne plus se laisser guider par ses émotions, et cela, avec des accents de maître bouddhiste enseignant à son disciple d'être à lui-même sa propre lumière : « L'âme d'un être comme vous doit lutter et rester maîtresse du logis. Rappelez-vous que vous avez tiré de vous-même de grandes forces et de grandes lumières. » Machine à devoir, machine à sermon, George Sand est aussi une machine à courage. Nohant, ses enfants, et, dans une certaine mesure, Frédéric Chopin, sont entretenus grâce aux travaux forcés littéraires de celle qui, avec une vaillance sans défaut, noircit du papier pendant des nuits entières. Elle donne une suite à *Consuelo*, et c'est *la Comtesse de Rudolstadt*.

La renommée de Sand ne cesse de s'étendre, franchit les frontières, éditeurs et revues se disputent ses textes. Début octobre 1843, elle répond à l'un de ces demandeurs empressés, Pierre-Jules Hetzel, par un cérémonieux : « Monsieur, je ferai mon possible pour vous satisfaire. » Pierre-Jules deviendra rapidement « mon cher Hetzel » et c'est lui qui publiera, plus tard, les *Œuvres illustrées* de Sand. Comme elle en avait prévenu Buloz, elle n'est pas en peine de placer sa prose.

Fin octobre, le « petit », puisque c'est ainsi que Sand désigne Chopin à ses intimes, doit regagner Paris seul. George alerte aussitôt ces mêmes intimes qu'elle charge de veiller à ce que Frédéric prenne le matin sa tasse de chocolat ou de bouillon. Il est en bonne santé à Nohant parce qu'il y mène une vie aussi réglée que celle de George. Certes, les soins constants de la romancière n'ont pas réussi à faire pousser « l'ombre d'un mollet » au musicien, comme elle l'explique plaisamment à Delacroix. Enfin, heureusement que son « petit » s'en va à Paris en compagnie de son « grand » Maurice. Il est entendu que si Frédéric tombe malade, Maurice prévient immédiatement George et promet de coucher dans la chambre du malade. On ne sait pas comment Sand est toujours parvenue à faire admettre ses amants à ses enfants qui ont raffolé de Michel, logé chez Didier, voyagé avec Malefille. Et maintenant, à l'exemple de leur mère, ils entourent Chopin de soins. Ce fragile équilibre ne peut être que l'œuvre d'une Sand capable de persuader chacun qu'il est le plus aimé et qu'il doit aimer ce qu'elle aime...

Privés de la chaleur de cet amour, Frédéric et Maurice succombent au froid et à l'humidité de Paris. Maurice s'efforce de rassurer sa mère. « Nous sommes malades plus moralement que physiquement. » En fait, ni Maurice ni Frédéric ne peuvent se passer de George. Pour compliquer la situation, Chopin ne veut pas que Sand sache qu'il est malade. Chacun fait assaut de délicatesse pour rendre supportable l'absence. « Il me manque autant que je lui manque. J'ai besoin de veiller sur lui, autant qu'il a besoin de mes soins. Sa figure me manque, sa voix, son piano, sa petite tristesse, et jusqu'au bruit déchirant de sa toux me manquent. Pauvre ange ! Moi, je ne lui manquerai jamais, sois-en sûr, et ma vie lui est consacrée pour toujours », écrit George Sand, le 18 novembre 1843, à Albert Grzymala qui peut noter le changement de ton de cette lettre avec celle de fin mai 1838... Sand hésitait à s'engager dans « une course dans les étoiles » avec Chopin dont elle se croit maintenant l'éternel soleil.

Sand est retenue à Nohant par le projet de fonder un journal, *l'Éclaireur de l'Indre* avec ses amis Duvernet, Néraud, Planet et Duteil. Saisie d'enthousiasme, elle considère comme « un devoir social » de rendre à la province, et à la sienne particulièrement, un éclat perdu au profit de Paris. « Il y a nécessité urgente à décentraliser Paris, moralement, intellectuellement et politiquement. La presse parisienne, absorbée par ses propres agitations, ou fatiguée de combattre sur une trop vaste arène, abandonne en quelque sorte la province à ses luttes intérieures. »

Les luttes intérieures de la province, Sand les connaît, et dans leurs pires horreurs, comme l'affaire Fanchette. Fanchette, une retardée mentale de quinze ans, a été abandonnée dans la campagne berrichonne par les religieuses, peu charitables, qui l'élevaient. Sand écrit aussitôt une brochure, *Fanchette*, pour sauver cette malheureuse, « souillée » par on ne sait qui, de l'abjection.

Entre la création de *l'Éclaireur de l'Indre* et le sauvetage de Fanchette mené à bien par la seule force de sa plume et de ses démarches, Sand trouve encore le temps de revoir les baux avec ses fermiers et de visiter, comme au temps de Deschartres, les champs, les bergeries et, malgré son aversion des cochons, les porcheries. La châtelaine de Nohant n'esquive aucun de ses devoirs. Ce n'est que le 29 novembre qu'elle peut quitter le Berry pour retrouver les siens, un Chopin souffreteux, un Maurice blagueur, qui ont survécu, tant bien que mal, à son absence.

À la joie de retrouver ses deux enfants préférés s'ajoute celle d'avoir la confirmation qu'elle ne s'est pas trompée avec son poète-maçon de Toulon, Charles Poncy. Son deuxième recueil de poèmes, *le Chantier*, est digne du premier, *Marines*. Elle exulte : « Je ne m'étais donc pas trompée, vous serez, et vous êtes déjà un grand poète. Bien des gens, malgré une approbation prononcée pour votre premier volume, me raillaient de " mon engouement pour mon maçon ". Eh bien, " mon maçon " a très bien justifié mon engouement. »

Il faudrait un jour réunir, en une plaquette, les

lettres de George Sand à Charles Poncy. On serait étonné de la hauteur de leurs considérations. C'est à Poncy qu'elle réserve l'aveu de sa croyance dans les vies antérieures et futures. « Le temps ne paraît long qu'à nous. Aux yeux de Dieu, il n'existe pas. Nos siècles ne comptent pas dans l'éternité, et nous sommes vivants et agissants avec Dieu dans l'éternité, car nous mourons pour renaître et progresser. Chaque existence est la récompense ou le châtiment de celle qui l'a précédée. Chaque vertu amasse pour notre prochaine réapparition sur la terre un trésor de dédommagement et de force nouvelle. Soyez sûr que vous avez déjà vécu de tout temps sur la terre, et que votre génie poétique est la récompense de quelque belle action, de quelque noble dévouement, dont vous ne vous souvenez pas. » Il y a du maître bouddhiste en George Sand, comme on l'avait déjà constaté dans des conseils pour ramener au calme Charlotte Marliani.

Après avoir complimenté Poncy, Sand l'incite à la modestie puisque « quand nous créons quelque chose (...), c'est Dieu qui vibre, qui parle, qui agit en nous ». Ces fameuses « vibrations » que l'on découvre aujourd'hui étaient déjà connues de George Sand qui en savait plus sur le bon usage de l'univers que beaucoup de ses illustres contemporains.

BOHÈME BOURGEOISE ET FLUCTUATIONS DU CERCLE DE FAMILLE
(janvier 1844-décembre 1846)

> Mais sans souffrir de rien précisément je souffre de tout, parce que j'ai la faculté de comprendre où est le mal de ce monde.
>
> Nohant, le 18 octobre 1845

En janvier 1804, George Sand envoie une « lettre circulaire », autrement dit un tract publicitaire, pour annoncer la fondation de *l'Éclaireur de l'Indre* qui, entre-temps, est devenu *l'Éclaireur de l'Indre et du Cher*. Dans ce texte qu'elle signe, Sand ne cache pas sa satisfaction de compter sur « l'approbation et le concours de M. de Lamartine, de M. Louis Blanc, de M. de Latouche et de plusieurs autres grands et nobles écrivains ».

Il est piquant de retrouver dans cette liste de noms destinés à soutenir le journal que fonde George avec ses amis le nom de l'ancien directeur du *Figaro*, M. de Latouche, qui présida aux débuts de celle qui s'escrimait à écrire des « bigarrures ».

Piquante aussi sa condamnation de Musset, dans une lettre du 26 janvier 1804, à Charles Poncy qui a osé envoyé un exemplaire de son dernier recueil de poèmes, *le Chantier*, à l'auteur des *Nuits*. « Un exemplaire à Musset ! Il méprise profondément les ouvriers poètes, et à moins qu'un miracle ne se fasse en lui, il crachera sur votre volume. Il est devenu talon rouge et conservateur, à la fois marquis et juste milieu, aussi n'a-t-il plus le feu sacré qui lui inspirait autrefois des chants sublimes, il est mort. » Musset est enterré avant l'heure, et avec quel éloge funèbre !

Une autre mort, réelle celle-là, endeuille, en mai 1844, le foyer de Sand : le décès de Nicolas Chopin, père de Frédéric. Brisé de douleur, le musicien ne veut plus voir personne, sauf George. Le couple se réfugie à Nohant. Nohant refuge, et remède, au malheur. Chopin domine son chagrin et compose, « tout en disant comme de coutume qu'il ne peut rien faire que de détestable et de misérable ».

Cet été-là, la châtelaine de Nohant ajoute, à ses multiples occupations quotidiennes, la fabrication de confitures de prunes, une quarantaine de pots qu'elle offre à son ami, Jules Néraud. Elle donne son secret pour réussir cette confiture : « Il faut la faire soi-même et ne pas la quitter d'un instant. *C'est aussi sérieux que de faire un livre.* » C'est moi qui souligne cette dernière phrase. Sand a raison... Les confitures, comme n'importe quelle autre œuvre d'art, nécessitent une attention constante.

Pendant qu'elle surveille ses confitures, George Sand en oublie un peu Maurice qu'elle a fait exempter du service militaire et qui est à Paris où il devient, en août 1844, l'amant de Pauline Viardot. Voilà qui agrandit le cercle de famille. « Je l'aime sérieusement », avoue Pauline à George à qui elle demande d'écrire « à double entente » à Saint-Petersbourg où elle s'en va chanter. Louis Viardot ne doit pas être mis au courant de cette liaison entre le vrai fils de George et sa fille adoptive. Dans cette bohème bourgeoise que représentent Sand et Viardot, un mari trompé est toujours un mari trompé. Mieux vaut éviter esclandres et scandales. Ce qui importe, c'est que personne ne soit malheureux...

La compassion toujours en éveil de George Sand est attirée par le prince Louis Napoléon Bonaparte qui, après deux tentatives de retour en France, deux échecs, a été condamné à l'emprisonnement perpétuel au fort de Ham. Le 26 novembre, elle écrit à ce Bonaparte que l'on dit acquis aux idées avancées : « Le peuple est comme vous dans les fers. Le Napoléon d'aujourd'hui est celui qui personnifie les douleurs du peuple comme l'autre personnifiait ses gloires. » Cette comparaison a dû plaire au neveu de Napoléon Ier qui saura s'en souvenir quand il sera Napoléon III.

Au printemps 1845, George Sand supporte de

moins en moins la jalousie de Frédéric Chopin, et s'en plaint de plus en plus. Jalousie qui n'est pas sans fondement. Il est à peu près certain que, sous le règne de Frédéric, et vraisemblablement au mois de février 1845, George a été la maîtresse de Louis Blanc, un journaliste-écrivain, un populaire homme politique, à qui elle adresse un billet qui commence par « Mon cher ange » et se termine par « Dors bien, toi. Je t'aime ». On sait que George Sand n'ignore rien du sexe des anges.

Chaque passade avec un ange étant un reflet d'éternité, sainte Tranquille se garde bien de confondre les galanteries et l'amour, comme elle le rappelle à Marie des Rozières, qui a été l'élève de Chopin et qui est maintenant la maîtresse de piano de Solange : « Mon enfant, vous ne serez aimée d'amour que quand vous serez infiniment respectée. » On n'a jamais manqué de respect à George Sand. Sauf ses anges, le temps d'un embrasement céleste.

À mesure que le temps passe, les sermons de Sand se teintent de sévérité. Pierre Leroux, comme Marie des Rozières, en fait les frais. George est lasse de payer les chimères du « sublime bohémien ». Celui que Victor Hugo avait surnommé « le filou-sophe » provoque l'indignation de sa protectrice : « Qui me prouvera que je doive laisser les miens exposés à se faire bandits ou prostituées pour servir la famille de Leroux et lui, véritable sybarite intellectuel, qui ne veut faire que ce qui l'enthousiasme et travailler qu'à ce qui contente pleinement son esprit ? »

La sublime bohémienne, c'est Sand qui, malgré ses plaintes justifiées contre Pierre Leroux, réussit à être châtelaine berrichonne et socialiste parisienne, réussit ses confitures et ses romans comme *Jeanne* ou *le Meunier d'Angibault*, réussit à apaiser les jalousies de Chopin, à protéger les amours de Maurice et de Pauline et à endiguer les humeurs fantasques de Solange.

La seule chose qu'elle ne réussisse pas, c'est à

rester trois heures sans fumer. À son cousin René de Villeneuve avec qui elle vient de renouer, après la brouille de 1822, elle écrit, le 17 juillet 1845 : « J'ai un abominable défaut. Je fume des cigarettes ! bien petites, bien fades, bien misérables auprès de celles que consomment certaines " lionnes " d'aujourd'hui. (...) Et pourtant, si je reste trois heures sans fumer, je tombe dans un état de torpeur (...). Voilà mon plus grand vice, est-ce que vous le pourrez tolérer ? Je l'ai contracté en travaillant la nuit pour combattre le sommeil (...). » Révélation qui n'a pas dû surprendre l'austère M. de Villeneuve : il faut bien que la fille de l'infréquentable Sophie-Victoire Dupin ait un « abominable » défaut. Les femmes ne fument pas chez les Villeneuve.

En septembre 1845, parvenue au milieu de sa vie, George Sand dresse pour Charles Poncy le bilan suivant : « Nous avons une petite aisance qui nous permet de faire disparaître la misère autour de nous (...). Nous avons donc eu une sorte de bonheur relatif et mes enfants le goûtent avec la simplicité de leur âge. »

Ce bonheur est vraiment relatif, puisque, un peu plus tard, à l'une de ses correspondantes, Éliza Tourangin, elle avoue : « Sans souffrir de rien précisément je souffre de tout, parce que j'ai la faculté de comprendre où est le mal de ce monde. » En quoi George Sand rejoint ses précédentes incarnations, Aurore Dupin et Aurore Dudevant, qui auraient pu prononcer exactement le même aveu que précède cette explication : « Au fond du cœur, je suis plus triste que le temps qu'il fait, et n'échappe au spleen intérieur et profond qui a fait sa proie de toute ma vie que par le travail et une certaine activité du corps. »

Ce bilan intimiste adressé à Éliza Tourangin est plus proche de la vérité que celui adressé à Charles Poncy. Le spleen, la tristesse, le dégoût de soi et des autres auront ravagé celle qui offre le spectacle de ses réussites diverses à ses contemporains à la fois éblouis et envieux.

George Sand souffre particulièrement d'apprendre qu'Augustine Brault, fille de sa cousine germaine, Adèle, est pressée par ses parents d'accepter ce que l'on nommait alors un protecteur, c'est-à-dire un monsieur assez riche pour assurer la fortune de sa protégée, et celle de ses parents. En échange de cette faveur, le protecteur pouvait user, à discrétion, du corps de sa jeune protégée. C'était l'une des formes les plus subtiles, les plus courantes, de la prostitution à l'usage des familles pauvres. Le dix-neuvième siècle abonde en exemples de cette pratique qui ne s'arrêta qu'au début du notre siècle, avec la guerre de 1914-1918.

George Sand, qui ne saurait tolérer ce genre de protection dans sa propre famille, persuade Adèle de laisser Augustine venir séjourner à Nohant. Elle ne cache pas à Adèle qu'Augustine, qui a vingt et un ans, pourrait être une épouse idéale pour Maurice, qui en a vingt-deux. Certes, Maurice est toujours amoureux de Pauline Viardot, mais cet amour n'est pas indestructible. Et puis, Maurice n'est pas apte aux amours illicites. « Il n'est heureux qu'à la maison, au travail et dans les habitudes retirées et régulières. Ce tempérament heureux fait présager qu'il doit trouver dans Augustine tout ce qu'il peut désirer de sécurité, de douceur, de gaieté et de simplicité. » George promet à Adèle que si Maurice n'épouse pas Augustine, « il la respectera comme sa sœur ».

Augustine arrive à Nohant, début septembre 1845, et s'y « amuse comme une enfant en vacances » au contentement de George qui ne veut pas livrer ce trésor de Maurice à n'importe qui, et avoir aussi n'importe qui pour belle-fille. Avec Augustine, la joie et la paix du ménage semblent assurées !

Une paix que menacent les premières dissensions apparaissant, en octobre 1845, entre Frédéric Chopin et Maurice Dupin. Frédéric voudrait rentrer à Paris, Maurice ne veut pas. Le 15 octobre, George fait part à Marie des Rozières de ces dissensions et de ses propres réticences : « Nous pensons à rester ici jusqu'à la fin de novembre. Je ne sais pas si Chopin ira jusqu'au bout. Les jours de soleil il s'égaye, mais les grands jours de pluie, il devient sombre et ennuyé à mourir. Il ne s'amuse pas de tout ce qui m'occupe et me plaît à la campagne. Alors je voudrais le transporter à Paris d'un coup de baguette. Mais, d'un autre côté, je sais qu'il s'ennuie sans moi là-bas. Je lui ferais volontiers le sacrifice de mon amour de la campagne, mais Maurice n'est pas de cet avis-là, et si j'écoutais Chopin plus que Maurice, on jetterait de hauts cris. Voilà comme tout ne va pas de soi-même dans les familles les mieux unies. »

Sand ne voit jamais « sans terreur » s'approcher l'hiver et sonner l'heure du retour à Paris. Ah, si elle s'écoutait, George ne bougerait plus de Nohant où elle peut travailler sans être dérangée par « ces ennuyeux qui viennent bâiller chez vous une heure ou deux ». Le 21 octobre, elle termine *le Péché de M. Antoine* et le 1ᵉʳ novembre, elle achève *la Mare au diable*. « J'ai fini mon petit roman, je l'ai fait en quatre jours, et cela m'a remise en goût de travail. »

Ce « goût de travail » ne quitte guère sainte Tranquille, capable d'écrire *la Mare au diable* en quatre jours sans s'étonner d'une telle prouesse. Elle en profite, le 4 novembre, pour rendre hommage à son cousin, René de Villeneuve. « Je me souviens toujours que c'est vous, le premier, qui m'avez conseillé d'écrire des romans, en me disant que c'était très facile et que cela faisait une occupation agréable. » Et elle ajoute : « C'est facile, en effet, quand on n'y met pas de prétention, et le charme de cette occupation, c'est je crois qu'elle vous fait oublier souvent la vie réelle pour le monde des rêves. » Adorable simplicité.

Plus tard, vers le 19 novembre, c'est en évoquant ses souvenirs de famille dans une lettre à ce même Villeneuve qu'elle aura l'idée de raconter l'histoire des siens dans ce qui deviendra *Histoire de ma vie*. Le cousin René est donc à l'origine de la carrière de Sand romancière et de Sand mémorialiste. Grave responsabilité pour cet ultraconservateur !

Le 9 décembre 1845, George rentre à Paris, malgré son aversion grandissante pour « cette ville de boue et de vices ». De ce cloaque, elle parvient à arracher sa cousine, Augustine Brault, qui, fin janvier 1846, s'installe définitivement chez sa cousine. Comme Frédéric a été son deuxième fils, Augustine sera sa deuxième fille, ou sa troisième, si l'on compte Pauline Viardot. L'insatiable instinct maternel de George Sand trouve son compte dans ces parentés imaginaires et elle signe ses lettres à Charles Poncy « votre vieille mère ». Elle rêve que Poncy vienne à Nohant pour... y installer le calorifère. Le calorifère, comme le mariage de Maurice, appartient aux obsessions majeures de celle qui, en cela, demeure la bourgeoise Mme Dudevant.

Augustine se révèle une bonne acquisition, et une bonne compagne qui stimule la paresseuse Solange que l'on a retirée de sa pension, « ces demoiselles travaillent beaucoup maintenant, elles prennent des leçons toute la journée », et particulièrement des leçons de chant avec Manuel Garcia, le frère de Pauline Viardot. On reste en famille...

Solange a seize ans, l'âge du bal. En février 1846, George Sand domine sa répugnance à ce genre de divertissement et, pendant le carnaval, conduit Solange et Augustine au bal de l'hôtel Lambert. Dans cette cohue de trois mille cinq cents personnes, « mes filles étaient fort jolies et ont été très remarquées ».

Aller au bal, entrer dans le monde, marque, pour une jeune fille, le début de la chasse au mari, puisque le mariage est alors la seule issue possible pour quitter honorablement sa famille. On n'est pas là uniquement pour danser, mais pour attirer l'attention des prétendants. Le sculpteur Jean-Baptiste Clésinger, trente-deux ans, a-t-il « remarqué » à l'un de ces bals, la blonde, la belle Solange ? Paris est un village et Clésinger sait que, s'il veut la fille, il doit d'abord séduire la mère. Le 16 mars 1846, il demande à Sand la permission de baptiser l'une de ses statues *Consuelo*. Flattée, la romancière accepte. Remerciements dithyrambiques du sculpteur qui évoque le « grand cœur » et la « belle âme » de l'auteur de *Consuelo*. Sand mord à l'hameçon et invite Clésinger à venir au 5, square d'Orléans. Le loup est dans la bergerie et n'a plus qu'à attendre le moment opportun.

Les prétendants ne manquent pas à Solange. Sur les rangs, un neveu de Charlotte Marliani que Mlle Dudevant repousse à cause de sa figure. Ce qui fait dire à sa mère : « Je vois que Solange se fait des idées de perfection pour son mari, dont il faudra qu'elle rabatte beaucoup. (...) Jusqu'à présent, elle croit que les dieux de l'Olympe viendront briguer sa main. Elle ignore que les dieux ne sont pas de ce monde. »

Le 4 mai 1846, Sand signe un traité avec le journal *le Courrier français*, à qui elle vend, pour 8 000 francs, un roman, *Lucrezia Floriani*, qui y paraîtra en feuilleton, du 25 juin au 14 juillet, et du 28 juillet au 17 août. C'est, transposée, l'histoire de ses amours avec Chopin, et surtout de ses griefs contre le musicien, principalement son incessante jalousie. « Un jour, Karol fut jaloux du curé qui venait faire une quête. Un autre jour, il fut jaloux d'un mendiant qu'il prit pour un galant déguisé. » Elle travestit Frédéric Chopin en prince Karol, un ange adolescent, mais insupportable : « Il était véritablement insupportable, parce qu'il voulait raisonner et soumettre la vie réelle, à laquelle il n'avait jamais rien compris, à des principes qu'il ne pouvait définir. (...) Il était persifleur, guindé, précieux, dégoûté de tout. Il avait l'air de mordre, tout doucement, pour s'amuser, et la blessure qu'il faisait pénétrait jusqu'aux entrailles. (...) Il se renfermait dans un silence dédaigneux, dans une bouderie navrante. »

Aucun des défauts de l'ange polonais n'a échappé

à la romancière. Chopin, dans la vie quotidienne, par sa jalousie, ses dégoûts, ses silences, ses bouderies, se serait-il rendu insupportable à George en ce printemps 1846 ? On reste confondu par ce règlement de comptes que Sand a épargné à ses autres amours. Elle considérait Musset comme mort, et se gardait de trahir les secrets du Musset intime qu'elle avait connu à Paris, à Fontainebleau et à Venise.

Avec Chopin, c'est l'étalage et le déballage. Face au prince Karol, Sand s'est déguisé en Lucrezia Floriani. Elle ne s'est pas non plus donné le beau rôle en cette actrice de trente ans, « dont les mœurs imprudentes, les dévouements effrénés, la faiblesse de cœur et l'audace d'esprit semblaient une violente protestation contre tous les principes du monde et de la religion officielle ».

Quand, un soir, Sand fait la lecture de *Lucrezia Floriani* à Chopin et à Delacroix, personne ne se reconnaît, ou ne veut se reconnaître. Delacroix racontera plus tard : « J'étais au supplice pendant cette lecture. Le bourreau et la victime m'étonnaient également. Mme Sand paraissait absolument à l'aise et Chopin ne cessait d'admirer le récit. »

Inconscience de Sand ou extrême courtoisie de Chopin ? Leur absence de réaction, pendant cette lecture, nous surprend encore autant que Delacroix l'a été. Il faut admettre qu'un Frédéric Chopin n'appartient pas au commun des mortels. Ne s'étonne-t-il pas de « suer » pendant les fortes chaleurs à Nohant ? Le 18 juin 1846, George Sand prévient Marie des Rozières que « Chopin est tout étonné de suer. Il en est désolé, il prétend qu'il a beau se laver, qu'il empeste ! Cela nous fait rire aux larmes de voir un être aussi éthéré ne pas vouloir consentir à suer comme tout le monde, mais ne parlez pas de ça, il en serait furieux. »

Dans cette même lettre, George raconte à Marie qu'elle a conduit ses filles aux courses de Mézières-en-Brenne, « ces demoiselles ont trouvé là une cour, fort du goût de Miss Solange ». Parmi cette cour, se détache un gentilhomme berrichon de vingt-quatre ans, Fernand de Préaulx. Un bon garçon, prêt à se soumettre aux caprices de Miss Solange. Le contraire d'un Clésinger qui poursuit ses manœuvres d'encerclement et médite d'envoyer à Nohant une copie de son *Faune.*

Le sculpteur fait faire son éloge par un ami commun : « C'est un homme d'une nature saintement enthousiaste, il mange et dort peu, la gloire est son grand besoin. » Dans l'atelier de Clésinger, on ne lit, et à haute voix, que les œuvres de George Sand, comme *Valentine* ou *la Mare au diable.* Cet ami commun, le capitaine Stanislas d'Arpentigny, seconde Clésinger avec une vigueur militaire et ne craint pas les considérations un peu trop familières, concernant Solange et Augustine, comme : « J'espère que ces demoiselles ne nous reviendront point trop hâlées, une femme se doit d'être pure devant Dieu et blanche devant les hommes. » Les temps ont bien changé qui sont devenus ceux du bronzage universel !

Pendant cet été 1846, le dernier été que Frédéric Chopin passe à Nohant, l'accord entre le musicien et la romancière se dégrade. Le renvoi d'un couple de vieux domestiques motive une scène entre la châtelaine et son invité. « Chopin est effaré de ces actes tardifs de rigueur. Il ne conçoit pas qu'on ne supporte pas toute la vie ce qu'on a supporté vingt ans. Je dis, moi, que c'est parce qu'on l'a supporté vingt ans qu'on a besoin de s'en reposer. »

En ces raisons, Chopin trouve-t-il matière à réflexion sur les limites de la patience de Sand ? En ce renvoi, Chopin pressent-il le sien ? Il essaie de corriger sa jalousie, ses susceptibilités, ses silences qui rendent la vie quotidienne difficile. George se fait l'écho, fin juillet 1846, de tels efforts : « Il est très gentil cette année depuis son retour. J'ai bien fait d'avoir un peu de colère qui m'a donné un jour de courage pour lui dire ses vérités et le menacer de m'en lasser. Depuis ce moment, il est dans son bon sens, et vous savez comme il est bon, excellent, admirable, quand il n'est pas fou. »

Il est vrai que, depuis le séjour à Majorque, les enfants, Maurice et Solange, ont grandi et sont en âge de se marier. Frédéric, lui, est resté un enfant. Maurice et Solange sont des adultes. Ce qu'ils supportaient, enfants, de l'enfant Frédéric, ils ne le supportent plus maintenant. Pour Maurice, Chopin est un intrus dans le cercle de famille, un indésirable. Pour Solange, Chopin est un objet de coquetterie, un moyen de montrer son pouvoir à sa mère. Mlle Dudevant a su amener Fernand de Préaulx à ses pieds. Pourquoi pas Frédéric Chopin ?

La rumeur d'un possible mariage de Solange avec Fernand se répand. Il est temps d'avertir, en novembre, M. Dudevant qui, mis devant le fait en train de s'accomplir, répond placidement qu'il ne connaît guère Solange qu'il a quittée depuis une dizaine d'années et dont il n'a reçu depuis qu'une demi-douzaine de lettres. Il refuse de participer à la dot de sa fille, à qui George veut donner l'hôtel de Narbonne. Il n'en assure pas moins Solange qu'elle pourra venir, tant qu'elle voudra, à Guillery, où elle trouvera « bon gîte, bonne table, et bonne mine d'hôte ».

Une certaine désinvolture est dans l'air. Et à la désinvolture (explicable) de Casimir correspond la désinvolture (plus inattendue) de George à l'égard de Frédéric : « Chopin se plaint beaucoup, comme tous les ans à l'automne. Il tousse un peu plus, le matin, et voilà tout. » Ce « et voilà tout » sonne comme une condamnation. Était-ce hier que Sand affirmait aimer jusqu'à la toux de Chopin, jusqu'à en avoir mal dans sa propre poitrine ?

Le 30 décembre 1846, Chopin qui est à Paris envoie ses vœux à Sand résolument blottie à Nohant : « Soyez heureuse et tous heureux dans l'année qui vient et quand vous pouvez, écrivez-moi, je vous prie, que vous allez bien. » Elle va très bien, George Sand, en ce 30 décembre, elle qui vante les plaisirs de l'hiver à la campagne à son éditeur, Pierre-Jules Hetzel : « Pour moi, c'est un grand plaisir de voir de la neige, de la vraie neige blanche et de sentir du vrai vent qui vous vient en plein nez de tous les bouts de l'horizon. (...) Et puis le coin du feu et les longues soirées sont charmantes quand on est sûr de pouvoir en disposer d'un bout à l'autre, sans visiteurs et sans *bavards*. »

Dans ces bavards soulignés par Sand, faut-il inclure Chopin qui, quand il ne boudait pas en silence, savait être le plus brillant des causeurs et le plus drôle des imitateurs ?

Bohémienne immobile, Sand est une adepte du voyage entre quatre murs. Elle aime attirer sa proie dans son cercle de famille. La proie dévorée, ou changée en roman, elle continue à creuser imperturbablement son sillon de Nohant à Paris, et de **Paris** à Nohant. Sans quitter sa table de travail, elle parcourt un seul univers, le sien. Un univers très simple où règnent ses enfants, les vrais et les faux. Quoi qu'il arrive, les vrais finissent toujours par l'emporter sur les faux qui doivent alors céder la place.

LE DRAME À NOHANT
(janvier-décembre 1847)

Je sais de quoi ma fille est capable en fait de calomnie, je sais de quoi la pauvre cervelle de Chopin est capable en fait de prévention et de crédulité. (...) Je ne donnerai plus ma chair et mon sang en pâture à l'ingratitude et à la perversité.

Nohant, le 26 juillet 1847

À Nohant, 1847 commence comme 1846 s'est terminé : dans la joie de faire du théâtre. « Nous avons imaginé de jouer la comédie tous les soirs entre nous, sans aucun spectateur. Nous sommes six, mes deux enfants, ma fille adoptive, Lambert, l'ami de Maurice, jeune peintre rempli d'esprit et de gaieté, mon futur gendre et moi. Nous avons fait un théâtre, peint des décors, fabriqué des costumes. En cinq minutes, on installe ce théâtre dans le salon, en une demi-heure on s'habille. La pièce que j'écris durant le dîner et qui est nouvelle tous les soirs est lue et apprise au dessert. C'est un canevas stupide sur lequel chacun improvise son dialogue, quelquefois même ce sont des pantomimes que je conduis au piano. Cela dure jusqu'à minuit, après quoi on soupe, on rit, et on va se coucher. »

Les chambres sont glaciales et Sand se plaint de n'avoir dans la sienne que douze degrés, ce qui n'est pas suffisant pour y écrire cinq ou six heures de suite. Ah, si Nohant avait un calorifère... La frénésie des soirées fait oublier le froid des nuits.

Fernand et Solange s'aiment et roucoulent sous les yeux indulgents de George Sand qui, audacieuse innovation pour l'époque, consent à ce que deux fiancés vivent sous le même toit. La Châtre, pourtant habituée aux audaces de la châtelaine de Nohant, en blêmit. Quel exemple ! Quel laisser-aller ! Quel manque de façons ! Quelle insulte aux bienséances ! Pour prévenir, ou atténuer, de telles critiques, Sand précise que cette union est semblable à celle qu'elle a dépeinte dans *Mauprat*, entre

Edmée et Bernard. Elle ne tarit pas d'éloges sur son futur gendre, « bon comme un ange ». Voilà Fernand élevé au grade d'ange, et « simple comme la nature, habillé comme un garde-chasse, beau comme un antique, chevelu comme un sauvage ».

Fernand de Préaulx n'a qu'un défaut : il est légitimiste. Sand n'en est plus à une bravade près. Elle, la républicaine, aura un gendre royaliste !

Le 7 février 1847, Sand et ses enfants, parmi lesquels compte désormais Fernand, arrivent à Paris pour préparer les noces. Le 18 février, George et Solange rendent visite à Jean-Baptiste Clésinger qui doit faire leur buste. Le 19, la romancière remercie le sculpteur, qui, fidèle à sa promesse, a envoyé une copie en bronze de son *Faune*. Touchée par ce don, Sand affirme à Clésinger qu'elle sera toujours fière d'avoir apprécié ce chef-d'œuvre, et son auteur, avant qu'ils n'aient reçu la consécration de la foule.

Pendant les séances de pose, Solange est sensible à l'atmosphère de l'atelier, « toujours plein de jeunes gens, on y rit, on y chante, on y peint, on y fume » et à celui qui y règne en rêvant à la gloire. Partager l'imminente gloire de Clésinger, être sa muse comme sa mère l'a été de Musset et de Chopin, voilà une tentation qui rend singulièrement sans attrait Fernand de Préaulx. Aller s'enterrer dans une province, avec un gentilhomme désargenté, car Fernand n'a pas de fortune, alors que, Clésinger s'étant déclaré, Solange pourrait être l'une des reines de Paris !

Le 26 février, Mlle Dudevant demande un temps de réflexion à Fernand et reprend sa parole. Tête basse, avec encore un peu d'espoir au cœur, Fernand regagne le Berry et écrit à Sand qu'il « aspire ardemment » au bonheur de la « nommer sa mère ». S'étant aperçu de son inculture, il annonce qu'il va lire le seul livre qu'il possède en son château, les *Caractères* de La Bruyère. Pauvre Fernand !

Si Fernand de Préaulx n'est pas riche, Jean-Baptiste Clésinger ne l'est pas davantage, et a seulement l'habileté de cacher son impécuniosité. Il dépense plus qu'il ne gagne. Il a des dettes, il boit, il est brutal, il bat sa maîtresse, dit-on. Sa réputation est tellement déplorable que Sand finit par s'en alarmer et réclame des explications à Clésinger le 13 mars. Le futur gendre réussit à convaincre sa future belle-mère qu'il s'agit là de calomnie. « Calomnie », répète Sand, convaincue. Et elle ajoute : « Je le sais homme de cœur. » C'est un homme de cœur, presque un ange. Donc tout est dit pour George Sand qui regagne Nohant le 6 avril 1847.

Le 13 avril, Clésinger y surgit, décidé à obtenir, sans plus tarder, la main de Solange. Le 14, sainte Tranquille note : « Notre enragé sculpteur est ici. L'idylle fleurit à La Châtre ; la grande princesse s'est humanisée jusqu'à dire oui. (...) Ils me paraissent enchantés tous les deux. Je le suis par conséquent. »

Tel un César d'atelier, Clésinger est venu à Nohant, il a vu, il a vaincu. La volonté de cet homme a plu à George Sand qui ne s'en cache pas. « Cette tension de la volonté, sans fatigue ni défaillance, m'étonne et me plaît. Pour mon compte, tu sais que je procède par volonté lente et couvée. Mais j'admire cette puissance et j'y vois le salut certain de l'âme inquiète de ta sœur. Elle marchera droit avec lui, et elle sera cependant heureuse, parce qu'il aime passionnément ce qu'il a créé par sa conquête », écrit Sand à Maurice, le 16 avril. Elle ne saurait se tromper davantage, et persiste dans son aveuglement, annonçant à Charles Poncy, le 18 avril : « Le travail et l'émotion prennent tous mes jours et toutes mes nuits. J'ai presque supprimé le sommeil, de mon existence. » Quand trouverait-elle le temps de dormir ? C'est le 15 avril qu'elle a commencé *Histoire de ma vie*. L'usine Sand ignore les interruptions. Subissant les pressions de Solange et de Clésinger, elle espère que, après leur mariage, « le calme se fera enfin ». Elle se trompe encore.

Dans la précipitation de ces noces, chacun ne voit

que son intérêt. Sand n'est pas fâchée de se débarrasser de sa fille. Solange n'est pas mécontente de
quitter sa mère qu'elle juge trop tyrannique pour
suivre un époux qu'elle pense mener au gré de ses
caprices. Et Clésinger, qui croit George plus riche
qu'elle ne l'est et Solange plus docile qu'elle n'y
paraît, pense faire une bonne affaire et pouvoir
régler ses dettes les plus criardes avec la dot de son
épouse.

La châtelaine de Nohant a baptisé Clésinger
Méphisto. Pas complètement aveuglée, ou en un
ultime sursaut de lucidité devant l'imminence de la
cérémonie, elle craint un peu le choc de ce Méphisto
avec sa diablesse de fille. Elle prévoit que ce sera
« un rude attelage à gouverner ». Mais « il n'est plus
temps de reculer ».

À Nohant, le 19 mai, Solange épouse Clésinger
pour le meilleur, et surtout pour le pire. De Paris,
Chopin, que Sand a tenu éloigné de ces diverses
tractations, se contente d'envoyer ses vœux de bonheur : « Personne plus que moi parmi vos amis, vous
le savez bien, ne fait de vœux plus sincères pour le
bonheur de votre enfant. » Cela, Sand n'en doute
pas, pas plus qu'elle ne doute de l'opposition de
Chopin à ce mariage trop rapide avec un rapin dont
la mauvaise réputation parisienne n'a pas encore
franchi les frontières du Berry. Face à une possible
réaction de Frédéric, George ne cache pas ses
craintes à Marie de Rozières. « Je crains que le
mariage de Solange ne lui déplaise beaucoup et que
chaque fois que je lui en parle il n'ait une secousse
désagréable. Pourtant je n'ai pas pu lui en faire
mystère et j'ai dû agir comme je l'ai fait. Je ne peux
pas faire de Chopin un chef et un conseil de famille,
mes enfants ne l'accepteraient pas, et la dignité de
ma vie serait perdue. »

Dignité, le grand mot est lâché. À quarante-trois
ans, Sand aspire à cette dignité qu'elle pense avoir
acquise par son travail. Depuis qu'elle est sur terre,
elle brave les conventions. Elle estime que le temps

des bravades est terminé et qu'il vaut mieux que son amant ne se mêle pas du mariage et n'y assiste pas.

La présence de M. Dudevant aux noces de Solange serait une raison supplémentaire pour expliquer l'absence de l'amant de Mme Dudevant. Le duo Casimir-Frédéric n'aurait certainement pas manqué de saveur. Il faudra attendre le siècle suivant pour voir se mêler aux noces des enfants les maîtresses et les amants des parents...

Vis-à-vis de Chopin, Sand n'a quand même pas la conscience tranquille puisqu'elle éprouve le besoin d'écrire à Albert Grzymala une longue lettre justificative dans laquelle on peut voir les préludes à une proche rupture. George ne demande plus à Albert si Frédéric est apte à la « course aux étoiles » et à « l'embrasement céleste ». Il ne l'est visiblement pas, « il y a sept ans que je vis comme une vierge avec lui et avec les autres. (...) Je sais que bien des gens m'accusent, les uns de l'avoir épuisé par la violence de mes sens, les autres de l'avoir désespéré par mes incartades. (...) Lui, il se plaint à moi de ce que je l'aie tué par la privation, tandis que j'avais la certitude de le tuer si j'agissais autrement. (...) Je suis arrivée au martyre. »

Ce martyre, George l'oublie, le 29 mai, pour envoyer des bulletins de victoire à ses proches et à ses amis. Y revient le même refrain sur le bonheur de Solange et de Clésinger : « Ils s'adorent ». Une telle réussite ne peut qu'inciter Sand à marier Augustine qui s'est attachée à elle « comme le lierre à son arbre ». Un ami de Delacroix, le peintre Théodore Rousseau, est agréé comme prétendant. George a donné en dot à Solange l'une de ses propriétés de Paris, l'hôtel de Narbonne, estimé à 200 000 francs. Elle veut donner, sur sa propriété littéraire, 100 000 francs à Augustine.

Dès qu'ils apprennent ce projet qu'ils jugent d'une prodigalité excessive, Jean-Baptiste et Solange Clésinger ne reculent devant rien pour le faire échouer, même pas devant une lettre anonyme. Augustine y est traitée d'intrigante, et accusée d'avoir été la maîtresse de Maurice. Submergé par ce torrent de boue, Théodore Rousseau renonce à épouser Augustine Brault. Digne réponse de Sand, le 10 juin, à Rousseau : « Nous sommes des femmes, et pour cela nous ne sommes pas faibles, et nous ne répondons pas aux hommes qui se croient forts ce que nous pourrions leur répondre. Vous avez des soupçons et sur la franchise de la mère et sur la pureté de la fille qui veulent le mariage. (...) Il est des soupçons qu'on ne pardonne pas et qui tuent l'amour et l'amitié du même coup. »

Sand a quitté le sublime pour la dignité et elle y est aussi à l'aise. Dans la perfection d'une dignité semblable à celle qu'elle admirait tant chez Mme Dupin de Francueil, George Sand puise une consolation à la déception causée par l'échec du mariage d'Augustine. Une contrariété plus grande encore l'attend.

Un mois après son mariage avec Solange, Clésinger, devant l'urgence de ses dettes, demande à Sand d'hypothéquer Nohant. Elle refuse net. « Je refuse comme je refuserai toujours de grever Nohant d'une obole. C'est le refuge de ma vieillesse, c'est le patrimoine de Maurice. »

Ce refus irrite tellement les Clésinger qu'ils empoisonnent l'atmosphère de Nohant par leur conduite et leurs propos. Sand, Augustine, Maurice, et l'ami de ce dernier, Lambert, font serment de ne pas répondre aux provocations des Clésinger qui en profitent pour multiplier les incidents, les injures contre Augustine, ou contre Maurice qu'ils traitent d'abruti. Maurice ! Abruti ! C'en est trop ! On ne touche pas à Maurice, et le 10 juillet, George prie sa fille et son gendre de déguerpir sans autre forme de procès.

Le lendemain, les Clésinger obtempèrent et font leurs bagages. Le sculpteur emballe les deux statues offertes à sa belle-mère, *le Faune* et *Mélancolie*. Armé d'un marteau, il cloue lui-même les planches des caisses quand Solange surgit pour se plaindre : Lambert a refusé de la saluer. Clésinger ordonne à Lambert de saluer Solange. Lambert répond qu' « il n'a pas besoin qu'on le lui dise, qu'il n'y manque jamais ». Clésinger et Lambert en viennent aux mains, Maurice intervient pour les séparer. Alertée par le bruit de la bagarre, Sand accourt et voit Clésinger menacer Maurice d'un coup de marteau. Elle s'élance, gifle son gendre qui riposte par un coup de poing. On désarme le sculpteur et Solange dit suavement à son époux : « Mon ami, rentrez chez vous, vous avez frappé ma mère, vous vous êtes mis dans votre tort. »

Les Clésinger se retirent dans leur chambre où ils dînent de bon appétit. Ils quittent ensuite Nohant pour s'arrêter à La Châtre, à l'auberge, où, pendant deux jours, ils racontent, à leur façon, le drame, et vitupèrent contre une mère indigne, un frère idiot, et une infâme Augustine. Puis, Solange prend congé des badauds venus écouter le dernier scandale de la famille Dudevant, en lançant, du haut de sa calèche, ce cri du cœur : « Voici le plus beau jour de ma vie. »

Sand est anéantie. Elle a perdu Solange. Elle perd maintenant Chopin qui a pris le parti de Solange. « Chopin qui allait venir ici et qui tout à coup n'y vient plus (...), Chopin tout changé, tout transformé à mon égard, ne se mourant plus du tout de cet éternel amour que ses amis me reprochaient de ne pouvoir partager et me déclarant tout net que je suis une mauvaise mère, que Solange a parfaitement raison, que lui ne l'abandonnera pas. »

Ainsi, pour ne pas abandonner Solange, Frédéric abandonne George qui, dans sa colère, en oublie sa dignité et balaie d'un trait de plume ses neuf ans de liaison avec Chopin « qui est trop malade pour n'être pas réduit à l'amour platonique ». Saisie d'une exultation affreuse, elle piétine ce qu'elle a aimé. « Pour moi, quel débarras ! quelle chaîne rompue ! Toujours résistant à son esprit étroit et despotique, mais toujours enchaînée par la pitié et la crainte de le faire mourir de chagrin, il y a neuf ans que, pleine de vie, je suis liée à un cadavre. » Neuf ans passés à prodiguer des bouillons, des tisanes, des cataplasmes à ce cadavre ingrat! Et maintenant, quelle délivrance, quelle résurrection pour elle qui va enfin pouvoir se « donner la joie de penser et de parler, sans crainte que le mot le plus innocent ne soit un assassinat » ! Elle s'y livre déjà dans cette lettre du 26 juillet 1847, véritable règlement de comptes qu'elle adresse à son ami, Emmanuel Arago.

Comme toutes les mères déçues, Sand gémit : « Mon Dieu, je n'avais rien fait pour mériter une telle fille. » Sagement, Emmanuel Arago répond : « Il fallait s'attendre à ce qui est arrivé. (...) Solange n'aime qu'elle-même (...) son égoïsme est féroce (...) parlons de Chopin. (...) Depuis plusieurs années, il était fasciné par elle, et souffrait d'elle avec plaisir ce qui l'aurait exaspéré de la part de tout autre. J'ai vu, bien vu, qu'il avait, pour elle, un sentiment profond qui ressemblait d'abord à de l'affection paternelle et qui s'est transformé, peut-être à son insu, lorsque d'enfant elle devint jeune fille, et de jeune fille, femme. »

Chopin fasciné par Solange, fascination qui ne date pas d'hier. Comme toujours, dans ce genre d'infortune, Sand est la dernière informée et n'en croit pas ce que ses yeux lisent. Mais elle doit se rendre à l'évidence, Emmanuel Arago a raison. Il n'y a plus qu'à s'incliner et à écrire à Frédéric Chopin, le 28 juillet, une lettre de rupture, une lettre qui sera la dernière et qui se termine par : « Adieu mon ami, que vous guérissiez vite de tous maux, et je l'espère maintenant (j'ai mes raisons pour cela), et je remercierai Dieu de ce bizarre dénouement à neuf années d'amitié exclusive. Donnez-moi quelquefois de vos nouvelles. Il est inutile de jamais revenir sur le reste. »

Après quoi, George Sand tombe malade et souffre pendant huit jours de migraines atroces qui ressemblent à une congestion cérébrale. Puis, usine oblige, elle se remet au travail, à un roman, *Clelio Floriani*, qui deviendra *le Château des désertes*. En écrivant, elle ne trouve pas l'apaisement souhaité, l'oubli des récentes horreurs, et elle se fait l'écho des calomnies que Solange répand sur son compte à Paris. « Chaque jour m'apporte de loin un trait de la vengeance et de l'aversion que cette malheureuse et criminelle enfant porte, la tête haute, et qui se traduisent en diffamations adroites, perfides, contre sa famille et contre moi-même, qui n'ai vécu que pour elle et pour Maurice. (...) Elle se pose comme une victime de mon injuste préférence pour son frère et pour sa cousine ! Elle salit le nid d'où elle sort, en supposant et en disant qu'il s'y commet des turpitudes. Elle ne m'épargne pas non plus, moi qui me suis fait l'existence d'une religieuse, et elle le sait si bien ! »

Elle passe ses jours et ses nuits « dans des réflexions et des angoisses à faire pitié ». Mais qui a pitié de George Sand ? Personne, sauf Maurice qui « ne veut pas se marier à ce qu'il prétend, parce que jamais il n'aimera une femme autant que sa mère ». Comblée par cet aveu, Sand n'en espère pas moins que Maurice changera d'avis. Soutenue par l'affection de son fils, d'Augustine et de quelques fidèles comme Emmanuel Arago, George Sand barbouille inlassablement du papier, activité qu'elle résume en une jolie formule, « noircir bien du papier pour me dénoircir l'esprit ».

Dans ces ténèbres, une éclaircie. En novembre 1847, un Polonais, Charles de Bertholdi, professeur de dessin, demande la main d'Augustine qui, échaudée, demande un délai de réflexion. George et Augustine ont appris qu'il ne sert à rien de précipiter les mariages...

En ce même mois de novembre, l'incroyable se produit. Quatre mois après le drame, Solange revient à Nohant, comme si rien ne s'y était passé. Elle y est amenée par les amis Duvernet. Plus princesse que jamais, enceinte, « fraîche, rose, grasse », Solange verse trois ou quatre larmes, pas davantage, et daigne embrasser sa mère, puis son frère. George dit à Solange que, en cas de malheur, elle sera là, prête à l'aider. Solange répond qu'elle n'aura pas besoin de son aide puisqu'elle ne connaîtra jamais le malheur avec Clésinger. « Tant mieux », conclut George pour mettre fin à cet entretien sans issue.

Les Duvernet, qui espéraient une réconciliation en règle, sont déçus et suggèrent à Solange de demander pardon à sa mère. « Pardon de quoi ? Je n'ai rien fait, ma mère n'a rien à me reprocher, je ne lui demande rien. Je ne suis pas venue pour lui demander quelque chose », s'insurge Solange qui ment et qui sait parfaitement qu'elle est venue demander de l'argent à sa mère. Les Clésinger, perdus de dettes, n'étaient revenus à La Châtre que pour soutirer de l'argent à Sand qui, si elle a consenti à recevoir sa fille, a refusé de recevoir son gendre.

Leur coup manqué, les Clésinger retournent à Paris puiser dans la bourse de Chopin, ce que n'ignore pas Sand. « Je sais par eux-mêmes que Chopin les entretient. Clésinger l'a dit à tout le monde. La bourse de Chopin est inépuisable pour eux. » Quelle amertume, quelle humiliation pour George, une de plus. « J'aurais commis des fautes, des crimes, Chopin n'aurait pas dû y croire, il n'aurait pas dû les voir. Il y a un certain point de respect et de gratitude où nous n'avons plus le droit d'examiner des êtres qui nous deviennent sacrés. Eh bien, Chopin, loin de garder cette religion, l'a perdue et profanée. Il m'a rêvé et inventé des torts dont je n'ai même pas eu la pensée. » Chopin prête sa bourse aux Clésinger, et ses oreilles à leurs calomnies. Cela, c'est impardonnable pour Sand qui, pourtant, pardonne : « Je pardonne donc à Chopin du fond de mon cœur, comme je pardonne à Solange, bien plus coupable encore, à Grzymala, faible et frivole, à Mlle de Rozières, bête comme une oie. »

Ce pardon est sincère. Sand veut donner « un grand coup de collier » pour sauver Solange « d'une catastrophe à prévoir ». Ce « coup de collier », c'est *Histoire de ma vie* qu'elle a déjà entreprise et qu'elle définit, en décembre 1847, comme « une série de souvenirs, de professions de foi, de méditations ». Puis, quittant les sommets de l'inspiration, elle retombe à pieds joints dans la réalité : « Solange ne devrait pas s'attendre à être très riche, puisque je ne le suis pas. »

Sand vit avec les apparences de la richesse, tenant table ouverte à Nohant. Elle mène la vie de château, sans en avoir la fortune correspondante. D'où les incessantes demandes d'argent à son éditeur, Hetzel, et les flots de copie qu'elle répand pour maintenir ce navire en perdition qu'est toujours ce Nohant qui rapporte alors seulement 7 800 francs par an.

Le 31 décembre 1847, après une année durement remplie, marquée par la rupture avec Solange, la rupture avec Chopin, la signature du traité pour *Histoire de ma vie*, George Sand n'a plus qu'un désir, qu'elle exprime ainsi à Jean-Baptiste Clésinger : « Rendez ma fille heureuse, c'est tout ce que je vous demande. »

GUIGNOLS À PARIS
ET MARIONNETTES À NOHANT
(janvier-décembre 1848)

> Je te l'ai déjà dit : Les révolutions ne
> sont pas des lits de roses. Ce sont au
> contraire des lits d'épines.
> Nohant, le 3 novembre 1848

Bonne, profondément bonne, George Sand non seulement pratique le pardon des offenses, mais veille encore au bonheur de celle qui l'a le plus offensée, Solange, à qui elle constitue une rente de 2 500 francs par an. Elle lui annonce l'envoi du premier semestre, 1 200 francs. Solange prend de haut ce qu'elle considère comme une aumône insuffisante : « 1 200 francs n'empêcheraient chez moi ni une saisie, ni une vente forcée ; cela ne servirait même pas à me procurer tout ce qu'il manque dans ma maison. Ce serait un grain de sable dans la mer. » Mme Clésinger prie donc sa mère de garder cette somme.

« Une rente de 2 500 francs n'était pas un grain de sable dans la mer. Tu n'as point été élevée dans une telle opulence que tu puisses parler comme un M. de Rothschild. Avec 2 500 francs par an, il y a de quoi nourrir, entretenir, élever un enfant. Tu vas en avoir un et le premier semestre de cette pension pourra payer la layette ou la nourrice. (...) Pour te faire cette rente, j'ai donné congé de mon appartement de Paris ainsi que de l'atelier de Maurice, et je t'ai envoyé d'avance le fruit d'une économie qui n'est pas encore réalisée puisque mon terme ne finit qu'au mois d'avril », répond Mme Sand avec cette dignité qu'elle semble avoir prise comme règle de conduite. Ce qui ne l'empêche pas, devant ses intimes, d'accuser le coup et de gémir : « C'est affreux d'aimer un marbre. » Le sculpteur a épousé un marbre, il y aurait de quoi en rire, si les pleurs, en cette triste affaire, ne l'emportaient sur le rire.

À la révolte de Solange et de Chopin — on ne peut pas parler de la révolte des anges — qui a bouleversé sa famille, George Sand voit se succéder une révolution qui ravage Paris et les provinces. Fin février 1848, Louis-Philippe abdique, les Tuileries sont pillées, les rues de la capitale ensanglantées par des combats.

Le 24 février, un gouvernement provisoire est constitué, certains de ses membres, comme Ledru-Rollin ou Louis Blanc, sont des amis de Sand. Le 26 février, les Ateliers nationaux sont créés pour donner du travail aux ouvriers. Le 29, les titres de noblesse sont abolis. Il se passe trop de choses à Paris pour que George Sand reste davantage à Nohant. Le 1er mars, George fait son entrée dans la capitale et y retrouve Maurice, intact ; il a traversé ces journées d'émeute sans une égratignure, Dieu soit loué ! Maurice loge dans un petit appartement au 8, rue de Condé. Sa mère s'y installe et vit les événements, au jour le jour.

Le 2 mars, la journée légale de travail est fixée à dix heures. Le 3 mars, George fait le point de la situation. « Le Gouvernement est bon et honnête, le peuple excellent. » Ce même jour, elle publie une *Lettre à la classe moyenne*. Elle se grise de politique comme elle se grisait d'embrasement céleste. Elle est reçue par les membres du gouvernement, elle participe à quelques délibérations, et, par son silence, approuve le refus de nommer commissaire son ex-roi Michel. Ce n'est pas pour se venger des souffrances infligées par « les bras de fer » de l'avocat, mais parce que « Michel a abandonné la démocratie, en haine de la démagogie ». Et puis, « Michel est riche, il est ce qu'il a souhaité, ce qu'il a choisi d'être ». Michel, amen !

Le 4 mars, Sand rencontre Chopin dans l'escalier de Mme Marliani. Le 5, Chopin raconte à Solange cette rencontre dont il ignore qu'elle est la dernière : « J'ai dit bonjour à madame votre mère et ma seconde parole était s'il y avait longtemps qu'elle a reçu de vos nouvelles. " Il y a une semaine, m'a-t-elle répondu. — Vous n'en aviez pas hier, avant-hier ? — Non. — Alors, je vous apprends que vous êtes grand-mère, Solange a une fillette, et je suis bien aise de pouvoir vous donner cette nouvelle le premier. " J'ai salué et je suis descendu l'escalier (*sic*). Combes l'Abyssinien (qui du Maroc est tombé droit dans la révolution) m'accompagnait, et comme j'ai oublié de dire que vous vous portiez bien, chose importante pour une mère surtout (maintenant, vous le comprendrez facilement, mère Solange), j'ai prié Combes de remonter, ne pouvant pas grimper moi-même, et dire que vous allez bien et l'enfant aussi. J'attendais l'Abyssinien en bas quand madame votre mère est descendue en même temps que lui et m'a fait avec beaucoup d'intérêt des questions sur votre santé. (...) Elle m'a demandé comment je me portais ; j'ai répondu que j'allais bien, et j'ai demandé la porte au concierge. » Frédéric Chopin salue George Sand et s'éloigne. Frédéric et George se quittent pour toujours, dans la froideur d'un salut de courtoisie...

La fille de Solange et de Clésinger, Jeanne-Gabrielle, est née le 28 février, à Guillery, chez M. Dudevant. Elle y meurt le 6 mars. Ce décès vaut à Mme Clésinger une lettre « assez affectueuse » de sa mère. Quand il apprend ce retour d'affection, Chopin s'en réjouit et plaint son ancienne compagne. « Elle est bien à plaindre, c'est un grand coup pour elle, j'en suis sûr, et je ne doute qu'elle ne fasse tout ce qu'elle pourra pour vous. » Voilà la preuve que Chopin, s'il a choisi le parti de Solange, ne s'est pas rangé pour autant parmi les ennemis de Sand, comme cette dernière avait tendance à le penser, à le dire, et à l'écrire... Et quoi qu'en pense Chopin, la joie causée par la révolution de 1848 l'emporte sur la peine causée par la mort de Jeanne-Gabrielle.

Le 8 mars, George Sand écrit à Charles Poncy. « J'ai le cœur plein et la tête en feu. Tous mes maux physiques, toutes mes douleurs personnelles sont oubliés. Je vis, je suis forte, je suis active, je n'ai plus que vingt ans. » L'amour vieillissait George, la politique la rajeunit. Chacun trouve sa fontaine de jouvence où il peut, et sa source d'oubli.

Le 17 mars, elle répète à Pauline Viardot : « Ah ! nous serons républicains quand même (...). C'est la pensée, le rêve de toute ma vie qui se réalise (...). Mes chagrins personnels, qui étaient arrivés au dernier degré d'amertume, sont comme oubliés ou suspendus... » Sand, prodigieuse abeille qui fait son miel de tout, y compris des révolutions.

Le 22 mars, pour la première fois dans sa *Correspondance*, apparaît le nom d'Alexandre Manceau, un ami de Maurice. « On a couru chez Manceau, pas de Manceau. » À partir de 1850, Sand n'aura plus à courir chez celui-ci, qui s'installera à Nohant...

Ayant retrouvé la légèreté de la vingtième année, George court beaucoup et partout. Le 23 mars, elle se déclare « occupée comme un homme d'État. J'ai fait déjà deux circulaires gouvernementales aujourd'hui, une pour le ministère de l'Instruction publique, et une pour le ministère de l'Intérieur ». Elle rédige des bulletins, elle persuade Ledru-Rollin de demander à Pauline Viardot de chanter *la Marseillaise*. Pauline chantera *la Jeune République*. Sand se mêle de tout. Elle est aussi infatigable que sa plume qui galope sur le papier. Toutes deux sonnent la charge, le 28 mars : « La république, c'est la vie. Elle est perdue si les vrais amis du peuple s'endorment. Elle est sauvée si nous sommes tous là. Debout ! debout ! »

Elle est obsédée par la république et prête à tout pour sa sauvegarde.

Elle multiplie les avertissements, les appels à la vigilance, et dans son seizième bulletin, elle incite les ouvriers à l'émeute et aux barricades si la démocratie était menacée. Les ouvriers n'entendront que trop cet appel et Sand sera rendue responsable des désordres de juin durement réprimés par le général Cavaignac.

Elle apprend, avec stupéfaction, que, à la mi-mars, les ouvriers de La Châtre ont manifesté à Nohant aux cris de « À bas Mme Dudevant, à bas Maurice Sand, à bas les communistes ». Le peuple ne serait-il pas aussi « excellent » que le suppose la châtelaine de Nohant ?

En avril 1848, un club de femmes propose la candidature de George Sand à l'Assemblée nationale. L'intéressée qualifie cette prétention de « ridicule » et en profite pour affirmer son opposition à la participation des femmes à la vie politique. « Quelques femmes ont soulevé cette question : Pour que la société soit transformée, ne faut-il pas que la femme intervienne politiquement, dès aujourd'hui, dans les affaires politiques ? J'ose répondre qu'il ne faut pas, parce que les conditions sociales sont telles que les femmes ne pourraient pas remplir honorablement et loyalement un mandat politique. La femme étant sous la tutelle et dans la dépendance de l'homme par le mariage, il est absolument impossible qu'elle présente des garanties d'indépendance politique à moins de briser individuellement, et au mépris des lois et des mœurs, cette tutelle que les mœurs et les lois consacrent. » Bref, avant de siéger à l'Assemblée nationale, la femme doit obtenir d'abord, Sand en est consciente, « l'égalité civile, l'égalité dans le mariage, l'égalité dans la famille ». En 1848, on en est loin, très loin... Et Sand prévoit le pire pour la femme député : « À quelles ridicules attaques, à quels immondes scandales peut-être, donnerait lieu une pareille innovation ? Le bon sens la repousse, et la fierté que votre sexe devrait avoir vous fait presque un crime de songer à en braver les outrages. » Là-haut, bonne-maman et ses amies, les vieilles comtesses, doivent applaudir cette tirade en faveur du maintien des convenances.

George Sand vit dans ce tumulte politique comme un poisson dans l'eau. Le 20 avril, du haut de l'Arc de triomphe et en compagnie des membres du gouvernement provisoire, elle assiste à la fête de la

Fédération. « La fête de la Fraternité a été la plus belle journée de l'histoire. Un million d'âmes, oubliant toute rancune, toute différence d'intérêt, pardonnant au passé, se moquant de l'avenir, et s'embrassant d'un bout de Paris à l'autre au cri de " Vive la fraternité ", c'était sublime. »

Avec Aurélien de Sèze, George Sand avait atteint le sublime sentimental. Avec Alfred de Musset, le sublime poétique. Avec Michel de Bourges, le sublime sensuel. Avec Frédéric Chopin, le sublime musical. Avec le gouvernement provisoire, elle atteint le sublime politique, et n'en perd pas pour autant le sens des réalités. Elle obtient pour Clésinger une commande, celle de la statue du Champ de Mars, et pour Charles de Bertholdi, qui vient d'épouser Augustine Brault, un poste de percepteur à Ribérac. Il faut reconnaître que Sand ne demande rien pour elle-même, si ce n'est de satisfaire sa faim de sublime. Le 18 mai, elle revient à Nohant, rassasiée, voire dégoûtée. La bourgeoisie s'est, une fois de plus, approprié la révolution. Le gouvernement provisoire a été dissous le 6 mai.

L'apprentie sorcière de la révolution de février 1848 contemple ses enchantements brisés et ses philtres évaporés. Elle a cru en la révolution, comme elle avait cru en l'amour. Elle ne croit plus à rien, même pas à l'art. « Je ne sais plus ce qu'est l'art et le soin de cultiver son propre talent », soupire-t-elle. Après tout, elle pourrait être arrêtée comme l'ont été certains de ses amis, un Barbès, par exemple. Elle se rassure d'un : « On ne fera pas la ridicule et odieuse bêtise de persécuter une femme qui n'est jamais sortie de son rôle de femme, pas plus en politique qu'en littérature. » Elle plaide non coupable et donne pour preuve de son innocence son ignorance : « Je ne comprenais rien à ce qui se passait. » Elle comprend que la possibilité d'un Âge d'Or est irrémédiablement révolue et déplore les malheurs du peuple : « Nous aimons le peuple comme notre enfant. Nous l'aimons comme l'on aime ce qui est malheureux, faible, trompé et sacrifié. » Bref, le monde, et particulièrement Paris, ne sont qu'une pétaudière, et Sand remercie Dieu d'avoir Nohant : « Je remercie Dieu d'avoir un Nohant pour y oublier tout cela. »

À Nohant, elle est dans une telle gêne qu'elle est prête à céder à Hetzel pour 3000 francs sa *Petite Fadette* dont elle aurait obtenu, sans peine, 5000 francs avant la révolution. Ah, les révolutions ne favorisent guère les arts, ni les artistes ! Pour en finir avec celle de février 1848, Sand prononce, le 6 septembre, l'une de ses plus fermes déclarations de foi : « Je serai jusqu'à ma dernière heure du parti des victimes contre les bourreaux. » On ne saurait être plus clair. La première victime de cette révolution, c'est elle, Sand : « Fatigue, privations, douleurs, déceptions, reproches, diffamations[1] et calomnies, j'ai tout subi sans seulement y prendre garde. »

En novembre, elle établit un triste bilan de l'année écoulée, avec cet éternel refrain : « La bourgeoisie l'emporte, direz-vous, et il est tout simple que l'égoïsme soit à l'ordre du jour. » Elle reconnaît volontiers que « les chefs socialistes ne sont ni des héros ni des saints. Ils sont entachés de l'immense vanité et de l'immense petitesse qui caractérisent les années du règne de Louis-Philippe. » Elle n'a plus aucune illusion sur les hommes qu'elle a tant admirés. « Voilà Leroux qui bat la campagne. Cavaignac ne sait pas ce que c'est que la France. Le prince Louis[2] n'a pas de cervelle. Proudhon manque de quelque chose. » Elle n'a qu'une consolation, dont

---

1. Dans ces diffamations, Sand inclut certainement une brochure signée par Brault, le père d'Augustine qui ne désarme pas depuis le mariage de sa fille avec Bertholdi. Brault aurait dépensé 20000 francs pour l'éducation musicale d'Augustine et il accuse Sand d'avoir détruit cette carrière de cantatrice. Il réclame 80000 francs de dommages et intérêts, qu'il n'obtient pas.
2. Le prince Louis Napoléon Bonaparte, le futur Napoléon III.

elle ne se prive pas : « Je fais souvent des châteaux en Espagne, c'est la ressource des âmes brisées. »

Le 8 décembre 1838, George demande à Pauline Viardot des nouvelles de Chopin : « Je l'aime toujours comme mon fils quoiqu'il ait été bien ingrat envers sa mère. » Si Maurice lisait ces lignes... et s'il lisait celles qui suivent : « Il me semble même que cette histoire de ma vie que j'écris est mon testament et quand je l'aurai finie, je pourrai dire comme je ne sais plus quel poète mourant à qui l'on demandait comment il se trouvait : toujours plus tranquille. » Combien de fois, déjà, pendant sa vie, Sainte Tranquille aura aspiré à cette mort et à cette tranquillité qu'elle a tendance à confondre ! Ni sainte, ni tranquille, elle aura souffert de cette hypersensibilité qu'elle reprochait tant à Chopin dont la santé, d'après Pauline, décline lentement, entre des crachements de sang et des quintes de toux.

Privée de George, sa vigilante infirmière, Frédéric oublie son bouillon du matin et son cataplasme du soir. « Il parle de vous avec le plus grand respect, et je persiste à affirmer qu'il n'en parle jamais autrement », précise Mme Viardot à Mme Sand qui persiste à penser que Chopin prête une oreille trop complaisante aux ragots de Solange.

Le 10 décembre 1848, l'ancien prisonnier du fort de Ham, le prince Louis Napoléon Bonaparte, est élu président de la République. Élection que Sand traite de « belle folie » et de « belle bêtise ». Elle prophétise : « L'homme qui a fait les équipées de Strasbourg (...) aura une fin misérable [1]. »

Autre fin misérable et prévisible, celle d'Hyppolite Chatiron qui meurt le 23 décembre, tué par sa « passion du vin ». « Ce pauvre ami de mon enfance était fini pour moi depuis longtemps, et, depuis le mariage de ma fille, je ne l'avais pas vu. »

---

1. Après la défaite et la capitulation de Sedan, Napoléon III mourra en exil, en Angleterre, en 1873.

Hyppolite, comme Chopin, avait pris le parti de Solange, donc n'existait plus aux yeux de Sand. George pardonne mais n'oublie pas. Elle ne figure pas sur le faire-part de la mort de Chatiron alors que les Clésinger y figurent. Mesquinerie qui n'affecte plus George Sand, qui contemple la vie comme un songe dont les acteurs sont des fous. Ruptures, disparitions, révolutions, tout cela ne vaut pas un bon spectacle de marionnettes comme Maurice et son ami Lambert savent en offrir à George qui s'amuse à voir « gesticuler tout ce monde de guignols ». Il est impensable qu'elle ne fasse pas de rapprochements entre les marionnettes de Nohant et les guignols de la politique parisienne.

L'AVÈNEMENT D'ALEXANDRE MANCEAU
(janvier-juillet 1850)

> Je suis comme transformée, je me porte bien, je suis tranquille, je suis heureuse ; je supporte tout ; même son absence, c'est tout dire, moi qui n'ai jamais supporté cela.
>
> Nohant, fin avril 1850

Les efforts déployés par Maurice, Lambert et leurs marionnettes ne parviennent pas à arracher George Sand à son spleen habituel que renforcent les désillusions de 1848. « Combien la vie est triste et pleine d'amers enseignements, écrit George à Charles Poncy, le 9 janvier 1849. Sans argent frais, elle n'a pas 100 francs devant elle, elle se prive de feu dans sa chambre et passe l'hiver en chaussons, « faute de souliers ». Elle supporte ces privations sans se plaindre, sauf une qu'elle déplore : le manque de musique. Depuis que Chopin n'est plus là, plus de musique. Elle essaie, vainement, de suppléer à cette double absence en jouant sur son piano *le Mariage secret* de Cimarosa et *Don Juan* de Mozart. Elle voudrait avoir quinze ans et consacrer sa vie à la musique. À la place de quoi, elle entre dans sa quarante-cinquième année et travaille à l'*Histoire de ma vie*.

Le 20 mai 1848, elle apprend la mort de Marie Dorval — « Quelle affreuse douleur pour moi. » Marie en qui elle voyait une vraie sœur, un double idéal.

Peu après, elle apprend une autre mauvaise nouvelle : Chopin est mourant. Elle n'y croit pas. « J'ai encore l'espérance qu'il vivra, je l'ai vu tant de fois comme s'il était sur le point d'expirer que je ne désespère jamais de lui », note-t-elle le 19 juillet. Optimisme excessif : Chopin meurt peu après, à Paris, le 17 octobre. Sand se dit « affectée profondément ». La preuve ? Elle reste quatre jours sans écrire, quatre jours pendant lesquels elle n'est

« bonne à rien ». Et le pire, c'est que le dernier regard de Chopin aura été pour Solange qui le veillait et que les dernières mains qui auront touché son visage auront été celles de Clésinger. En effet, c'est à Clésinger que l'on doit le masque mortuaire du musicien.

« Le pauvre enfant ! » gémit George qui doit dissimuler son chagrin pour ne pas peiner Maurice qui « perd la tête » dès que sa mère a « l'air triste et souffrant ».

Mort d'Hyppolite Chatiron, mort de Marie Dorval, mort de Frédéric Chopin, mort du régime démocratique qu'elle avait rêvé, la vie de Sand ne serait alors qu'une suite de deuils si, en novembre 1849, ne triomphait à l'Odéon une adaptation théâtrale de son roman *François le Champi*. C'est pour Sand l'amorce d'une résurrection. On applaudit son nom qui, après l'échec de la révolution de 1848, était devenu « un épouvantail ». Louis Viardot ne s'y trompe pas qui, le 24 novembre, écrit à George : « On vous a tellement identifiée, et tellement insultée avec l'opinion républicaine, que c'était un triomphe pour nous tous. »

À Nohant, l'auteur de *François le Champi* reçoit des bulletins de victoire signés par Mme Marliani, par François Rollinat et par l'acteur Pierre Bocage qui dirige l'Odéon et qui a été l'artisan de ce succès, Bocage à qui elle avoue simplement : « J'ai beau me tâter, je ne me sens pas enivrée du succès. »

Fin décembre 1849, arrivent à Nohant un musicien allemand, Hermann Müller-Strübing et le graveur Alexandre Manceau. Hermann a trente-sept ans, c'est un helléniste distingué, un révolutionnaire éminent, un ami des Viardot. Il est grand et fort. Alexandre a trente-deux ans. Ce graveur sur cuivre n'est ni grand, ni fort. C'est donc avec Hermann que George choisit d'avoir d'abord une aventure...

Elle en est tout étonnée et ne cache pas son étonnement, le 29 décembre, à son éditeur, Pierre-Jules Hetzel : « C'est la première fois que je m'associe à un homme robuste au moral et au physique. Jusqu'ici j'ai comme cherché la faiblesse par un instinct maternel qui n'a fait de moi qu'une gâteuse d'enfants, et une maman dont on connaît trop la faiblesse. On est dominé toujours par les êtres faibles. »

George ne veut plus être dominée, et surtout pas par celui qui a succédé à Chopin, Victor Borie. On ne sait pas grand-chose de cette liaison qui a duré de l'été 1847 à la mi-décembre 1849, et qui a valu à Boris le surnom de « Pôtu »[1]. Journaliste, ami de Pierre Leroux, il est condamné le 19 décembre, par la cour d'assises de l'Indre, pour avoir « excité les citoyens à la haine les uns envers les autres », à un an de prison et à une amende de 2 000 francs. Il préfère s'enfuir à Bruxelles, quittant Nohant et sa châtelaine, sans trop de regrets de part et d'autre, semble-t-il.

Le successeur de Chopin est, à son tour, rapidement remplacé par Hermann Müller-Strübing, car, comme l'explique Sand à Hetzel dans sa lettre du 29 décembre : « Je ne veux pas, je ne peux pas vivre sans aimer. » On s'en doutait un peu, et, entre la fuite de Borie et la conquête de Müller, George n'aura passé qu'une dizaine de jours sans « aimer »...

Le 10 janvier 1850, George Sand, comblée, célèbre en Hermann « la perfection du dévouement et de la bonté ! (...) Il ne lui manque que d'être français, d'avoir la pensée prompte et de pouvoir parler cette langue qu'il sait pourtant mieux que moi. Mais le Pôtu m'impatientait parce qu'il ne voulait pas être ce qu'il pouvait être, et celui-ci veut tant qu'il peut ».

Grâce à Hermann, la gaieté revient à Nohant où l'on joue la comédie, chaque soir, avec Manceau qui

1. Si vous voulez en savoir plus sur Alexis-Pierre-Victor-Louis-André Borie, lisez la note que Georges Lubin consacre à ce « Pôtu » aux pages 774 et 775 du tome VIII de la *Correspondance*.

s'improvise chef de troupe. On joue des adaptations des pièces de Shakespeare. Maurice est excellent en Falstaff et Manceau, tout ému, fait ses débuts en Prince de Galles. « Il a bien joué cependant, il a beaucoup de distinction », remarque Sand. On s'amuse tellement, les soirées sont tellement réussies que l'on se couche parfois à six heures du matin.

Sand est de plus en plus tentée par le théâtre qu'elle est prête à considérer comme un grand art. Le 3 février, elle annonce à Pierre Bocage : « Je veux faire de l'art. On peut toujours se passer d'argent et de succès quand on se sent artiste pour de bon. On ne peut se passer de chercher sa jouissance intime dans son œuvre et le public en me sifflant, ou en m'applaudissant, ne peut ni augmenter ni diminuer le plaisir que j'ai trouvé dans mon travail. » Un plaisir qu'elle n'a pas connu longtemps avec Hermann, plus doué pour prodiguer des leçons de philosophie que des embrasements célestes ! La rupture s'accomplit sans drame et Hermann reste à Nohant comme un frère, comme un ami. « Nous sommes deux amis, deux hommes », explique Sand, en ce même 3 février, à Hetzel qui doit trouver que la vie sentimentale de sa correspondante est encore plus variée que l'intrigue de certains de ses romans...

Pour justifier sa présence à Nohant, Hermann traduit en allemand des chapitres d'*Histoire de ma vie*, et cela, à l'entière satisfaction de George Sand. Sans rechigner, ni montrer de l'humeur ou de la jalousie, il laisse la place à Alexandre Manceau qui devient ainsi l'homme à tout faire de Nohant, comme l'avoue Sand à Hetzel, fin avril 1850 : « C'est un ouvrier qui fait son métier en ouvrier, parce qu'il veut et sait gagner sa vie. Il est incroyablement artiste par l'esprit. Son intelligence est extraordinaire, mais ne sert qu'à lui, à moi par conséquent. Il ne sait rien, mais il devine tout, questionnant toujours, il me prouve à moi combien son esprit travaille intérieurement. Il ne sait pas l'orthographe, mais il sait faire des vers. C'est un détail qui le peint tout entier. »

À quoi bon énumérer à Hetzel les qualités de Manceau ? Un triomphant « Oui, je l'aime, lui ! » suivi d'un non moins triomphant « Il aime, voyez-vous, comme je n'ai vu aimer personne » valent toutes les explications que la romancière s'efforce de donner à son éditeur. Elle reconnaît à Manceau deux grands défauts : « Il est à la fois violent et calculé. Violent, il blesse affreusement ; calculé, il s'impose et cherche la domination. » Mais « tous les défauts qu'il a avec les autres disparaissent dans le tête-à-tête ? Là, c'est à la fois un chat caressant et un chien fidèle, et tout son calcul, toute son intrigue n'a pour but que d'obtenir l'approbation de l'être qu'il aime ». Autrement dit, Manceau a la patience de conduire Sand jusqu'à l'approbation suprême, jusqu'à l'embrasement céleste.

En plus, Manceau est aux petits soins avec celle qu'il appelle, respectueusement, devant tout le monde, Madame. Il s'empresse d'apporter un verre d'eau à George, ou d'allumer sa cigarette. Quand George est malade, elle guérit en voyant Manceau préparer son oreiller et apporter ses pantoufles. La passion à domicile, la passion en pantoufles, c'est, au fond, ce que cherchait la descendante des « dames d'opéra » et qu'elle a trouvée en Manceau. Finies, les escapades à Venise ou à Valldemosa, finies, les chevauchées nocturnes. Dieu qu'on est bien chez soi, avec un Manceau à ses pieds ! « Je suis comme transformée, je me porte bien, je suis heureuse, je supporte tout, même son absence, c'est vous dire, moi qui n'ai jamais supporté cela. »

La châtelaine de Nohant, qui a toujours voulu prouver son amour pour le peuple, ne saurait en donner une preuve plus éclatante qu'en prenant un amant dans le peuple, un amant ouvrier...

Les débuts de cette liaison sont marqués par la création de *la Véritable Histoire de Gribouille*, que Manceau, promu secrétaire de l'auteur, recopie patiemment et que Maurice illustre. Sand écrit, Manceau recopie, Maurice illustre. C'est donc aussi simple que cela, le bonheur ? « Oui, je suis heureuse, très heureuse », confirme George à Hetzel, en juillet 1850. Elle a célébré son quarante-sixième anniversaire par le constat de ce bonheur : « J'ai quarante-six ans, j'ai des cheveux blancs, cela n'y fait rien. On aime les vieilles femmes plus que les jeunes, je le sais bien maintenant. Ce n'est pas la personne qui a à durer, c'est l'amour ; que Dieu fasse durer celui-ci, car il est bon ! »

DE LA BOUDERIE AU COUP D'ÉTAT
(août 1850-décembre 1851)

> Depuis trois ans, je puis jurer devant Dieu que, sans perdre mon utopie qui, vous le savez, est chrétienne et douce comme mes instincts, je n'ai pas remué un doigt contre la société officielle. J'ai passé tout mon temps à faire de l'art...
>
> Nohant, le 13 janvier 1852

Le bonheur pour Sand, comme pour les autres humains, est rarement un état permanent. À peine a-t-elle répété sur tous les tons, à Hetzel, en juillet 1850 : « Oui, je suis heureuse, très heureuse », que, le 7 août, elle écrit à ce même Hetzel : « Je suis malade de chagrin. J'ai perdu ma vieille amie, Mme Marliani. (...) Je cache mon chagrin à ceux qui m'aiment. Car toute affection est jalouse, même des morts. Mais dans le secret de mon cœur, je souffre plus que je ne puis le dire. »

On comprend que George ne puisse guère parler de cette pauvre Marliani, indissolublement liée à l'affaire Chopin, au séjour à Majorque et au phalanstère du square d'Orléans, à Alexandre Manceau qui pourrait en prendre ombrage.

Son amour pour Manceau, et l'amour de Manceau, ne l'empêchent pas d'être écœurée, complètement écœurée par la situation politique : « Cette révolution avortée, ces intrigues de la bourgeoisie, ces exemples d'immoralité donnés par le pouvoir, cette impunité assurée à toutes les apostasies, à toutes les trahisons, à toutes les iniquités, c'est en fin de compte l'ouvrage du peuple qui l'a souffert et qui le souffre. »

Combien de fois Sand aura-t-elle employé le verbe souffrir ? Elle souffre d'avoir perdu sa foi dans le peuple. Elle est moralement anéantie, et, à ceux qui, comme Pierre Bocage, vantent sa force, elle réplique avec lucidité : « Vous dites que je suis de force à briser les plus forts. Vous me vantez ! Je n'ai jamais brisé personne, je me suis brisée moi-même. »

323

Cet état d'écœurement dure plus que d'habitude et se change en bouderie, comme elle l'avoue, le 16 novembre 1850, à Émile de Girardin : « Je boude. Je boude contre le peuple, contre le parti, contre ma cause, contre moi-même si vous voulez. (...) Que voulez-vous ? les journées de juin 1848[1] m'ont porté un coup dont je ne suis pas revenue et je suis misanthrope depuis ce temps-là. » Elle l'était déjà, et bien avant la révolution de 1848 !

La bouderie accentue un mal dont Sand pâtit de façon chronique : la constipation. Elle se dit « constipée de naissance » et en « souffre en ce moment plus que de coutume », pestant contre le manque de confort, à Paris, des cabinets. À Nohant, au moins, elle souffre, et boude, au chaud. Le calorifère, qui est enfin installé, « chauffe toute la maison ».

Début janvier 1851, à Paris, Maurice croise, par hasard, dans la rue, Solange Clésinger et sa deuxième fille qui porte les mêmes prénoms que la première, trop tôt disparue, Jeanne-Gabrielle. Cette Jeanne-Gabrielle numéro deux est née le 18 mai 1849. Sand ne la connaît toujours pas, elle boude les Clésinger plus que quiconque. Quand elle apprend que, après cette rencontre, Maurice s'est laissé entraîner à dîner en leur compagnie, elle laisse éclater le plus affreux des soupçons : « Je n'aime pas que tu manges chez eux. N'y mange pas. Clésinger est un fou. Solange est sans entrailles. Tous les deux ont une absence de moralité qui les rend capables de tout, dans certains moments. (...) Ils ont tout intérêt à ce que tu n'existes pas, et pour eux, l'intérêt avant tout. » Bref, George accuse sa fille et son gendre de vouloir attenter aux jours de Maurice.

Pour oublier cette menace, Sand fête les Rois en tête à tête avec Manceau. Ils vident, à eux deux, une demi-bouteille de vin de Champagne. Elle fête

---

1. Dissolution des Ateliers nationaux, Paris en état de siège, morts de Mgr Affre et de divers représentants du peuple.

ensuite le succès de sa pièce, *Claudie,* que Bocage interprète magnifiquement au théâtre de la Porte-Saint-Martin, « succès de larmes, succès d'argent. Tous les jours salle comble, pas un billet donné, pas même une place pour Maurice ».

Le 31 janvier 1851, Solange et sa fille, Jeanne-Gabrielle, dite Nini, arrivent, sans crier gare, à Nohant et en repartent le 5 février. Solange, qui n'est plus revenue à Nohant depuis novembre 1847, embrasse sa mère avec « assez de tendresse mais trop d'aplomb ». Un aplomb que Sand n'apprécie guère, pas plus qu'elle n'a aimé cette intrusion grâce à laquelle pourtant elle a enfin connu Nini, une Nini de sept mois.

George a le pardon aisé, mais la rancune tenace. Après dix ans de solide brouille avec Buloz, elle consent à ce que son roman, *le Château des désertes,* paraisse dans *la Revue des Deux Mondes.* « Je me félicite que votre nom reparaisse dans *la Revue,* après dix ans d'absence », se réjouit Buloz.

Le 23 mars, Bocage joue *Claudie* à La Châtre. C'est un triomphe auquel participe George Sand et dont *l'Écho de l'Indre* rend compte : « G. Sand assistait à la représentation de son œuvre : les applaudissements ont éclaté à son entrée dans la salle, les regards du public sans cesse tournés vers sa loge ont dû lui dire la reconnaissance et les sympathies d'un pays dont elle est la gloire. » Comme elle avait été la gloire du couvent des Anglaises, après en avoir été la honte, George Sand est la gloire du Berry, après en avoir été aussi la honte, celle qui courait les bois et les champs avec des garçons, et habillée en garçon...

En même temps que cet hommage des Berrichons, Sand reçoit l'hommage de ses pairs. « Vous êtes le génie de la France », lui écrit Michelet. Elle en est, en tout cas, la conscience.

La gloire de Sand ne se limite pas à La Châtre, elle est européenne et même universelle. Elle est lue à Paris comme à Saint-Pétersbourg, ou à São

Paulo, dans l'hémisphère Nord comme dans l'hémisphère Sud. La preuve ? Le sauvetage d'Edmond Plauchut.

Plauchut, journaliste républicain, s'exile volontairement après l'échec de la révolution de 1848. Pendant ses errances, il fait naufrage aux îles du Cap-Vert. Il a tout perdu, sauf deux lettres de Sand qu'il avait reçues autrefois et précieusement conservées. Grâce à ces deux lettres, il trouve un appui sans faille auprès d'un jeune, et riche, Portugais, Francisco Cardozzo de Mello, fervent admirateur de la romancière. Rentré en France, Edmond Plauchut raconte son sauvetage à Sand qui, le 11 avril, y voit « quelque chose de providentiel entre Dieu, vous et moi ».

En échange de son aide involontaire, la châtelaine de Nohant réclame à Plauchut des papillons, « les plus humbles, les plus chétifs » pour sa collection. La passion de l'entomologie vient de saisir George Sand qui, on ose l'espérer, fait une différence entre les ailes de ses papillons et celles de ses anges...

Le 30 avril, George écrit à Solange, qu'elle a renoncé à amender : « Tu t'amuses, tant mieux. Moi, je travaille, et comme ça m'amuse plus que tout, nous faisons bien toutes les deux. » Sur cet « amusement » qu'est l'écriture, Bocage reçoit, au même moment, une autre version qui semble plus conforme à la vérité : « On voit bien que ce n'est pas votre état, d'écrire. Et les yeux, et la migraine, et la tension d'esprit ! » Il en est de la « facilité » de Sand à écrire comme de sa « frigidité » en amour : des légendes...

Que cela l'amuse, ou non, d'écrire, George Sand, chaque nuit, s'enferme avec sa plume, son encrier et ses feuilles de papier. Sur sa table de travail, un verre d'eau sucrée préparé par Manceau. Elle s'est créé à Nohant un cercle enchanté dont elle ne veut plus sortir, même pour aller à Paris assister à la création de l'une de ses pièces, *Molière*. Elle préfère en lire dans les journaux des comptes rendus que signent Paul de Musset, ou Théophile Gautier.

Quand elle s'arrache à Nohant pour un bref séjour

à Paris, elle recommande à la bavarde Solange le silence sur sa venue : « Ne dis à personne, pas même à ton bonnet de nuit, que je vais à Paris. Tu sais que cela fait sortir de terre des milliers de gens inconnus, méconnus, incompris avec des manuscrits dans leurs poches, et qui me découvrent avec un art incompréhensible. Et puis cela me forcerait à faire des visites que je n'aurai pas le temps d'entreprendre. » Sainte Tranquille est, plus que jamais, farouchement opposée à tout ce qui pourrait troubler sa sainte tranquillité.

C'est en juin 1851 qu'elle fait à Pierre Bocage une déclaration politique destinée à devenir fameuse : « Je suis communiste comme on était chrétien en l'an 50. C'est pour moi l'idéal des sociétés en progrès. » Le communisme de sa mère doit divertir Solange qui séjourne à Nohant, en juillet, avec Nini, promue au rang de « petite merveille » par Sand. Solange abandonne brusquement Nohant et sa fille pour rejoindre son mari. Ce départ rend Nini boudeuse. Sa grand-mère, que les événements ont également rendue boudeuse, comme on le sait, n'en réprimande pas moins la « merveille » d'un : « N'est-ce pas que ça t'ennuie de bouder ? » La petite répond : « Ça ennuie Nini » et embrasse sa grand-mère. L'amour passion que George Sand va porter à Nini commence à cet instant. Aussi, quand, à la fin juillet, elle doit rendre Nini à Solange, elle fait cette remarque dont les Clésinger ne tiendront, hélas, aucun compte : « C'est très grave d'avoir la garde d'un petit enfant, il ne faudrait jamais le perdre de vue. »

Manceau, par jeu, se pose en amoureux de Nini et craint déjà « ses caprices dans leur ménage ». « Je lui fais observer que quand elle sera en âge de l'épouser, il sera lui-même en enfance », observe paisiblement Sand avec son implacable bon sens.

Le 14 août 1851, elle écrit sa première lettre à Alexandre Dumas fils qui a vingt-sept ans et qui sera l'un de ses amis de prédilection, l'un de ses fils imaginaires. Les Dumas père et fils représentent pour George Sand ce monde de la scène qu'elle implante à Nohant où l'on inaugure une salle de théâtre. Ce qui fait dire à sa châtelaine, en octobre : « Nohant n'est plus Nohant, c'est un théâtre, mes enfants ne sont plus mes enfants, ce sont des artistes dramatiques ; mon encrier n'est plus une fontaine de romans, c'est une citerne de pièces de théâtre, je ne suis plus Mme Sand, je suis un premier rôle marqué. »

La troupe comprend une vingtaine d'acteurs parmi lesquels Sand, Maurice, Manceau, Lambert, les Duvernet, les Fleury et autres, en tout une vingtaine d'acteurs improvisés, se partagent les rôles, premiers ou secondaires, dans une parfaite entente et bonne humeur. Une cinquantaine de personnes, amis intimes, domestiques, paysans du voisinage composent le public.

On joue une pièce de Sand, *Victorine*, une de Lambert, *la Belle Anglaise*, une autre de Maurice, *la Cour du prince Irénéus*. Les auteurs qui sont aussi les acteurs sont également applaudis.

Le 14 novembre, George quitte Nohant et son théâtre pour assister, à Paris, à la représentation de son *Mariage de Victorine* au Gymnase. C'est un succès. « C'est un succès plus grand que la bêtise du public ne le comporte », note son auteur, le 27 novembre.

Le succès de *Victorine* est arrêté net par le coup d'État du 2 décembre 1851. Dans la nuit du 1er au 2 décembre, les députés de l'opposition sont arrêtés à leur domicile. Quand Paris s'éveille, au matin du 2, le prince-président Louis Napoléon Bonaparte a dissous l'Assemblée nationale et rétabli le suffrage universel.

Dès le 2 décembre, Sand rassure Maurice resté à Nohant : « Je parie que l'on dit en Berry que tout est à feu et à sang ici. Il n'y a rien encore. » Le 4, alors que des fusillades éclatent sur les Boulevards, Sand, Manceau, Solange et Nini quittent Paris pour arriver à Nohant le 6.

De Nohant, George s'inquiète pour ses amis demeurés dans la capitale, et particulièrement pour son éditeur, Pierre-Jules Hetzel, prié de quitter la France dans les quarante-huit heures. « Votre absence est ma ruine », écrit Sand à l'exilé, le 12 décembre. Malgré cette ruine, elle envoie 200 francs à Delacroix afin qu'il envoie l'un de ses tableaux, « un Turc, un lion, un cheval, une odalisque », qui constituera les étrennes de Maurice. Le coup d'État ne fait pas oublier à Sand ses obligations de mère dont la première est de combler son fils. Heureux Maurice qui reçoit un Delacroix pour ses étrennes.

NOTRE-DAME DES GRÂCES
(janvier 1852-avril 1853)

> Il en est d'autres, moins résignés, sans doute, moins désintéressés, peut-être, il en est probablement d'aigris et d'irrités qui, s'ils me voyaient en ce moment implorer grâce pour tous, me renieraient un peu durement.
>
> Nohant, le 20 janvier 1852

Après le coup d'État du 2 décembre 1851, les arrestations des opposants au nouveau régime se multiplient. George Sand craint d'être arrêtée et fait part de ses craintes à son cousin, René de Villeneuve, le 13 janvier 1852. « Mon tour va venir bientôt, demain peut-être. Peut-être, quand vous recevrez cette lettre, serai-je arrêtée et en route pour être transportée. Autour de moi mes amis d'enfance, les gens les plus modérés, les plus ennemis des prises d'armes, sont en prison ou en fuite. C'est une nouvelle terreur organisée. Cependant je crois encore au prince Louis. »

Le 20 janvier, elle écrit au prince Louis Napoléon Bonaparte, au prince-président, pour lui demander une audience. Dans cette lettre, elle laisse parler son cœur, comme elle l'avait fait autrefois, avec celui qui fut prisonnier au fort de Ham, et cela donne des cris — « La politique fait de grandes choses, mais le cœur seul fait des miracles » —, des appels — « Amnistie, amnistie, bientôt mon prince ! » —, dont la justesse et la sincérité ne peuvent que toucher, momentanément, celui qui en est l'objet, et qui, peut-être, en même temps, sourit à cet habile, quoique énorme, flatterie : « Je vous ai toujours regardé comme un génie socialiste. »

Le 29 janvier 1852, le prince-président reçoit chaleureusement son ancienne correspondante, l'assure de son amitié et de son admiration, et avec une écrasante habileté, instaure un dialogue de sourds. « Demandez-moi tout ce que vous voudrez, pour qui vous voudrez », dit-il. Il offre des grâces particulières pour les amis de Sand. Sand ne veut entendre parler que d'une grâce générale. Le duo entre ces deux personnages qui comptent parmi les plus célèbres de la France, le duo entre le pouvoir et la littérature tourne court. Le miracle de l'amnistie réclamé par la romancière n'a pas lieu. Le prince-président se contente de recommander George Sand à son ministre de l'Intérieur, Persigny.

Forte de cette recommandation, Sand sauve ceux qui peuvent l'être et se dépense sans compter pour obtenir la libération de ses amis emprisonnés, ou sur le chemin de la déportation à Cayenne, ou en Algérie. Elle fait ce qu'elle estime être son devoir, sans se soucier des conséquences. Elle est vite accusée de se compromettre avec le nouveau régime. Sa visite au prince-président n'est pas passée ina-perçue et *la France napoléonienne* en rend compte : « Mme Sand, dont toute la France connaît les opinions, n'a pas voulu bouder contre le président, qui l'a reçue avec des égards dus à une femme de génie. La démarche de Mme Sand à l'Élysée était d'ailleurs inspirée par le mobile le plus respectable. Elle venait solliciter la clémence de Louis Napoléon pour ses amis politiques tombés en disgrâce. »

Comme il y eut, pendant l'autre Terreur, une Notre-Dame de Thermidor, Sand devient une Notre-Dame des Grâces. Elle fait le bien non seulement pour ses amis, un Émile Aucante, un Alphonse Fleury, un Ernest Perigois, mais aussi pour des inconnus. Elle n'en récolte souvent qu'ingratitude. Certains, qui ne veulent rien devoir à la clémence d'un Louis Napoléon Bonaparte — ce serait recon-naître qu'il existe —, refusent de profiter de la grâce obtenue et accusent Sand de trahison. « Pour récom-pense, on m'a dit et on m'écrit de tous côtés : Vous vous compromettez, vous vous perdez, vous vous déshonorez, vous êtes bonapartiste ! Demandez et obtenez pour nous, mais haïssez l'homme qui accorde. »

George Sand est incapable d'une telle conduite. Et

puis, elle ne peut pas haïr puisque la haine est un sentiment qu'elle ignore. Elle ignore aussi, elle qui aime tant le sublime, qu'elle est, dans son entreprise de sauvetage, sublime sans aucune pose, naturellement. Sublime et découragée.

À Hetzel qui, lui aussi, persiste dans son exil en Belgique, Notre-Dame des Grâces laisse voir son découragement, le 22 février. « Ici rien ne tient à rien. Les grâces ou justices qu'on obtient sont, la plupart du temps, non avenues grâce à la résistance d'une réaction plus forte que le président et aussi à un désordre dont il n'est plus possible de sortir vite, si jamais on en sort. La moitié de la France a dénoncé l'autre. » Ces horreurs de la délation se reverront en France, au siècle suivant, pendant les années quarante...

Une consolation pour Sand, deux jours plus tard, le 24 février, elle reçoit une lettre signée par les détenus à la prison de Châteauroux, une lettre de remerciement pour les démarches qu'elle a entreprises pour leur libération. Le 25 février, vaincue par tant de fatigues et d'émotions, George tombe malade, subissant des « suffocations assez effrayantes ». Elle suffoque surtout de voir la France tomber dans l'esclavage et devenir la proie de Napoléon III et de ses séides.

Depuis le coup d'État, « Paris est un chaos, et la province une tombe ». Cette catastrophe nationale se double pour Sand d'un désastre privé : les Clésinger se déchirent, se livrent « une guerre absurde », sans aucune dignité, cette dignité à laquelle elle tient tant et qu'elle acquiert, jour après jour, nuit après nuit, par son travail.

Remise de ses suffocations, Sand recommence à vivre, donc, à écrire. En avril 1852, elle signe un contrat pour un roman, *Mont-Revêche*, non sans récriminer : « C'est un peu court 1 centime par pied de mouche et 500 000 pieds de mouche c'est bien long pour 5 000 francs ! Enfin si c'est le tarif du moment... » Il faut bien accepter ce tarif, puisque

Nohant est un rocher de Sisyphe financier qu'il faut rouler sans répit. Ce n'est pas Maurice qui aidera sa mère à surmonter ses difficultés d'argent. À vingt-neuf ans, Maurice continue à jouer les étudiants. Il multiplie les séjours à Paris et sa mère, en ce mois d'avril, se plaint du « flou » de la carrière artistique de son fils qui ne sait pas encore s'il veut être peintre, dessinateur, ou auteur de théâtre.

De Solange Sand n'attend, comme d'habitude, que des complications. Mme Clésinger a quitté son mari pour se réfugier dans une pension minable. Elle s'en plaint à sa mère. « Est-ce ainsi que vont se passer les plus belles années de ma vie ? (...) Et l'on s'étonne que de pauvres filles sans esprit et sans éducation se laissent entraîner au plaisir et au vice. »

Verte réponse de Sand : « Je ne suis pas née princesse comme toi et j'ai établi mes relations suivant mes goûts simples et mes instincts de retraite et de tranquillité. (...) Ce n'est pas d'ailleurs si facile que tu crois de se déshonorer. Il faut être plus extraordinairement belle et spirituelle que tu ne l'es pour être poursuivie ou seulement recherchée par les acheteurs. (...) Les hommes qui ont de l'argent veulent des femmes qui sachent le gagner, et cette science te soulèverait le cœur d'un tel dégoût que les pourparlers ne seraient pas longs. (...) Marche droit ; c'est ennuyeux selon toi. Selon moi, c'est agréable et sain. »

La crainte de voir sa fille suivre les traces galantes d'une Marie Rainteau ou d'une Sophie-Victoire inspire à celle qui a suivi tant de chemins de traverse l'éloge du droit chemin.

Pour son fils et sa fille qui vivent à ses crochets, George Sand résume leur précaire situation financière : « Nous avons pour trois 7 000 francs de rentes. Le reste sort de mon cerveau. » Le cerveau de Maurice et la cervelle de Solange ne se seront guère fatigués à trouver des solutions pour aider leur mère !

Ayant, en avril, réglé ses comptes avec Solange, Sand règle, en mai, ceux de Maurice qu'elle accuse de perdre son temps, et de jouer les enfants gâtés. En plus, Maurice accuse Manceau de perdre son temps.

Autre verte réponse de Sand : « Tu te plains du temps qu'il perd à autre chose, qu'est-ce que cela te fait ? Tu ne peux le considérer comme un manœuvre à ta solde, puisque tes avances sont nulles ; mais moi je peux le considérer comme un ami et un serviteur volontaire qui me rend mille petits services très profitables (...) Je disais donc que tu aurais tort de lui reprocher cela, puisque j'en profite, et que tu ne peux trouver très bien et très bon qu'on m'allège une partie des soins qui m'écrasent et auxquels ma santé ne suffit plus. »

Devant tant de verdeur, Maurice et Solange doivent se demander quelle mouche a piqué leur mère, qui, devant ces insolubles problèmes d'argent, se dit prête à se retirer en Amérique, puis en Suisse. Menaces que ses enfants ne peuvent prendre au sérieux, et pour cause. Sand est une nourrice-née qui succombe sous les bouches à nourrir. « J'ai trente amis sur le dos et je ne viens pas à bout de les nourrir. »

Le 17 juin 1852, Solange et Nini arrivent à Nohant. Voilà deux bouches supplémentaires, mais Sand ne s'en plaint pas. Nini reste en extase devant sa grand-mère qu'elle regarde écrire, sans la déranger. Sand rend extase pour extase et trouve Nini « adorable de gentillesse et de grâce ». Quant à Solange, « elle a mangé tant de vache enragée dans le mariage qu'elle apprécie enfin la tranquillité de notre intérieur ». Pas autant que le croit sainte Tranquille. Solange passe son temps à errer, sans but, dans Nohant, à monter, et à descendre, les escaliers pour échouer dans l'atelier de Maurice, se laisser tomber sur une chaise et soupirer : « Ah ! qu'on s'ennuie ici ! »

Le 3 août 1852, Tony Johannot, qui illustrait les œuvres de George Sand, meurt. Maurice brigue aussitôt sa succession auprès de Hetzel. Ce dernier déchaîne une tempête en prétendant que Maurice ne sait pas dessiner. « Il dessine mieux que Johannot et il ne lâche pas les choses », insiste Sand.

Pour avoir osé douter du talent de Maurice, Hetzel tombe en disgrâce, il « n'est plus, depuis longtemps, ni un éditeur, ni un libraire, c'est un courtier d'affaires ». En tout cas, Hetzel n'est pas pressé de prendre Maurice pour illustrateur. C'est compter sans la ténacité de Sand et sa méthode de harcèlement continu, « tout le monde dira : l'auteur a un fils qui dessine. Pourquoi ne dessine-t-il pas pour sa mère ? Il faut donc qu'il n'ait pas l'ombre de talent, puisque sa mère ne le choisit pas et ne l'impose pas. » De guerre lasse, Hetzel finit par céder et Maurice illustre une partie des œuvres de sa mère, dont le *Château des désertes,* qu'elle vient de terminer.

Dans sa traversée des déserts éditoriaux, familiaux et politico-financiers, George Sand trouve une oasis en Nini, « mignonne comme un petit ange ». Petit ange, le grand mot est lâché qui suffirait à prouver que Sand est véritablement amoureuse de sa Nini.

Depuis que Mme Clésinger est retournée à Paris se battre avec M. Clésinger par avocats interposés, les époux ayant décidé de se séparer, Nini, soumise à l'unique influence de sa grand-mère, se comporte donc comme un ange. Nini prend ses clystères sans se plaindre, à condition que la seringue soit ornée de fleurs et de rubans, et que Manceau siffle un air pendant la durée de l'opération. Incomparable Nini.

Le 6 septembre 1852, George Sand annonce à Émile de Girardin : « Je commence, à quarante-huit ans, un nouvel état : le théâtre. On ne veut pas m'y laisser prendre ma place. Je veux la prendre, je la prendrai. » On ne saurait être plus déterminée que Sand se lançant à l'assaut de la scène parisienne dont elle espère tirer assez de revenu pour arranger Nohant. « Tout ce travail me ruine, surtout l'atelier

338

de Maurice qui tourne à la cathédrale. Mais j'arrive-rai à installer tout mon monde. » Nourrir, loger son monde, Sand aurait fait une excellente patronne de pension de famille, si ses pensionnaires avaient été payants. Elle a élevé la gratuité de son hospitalité jusqu'à un art de vivre loué par ceux ou celles qui ont eu le privilège de séjourner à Nohant. Mais cette splendeur a un prix que Sand est prête à payer : écrire des pièces de théâtre.

En novembre 1852, un sénatus-consulte procla-mant Louis Napoléon empereur des Français est ratifié à une énorme majorité. À Nohant, sur 180 votants, l'on a compté 181 « oui » (sic) !

Un an après le coup d'État, l'Empire est proclamé le 2 décembre 1852. Sand espère que cette procla-mation coïncide avec l'amnistie qu'elle espère encore et pour laquelle elle a tant lutté. Elle est bien déçue, pas d'amnistie, et sa déception accentue ses malaises du retour d'âge qu'elle appelle « la crise de l'âge », et qui se manifestent par d'accablantes, d'imaginaires transpirations dont elle est la pre-mière à se moquer.

En janvier 1853, à Hetzel qui, malgré sa disgrâce, reste l'un de ses confidents préférés, Sand fait l'éloge de Manceau : « Manceau est l'inséparable, le plus fidèle ami qu'il y ait au monde, piochant toujours pour lui, pour moi, pour tout. Quand il a gravé plusieurs heures par jour, tant que ses yeux y voient clair, il me tient mes comptes, il surveille mes ouvriers, il me fait des copies, il torche Nini, il subit les taquineries de Solange, (...) il me soigne quand je suis malade, il panse les plaies dans le village, il fait des alphabets pour les enfants, des cartons pour Maurice, des plans pour les travaux du maçon, du peintre, etc. Je ne peux vous dire que la centième partie de ce qu'il fait. » George omet la plus impor-tante activité de Manceau, et la plus secrète, qu'Het-zel doit aisément deviner.

Michel meurt le 16 mars. Qu'importe ? Manceau est là, à Nohant, bien vivant. Il se démène comme un diable pour que l'atelier de Maurice soit prêt. « Le fait est que ce pauvre garçon y met une ardeur, une passion de bien faire et de te faire plaisir, qui méritera une bonne embrassade de ta part », suggère Sand à son fils, le 18 avril. On sent que Sand ne ménage aucun effort pour rendre Manceau aimable à Maurice. Notre-Dame des Grâces ne veut pas se changer en une Notre-Dame des Crises, qu'il s'agisse de crise nationale ou familiale...

UNE LUMIÈRE NOMMÉE NINI
(mai 1853-janvier 1855)

> Ainsi on m'a fait bien de la peine et bien du mal en m'ôtant ma petite-fille, et avec des procédés qui m'ôtent l'espoir et même le désir de la ravoir.
>
> Nohant, le 15 juillet 1854

En juillet 1853, pour son quarante-neuvième anniversaire, George Sand confirme à son homme d'affaires, et ami, Émile Aucante, son unique préoccupation : laisser à ses enfants le fruit de son travail, « sauver Solange de ses désastres et assurer à Maurice une existence indépendante. » Son humeur contre son fils et sa fille n'a été que passagère, et elle songe, avant tout, à leur avenir. La « crise de l'âge » n'est certainement pas étrangère à ces dispositions. George aime l'ordre et déteste l'imprévu.

Cet imprévu, et ces désordres, dans lesquels Solange se complaît, plus que jamais ! Elle vient de se réconcilier avec Clésinger qui, sans crier gare, tombe à Nohant pour récupérer sa femme et sa fille, le 1ᵉʳ juillet. Le 10, George, avec modération, exprime à Solange ses regrets d'une telle conduite : « Je travaille à me déshabituer de ma Ninette. Il m'en coûte beaucoup, mais si tu ne dois pas la garder et t'en occuper sérieusement, je ne désire pas ne l'avoir qu'en passant, pour en être brusquement séparée tout d'un coup et la reprendre, la quitter, sans raison majeure et sérieuse. J'ai le malheur de m'attacher aux êtres dont j'ai la charge et je n'aime pas du tout l'imprévu. »

Elle conjure Solange de consacrer sa vie à Nini. Autant prêcher dans le désert... Elle se refuse à admettre l'absence de cœur d'une Solange uniquement préoccupée d'elle-même, comme elle se refuse à supporter la domination d'un Pierre-Jules Hetzel. En conflit avec Hetzel, comme elle l'avait été avec Buloz, et quel auteur ne l'est pas, un jour ou l'autre, avec son éditeur, George Sand affirme son incompétence dans les affaires de l'édition. « Vous me criez : " Mais comprenez donc ! " Je fais de grands efforts, je comprends un instant, ou je crois comprendre, et puis je ne comprends plus, ou j'oublie radicalement ce que j'ai compris. Et chaque fois qu'une lettre d'explications m'arrive, c'est à recommencer », écrit-elle à Hetzel, le 2 octobre 1853. Elle vit dans « un monde de roman, de théâtre ou de fictions quelconques » qui la transporte « hors du positif et de l'intérêt personnel ».

Pour être délivrée de ses soucis d'affaire, elle a donc choisi Émile Aucante qui, né à La Châtre en 1822 et ayant été clerc chez un avoué, est « versé dans la chicane ». Aucante sait faire comprendre à Sand ces affaires qu'elle ne comprend pas. « Il me résume les choses, et il me laisse les trancher d'un mot. Cela simplifie ma vie extrêmement. Il me dépêtre des finasseries des paysans, où je ne voyais jamais clair, il prend connaissance des offres qu'on me fait... »

Aucante est un vrai trésor. Mais il est un trésor qui, pour Sand, domine tous les autres : Nini. Nini qu'elle ramène triomphalement à Nohant, début décembre 1852. Nini qui, ô merveille, a pissé dans le wagon juste avant d'arriver à Châteauroux. Nini qui déballe ses poupées avec des transports de joie. Nini qui ne veut plus quitter Nohant « jamais, jamais ». Tout ce que dit, et fait, Nini plonge sa grand-mère dans le ravissement. Nini « est un véritable petit amour, jolie, drôle et caressante. J'avoue que je suis son esclave ». Même avec Nini, George ne peut s'empêcher d'employer le langage des passions d'autrefois. L'esclavage, le bonheur dans l'esclavage, réapparaissent sous sa plume, comme au temps du roi Michel...

À Nohant, la présence de Nini ne dérange en rien les habitudes de Sand que Manceau énumère gravement au photographe Nadar. « Elle se lève assez tard, déjeune, fait du jardinage avec passion, écrit, dîne, passe la soirée au salon, en famille, à broder, remonte chez elle, et travaille habituellement jusqu'au petit jour. » Sand n'a plus rien à cacher et s'en réjouit : « Mon cœur est transparent comme ma vie. » Le 24 décembre, elle est sacrée, dans une lettre, « Notre-Dame de Nohant » par Alexandre Dumas père. À ce « Chère Notre-Dame de Nohant », elle répond, le 27, par un amusant « Je ne suis pas aux cieux » !

En janvier 1854, Notre-Dame de Nohant décerne enfin à Manceau le titre d'ange qu'elle avait accordé à tous ses autres amants, « Manceau toujours bon comme un ange et me soignant comme si j'en étais un. » Cette trinité d'anges, George, Manceau et Nini, ne contribuent pas peu à faire de Nohant un morceau de paradis sur terre.

La grand-mère et la petite-fille, malgré la neige, jardinent et construisent un Trianon de lierre et de rocaille. À travers Nini, Sand recommence son enfance, avec les mêmes occupations accomplies avec Mme Dupin de Francueil et Sophie-Victoire qui ne sont plus là...

Trianon devient « colossal » et Nini le trouve « pistorèque ». « Nini dit toutes les bêtises du monde », note Sand avec une satisfaction qu'elle ne dissimule pas. Nini, « c'est toute la gaieté de la maison », une gaieté entretenue par Manceau qui sait tellement se mettre à son niveau qu'elle demande à sa grand-mère : « Bonne-maman, est-ce que je suis encore plus bête que lui ? » On aimerait savoir ce que ressentait Sand en s'entendant appeler « bonne-maman » par une Nini de cinq ans...

On peut ranger les mois que passe Nini à Nohant, de décembre 1853 à mai 1854, parmi des mois de parfait bonheur dans la vie de Sand. Hélas, le 7 mai, Clésinger arrache Nini à sa grand-mère, avec des torrents d'insultes contre Solange. Le 3 mai, Clésinger a découvert des lettres qui prouvent, de façon irréfutable, que Solange est la maîtresse de son cousin, Gaston de Villeneuve. Sand, bien qu'elle juge « injurieuse » la conduite de son gendre à son égard, ne veut que « le bien de l'enfant » et se dit prête, pour atteindre ce but, à toutes les humiliations. « On m'a repris Nini que je m'habituais à croire à moi et dont on se fait une pomme de discorde et un prétexte à procès », se plaint George qui sait trop ce qu'il en coûte d'être « une pomme de discorde » dans la famille ! En plus, elle ignore où se trouve Nini que son père cache à Dole, puis à Besançon. Elle est « en proie à de poignantes inquiétudes ». Alors, elle applique le seul remède qu'elle connaisse contre le chagrin, le travail : « Je me distrais de tous les chagrins par un travail assidu. » Elle ajoute : « Mais se distraire, ce n'est pas se consoler. » Et ce n'est pas un bain dans la rivière qui pourrait la consoler de l'absence de Nini, des frasques de Solange, des duretés de Clésinger. Elle se plaît pourtant dans ces bains où elle retrouve « une innocence primitive ».

Le 15 décembre 1854, Solange annonce à sa mère qu'elle a gagné son procès contre Clésinger, qu'elle a obtenu la séparation et que Nini sera confiée à « Mme George Sand ». Clésinger a perdu : il ne payait pas la pension où il avait mis Nini à Paris et a échappé, de justesse, à la prison pour dettes. « Quel bonheur, n'est-ce pas ? Quel bonheur inespéré, un vrai miracle », clame Solange à sa mère qui, pour une fois d'accord avec sa fille, répond : « Quel bonheur (...), j'irai chercher Nini moi-même s'il le faut. »

Malheureusement, l'avocat de Clésinger, Eugène Bethmont, se fait un malin plaisir de susciter des obstacles pour retarder la remise de Nini à sa grand-mère. Bethmont, qui a été aussi l'avocat de Casimir Dudevant et qui a été plusieurs fois ministre pendant le gouvernement provisoire de 1848, déteste George Sand. Cette dernière apprend que Nini a la fièvre scarlatine.

Le 23 décembre 1854, celle qui n'est plus qu'une « bonne-maman » folle d'inquiétude écrit à Bethmont : « Jeudi dernier, un de mes amis a été à la pension Villeneuve pour voir ma petite Jeanne. On lui a dit qu'elle avait la fièvre scarlatine. Il y est retourné le lendemain vendredi, même réponse. Le même jour, vendredi, l'enfant a été vue boulevard des Capucines, 29, avec son père, à une fenêtre. » Sand en conclut que, s'il en est ainsi, « l'enfant vue à la fenêtre avec la fièvre scarlatine serait en danger de mort ».

Sand ne se trompe pas. Dans la nuit du 13 au 14 janvier 1855, Nini meurt. Le 16, elle est enterrée à Nohant, en présence de Sand, de Solange, de Maurice et de Manceau. Le 17, Sand annonce à Hetzel : « Ma petite-fille est morte, assassinée par son père et M. Bethmont, qui l'ont maintenue par méchanceté d'amour-propre dans une pension détestable à Beaujon où elle a eu une scarlatine mal soignée et rentrée. Je ne dis pas cela par exaltation de douleur, je le prouverai à toute la terre. » Sand n'a rien à prouver. Il n'est que trop vrai que Clésinger a réussi à faire sortir de sa pension Nini, le temps d'une promenade sur les Boulevards. Avec la fatale conséquence que l'on sait. Ce même 17 janvier, George Sand écrit à Bethmont : « Monsieur, vous avez gagné votre cause. Ma petite-fille est morte. »

Dans le cimetière de Nohant, Nini a rejoint la grand-mère et le père de Sand. Une Sand qui se demande comment elle va pouvoir vivre maintenant sans Nini, « ma vie de tous les instants, la joie, la lumière de la maison ». Une lumière nommée Nini...

ROME-NOHANT-GARGILESSE
(février 1855-juin 1858)

> Elle a pu et dû se tromper quelque-
> fois et avec violence, mais toujours
> avec sincérité. Personne n'a joué plus
> franc à ce jeu si périlleux de la vie. (...)
> Elle est femme et très femme (...).
>
> Sainte-Beuve,
> à propos de George Sand,
> le 10 août 1855

Après la mort de Nini, George Sand retrouve sa vieille compagne, la douleur. Mais George se demande si elle va pouvoir supporter l'intensité de cette douleur qui n'a rien à voir avec celles qu'elle a déjà subies. Une douleur est toujours nouvelle et ne vient jamais du côté où on l'attend...

Début février 1855, George tombe malade et on doit la saigner deux fois. Chaque jour, retirée dans sa chambre, sans témoin aucun, elle pleure. Elle succombe à sa crise quotidienne de larmes, tout en la déplorant.

Après la mort de Chopin, Sand était restée quatre jours sans écrire. Après la mort de Nini, les jours passent sans que Sand puisse reprendre la plume. Elle qui a toujours puisé sa force de résurrection dans son encrier refuse ce remède habituel. Son esprit ne peut se fixer dans la composition d'un roman ou d'une pièce de théâtre. Son esprit, son âme et son cœur sont obnubilés par le souvenir de Nini. Un mois après cette disparition, elle essaie de s'en consoler en se répétant : « Je sais bien que ma Jeanne n'est pas morte (...). Je sais bien que je la retrouverai et qu'elle me reconnaîtra (...). Elle était une partie de moi-même et cela ne peut être changé. »

Comme *la Presse* s'apprête à publier en feuilleton *Histoire de ma vie*, elle doit en corriger les épreuves. Faible occupation pour une douleur si grande. Maurice s'inquiète de la prostration dans laquelle est tombée sa mère et suggère, pour faire diversion, un voyage en Italie. Sans le sou, elle doit accepter un prêt de Manceau pour rendre ce départ possible. Elle est aussi alarmée que Maurice de son inaction : « Ce qui m'effraye le plus (...), c'est de me sentir incapable de travailler depuis la mort de cet enfant. »

Le 11 avril 1855, George, Maurice et Manceau partent en Italie. Sand est déçue par Rome : « La ville est immonde de laideur et de saleté. C'est La Châtre centuplée en grandeur. » Elle trouve que Frascati et Valldemosa se ressemblent, et face aux arbres et aux paysages de Frascati, elle manifeste un peu de cet enthousiasme qu'avaient engendré, aux premiers jours, les beautés de Valldemosa. Mais comme elle déplorait la présence des « odieux insulaires » des Baléares, elle regrette qu'il y ait autant d'Italiens en Italie, « presque tous des voleurs ou mendiants ».

George ne peut toutefois s'empêcher d'être sensible aux splendeurs du printemps romain, comme elle le fut, autrefois, à celles du printemps vénitien. « Nous cueillons des anémones de toutes couleurs, des cyclamens, des hépatiques ravissantes en plein bois et en plein champ. Tous les arbres sont en fleurs... » Elle cueille des fleurs, elle marche, elle mange, elle boit, elle en est réduite à l'état de « brute absolue ». Pas autant qu'elle le dit : une « brute absolue » ne continuerait pas à souffrir comme elle souffre. Son chagrin est toujours là. Dès qu'elle est seule, pendant que Maurice et Manceau s'amusent à faire des croquis, elle retrouve sa Nini. « Car j'avais arrangé ma vie pour elle et il m'en coûte d'en reprendre l'usage pour mon propre compte. »

En mai, Sand revient d'Italie, « très bien portante » et se remet au travail, vaillamment. Le 21 juillet 1855, elle signe avec Hachette un traité pour dix romans dans la bibliothèque des Chemins de Fer. C'est une façon comme une autre de célébrer son cinquante et unième anniversaire.

Le 5 décembre 1855, elle refuse une entrevue à Clésinger d'un : « Je ne veux pas vous voir. Le lien qui existait entre nous est brisé, et c'est vous qui l'avez voulu. »

Aux veilles du premier anniversaire de la mort de Nini, George Sand qui est à Paris écrit à Solange qui veut se rendre à Nohant : « Laisse-moi te déconseiller ce voyage. Il te fatiguera et te fera du mal. L'âme de notre chère enfant est avec nous, partout et à toute heure. Sa tombe n'est qu'un objet à respecter. Le respect des tombeaux, oui, mais pas le culte. »

Solange ne tient pas compte de ces conseils. Elle passe deux jours à Nohant. Elle veut faire poser une croix sur la tombe de Nini. Sand s'y oppose [1].

En fait, George ne supporte plus la présence de Solange à Nohant, une Solange que, dans le secret de son cœur, elle doit rendre aussi responsable de la mort de Nini. Après tout, si Solange avait « marché droit » comme le souhaitait sa mère, et avait consacré sa vie à Nini, Nini serait encore en vie... Aussi, chaque fois que Solange veut venir à Nohant, George oppose un refus qu'elle essaie de rendre plausible, prétextant l'absence d'une cuisinière, ou sa propre absence.

En mars 1856, Sand entraîne Manceau pendant quelques jours à Fontainebleau. Dans la vie sentimentale de George, Fontainebleau semble une halte obligatoire, c'est « un pays plus beau, ne vous en déplaise, que la campagne de Rome ».

Le 11 mai 1856, au beau milieu d'une lettre à Émile Aucante, George Sand change d'écriture et s'en expliquera plus tard à Pauline Viardot : « Habituez-vous à mon écriture changée. » Son graphisme penché se redresse nettement et brusquement. Sand est imprévisible, y compris dans ce changement que rien ne laisse présager et qui survient après un mot, « laissez » [2].

Avec cette écriture droite qu'elle conservera jus-

---

1. Elle n'y consentira qu'en décembre 1856.
2. Cf. note de Georges Lubin dans le treizième volume de la *Correspondance*, page 613.

qu'à la fin de sa vie, elle couvre inlassablement des feuillets qui deviennent des romans comme *la Daniella*, ou *les Beaux Messieurs de Bois-Doré*, et des pièces de théâtre, comme *Claudie*. Sa fécondité provoque l'admiration de Hetzel qui, le 10 mars 1857, salue, en même temps, son « éternelle jeunesse » et ajoute : « *Daniella* est pleine d'amour ! Comment faites-vous pour garder vos soleils ? »

Cette fécondité n'est pas exactement celle que souhaite Sand qui soupire : « Redevenir grand-mère est encore mon rêve le plus doux. » Mais pour cela, il ne faut plus compter sur Solange qui mène une vie de plus en plus galante, incompatible avec la procréation, et il faudrait que Maurice se marie.

« Il faut marier Maurice » devient le refrain de ces années-là. George lance son fils sur le marché matrimonial comme un produit dont les perfections devraient attirer les clientes. Il a une dot, des rentes, des qualités, franchise, gaieté, bonté. Il ne paraît pas ses trente-trois ans. Et puis le temps passe, Sand pourrait disparaître. « Mon rêve, c'est de ne pas le laisser seul après moi. Il a tant concentré sur moi ses affections que l'idée de lui manquer m'effraie. Si je le voyais mari et père, je regarderais ma tâche comme accomplie. Jusqu'ici, elle ne l'est pas. »

À travers le mariage de Maurice, c'est son éternel besoin d'aimer qu'elle pourrait satisfaire avec ses petits-enfants. « Il me semble que je suis morte si la vie ne repousse pas sur notre arbre. » On reconnaît là le langage d'une amie des arbres. Car sa passion des arbres est intacte et se ravive, en mars 1857, à la lecture d'*Un été au Sahara* d'Eugène Fromentin. Elle assure son auteur qu'il s'agit d'un chef-d'œuvre. Elle l'assure aussi qu'elle n'ira jamais au Sahara parce qu'il n'y a pas d'arbres : « J'ai la passion des arbres et je n'aime pas les plaines. »

Le 2 mai 1857, Alfred de Musset meurt. Il était mort depuis longtemps pour George, celui qui, pendant l'été 1835, avait écrit à Alfred Tattet : « Si vous voyez Mme Sand, dites-lui que je l'aime de tout mon cœur, que c'est encore la femme la plus femme que j'aie jamais connue. »

Quinze jours après la mort de son frère, Paul de Musset vient voir George Sand, « de la part du mourant, disait-il, lui demander ce qu'elle comptait faire des lettres ; qu'à son heure dernière, il s'en était vivement préoccupé et avait désiré que tout fût brûlé ». George et Paul ne parviendront pas à se mettre d'accord sur le mode d'exécution de ce vœu[1].

Paul de Musset aurait pu, comme Pierre-Jules Hetzel, demander à George Sand : « Comment faites-vous pour garder vos soleils ? » On peut imaginer la réponse que l'on peut déduire de sa conduite : plus George avance en âge, plus elle vit dans l'instant présent. C'est ainsi que, en juin 1857, elle découvre, dans les environs de Nohant et en compagnie de Manceau, « un paradis terrestre », Gargilesse, « un pays féerique ». Manceau y a pris deux papillons, un Algira et un Gordius.

Le charme de Gargilesse est si fort que, un mois plus tard, en juillet, Manceau y acquiert une maison qu'il baptise, en souvenir du premier papillon rencontré, villa Algira. « Manceau est propriétaire. Manceau dit ma maison, mon mur, ma cour, mon rocher, mon ruisseau », s'exclame Sand. Elle appelle Manceau « mon fidèle tête-à-tête ». Ce tête-à-tête suffit à sa quiétude.

À Gargilesse, Sand et Manceau peuvent vivre comme n'importe quel couple heureux, uni, loin des curieux, des visiteurs, des quémandeurs qui ont envahi, peu à peu, Nohant. Rançon d'une gloire que Sand se refuse à payer. Elle s'enfuit, chaque fois qu'elle le peut, à Gargilesse. « Ma vie, d'ailleurs, tourne au Gargilesse, avec un attrait invincible. Cette vie de village, pêle-mêle, avec la véritable

_____

1. On sait que ce vœu n'a pas été respecté et que les lettres d'amour de George Sand et d'Alfred de Musset figurent maintenant dans les anthologies comme celle de Jacques de Lacretelle, *L'Amour sur la place* (Perrin).

rusticité me paraît beaucoup plus normale que la vie de château qui est bien compliquée pour moi. N'avoir à s'occuper de rien au monde en fait de choses matérielles m'a toujours paru un idéal et je trouve cet idéal dans ma chambrette où il y a tout juste la place de dormir, de se laver, et d'écrire », écrit-elle, exactement un an plus tard, en juin 1858.

Il y a, en Sand, une perpétuelle aspiration à la vie de bohème, comme celle qu'elle a menée, pendant quelques mois à Paris, quand elle était encore une jeune baronne Dudevant, ou comme celle qu'elle prête à certains de ses personnages, une Consuelo, par exemple. Aspiration qu'elle satisfait pleinement à Gargilesse où elle oublie enfin qu'elle est la châtelaine de Nohant, ou cette George Sand tantôt adulée, tantôt insultée. Et pour les gens de Gargilesse, elle est simplement « une étrangère qui n'est pas du bourg, mais qui s'y plaît tout de même ».

Gargilesse ou les délices de l'anonymat.

MILLE RIENS INTIMES
(été 1858-printemps 1862)

> Vous me demandez où je suis : tou-
> jours à la campagne, faisant de l'his-
> toire naturelle et mille riens intimes
> avec mon fils, qui a fait l'été dernier
> un grand voyage. Je cultive pour mon
> compte mon « petit jardin littéraire »,
> comme dit Dumas, et l'expression me
> plaît beaucoup à moi qui suis éprise
> de botanique. Mes romans sont des
> pages d'herbier (...)
>
> George Sand à Victor Hugo,
> le 22 février 1862

C'est à Gargilesse que George Sand écrit *Elle et Lui*. Elle y raconte ses amours avec Alfred de Musset, mort voilà un an maintenant. La mort d'Alfred, qui n'a pas affecté sentimentalement George, n'en a pas moins déclenché en elle un puissant réflexe créateur. Sand compose six cent vingt pages en vingt-cinq jours, ou plutôt, en vingt-cinq nuits puisqu'elle écrit la nuit. « Cette fois sans aucune fatigue, pouvant travailler le soir après des courses assez rudes. La chaleur devient dure... »

L'été 1858 est torride. La dame de Gargilesse se rafraîchit par de fréquents bains dans la rivière, et par l'usage d'une eau portant son nom, l'Eau George Sand, qui a obtenu une médaille d'honneur, et l'approbation de la romancière qui apprécie sa finesse, sa distinction, et la trouve même « très salutaire pour les personnes qui comme moi craignent les parfums trop concentrés ». À la création de ce parfum portant son nom, on aura un exemple supplémentaire de la gloire de Sand à son époque ! Une gloire que la publication de *Elle et Lui* va encore augmenter.

Nées à un dîner de *la Revue des Deux Mondes*, les amours de George Sand et d'Alfred de Musset retournent, un quart de siècle plus tard, à cette même revue qui publie *Elle et Lui*, en feuilleton. Le 14 août, après en avoir lu le manuscrit, François Buloz écrit à son auteur : « J'ai lu votre roman autobiographique. Pour moi qui connais les faits, qui vous ai même toujours défendue verbalement à l'endroit d'Alfred, je vous trouve dans la vérité et la modération dans le portrait que vous tracez. »

Hetzel, lui, accuse Sand d'être trop indulgente pour Musset : « Ceux qui ne l'ont pas connu (...) ne sauront pas que ce portrait est sublime de clémence et que le malheureux qu'il idéalise pour tous ceux qui l'ont vu de près — s'il fut un amant exécrable — fut un pire ami, un frère pire, un citoyen pire encore (...) Il était né empoisonné, il était naturellement pourri. »

Les amours de Sand et de Musset qui s'étaient pratiquement déroulées sur la place publique y reviennent donc avec cette publication d'*Elle et Lui* dans *la Revue des Deux Mondes,* en janvier 1859. Les salons en frémissent, on jase dans les cafés, les lecteurs d'*Elle et Lui* se partagent en partisans de Sand et défenseurs de Musset.

Pour aviver ces dissensions, Paul de Musset publie, à son tour, ce qu'il croit être la version des faits, dans *Lui et Elle.* Louise Colet, femme de lettres spécialisée dans la conquête des écrivains et qui a été l'une des dernières maîtresses de Musset, donne elle aussi sa version des amours vénitiennes dans *Lui.*

Avec *Elle et Lui, Lui et Elle,* et *Lui,* George Sand défraye, une fois de plus, la chronique. Elle croit pourtant, à cinquante-cinq ans, avoir atteint ce qu'elle nomme « l'âge de l'impersonnalité ».

Le 4 mars 1859, elle vante les charmes de cet âge. « Moi j'ai cinquante-cinq ans et je ne vois rien de triste dans la vieillesse. Au contraire, je trouve que c'est l'âge de sentir plus que jamais les belles et bonnes œuvres de Dieu. » Parmi ces « œuvres de Dieu », elle ne peut que ranger « le sage, l'intelligent, l'incomparable Manceau ». Ce « bon Manceau » qui « montre un courage à toute épreuve » résiste à l'épreuve du temps. Il est absolument indispensable à celle qu'il continue à nommer

« Madame » en public, et dans les agendas intimes qu'ils tiennent ensemble depuis 1852. Il tient à être un hôte payant de Nohant, et règle, depuis janvier 1859, une pension de 1 200 francs par an, « malgré moi comme vous pouvez en croire », précise Sand à son homme d'affaires, Émile Aucante.

Maurice se montre enfin d'humeur matrimoniale. Il a beaucoup tardé et son âge, trente-six ans, est un handicap auprès des jeunes filles qui doivent appréhender aussi d'avoir pour belle-mère une George Sand et pour belle-sœur une Solange ! Sur ce dernier point, Sand est sans illusion aucune, « je sais que dans toutes les familles, Solange est un épouvantail qui a déjà été fatal ». Folle Solange à qui sa mère prêche vainement la sagesse : « Vis de peu ou apprends à travailler. » Comment faire comprendre à Solange que George se tue de travail, ne prenant jamais d'exercice. « C'est le repos du corps et l'activité continuelle de l'esprit qui me tuent », lance-t-elle à sa fille qui a le diable au corps et n'exerce son esprit qu'aux dépens des autres.

En juin 1859, George Sand fait une escapade en Auvergne. Elle visite Saint-Nectaire, Limagne, Issoire, Espaly, la Roche-Lambert, la Montagne de Denise, la Chaise-Dieu et en ramène un roman, *Jean de la Roche*, qu'elle termine le 28 août. Ainsi, les perfections de Manceau, les fiançailles toujours rompues de Maurice, les liaisons tapageuses de Solange ne détournent pas George Sand de son occupation préférée, écrire.

Quand elle n'écrit pas, George se livre à son autre occupation préférée : faire la charité. Elle représente, en sa personne et en son pays, une préfiguration de ce qui sera plus tard la Sécurité sociale... Comme la Sécurité sociale, elle connaît des difficultés de paiement. Mais, quand sa bourse est plate, et elle l'est souvent, la châtelaine de Nohant n'hésite pas à mendier pour ses innombrables protégés. Elle sait émouvoir les plus grands qui, en général, ne brillent guère par leur compassion envers les petits.

Pour atteindre l'impératrice Eugénie, George Sand s'adresse à l'un de ses secrétaires particuliers, Albert Damas-Hinard, à qui elle écrit le 10 octobre 1859 : « D'ailleurs l'impératrice aime faire le bien pour le bien. Je n'ose pas lui écrire pour une si obscure infortune. Mais je suis sûre que si vous la lui révélez, elle dira tout de suite oui. » Cette « obscure infortune » désigne un aveugle, un poète-tisserand de quatre-vingts ans, le père Magu, qui habite à Lizy-sur-Ourcq, dans les environs de Nohant, et qui y vit avec 19 sous par jour. « Il fume de l'herbe pour tromper son besoin de fumer du tabac. » L'impératrice se laisse attendrir par ce dénuement et accorde, de suite, les 1 000 francs que Sand souhaitait pour le père Magu.

Après avoir célébré, en mars 1859, les avantages de la vieillesse, George, en décembre de cette même année, en dénonce les ravages avec un entrain tel que cela tourne, malgré tout, à une nouvelle célébration. « Nous sommes vieux, nous sommes laids. Maurice engraisse, Manceau est chauve, moi j'ai cent ans. Qu'est-ce que ça fait si nous nous aimons assez pour nous trouver très gentils les uns les autres ? »

Sand prétend avoir vieilli brusquement et atteint sa centième année quand elle a appris que, le 9 décembre 1859, à la cour d'assises d'Indre-et-Loire, Angélina Lemoyne, seize ans, accusée d'infanticide, a répondu, pour sa défense : « J'avais lu les romans de George Sand et j'étais partagée entre la douleur que j'éprouvais de ma chute et le bonheur d'avoir élevé jusqu'à moi un domestique. » Le père de l'enfant assassiné était un domestique d'Angélina. L'affaire Lemoyne fait grand bruit, autant que les parutions successives d'*Elle et Lui*, *Lui et Elle*, et *Lui*. Il ne s'agit plus là de littérature seulement, mais d'un infanticide provoqué, peut-être, par la lecture de « romans les plus détestables et les plus dangereux », voilà comment le procureur général définit les romans de George Sand qui réagit d'abord avec violence, se plaignant hautement des « lâches injures » dont elle est l'objet. Puis, elle renonce à poursuivre ceux qui, à la suite du procureur général, l'accablent, et dénoncent son influence néfaste sur une certaine jeunesse, comme elle s'en explique à Hetzel, dans une lettre du 23 décembre. « Il n'y a pas deux jours par an où je me sente en veine de me défendre. (...) Au fond, ce n'est pas à moi que l'on fait la guerre. C'est à la foi que nous avons (...) vous, moi, et tous ceux, grands et petits, qui regardent vers l'avenir. C'est l'honneur de la lumière qui fait crier tous ces aveugles. »

C'est dans cette lettre du 23 décembre que se trouve l'un des plus bouleversants aveux contenus dans la *Correspondance* : Nini, l'inoubliable Nini continue à vivre, et de quelle intense façon, en sa bonne-maman. « Figurez-vous que ma petite-fille vit toujours en moi ; je ne la crois pas, je ne la sens pas morte. J'y pense à chaque instant comme si elle était là. Je la vois grandir, j'entends sa voix changer, je me dis, elle a aujourd'hui tel âge. Seulement elle est absente, elle ne peut plus me consoler, elle est partie. La douleur est pour moi, le bonheur est pour elle, c'est elle qui m'aide à vivre... »

Après cet accès d'émotion, George commande les truffes, les dindes, les huîtres nécessaires aux fêtes de Noël, et attend, avec résignation, Solange qui veut commencer, en sa compagnie, à Nohant, l'année 1860. Solange qui se pique d'écrire comme sa mère et qui, comme sa mère, autrefois, demande des conseils à Sainte-Beuve. Solange qu'elle a qualifiée dans un accès de colère, le 30 octobre 1858, comme son pire ennemi. « Mon pire ennemi en ce monde est ma fille. »

Est-ce à cause de cette importune présence ? En ce début 1860, Sand n'est guère encline à l'optimisme : « Demain sera comme aujourd'hui et comme hier. Je ne suis plus d'âge à me faire illusion. La vie de l'artiste convaincu est le supplice de saint Laurent. C'est un gril où l'on vous retourne d'un flanc sur l'autre. »

Le 17 mars 1860, Maurice Dudevant-Sand est promu chevalier de la Légion d'honneur sur intervention de l'un de ses amis, le prince Jérôme Napoléon, et non comme auteur d'une histoire du théâtre, *Masques et bouffons*, que sa mère a présentée comme « une des séries de son immense labeur ». Il faut tout l'aveuglement d'une mère pour croire Maurice capable d'un « immense labeur ».

Solange feint de croire que Maurice porte la croix qui aurait dû être attribuée à sa mère et s'empresse de surnommer son frère « la croix de sa mère ». Sand, que cette distinction fait exulter — « il paraît qu'on ne parle que de ça » — s'indigne et défend son Maurice, « un si brave garçon », et qui « n'a pas volé une récompense honorifique que tant d'autres déshonorent ». Mon Dieu que les gens, et Solange en particulier, sont méchants !

Pour oublier tant de malignité, George Sand se réfugie dans sa nouvelle passion : la minéralogie. Elle envie l'impassibilité des pierres et des cailloux qu'elle étiquette inlassablement, en compagnie de Manceau. Elle cède à « l'empire des études géologiques et botaniques » et à la passion de s'instruire. « Cette passion est ridicule à cinquante-six ans, mais elle m'a tourmentée toute ma vie sans pouvoir être satisfaite, faute de temps. Elle ne fait de mal à personne, et bien que le roman m'amuse beaucoup, la réalité du beau, la nature me semble bien préférable à tout ce qui peut sortir de mon cerveau. »

À cinquante-six ans, George Sand dévore *la Flore du centre de la France* par Alexandre Boreau et *la Physiologie végétale, ou exposition des forces et des fonctions vitales des végétaux* par Augustin Pyrame de Candolle comme elle dévorait les évangiles socialistes de Pierre Leroux, un Leroux qu'elle vient de revoir, vieilli, lui aussi, amer et amaigri, n'ayant plus qu'une seule dent dont il se sert encore pour mordre son prochain. Retrouvailles sans lendemain. George Sand n'a plus de temps à perdre. Elle est, plus que jamais, une éternelle étudiante et manifeste une soif inextinguible de connaissances. « Je cours vers la soixantaine, et j'ai mon éducation à faire ! Il n'y a vraiment pas de temps à perdre, si je veux connaître pendant quelques années le bonheur de n'être plus un crétin ! »

Cette passion de s'instruire, et d'en avoir le temps, cette marche inéluctable vers la soixantaine qui entraîne une peur de l'avenir conduisent Sand à signer, en octobre 1860, deux traités avec des éditeurs, l'un de cinq ans avec Buloz, l'autre de dix ans avec Michel Lévy. Elle s'assure des revenus confortables, dans les 25 000 francs par an, dont les paiements ne doivent pas être interrompus, même en cas de maladie, elle a beaucoup insisté sur ce dernier point.

Mis devant le fait accompli, Hetzel s'estime trahi et se fâche « à mort » avec Sand que cette brouille n'émeut pas outre mesure. Hetzel n'a jamais vu en elle « qu'un écrivain dont il pouvait spéculer », prétend-elle.

Le 27 octobre, George est terrassée par une fièvre typhoïde. Maurice et Manceau se relaient à son chevet. Elle délire pendant plusieurs jours de suite et manque mourir. « Oui, j'ai été près des sombres bords, comme disaient nos pères, mais je n'y ai rien vu de sombre. » Elle décide de passer sa convalescence dans le Midi.

Le 15 février 1861, George, Manceau et une servante plus que dévouée, Marie Caillaud, dite « Marie-des-poules », quittent Nohant pour Toulon où ils retrouvent Maurice. Avant son départ, la consciencieuse Sand a terminé un roman, *Valvèdre*, et peut contempler à son aise les beautés de Tamaris où elle s'installe dans une maison « jaune rosé ». Les « commodités » sont en plein champ. « Le pays me rappelle Majorque », écrit-elle à Solange, sans autre commentaire.

Comme à Majorque, il pleut. Ce n'est plus Chopin qu'elle a, à ses côtés, mais Manceau.

Comme Chopin, Manceau commence à tousser. Sand ne s'en inquiète pas outre mesure et met cette toux sur « la conséquence des fatigues de l'installation dont il prend toujours la plus grosse part ».

Après la pluie, le beau temps. Sand retrouve de vieux amis : Charles Poncy qui vient en voisin de Toulon, Jules Boucoiran qui, lui, accourt de Nîmes, et une vieille connaissance : l'éblouissant printemps méditerranéen.

À Tamaris, comme à Nohant, George Sand exerce sa charité. Au père Magu de Lizy-sur-Ourcq succède le père Quiquisolles, un vieux pêcheur infirme qui a perdu sa barque dans un naufrage et qui a besoin, comme le père Magu, de 1 000 francs. Sand implore, une fois de plus, Albert Damas-Hinard qui, à son tour, sollicite l'impératrice Eugénie qui accorde la somme souhaitée.

George Sand ne craint jamais de tendre la main pour les autres. Si elle a obtenu des grâces de Napoléon III et de l'argent de l'impératrice Eugénie, George Sand ne veut rien pour elle-même. Aussi, quand elle ne reçoit pas le prix de l'Académie française qu'elle espérait et que l'Empereur offre, à la place, 20 000 francs, elle refuse dignement cette somme et s'en explique à Buloz, le 9 mai 1861 : « Dans plus d'une circonstance, j'ai trouvé l'Empereur généreux, l'impératrice charitable et bonne. Je ne leur ai jamais rien demandé pour moi et je n'ai besoin de rien. (...) J'entends bien que mon refus soit un remerciement sans fausse fierté et sans la moindre nuance d'ingratitude. »

Et voilà que le 13 mai 1861, le sage, le casanier Maurice, poussé par on ne sait quel démon de l'aventure, s'en va faire un tour en Algérie. Sand s'efforce de cacher son anxiété, quitte Tamaris le 29 mai et revient à Nohant pour y apprendre, le 8 juin, que Maurice, non content d'être allé se perdre en Afrique, veut maintenant découvrir l'Amérique !

366

Il y est invité par le prince Jérôme Napoléon qui y va sur son yacht. Ni le renom du prince, ni l'état – excellent — du yacht ne rassurent cette mère aux abois. « Le cœur crie tout bas », soupire George qui, le 26 juin, accorde sa permission pour ce voyage lointain à son grand fils de trente-huit ans. Enfin, le sacrifice étant accompli, Solange aurait-elle raison et Maurice serait-il « la croix de sa mère » ? Elle rassure, le 11 août, son très cher enfant : « Tu auras à me remercier et à me complimenter d'avoir été si raisonnable, moi qui le suis si peu quand tu es absent ! »

Pour rendre supportable l'absence de Maurice, elle reçoit à Nohant son ami, le graveur italien Luigi Calamatta, et sa fille, Lina, une petite beauté de dix-neuf ans qui ferait une idéale belle-fille. Ah, pourquoi Maurice est-il absent ?

Pour ne pas sombrer dans son spleen habituel, elle admire « tous les bons mots que Manceau m'a débités pour me faire rire ». À Alexandre Dumas fils dont elle soigne, par lettre, l'hypocondrie, elle ne cache pas ce qu'elle doit à Manceau : « En voilà un que vous pouvez estimer sans crainte de déception ! Quel être tout cœur et tout dévouement ! C'est bien probablement les douze ans que j'ai passés avec lui du matin au soir qui m'ont définitivement réconciliée avec la nature humaine. »

Elle accorde aussi son estime, et sa protection, à un jeune homme de dix-sept ans, Francis Laur qui, depuis l'âge de quatorze ans, est secrétaire de Charles Duvernet. Elle fait poursuivre ses études à Francis qu'elle met en garde contre « les aventures de la vie parisienne » et qu'elle engage vivement à se cultiver : « Il te faut beaucoup lire, c'est un grand bien. » Elle joint l'exemple à la parole et lit beaucoup pour oublier que son Maurice est en Amérique, chez les sauvages des Grands Lacs. « Il est content. Je le suis pour lui. Mais non pour moi comme bien vous pensez. » Dans ses pires cauchemars de mère poule, Sand ne pouvait imaginer que son fils irait un jour chez les sauvages des Grands Lacs... Elle en perd le sommeil. Le 22 septembre, elle montre son impatience : « Je commence à être à bout de mon courage et à ne plus dormir. » Enfin, Maurice revient à Nohant le 12 octobre. George se dit « écrasée de soulagement ». Soulagement qui va de pair avec une inquiétude provoquée par la persistante toux de Manceau. Dans les agendas où Sand et Manceau, à tour de rôle, notent les événements du jour, cette toux apparaît de plus en plus fréquemment.

Moins inquiétante certes, mais irritante quand même, l'insistance de Solange à vouloir s'installer dans les environs de Nohant. George s'y oppose. Les désordres de la fille ne rappelleraient que trop ceux de la mère. La châtelaine de Nohant a conquis, dans le Berry, une respectabilité qu'elle ne veut pas voir ternie par le défilé des amants que l'on prête à sa fille.

N'ayant pas réussi à se faire une place dans le monde, Solange est entrée dans le demi-monde, comme elle en avait menacé sa mère. Elle a suivi les traces de ses ancêtres, les dames d'opéra, et se fait entretenir par des amants aussi riches et généreux que ceux de sa mère furent pauvres. Cela, Sand veut l'ignorer : « J'entends ne pas savoir comment tu arranges ta vie intime, et pour cela faire, je ne veux pas que tu demeures près de Nohant. » Solange se cabre et répond : « Voilà de bien dures paroles, ma chère mère, sur un sujet qui n'en vaut guère la peine. » Après quoi, commencent entre la mère et la fille une brouille, un silence qui durent quatre ans.

Solange est remplacée par le « deuxième fils » de George Sand, Alexandre Dumas fils, à qui elle dédie sa pièce *le Drac*. En 1861, elle n'a écrit que quatre pièces de théâtre et s'excuse de ce qu'elle considère comme une baisse de sa fécondité...

Éternelle étudiante, George est aussi une éternelle maman qui a besoin de nourrissons à qui donner le meilleur d'elle-même. Elle prodigue à Alexandre

Dumas fils des leçons de vie, et grande leçon que celle-là, par exemple : « À votre âge[1], j'étais aussi tourmentée et plus malade que vous, au moral et au physique. Lasse de creuser les autres et moi-même, j'ai dit un beau matin : Tout ça m'est égal. L'univers est grand et beau. Tout ce que nous croyons plein d'importance est si fugitif que ce n'est pas la peine d'y penser. Il n'y a dans la vie que deux ou trois choses vraies et sérieuses, et ces choses-là, si claires et si faciles, sont précisément celles que j'ai ignorées et dédaignées, *mea culpa*. Mais j'ai été punie de ma bêtise, j'ai souffert autant qu'on peut souffrir, je dois être pardonnée. Faisons la paix avec le bon Dieu. Si j'avais eu l'orgueil incurable, c'était fait de moi, mais j'avais ce que vous avez, j'avais la notion du bien et du mal, chose devenue très rare en ce temps-ci, et puis je ne m'adorais pas, et je me suis oubliée. »

Avec Maurice, son oubli de soi est complet. Elle aide son fils à rédiger le livre qu'il tire de son voyage en Amérique, *Six Mille Lieues à toute vapeur*. Cette aide est si constante, si puissante que Georges Lubin n'hésite pas à en conclure malicieusement : « Il va falloir rajouter *Six Mille Lieues à toute vapeur* à la liste des œuvres de George Sand[2]. » C'est à croire que Sand écrit des deux mains. De l'une, elle rédige son nouveau roman, *Tamaris,* et de l'autre, *Six Mille Lieues à toute vapeur*. La mère et le fils excellent à utiliser leurs séjours en terres plus ou moins lointaines pour en alimenter leur inspiration.

Alexandre Dumas fils n'est pas un ingrat. En échange des leçons de vie, il conduit à Nohant, en septembre 1861, un peintre de trente-six ans, Charles Marchal, qui exécute les portraits de Sand, de Manceau et de Maurice. Il semble que George ait apprécié l'homme aurant que le peintre. Marchal est

---

1. Dumas fils a alors trente-sept ans.
2. Seizième volume de la *Correspondance*, page 674.

rapidement enrôlé dans la cohorte des anges et le ton des lettres qu'il reçoit laisse entendre que des embrasements célestes n'ont pas tardé à se produire ! Dès le 30 novembre, Sand relance Marchal. « Mon doux bibi, vous êtes joli comme un amour d'avoir donné de vos nouvelles. (...) Je vois, gros gueux, que vous êtes un coquet avec les autres, et que vous ne gardez pas vos séductions pour moi toute seule. (...) Je vois, énorme scélérat, que vous oubliez vite Nohant qui a la folie de raffoler de vous. » Sous les apparences de la vérité et du badinage, c'est la vérité qui se manifeste, c'est Sand qui « raffole » de Marchal, de sa rondeur et de ses rondeurs.

Le 3 janvier 1862, Sand renouvelle à Marchal l'expression de ce que l'on pourrait considérer comme des sentiments empressés. « Mon gros amour, on vous embrasse et on vous aime. (...) Enfin revenez vite, mon gros chérubin, pour nous rendre à tous espoir et santé. »

La santé de Manceau donne de sérieuses inquiétudes à Sand. Cette toux qui augmente de jour en jour serait-elle semblable à celle qui a emporté Chopin ? Sand n'a vraiment pas de chance avec la santé de ses amants et il ne faut pas s'étonner qu'elle apprécie la « forte vitalité communicative » de Marchal qui joue les consolateurs rapides, efficaces et discrets.

Manceau qui ignore tout de cette passade raffole lui aussi de Marchal. Tout est donc pour le mieux à Nohant où les passions secrètes, Manceau ou Marchal, voisinent avec les passions affichées, la botanique ou la minéralogie. Chacun s'y livre paisiblement à ses occupations préférées, comme le confirme George Sand à Victor Hugo, le 22 février 1862 : « Vous me demandez où je suis : toujours à la campagne, faisant de l'histoire naturelle et mille riens intimes avec mon fils. »

Sand sait profiter des « mille riens intimes » comme personne, et avec d'autres que son fils. Au fond, c'est quelqu'un de très simple qui se dissimule sous une couverture de complexité. Sa simplicité étonne les frères Goncourt qui, le 30 mars 1862, rendent visite à George qui habite maintenant à Paris, au quatrième étage du 2, rue Racine. Edmond et Jules remarquent son « aspect spectral, automatique », sa « dignité de pachyderme » et en concluent très injustement : « C'est la banalité dans son paroxysme. »

Les frères Goncourt sont quand même séduits par la « figure délicate, douce, fine, calme » de Sand et par son teint d'ambre. Le charme de George agit sur ces deux grognons, un charme que les années qui passent n'ont pas atténué et dont Charles Marchal constitue l'ultime conquête. Oui, à cinquante-huit ans, George ne refuse aucun de ces « mille riens intimes » qui rendent la vie tellement agréable...

LE SOURIRE DU BOUDDHA
ET L'OR DU BON DIEU
(avril 1862-juillet 1863)

> Oui, c'est ici qu'il faut se dire qu'aujourd'hui se compose de demain autant que d'hier...
>
> Nohant, le 4 avril 1863

Le lendemain de la visite des Goncourt, le 31 mars 1862, George Sand abandonne sa « dignité de pachyderme » pour une extrême exaltation. Elle fait à Lina Calamatta une demande en mariage qui ressemble à une déclaration d'amour : « Crois au bonheur. Il n'y en a qu'un dans la vie, c'est d'aimer et d'être aimée. Nous sommes deux qui n'aurons pas d'autre but et pas d'autre pensée que de te chérir et te gâter. »

Lina ne doit pas s'y tromper, et ne s'y trompe pas, c'est Maurice et George qu'elle épouse en même temps...

Ce mariage n'a pas été réglé, comme celui de Solange, en quelques semaines. Il est le fruit d'une longue, d'une intense préméditation. Cela fait trente ans que George connaît les parents de Lina, des artistes. Trente ans qu'elle apprécie les gravures de M. Calamatta, les peintures de Mme Calamatta, et leur meilleure œuvre, qu'elle a vue naître, grandir, et embellir : Lina.

Lina est née à Paris le 26 juin 1842 et a eu pour parrain le peintre Ingres. Lina a juste vingt ans en 1862 et semble n'avoir été mise au monde que pour assurer le bonheur de Maurice, donc celui de George. Maintenant, le moment est venu d'unir les vingt printemps de Lina aux trente-neuf étés de Maurice.

Ce projet de mariage doit être tenu secret, sauf pour Émile Aucante à qui George le dévoile, le 17 avril. « Voici le secret qui n'est et ne doit être encore confié à personne, c'est un mariage de pure convenance de goût et de cœur (...). Tout s'est fait par correspondance et tout le monde est d'accord. »

Accord secret, accord parfait. Dans sa joie, George ne peut se retenir de partager son secret avec quelques intimes parmi lesquels Alexandre Dumas fils et l'acteur Pierre Bocage, l'un de ses anciens amants, qui triomphe à l'Ambigu dans l'une de ses pièces, *les Beaux Messieurs de Bois-Doré*.

Le secret cesse bientôt de l'être, le cercle des intimes s'élargit, et Sand, plus infatigable épistolière que jamais, écrit une trentaine de lettres pour annoncer l'heureux événement à l'univers entier, et en particulier, à Sainte-Beuve, à Pierre-Jules Hetzel, à Charles Poncy, à Jules Boucoiran, à Victor Hugo, à Eugène Fromentin, et au cousin René de Villeneuve que l'on allait oublier, et Jules Janin, et Barbès, et Eugène Delacroix... qui offre en cadeau de mariage un pastel, *le Centaure*. George, une fois de plus comblée, ne tarit pas d'éloges sur cette Lina, « une petite Romaine pur sang (...) crépue, mignonne, fine, une voix charmante » et « franche, intelligente et pas dévote, qualité rare en ces temps-ci ; artiste dans ses idées et ses habitudes, ne demandant pas à rouler carrosse et à faire la roue ».

Pas de noces tapageuses : la mère de Lina qui vit avec un amant — il n'y a pas de famille parfaite — ne sera pas là. Non plus que Solange qui persiste dans sa brouille et qui a refusé, à Paris, de recevoir sa mère, puis son frère.

Pas d'église non plus : Maurice et Lina se contentent d'un mariage civil, célébré à Nohant, le 17 mai 1862. Le 25, George confie à son fidèle Poncy : « Nous sommes dans l'ivresse. Elle est adorable, c'est le soleil sur nous. »

L'ivresse doit être générale puisque Marie d'Agoult daigne envoyer un mot de félicitations à George Sand qui remercie en l'assurant de la pérennité de ses sentiments. « Quand on s'est franchement aimés, je crois qu'on s'aime toujours, même pendant le temps où l'on croit s'être oubliés. Moi, je ne sais plus trop ce qui s'est passé. *La vie est toujours pour moi l'heure présente.* » C'est moi qui souligne cette phrase, reflet de l'art de vivre et de la prodigieuse vitalité de son auteur.

Ombre à ce bonheur : l'incessante toux de Manceau. En août 1842, Sand appelle, en consultation, trois médecins qui « ne lui trouvent aucun mal dangereux et considèrent ce catarrhe chronique comme un brevet de longévité ».

Ce « catarrhe chronique » n'est autre que la tuberculose. Cette toux de Manceau, Sand en rend compte dans les mêmes termes que Mme de Sévigné évoquant la toux de sa fille, Mme de Grignan. Sand, comme Sévigné, affirme : « Sa toux me déchire la poitrine. »

Manceau tousse, Maurice et Lina sont heureux, Sand compose *Mademoiselle La Quintinie*, et prévient Buloz qu'il s'agit là d'un roman « dangereux » parce que anticlérical. Buloz la rassure et l'encourage. « Vous êtes un maître dans l'art d'écrire, et vous trouverez bien le moyen de tout dire sans que nous tombions sous les mains du pouvoir et du parti clérical. »

En janvier 1863, Lina est enceinte et George s'en réjouit. « Ma Lina s'arrondit, elle est haute comme un chat, elle va devenir une boule. Elle chante comme un rossignol. » Lina a toutes les qualités, et, en plus, elle chante comme une Consuelo. Son dieu, c'est Rossini, et sa déesse, c'est George Sand qu'elle admire depuis qu'elle est enfant. C'est à se demander si Lina n'a pas épousé Maurice à défaut de pouvoir se marier avec sa mère...

Ce 27 janvier, paraît dans *la Presse* un article élogieux de Sand sur le roman de Gustave Flaubert, *Salammbô*, qui a été passablement éreinté par la critique. « Tout ce que j'avais lu sur *Salammbô* avant de lire *Salammbô* était injuste ou insuffisant, écrit-elle à Flaubert, le 28. J'aurais regardé le silence comme une lâcheté, ou comme une paresse, ce qui se ressemble beaucoup. Il m'est indifférent d'avoir à ajouter vos adversaires aux miens. Un peu plus, un peu moins... » Ainsi commence l'amitié[1] entre George Sand et Gustave Flaubert. L'initiative en revient à George qui, dès cette première lettre du 28 janvier, appelle Gustave « mon cher frère ».

Flaubert, qui a alors quarante-deux ans, est déjà l'auteur de *Madame Bovary* et de *Salammbô* qui a paru en novembre 1862. Il aime l'art, l'exotisme, la beauté sous toutes ses formes. Son « Madame Bovary, c'est moi » est loin d'être une boutade. Il y a beaucoup d'Emma en Gustave, beaucoup plus qu'on ne croit...

L'amitié, entre écrivains, est rarissime. Celle de Sand et de Flaubert est exemplaire. S'il existe un paradis des vrais amis, George et Gustave doivent, en ce moment, s'y prélasser et poursuivre leurs discussions sur l'art, l'argent, la tendresse, le style. Ce paradis doit exister. De toute façon, Sand ne croit pas à l'enfer comme elle l'affirme hautement et clairement à l'une de ses innombrables correspondantes, Marie-Sophie Leroyer de Chantepie. « Le dogme de l'enfer est une monstruosité, une imposture et une barbarie. »

De plus en plus, Sand se passionne pour les problèmes que pose, en ce monde, la coexistence du bien et du mal. Le 1er février, elle expose à Émile de Girardin l'une de ses théories : « Notre indignation contre le mal s'apaisera complètement le jour où nous aurons bien compris et bien senti ce qu'est la liberté sans limites. Dès lors, le mensonge nous devient indifférent, nous sommes si forts et si libres que nous n'y répondons plus que par un sourire. »

Ce sourire, face au bien et au mal, c'est le sourire du Bouddha. Et c'est avec ce même sourire qu'elle doit dire à Lina : « Aimer réellement, c'est entrer dans l'infini. » Ce n'est pas seulement dans l'infini

---

1. Lire l'histoire de cette amitié dans la *Correspondance Flaubert-Sand*, parue chez Flammarion.

qu'entre George Sand, mais dans l'âge des convictions profondes. « J'ai un grand bonheur, c'est d'être arrivée avec l'âge à des convictions aussi fortes que mes doutes d'autrefois étaient profonds et douloureux. »

Sa connaissance de la vie, durement acquise par l'expérience, elle l'enseigne de cette façon : « Ne vous plaignez pas du travail ingrat et acceptez-le comme une bonne chose, les trois quarts de la vie sacrifiés à un devoir quelconque font le dernier quart très fort et très vivant. » Sand en est la vivante preuve, épanouie dans le dernier quart de sa vie, plus qu'elle ne l'a été au temps de sa jeunesse folle... À cinquante-neuf ans, au hasard de ses lettres, elle établit de brefs bilans. « J'ai un peu coulé comme un ruisseau qui ne sait pas trop où il va, et qui suit sa pente sans la choisir. J'ai fait des tours et des retours, ce n'est pas ma faute. Je n'étais préoccupée que du besoin de me clarifier et chaque nouvel horizon me semblait être celui où je pouvais m'arrêter. L'âge m'a appris qu'on ne s'arrête pas... »

Elle s'arrête pourtant, le temps de prendre conscience que les amours éphémères, les passions rapides ont laissé la place aux sûres affections et aux sentiments modérés ou à la sagesse.

Pour Édouard Rodrigues, un riche financier qu'elle a réussi à intéresser à l'un de ses protégés, Francis Laur, dont il finance les études, Sand pose les grands problèmes de l'égalité et de la fraternité entre les hommes, atteignant ces sommets que sont la tolérance, l'absence de mépris envers le prochain. Elle a de saisissantes formules comme : « Dès qu'on crée des inférieurs, on se fait inférieur soi-même. »

George Sand est passée, et non sans peine, des embrasements célestes aux idées célestes. Quand elle quitte ces sommets, elle entraîne Édouard Rodrigues vers les bonnes réalités de Nohant : « C'est une adoration que nous avons ici les uns pour les autres et cela nous rend bêtes et casaniers au possible. » Les beaux étés de Nohant n'ont pas été, comme on l'a cru, ceux passés en compagnie de Liszt ou de Chopin, mais ceux qu'elle vit maintenant, dans les années soixante avec Manceau, Maurice, et Lina, et sans que ce bonheur soit troublé par Solange, trop occupée à courir les amants et les villes d'eaux.

De mars à mai 1863, *Mademoiselle La Quintinie* paraît « sans encombre » dans *la Revue des Deux Mondes*. Sand et Buloz respirent, leur crainte des réactions et du pouvoir contre ce roman étaient sans fondement aucun. Et pourtant, l'héroïne, Lucie La Quintinie préférait son époux à son directeur de conscience, ce qui était, pour l'époque, véritablement révolutionnaire.

Sand songe à tirer de ce roman une pièce, quoiqu'elle reconnaisse qu'elle n'est pas trop douée pour le théâtre. « Je n'ai pas d'éléments de succès dans mon talent seul. Je n'ai pas ce qu'il faut. Je n'ai que des idées, je ne sais pas m'en servir (...). »

Le vrai, le seul théâtre est celui de Nohant où se passe un événement qui éclipse tous les autres. Le 14 juillet 1863, « jour anniversaire de la prise de la Bastille » comme se plaît à le souligner la descendante des Delaborde et des Cloquard, François Marc Antoine, fils de Maurice et de Lina, naît à six heures du matin. Le nouveau-né regarde sa grand-mère qui l'a reçu dans son tablier « d'un air attentif et délibéré ». La grand-mère en tire aussitôt les conclusions qui s'imposent : « Il est superbe et très précoce. » On s'arrache le bébé et Manceau n'est pas le dernier à vouloir le prendre dans ses bras.

Parvenue à une entière félicité, George Sand ne supporte plus l'existence d'un seul malheureux et pratique la meilleure charité qui soit, la charité anonyme. « Je sais des gens réduits à la dernière extrémité à qui j'envoie de temps en temps par la poste un billet de banque anonyme. Ils le reçoivent, ils s'en servent, cela les sauve du dernier désespoir. »

Pour désigner cet argent destiné aux charités, elle a une jolie trouvaille : « Cela ne s'appelle plus de l'argent, mais l'or du Bon Dieu. » Cet or du Bon Dieu, Sand le répand sans compter et l'accompagne d'un sourire, le sourire du Bouddha.

LA DAME DE PALAISEAU
(août 1863-août 1865)

> Me voilà seule depuis deux nuits auprès de ce pauvre endormi qui ne se réveillera plus. Quel silence dans cette petite chambre où j'entrais sur la pointe des pieds à toute heure du jour et de la nuit !
>
> Palaiseau, le 22 août 1865

L'or de Dieu est le seul qui ne se dévalue pas : il produit même des intérêts inattendus, comme l'entrée de Francis Laur à l'École des mines de Saint-Étienne. Le 3 août 1863, George Sand se réjouit de ce succès qui est un peu le sien.

Le 13, Eugène Delacroix meurt. Maurice en est très peiné, et George aussi qui renouvelle, à cette occasion, sa foi en l'espoir d'une rencontre dans une autre vie. « L'absence et la mort ne diffèrent pas beaucoup, donc, on ne se quitte pas, on se perd de vue, mais on sait bien que n'importe où, on se retrouvera. » Pour George, Eugène reste présent, debout dans son atelier, la palette à la main et une longue écharpe de laine rouge autour du cou...

En septembre, George est distraite de ce nouveau chagrin par Alexandre Dumas fils et Théophile Gautier qui séjournent ensemble à Nohant où ils rejoignent un autre invité, Charles Marchal... Gautier a laissé de la châtelaine de Nohant un portrait dont la justesse tranche avec celui, caricatural, laissé par les Goncourt, plus soucieux de l'effet à produire que de la vérité. La « dignité de pachyderme » évoquée par les Goncourt devient, sous la plume de Gautier, l'image de la tranquillité. « Madame Sand est la tranquillité même. Elle roule sa cigarette, la fume et parle peu car elle travaille toutes les nuits jusqu'à trois ou quatre heures du matin et jusqu'à midi, une heure, elle est comme une somnambule puis elle commence à s'éveiller et rit des calembours de Dumas qu'elle

385

ne comprend qu'après tout le monde. Il est impossible d'être meilleure femme et meilleur garçon à la fois. »

Sainte Tranquille, si elle avait pu lire cette lettre adressée à Ernesta Grisi, aurait été certainement contente de voir son droit à la tranquillité reconnu, et elle aurait aussi certainement approuvé l'excellence de cette définition : « Il est impossible d'être meilleure femme et meilleur garçon à la fois. »

Si elle s'écoutait, George passerait son temps à jouer avec Marc, son petit-fils qui « pousse comme un rosier ». Mais l'écrivain l'emporte sur la grand-mère et elle écrit une pièce, *le Marquis de Villemer*, à laquelle Alexandre Dumas fils apporte une discrète, une efficace collaboration.

En novembre, trois crises de coliques bilieuses ne parviennent pas à abattre la vitalité de Sand qui se soigne avec de la teinture de castoréum et qui ne cache pas son émerveillement devant ses propres résurrections : « J'ai été très malade hier, et je me porte très bien aujourd'hui. Je suis comme cela, tout de suite par terre et tout de suite debout. Aussi, après avoir passé ma jeunesse à croire que je ne pourrais pas vivre, je passe ma vieillesse à croire que je ne peux pas mourir. C'est plus gai... »

La mélancolique Sand a des accès de gaieté dont elle s'émerveille aussi, comme elle continue à s'enchanter des bienfaits de son âge. « C'est excellent d'être vieux. C'est le meilleur âge, c'est celui où l'entendement voit clair. Tant pis si les yeux s'éteignent. On approche de la belle grande lumière. » Cette « belle grande lumière » évoquée par Sand le 3 novembre 1863 serait-elle cette lumière primordiale chère aux bouddhistes, aux mystiques et aux chercheurs de l'ultime vérité ? Sand se contente de l'évoquer comme une récompense et n'en dit rien de plus. Elle retrouve un peu de cette lumière dans l'éclat des roses de Nohant, « fille de Dieu et des hommes » dont elle compose un éloge pour Alphonse Karr, le 10 décembre. Elle a bien du mérite à vanter ces fleurs alors qu'une terrible crise vient de ravager Nohant qui a déjà connu bien des tempêtes. Cette fois, pas de tempête, pas de marteau brandi par un Clésinger fou de rage et de rhum, pas de hurlements d'une Solange endiablée, pas de cris de Sophie-Victoire, pas de sanglots de Mme Dupin de Francueil, tout se passe dans le calme, et la froideur, de l'inéluctable : Maurice ne veut plus de Manceau. Maurice ne supporte plus Manceau, comme il ne supportait plus Chopin.

Le 23 novembre 1863, Maurice a demandé à Manceau de quitter Nohant. Et, à sa stupéfaction, il a appris, le lendemain, que sa mère préférait quitter Nohant, son Nohant, plutôt que d'abandonner Manceau, son Manceau. Vingt-quatre heures de réflexion ont suffi à George Sand pour comprendre que la compagnie de l'irremplaçable Manceau comptait plus que tout le reste. Le sacrifice s'accomplit « sans rancune, ni fâcherie ». Tout le monde se dit d'accord pour cette séparation. Maurice et Lina craignant pour leur enfant la contagion d'un Manceau poitrinaire, et Sand se croyant délivrée des charges écrasantes de Nohant. Elle pense pouvoir se retirer à Gargilesse, et y vivre à l'économie.

Début janvier 1864, Sand, qui a horreur des dettes, s'aperçoit que, malgré son labeur incessant, elle doit à *la Revue des Deux Mondes* l'équivalent d'une année de travail, soit 15 400 francs. Elle en est atterrée et demande à Buloz d'aviser. Généreusement, Buloz réduit la dette et les feuilles à fournir annuellement par Sand qui pousse un soupir de soulagement et de reconnaissance.

Maurice, de son côté, a fait ses comptes qui sont très simples : Nohant coûte plus qu'il ne rapporte. Sand rêve à nouveau à la maison déserte, à l'intangible retraite où elle n'aurait plus de lettres à écrire, de services à rendre, ni de domestiques à nourrir et à payer.

Dans l'espoir de trouver cette retraite idéale, Sand et Manceau se rendent dans les environs de Paris, du côté d'Orsay et de Palaiseau, le 31 janvier. Le 7 février, le couple se décide pour une « charmante » maison à Palaiseau.

Le 27 février, la représentation du *Marquis de Villemer* à l'Odéon tourne à l'événement, et au triomphe. Tout Paris, de l'Empereur à l'étudiant, de l'impératrice à la concierge, veut assister à cette pièce dans laquelle une demoiselle de compagnie réussit à se faire épouser par le fils de la maison. Devant l'audace d'un tel sujet, le Tout-La Châtre doit encore frémir. Que voulez-vous, on ne change pas une Mlle Dupin, une Mme Dudevant, une George Sand !

Pour *le Marquis de Villemer*, salle comble, « et il y en aura autant à la porte. De mémoire d'homme, l'Odéon n'a connu une pareille rage ». Pour Maurice et Lina restés à Nohant, George rend compte, à chaud, du succès, à deux heures du matin, le 1er mars. « Mes enfants, je reviens escortée par les étudiants aux cris de " Vive George Sand, Vive *Mademoiselle La Quintinie*, À bas les cléricaux. " C'est une manifestation enragée en même temps qu'un succès comme on n'en a jamais vu, dit-on, au théâtre. »

L'Empereur « a pleuré ouvertement », Flaubert « pleurait comme une femme », Marchal menaçait d' « étriper les récalcitrants ». Sainte Tranquille n'en perd pas la tête pour autant et précise à Maurice et à Lina : « Je vous raconte tout ça pour vous amuser. Si vous voyiez mon calme au milieu de tout ça, ça vous ferait rire, car je n'ai pas été plus émue de peur et de plaisir que si ça ne me regardait pas. (...) Il faut voir le personnel de l'Odéon autour de moi, je suis le bon Dieu. »

Au lendemain de ce succès, seul Manceau perd la tête devant l'afflux des visiteurs qui viennent sonner chez le Bon Dieu de l'Odéon. Rôle qui n'enchante guère Sand qui revient, le 16 mars, à Nohant pour y constater que Maurice et Lina se déclarent inaptes à gouverner l'ingouvernable Nohant, promu alors au rang de maison de famille où l'on viendra se reposer entre deux séjours à Paris. Un strict gardiennage remplacera le coulage habituel.

À l'annonce que Sand quitte Nohant pour Palaiseau, les artisans et ouvriers de La Châtre adressent à leur « chère et illustre compatriote » une lettre collective pour exprimer leur désolation. « Et ce n'est pas seulement, croyez-le bien, les bienfaits que votre main a toujours semés autour d'elle qui leur rendent cette privation douloureuse. Votre génie est une lumière qui brille sur le monde entier, mais votre cœur a toujours su se faire entendre des âmes simples et populaires. (...) Nous vous devons la patience et l'espoir. »

En lisant cette lettre, Sand, « vivement touchée », laisse entendre qu'elle est largement payée des « petites persécutions » de La Châtre.

En ce printemps 1864, Notre-Dame de Nohant, comme l'avait surnommée Alexandre Dumas père, se change en Notre-Dame de Palaiseau. Le 12 juin, George annonce à Maurice : « Me voilà installée à Palaiseau, après avoir bien dîné et contemplé la maisonnette qui est ravissante de propreté et de confortable. (...) J'ai une bonne chic, le jardinet est charmant quoi qu'en dise Manceau, c'est une assiette de verdure avec un petit diamant d'eau au milieu, le tout placé dans un paysage admirable. »

Sand a trouvé à Palaiseau, comme à Gargilesse, un beau paysage, et un isolement complet qui favorise son travail. Pour distraction, promenade à travers les champs de blé. Elle peut marcher trois heures dans les collines, « sans rencontrer une âme, ou un animal ». Et quand elle croise des paysans, « ils vous disent bonjour comme à Gargilesse ». Que demander de plus ?

Le 18 juin, Maurice, Lina et leur fils Marc quittent Nohant pour Guillery où M. Dudevant manifeste quelque impatience de connaître son petit-fils. Le 3 juillet, George apprend que Marc a des coliques et supplie ses parents de ne pas donner « trop de fruits » à ce « petit ventre ». Le 10 juillet, son inquiétude augmente : Marc a la dysenterie. Le 14 juillet, pour son premier anniversaire, Marc va mieux. Ce mieux ne continue pas et Marc meurt le 21 juillet. « Malheureux que nous sommes », s'écrie sa grand-mère accourue à Guillery, où elle a retrouvé M. Dudevant, « aussi affecté qu'il peut l'être » et qui lui témoigne « beaucoup d'amitié ». Il est vrai que M. et Mme Dudevant ne se revoient plus qu'aux enterrements...

George est très affectée. « Je pleure en dormant, en marchant, en travaillant, et la moitié du temps sans penser à rien, comme en état d'idiotisme. » Dès qu'il apprend le deuil qui frappe son amie, Victor Hugo, toujours en exil à Jersey, lui écrit : « Vos deuils sont les miens, par la même raison qui fait que vos succès sont mes bonheurs. Grande âme, je souffre en vous. Je crois aux anges, j'en ai dans le ciel, j'en ai sur la terre. » George Sand n'avait donc pas l'exclusivité de ces anges qui peuplaient sa vie, comme celle de Victor Hugo...

La mort de Marc n'affecte pas George autant que la mort de l'inoubliable Nini. Dès septembre, George s'offre une récréation en compagnie du « gros Marchal » avec qui elle court « le long de la Creuse et sur les rochers ». Pas plus que Hugo, Sand ne renonce à ces « plaisirs que l'on nomme, à la légère, physiques ». La toux de Manceau, comme celle de Chopin, ne favorise pas les embrasements célestes. Le « gros Marchal » est là pour suppléer à ce manque.

Sand sait, et répète, que se distraire, ce n'est pas se consoler. Après son intermède à Gargilesse avec Marchal, elle soupire : « Hélas et courage, voilà toute ma vie. »

Pendant que George court le long de la Creuse, des rochers et des étoiles, Manceau aménage la maison de Palaiseau qu'il vient d'acheter. « Il a acquis la maison que j'habite et il m'en a fait une bonbonnière des plus simples et des plus commodes. »

À la « bonbonnière » de Palaiseau correspond un nouveau pied-à-terre parisien, au 97, rue des Feuillantines, actuellement 90, rue Claude-Bernard, dont le dénuement, le mauvais goût horrifient le photographe Nadar. L'ameublement s'y veut algérien, avec deux ou trois poteries kabyles, et, en guise de lustre, un œuf d'autruche. « Comment pouvez-vous vivre au milieu de ces horreurs ? » demande Nadar. « Fort bien », répond Sand qui, en décoration, ne voit pas plus loin que le bout de son encrier, ou que le nez de Manceau.

Pour tous les détails de la vie pratique et quotidienne, George a pris l'habitude de compter sur Manceau comme Maurice comptait sur elle. Son fils ne s'habitue pas à son absence, ce qu'elle déplore. « Je sais qu'il y a pour Maurice un grand chagrin de cœur et un grand mécompte d'habitude à ne m'avoir pas toujours sous la main pour songer à tout, à sa place. Mais il est temps pour lui de se charger de sa propre existence et le devoir de sa femme est d'avoir de la tête et de me remplacer. »

Le 11 février 1865, George se plaît à constater que son engouement pour Palaiseau continue. « J'ai un charmant pays sous les yeux et du soleil plein mon cabinet de travail. (...) J'ai un bon et fidèle compagnon à mes côtés (...). » Pour combien de temps encore ?

Manceau ne guérit pas et note sur l'agenda, le 21 avril : « Le 3 mai, c'est mon anniversaire. C'est peut-être le dernier, hein, Bon Dieu ? » Il ne peut que se rendre à l'évidence : sa santé se dégrade. Il perd l'appétit, le sommeil, les forces. Il s'essouffle vite, il souffre d'une fièvre aussi tenace que sa toux.

En ce printemps 1865, tout va mal pour George Sand : Manceau étouffe, il a grêlé à Nohant, et à Guillery, M. Dudevant est sous l'emprise d'une servante-maîtresse, Jenny, dont il a eu une fille, Rose, qui a maintenant dix-sept ans et dont il veut faire sa légataire universelle. L'héritage de Maurice et de Solange semble bien compromis.

Enfin, une bonne nouvelle : Lina est à nouveau enceinte. « Ah ! Dieu veuille », se contente de commenter Sand.

Le 26 mai 1865, Manceau note sur l'agenda : « Il paraît que je vais bien. C'est à crever de rire. » Quelqu'un qui ne rit pas, c'est George, qui se rend parfaitement compte que Manceau est perdu, mais qui fait tout pour le sauver, ne perdant pas l'espoir d'un miracle. « On essaie de tout sans succès », confirme-t-elle au Dr Darchy, le 1er juin. Le 27, elle confie à Hetzel : « Je suis dans le chagrin plus que jamais. L'état de mon pauvre ami s'aggrave de jour en jour. Les médecins disent qu'il n'y a pas de maladie sans ressources, et en attendant ils ne le tirent pas d'un dépérissement qui a fait des progrès inquiétants. Son moral est tout abattu, son caractère tout changé. Je vis dans les larmes. »

Par surcroît de malchance, elle a fait une chute et s'est abîmé une jambe. La série noire, quoi. Triste situation dont s'irrite Manceau. « Il s'en prend à moi de ce qu'il ne guérit pas, de ce que les médecins ne sont pas sérieux. » À cette irritation de ne pas guérir, s'ajoute pour Manceau la désolation de ne pouvoir soigner Sand handicapée par sa jambe blessée. Chacun fait assaut de dévouement et ne réussit qu'à accentuer la peine de l'autre.

Sand fait appel à un nouveau médecin, le Dr Fuster, qui préconise un nouveau traitement. Fuster vient à Palaiseau le 8 juillet pour une consultation de la dernière chance. Le 10, Sand se laisse aller au désespoir. « C'est une grande âme qui s'éteint, toute une vie de dévouement et d'oubli de lui-même, quinze ans de dévouement exclusif pour moi et ma famille ! C'est la moitié de ma vie qui me quitte, hélas ! » Puis, le 20, elle reprend espoir en constatant une légère amélioration : « Mon pauvre malade commence à aller un tout petit peu mieux et voilà que j'espère ! »

Le 9 août, Sand ne cache pas à Maurice les progrès du mal qui emporte inexorablement Manceau :

« Depuis deux jours il garde le lit et ne se lève que pour les repas, il s'affaiblit et s'éteint de jour en jour, et il le dit sans cesse d'une manière navrante. (...) Je perds encore une fois l'espérance. Et je t'assure qu'il faut du courage pour le lui cacher. » Que Maurice n'accoure pas immédiatement au secours de sa mère en lisant ces lignes passe l'entendement !

Le 16 août, toujours à Maurice qui joue les sourds et les aveugles : « Enfin ! je vis sous le coup de cette agonie avec un courage qui me fait voir qu'on peut tout supporter quand on le doit. Je ne suis pas malade, je travaille à bâtons rompus, mais je travaille. »

Le 21 août, Manceau meurt et, le jour même, Sand écrit à son fils : « Notre pauvre ami a cessé de souffrir. Il s'est endormi à minuit avec toute sa lucidité. (...) Je suis brisée de toute façon, mais après l'avoir habillé et arrangé moi-même sur son lit de mort, je suis encore dans l'énergie de volonté qui ne pleure pas. »

Maurice daigne enfin accourir et assiste, le 23 août, à l'enterrement civil de Manceau, au cimetière de Palaiseau. Sont également présents, entre autres, Alexandre Dumas fils, Charles Marchal et Francis Laur.

Le 27 août, George Sand retourne à Nohant, en compagnie de son fils. Elle a perdu « cet être qui était ma vie ». Elle s'étonne de vivre encore...

UNE MÈRE COURAGE
(septembre 1865-mai 1868)

Je suis très active, je supporte la
solitude sans amertume, je travaille.
Palaiseau, le 16 octobre 1865

Manceau qui, pendant exactement quinze ans, a
suivi Sand comme son ombre, ou plutôt comme un
fidèle soleil, montre dans son testament qu'il était
véritablement une « grande âme » : « Je lègue à
Mme Amantine Aurore Dupin (femme Dudevant)
George Sand : la propriété de toute la fortune
mobilière que je laisserai lors de mon décès, et aussi
la jouissance, sa vie durant, de tout ce que je
posséderai en immeubles, donnant la nue-propriété
de ces immeubles à son fils, Maurice Dudevant. »
C'est donc Maurice, qui a chassé Manceau de
Nohant, qui, finalement, hérite de son ancien ami.
En échange, il accepte de verser une rente aux
parents de Manceau. Machine à écrire, machine à
courage, Sand écrit une trentaine de lettres pour
annoncer son nouveau malheur et note dans son
Journal : « Mon fils est mon âme même. Je vivrai
pour lui, j'aimerai les braves cœurs. — Oui, oui,
mais toi... Toi qui m'as tant aimée ! Sois tranquille,
ta part reste impérissable. »

Un peu avant la mort de Manceau, le 10 août,
Sand avait écrit : « C'est la moitié de ma vie qui me
quitte. » La moitié seulement. Maurice reste le
principe vital de George qui n'en veut pas à son fils,
ni à sa belle-fille, de l'avoir laissée supporter seule
cette interminable agonie, bien au contraire. « Je
fais provision de courage en pensant à vous et en me
disant que j'aurai supporté cette épreuve, sans vous
la faire subir. »

Toute-puissance de l'instinct maternel en Sand,
en ce qui concerne Maurice. Aussi, quand Buloz, en

octobre 1865, ose refuser un roman de son fils, *le Coq aux cheveux d'or*, la mère en furie l'emporte sur l'amante en deuil. Elle n'est plus « brisée de toute façon » pour invectiver ce misérable Buloz. « Je vous dis que *le Coq* est un bijou et je proteste contre vos critiques, vous tuez Maurice (...) Vous m'éteignez complètement, je n'ai plus de cœur à rien. » Aveuglée par sa colère, George trouve que son fils a plus que du talent, « il a du génie ».

Autre sujet de rage, Solange. Sand n'ignore plus, comme elle l'apprend à Charles Poncy, que sa fille est « une femme payée et entretenue ». Elle fermait les yeux sur ces débordements, mais elle ne peut rester sourde à la rumeur : Solange mène un train de vie infiniment supérieur à ses rentes. « Elle a 3 000 francs de pension et elle ne travaille pas. (...) Il faut au moins 20 000 francs par an pour la vie qu'elle mène ; où les prend-elle ? Je ne le sais que trop à présent que tout le monde le sait. (...) Moi, je n'accepte pas la prostitution et rien n'existe plus entre moi et une personne qui a pris ce chemin-là. (...) Elle a préféré le libertinage et ses profits. Je vous répète que je ne la connais plus, d'autant qu'il n'y a chez elle ni affection, ni respect pour moi », écrit-elle, le 14 octobre, à Charles Poncy qui a eu l'imprudence de laisser sa fille devenir l'amie de Solange.

Solange a repris, comme sa grand-mère Delaborde et son arrière-arrière-grand-mère Rainteau, les chemins de la galanterie. Tradition familiale que George Sand oublie, s'efforce d'oublier, par son travail quotidien.

Le 16 octobre 1865, de retour à Palaiseau, cette indomptable de soixante et un ans repart à zéro. « Je vais recommencer à gagner ma vie au jour le jour, et si je me porte bien, tout ira bien. J'ai trouvé beaucoup de courage dans la résignation. (...) Je suis très active, je supporte la solitude sans amertume, je travaille. »

Le refus de l'amertume, le travail, voilà les sources où cette Mère Courage puise ses forces, son éternelle jouvence. Elle apprend à vivre sans Manceau, à aller seule dans les rues, à dîner seule au restaurant, à payer les fiacres, « j'apprends tout comme un enfant et l'ordre me revient ». Elle n'est pas aussi seule qu'elle le dit, et Charles Marchal a repris son rôle de consolateur. Le 20 octobre, en sa compagnie, elle entend à l'Opéra l'*Africaine*. Dès le 25, elle relance Marchal : « Dites-moi si nous recommençons notre orgie de musique. C'était bien bon, et ça fait du bien. » On peut se demander s'il a été, ce soir-là, seulement question de musique entre George et Charles ! Sand, à sa façon, préfigure les jeunes femmes de soixante ans [1] qui, aujourd'hui, ne craignent pas d'exhiber leurs jeunes amants comme une insolite Légion d'honneur...

Le 31 décembre 1865, de retour à Nohant où l'on vit dans l'attente de l'accouchement de Lisa, George évoque, le plus naturellement du monde, pour Charles Marchal « la vitalité si diverse et si intense » de Manceau. Elle reconnaît que sa perte est plus supportable qu'elle ne s'y attendait. « Tout cela n'est pas si navrant à mon âge que si j'avais vingt ans de moins. (...) J'ai fait les trois quarts de la route. Il ne faut pas faire d'embarras et de plaintes pour un bout de chemin qui sera peut-être plus facile qu'on ne croit. (...) Je t'embrasse et je t'aime de tout mon cœur. »

Sand, plus que jamais, pratique la politique de l'heure présente. Comment pourrait-il en être autrement puisque, à la mort de Manceau, le 21 août 1865, à Palaiseau, succède, le 10 janvier 1866, à Nohant, la naissance de la fille de Maurice et de Lina, qui, comme sa grand-mère, reçoit le prénom préféré des Kœnigsmark, Aurore. « Mlle Aurore Sand est née cette nuit. Elle est superbe », proclame inlassablement George Sand à ses amis. D'abord à

_____

1. Quand, en 1973, je publiais mon roman, *Une jeune femme de soixante ans*, je pensais qu'il s'agissait là d'un phénomène purement contemporain...

Charles Marchal et à Alexandre Dumas fils, Marchal à qui elle fait mesurer la faveur de compter parmi les premiers avertis d'un tel événement : « Moi je tiens à ce que tu constates que j'ai pensé à toi et à Alexandre, *avant tous les autres*. » Elle souligne ce « avant tous les autres » d'un trait de plume énergique afin que Marchal ne s'y trompe pas : il est bien l'actuel favori de la reine Sand.

Tout Nohant repose à nouveau sur les épaules de George qui ne s'en plaint pas, oh non ! Lina, fiévreuse, est veillée par son mari et par son père. « Mais ce sont des hommes, ça ne pense à rien, ça ne prévoit pas, ça n'ose rien », note Sand avec une satisfaction non dissimulée. Elle, elle est une femme qui pense, qui prévoit, qui ose. Elle ose même dire que, quatre jours après sa naissance, Aurore ne supporte pas qu'on l'appelle *baby* : elle est « déjà résolue et antibritannique ». Très précoce Aurore...

Pendant les dix jours qui suivent la naissance de sa petite-fille, celle qui est enfin redevenue une « bonne-maman » multiplie ses rôles : elle est, tour à tour, sage-femme, nourrice, berceuse, garde-malade. La grand-mère qui triomphe en elle trouve quand même le temps de s'inquiéter pour Charles Marchal qui la laisse sans nouvelles. « Je ne sais pas pourquoi je suis inquiète de toi, mon cher gros. (...) Dis-moi que tu te portes bien. » Le « cher gros » se porte bien, court les actrices, et ne peut, comme Manceau, se consacrer entièrement à Sand qui, indulgente et sans jalousie aucune, comprend.

Dans le désert laissé par Manceau, Marchal représente l'oasis, le verre d'eau qui étanche une soif passagère. Il n'est plus question de passion, mais de plaisir. Marchal, entre deux passades avec des actrices, ou des modèles, consacre un peu de son temps, et de ses talents d'alcôve, à George qui n'en demande pas davantage. Certes, Marchal n'est pas toujours disponible et Sand sait s'en plaindre aimablement : « On ne te trouve jamais chez toi, surtout quand il pleut. Tu es de la race des grenouilles, tu mets le nez dehors quand le nuage crève. » Elle sait aussi prier sans en avoir l'air : « Je ne te dis pas de venir à Palaiseau. Tu n'auras pas le temps. Si tu l'avais par hasard, tu ne serais pas flanqué à la porte à coups de pied. » On admirera combien George Sand pratique, avec Charles Marchal, un art qu'elle connaît bien : l'euphémisme. Parfois, elle se fait plus insistante : « Viens si tu peux. Tu me feras grand bien. Tu sais que pour moi je ne demande pas souvent qu'on m'aide à prendre le dessus. Mais ici, je broye du noir. » C'est que le souvenir de Manceau est toujours là, dans cette maison de Palaiseau qui devait être la maison de leur bonheur à deux, loin de la famille et des importuns. Quand Sand consulte les brouillons de son roman, *Mont-Revêche*, pour en tirer une pièce, elle ne peut s'empêcher d'évoquer celui qui recopiait tout ce qu'elle écrivait...

Bref, George considère Charles comme une distraction des plus appréciables, sans plus. Car il n'est pas facile d'être, de son vivant, un monument, un panthéon des gloires défuntes où brillent particulièrement les noms de Musset et de Chopin. Ce qui suffirait à décourager les amateurs peu soucieux de subir la comparaison avec d'aussi illustres ombres. Le « cher gros » Marchal ignore ce genre de scrupules et pratique l'amour sainement, gaiement, comme c'est l'usage dans les ateliers d'alors. Gaudriole et calembour peuvent égalememment conduire aux embrasements célestes. À soixante ans passés, George Sand découvre qu'il peut être agréable de considérer l'amour uniquement comme le contact de deux épidermes. Il était temps.

Sand, ce monument physiquement caressé par Marchal, l'est aussi, abstraitement, par ses pairs. Sainte-Beuve, Gustave Flaubert, Théophile Gautier, les frères Goncourt et autres écrivains qui se réunissent pour dîner au restaurant Magny pressent leur consœur d'être des leurs. Sand finit par accepter et dîne en leur compagnie, pour la première fois, le 12 février 1866. Compte rendu de ce mémorable dîner par Sand dans son agenda qu'elle tient toute seule, maintenant, sans l'aide de Manceau. « Premier dîner chez Magny avec mes petits camarades. Ils m'ont accueillie on ne peut mieux, ils ont été très brillants, sauf le grand savant Berthelot qui seul a été, je crois, raisonnable. (...) On paie 10 francs par tête, le dîner est médiocre, on fume beaucoup, on parle en criant à tue-tête et chacun s'en va quand il veut. J'étais rentrée à dix heures et demie. » Compte rendu de ce même dîner par les Goncourt dans leur Journal : « Mme Sand vient aujourd'hui dîner à Magny. (...) Ce qui me frappe chez la femme-écrivain, c'est la délicatesse merveilleuse des petites mains, perdues, presque dissimulées dans des manchettes de dentelle. »

La « délicatesse » de ces « petites mains » n'est qu'apparente : elles sont capables de mener à bien, et en même temps, les douze travaux d'Hercule! Toujours sur la brèche, Sand écrit, lit, brode, étudie, rend visite à la princesse Mathilde, entend la Bohème de Puccini, Orphée aux enfers d'Offenbach, et démontre à Buloz que ses « accès de colère » ne sont que des « retours de vitalité ». Elle se tourmente pour les rhumes d'Aurore qui, comme son père, manifeste une fâcheuse tendance à s'enrhumer. « J'ai dit et dis encore que l'on doit faire prendre l'air aux enfants et les y habituer le plus tôt possible. Vous tenez la vôtre enfermée, aussitôt qu'elle sort, elle s'enrhume, la nourrice aussi, c'est inévitable. »

« Accès de colère » ou « retours de vitalité », ses démêlés avec Buloz reprennent de plus belle quand elle apprend que c'est le caissier de la Revue des Deux Mondes, Gerdès, qui lit ses manuscrits, et ceux de Maurice. Le 21 mai 1866, elle blâme, dans son agenda, une telle pratique : « Quel temps! quelle crotte! c'est comme ça. Patience, je n'ai plus tant d'années à vivre. J'en ris au Magny avec les amis qui me trouvent longanime. »

À force de vivre dans l'heure présente, Sand a retrouvé le bonheur. « Je suis aussi heureuse ainsi qu'il m'est permis de l'être. Ma vie est très simplifiée et beaucoup plus libre. » Elle compense l'insuccès de sa pièce, *Don Juan de village*, par un séjour, en août 1866, chez Gustave Flaubert, à Croisset, « un endroit délicieux, et notre ami Flaubert mène là une vie de chanoine, au sein d'une charmante famille ».

George et Gustave ont l'un en l'autre une inébranlable confiance. C'est à Flaubert que vont les confidences les plus intimes, comme celles sur les vies antérieures. À l'auteur de *Salammbô* qui affirmait « posséder des souvenirs qui remontent aux pharaons » l'auteur de *la Mare au diable* répond plus modestement : « Moi je crois que j'étais végétal ou pierre. » Sa passion pour les arbres et les minéraux s'expliquerait mieux ainsi.

Son amour des animaux s'étend jusqu'à Marchal, « mon lapin rose qui est gras comme trois cochons ». Ange consolateur, Marchal a droit, le 19 novembre 1866, à cette déclaration : « Pourvu que je sois avec toi et que j'aille devant moi, tout me botte. (...) Il me semble que je recommence ma vie et que je vois tout pour la première fois. Pourquoi ça ? Je n'en sais absolument rien. Pourquoi rajeunir à soixante-trois ans, pour tomber tout à coup en enfance, peut-être dans peu ? »

Sand a appris que, pour garder son bonheur, il vaut mieux ne pas se poser certaines questions. Elle se contente donc de rajeunir à soixante-trois ans, avec Charles Marchal, qui en a alors quarante et un. Elle veille à ce que son « cher gros » ne perde pas trop son temps en mondanités chez la princesse Mathilde et recommande maternellement « le travail avant tout ». Elle peut, sans peine, se donner en exemple puisqu'elle n'a jamais laissé le plaisir l'emporter sur le travail. Elle travaille ferme, elle « pioche » comme elle dit, et se souvient que, à la voir tant « piocher », ce « pauvre Manceau » l'avait surnommée « le cantonnier ».

Un cantonnier qui, le 9 janvier 1867, fait à Gustave Flaubert cette simple déclaration de foi : « Je me désintéresse prodigieusement de tout ce qui n'est pas mon petit idéal de travail paisible, de vie champêtre et de tendre et pure amitié. » À vingt ans comme à soixante-trois, George Sand reste fidèle à ses goûts profonds. Elle a atteint maintenant son idéal de « travail paisible » et de « vie champêtre ». Quant à la « tendre et pure amitié » à laquelle elle aspirait en Aurélien de Sèze, c'est Gustave Flaubert qui l'incarne, et à qui elle apprend qu'il n'y a qu'un sexe, et non deux, comme on le croit généralement, « pour les gens forts en anatomie : il n'y a qu'un sexe. Un homme et une femme, c'est si bien la même chose que l'on ne comprend guère les tas de distinctions et de raisonnements subtils dont se sont nourries les sociétés sur ce chapitre-là. J'ai observé l'enfance et le développement de mon fils et de ma fille. Mon fils était moi, par conséquent femme, bien plus que ma fille qui était un homme pas réussi ».

Maurice féminin, Solange masculine, Sand n'est pas une mère aussi aveugle que je l'ai prétendu... George se plaît dans ce jeu des métamorphoses et y inclut Marchal qui, en février 1867, de « petit lapin rose » qu'il était devient « petit lapin bleu », sans que l'on sache pourquoi...

En ce même mois de février, George Sand succombe sous l'excès de la correspondance, et des correspondants qui, en huit pages, lui racontent leurs infortunes et demandent conseil. Pour la première fois de sa carrière d'épistolière infatigable, elle ne répond pas à une lettre et charge son neveu, Oscar Cazamajou, d'y répondre à sa place. Passager accès de mauvaise humeur.

Ni la « pioche » quotidienne, ni les séances de gymnastique voluptueuse avec Charles Marchal, ni les échanges d'esprit avec Gustave Flaubert ne détournent cette chercheuse de son but suprême : acquérir la sagesse. Par crainte de perdre sa petite fille Aurore, comme elle a perdu Nini, sa Nini, elle ne se livre pas entièrement à l'adoration de sa « chère enfant ». « Je n'ose pas l'adorer. Il m'a été si cruel de perdre les autres. Elle est forte et bien portante, mais je ne peux croire à aucun bonheur, bien que je paraisse toujours avec mes enfants l'espérance en personne. »

Si elle a souvent la tête dans les nuages, George Sand n'en garde pas moins les pieds sur terre. Les craintes de voir M. Dudevant déshériter complètement Maurice et Solange au profit de Rose, sa fille naturelle, se précisent. Bien qu'elle soit en plein dans la composition d'un roman, *Cadio*, qui se passe en Vendée de 1793 à 1795, et qu'elle en perde « le manger et le dormir », Mme Dudevant ne perd pas de vue les intérêts de ses enfants et démontre, avec une belle inconscience, que « la vie de M. Dudevant n'a pas cessé d'être scandaleuse ».

Intrigues et procès aboutissent, en juillet 1867, à un arrangement. M. Dudevant est reconnu « usufruitier » de ses propriétés dont, à sa mort, hériteront Maurice et Solange.

L'Exposition universelle bat son plein à Paris, témoignant de la prospérité de la France. Ce qui ne manque pas d'inquiéter la Prusse. Planent des menaces d'une guerre que prévoit Sand qui, le 28 août, écrit à Barbès : « Que la guerre s'allume sur une grande ligne, avant peu, je le crois. » Elle s'allumera, cette guerre, exactement trois ans plus tard...

Le lendemain, George Sand ajoute à son testament un codicille par lequel elle confie à Maurice le soin de s'occuper des papiers et correspondances qu'elle laissera après sa mort. Elle écarte ainsi Solange dont elle craint les malveillances à son égard, et les inévitables indiscrétions. « Nul ne peut nourrir l'espérance de supprimer le passé », soupire-t-elle sans illusion aucune. On ne peut pas non plus supprimer Solange qui, le 16 février 1858, est sur le quai de la gare de Toulon pour y accueillir sa mère qui vient séjourner sur la Côte d'Azur, chez l'une de ses nouvelles amies, Juliette Adam. Sand embrasse sa fille du bout des lèvres, demande : « Comment te portes-tu ? » et passe, en écoutant à peine la réponse. Maurice imite la conduite de sa mère et salue sa sœur avec la même ostensible froideur. Solange doit comprendre, et elle le comprend, que ni sa mère ni son frère n'admettent sa situation de « femme entretenue »...

Lina n'est pas du voyage : elle est sur le point d'accoucher. Elle accouche plus tôt que prévu, le 11 mars 1868, d'une deuxième fille, Gabrielle. Le 14, George et Maurice se précipitent à Nohant pour y admirer cette deuxième Aurore « brune comme Lolo, avec de grands yeux noirs comme Lolo, c'est une Lolo numéro deux ». Aurore est appelée familièrement Lolo. Lolo numéro un est en extase devant Lolo numéro deux. Elle se dit « enseigne », c'est-à-dire « enceinte », à l'émerveillement de sa grand-mère qui trouve cette Lolo de deux ans encore plus précoce que ne l'était Nini.

Après cette naissance qui n'est pas prématurée comme on l'a craint à Nohant, Lina s'est simplement trompée de quelques semaines, George se livre à ses habituels tourbillons de joie épistolaire pour annoncer l'heureux événement, ce qui ne l'empêche pas de prêcher le calme à Juliette Adam et d'en donner la recette : « Un grand détachement des petites choses qui prend à son heure, quand on se laisse faire sans dépit et sans regret. (...) Dépensez-vous mais sans vous dévaster. »

Pour Sand, ce calme est le commencement de la sagesse. Elle avance ainsi à petits pas, vers la grande sagesse, vers le détachement suprême. Apprenant qu'Alexandre Dumas fils s'enrichit, elle ne s'en réjouit pas, au contraire. « Je plains Alexandre de s'enrichir. C'est une complication dans l'existence. » Elle tend vers l'ascétisme et devient encore plus sobre qu'elle ne l'était. À Paris, ou à Palaiseau, elle déjeune avec deux œufs et une tasse de café. Elle dîne d'un peu de poulet, ou de veau, avec des légumes. À Nohant, elle vit de galette et de piquette. Elle pratique ce régime quand elle est seule, évidemment. Et elle l'est rarement. Ses invités, parmi lesquels Théophile Gautier, vantent l'excellence, et l'abondance (parfois excessive en gibier) de la table à Nohant [1].

Au printemps 1868, Sand, abandonnant sa sauvagerie, sa crainte des inconnus, consent à rencontrer, présenté par Émile de Girardin, Alphonse Daudet, « un jeune auteur nîmois », le 29 mai. Ce même jour, elle relance Charles Marchal : « Je serai chez moi demain, toute la journée. Si tu as un moment, viens me dire adieu. » Car elle déménage, elle va occuper, au 5, rue Gay-Lussac, un entresol orné d'un Delacroix, *la Nuit de Walpurgis*, de bronzes chinois, de vieilles porcelaines et de l'inévitable œuf d'autruche qui a tant choqué Nadar. À propos de cet œuf, Georges Lubin précise, à la page 860 du vingtième tome de la *Correspondance*, que, « en réalité, c'était un moulage d'un œuf d'æpyornis, échassier des temps préhistoriques »...

---

1. Voir l'album de Christiane Sand, *À la table de George Sand*, Éd. Flammarion.

UN EXEMPLE
DE PAISIBLE SIMPLICITÉ
(juin 1868-décembre 1869)

> Simplifier sa vie à mesure qu'on a moins de besoins dans la vie est une chose sage et facile, à portée de tout le monde.
>
> Paris, mai 1869

George Sand, sexagénaire, savoure son hiver, et apprend que « la vie se passe à apprendre ». Considérant la famille comme « une douce prison », elle vit à Nohant dans un grand calme, sans ouvrir un journal. Chaque jour de cet été 1868, elle se plonge dans l'Indre, ou dans la botanique. Elle écrit des articles sur la sensibilité des plantes : « Qui vous dit que la plante coupée ou brisée ne souffre pas ? » Pour Sand, de la plante à l'étoile, tout vit, aime, souffre et meurt. Quant à elle, elle « se porte comme trois Turcs » et ne ressent aucunement les effets de l'âge.

Refusant obstinément d'admettre qu'elle est née un 1er juillet, elle écrit, le 5 juillet 1868 : « J'ai aujourd'hui soixante-quatre printemps. Je n'ai pas encore senti le poids des ans. Je marche autant, je travaille autant, je dors aussi bien. Ma vue est fatiguée aussi ; je mets depuis si longtemps des lunettes que c'est une question de numéro, voilà tout. Quand je ne pourrai plus agir, j'espère que j'aurai perdu la volonté d'agir. Et puis, on s'effraie de l'âge avancé, comme si on était sûr d'y arriver. On ne pense pas à la tuile qui peut tomber du toit. Le mieux est de se tenir toujours prêt et de jouir des vieilles années mieux qu'on n'a su jouir des jeunes. On perd tant de temps et on gaspille tant la vie à vingt ans. Nos jours d'hiver comptent double ; voilà notre compensation. » Avouez que l'on ne saurait mieux dire et que George Sand donne là, sans en avoir l'air, une leçon de bien-vieillir... Elle est aussi virulente à soixante-quatre ans qu'à quarante et son

anticléricalisme atteint alors des sommets, particulièrement contre les frères des écoles chrétiennes
qui, selon elle, « violent les petits garçons par
centaines » ! Immédiatement après avoir fait cette
constatation, elle célèbre la bonté de Dieu. « Dieu
est la bonté infinie et ne damne personne. Il n'y a
que l'ignorance. » Comme les bouddhistes dont elle
est, sans le savoir, très proche, George Sand croit
que le mal vient de l'ignorance des pauvres
humains. « Il n'y a pas d'esprit du mal dans l'univers, Dieu ne le permettrait pas. Il n'y a que de
l'ignorance, et Dieu ordonne à l'homme de combattre l'ignorance et les superstitions du passé. »

Bel été 1868. George ne se lasse pas de contempler,
et d'apprécier, la paix qui règne à Nohant. Maurice
écrit un roman, Lina fait des confitures, Lolo et
Gabrielle pépient comme des oiseaux. Comment
peut-on se plaire dans la fiction alors que la réalité
est tellement agréable ? Sand ne cesse de se poser
cette question, et d'en discuter, par lettres, avec
Flaubert, à qui, le 21 décembre, elle lance ce cri que
certains sentimentaux devraient prendre pour
devise, ou pour signe de ralliement : « Méprise-moi
profondément, mais aime-moi toujours. »

L'amour est indispensable à George qui débute le
premier jour de l'année 1869 par cette affirmation
d'adoration : « Aurore est toujours l'être adoré
autour duquel tout gravite. » Pour ses étrennes, elle
a offert à Aurore-Lolo « une poupée presque aussi
grande qu'elle ». Grand-mère modèle, elle habille
les poupées qu'elle donne à sa petite-fille. Avec
Aurore Dudevant-Sand, celle qui fut Aurore Dupin
connaît « le bonheur d'être paisible et de s'amuser
de tout ». Les deux Aurore se contemplent, éblouies,
l'une en sa fin, l'autre en son commencement...

Le 8 mars 1869, le père de Lina meurt à Milan.
« Voilà comment le malheur vous tombe sur la tête
au milieu du calme et de la joie », commente Sand
que cette mort plonge dans des abîmes de réflexion :
« Mourir sans souffrance, en dormant, c'est la plus

belle des morts, et c'est celle de Calamatta (...) Mourir ainsi, ce n'est pas mourir, c'est changer de place au gré de la locomotive. Moi qui ne crois pas à la mort, je dis : Qu'importe tôt ou tard ? (...) Je ne crains que les infirmités qui font durer une vie inutile et à charge aux plus dévoués. » Elle fait part de ces réflexions-là à Alexandre Dumas fils qui, éperdu d'admiration pour son amie, lui répond : « Vous êtes, vous, la seule parmi les femmes de tous les temps, passés, présents ou futurs. »

Lourde responsabilité pour George Sand d'être « la seule femme » selon Alexandre Dumas fils, ou « la femme la plus femme... » selon Alfred de Musset. Il y aurait de quoi en être grisé. Sand ne l'est pas. Elle doit chaque jour affronter le malheur qui est la chose du monde la mieux partagée. Chaque jour, elle reçoit vingt lettres dont dix-neuf sont des appels au secours auxquels elle s'efforce de répondre. Cette correspondance que Sand considère maintenant comme un « fléau » qui dévore son temps appartient à ce qu'elle nomme elle-même « les horreurs de la célébrité ».

Harcelée par des inconnus, George Sand l'est aussi, mais agréablement en ce cas, par Aurore-Lolo et ses incessantes questions sur Dieu, les étoiles, les animaux. Du haut de ses trois ans, Aurore demande à sa grand-mère pourquoi elle écrit tant. « Pour avoir de l'argent », répond Sand avec sincérité et simplicité. « Ah oui, pour tes petites-filles », commente la pratique Aurore.

La maison de Palaiseau est vendue 35 000 francs qui sont transformés en rente pour Maurice. L'après-Manceau est bien terminé. Son remplaçant, Charles Marchal, après avoir été successivement lapin rose et lapin bleu, prend, en mai 1869, une nouvelle couleur, le vert : « Quand te verrai-je, mon cher lapin vert ? » Marchal serait-il devenu aussi inaccessible, aussi vert que les raisins convoités par le renard dans la fable de La Fontaine ? Le peintre semble beaucoup se faire prier par la romancière qui, pourtant, offre de se plier à ses horaires et à son seul désir : « Si je savais le jour où tu viendras, je me garderais libre. »

En attendant Marchal, Sand s'occupe de placer l'*Éducation sentimentale*, que Flaubert vient de terminer, chez l'éditeur Lévy, et dans les meilleures conditions. Content, Flaubert annonce à sa nièce : « Je compte tirer à Lévy un supplément de 5 à 6 000 francs. C'est à la mère Sand que je devrai cela. » L'auteur de l'*Éducation sentimentale* doit beaucoup plus que « cela » à cette « mère Sand » qui le soutient constamment dans les affres de la création et de la dépression...

Entre les romans qu'elle écrit, et ceux des autres qu'elle lit, George constate, sans amertume aucune : « Je n'ai pas eu une minute à moi aujourd'hui. » Et pourtant, elle simplifie sa vie, la vente de la maison de Palaiseau en est une preuve. « Simplifier sa vie, à mesure qu'on a moins de besoins dans la vie, est une chose sage et facile, à la portée de tout le monde. (...) La vie est trop courte pour qu'on la passe à changer de domicile et c'est vers celui de mes enfants que j'irai le plus souvent. »

C'est en effet à Nohant que George Sand séjourne de plus en plus longuement, Nohant qui, sous l'influence de Maurice et de Lina, se change en ferme modèle. « Maurice veut du beau bétail et il s'en paie. Lina s'est payé une bande d'oies, de canards et de poules. » Devant le spectacle de Maurice et de Lina jouant aux paysans, Sand se laisse envahir par une béatitude inaccoutumée. « Ici on va sur des roulettes. (...) J'engraisse. Je ne pense à rien. Je suis au comble de mes vœux. »

Après avoir été dans le Berry un objet de scandale, la châtelaine-douairière de Nohant n'est plus qu'un exemple de paisible simplicité, ou de tranquille félicité, seulement interrompue par les supportables disparitions d'amis d'autrefois. Le 13 octobre 1869, Sainte-Beuve meurt à Paris. Et le 16, son enterrement se termine en une manifestation muette en faveur de Sand qui a tenu à rendre les derniers devoirs à celui qui fut le confident de ses amours avec Prosper Mérimée et avec Alfred de Musset. « La chose finie, j'ai quitté tout ce monde officiel pour aller retrouver ma voiture, alors en rentrant dans la vraie foule j'ai été l'objet d'une manifestation dont je peux dire que j'ai été reconnaissante, parce qu'elle était tout à fait respectueuse et pas enthousiaste ; on m'a escortée en se reculant pour me faire place et en levant tous les chapeaux en silence. » La célébrité ne comporte pas que des horreurs, comme le montre la spontanéité de cet hommage.

Le 26 novembre 1869, à Louis Ulbach, homme de lettres, qui veut inclure George Sand dans sa série intitulée « Nos contemporains », elle conseille de lire *Histoire de ma vie* et trace un bref autoportrait en forme de mise au point. « Je ne suis qu'une bonne femme à qui on a prêté des férocités de caractère tout à fait fantastiques. On m'a aussi accusée de n'avoir pas su aimer passionnément. Il me semble que j'ai vécu de tendresse et qu'on pouvait bien s'en contenter. »

Toujours en novembre, la parution de *l'Éducation sentimentale* provoque de tels éreintements que Sand vole au secours de son ami, dans une lettre d'abord — « Tout cela est d'un maître et ta place est bien conquise pour toujours » —, puis dans un article qui reflète son enthousiasme.

Est-ce en signe de remerciement ? Gustave Flaubert consent à quitter son ermitage de Croisset pour passer les fêtes de Noël à Nohant. Il y est entouré, congratulé, fêté. Il en repart le 28. Le 30, le « vieux troubadour » écrit à son « cher maître » : « Pendant toute la route je n'ai pensé qu'à Nohant. Je ne peux pas vous dire combien je suis attendri de votre réception. Quels braves et aimables gens vous faites tous ! Maurice me semble l'homme heureux par excellence. Et je ne puis m'empêcher de l'envier, voilà ! »

MALGRÉ TOUT...
(1er janvier-5 septembre 1870)

On vous lira malgré tout, croyez-moi. Du reste les nouvelles sont un peu meilleures. On a réussi à se concentrer en repoussant l'ennemi et en lui faisant éprouver de grandes pertes.

François Buloz à George Sand,
le 17 août 1870

On pourrait faire un recueil avec les prophéties de George Sand qui, à mesure qu'elle avance en âge, voit son don de voyance, ou de clairvoyance, augmenter. Au commencement de ce qui sera l'année terrible, 1870, Sand écrit, le 4 janvier, à Barbès : « La fin du pouvoir personnel, plus ou moins proche, est inévitable, fatale. »

Face à cette inexorable fin du second Empire, la romancière songe à assurer son avenir et signe, le 25 janvier, avec l'éditeur Michel Lévy, un traité par lequel elle engage sa production littéraire pour dix ans, moyennant la somme forfaitaire de 125 000 francs, payables par mensualités. Malgré ses plaintes, Buloz et Hetzel en savent quelque chose, Sand sait faire apprécier sa prose à son plus juste prix, et ce n'est que justice.

Fin janvier, George reçoit en cadeau un petit flacon d'ylang-ylang, une essence tirée d'un arbre qui porte ce nom et qui pousse à Madagascar et en Indonésie. L'amie des arbres aime ce parfum d'arbre...

Le 2 février, retenue à Paris par la répétition de sa pièce l'Autre, elle écrit sa première lettre à sa petite-fille Aurore en forme de déclaration d'amour. « Ma Lolo adorée, je t'aime et je rêve à toi la nuit. » La grand-mère, en George Sand, se comporte exactement comme l'amoureuse d'autrefois, celle qui envoyait à Musset, ou à Michel, des messages d'adoration, de jour comme de nuit.

Loin de Nohant, et de sa Lolo, George dépérit et tombe malade. Ce qui ne l'empêche pas, soutenue par Charles Marchal, d'assister, à l'Odéon, au triomphe de *l'Autre*, le 25 février. Elle a terminé, et livré, un roman, *Malgré tout*, qui paraît dans *la Revue des Deux Mondes*. Ayant accompli ses devoirs d'écrivain, elle peut retourner à Nohant, le 5 mars, avec, en poche, une lettre de Victor Hugo qui la félicite pour le triomphe de *l'Autre*. « Encore un triomphe. (...) Vous mettez votre suprême esprit au service de la justice, vous combattez, ô guerrière divine, toutes les vieilles démences, toutes les vieilles cruautés. Triomphez, moi j'applaudis. »

La « guerrière divine » trouve Nohant changé en hôpital. Tous ses habitants y ont la grippe, les maîtres comme les domestiques. Le plus atteint est Maurice qui souffre d'une angine couenneuse. Sa mère en perd le sommeil et fait venir de Paris l'éminent Dr Favre qui soigne, et guérit, Maurice. Sand promet de bénir le sauveur de son fils jusqu'à la fin de ses jours.

En même temps que la maladie de Maurice, tombent sur la tête de George les foudres impériales. L'impératrice Eugénie a cru se reconnaître en l'un des personnages de *Malgré tout*, Mlle d'Ortosa. Les ambitions matrimoniales de Mlle d'Ortosa ne sont pas sans rappeler celles de Mlle de Montijo. « Je veux épouser un homme (...) portant avec éclat dans le monde un nom très illustre. Je veux aussi qu'il ait la puissance, je veux qu'il soit roi, empereur, tout au moins héritier présomptif ou prince régnant. (...) Un jour viendra où je serai aussi utile à un souverain que je peux l'être aujourd'hui à une femme qui me demanderait conseil sur sa toilette. J'ai l'air d'attacher une grande importance à des choses futiles, on ne se doute pas des préoccupations sérieuses qui m'absorbent, on le saura plus tard ; quand je serai reine, grande-duchesse..., ou présidente d'une république... »

Il est facile de reconnaître là les ambitions politiques d'Eugénie de Montijo, et de remplacer « présidente de la république » par « impératrice ». Une impératrice qui pousse de hauts cris et que révolte ce qu'elle considère comme une ingratitude de Sand à qui elle a donné, sans compter. « Comment ! moi que tout le monde attaque maintenant ! Je n'aurais jamais cru ça ! et je voulais la faire nommer à l'Académie ! Mais que lui ai-je donc fait ? » L'impératrice est « désolée », et l'empereur, « prostré ». Ils ne comprennent rien à ce qu'ils considèrent comme une inexcusable perfidie. Napoléon III et son épouse n'ont pas cessé de prodiguer des marques de bienveillance à George Sand et de répondre à chacun de ses appels. La romancière serait-elle vraiment une ingrate ? Eugénie en appelle à sa confidente, Mme Cornu, qui, à son tour, en appelle à l'un des admirateurs de l'impératrice, Gustave Flaubert.

Coincé entre son admiration pour Eugénie et son amitié pour George, Gustave s'entremet. Il n'est pas question pour Sand de faire paraître un démenti dans les journaux qui, déjà, se sont emparés de l'affaire. Mais elle consent à écrire une lettre d'explication à Flaubert qui montrera cette lettre à Mme Cornu qui la transmettra à l'impératrice. La « guerrière divine » y jure n'avoir tracé en Mlle d'Ortosa « qu'une figure de fantaisie », et non un portrait satirique comme on le prétend. Et cela pour deux bonnes raisons : elle ne fait pas de satire et elle ne fait pas de portrait. Elle « invente », c'est son métier. C'est un peu léger comme défense, et assez peu convaincant. Mais l'empereur et l'impératrice doivent s'en contenter. Ils ont d'autres préoccupations plus importantes. Un sénatus-consulte destiné à modifier la Constitution dans un sens libéral, et avec consultation populaire le 8 mai, est voté ce 20 avril.

Ce projet de plébiscite indigne George Sand : « Nous entrons certainement dans le césarisme absolu par le plébiscite qui donnera pleins pouvoirs à l'Empereur. » En quoi elle ne se trompe pas. Résultat de la consultation du 8 mai 1870 : 7 350 000 « oui » pour 1 538 000 « non ».

Deux mois et demi plus tard, le 16 juillet, la France déclare la guerre à la Prusse. « Paris est rugissant d'enthousiasme. Ce n'est pas la même chose en province », écrit à Juliette Adam en ce même 16 juillet Sand qui, à Nohant, ne voit autour d'elle que complète consternation et familles tremblant pour leurs enfants. « Les jeunes gens ne sont pas soutenus par l'enthousiasme de la patrie en danger. (...) Je suis très triste, et cette fois, mon vieux patriotisme, ma passion pour le tambour ne se réveillent pas. (...) Tout le monde devient fou. Il faut en prendre son parti et avaler la décadence jusqu'à la lie. »

Comme si cette guerre ne suffisait pas, la sécheresse dévaste la France, et particulièrement le Berry. « Nous avons ici des 40 et 45 degrés de chaleur à l'ombre. On incendie les forêts : autre stupidité barbare. Les loups viennent se promener dans notre cour où nous les chassons la nuit, Maurice avec un revolver, moi avec une lanterne. Les arbres quittent leurs feuilles et peut-être la vie », note Sand pour Flaubert, le 26 juillet. Elle ne décolère pas contre cette « guerre infâme ». À travers cette guerre contre la Prusse, ce sont toutes les guerres que condamne Sand que nos modernes pacifistes devraient prendre pour patronne. « Trouver charmant que l'on se tue pour savoir qui est le plus fort me semble sauvage et cruel. » Elle voudrait s'enfuir sur une autre planète, à condition d'y retrouver les siens.

Devant les inévitables, les inutiles horreurs de la guerre, la colère de George Sand se change en fureur. « France et Prusse s'égorgent pour des questions qu'elles ne comprennent pas. » Il n'y a rien d'autre à faire qu'à attendre les événements et cette passivité pour l'active George est insupportable, « cette morne attente est terrible ». Sa fureur personnelle reflète celle de la province contre le gouvernement de Paris.

Dès le 13 août, reprise par son esprit de prophétie, la pythie de Nohant prédit : « Je crois l'Empire perdu, fini. Les mêmes hommes qui ont voté le plébiscite avec confiance voteraient aujourd'hui la déchéance avec unanimité. » Le 18, elle prévient son ami, le prince Jérôme Napoléon, de l'imminence de cette déchéance.

La désorganisation la plus complète règne en France. Sur le front, les états-majors n'ont même pas de cartes. Des troupes entassées à Châteauroux et à Bourges vivent de la charité publique, en attendant... quoi ? Personne ne le sait !

Tout s'effondre, sauf le pouvoir de Sand sur ses lecteurs. Au nom des abonnés à *la Revue des Deux Mondes*, Buloz supplie Sand d'envoyer sa copie. « On vous lira malgré tout, croyez-moi. » Rassurée de ce côté-là, elle envoie, par la poste, les deux dernières parties de *Césarine Dietrich*. Oui, malgré tout, elle continue à écrire, et à ouvrir grandes les portes de Nohant à ses amis de Paris, comme les Lambert qui pourraient, s'ils le désiraient, y chercher refuge. À Charles Marchal, elle demande, plus que jamais : « Où es-tu et où en es-tu ? » Marchal ne veut pas quitter Paris, et, comme le reste de la France, attend.

Le 2 septembre, l'armée française capitule à Sedan. L'Empereur est prisonnier. Le 3, sa déchéance est proclamée, suivie, le 4, par la proclamation de la république que Sand, le 5, salue ainsi : « La voilà donc revenue sans coup férir, cette pauvre chère république ! Puisqu'elle peut renaître (...), espérons qu'elle est viable cette fois. »

L'incorrigible optimiste qu'est George Sand espère, malgré tout, en ces veilles du siège de Paris. « Malgré tout », cela pourrait être l'une de ses devises...

AUX PRISES AVEC LE CHAOS
(7 août 1870-6 juillet 1871)

Quant à la Commune, ce n'est pas, selon moi, une révolution, mais bel et bien un crime qui relève du droit commun.

Le désastre de Sedan a, au moins, fait une heureuse : George Sand qui voit dans ce désastre renaître la république. Elle clame son bonheur à ses amis, et dans un article qui paraît dans *le Temps* du 7 août : « Paris aura proclamé la république sans effusion de sang ; je n'osais le rêver ! »

Saisies par la contagion républicaine de leur grand-mère, Lolo et sa sœur Gabrielle, dite Titite, crient « Vive répubolicolique ». Il est vrai qu'elles pensent qu'il s'agit là d'un bonbon, le bonbon république dont s'était délectée autrefois, quand elle était perle du district, leur arrière-grand-mère, Sophie-Victoire Delaborde...

Cet enthousiasme pour la république n'est pas partagé par La Châtre que Sand surnomme alors « Trou-cochon », ni par Gustave Flaubert qui, le 10, précise ses positions, et son opposition à son amie. « Et vous m'affligez, vous, avec votre enthousiasme pour la république. » Mais la république ne réussit pas à brouiller le vieux troubadour avec son cher maître.

Joignant le geste aux paroles, George remet 1 000 francs à titre de souscription patriotique au gouvernement de la Défense nationale. Le 9 septembre, elle continue à montrer son optimisme : « J'ignore si nous aurons la guerre civile. J'espère que non. » Elle n'a pas peur pour l'avenir de la France, elle ne craint que les rôdeurs qui se multiplient dans le Berry. Là-dessus, les malheurs publics faisant généralement oublier les dissensions personnelles, Solange, bravant l'interdiction de sa mère de se présenter à Nohant sans prévenir, y tombe sans crier gare, alors que la famille termine tranquillement de dîner. « Ce soir, au dessert, Solange nous arrive tout effarée, disant que tout est perdu, ne songeant qu'à effrayer, à consterner, à tout blâmer et critiquer, comme toujours, elle est forte comme un diable, elle va et vient d'un bout de la France à l'autre comme nous allons à Vic. »

Tout est perdu pour Solange, rien ne l'est encore pour George. La mère et la fille ne sont jamais d'accord, même dans les pires moments. Les malheurs publics ajoutent encore à leurs dissensions personnelles, Solange s'enfuit à Cannes, elle est remplacée par une épidémie de variole qui ravage Nohant et ses environs.

Lina et ses deux filles se réfugient à Saint-Loup, dans la Creuse, chez des amis, les Maulmond. Stoïque, Sand corrige les épreuves de son roman, *Césarine Dietrich*, et pratique, sans relâche, ce qu'elle considère comme l'un de ses principaux devoirs : la charité. Elle assure Marguerite Thuillier, une actrice dans le besoin, que tant qu'elle aura quatre sous, il y en aura deux pour Marguerite. Pour pouvoir exercer ses charités qui sont innombrables et qui ne se limitent pas à la seule Marguerite Thuillier, George Sand « pioche » sans arrêt pour *la Revue des Deux Mondes*, sans savoir comment elle parviendra à expédier sa prose, les services de la poste étant aussi désorganisés que les autres services d'un État qui s'effondre.

Depuis le 18 septembre, le siège de Paris qui devait imprégner de façon ineffaçable les mémoires du temps avec son cortège d'héroïsme, d'humiliation, de famine — on ira jusqu'à manger des rats —, est commencé. Le 7 octobre, deux ballons quittent la capitale encerclée. L'un s'appelle Barbès, l'autre George Sand. George envie [1], peut-être, ce ballon qui

---

1. On ne peut s'empêcher de songer à une similitude de situations, à Marie-Antoinette qui, en 1785, regardait voguer, libre dans les airs, un ballon nommé Marie-Antoinette.

porte son nom et qui, libre, vogue dans les airs, hors d'atteinte alors qu'elle est à Nohant, prisonnière de sa famille et surtout de Maurice qui refuse de s'enfuir comme une Solange. Sous-lieutenant des pompiers, il aspire à être lieutenant-colonel de l'une des légions de l'Indre, et à servir son pays. Comme il n'est pas question de quitter Maurice en un instant aussi critique, Sand reste à Nohant où, l'épidémie de variole conjurée, reviennent Lina et ses deux filles. Lolo et Titite jouent maintenant à la guerre et aux Prussiens.

Pour calmer les ardeurs belliqueuses de son fils, la descendante du maréchal de Saxe et du colonel Dupin obtient du Dr Vergne, oncle du général Vergne, un certificat prouvant que « M. Maurice, dans son état actuel de santé, et dans cette saison, est absolument hors d'état d'être appelé à un service militaire actif, très actif, vu les circonstances ; le demander, s'y exposer, c'est folie. »

Après tout, il n'y a que l'intention qui compte ! Il n'est pas question de sacrifier Maurice sur les autels de la patrie. Sand préfère laisser réquisitionner ses chevaux, tout en insistant pour garder deux juments afin de permettre à Lina et à ses deux filles de fuir, si besoin était, ce qu'elle désigne pudiquement par « les cruautés de l'ennemi ».

Les Prussiens déferlent, multipliant les vols et les viols auxquels George ne veut pas croire complètement. « Les Prussiens et les Allemands commettent-ils toutes les atrocités qu'on raconte ? Il m'est impossible de le croire. (...) Entre ces actes de vandalisme et la férocité qu'on impute à ce peuple allemand si bon chez lui, il y a un abîme, et il me faudrait le voir pour le croire. »

On se rassure comme on peut. George ne peut pas croire que les Prussiens commettraient de telles atrocités dans son intangible Nohant. N'importe, mieux vaut se préparer à toute éventualité et préserver du pire Lina, Lolo et Titite. Quant à elle, George, c'est sans aucune hésitation qu'elle donnerait sa vie pour sauver celle des siens. Tristes pensées, triste Noël 1870 et triste jour de l'an 1871. Tristesse renforcée par les rigueurs d'un froid intense.

Clésinger, avant de partir à la guerre, a supplié sa belle-mère de quitter Nohant pour se réfugier à Cannes, chez Solange. Sand n'a pas répondu à celui qu'elle considère comme l'assassin de Nini. Heureuse Nini : George en vient à envier le sort des morts qui jouissent enfin de « ce calme éternel des lois comprises et acceptées ».

En ce début 1871, George Sand admet qu'elle est « comme tout le monde, aux prises avec le chaos ». Elle ne comprend plus rien. Elle a l'impression de marcher dans les ténèbres, dans les batailles, on se bat à Bapaume, à Villersexel, au Mans, dans les alentours de Paris assiégé.

Depuis le 15 septembre 1870, elle tient son Journal qu'elle publiera chez Lévy, l'année suivante sous le titre *Journal d'un voyageur pendant la guerre*. Dès le début de la mêlée, en ce 15 septembre, elle devine que l'ennemi cessera un jour de l'être : « De cette étreinte furieuse de deux races sortira un jour la fraternité, qui est la loi future des races civilisées. » Cela s'appellera, au siècle suivant, les États-Unis d'Europe...

Précieux *Journal* où les aveux personnels — « J'aime l'eau avec passion, et le vin me répugne » — alternent avec des considérations générales : « Nous sommes difficiles à satisfaire en tout temps, nous autres Français. Nous sommes la critique incarnée, et dans les temps difficiles, la critique tourne à l'injure », et l'omniprésence de la guerre sur la terre et dans les esprits.

« 4 janvier 1871, lettre de Paris. Nous voulons bien mourir, surtout mourir, disent-ils. Ce peu de mots en dit beaucoup : ils sont désespérés !... comme nous.

« 7 janvier. Depuis douze jours, on bombarde Paris. Le sacrilège s'accomplit. La barbarie poursuit son œuvre (...) La France est ruinée, pillée, ravagée à la fois par l'ennemi implacable et les amis funestes.

« 8 janvier. (...) Pauvre France ! Il faudrait pourtant ouvrir les yeux et sauver ce qui reste de toi !

« 9 janvier. Neige épaisse, blanche, cristallisée, admirable. Les arbres, les buissons, les moindres broussailles sont des bouquets de diamants : à un moment, tout est bleu. Chère nature, tu es belle en vain ! Je te regarde comme te regardent les oiseaux qui sont tristes parce qu'ils ont froid. »

Bloquée à Nohant par la neige et par le froid, George Sand apprend que Pierre Leroux se meurt de misère à Nantes. Oubliant leurs différends, elle essaie, encore une fois, de porter secours à son philosophe, son Platon socialiste, qui s'éteint le 12 avril.

Le 17 janvier 1871, Paris est bombardé et George éprouve pour sa ville natale un regain d'amour. « Pauvre Paris ! c'était la moitié de mon âme. C'est là que je jouissais de la civilisation avec quelques amis qui l'appréciaient en la critiquant. » Elle non plus n'avait pas épargné les diatribes à ce Paris où elle s'étiolait et dépérissait ! Sand n'échappe pas à la terrible règle générale qui veut que l'on apprécie mieux ce que l'on a perdu... Elle s'inquiète pour ses amis restés dans la capitale. « Tous mes chers amis sont sur la brèche, héroïques ! Les retrouverai-je tous ? M'en restera-t-il un seul ? » Et ce seul ami sera-t-il, au moins, Charles Marchal ? Rien n'est moins sûr. Marchal participe vaillamment à la défense de Paris et recommande sa mère et sa maîtresse à George qui note dans son agenda : « Pauvre cher Marchal, quelle atroce position ! »

À ce détail, à cette recommandation, on peut mesurer la liberté qui réglait les rapports de Sand et de Marchal. Depuis son apprentissage de la camaraderie voluptueuse avec Casimir Dudevant, George n'a pas cessé de faire des progrès et Charles en est le dernier bénéficiaire...

Le 29 janvier 1871, Paris capitule et un armistice est signé que Sand accueille avec une joie prudente : « Je ne sais pas si c'est la paix, je ne sais quel avenir, quelles luttes intestines, quels nouveaux désastres nous menacent encore, mais on ne vous bombarde plus, mais on ne tue plus les enfants dans vos rues, mais le ravage et la désolation sont interrompus, on pourra ramasser les blessés, soigner les malades... C'est un répit dans la souffrance intolérable. »

En ce 29 janvier, il s'agit bien d'un répit. La France est, plus que jamais, divisée. Les élections du 8 février donnent la majorité aux conservateurs favorables à la paix. Adolphe Thiers en est l'idole et devient le chef du pouvoir exécutif de la république. La minorité républicaine que représente Gambetta est pour la poursuite de la guerre.

Le divorce entre Paris qui veut la guerre à outrance et la province qui veut la paix à tout prix est complet. George, qui souhaite aussi la paix, se lamente sur tant de dissensions : « Ah ! que Dieu nous envoie la paix ! Je ne suis qu'une faible femme, la souffrance des autres m'est intolérable, et mon cœur a tant saigné que je ne sais pas s'il vit encore. »

Dieu merci, il vit encore, ce cœur, pour se réjouir, le 13 février, de savoir que Charles Marchal est sain et sauf. « Lettre de Marchal, enfin ! il va bien, il n'a souffert de rien, il a fait son devoir, il est très rouge. » Le lapin rose, bleu, puis vert est devenu rouge, politiquement rouge. Qu'importe ? Le « cher gros » est rouge, mais en vie.

Une mort qui ne cause pas un extrême chagrin à George Sand, c'est celle, le 8 mars 1871, de Casimir Dudevant. Voici sa brève oraison funèbre : « Mon pauvre mari, absent de corps, de cœur et d'esprit depuis des années, a fini de végéter. Il ne souffrait pas, il ne vivait pas. » Elle s'indigne ensuite qu'un journal ait osé décerné des louanges au défunt qui avait « souillé la maison par mille orgies ». Mille orgies, c'est beaucoup pour désigner la servante-maîtresse à laquelle M. Dudevant semble avoir été fidèle[1].

Vingt jours plus tard, le 28 mars, la Commune de Paris est officiellement proclamée. Thiers et son gouvernement se retirent à Versailles. Désabusée, Sand commente : « J'avais prévu tout cela. Mais c'est une triste chose que d'avoir raison quand c'est le désastre qui vous la donne. » Elle prévoit les souffrances du peuple qui vont s'ensuivre. « Pauvre peuple ! il commettra des excès, des crimes, mais quelles vengeances vont l'écraser ! »

À Gustave Flaubert, à Alexandre Dumas fils, elle crie son dégoût des événements. Elle en a même une crise de vomissements. Et toujours son souci d'avoir des nouvelles de Charles Marchal. « Je ne sais pas ce que devient notre gros Marchal dans la bagarre, s'il y est encore », interroge-t-elle le 16 avril. Pauvre Marchal. Pauvre Sand qui apprend à vivre sans argent dans un pays ruiné, c'est-à-dire à crédit, elle qui a le crédit en horreur. Elle manque de cigarettes et réclame à son ami Plauchut : « Un millier de cigarettes de la régie Maryland pur. À La Civette, ils savent ce qu'il me faut. Mais Dieu sait si vous n'en manquez pas à Paris. Ici cela est devenu un mythe depuis longtemps. » Et voilà qu'un manuscrit de Sand, *Francia*, destiné à *la Revue des Deux Mondes*, se perd, angoisse, puis est retrouvé, allégresse. Mais

---

1. En mai 1869, le baron Dudevant avait écrit à Napoléon III pour demander la Légion d'honneur en récompense pour ses services depuis 1815 (on se demande lesquels) et aussi en invoquant « des malheurs domestiques qui appartiennent à l'histoire. Marié à Lucile Dupin, connue dans le monde littéraire sous le nom de George Sand, j'ai été cruellement éprouvé dans mes affections d'époux et de père ». Napoléon III se garda bien de donner suite à cette insolite demande. S'il avait fallu offrir la Légion d'honneur à tous les maris trompés de France et de Navarre...

quel est ce pays où l'on manque de tabac, où l'on égare les manuscrits, et où l'on se bat entre Français sous le regard des Prussiens ?

Entre la Commune de Paris et le gouvernement de Versailles, entre les Communards et les Versaillais, il y a des abîmes de haine et d'incompréhension qui ne peuvent être comblés que par des morts. Les Communards n'ayant pas réussi à vaincre les Versaillais refluent à Paris et c'est, du 22 au 28 mai 1871, la semaine sanglante. Les Versaillais doivent reconquérir Paris rue par rue. Devant cette implacable avance, les Communards massacrent prisonniers et otages, et incendient les Tuileries. Paris brûle-t-il ? Paris brûle. Après le palais des Tuileries, c'est au tour du palais de la Légion d'honneur, du Conseil d'État, du Palais-Royal, de l'Hôtel de Ville, du Palais de justice, de la bibliothèque du Louvre d'être la proie des flammes. Incendies et luttes durent jusqu'au 28 mai qui voit la victoire des Versaillais. Dès le 29, George Sand s'élève, avec violence, contre les excès de la Commune. « Et pourquoi vouloir brûler Paris, anéantir la population ? C'est une folie furieuse, odieuse, et qui, s'il était possible, tuerait jusqu'à la pitié qu'on doit aux vaincus. (...) Nous nous attendons demain à apprendre les cruautés atroces de la dernière heure. Les représailles seront cruelles aussi. »

Et Sand, une fois de plus, ne se trompe pas. Les représailles sont terribles et aux atrocités des Communards correspondent celles des Versaillais.

Sand est anéantie. Son Paris n'est plus Paris, c'est « un repaire de bandits de toutes les nations, opprimant un troupeau de couards et d'imbéciles, et finissant par vouloir détruire l'asile qu'il a souillé ! »

Paris est défiguré, et la France ne vaut guère mieux. Par le traité de Francfort qui, le 10 mai, a mis fin à la guerre avec l'Allemagne, la France perd l'Alsace, une partie de la Lorraine et doit payer une indemnité de 5 milliards. Les plus noires prédictions de George Sand sont accomplies. Cette guerre, comme toutes les guerres, n'aura apporté que ruines, deuils et désordres.

Le 13 juin, à l'intention de son amie Juliette Adam qui l'accuse de n'être plus la passionnée de 1848, Sand fait le point : « La France est une grande ambulance. » Elle voit le salut dans un « libéralisme qui sera sec, froid et borné ». Ce sera le libéralisme de M. Thiers. Et elle ajoute : « Ce ne sera pas un idéal, mais il faudra l'accepter ou périr dans la boue et le sang de l'Internationale. » Elle a perdu, et définitivement, ses illusions sur les vertus de l'Internationale et du communisme !

Au fond, George Sand ne veut plus des excès de la Commune, ni de ceux des légitimistes. La coupe des horreurs est pleine et elle s'en détourne. Quoi qu'en pense Juliette Adam, elle se retrouve dans le même état d'esprit qu'aux lendemains de la révolution ratée de février 1848. En juin 1871, comme en juin 1848, Sand répète : « Les partis, j'en ai plein le nez, je n'en veux plus. Je tiens pour crétins ou insensés tous ceux qui se donnent à des personnalités. Comme au lendemain de juin 48, le dégoût me jette dans l'isolement. »

On l'accuse de n'être plus assez républicaine et de trop croire en M. Thiers. Et pourquoi pas, réplique-t-elle, pratique, si M. Thiers peut aider la France à se relever et à faire renaître Paris de ses cendres ? Oui, elle croit « à la sincérité, à l'honneur, à la grande intelligence de M. Thiers et du noyau modéré qui joint ses efforts aux miens ». Ce langage n'est évidemment plus le langage de celle qui, au printemps 1848, invitait les ouvriers à défendre la liberté en montant sur les barricades. Les barricades du printemps 1871 comportent plus de cadavres que de pierres. Sand s'en détourne, tout en reconnaissant que ce n'est pas de gaieté de cœur qu'elle, la passionnée, est devenue une modérée : « Il n'en est pas moins triste de reconnaître qu'il faut passer absolument par cette grande modération qui est un instrument de progrès lent et froid, au lieu de pouvoir compter sur les forces vives et jeunes de l'esprit public ! Que de moyens et de puissances il va falloir enchaîner par crainte du désordre et de la démence. »

Maintenant, George Sand rejoint Mme Dupin de Francueil qui, après avoir été acquise aux idées nouvelles, déplorait que la Révolution n'ait apporté que la vieillesse et la laideur. Convertie à d'autres idées nouvelles, George parvient aux mêmes conclusions que sa bonne-maman...

LE SPHINX DE NOHANT
(août-septembre 1871)

> Malgré vos grands yeux de sphinx,
> vous avez vu le monde à travers une
> couleur d'or. Elle venait du soleil de
> votre cœur.
>
> Gustave Flaubert à George Sand,
> le 8 septembre 1871

Après l'année terrible, George Sand, à soixante-huit ans, refuse de se changer en mur des lamentations. Elle sait que se plaindre ne sert à rien. Si elle se dit déchirée par les malheurs de son pays, et elle l'est véritablement, elle n'a à déplorer, dans sa famille et parmi ses amis, aucune perte due à la guerre, à la Commune, ou aux représailles qui ont suivi. Même son appartement de la rue Gay-Lussac est intact. Elle espère que « c'est fini à présent, et que de longtemps, nous ne reverrons pareille chose ». Pour se persuader que ces horreurs sont terminées, elle répète à Charles Poncy : « La voilà vaincue, cette chimérique insurrection. (...) Je ne sais ce que la France peut subir de plus douloureux, elle a eu la dernière des humiliations, le ridicule après l'odieux. C'est un malheur pour ceux qui aiment l'égalité et qui ont cru aux nobles instincts des masses, et j'étais de ceux-là ! » Il en coûte à George Sand d'admettre que tous les hommes ne naissent pas libres et égaux, que tous les hommes ne sont pas également des anges... Elle reconnaît, de bon cœur, ses erreurs, quitte à retomber dans d'autres. Mais tomber, puis se relever, n'est-ce pas cela, vivre ?

Des journaux ayant annoncé sa mort, la châtelaine-douairière de Nohant clame bien haut qu'elle est toujours là et qu'elle n'a aucune intention de quitter cette « vallée de larmes ». Elle est en vie, et plus forte que jamais. On dirait qu'elle puise dans l'adversité des forces nouvelles : « Plus je vieillis, plus j'acquiers des forces physiques. » Renaissant, une fois de plus, de ses cendres, ou des cendres de Paris, George Sand est un parfait exemple de phénix à visage humain. Et puis, elle ne veut plus entendre parler de politique, « il n'y a plus rien à en dire, tout a été dit, écrit, publié : le vrai et le faux », ni de république qu'elle considère comme perdue par ceux-là mêmes qui la réclamaient à grands cris, « ils ont perdu et ils perdront toujours la république, absolument comme les prêtres ont perdu le christianisme ».

À ceux ou à celles qui, comme Juliette Adam, estiment qu'elle n'est plus « assez républicaine », elle répond qu'elle ne l'est pas à leur manière. Et voilà. Politique, république, des mots, des mots, des mots auxquels elle a trop cru et trop sacrifié. Ce qu'elle veut maintenant ? Travailler comme d'habitude, apprendre jusqu'à son dernier jour, et savourer pleinement les fruits de son âge.

Le 23 juillet 1871, elle établit pour Gustave Flaubert son bilan de santé : « J'ai une santé de fer et une vieillesse exceptionnelle (...). Le jour où j'ai résolument enterré la jeunesse, j'ai rajeuni de vingt ans. Tu me diras que l'écorce n'en subit pas moins l'outrage du temps. Ça ne fait rien, le cœur de l'arbre est fort bon et la sève fonctionne dans les vieux pommiers de mon jardin qui fructifient d'autant mieux qu'ils sont plus racornis. »

George Sand aime à se comparer aux arbres qu'elle aime. C'est à se demander si elle appartient encore au genre humain, et si elle n'a pas secrètement opté en faveur du règne végétal... L'arbre Sand, inconnu des botanistes. Mais non, mais non, Sand n'est pas un arbre, même si elle considère les arbres de Nohant comme des frères. Elle préfère les ombrages de Nohant à ceux des Champs-Élysées. « Moi, je ne veux pas voir Paris. Je n'ai pas quitté Nohant, je ne le quitterai pas cette année. (...) J'aime mieux l'ombrage de mes tilleuls et la possession de moi-même, de mon jugement, de ma liberté et de ma dignité. Ceux qui vont à Paris et qui ont du cœur ne décolèrent pas. Que voulez-vous ? on liquide tout, de la cave au grenier. »

La femme pratique en George Sand ne perd jamais ses droits. George considère que la guerre n'a été qu'un immense gâchis et la Commune, un inutile gaspillage. Elle aspire à l'ordre et à la tranquillité. Mettant à profit cette période de bouleversements et de changements, elle rompt avec *la Revue des Deux Mondes*, sans se fâcher pour autant avec Buloz à qui elle explique qu'elle ne veut plus être liée par un traité. Ce qui ne l'empêche pas de s'engager à donner deux articles par mois au journal *le Temps*. Buloz pousse des cris d'éditeur lésé mais doit s'incliner devant la volonté de Sand qui veut pleinement exercer son privilège de placer sa production où elle veut, quitte à travailler « comme un vieux nègre ». Qu'importent l'indignation de Buloz, les dévastations de Paris ? Ce qui compte, en ce mois de septembre 1871, c'est que ses deux petites-filles soient « si bien pourvues de beaux yeux qu'elles ne pourront jamais être laides ». En beaux yeux, George Sand s'y connaît, et sait combien un Alfred de Musset ou un Frédéric Chopin, pour ne nommer que ces deux-là, ont été sensibles à son regard dont semblent avoir hérité Lolo et Titite.

Le 8 septembre 1871, George Sand et Gustave Flaubert s'écrivent, en même temps, sans le savoir, et, sans le savoir, se répondent, coïncidence qui montre la perfection de leur amitié. Le 8, Sand écrit à son troubadour : « Tu vois que je suis écœurée comme toi et indignée, hélas ! sans pouvoir haïr ni le genre humain ni notre pauvre cher pays. » Comme s'il avait lu à distance, Flaubert écrit à son maître : « Ah ! chère bon maître, si vous pouviez haïr ! C'est là ce qui vous a manqué : la haine. Malgré vos grands yeux de sphinx, vous avez vu le monde à travers une couleur d'or. Elle venait du soleil de votre cœur. »

Piquée par ce mot de haine, par cette possibilité de haïr, George Sand bondit et réplique à Gustave

Flaubert, le 14 septembre : « Eh quoi, tu veux que je cesse d'aimer ? Tu veux que je dise que je me suis trompée toute ma vie, que l'humanité est méprisable, haïssable, qu'elle l'a toujours été, qu'elle sera toujours ainsi ? Et tu me reproches ma douleur comme une faiblesse, comme le puéril regret d'une illusion perdue ? »

Revendiquant le droit à ses anciennes erreurs, et aux nouvelles, Sand transforme sa lettre du 14 septembre 1871 à Flaubert en une apologie de l'amour dans ce qu'il a de plus noble, en une *Réponse à un ami* qu'elle publie dans *le Temps* du 3 octobre et qui s'adresse à la France entière : « Français aimons-nous, mon Dieu, mon Dieu ! Aimons-nous ou nous sommes perdus. »

Appel qui n'a toujours pas été entendu... On remarquera que l'anticléricale Sand invoque de plus en plus Dieu dans l'espoir d'un miracle qui rendrait à Paris ses beautés et sa suprématie. « Ce pauvre Paris représente-t-il encore la France ? L'Empire en avait fait un bazar et un égout. La Commune en a fait un égout et une ruine. Les cléricaux voudraient bien en faire un couvent et un cimetière. » On ne saurait être plus sévère, plus lucide que George Sand en cet automne 1871... Elle n'a pratiquement plus aucune illusion, même si elle prêche, comme dans sa *Réponse à un ami*, l'entente par-dessus tout, l'entente malgré tout, et surtout malgré les partis dont les dissensions ont conduit la France à la défaite. Elle en vient même à condamner cette Révolution de 1789 qu'elle avait tant admirée. « Toute la Révolution de 89 se résume en ceci, acquérir les biens nationaux, ne pas les rendre », décrète-t-elle, péremptoire, à Solange qui, élevée dans le culte de 89, doit se demander si cette affirmation émane bien de sa mère. À la faveur des désastres de la guerre et de la Commune, Solange est rentrée, un peu, en grâce. Les deux femmes échangent des considérations botaniques, des fleurs, et trouvent là un semblant d'accord. À George qui, pour le moment, refuse de se rendre dans la capitale avilie, Solange donne raison : « C'est-à-dire que ce n'est plus Paris du tout (...) La ville est morne, triste, éteinte. »

George Sand poursuit son règlement de comptes envers les révolutions, et envers elle-même. Au poète Alfred Gabrié, elle définit, le 21 octobre, ses nouvelles positions : « Je hais le mal répandu et je ne veux plus de cette thèse : " Faisons le mal pour amener le bien ; tuons pour créer. " Non, non ; ma vieillesse proteste contre la tolérance où ma jeunesse a flotté. Les événements multiples qui viennent de s'accomplir doivent nous faire faire un grand pas en avant. Il faut nous débarrasser des théories de 93 ; elles nous ont perdus. Terreur et Saint-Barthélemy, c'est la même voie. (...) Maudissez tous ceux qui creusent des charniers. La vie n'en sort pas. C'est une erreur historique dont il nous faut nous dégager. Le mal engendre le mal. »

À ce « mal engendre le mal » répondra « la violence engendre la violence » que lancera Gandhi, au siècle suivant. Ennemie résolue du mal, Sand répète : « J'ai la passion du bien. » Tout est passion chez George : elle découvre, avec ravissement, que Lolo a hérité de sa passion des lettres : Lolo « qui est si fière d'écrire et de recevoir des lettres que cela devient une passion ». Précoce épistolière, Aurore-Lolo n'a que cinq ans...

Fidèle en amitié, George Sand est restée en correspondance avec le prince Jérôme Napoléon qui est le parrain de l'incomparable Aurore. À la chute de l'Empire, le prince Jérôme s'est réfugié à Londres où il a oublié les malheurs de la France et ceux de sa famille en compagnie de danseuses, ou de courtisanes comme Cora Pearl. C'est donc au prince Jérôme qu'elle adresse de Nohant, le 28 décembre 1871, l'un de ses derniers messages de l'année : « Enterrons vite cette affreuse et déplorable année, mon cher et grand ami, et demandons à Dieu et aux hommes une meilleure. Avec, ou sans espoir, il faut s'embrasser et s'aimer. »

George Sand semble avoir perdu toutes ses croyances, sauf sa foi, immuable, en l'amour. Le sphinx de Nohant sait que l'amour ne meurt pas, ne peut pas mourir...

LES SUPRÊMES VOLUPTÉS
(1er janvier 1872-24 mars 1876)

> Il y a tant de choses plus amusantes
> que la littérature.
> Nohant, le 29 janvier 1874

Le 1ᵉʳ janvier 1872, George Sand s'accorde un jour de repos bien mérité. Elle vient de terminer un roman, *Nanon*, qu'elle n'aime pas. « Je ne l'aimais pas, cette *Nanon*. J'ai eu de la peine à ne pas la jeter au feu. Plus on vieillit, plus on devient difficile et peu content de soi-même. » *Nanon* n'en paraîtra pas moins en feuilleton dans *le Temps*, nécessité financière oblige...

Le 6 janvier, jour des rois, est un jour faste pour George. Elle reçoit enfin des nouvelles de Charles Marchal, son lapin bariolé, à qui elle avoue : « J'ai été moi, très inquiète de toi, l'année dernière. Mais on m'a rassurée et j'ai eu de tes nouvelles assez souvent par nos amis. » On peut en déduire que le « cher gros » n'est pas un épistolier enragé, ou que la conversation par écrit n'est pas son langage... Elle dresse pour le peintre son portrait en grand-mère modèle. « Je passe tous les jours trois ou quatre heures avec Aurore à l'instruire et à l'amuser. Elle ne s'ennuie pas avec moi et j'arrive, même en travaillant, à n'avoir pas de plus chère compagnie. (...) Je me plonge dans le sentiment maternel et dans le travail pour échapper à la réflexion navrante. Je n'ai pas encore le courage de revoir Paris que j'aimais tant et qui est si changé! Et pourtant je voudrais bien revoir toi et ceux que j'aime toujours. » Faut-il voir en cet espoir de retrouvailles la promesse d'un embrasement céleste ? On peut être une grand-mère modèle et ne pas renoncer à la « course dans les étoiles », comme elle disait, au temps de Chopin...

447

En ce début janvier 1872, George Sand apprend que l'empereur du Brésil, Don Pedro d'Alcantara, souhaite, lors de sa visite en France, la rencontrer. Ce désir qui donne une idée de l'étendue de la gloire de l'écrivain à son époque ne trouble guère celle qui en est l'objet. George décline l'invitation de « ce Brésilien », alléguant sa vieillesse et sa timidité. « J'ai passé ma vie à cacher ou à effacer ma personne. L'éclat d'une grande existence appartient à Don Pedro. Les rêveurs comme moi oublient, dans l'ombre et le silence, l'art de parler. »

On ne saurait envoyer promener un empereur avec autant d'humilité suave. Sand pratique le snobisme à l'envers. Elle se serait dérangée pour un pauvre paysan brésilien. Elle ne se dérange pas pour un empereur à qui elle laisse entendre que « s'il voulait parcourir la France en simple particulier, il trouverait à Nohant la cordiale et respectueuse hospitalité du paysan ». Et c'est ainsi que l'empereur du Brésil et la châtelaine-douairière de Nohant ne se rencontrèrent pas. C'est dommage... Mais George Sand est payée pour savoir que la fréquentation des grands de ce monde n'apporte généralement que des ennuis et des importunités. Elle ressent un « immense besoin d'être calme pour réfléchir et chercher ». Elle a aussi besoin d'un « nid intérieur », c'est-à-dire « le petit sanctuaire, la petite pagode intellectuelle (...) que l'âme se bâtit, qu'elle orne à sa guise et où elle entre de temps en temps pour s'absorber et se refaire ». C'est exactement cette nécessité du « nid intérieur » que préconiseront, à la fin du siècle suivant, les adeptes du Nouvel Age. George Sand aurait pu faire graver sur sa carte de visite : « Précurseur en tout ».

Pour le carnaval de 1872, on danse en famille à Nohant et Maurice danse tellement qu'il en tombe malade. Ah, les angines de Maurice, auront-elles fait souffrir sa mère, qui vit dans une terrible crainte qu'elle exprime à Gustave Flaubert, dans la nuit du 28 au 29 février, à trois heures du matin : « Ah ! mon cher vieux, que j'ai passé douze tristes jours, Maurice a été très malade. Toujours ces affreuses angines qui d'abord ne paraissent rien et qui se compliquent d'abcès (...). J'espère que nous allons revivre sans rechutes nouvelles. Il est l'âme et la vie de la maison. Quand il s'abat, nous sommes mortes, mère, femme et filles. Aurore dit qu'elle voudrait bien être malade à la place de son père. Nous nous aimons passionnément nous cinq, et la sacro-sainte littérature, comme tu l'appelles, n'est que secondaire pour moi dans la vie. J'ai toujours aimé quelqu'un plus qu'elle, et ma famille plus que ce quelqu'un. » Voilà qui remet les passions de Sand à leur juste place : personne n'a compté autant que sa famille, et dans cette famille, une seule et unique personne, Maurice, « l'âme et la vie de la maison ».

George Sand ne pense pas un instant que l'âme véritable de Nohant, c'est elle. Son humilité envers sa personne et son œuvre ne connaît pas de bornes. En avril 1872, elle écrit à Hyppolite Taine : « Je m'en prends à moi. Je me dis que si j'avais eu plus de talent, j'aurais mieux fait accepter mon idéalisme. De là des accès de découragement qui ne sont point une modestie cherchée, mais un véritable remords de n'avoir pas mieux employé ma vie, d'avoir trop flâné, trop rêvé, trop joui de mes contemplations et pas assez travaillé à m'élever et à m'instruire. J'ai trop admiré la mer et contemplé le flot, j'ai mal tenu le gouvernail. » Si quelqu'un ne mérite pas ce reproche de flânerie, c'est bien George Sand !

Son humilité n'a d'égale que sa délicatesse à pratiquer la charité. Quand elle apprend, le 6 avril, la mort de la mère de Gustave Flaubert, elle met spontanément à la disposition de son ami « les « quelques sous » qu'elle vient de gagner. Cette offre attendrit Flaubert « jusqu'aux larmes ! Je n'ai pas besoin d'argent (...), quel excellent être vous faites ! Je n'ai pas besoin d'argent, présentement ! Merci. Mais si j'en avais besoin, c'est bien à vous que j'en demanderais. »

Aux horreurs de l'année terrible, succède ce que George appelle « l'horreur des affaires personnelles ». Elle consent enfin à se rendre à Paris, le 29 mai, contrainte et forcée par cette « horreur des affaires personnelles », c'est-à-dire la lecture de *Nanon*, une pièce qu'elle a tirée de son roman, et de *Mademoiselle La Quintinie*, aux directeurs de l'Odéon.

Dès son arrivée, elle s'aperçoit que son quartier est « très dépeuplé » et que « le mouvement des rues » y a « diminué de moitié ». Si Paris a changé, elle constate que Pauline Viardot « est toujours aussi jeune de tournure et charmante de manières ». Elle retrouve ses amis, les anciens, comme les Lambert, et les nouveaux, comme les Adam. Elle court, avec ou sans Charles Marchal, les théâtres, applaudit Sarah Bernhardt dans *Ruy Blas* et, le 11 juin, assiste à la représentation du *Chandelier* d'Alfred de Musset. « J'ai été ce soir au Français voir le *Chandelier* de Musset. C'est charmant. » Aucun autre commentaire. Le passé est définitivement passé.

Elle est, à peine, plus prolixe sur Frédéric Chopin, apportant à un ami les précisions suivantes : « Tu n'as pas compris Chopin si tu n'y as vu que le côté déchirant. Il avait aussi le côté naïf, sincère, enthousiaste et tendre. Ce n'était pas un génie incomplet. »

Comme ils sont loin, les orages de la passion mis en vers par Musset et en musique par Chopin. Les seuls orages que connaisse maintenant George Sand, ce sont ceux qui frappent Nohant et noient ses jardins, comme elle l'annonce à Gustave Flaubert dans sa lettre du 5 juillet 1872 qui tient à la fois du bulletin de santé et du bulletin météorologique. « C'est aujourd'hui que je veux t'écrire. Soixante-huit ans. Santé parfaite, malgré la coqueluche qui me laisse dormir depuis que je la plonge tous les jours dans un petit torrent furibond, froid comme glace. (...) Nous avons eu des orages terribles, le tonnerre est tombé dans notre jardin, et notre ruisseau d'Indre est devenu un gave des Pyrénées, ce n'est pas désagréable. »

À soixante-huit ans, George Sand a attrapé la coqueluche de son Aurore, et comme tout ce qui vient d'Aurore est une bénédiction, elle ne s'en plaint pas. Elle constate simplement « à mon âge, c'est rude » et se contente de noyer sa coqueluche dans les eaux glacées de l'Indre. Étrange remède qui, une fois de plus, scandalise ses contemporains de La Châtre qui doivent penser : « Voilà bien les façons de Mme Dudevant. » Consciente de l'originalité de sa cure, George précise à Gustave : « Le médecin trouve que c'est fou, je le laisse dire aussi, je me guéris pendant que ses malades se soignent et crèvent. Je suis de la nature de l'herbe des champs, de l'eau et du soleil, voilà tout ce qu'il me faut. » On ne saurait mieux se définir. C'est vrai que, à la fin de sa vie, se dépouillant de tout ce qui n'est pas sa nature profonde, George Sand redevient aussi simple que l'herbe des champs, ou que l'enfant Aurore qui gambadait dans les champs de Nohant...

C'est aussi un peu de son enfance qu'elle retrouve en écrivant les *Contes d'une grand-mère* qu'elle compose d'abord à l'usage de ses petites-filles avec qui elle part en vacances, fin juillet, à Cabourg, au grand hôtel de la Plage [1]. Ce sont les délices de Cabourg, « les coquilles qu'on ramasse, les vagues qu'on attend, les puits qu'on creuse dans le sable avec les petites pelles, et que la mer vient remplir, c'est un délire perpétuel ». Grâce à ce délire, les deux Aurore, la grand-mère et la petite-fille, toussent de moins en moins et leur coqueluche n'est bientôt plus qu'un mauvais souvenir.

Parmi les délices de Cabourg, la balançoire. « Il y a aussi la balançoire où Lolo s'est lancée avec

---

1. Voir note de Georges Lubin, à la page 2 de son introduction au vingt-troisième volume de la *Correspondance :* « Le même dont Marcel Proust sera le client attitré pendant plusieurs années (...). »

passion. » Comme sa grand-mère, Aurore n'agit que par passion. De retour à Nohant, George Sand ne peut que constater : « Ma passion dominante, c'est mon Aurore. Ma vie est suspendue à la sienne, elle a été si gentille en voyage, si gaie, si reconnaissante des amusements qu'on lui donnait, si attentive à ce qu'elle a vu et curieuse de tout avec tant d'intelligence, que c'est une société véritable et une société sympathique à toute heure. » C'est à peu près en ces mêmes termes que George évoquait la présence de Nini, quand Nini était en vie. Nini perdue, puis retrouvée en Aurore, la grand-mère laisse éclater cette action de grâce : « Mon Dieu, que la vie est bonne quant tout ce qu'on aime est vivant et grouillant ! »

Son seul « point noir », c'est Gustave Flaubert qui est toujours triste, qui refuse de regarder le soleil, et qui refuse aussi une invitation à séjourner à Nohant, sous prétexte qu'il a trop vagabondé cet été. « On n'est pas assez littéraire pour toi, chez nous, je le sais », reconnaît George en soupirant de regret, et en insistant sur son manque : « Ah ! que je suis peu littéraire ! »

Les baignades dans l'Indre, les spectacles de marionnettes, les calembours à la mode de Nohant, n'amusent qu'un moment Gustave Flaubert qui, tel son saint Antoine, ne veut pas se prêter aux divertissements. Il termine sa *Tentation de saint Antoine*. « Viens donc me lire *Saint Antoine* », demande Sand qui n'hésite pas à reconnaître la supériorité de l'œuvre de Flaubert sur la sienne : « Tu veux écrire pour les temps. Moi je crois que dans cinquante ans je serai parfaitement oubliée et peut-être durement méconnue. C'est la loi des choses qui ne sont pas de premier ordre et je ne me suis jamais crue de premier ordre. » Elle n'en continue pas moins à écrire contes, romans, pièces de théâtre et maintenant Maurice la gronde quand elle veille trop...

Ces tendres reproches qu'elle supporte de Maurice, elle ne les admettrait pas de Solange à qui elle a permis de s'installer dans le Berry et d'y acquérir le château de Montgivray. On voisine le moins possible. Quand elle sait sa fille à Paris, George la charge de commissions comme l'achat d'un chapeau ou de jarretières qui peut donner une illusion d'intimité. Mais c'est Lina qui est sa vraie fille, Lina à qui elle apprend fièrement qu'elle sait réparer le ressort d'un dentier qu'elle s'est offert, lors d'un séjour à Paris, en mai 1873. Ce dentier qui pourrait provoquer des plaintes sur les infortunes de la vieillesse n'est que prétexte à rire pour Sand qui affirme : « Le rire est un grand médecin. » Comme elle aime rire, et comme elle salue d'un tonique éclat de rire son entrée dans sa soixante-neuvième année !

L'unique chose qui ne fasse pas rire George Sand, c'est *la Revue des Deux Mondes*. « Oh ! *la Revue des Deux Mondes !* tout ce qu'il y a de plus rechigneux, je ne dirai pas de plus difficile ! Ils se connaissent en littérature comme moi en géométrie, mais affectent de tout dédaigner », écrit-elle le 17 janvier 1874 à Juliette Adam. C'est à se demander si Sand ne garde pas rancune à la revue d'avoir organisé certain dîner où elle rencontra Alfred de Musset... En tout cas, à soixante-neuf ans, la romancière découvre : « Il y a tant de choses plus amusantes que la littérature ! » Et parmi ces amusements, les dendrites. D'après Littré, ce terme de minéralogie signifie : « Pierre arborisée. On appelle ces pierres figurées dendrites, quand elles représentent des arbres. »

À partir de ces dendrites qu'elle réussit à imprimer « au naturel » avec un peu d'eau et de terre de Sienne sur une feuille de papier, George Sand se livre aux voluptés de l'aquarelle et aux délires de son imagination, voyant à travers cet arbre de pierre, des bois, des forêts, des lacs, des collines. « J'accentue ces formes vagues produites par le hasard », explique-t-elle. Quand les rhumatismes paralysent son bras droit, elle fait ses « petits barbouillages d'aquarelles avec la main gauche ». Jusqu'à la fin, Sand reste cette intrépide dont la volonté vient à bout de tout, y compris des rhumatismes. Pour son soixante-dixième anniversaire, elle guérit de sa crise et récupère l'usage de sa main droite. Elle peut reprendre sa correspondance et le premier à bénéficier de cette reprise, c'est Gustave Flaubert qui gémit sous les attaques dont sa *Tentation de saint Antoine* est l'objet et à qui elle conseille : « Tu devrais faire comme moi et ignorer la critique quand elle n'est pas sérieuse et même quand elle l'est. (...) Tu attaches (...) trop d'importance au détail des choses humaines et tu ne te dis pas qu'il y a en toi-même une force naturelle qui défie les si et les mais du bavardage humain. Nous sommes de la nature, dans la nature, par la nature et pour la nature. Le talent, la volonté, le génie, sont des phénomènes naturels comme le lac, le volcan, la montagne, le vent, l'astre, le nuage. (...) Le difficile, quand on voyage, c'est de trouver la nature parce que l'homme l'a arrangée et presque partout gâtée (...). » Profondes paroles. Mais si George Sand trouvait déjà la nature « gâtée » à la fin du siècle dernier, que dirait-elle alors, aujourd'hui, en notre fin de siècle, elle qui, déjà, dénonçait le dépeçage de la forêt de Fontainebleau et la disparition des arbres : « Si on n'y prend garde, l'arbre disparaîtra et la fin de la planète viendra par dessèchement sans cataclysme nécessaire, par la faute de l'homme. N'en riez pas, ceux qui ont étudié la question n'y songent pas sans épouvante. »

George a communiqué son amour de la nature à Maurice qui, après avoir fêté le soixante-dixième anniversaire de sa mère, s'en va dans le Cantal pour y traquer, sur les hauteurs, le soir, « des papillons microscopiques ». Elle pousse le grand, l'éternel cri de la mère aux aguets : « Ne t'enrhume pas surtout. » En plus, on annonce des orages sur le Cantal alors que Maurice laisse Nohant sans nouvelles pendant trois jours. Ah, les mères, quel calvaire ! Même quand leur fils a passé la cinquantaine, ce qui est le cas de Maurice qui a cinquante et un ans...

Heureusement qu'Aurore est là pour consoler George de la courte absence, du 10 au 27 juillet, du chasseur de papillons du Mont-Dore. Avec satisfaction, Sand note que sa Lolo « a comme son père le goût des choses innocentes, les bêtes et les plantes, les eaux et les roches ». C'est ce goût des choses innocentes qui avait uni autrefois M. Dupin de Francueil à la veuve d'Antoine de Horn, et cela semble devenu une tradition de famille.

Dans le domaine des plaisirs innocents, il faut inclure la photographie que Sand étudie le 21 août 1874 : « J'en suis encore à la mise au point. C'est le plus important et le plus difficile. Le reste est une question de cuisine. » George ne persévère pas longtemps dans la photographie qu'elle ne considère pas comme une volupté, ni même comme un art. Elle y renonce en novembre. « Il y a trop de choses à laver, à essuyer, à ne pas embrouiller pour qu'il ne soit pas nécessaire de s'y mettre tout entier pendant plusieurs jours. »

C'est un luxe que George Sand ne peut s'offrir. Elle ne peut pas consacrer plusieurs jours de suite à la photographie. Bien qu'elle ne produise plus qu'un roman par an, elle reste la prisonnière de son encrier et de sa table de travail. Aucun amour, aucun malheur n'ont pu la détourner longtemps de ses griffonnages, alors, la photo, vous pensez ! Elle continue à écrire, mais elle n'a plus aucune envie de publier. « J'ai fait tant de romans que je suis bien rassasiée de publicité. » Dès novembre 1874, elle ne pense plus qu'à assurer l'avenir d'Aurore et de Gabrielle. Elle sait bien que ce n'est pas avec le « grand travail » entrepris par Maurice, un *Catalogue raisonné des lépidoptères du Berry et de l'Auvergne*, que ces demoiselles pourront tenir leur rang et avoir une dot. Elle calcule que « mon traité avec Lévy me donne de quoi vivre sans écrire ; si je lui laissais quatre ou cinq ouvrages inédits, il en tirerait évidemment au profit de mes petits-enfants un meilleur profit que je ne saurai le faire moi-même. » Elle a, sa vie durant, travaillé pour les siens, poussant l'abnégation jusqu'à continuer à assumer ce qu'elle considère comme son premier devoir, en laissant ces inédits qu'elle engrange, patiente comme une fourmi, et toujours démunie comme une cigale. Elle est incapable de résister à l'appel d'un miséreux. Aux uns, elle donne son argent, aux autres, comme Gustave Flaubert, de bonnes paroles.

À Flaubert qui geint comme Musset ou comme Chopin, pour un oui ou pour un non, elle répète ce qu'elle disait à Alfred ou à Frédéric : « Je t'aime d'autant plus que tu deviens plus malheureux. » Elle essaie vainement d'enseigner à son ami sa conception du bonheur, « le bonheur, c'est-à-dire l'acceptation de la vie quelle qu'elle soit » à laquelle elle joint cette belle formule, « c'est à nous de déblayer nos nuages ».

À Flaubert qui admire tant de sérénité, elle répond, le 16 janvier 1875 : « Ma sérénité (...) ne vient pas de mon fond, mais de la nécessité où je suis de ne plus penser qu'aux autres. Il n'est que temps, la vieillesse marche et la mort me pousse par les épaules. Je suis encore, sinon nécessaire, du moins extrêmement utile aux miens tant que j'aurai un souffle, pensant, parlant, travaillant pour eux. »

George Sand peut alors considérer sa vie dans son unité profonde : le travail. Elle a passé infiniment plus de temps à sa table de travail que sur le divan des alcôves. Elle n'écrit plus la nuit, mais le jour, entre deux leçons à Aurore. Écrire, enseigner, comme autrefois à Valldemosa. Sa vie se sera accomplie dans la rigoureuse répétition des mêmes actes. Force de l'habitude où elle puise de profonds plaisirs.

L'habitude conserve une certaine fraîcheur à l'âme, et, telle une débutante, George Sand remercie pour son « encouragement » Marius Topin qui a fait paraître dans la Presse du 13 avril 1875 l'article suivant : « En tête des romanciers contemporains, nul, sinon Mme Sand elle-même, ne s'étonnera de nous voir placer la femme célèbre, dont une carrière ininterrompue, durant quarante années, n'a pas tari l'imagination féconde et qui, par la variété du dialogue, par la beauté sereine et majestueuse des récits, par la fidélité dans la peinture des mœurs et des caractères, par l'exactitude merveilleuse des descriptions, enfin par l'éloquence impétueuse de la passion, a eu le rare privilège d'obtenir à la fois les suffrages de la foule et l'appréciation des délicats. »

Avoir les « suffrages de la foule » et « l'appréciation des délicats », que peut-on souhaiter de plus ? « À mon âge on en a peut-être plus besoin que dans la jeunesse, car on doute de soi encore plus », répond « Mme Sand » à Maurice Topin.

C'est avec un scrupule accru que, en ce printemps 1875, elle veille à l'édition de ses œuvres complètes et reprend ses feuilletons dans *le Temps*. Elle publie ses contes dans *la Revue des Deux Mondes*, en s'étonnant de « faire court ». Ses lettres ont aussi tendance à plus de brièveté.

En novembre 1875, sa dégradation physique, rhumatismes et douleurs d'entrailles, s'accentue : « Je ne peux plus marcher, moi qui aimais tant à me servir de mes pattes, sans risquer d'atroces douleurs. Je patiente avec ces misères, je travaille d'autant plus et je fais de l'aquarelle à mes heures de récréation. » Elle traite ses maux avec philosophie : « Ça passera, tu sais que c'est toute ma philosophie. » Sur l'impermanence des choses et des êtres, George Sand en sait autant qu'un maître zen ! Elle garde un ultime souhait : elle voudrait bien vivre assez pour marier Aurore, reprenant à son compte ce qui avait été l'ultime ambition de Mme Dupin de Francueil qui, elle aussi, avait voulu marier son Aurore.

Fin décembre 1875, la pythonisse de Nohant interroge l'avenir pour elle, et pour son ami Flaubert : « Que ferons-nous ? Toi à coup sûr, tu vas faire de la désolation et moi de la consolation. Je ne sais à quoi tiennent nos destinées. Tu les regardes passer,

tu les critiques, tu t'abstiens littérairement de les
apprécier, tu te bornes à les peindre en cachant ton
sentiment personnel avec grand soin, par système.
Pourtant on le voit bien à travers ton récit et tu
rends plus tristes les gens qui te lisent. Moi, je
voudrais les rendre moins malheureux. » Et moins
dupes d'une politique qu'elle considère enfin comme
une comédie : « La politique est une comédie en ce
moment. Nous avons eu la tragédie, finirons-nous
par l'opéra, ou par l'opérette ? Je lis consciencieuse-
ment mon journal tous les matins, mais hors ce
moment-là, il m'est impossible d'y penser et de m'y
intéresser. C'est que tout cela est absolument vide
d'un idéal quelconque, et que je ne puis m'intéresser
à aucun des personnages qui font cette cuisine. Tous
sont esclaves du fait, parce qu'ils sont nés esclaves
d'eux-mêmes. »

Ces lignes de décembre 1875 pourraient avoir été
écrites ce matin même. Actualité de certains textes
de George Sand...

Noël 1875. Sapin, loteries, folies d'Aurore et de
Gabrielle. « Lina déploie tous ses talents culinaires
et Maurice arbore tous les prestiges de son théâtre. »
Au fond, George Sand n'aime que les voluptés
domestiques. Elle n'a jamais été aussi heureuse
qu'entourée de son cher fils, de sa chère belle-fille, et
de ses chères petites-filles dans son cher Nohant.
Elle sait que le bonheur est dans la limitation des
désirs, et non dans leur extension. Jouir pleinement
de ce que l'on possède sans en être jamais rassasiée,
telle est désormais sa règle de conduite.

Le 9 janvier 1876, George Sand apprécie le spectacle de Nohant sous la neige et sous le clair de lune.
« Que Nohant est beau dans ce moment-ci ! C'est une
vraie nappe de neige avec les pins et les cèdres
blancs jusqu'aux pointes des rameaux. Avec cela un
beau clair de lune tous les soirs. Quand on a les yeux
pleins de la lumière rougeâtre des appartements et
qu'on regarde dehors cette douce clarté bleue on est
comme rafraîchi et enchanté par cet autre monde

féerique dont une vitre nous sépare. On en a toute la poésie sans en sentir la morsure. La vie est comme cela pleine de petits plaisirs innocents et qui ne coûtent rien. »

On pourrait considérer ce retour aux « petits plaisirs innocents » comme un retour à l'enfance, et cela enlèverait à l'expression « retomber en enfance » tout le mépris qu'elle peut contenir. Sand retombe en enfance, redevient cet enfant qu'elle n'a jamais cessé d'être, et dont elle n'a jamais cessé de proclamer l'existence, « restée enfant à bien des égards », combien de fois en aura-t-elle fait l'aveu, à quelques variantes près ? Revendiquer son droit à une enfance permanente, telle aura été l'une des principales, et secrètes, luttes de George Sand.

Aurore Dupin et George Sand enfin réconciliées se rejoignent en ce 9 janvier 1876 face au spectacle de Nohant sous la neige et le clair de lune. Il ne sert à rien de courir à Venise ou à Valldemosa, tout est là, sous ses yeux, mirage de neige et de lune. Comme certain sage chinois, elle pourrait dire :

Sans passer le pas de ta porte
Tu peux connaître l'univers

George Sand pratique ce qu'une Alexandra David-Néel baptisera, au siècle suivant, « un ascétisme épicurien ». Ses multiples voluptés, ce sont les lettres, les confitures, les contes, la tapisserie, l'aquarelle. Toute la panoplie de la dame qui sait vieillir, sans déchoir. « Je fuis le cloaque et je cherche le sec et le propre, certaine que c'est la loi de mon existence. » Une existence qui s'achève dans le détachement, la sérénité et la charité.

Une charité qu'elle s'efforce d'apprendre à l'un de ses amis à qui elle recommande une actrice, Marguerite Thuillier, dont elle s'est déjà beaucoup occupée, avec cette charmante formule : « Je vous lègue cette infortune », faisant ainsi un cadeau très précieux en ayant l'air d'implorer une faveur. « Marguerite Thuillier (...) vend ses nippes pour subsister. Quand elle n'aura plus rien à vendre ? Je ne l'abandonnerai pas, mais je suis si vieille ! Savez-vous que je vais sur mes soixante-douze ans ? Prenez-la sous votre protection, je vous lègue cette infortune. Une femme de théâtre charmante et célèbre qui ne s'est jamais vendue, bien qu'elle ait débuté enfant et qu'elle ait vécu sur les planches, vous n'en trouverez pas beaucoup. » En écrivant ces lignes, le 2 février 1876, au marquis de Chennevières, en évoquant « une femme de théâtre (...) qui ne s'est jamais vendue », George Sand pense-t-elle à ses ancêtres, les dames d'opéra, ou à sa mère, qu'un riche tira du théâtre où elle jouait pour « la jeter dans une abjection plus grande encore ? » Bah ! à quoi bon penser au passé quand le présent est là, simple et tranquille. « Ma vie présente serait de médiocre intérêt pour les biographes, car c'est toujours la même chose : pioche continue, avec le ramage de mes petites-filles autour de moi. »

La « pioche », le travail s'interrompent pour laisser la place aux folies familiales du carnaval à Nohant. Cédant aux prières de ses petites-filles, la châtelaine-douairière se costume « en Turc avec un faux nez et en Pierrot avec la figure enfarinée ». On danse à la cuisine, et au matin, « on court dans le jardin sur un tapis de violettes invraisemblable. Il y en a partout, le pré, le bois, le sable des allées en sont jonchés et elles embaument. Les abricotiers fleurissent, et malgré de fréquentes giboulées et de grosses bourrasques, il fait chaud et nous avons des heures de beau soleil. »

George Sand ne sait pas résister à l'appel de ce printemps précoce et de ses rapides soleils. Elle ne va pas assister à Paris, au Théâtre-Français, le 7 mars, à la reprise de sa pièce, *le Mariage de Victorine*. Mais elle veille à ce que tous ses amis y soient invités, donnant leur adresse à M. Perrin, directeur du Français. Figurent parmi les premiers de cette liste Pauline Viardot, 50, rue de Douai,

Gustave Flaubert, 11, rue du Faubourg-Saint-Honoré et Charles Marchal, 11, place Pigalle.

La veille de cette reprise, elle écrit à Charles Marchal : « J'ai prié M. Perrin de t'envoyer pour demain mardi un orchestre pour *le Mariage de Victorine*. Je t'embrasse et t'aime toujours et tout Nohant aussi. » C'est l'ultime déclaration du sphinx de Nohant à son lapin bariolé.

Le 9 mars, George Sand apprend la mort de Marie d'Agoult survenue le 5 à Paris. Elle ne manifeste aucune émotion à la nouvelle du décès de son amie-ennemie. Il y avait si longtemps que Marie n'appartenait plus au monde de George...

Le 22 mars, George pratique la suprême volupté des vieilles dames : elle ajoute un codicille à son testament, en faveur, évidemment, de Maurice qui reste seul propriétaire de Nohant et de ses dépendances, Solange devant se contenter du domaine de La Porte.

Si elle ne s'intéresse plus à la politique et à ses comédiens, George Sand suit attentivement les débuts de ses jeunes confrères, comme ceux d'Émile Zola. Flaubert recommande à son amie la lecture de *Son Excellence Eugène Rougon*, et Sand obtempère. « Dis donc à M. Zola de m'envoyer son livre. Je le lirai certainement avec grand intérêt. » Ce qu'elle fait, trouvant *Son Excellence*, « très vivant et très puissant » quoique « un peu brutal parfois ».

Fin mars, celle qui ne se plaint jamais reconnaît du bout des lèvres : « Je suis toujours couci-couça. » Elle est soignée, et dorlotée, par Aurore, ce qui rend supportable, et presque agréable, son mauvais état de santé. « Je n'ai pas souvent un jour sans douleurs mais je m'y habitue et n'y songe guère. Me voilà bien vieille et d'autres à mon âge sont plus éprouvés. » Et d'autres n'ont pas à leurs côtés une Aurore qui, comme sa grand-mère, est une infirmière-née.

Le 23 mars, à l'un de ses nouveaux protégés, Henri Amic, un garçon de vingt-trois ans qui veut être « littérateur », elle prodigue des conseils qui pour-

461

raient encore servir aujourd'hui aux débutants : « On vous distrait parce qu'il vous plaît de vous laisser distraire. Quand on veut s'enfermer, on s'enferme, quand on veut travailler, on travaille au milieu du bruit, il faut même s'y habituer comme on s'habitue à dormir à Paris au milieu du roulement des voitures. Vous voulez être littérateur, je le sais bien. Je vous l'ai dit : vous pouvez l'être si vous apprenez tout. L'art n'est pas un don qui puisse se passer d'un savoir immense étendu dans tous les sens. Mon exemple vous est pernicieux peut-être. Vous vous dites : voilà une femme qui ne sait rien et qui s'est fait un nom et une position. Eh bien, cher enfant, je ne sais rien, c'est vrai, parce que je n'ai plus de mémoire, mais j'ai beaucoup appris et à dix-sept ans je passais mes nuits à apprendre. »

Tout au long de cette lettre, George Sand affirme sa croyance au pouvoir de la volonté et termine sa profession de foi en suppliant Henri Amic de ne pas dire « ce mot honteux : Je ne peux pas ».

Sand n'est pas loin de penser que, par la seule force de la volonté, on peut ne pas mourir...

LES DERNIÈRES FOIS
(25 mars-10 juin 1876)

La mort de la pauvre mère Sand m'a fait une peine infinie. J'ai pleuré à son enterrement comme un veau, et par deux fois : la première en embrassant sa petite-fille Aurore (dont les yeux, ce jour-là, ressemblaient tellement aux siens que c'était une résurrection) et la seconde, en voyant passer devant moi son cercueil... Pauvre chère grande femme !... Il fallait la connaître comme je l'ai connue pour savoir tout ce qu'il y avait de féminin dans ce grand homme, l'immensité de tendresse qui se trouvait dans ce génie... Elle restera une des illustrations de la France et une gloire unique.

Flaubert à Tourgueniev,
le 25 juin 1876

Le 25 mars 1876, George Sand, « après des crampes d'estomac à en devenir bleue, et cela avec une persistance atroce », se sent mieux.

Le 5 avril, elle envoie à Gustave Flaubert sa dernière lettre qui se termine par un affectueux : « Je t'embrasse et je t'aime. Quand donc me feras-tu lire du Flaubert ? » Heureuse femme qui, pendant son existence, a pu demander à Chopin de jouer pour elle ses mazurkas, et à Flaubert de lui lire sa *Tentation de saint Antoine !*

Le 26 avril, elle adresse des remerciements à un débutant qui promet, Anatole France, dont elle a reçu le recueil de poèmes, *les Noces corinthiennes*, qu'elle juge « beau et frais comme l'antique ». France y malmène la religion chrétienne. Sand l'encourage fortement dans cette voie, dénonçant, encore une fois, « l'œuvre malsaine du christianisme, cette fausse interprétation de la parole de Jésus, plus que jamais torturée et calomniée de nos jours ». Les dames du couvent des Anglaises frémiraient si elles pouvaient lire ces lignes de leur ancien bon petit diable qui voulait entrer en religion...

Début mai, George Sand est réveillée, un matin, par les baisers de M. Claymore. Qui est ce M. Claymore ? Un petit chien, « un griffon gros comme deux fois le poing », George en avait envie et l'a reçu, en cadeau, d'Henri Amic. « Le chien est un vrai bijou, mais la tendre amitié que vous me témoignez est un vrai trésor. » Jusqu'à ses derniers jours, cette séductrice malgré elle suscite l'intérêt, l'amitié, le dévouement des jeunes gens.

George partage son amour de Claymore avec Aurore qui est « folle de ce toutou ». Aurore, dans le domaine des sentiments, semble aussi portée aux excès que le fut sa grand-mère en son temps.

Le 16 mai, les crises reprennent Sand « plus fréquentes, mais moins aiguës ». Douleurs d'entrailles suffisantes pour l'empêcher de travailler. On mesure, à cet empêchement, la gravité du mal. Le 22 mai, elle envoie au *Temps* son dernier feuilleton inspiré par *Dialogues et fragments philosophiques* de Renan. Dans ce texte éclate l'évidence de son don prophétique. « Nous voici donc lancés dans des guerres atroces où vous régnerez par la terreur, et votre science de destruction augmentant toujours, chaque nouvelle guerre sera plus meurtrière que les autres, jusqu'à ce que vous restiez seuls en face de vos instruments formidables, n'ayant plus d'autre ressource que de faire sauter la planète pour finir. »

Le 28 mai, elle adresse au Dr Favre un minutieux compte rendu de son état général : « L'état général n'est pas détérioré et malgré l'âge (soixante-douze ans bientôt), je ne sens pas les atteintes de la sénilité. Les jambes sont bonnes, la vue est meilleure qu'elle n'a été depuis vingt ans. Le sommeil est calme, les mains sont aussi sûres et aussi adroites que dans la jeunesse. Quand je ne souffre pas de ces cruelles douleurs, il se produit un phénomène particulier sans doute à ce mal localisé, je me sens plus forte et plus libre dans mon être que je ne l'ai peut-être jamais été. J'étais légèrement asthmatique, je ne le suis plus. Je monte les escaliers aussi lestement que mon chien, mais les évacuations naturelles étant presque absolument supprimées depuis plus de deux semaines, je me demande où je vais et s'il ne faut pas s'attendre à un départ subit un de ces matins. J'aimerais mieux le savoir que d'être prise par surprise. Je ne suis pas de ceux qui s'affectent de subir une grande loi et qui se révoltent contre les fins de vie universelle ». On ne saurait montrer plus de sérénité face à l'inéluctable. Et si George Sand exprime au Dr Favre un souhait de guérison, c'est uniquement parce qu'elle se sent « encore utile aux siens ». Il y a longtemps qu'elle a renoncé à vivre pour elle-même.

Le 30 mai au matin, celle que l'on peut considérer comme la Sévigné du dix-neuvième siècle met un point final à sa correspondance par une lettre, la dernière écrite de sa main, à son neveu, Oscar Cazamajou. En voici les ultimes lignes : « Ne t'inquiète pas. J'en ai vu bien d'autres et puis j'ai fait mon temps, et ne m'attriste d'aucune éventualité. Je crois que tout est bien, vivre et mourir, c'est mourir et vivre de mieux en mieux. Ta tante qui vous aime. »

George Sand vient de conjuguer le verbe « aimer » pour la dernière fois. C'est le dernier mot qu'elle trace, et c'est certainement celui qu'elle a le plus employé dans son œuvre, et dans sa vie.

Ce même 30 mai, vers trois heures de l'après-midi, George s'étend sur un canapé « en proie à de vives douleurs ». Elle fait appeler Maurice qui fait appeler leur vieil ami, le Dr Gustave Papet. Papet dit à Maurice : « Elle est perdue. » Nuit atroce pour la malade qui pousse des cris que l'on entend du fond du jardin.

Dans les jours qui suivent, un, deux, trois, quatre, cinq, six médecins se relaient, se consultent, sans parvenir à sauver Sand, ni même à atténuer ses souffrances. Atteinte d'une occlusion intestinale, George ne pense qu'à épargner aux siens le spectacle de ses souillures et répète inlassablement : « Que Maurice ne me voie pas souffrir, épargnez-lui cette peine et que les petites ne viennent pas. »

Le 7 juin, elle consent à dire adieu à ses petites-filles. « Oh ! mes adorées, je vous aime ! je vous aime ! »

Dans la nuit du 7 au 8 juin, elle est veillée par Lina, et par Solange que son frère a avertie par un télégramme de l'état désespéré de leur mère. Télégramme qui se terminait par : « Viens si tu veux ». Et Solange est venue.

Sur les trois heures du matin, Maurice se présente à l'entrée de la chambre à sa mère qui le repousse d'un « Non, non, va-t'en. » C'est la dernière preuve d'amour que George donne à Maurice à qui elle veut éviter la peine d'assister à son agonie.

Ensuite, Lina et Solange entendent l'agonisante réclamer la mort à plusieurs reprises. « Mon Dieu, la mort, la mort. » Au matin, toujours consciente, elle murmure : « Adieu, adieu, je vais mourir. Adieu Lina, adieu Maurice, adieu Lolo... ad... », et puis, « laissez verdure ».

Maurice n'est pas là pour entendre cet adieu. Accablé de fatigue et de chagrin, il dort dans sa chambre quand, le 8 juin 1876, à neuf heures trente du matin, sa mère rend le dernier soupir.

Aurore et Gabrielle sont chargées de réveiller leur père pour lui annoncer le décès. Entre deux sanglots, Maurice s'écrie : « Ma mère, ma mère, la vie pour nous est finie. »

George Sand, qui voulait être enterrée civilement, l'est, sur intervention et pression de Solange, religieusement, le 10 juin au cimetière de Nohant. Elle y rejoint bonne-maman et Nini devant sa famille et ses familiers en pleurs. Gustave Flaubert, Alexandre Dumas fils, Ernest Renan sont là et remarquent l'absence de Charles Marchal et de l'éditeur Hetzel. Ils écoutent le message de Victor Hugo que lit Paul Meurice et qui débute par : « Je pleure une morte et je salue une immortelle. »

Un témoin de la cérémonie, l'avocat Henry Harrisse, rapporte : « Ce cimetière inculte, toutes ces paysannes enveloppées de manteaux, agenouillées et priant dans l'herbe humide ; le ciel gris, la pluie fine et froide qui vous fouettait le visage, le vent bruissant à travers le cyprès et se mêlant aux litanies du vieux chantre, me touchèrent bien plus que cette rhétorique. Et cependant je ne pouvais m'empêcher de dire, à part moi, que la nature, en ce triste moment, devait bien à George Sand un dernier rayon de soleil. »

Qu'importe maintenant la pluie et le soleil à George Sand ? Croyant à la réincarnation, elle sait qu'elle recommence un interminable cycle, avant de retomber sur terre sous forme de pluie et de soleil. Chère George Sand...

Paris, le 16 janvier 1991, midi

REMERCIEMENTS

Pendant que j'écrivais *Chère George Sand*, trois ouvrages n'ont pas quitté ma table : *Lélia ou la Vie de George Sand*, d'André Maurois (Hachette), *George Sand ou le Scandale de la liberté*, de Joseph Barry (Seuil), *George Sand*, de Pierre Salmon (Éditions de l'Aurore). Que les auteurs de ces biographies, vivants ou morts, soient ici remerciés de leur aide.

Je remercie également ceux et celles qui, à des titres très divers, m'ont aidé dans cette tâche et dont voici les noms par ordre alphabétique : Carlos de Angulo, Josée de Chambrun, Anne Chevereau, Isabelle Courcelle, Jean Courrier, Dicta Dimitriadis, Michèle Gautheyrou, Jean Miot, Anne Muratori-Philip, Liliane de Rothschild, Gabrielle de Talhouêt, Olenka de Veer.

Pendant que j'écrivais *Chère George Sand*, deux de mes meilleures amies sont parties pour un monde que l'on espère, sans peine, meilleur que le nôtre : Belly Sirakian, qui soutenait mon travail par ses voyances et son affection, et Maria Gracia Marti Requena, qui me délivrait des soucis du quotidien, avec le sourire...

TABLE DES MATIÈRES

474

Cet ouvrage a été composé
par l'Imprimerie BUSSIÈRE
et imprimé sur presse CAMERON
dans les ateliers de la S.E.P.C.
à Saint-Amand-Montrond (Cher)
en avril 1991